# Gazetteer and business directory of Broome and Tioga counties, N.Y. for 1872-3

## Hamilton Child

# GAZETTEER

AND

# BUSINESS DIRECTORY

OF

## BROOME AND TIOGA COUNTIES, N. Y.

FOR

## 1872-3.

COMPILED AND PUBLISHED BY

# HAMILTON CHILD.

AUTHOR OF WAYNE, ONTARIO, SENECA, CAYUGA, TOMPKINS, ONONDAGA, MADISON, CORTLAND, CHEMUNG, SCHUYLER, ONEIDA, STEUBEN, ORLEANS, NIAGARA, GENESEE, CHENANGO, MONROE, HERKIMER, SARATOGA, MONTGOMERY AND FULTON, ALBANY AND SCHENECTADY, RENSSELAER, WASHINGTON, WYOMING, COLUMBIA, ULSTER, SCHOHARIE, OTSEGO, SULLIVAN, LEWIS, St LAWRENCE AND OTHER COUNTY DIRECTORIES.

Permanent Office, 23 & 24 E. Washington St., Syracuse, N. Y.

"He that has much to do, will do something wrong, and of that wrong must suffer the consequences, and if it were possible that he should always act rightly, yet when such numbers are to judge of his conduct, the bad will censure and obstruct him by malevolence, and the good sometimes by mistake."—SAMUEL JOHNSON.

## SYRACUSE:

PRINTED AT THE JOURNAL OFFICE, 23 & 24 E. WASHINGTON STREET.
1872.

# WAYMAN'S HARNESS SHOP!

MANUFACTURER AND DEALER IN ALL STYLES OF

## HEAVY AND LIGHT HARNESS,

Made exclusively from OAK TANNED LEATHER.   Also Dealer in

*Saddles, Trunks, Valises, Whips, Curry Combs, Cards,*
*Zinc Collar Pads, Sleigh Bells, Blankets, Robes, &c.*

30 Years Experience in the Business.   ☞ REPAIRING Neatly Done.

## WILLIAM WAYMAN, - NICHOLS, N. Y.

# INTRODUCTION.

In presenting to the public the "Gazetteer and Business Directory of Broome and Tioga Counties," the publisher desires to return his sincere thanks to all who have so kindly aided him in obtaining the information it contains, and rendered it possible to present it in the brief space of time in which it is essential such works should be completed. Espccially are our thanks due to the several editors of the papers published in the Counties, for the uniform kindness they have evinced in calling public attention to the author's efforts; and for essential aid in furnishing material for the work. Many others have placed us under similar obligations, but as credit has been given in most of such cases, as well as in works from which we have quoted, in connection with the substance of the information gleaned from each, we omit special mention here; while still others have kindly volunteered their assistance, to all of whom we tender our grateful acknowledgment.

That errors have occurred in so great a number of names and dates as are here given is probable; and that names have been omitted which should have been inserted is quite certain. We can only say that we have exercised more than ordinary diligence and care in this difficult and complicated feature of book making. Of such as feel aggrieved in consequence of errors or omissions we beg pardon, and ask the indulgence of the reader in marking such as have been observed in the subsequent reading of the proofs, and which are found in the *Errata*, following the *Introduction*.

It was designed to give a brief history of all the Church organizations in the Counties, but owing, in some cases, to the negligence of those who alone were able to give the necessary information, and in others, to the inability of any one to do so, we have been obliged to omit many or indefinitely delay the completion of the work.

We would suggest that our patrons observe and become familiar with the explanations at the commencement of the Directory.

The map of the Counties was engraved with great care by Weed, Parsons & Co., of Albany, and will, it is believed, prove a valuable acquisition to the work.

The *Advertisers* represent some of the leading business men and firms of these and other counties; and we most cheerfully commend them to the patronage of those under whose observation these pages may come.

While thanking our patrons and friends generally for the liberality and cordiality with which our efforts have been seconded, we take this occasion to express the hope that the information found in these pages will not prove devoid of interest and value, though we are fully conscious that the brief history of the Counties the scope of the work enables us to give, is by no means an exhaustive one, and can only hope that it may prove a nucleus and incentive to future historians, who will be the better able to do full justice to the subject, and leave our work to secure that favor which earnest endeavor ever wins from a discriminating public

HAMILTON CHILD.

# ERRATA.

## ADDITIONS AND CORRECTIONS.

**Stamp Duties.**—All Stamp Duties enumerated in this work, will be abolished on and after October 1st, 1872, with the exception of the two cent stamp on Bank Checks, which will still remain in force.

**Postal Rates and Regulations**—The postage on Circulars is now one cent for every two ounces or fraction over two ounces. On Books, two cents for every two ounces. On Newspapers, one cent if under two ounces, and one cent for every two ounces or fraction over two ounces On Packages of Merchandise not exceeding twelve ounces and containing no writing, done up so they may be examined, two cents for each two ounces Unpaid postage will be charged double rates.

### GAZETTEER—Tioga County.

**County.**—THE CANDOR FREE PRESS was started at Candor, in Josiah Rich's law office, in November, 1867, by Clizbe & Mandeville, and after six weeks was purchased by the junior partner, J D Mandeville who after a time removed it to Holmes Building, in South Candor, where it was burned out in the fall of 1868, and after a few months revived and continued by Mr Mandeville in the basement of the Eagle Hotel, until October 13, when it was purchased by Graves & Shepardson, of Owego, who continued it until the following February, when it was moved into the third story of Tuttle & Bogert's brick block, on the site of the burnt office, and purchased by Benj B F Graves, its present editor and proprietor In December, 1870, it was removed to Spaulding & Heath's building, second door above the Post Office and Depot, in the center of the village, and in September, 1871, this building being needed for a banking house, a set of convenient and handsome rooms were fitted up in the second story of the next building north, where the office is at present located The paper was called *The Candor Press* until it came into the hands of Graves & Shepardson, when it was enlarged and the name changed to *The Candor Free Press.* It is the only paper in the County off from the Erie Railway, and the only representative of the north part of the County. It is neutral in politics.

### DIRECTORY--Broome County.

**Binghamton,** (Town )—*McGRAW, D C , (Binghamton,) prop Riverside Gardens, half a mile east of water works, producer and dealer in choice flowers and vegetable seeds, also green-house plants, ornamental shrubbery and trees, fruit trees and small fruits

**Binghamton City.**—*BINGHAMTON TIMES, (weekly, Thursday ) 38 Court, 3d floor, Purdy & Cronin, props. and publishers
Brown, Lewis lumber dealer rear of Gaylord Block, south side of Susquehanna River.
Campbell, E R , billiard room, 99 Washington, also lunch room, Lafayette Block, 8 Court
CRONIN, DAVID E , (Purdy & Cronin,) editor *Binghamton Times,* lawyer, Deutcher Advocate, 43 Court.
Hecox, Wm H , (Howland & Hecox,)
Howland & Hecox, (Ransom Howland & Wm H Hecox,) lawyers.

Patterson, R A , secretary Dean College.
Paul, Robert Rev , pastor Chapel of the Good Shepherd.
*PURDY & CRONIN, (E H Purdy & D L Cronin,) props. Binghamton Times, 38 Court, 3d floor
PURDY, E H , (Purdy & Cronin )
Riggs, T J , piano tuner, 52 Court
Rowe, O J., wholesale grocer and provision dealer, Chenango Block,
SHEPARD, E R & CO . manufs American fluting irons and shelf hardware, 101 Water
Stevens, A T , barber, over 69 Washington
Wheeler, W Lamont, physician, 39 Court

**Chenango.**—Chenango Valley Division, Sons of Temperance, (Chenango Bridge,) meets every Friday evening, in their hall, at the house of Walter Jewell.

**Colesville.**—DOOLITTLE, WARREN, (Ousquaga,) lot 54, Ham P , farmer 80 and, in Windsor, 22
MONROE, SAMUEL E , (Harpersville,) station agent.

**Deposit Village.**—Clark, James G., (Devereux & Clark )
Devereux, Alvin, (Devereux & Clark )
Devereux & Clark, (Alvin Devereux and James G Clark,) props Deposit Tannery

**Lisle.**—Collliar, Norris, (Lisle,) lot 441, blacksmith and farmer 175
Harrington, Wm., (Lisle,) confectionery, fruits &c
Northrop, Wm Mrs., (Lisle,) dress maker and agent for Weed Sewing Machine

**Sanford.**—MERRILL, JOHN, (Sanford,) great lot 11, F & N T, farmer 104
ROBBINS, SOLOMON, (Afton, Chenango Co,) farmer 137.
WELD, ALFRED R, (Center Village,) G & S L, farmer lessee of Mrs Graves, 200
WHEELER, BENJ F., (Sanford,) lot 39, L T 1, constable and farmer 110

**Triangle.**—Bixby, Frank, (Whitney's Point,) livery stable
ROWLAND, RANSOM, (Whitney's Point,) (*Howland & Hecox,*) lawyer, prest. of
village and farmer 2

### DIRECTORY--Tioga County.

**Berkshire.**—Walter, Joseph S, (East Berkshire,) S D 8, post master, physician
and farmer 87

**Candor.**—Herrick, Mason L, (Weltonville,) post master

**Owego.**—Brink D., (Owego,) confectionery and fruit, Lake
Decker, S. W. & Co., (Owego,) dry and fancy goods, millinery &c, under *Gazette*
office, Lake
Harris, Chas, (Owego,) prop Union House
Johnson, Jane, (Owego,) baker and confectioner
Livingston, A, (Owego,) dining saloon, Front
Moore, Theo F, (Owego,) (*Moore & Ross*)
Moore & Ross, (Owego,) (*Theo. F. Moore and John S Ross,*) carriage makers, North
Avenue near Erie Depot
Richardson, L D, (Owego,) general ticket agent, corner Broad and Fulton
Ross, John S, (Owego,) (*Moore & Ross*)

---

**The Candor Free Press,** published at Candor, N Y, by Benj B F. Graves is advertised on page 20 The *Free Press* is a good local paper and worthy of the patronage of the community in which it circulates As an advertising medium it commends itself to the business public. The Job office is fitted up with facilities for executing all kinds of work in good style.

**"The Buckeye,"** J. M. Childs & Co., proprietors, office 10 and 12 Fayette Street, Utica. It is hardly worth while to discuss the merits of this celebrated Mowing and Reaping Machine, at this late day So perfect and complete was the Machine as originally invented, that its principles have never been changed Improvements in parts, it is true have been made, as experience showed them to be requisite When it is understood that notwithstanding the great number of machines thrown upon the market for public favor, more than 180,000 of the "Buckeyes" have been sold, it will be universally conceded that the majority are in favor of this as a labor saving implement We will not attempt to detail its merits, but would recommend the reader to call and inspect the machine for himself, or send for a circular to J M Childs & Co, Utica Messrs C & Co., also keep on hand a full assortment of Agricultural Implements, such as Threshing Machines, Fanning Mills, Horse Rakes, Cultivators, Plows, Cider Mills, &c, &c Read their advertisement inside first cover

**Warren A. Hull,** General Blacksmith, Berkshire, N. Y., prints a card on page 398. Mr Hull is an adept at his business, and those patronizing him may be assured of having their work skillfully executed at reasonable rates.

**The Owego Gazette,** published at Owego, by Beebe & Kingman, is advertised on page 358 The name of the *Gazette*, is too familiar to the ears of our readers to need calling their attention to it For about 60 years this paper has paid its weekly visits to the home circles and business places of a large number of the residents of this section of the country Its continued extensive circulation is sufficient evidence of the popular favor in which it is held It is unnecessary to remind business men of its advantages as an advertising medium

**Dr. Kingsley,** of Rome, justly celebrated for the many cures he has effected of that most distressing disease, Cancer, publishes a notice on page 1 He is prepared to treat all scrofulous diseases, and others of long standing, and assures his patients that they will not be charged a heavy bill and dismissed without receiving any benefit Persons who cannot conveniently call upon him in person, can address him by letter, and will receive prompt attention Dr K is a graduate, with an experience of over fourteen years in the practice of medicine Let the afflicted give him a call

**Geo. W. Bingham** has established a Saw & Flouring Mill at Bingham's Mills, N. Y, on the Ithaca and Athens R R, where all kinds of Lumber, as well as Flour, Feed &c, can always be found. Those contemplating building would find it to their interest to give Mr B a call before purchasing their materials elsewhere If you want a good article of Flour and Feed, you can get it from Mr Bingham as cheap as from any one else. He also pays the highest cash price for Grain. Card on page 410.

# GENERAL CONTENTS.

# INDEX TO BUSINESS DIRECTORY.

## BROOME COUNTY.

## TIOGA COUNTY.

# INDEX TO ADVERTISEMENTS.

## Wall Paper, Window Shades Etc.
*(See also General Merchants )*

## Watches, Jewelry Etc.

## Wood Turning Etc.

## Woolen Mills.

# INDEX TO PUBLISHER'S NOTICES.

# Post Offices and Post Masters in Tioga Co.

| POST OFFICE | TOWN. | POST MASTER |
|---|---|---|
| Apalachin | Owego | Aaron Steele |
| Barton | Barton | Joseph Walhog |
| Berkshire | Berkshire | Carlisle P Johnson |
| Bingham's Mills | Barton | Geo W Bingham |
| Campville | Owego | S G Tonsley |
| Candor | Candor | John W McCarty |
| Catatonk | Candor | Frank W Truman |
| East Berkshire | Berkshire | Joseph S Walter |
| East Nichols | Nichols | Enoch White |
| Factoryville | Barton | Thomas Yates, jr |
| Flemingsville | Owego | Chas E Truman |
| Gaskill's Corners | Owego | Clark S Green |
| Halsey Valley | Tioga | Chas E Taylor |
| Hooper's Valley | Nichols | Emanuel Coryell |
| Jenksville | Newark Valley | Samuel M Avery |
| Ketchumville | Newark Valley | Seneca Ketchum |
| Newark Valley | Newark Valley | Jerome B Landfield |
| Nichols | Nichols | Henry Cady |
| North Barton | Barton | Edmund H Hoyt |
| North Spencer | Spencer | Rufus L Lake |
| Owego | Owego | Frank L. Jones |
| Richford | Richford | Chauncey D Rich |
| Smithsborough | Tioga | Delosa Goodenough |
| Sooth Owego | Owego | Benj F Hewitt |
| Spencer | Spencer | Sylvenus Shepard |
| Spencer Springs | Spencer | Wm H Pray |
| Strait's Corners | Tioga | David Strait |
| Tioga Center | Tioga | Forman S Higby |
| Waverly | Barton | Wm Polleys |
| Weltonville | Candor | Mason L Herrick |
| West Candor | Candor | John R Woodford |
| West Newark | Newark Valley | Herbert Richardson |
| Willseyville | Candor | Wakeman B. Smith |
| Wilson Creek | Berkshire | Anson M. Kimball |

# U. S. Internal Revenue Officers in Broome and Tioga Counties, 26th District, N. Y.

### ASSESSOR.

P O ADDRESS

Benjamin DeVoe ......... Binghamton

### ASSISTANT ASSESSORS.

Cyrus F. Hotchkiss, 4th Division ........... Binghamton
D. M Pitcher, 3d Division ........... Owego

### DEPUTY COLLECTOR

Horace E. Allen ........... Binghamton

### U S. GAUGER

Samuel Lee ........... Binghamton

# JOHN R. MURRAY,
## General Insurance Agent,

' Office over Corner Drug Store,

### WAVERLY, N. Y.

## Life, Fire & Lightning!

Farmers desiring RELIABLE INSURANCE will do well to apply at this office before insuring elsewhere. All Losses honorably adjusted and promptly paid.

# CAFFERTY HOUSE,

## COURT STREET Corner of WATER,

### BINGHAMTON, N. Y.

Refitted and newly furnished; first-class in every particular. Charges reasonable.

## CHARLES M. CAFFERTY, Proprietor.

ALSO FIRST-CLASS

# LIVERY STABLE,

*Where may be found splendid*

# HORSES

AND

# CARRIAGES,

*For Parties or for Private use.*

*Livery Stable on Water Street.*

# Post Offices and Post Masters in Broome Co.

| POST OFFICE. | TOWN | POST MASTER. |
|---|---|---|
| Belden | Coleaville | Nathaniel S. Wallace |
| Binghamton | Binghamton | Edward B Stephens |
| Cascade Valley | Windsor | Sabastia Comstock |
| Castle Creek | Chenango | James Bristol |
| Center Lisle | Lisle | Lewis S Smith |
| Center Village | Coleaville | Wm Tice |
| Chenango Bridge | Chenango | Chas H Jewell |
| Chenango Forks | Barker | Henry A Rogers |
| Choconut Center | Union | Justus Lewis |
| Colesville | Colesville | James E Jewel |
| Conklin Center | Conklin | Brewster C Johnson |
| Conklin Station | Conklin | Burtis J Bayless |
| Corbettsville | Conklin | Daniel J Murphy |
| Deposit | Sanford | J B Stow |
| Doraville | Colesville | Chas B Doolittle |
| East Maine | Maine | Russell F Chauncey |
| Glen Aubrey | Nanticoke | Wm H Riley |
| Glen Castle | Chenango | Geo. A Everett |
| Gulf Summit | Sanford | G S Williams |
| Harpersville | Colesville | Darius W. Pearsall |
| Hawleyton | Binghamton | Theodore H Gage |
| Hooper | Union | Frank Hooper |
| Kattelville | Chenango | Alonzo E. Kattell |
| Killawog | Lisle | John J Wheaton |
| Kirkwood | Kirkwood | John H Doubleday |
| Kirkwood Center | Kirkwood | Eli W Watrous |
| Lamb's Corners | Nanticoke | L LaRoy Brooks |
| Lisle | Lisle | Philotus Edmister |
| Maine | Maine | Francis H Marean |
| McClure Settlement | Sanford | Walter Hewitt |
| New Ohio | Colesville | Harvey F. Beardsley |
| Nineveh | Colesville | Franklin Edgarton |
| North Colesville | Colesville | Newel S Paddleford |
| North Fenton | Fenton | Melvin A Macomber |
| North Sanford | Sanford | Geo W Bixby |
| Osborne Hollow | Colesville | Isaac Craver |
| Ousquaga | Colesville | David B Guernsey |
| Port Crane | Fenton | James E Waite |
| Port Dickinson | Binghamton | G A Jewel |
| Randolph Center | Windsor | Joseph Brown |
| Riverside | Kirkwood | Tobias VanBuran |
| Sanford | Sanford | Samuel Whitney |
| Tracy Creek | Vestal | Wm W Davenport |
| Triangle | Triangle | E W Simmons |
| Union | Union | E C Mersereau |
| Union Center | Union | Jarvis O Howard |
| Upper Lisle | Triangle | A Austin |
| Vallonia Springs | Colesville | Andrew J Sande |
| Vestal | Vestal | Cornelius Merseran |
| Vestal Center | Vestal | Daniel M Clark |
| West Chenango | Chenango | A. Martin Hull |
| West Colesville | Colesville | Harrison H Carrol |
| Whitney's Point | Triangle | Chas. S Olmstead |
| Windsor | Windsor | P. A Russel |

**The Lisle Gleaner,** Eugene Davis, publisher, is advertised on page 294 The *Gleaner* is a neatly printed and worthy local paper Its Local and Miscellaneous columns are well sustained, and we cheerfully commend it to the favor of the citizens of Lisle and vicinity. All kinds of Job Work neatly executed at this office.

**Carrington & Porter,** Stove Dealers &c, at Binghamton, are extensive dealers in their line of business The business of this firm was established by *Carrington & Prendergast* about twenty years ago; afterward the firm was under the style of *Carrington, Prendergast & Carrington,* Prendergast subsequently went out, and *Carrington Brothers* continued the business until Mr Porter went in, when the firm was changed to *Carrington Brothers & Porter.* The next change was to the present style Since the begining, the store has been burned out three times Now all the goods are new and first-class Among their many styles of cook stoves, we take pleasure in mentioning the celebrated *Peerless,* of Boston, which took the first prize at the Paris Exposition, and a large number of first prizes in this country, and of which Mrs Henry Ward Beecher says, in an article to the *Christian Union,* "This is without exception the most complete and in all respects the most satisfactory of any we have ever tried" Messrs C & P are also agents for the Celebrated Herring's Fire and Burglar Proof Safes, Lawson's Diamond Hot Air Furnace &c, &c See their advertisement on Map.

**E. P. Holdridge,** Merchant Tailor and Clothier, at Owego, N Y, advertises on colored page 417 A man that studies his own interest will buy his clothing where he can buy the best and cheapest. "Money saved is money earned" Keep posted; buy where you can get the full value of your hard-earned money Better have your greenbacks in your pocket than shoddy on your back Mr Holdridge agrees to sell the best quality of goods from five to fifteen per cent cheaper than any other house can afford to. By buying in large quantities for cash, he saves a large profit and gives his customers the benefit of it Buy your goods where you can find the largest assortment to select from The mottoes of this house are "Not to be Undersold," "Large Sales, Small Profits and Honest Dealings" For anything in the line of Clothing or Gents' Furnishing Goods, our advice is, go to E P Holdridge's, where you will find the best goods at prices as low as the lowest

**G. F. Strait,** Candor, Tioga County, N Y., manufacturer of Lumber, Lath &c, advertises on page 196A Mr Strait keeps constantly on hand a good supply of Pine, Chestnut, Hemlock and Hardwood Lumber, Lath &c We commend Mr Strait to the favor of those needing Lumber for building purposes, as we can assure them of fair dealing at low prices He also deals in Ground Hemlock Bark, to which we would call the attention of tanners

**Burke, FitzSimons, Hone & Co.,** Importers, Jobbers and Retailers of Dry Goods, Fancy Goods and Woolens, Nos 53, 55 and 57 Main St, Rochester, publish a card on page 277 This House was established in 1849, since which time its success has been uninterrupted, each year increasing its amount of business. Their annual sales amount to the enormous sum of near $1,500,000, their trade extending from the Eastern portions of the State to the "Far West" Occupying, as they do, fully 40,000 feet of flooring in actual business departments, making this the largest establishment of the kind in the State, every portion of which is crowded with immense piles of goods from foreign countries, as well as of domestic manufacture, renders the facilities of this house for Jobbing equal to any in the country The firm are also proprietors of the "Genesee Falls Woolen Mills," where they manufacture 100,000 yards of goods annually.

**A Lady Artist.**—Miss Ella Wood, a lady possessing a rare fund of native talent for art, and who has by careful study and long practice attained an elevated position as an Artist, has located permanently in Binghamton, where she has taken rooms at Beecher's Photographic Studio, No 72 Court Street Miss Wood's talent is not of that narrow contracted kind, which would enable her to produce satisfactory results in but a single line of art She paints rapidly, and to the life, Portraits, Landscapes, Animals &c She paints in oil from original sketches, and is desirous of receiving orders for Portraits, a branch of her art which she especially excels in She also finishes Photographic Portraits in Water Colors or India Ink with great satisfaction to her patrons Our readers will consult their best interests by calling on Miss Wood and leaving their orders We are sure they will thank us for the advice. See her card on page 302.

**E. D. Robinson,** proprietor of Southern Tier Furniture Emporium, 88 Washington Street, Binghamton, N. Y., publishes a card on colored page 415 We would advise our patrons to visit the rooms of Mr Robinson and examine the elegant Parlor Furniture, Chamber Sets &c, there displayed, and learn prices, and they will become satisfied that here is the place to purchase. Indeed the rich and poor can here find any desirable style and price, accompanied by a corresponding quality. Mr R warrants all his goods and is bound not to be undersold.

**Misses Della and Theresa La-Grange,** of Waverly, N Y, have lately opened a Ladies' Hair Dressing Establishment at No. 8 Harnden's Block, up stairs, to which we call the attention of the fair sex Misses LaGrange propose keeping a complete stock of everything in the line of human hair goods, which they will offer at reasonable rates They will also make ornamental hair work to order Give them a call Card on page 20

**The Deposit Courier,** published by Chas. N. Stow, at Deposit. N. Y., is advertised on page 230 The *Courier* is a first-class local paper and enjoys an extended circulation The Job Department has facilities for executing Book and Job Printing equal to any office in the County, and at city prices We trust the citizens of Broom and Tioga Counties will accord it the patronage to which its merits entitle it

**O. D. Beman,** 89 Court Street, Binghamton, N. Y, Watchmaker, Engraver, Jeweler &c , prints a card on colored page 278, in which our readers may think Mr. B. makes some strong assertions; but we are assured he is prepared to substantiate any statement therein made to the satisfaction of any disinterested person. His instruments for obtaining the time directly from the sun or stars, as well as those for marking it, are as perfect as are made , and we have been informed that he has had opportunities of comparing his observations for time with those taken at the Albany Observatory, and they have never yet varied a single second We do not hesitate to recommend Mr. Beman to the favorable notice of our readers

**Horton Bros & Myer,** dealers in Hardware, Stoves, Furnaces, Tin Ware &c , at 32 Court St., Binghamton, are extensive dealers in these particular lines of goods The Hardware department has just been added, and consequently *everything* in that line is new and of the most approved styles Their Stove and Furnace department is supplied from several of the best manufacturers in the country Among their low priced goods in this line, we desire to mention the "Cabinet Range," made by *Richardson, Boynton & Co* , of New York, which is made with great care,—doors and covers fitted like the best first-class stoves, besides having other valuable improvements. In reality it is a first-class Range with a second-class price. Call and see it. See card, page 416.

**D. M. & E. G. Halbert,** Jobbers and Retailers of Dry Goods, Fancy Goods, Carpets, &c , &c , Nos 11 and 13 Court Street, Binghamton, publish a card on page 2 This House was established in its present location in the fall of 1865, since which time its success has been uninterrupted, each year increasing its amount of business. They have been obliged to enlarge their store until they now occupy two floors, 30 by 180 feet in area, as salesrooms, and a store room 30 by 40 feet, making 22,800 square feet of flooring The aggregate sales of this House amount to between $300,000 and $400,000 annually, with a steadily increasing business The proprietors hope by honest dealing and close attention to the wants of their customers to very materially extend their trade. We advise our readers to call and see them when visiting Binghamton, as theirs is the largest Dry Goods Store in the "Southern Tier"

**F. M. Snook,** Dentist, Waverly, N. Y., publishes a card on colored page 196A Dr Snook has one of the best arranged Dental offices to be found in the State. It occupies six rooms on the second floor of the Shipman Block, and was built from a design of his own, having special reference to the comfort and pleasure of his patients. His abilities as a Dentist are fully attested by his large and continually increasing practice He possesses all the modern facilities for doing good work, and we have no hesitation in commending him to the favor of those of our readers who may be so unfortunate as to require the services of one of the Dental profession Dr S is a member of the Sixth District Dental Society, as also of the New York State and National Dental Associations.

**Pratt & Comstock,** successors to W G Singhi, Photographers and dealers in Stereoscopes, Views, Pictures, Albums, Frames &c , Waverly, N. Y., advertise on page 415 Messrs P & C are prepared to take all kinds of Pictures known to the art, in the most approved style, and finish them up in oil, water colors, or India ink, if desired. It should be a matter of duty with every one to "secure the shadow ere the substance flies," and we know of none more competent to aid them in so doing than Messrs. Pratt & Comstock They also keep a fine assortment of Albums, Frames, Card Pictures, Stereoscopes &c , which it is worth while to call and examine.

**Albert R. Vail,** Deposit, N Y , keeps a general assortment of Dry Goods, Carpets &c , which he is prepared to dispose of in styles and quantities to suit customers His goods can be had at as low figures as at any other store. Give Mr Vail a call when in town. Card on page 20

**Royal & Rennie,** of Binghamton, dealers in Hardware, Stoves and House Furnishing Goods, publish an illustrated card on page 204 This firm are successors to Geo. M Harris, and they are determined by fair and liberal dealing to merit a continuance of the patronage so long bestowed upon their predecessor. They buy their goods in the best markets and will give patrons good bargains. Don't forget them when you want Hardware &c

**John R. Murray,** General Insurance Agent, over Corner Drug Store, Waverly, N. Y., advertises on page 16 He represents some of the best companies in existence, and will attend to Insurance of all kinds on as favorable terms as is consistent with safety. We can cheerfully recommend this Agency and the Companies it represents, to farmers and others desiring Insurance, for the prompt manner in which all losses are adjusted and paid.

# THE STATES,

THEIR SETTLEMENT, ADMITTANCE TO THE UNION, POPULATION,

SUFFRAGE LAWS, ETC.

---

*ALABAMA* was settled near Mobile, in 1702, by the French; was formed into a Territory by act of Congress, approved March 3, 1817, from the eastern portion of the Territory of Mississippi; framed a Constitution August 2, 1819, and was admitted into the Union December 14 of the same year. Area 50,722 square miles, or 32,462,080 acres — Population in 1860, 964,201, of whom 435,080 were slaves. Population in 1870 was 996,175 It is the chief cotton growing State of the Union. Male citizens who have resided one year in the State and three months in the county, are entitled to vote. An election for a Convention was held December 24, 1860, and a majority of over 50,000 votes cast for secession; the Convention met January 7, 1861, and on the 11th passed the ordinance of secession, by a vote of 61 to 39, which was followed on the 21st by the resignation of its members of Congress.

*ARKANSAS* was settled at Arkansas Post in 1685, by the French, and was part of the Louisiana purchase ceded by France to the United States, April 30, 1803. It was formed into a Territory by act of Congress, March 2, 1819, from the southern part of the Territory of Missouri; its western boundary was settled May 26, 1824, and its southern, May 19, 1828 Having adopted a Constitution, a memorial was presented in Congress, March 1, 1836, and an act for its admission into the Union passed June 15 of the same year Area 52,198 square miles, or 33,406,-720 acres. In 1860 its population was 435,450, of whom 111,115 were slaves. Population in 1870 was 473,174. It is an agricultural State, its staples being corn and cotton. Citizenship and residence in the State for six months, qualify voters in the county and district where they reside — January 16, 1861, its Legislature ordered a State Convention, which assembled, and on May 6, voted to secede, 69 to 1 January 4, 1804, a Convention assembled in Little Rock, which adopted a new Constitution, the principle feature of which consisted in a clause abolishing slavery. The Convention adjourned January 22. This body also inaugurated a Provisional Government. The Constitution was submitted to the people, and 12,177 votes cast for it, to 226 against it. The State was reorganized under the plan contained in the Amnesty Proclamation of President LINCOLN, in pursuance of which an election was held March 14, 1864 The vote required under the Proclamation was 5,405. About 16,000 votes were cast.

**B**

*CALIFORNIA* was settled at Diego in 1768, by Spaniards, and was part of the territory ceded to the United States by Mexico, by the treaty concluded at Guadaloupe Hidalgo, February 22, 1848 After several ineffectual attempts to organize it as a Territory or admit it as a State, a law was passed by Congress for the latter purpose, which was approved September 9, 1850 Area 188,981 square miles, or 120,947,784 acres. Population in 1870, 549,808 It is the most productive gold mining region on the continent, and also abounds in many other minerals. Male citizens of the United States, and those of Mexico who may choose to comply with the provisions of the treaty of Queretaro, of May 30, 1848, who have resided in the State six months and in the county or district thirty days, are entitled to vote.

*CONNECTICUT* was settled at Windsor, in 1633, by English Puritans from Massachusetts, and continued under the jurisdiction of that Province until April 23, 1662, when a separate charter was granted, which continued in force until a Constitution was formed, September 15, 1818 It was one of the original thirteen States, and ratified the United States Constitution, January 9, 1788. Area 4,674 square miles, or 2,991,360 acres. Population in 1870, 537,417, It is one of the most densely populated and principal manufacturing States in the Union Residence for six months, or military duty for a year, or payment of State tax, or a freehold of the yearly value of seven dollars, gives the right to vote.

*DELAWARE* was settled at Wilmington, early in 1638, by Swedes and Finns; was granted to William Penn, in 1682, and continued under the government of Pennsylvania until the adoption of a Constitution, September 20, 1776, a new one was formed June 12, 1792. It was one of the original thirteen States, and ratified the United States Constitution, December 7, 1787. Area 2,120 square miles, or 1,356,800 acres — Population, in 1860, 112,216, of whom 1,798 were slaves. Population in 1870 was 125,015. It is a grain and fruit growing State, with some extensive manufactories. Residence in the State one year, and ten days in the election district, with payment of a State or county tax assessed ten days prior to an election, gives the right to vote, except that citizens between twenty-one and twenty-two years of age need not have paid the tax.

*FLORIDA* was settled at St. Augustine, in 1565, by Spaniards; was formed from part of the territory ceded by Spain to the United States by treaty of February 22, 1819; an act to authorize the President to establish a temporary government was passed March 3, 1819, articles of surrender of East Florida were framed July 10, and of West Florida, July 17, 1821, and it was then taken possession of by General Jackson as Governor. An act for the establishment of a Territorial Government was passed March 30, 1822, and by act of March 3, 1823, East and West Florida were constituted one Territory. Acts to establish its boundary line between Georgia and Alabama were passed May 4, 1826, and March 2, 1831. After several ineffectual attempts to organize it into two Territories, or into a State and Territory, an act for its admission into the Union was passed March 3, 1845. Area 59,268 square miles, or 37,930,520 acres. Population, in 1860, 140,425, of whom 61,745 were slaves. Population in 1870 was 189,995. It is an agricultural State, tropical in its climate and products. Every male citizen, who has resided in the State two years and in the county six months, and has been enrolled in the militia (unless exempt by law,) is qualified to vote; but no soldier, seaman or marine can vote unless qualified before enlistment. Its Legislature called a Convention, December 1, 1860, which met January 3, 1861, and passed a secession ordinance on the 10th by a vote of 62 to 7.

*GEORGIA* was settled at Savannah, in 1733, by the English under General Oglethorpe. It was chartered June 9, 1732; formed a Constitution February 5, 1777, a second in 1785 and a third May 30, 1798.— It was one of the original thirteen States, and ratified the United States Constitution January 2, 1788. Area 58,000 square miles, or 37,120,000 acres. Population, in 1860, 1,057,286, of whom 462,198 were slaves. Population in 1870 was 1,174,832. It is a large cotton and rice growing State. Citizens of the State, six months resident of the county where voting, who have paid taxes the year preceding the election, are entitled to vote November 18, 1860, its Legislature ordered an election for a State Convention, which assembled and passed a secession ordinance January 19, 1861, by a vote of 208 to 89, and on the 23d of the same month its members of Congress resigned.

*ILLINOIS* was settled at Kaskaskia, in 1683, by the French, and formed part of the northwestern territory ceded by Virginia to the United States. An act for dividing the Indiana Territory and organizing the Territory of Illinois, was passed by Congress, February 3, 1809; and an act to enable it to form a State Constitution, Government, &c., was passed April 18, 1818; a Constitution was framed August 26, and it was admitted into the Union December 23 of the same year. Area 54,405 square miles, or 64,819,200 acres. Population, in 1870, 2,529,410. It is the chief "prairie" State, and the largest grain growing and second largest cattle raising State in the Union. All male inhabitants, who have resided in the State one year and election district sixty days, can vote in the district where actually residing.

*INDIANA* was settled at Vincennes, in 1690, by the French, and formed part of the northwestern territory ceded by Virginia to the United States. It was organized into a Territory May 7, 1800, from which the Territory of Michigan was set off in 1805, and Illinois in 1809 An act was passed to empower it to form a State Constitution, Government, &c., April 19, 1816, and it was admitted into the Union December 11 of the same year. Area 33,809 square miles, or 21,637,760 acres Population, in 1870, 1,655,675. It is an agricultural State, chiefly devoted to grain growing and cattle raising. A residence of one year in the State entitles males of 21 years of age to vote in the county of their residence.

*IOWA* was first settled at Burlington by emigrants from the Northern and Eastern States It was part of the region purchased from France; was set off from the Territory of Wisconsin and organized as a separate Territory June 12, 1838; an act for its admission as a State was passed and approved March 3, 1845, to which the assent of its inhabitants was to be given to be announced by Proclamation of the President, and on December 28, 1846, another act for its admission was passed. Area 50,914 square miles or 32,584,960 acres. Population, in 1870, 1,181,359. It is an agricultural State, resembling Illinois, and contains important lead mines Male citizens of the United States, having resided in the State six months and county twenty days, are entitled to vote

*KANSAS* was formed out of the original Louisiana purchase, and organized into a Territory by act of Congress, May 30, 1854, and after several ineffectual attempts was finally admitted into the Union in January, 1861. Area 78,418 square miles, or 50,187,520 acres. Population, in 1870, 379,-497. It is an agricultural State, with a soil of rich and deep black loam, except the central portion, which is partly a desert. The western portion is a fine grazing country, well wooded. Residence in the State six months, and in the township or ward thirty days, confers the right of suffrage on male citizens. It also abounds in minerals.

*KENTUCKY* was settled in 1775, by Virginians; formed into a Territory by act of the Virginia Legislature, December 18, 1789, and admitted into the Union June 1, 1792, by virtue of an act of Congress passed February 4, 1791. Area 37,680 square miles, or 24,115,200 acres.— Population in 1860, 1,155,684, of whom 225,483 were slaves. Population in 1870 was 1,320,407. It is an agricultural State, raising more flax and hemp than any other Loyalty, a residence of two years in the State and one in the county are the requirements to vote.

*LOUISIANA* was settled at Iberville, in 1699, by the French, and comprised a part of the territory ceded by France to the United States, by treaty of April 30, 1803, which purchase was erected into two Territories by act of Congress March 26, 1804, one called the Territory of Orleans, the other the District of Louisiana, afterwards changed to that of Missouri — Congress, March 2, 1806, authorized the inhabitants of Orleans Territory to form a State Constitution and Government when their population should amount to 60,000, a Constitution was adopted January 22, 1812, and the State admitted into the Union April 8 of the same year, under the name of Louisiana. Area 41,255 square miles, or 26,403,200 acres. Population in 1860, 708,002, of whom 331,726 were slaves. Population in 1870 was 734,420. It is the chief sugar producing State of the Union. Two years' residence in the State and one in the parish are the qualifications of voters. December 10, 1860, the Legislature ordered a State Convention to be held, which assembled and passed an ordinance of secession January 26, 1861, by a vote of 113 to 17. The people voted on the question, and on March 28 the following was announced as the result: For, 20,448, against, 17,296; a majority of 3,152. The Convention ratified the 'Confederate' Constitution March 11, 1861, by a vote of 107 to 7, and refused to submit it to the people by 94 to 10. On the 11th day of January, 1864, Maj. Gen Banks issued a Proclamation for an election of State officers and delegates to a Constitutional Convention, for the purpose of affecting a reconstruction of the State Government under the plan suggested in the Amnesty Proclamation of President Lincoln. The election was held on the 22d day of February, 1864. The officers thus elected were installed March 4. The total vote cast was 10,725. The vote requisite under the Proclamation, was 5,051. The Convention amended the Constitution so as to abolish slavery. The new Constitution was adopted by the people by a vote of 6,836 for, to 1,566 against.

*MAINE* was settled at York, in 1623, by the English, and was formerly under the jurisdiction of Massachusetts. October 29, 1819, the inhabitants of the District of Maine framed a Constitution; applied for admission December 8, 1819. Congress passed an act March 3, 1820, and it was admitted as a State March 15, of the same year. Area 31,766 square miles, or 20,330,240 acres. Population, in 1870, 628,719. It is largely engaged in the lumber trade and ship building. Citizens of the United

States, except paupers and persons under guardianship, who have resided in the State for three months next preceding the election, are entitled to vote.

*MARYLAND* was settled at St Mary, in 1634, by Irish Roman Catholics, having been chartered June 20, 1632  It was one of the original thirteen States ; formed a Constitution August 14, 1776, and ratified the Constitution of the United States April 28, 1788.  Area 11,124 square miles, or 7,119,260 acres.  Population in 1860, 687,049, of whom 87,189 were slaves.  Population in 1870 was 790,095.  It is mainly an agricultural State, producing grain and tobacco.  A residence of one year in the State, and six months in the county, gives the right to vote to every male citizen who takes the oath of allegiance prescribed in the Constitution.  January 28, 1864, a bill passed the Legislature submitting to the people the question of a Convention to revise the Constitution of the State  The popular vote on the question was as follows : For Convention, 32,203 ; against, 18,337.  The Convention assembled and adopted a Constitution abolishing slavery, which was submitted to and adopted by the people ; and in accordance with its provisions, on the 29th of October, 1864, the Governor issued his Proclamation declaring the slaves in that State free from the 1st day of November.

*MASSACHUSETTS* was settled at Plymouth, November 3, 1620, by English Puritans, and Charters were granted March 4, 1629, January 13, 1630, August 20, 1726, and October 7, 1731.  It was one of the original 13 States ; adopted a Constitution March 2, 1780, which was amended November 3, 1820, and ratified the Constitution of the United States February 6, 1788  Area 7,800 square miles, or 4,992,000 acres  Population in 1870, 1,457,351.  It is a largely commercial, the chief manufacturing and most densely populated State in the Union.  A residence of one year in the State, and payment of State or county tax, gives the right to vote to male citizens of 21 years and upward, except paupers and persons under guardianship.

*MICHIGAN* was settled at Detroit in 1670, by the French, and was part of the territory ceded to the United States by Virginia.  It was set off from the territory of Indiana, and erected into a separate Territory January 11, 1805 ; an act to attach to it all the territory of the United States west of the Mississippi river, and north of the State of Missouri, was passed June 28, 1834.  Wisconsin was organized from it April 30, 1836  In June of the same year an act was passed to provide for the admission of the State of Michigan into the Union, and a Constitution having been adopted, it was admitted January 26, 1837  Area 56,243 square miles, or 35,995,552 acres.  Population in 1870, 1,184,653  It is a grain growing and cattle rearing State, with rich and extensive mines of copper and iron in the Northern Peninsula.  In the vicinity of Saginaw, salt is extensively manufactured.  A residence in the State of six months preceding the election, entitles male citizens to vote.

*MINNESOTA* was settled about 1846, chiefly by emigrants from the Northern and Western States.  It was organized as a Territory by act of Congress approved March 3, 1849, and admitted into the Union February 26, 1857.  Area 95,274 square miles, or 60,975,536 acres  Population in 1870, 424,543 whites.  It is an agricultural State, chiefly devoted to Northern grains  The right to vote is extended to male persons of 21 years of age, of the following classes, if they have resided in the United States one year, the State four months, and the election district ten days : citizens of the United States, and those of foreign birth who have declared their intention to become citizens ; persons of mixed white and Indian blood who have adopted the customs of civilization, and those of pure Indian blood who have been pronounced capable by any district court of the State

*MISSISSIPPI* was settled at Natchez, in 1716, by the French, and was formed out of part of the territory ceded to the United States by South Carolina in 1787, and Georgia in 1802. It was organized as a Territory by act of Congress, April 7, 1789, and enlarged on the north March 27, 1804, and on the south May 14, 1812 After several unsuccessful attempts to enter the Union, Congress finally passed an act March 1, 1817, enabling the people of the western part of the Territory to form a State Constitution and Government, which being complied with August 15, it was admitted December 10 of the same year Area 47,156 square miles, or 30,179,840 acres Population in 1860, 791,305, of whom 436,631 were slaves. Population in 1870 was 842,056. It is the second cotton growing State of the Union Citizens who have resided one year in the State, and four months in the county, and having performed military duty or paid taxes, are entitled to vote. A Convention met January 7, 1861, and on the 9th passed an ordinance of secession by a vote of 84 to 15

*MISSOURI* was settled at Genevieve in 1763, by the French, and was part of the territory ceded by France by treaty of April 30, 1803. It was created under the name of the District of Louisiana, by an act approved March 26, 1804, and placed under the direction of the officers of the Indiana Territory, and was organized into a separate Territory June 4, 1812, its name being changed to that of Missouri; and was divided March 2, 1819, the Territory of Arkansas being then created An act authorizing it to form a State Constitution and Government was passed March 6, 1820, and it was admitted into the Union December 14, 1821. Area 67,380 square miles, or 43,123,200 acres Population in 1860, 1,182,012, of whom 114,931 were slaves. Population in 1870 was 1,691,-693 An act of gradual emancipation was passed July 1, 1863, by a vote of 51 to 30 On the 6th of January, 1865, a Constitutional Convention assembled in St Louis, and on the 8th of April adopted a new Constitution, declaring the State free, prohibiting compensation for slaves, and adopting many other radical changes On the 6th of June the Constitution was adopted by the people by a vote of 43,670 to 41,808, and pursuant to a Proclamation issued on the 1st of July, the Constitution went into effect July 4, 1865 It is an agricultural and mining State. Citizens of the United States who have resided in the State one year, and county three months, are entitled to vote. By an act passed by the Legislature of 1863, voting by ballot was adopted, and the *viva voce* system abolished.

*NEBRASKA* was settled by emigrants from the Northern and Western States, and was formed out of a part of the territory ceded by France, April 30, 1803 Attempts to organize it were made in 1844 and 1848, but it was not accomplished until May 30, 1854. Area 75,955 square miles, or 44,796,160 acres. Population in 1870 116,888, besides a few roving tribes of Indians A Convention adopted a State Constitution Feb 9, 1866, which was submitted to the people on the 22d of June, and adopted by a vote of 3,938 for, to 3,838 against, and State officers were elected. A bill was passed by Congress, July 27th, admitting the State, but the President withheld his signature. In Feb. 1867, Congress passed an act imposing certain conditions to admission, which were promptly accepted, and the territory became a State. It is an agricultural region, its prairies affording boundless pasture lands.

*NEVADA* was organized as a Territory March 2, 1861. Its name signifies snowy, and is derived from the Spanish word *nieve* (snow.) It comprises 81,539 square miles, or 52,184,960 acres, lying mostly within the Great Basin of the Pacific coast. Congress, at its session in 1864, passed an act which was approved March 21, to enable the people of the Territory to form a Constitution and State Government, in pursuance of which a Government was organized and the Territory admitted as a State by Proclamation of the President, October 31, 1864. At the time of its organization the Territory possessed a population of 6,857 white settlers. Population in 1870 was 42,456. The development of her mineral resources was rapid and almost without parallel, and attracted a constant stream of immigration to the Territory. As the population has not been subject to the fluctuations from which other Territories have suffered, the growth of Nevada has been rapid and steady. At the general convention election of 1863, 10,934 votes were cast During 1864 great accessions to the population were made. It is probably the richest State in the Union in respect to mineral resources. No region in the world is richer in argentiferous leads· It also contains an immense basin of salt, five miles square Quartz mills are a very important feature in mining operations. The State is barren for agricultural purposes, and is remarkably healthy.

*NEW HAMPSHIRE* was settled at Dover, in 1623, by English Puritans, and continued under the jurisdiction of Massachusetts until September 18, 1679, when a separate charter was granted. · It was one of the original thirteen States, and ratified the United States Constitution June 21, 1788; its State Constitution was framed January 5, 1776, and amended in 1784 and 1792. Area 9,280 square miles, or 5,939,200 acres. Population in 1860, 326,073; in 1870, 317,710, showing a decrease in ten years of 8,363. It is a grazing and manufacturing State. All male citizens, except paupers, are allowed to vote.

*NEW JERSEY* was settled at Bergen, in 1624, by the Dutch and Danes; was conquered by the Dutch in 1655, and submitted to the English in 1664, being held thereafter under the same grants as New York, until it was surrendered to the Crown in 1702 It was one of the original thirteen States, adopted a State Constitution July 2, 1776, and ratified the United States Constitution December 18, 1787 Area 8,320 square miles, or 5,324,800 acres. Population in 1870, 903,044. It is a grain and fruit growing region, its orchard and market products being relatively greater than those of any other State. A residence of one year in the State gives the right to vote, except to paupers, &c.

*NEW YORK* was settled at Manhattan, in 1614, by the Dutch; was ceded to the English by grants to the Duke of York, March 20, April 26, and June 24, 1664; was retaken by the Dutch in 1673, and surrendered again by them to the English, February 9, 1674. It was one of the original thirteen States; ratified the United States Constitution July 26, 1788; framed a Constitution April 20, 1777, which was amended October 27, 1801, and November 10, 1821; a new one was adopted November 3, 1846. Area 47,000 square miles, or 30,080,000 acres. Population in 1870, 4,370,846. It is the most populous, wealthy and commercial of the States. Male citizens of the United States, who have resided in the State one year, in the county four months, and election district thirty days, are entitled to vote.

*NORTH CAROLINA* was settled at Albemarle, in 1650, by the English, and was chartered March 20, 1663. It was one of the original thirteen States, and ratified the United States Constitution, November 21, 1789; its State Constitution was adopted December 18, 1776, and amended in 1835  Area 50,704 square miles, or 32,450,560 acres. Population in 1860, 992,622, of whom 331,059 were slaves. Population in 1870 was 1,016,954. It is an agricultural State, with some mines and extensive pine forests. Males of 21 years of age, having resided one year in any county in the State, may vote for a member of the House of Commons, but must own fifty acres of land to vote for a Senator. A State Convention passed an ordinance of secession May 21, 1861. An election for delegates to a State Convention took place September 21, 1865  The Convention assembled October 2. On the 2d of October it passed an ordinance forever prohibiting slavery. The Legislature ratified the Constitutional amendment December 1. An election was held on the first Thursday of November, for Governor, Members of Congress and the Legislature.

*OHIO* was settled at Marietta, in 1788, by emigrants from Virginia and New England; was ceded by Virginia to the United States October 20, 1783; accepted by the latter March 1, 1784, and admitted into the Union April 30, 1802. Area 39,964 square miles, or 25,576,960 acres  Population in 1870, 2,652,302. It is the most populous and wealthy of the agricultural States, devoted principally to wool growing, grain and live stock. A male of 21 years of age, who has resided in the State one year, and has paid or been charged with a State or county tax, is eligible to vote.

*OREGON*, although it had previously been seen by various navigators, was first taken possession of by Capt. Robert Gray, who entered the mouth of its principal river May 7, 1792, naming it after his vessel, the Columbia, of Boston  Exploring expeditions soon followed, and fur companies sent their trappers and traders into the region. In 1811 a trading post was established at the mouth of the Columbia river by the American Fur Company, who named it Astoria. For some time a Provisional Territorial Government existed, but the boundary remained unsettled until the treaty with Great Britain in 1846, when the 49th parallel was adopted. It was formally organized as a Territory August 14, 1848; was divided March 2, 1853, on the 46th parallel, the northern portion being called Washington and the southern Oregon. November 9, 1857, a State Constitution was adopted, under which it was admitted February 14, 1859, about one-third of it on the east being added to Washington Territory, its northern boundary following the Columbia river until its intersection with latitude 46° north  Area 102,606 square miles, or 65,667,840 acres. Population in 1870, 90,878. It is an agricultural State, possessed of a fertile soil, extensive pastures, genial climate, and is well wooded. Gold and other precious metals are found in considerable abundance.

*PENNSYLVANIA* was settled at Philadelphia, in 1681, by English Quakers, and was chartered February 28 of the same year. It was one of the original thirteen States, ratifying the United States Constitution December 12, 1787; adopted a State Constitution September 28, 1776, and amended it September 2, 1790. Area 46,000 square miles, or 29,440,000 acres. Population in 1870, 3,511,543. It is the second State in wealth and population, and the principal coal and iron mining region in the

Union. Residence in the State one year, and ten days in the election district, with payment of a State or county tax assessed ten days prior to an election, gives the right to vote, except that citizens between 21 and 22 years of age need not have paid the tax.

*RHODE ISLAND* was settled at Providence in 1636, by the English from Massachusetts, under Roger Williams. It was under the jurisdiction of Massachusetts until July 8, 1662, when a separate charter was granted, which continued in force until the formation of a Constitution in September, 1842. It was one of the original thirteen States, ratifying the United States Constitution May 29, 1790. Area 1,306 square miles, or 835,840 acres. Population in 1870, 217,356. It is largely engaged in manufactures. A freehold possession of $13; or, if in reversion, renting for $7, together with a residence of one year in the State and six months in the town; or, if no freehold, then a residence of two years in the State and six months in the town, and payment of $1 tax or military service instead, are the qualifications of voters.

*SOUTH CAROLINA* was settled at Port Royal, in 1670, by the English, and continued under the charter of Carolina, or North Carolina, until they were separated in 1729. It was one of the original thirteen States, ratifying the United States Constitution May 23, 1798; it framed a State Constitution March 26, 1776, which was amended March 19, 1778, and June 3, 1790. Area 29,385 square miles, or 18,806,400 acres. Population in 1860, 703,708, of whom 402,406 were slaves, an excess of 101,270 over the whites. Population in 1870, 705,789. It is the principal rice-growing State. Males residing in the State two years and district six months, and having a freehold of fifty acres of land, or have paid a State tax, are entitled to vote. December 17, 1860, a Convention assembled in Columbia, adjourned to Charleston, and on the 24th unanimously adopted an ordinance of secession, which was followed the next day by a Declaration of Causes claimed to be sufficient to justify the act. An election for delegates to a State Convention was held September 4, 1865. The Convention assembled September 13, and adjourned on the 28th. It repealed the ordinance of secession, abolished slavery, equalized the representation of the Senate and taxation throughout the State, giving the election of Governor and Presidential electors to the people, ordered voting in the Legislature by *viva voce*, endorsed the Administration unanimously, and directed a commission to submit a code to the Legislature for the protection of the colored population. The Legislature ratified the Constitutional Amendment November 13, 1865.

*TENNESSEE* was settled at Fort Donelson, in 1756, by emigrants from Virginia and North Carolina; was ceded to the United States by North Carolina, December, 1789, conveyed by the Senators of that State February 25, 1790, and accepted by act of Congress April 2 of the same year, it adopted a Constitution Feb. 6, 1796, and was admitted into the Union the 1st of June following. Area 45,600 square miles, or 29,184,000 acres. Population in 1860, 1,109,601, of whom 275,179 were slaves. Population in 1870 was 1,225,937. It is a mining and agricultural State, and is largely productive of live stock. Citizens of the United States who have resided six months in the county are entitled to vote. A military league was formed between the Governor, Isham G. Harris, and the rebel States, May 7, 1861, ratified the same day by the Senate by a vote of 14 to 6, and a Declaration of Independence submitted to the people, the election to be held June 8, the result of which was declared by the Governor, June 24, to be 104,913 for, and 47,238 against. This movement not being acceptable to the people of East Tennessee, which had declared against separation by a vote of 32,923 to 14,780, they, in a Convention held at Greenville, June 18–21, repudiated it. Andrew Johnson, Provisional Governor of the State, called a State Convention to be held in Nashville the second Monday in January. Delegates were elected, the Convention met, declared slavery forever abolished, prohibited compensation to owners of slaves, and abrogated the secession ordinances. These amendments of the Constitution were submitted to the people 22d of February, 1865, with the following result: For ratification, 22,197; rejection, 63. The United States Constitutional Amendment was ratified April 5, 1865.

*TEXAS* was first settled at Bexar, in 1694, by Spaniards, formed a part of Mexico until 1836, when she revolted from that Republic and instituted a separate Government, under which she existed until admitted into the Union by a joint resolution approved March 1st, 1845, imposing certain conditions, which were accepted, and a Constitution formed July 4 of the same year, and another joint resolution adopted by Congress, consummating the annexation, was approved December 29, 1845. Area 237,504 square miles, or 152,002,500 acres Population in 1860, 604,215, of whom 182,566 were slaves. Population in 1870 was 795,500. It is an agricultural region, principally devoted to grain, cotton and tropical fruits Male citizens of 21 years of age, who have resided in the State one year and district six months are entitled to vote. A Convention assembled at Galveston January 28, 1861, and on February 1 passed an ordinance of secession, by a vote of 166 to 7, to be submitted to the people February 23, and on March 4 they declared the State out of the Union, and Gov. Houston issued a Proclamation to that effect.

*VERMONT* was settled in 1724, by Englishmen from Connecticut, chiefly under grants from New Hampshire; was formed from a part of the territory of New York, by act of its Legislature March 6, 1769; framed a Constitution December 25, 1777, and was admitted into the Union March 4, 1791, by virtue of an act of Congress passed February 18 of the same year. Area 10,212 square miles, or 6,535,680 acres. Population in 1870, 330,582. It is a grazing region, producing more wool, live stock, maple sugar, butter, cheese and hay, in proportion to its population, than any other State Any citizen of the United States who has resided in the State one year, and will take the oath of allegiance, is entitled to vote.

*VIRGINIA* was settled at Jamestown, in 1607 by the English, and was chartered April 10, 1606, May 23, 1609, and March 12, 1612. It was one of the original thirteen States, ratifying the United States Constitution June 26, 1788; it framed a State Constitution July 5, 1776, which was amended January 15, 1830. The State was divided in 1863. Present area 37,352 square miles Population in 1860, 1,314,532, of whom 481,-410 were slaves Population in 1870 1,211,442 It is a large corn producing, and the chief tobacco growing State. Every male citizen of the age of 21 years, who has been a resident of the State for one year, and of the county, city or town where he offers to vote for six months next preceding an election, and has paid all taxes assessed to him, after the adoption of the Constitution, under the laws of the Commonwealth, after the re-organization of the county, city or town where he offers to vote, is qualified to vote for members of the General Assembly and all officers elective by the people. A Convention sitting in Richmond on the 17th of April, 1861, passed an ordinance of secession, by a vote of 88 to 55, which was submitted to the people at an election held May 23, the result of which was announced June 25 to be 128,824 for, and 32,134 against.

The State Government was re-organized by a Convention which met at Wheeling, May 11, 1861. Upon the division of the State in 1863, the seat of Government was removed to Alexandria. A State Constitutional Convention, March 10, 1864, adopted a section abolishing slavery.

*WEST VIRGINIA.*—On the passage of the ordinance of secession by the Virginia Convention, a Convention of the western and other loyal counties of the State was held at Wheeling, which assembled May 11, 1861, and on the 17th unanimously deposed the then State officers and organized a Provisional Government. On the 26th of November, 1861, a Convention representing the western counties assembled in Wheeling and framed a Constitution for West Virginia, which was submitted to the people on the 3d of May, 1862, and adopted by them by a nearly unanimous vote. The division of the State was sanctioned by the Legislature May 13, 1862, and ratified by Congress by an act approved December 31, 1862, conditioned on the adoption of an amendment to the Constitution providing for the gradual abolition of slavery, which was done on the 24th of March, 1863, by a vote of the qualified electors of the proposed State, 28,318 voting in favor of the amendment, and 572 against it.. In pursuance of the act of Congress, the President issued a Proclamation, April 20, 1863, admitting the State sixty days from the date thereof, and on the 20th of June the new State Government was formally inaugurated Area 24,000 square miles. Population in 1860, 350,599, of whom 12,754 were slaves. Population in 1870 was 441,094. It is a large corn producing State, and abounds in coal and other minerals. The Alexandria Legislature adopted the United States Constitutional Amendment February 9, 1865 Male citizens, residents of the State one year and county thirty days, unless disqualified by rebellion, are entitled to vote.

*WISCONSIN* was settled at Green Bay, in 1669, by the French; was a part of the territory ceded by Virginia, and was set off from Michigan December 24, 1834, and was organized into a Territory April 30, 1836. Iowa was set off from it June 12, 1838, and acts were passed at various times setting its boundaries. March 3, 1847, an act for its admission into the Union was passed, to take effect on the issuing of a Proclamation by the President, and by act of May 29, 1848, it was admitted into the Union. Area 53,924 square miles, or 34,511,360 acres. Population in 1870, 1,055,501. It is an agricultural State, chiefly engaged in grain raising and wool growing. Citizens of the United States, or foreigners who have declared their intention to become citizens, are entitled to vote. Colored citizens were admitted to the franchise, by a decision of the Supreme Court, rendered the 27th day of March, 1866, holding that, whereas an election was held in 1849, under the provisions of chapter 137, of that year, at which election 5,265 votes were cast in favor of the extension of the right of suffrage to colored men, and 4,075 against such extension, therefore, the section of said law conferring such right had been constitutionally adopted and is the law of the land.

# THE TERRITORIES,

### THEIR BOUNDARIES, AREA, PHYSICAL FEATURES, ETC

*ALASKA,* our new territory, recently purchased of Russia, comprehends all the north-west coast on the Pacific, and the adjacent islands north of the parallel of 50 degrees 40 minutes north, and the portion of the mainland west of the meridian (about 140° west) of Mount St. Elias   The area is computed at 481,276 square miles   The climate, although warmer than in the same latitude on the eastern coast, is too rigorous to admit of successful agricultural operations, and the chief value of the country and adjacent seas is derived from their fisheries and hunting grounds   The southern and central portions are mountainous; the northern portion along the Arctic ocean is quite flat, nowhere rising more than fifteen or twenty feet above the sea   The population is estimated at about 80,000, mostly Esquimeaux.

*ARIZONA* was organized by the Thirty-Seventh Congress, in the winter of 1863, out of the western half of New Mexico, the boundary between the two Territories being the 109th meridian (32d west from Washington,) and includes the greater portions of the valleys of Colorado and Gila, which two rivers drain its entire surface, with parts of Utah, New Mexico and Nevada, and yet convey, it is reported, a less volume of water to the sea than the Hudson at Albany.   The fertile Messilla Valley was left with New Mexico.   The Territory forms a block nearly square, and contains 126,141 square miles, or 80,730,240 acres.   Its white population in 1870 was 9,658   For agricultural purposes it is probably the most worthless on the Continent, owing to the absence of rains, but it is reputed to abound in silver mines.

*COLORADO* was organized March 2, 1861, from parts of Kansas, Nebraska and Utah, and is situated on each side of the Rocky Mountains, between latitude 37° and 41°, and longitude 25° and 32° west from Washington.   Area 104,500 square miles, or 66,880,000 acres.   Population in 1870 was 39,706, besides numerous tribes of Indians.   By an enabling act passed March 21, 1864, the people of the Territory were authorized to frame a State Constitution and organize a State Government, and a Convention accordingly met in 1865, and on the 12th of August adopted a Constitution, which was submitted to and adopted by the people September 5, and State officers elected November 14   A bill to admit the Territory as a State passed Congress, but was vetoed May 25, 1866.   It is said to be a superior grazing and cattle producing region, with a healthy climate and rich soil.   An extensive coal bed, and also gold, iron and other minerals abound.

*COLUMBIA.*—Originally the "*District of Columbia*" was ceded to the United States by Maryland and Virginia, in 1790, and became the seat of the National Government in 1800.   It was originally ten miles square, lying on both sides of the Potomac, thirty-six square miles having been taken from Virginia, and sixty-four square miles from Maryland.   By an act of Congress in 1846, that portion taken from Virginia was retroceded to that State. The 41st Congress, 1870–71, erected the District into a Territory. Until this year the District was governed directly by the Congress of the United States, and its inhabitants had no representation and no voice in the Federal elections. The cities of the Territory are Washington and Georgetown. Population in 1870 was 131,706.

*DAKOTA* was first settled by employees of the Hudson Bay Company, but is now being peopled by emigrants from the Northern and Western States. It was set off from the western portion of Minnesota when that Territory became a State in 1857, and was organized March 2, 1861. Area 148,932 square miles, or 95,316,480 acres. Population in 1870 was 14,181 whites, besides the roving tribes of Indians.

*IDAHO* was organized by the Thirty-Seventh Congress, at its second session, in the winter of 1863. Its name means 'Bead of the Mountains,' and it embraces the whole breadth of the Rocky Mountain region, and has within its bounds the head waters of nearly all the great rivers that flow down its either slope, but the greater portion lies east of the mountains. Its southern boundary is the 41st, its northern the 46th parallel of latitude. It extends from the 104th meridian on the east to the 110th on the west. Area 326,373 square miles, or 208,870,720 acres. Population in 1870, 14,998 besides the Indians. For agricultural purposes it is comparatively worthless, but abounds in gold and other valuable mines.

*MONTANA* was settled by emigrants from the Northern and Western States. Organized in 1864, with the following boundaries. Commencing at a point formed by the intersection of the 27° L. W from Washington with the 45° N L; thence due west on said 45th degree to a point formed by its intersection with the 34th degree W from Washington, thence due south along said 34th degree of longitude to its intersection with the 44th degree and 30 minutes of N. L.; thence due west along said 44th degree and 30 minutes of N. L. to a point formed by its intersection with the crest of the Rocky Mountains; thence following the crest of the Rocky Mountains northward till its intersection with the Bitter Root Mountains; thence northward along the crest of said Bitter Root Mountains to its intersection with the 39th degree of longitude W. from Washington; thence along said 39th degree of longitude northward to the boundary line of the British possessions, thence eastward along said boundary to the 27th degree of longitude W from Washington, thence southward along said 27th degree to the place of beginning. This makes it the northermost Territory next the States east of the Missouri Valley. It is a good mining and agricultural region. The population in 1870 was 20,594.

*NEW MEXICO* was formed from a part of the territory ceded to the United States by Mexico, by the treaty of Guadaloupe Hidalgo, February 2, 1848, and was organized into a Territory September 9, 1850 — Area 121,201 square miles, or 77,568,640 acres. Population in 1870 was 91,789, besides large tribes of warlike Indians. The principal resource of the country is its minerals.

*UTAH* was settled by the Mormons, and was formed from a part of the territory ceded to the United States by Mexico, by the treaty of Guadaloupe Hidalgo, February 2, 1848, and was organized into a Territory, September 9, 1850. Area, 106,382 square miles, or 68,084,480 acres. Population in 1870 was 86,786. Brine, sulphureous and chalybeate springs abound; limestone, granite, sandstone and marble are found in large quantities, iron is abundant, and gold, silver, copper, lead and zinc have been found  Not one-fiftieth part of the soil is fit for tillage, but on that which is, abundant crops of grain and considerable cotton are raised. A Convention was held at Great Salt Lake City, January 22, 1862, and a State Constitution formed, but it has not been acted on by Congress.

*WASHINGTON* was settled by emigrants from the Northern and Western States, and was organized into a Territory, March 2, 1853, from the northern portion of Oregon, to which was added another portion from the eastern part when the latter Territory was admitted as a State, February 14, 1859  Area 69,994 square miles, or 48,636,800 acres.  Population in 1870 was 23,901 besides numerous tribes of Indians.

*WYOMING* was organized in July 1868.  It lies between the 27th and 34th meridians of longitude west from Washington, and between the 41st and 45th parallels of latitude  The Territory is rich in mineral wealth, having large quantities of iron, coal, gypsum and building stone, besides vast quantities of gold, silver and copper  Salt springs of great value are found within its limits.  The western portion of the Territory embraces what is generally known as the "Sweet Water Mines."  The climate is healthy, and the Territory is rapidly filling up with an enterprising and hardy population.  The act of Congress organizing the Territory, provides that "There shall be no denial of the elective franchise or any other right, on account of color or race, and all persons shall be equal before the law." Population in 1870 was 9,118

# STAMP DUTIES.

*Schedule of Duties on and after March 1, 1867, with amendments to take effect Oct 1, 1870.*
*(See Note, at end of Schedule )*

**Stamp Duty**

Accidental injuries to persons, tickets, or contracts for insurance against, — exempt

Affidavits, — exempt.

Agreement or contract not otherwise specified ·

For every sheet or piece of paper upon which either of the same shall be written, — $0 5

Agreement, renewal of, same stamp as original instrument

Appraisement of value or damage, or for any other purpose : For each sheet of paper on which it is written, — 5

Assignment of a lease, same stamp as original, and additional stamp upon the value or consideration of transfer, according to the rates of stamps on deeds. (See Conveyance.)

Assignment of policy of insurance, same stamp as original instrument. (See Insurance.)

Assignment of mortgage, — exempt

Bank check, draft or order for any sum of money drawn upon any bank, banker or trust compa-

**Stamp Duty.**

ny at sight or on demand, — 2

When drawn upon any other person or persons, companies or corporations, for any sum exceeding $10, at sight or on demand, — 2

Bill of exchange, (inland,) draft or order for the payment of any sum of money not exceeding $100, otherwise than at sight or on demand, or any memorandum, check, receipt, or other written or printed evidence of an amount of money to be paid on demand or at a time designated · For a sum not exceeding $100, — 5

And for every additional $100 or fractional part thereof in excess of $100,

Bill of exchange, (foreign,) or letter of credit drawn in, but payable out of, the United States : If drawn singly, same rates of duty as inland bills of exchange or promissory notes.

If drawn in sets of three or more, for every bill of each set, where

Stamp Duty.

the sum made payable shall not
exceed $100 or the equivalent
thereof in any foreign currency   2
And for every additional $100, or
fractional part thereof in excess
of $100,   2
Bill of lading or receipt (other than
charter party) for any goods,
merchandise, or effects to be
exported from a port or place
in the United States to any foreign port or place,   10
Bill of lading to any port in British North America,   exempt.
Bill of lading, domestic or inland,   exempt.
Bill of sale by which any ship or
vessel, or any part thereof, shall
be conveyed to or vested in any
other person or persons :
When the consideration shall not
exceed $500,   50
Exceeding $500, and not exceed-
ing $1,000,   1 00
Exceeding $1,000, for every ad-
ditional $500, or fractional part
thereof,   50
Bond for indemnifying any person
for the payment of any sum of
money : When the money ultimately recoverable thereupon
is $1,000 or less,   50
When in excess of $1,000, for
each $1,000 or fraction,   50
Bond-administrator or guardian,
when the value of the estate
and effects, real and personal,
does not exceed $1,000,   exempt.
Exceeding $1,000,   1 00
Bond for due execution or per-
formance of duties of office,   1 00
Bond, personal, for security for
the payment of money. (See
Mortgage.)
Bond of any description, other than
such as may be required in legal proceedings, or used in connection with mortgage deeds,
and not otherwise charged in
this schedule,   25
Broker's notes. (See Contract.)
Certificates of measurement or
weight of animals, wood, coal
or hay,   exempt
Certificates of measurement of other articles,   5
Certificates of stock in any incorporated company,   25
Certificates of profits, or any certificate or memorandum showing
an interest in the property
or accumulations of any incorporated company : If for a sum
not less than $10 and not ex-
ceeding $50,   10
Exceeding $50 and not exceed-
ing $1,000,   25
Exceeding $1,000, for every ad-
ditional $1,000 or fractional
part thereof,   25
Certificate. Any certificate of damage or otherwise, and all other
certificates or documents issued by any port warden, ma-

Stamp Duty.

rine surveyor, or other person
acting as such,   25
Certificate of deposit of any sum of
money in any bank or trust
company, or with any banker
or person acting as such : If for
a sum not exceeding $100,   2
For a sum exceeding $100   5
Certificate of any other description than those specified,   5
Charter, renewal of, same stamp as
an original instrument.
Charter party for the charter of any
ship or vessel, or steamer, or
any letter, memorandum, or
other writing relating to the
charter, or any renewal or
transfer thereof · If the registered tonnage of such ship,
vessel, or steamer does not exceed 150 tons,   1 00
Exceeding 150 tons, and not exceeding 300 tons,   3 00
Exceeding 300 tons, and not exceeding 600 tons,   5 00
Exceeding 600 tons,   10 00
Check. Bank check,   2
Contract. Broker's note, or memorandum of sale of any goods
or merchandise, exchange, real
estate, or property of any kind
or description issued by brokers or persons acting as such ·
For each note or memorandum
of sale   10
Bill or memorandum of the sale
or contract for the sale of
stocks, bonds, gold or silver
bullion, coin, promissory notes,
or other securities made by
brokers, banks, or bankers,
either for the benefit of others
or on their own account · For
each hundred dollars, or fractional part thereof, of the
amount of such sale or contract,   1
Bill or memorandum of the sale
or contract for the sale of
stocks, bonds, gold or silver
bullion, coin, promissory notes,
or other securities, not his or
their own property, made by
any person, firm, or company
not paying a special tax as broker, bank or banker : For each
hundred dollars or fractional
part thereof, of the amount of
such sale or contract,   5
Contract (See Agreement.)
Contract, renewal of, same stamp
as original instrument.
Conveyance, deed, instrument or
writing, whereby any lands,
tenements, or other realty sold
shall be granted, assigned,
transferred, or otherwise conveyed to or vested in the purchaser or purchasers, or any
other person or persons, by his,
her or their direction, when the
consideration or value does not
exceed $500,   50

Stamp Duty

When the consideration exceeds $500, and not to exceed $1,000, 1 00

And for every additional $500, or fractional part thereof, in excess of $1,000, 50

Conveyance. The acknowledgment of a deed, or proof by a witness, exempt

Conveyance Certificate of record of a deed, exempt.

Credit, letter of Same as foreign bill of exchange

Custom-house entry. (See Entry.)

Custom-house withdrawals. (See Entry.)

Deed (See Conveyance Trust deed.)

Draft, payable at sight or on demand, 2

Draft, payable otherwise that at sight or on demand, for any sum not exceeding 100, 5

For every additional $100 or fractional part thereof in excess of $100, 5

Endorsement of any negotiable instrument, exempt

Entry of any goods, wares or merchandise at any custom-house, either for consumption or warehousing Not exceeding $100 in value, 25

Exceeding $100, and not exceeding $500 in value, 50

Exceeding $500 in value, 1 00

Entry for the withdrawal of any goods or merchandise from bonded warehouse, 50

Ganger's returns, exempt

Indorsement upon a stamped obligation in acknowledgment of its fulfillment, exempt

Insurance (life) policy: When the amount insured shall not exceed $1,000, 25

Exceeding $1,000, and not exceeding $5,000, 50

Exceeding $5,000, 1 00

Insurance (marine, inland, and fire,) policies, or renewal of the same. If the premium does not exceed $10, 10

Exceeding $10, and not exceeding $50, 25

Exceeding $50, 50

Insurance contracts or tickets against accidental injuries to persons, exempt.

Lease, agreement, memorandum, or contract for the hire, use, or rent of any land, tenement, or portion thereof: Where the rent or rental value is $300 per annum or less, 50

Where the rent or rental value exceeds the sum of $300 per annum, for each additional $200, or fractional part thereof in excess of $300, 50

Legal documents
Writ, or other original process, by which any suit, either criminal or civil, is commenced in any court, either of law or equity, exempt.

Stamp Duty.

Confession of judgment or cognovit, exempt

Writs or other process on appeals from justice courts or other courts of inferior jurisdiction to a court of record. exempt

Warrant of distress. exempt

Letters of administration. (See Probate of will )

Letters testamentary, when the value of the estate and effects, real and personal, does not exceed $1,000, Exempt

Exceeding $1,000, 5

Letters of credit. Same as bill of exchange, (foreign )

Manifest for custom-house entry or clearance of the cargo of any ship, vessel, or steamer, for a foreign port:
If the registered tonnage of such ship vessel, or steamer does not exceed 300 tons, 1 00

Exceeding 300 tons, and not exceeding 600 tons, 3 00

Exceeding 500 tons, 5 00

[These provisions do not apply to vessels or steamboats plying between ports of the United States and British North America.]

Measurers' returns, exempt.

Memorandum of sale, or broker's note. (See Contract )

Mortgage of lands, estate, or property, real or personal, heritable or movable, whatsoever, a trust deed in the nature of a mortgage, or any personal bond given as security for the payment of any definite or certain sum of money, exceeding $100, and not exceeding $500, 50

Exceeding $500, and not exceeding $1,000, 1 00

And for every additional $500, or fractional part thereof, in excess of $1,000, 50

Order for payment of money, if the amount is $10, or over, 2

Passage ticket on any vessel from a port in the United States to a foreign port, not exceeding $35, 50

Exceeding $35, and not exceeding $50, 1 00

And for every additional $50, or fractional part thereof, in excess of $50, 1 00

Passage tickets to ports in British North America, exempt

Pawner's checks, 5

Power of attorney for the sale or transfer of any stock, bonds or scrip, or for the collection of any dividends or interest thereon, 25

Power of attorney, or proxy, for voting at any election for officers of any incorporated company or society, except religious, charitable, or literary societies, or public cemeteries, 10

Power of attorney to receive or collect rent, 25

Stamp Duty.

Power of attorney to sell and convey real estate, or to rent or lease the same, 1 00

Power of attorney for any other purpose, 50

Probate of will, or letters of administration; where the estate and effects for or in respect of which such probate or letters of administration applied for shall be sworn or declared not to exceed the value of $1,000, exempt.

Exceeding $1,000, and not exceeding $2,000, 1 00

Exceeding $2,000, for every additional $1,000, or fractional part thereof, in excess of $2,000, 50

Promissory note For any sum less than $100, exempt.

For $100, and for each additional $100 or fractional part thereof, 5

Deposit note to mutual insurance companies, when policy is subject to duty, exempt

Renewal of a note, subject to the same duty as an original note.

Protest of note, bill of exchange, acceptance, check, or draft, or any marine protest, 25

Quit-claim deed to be stamped as a conveyance, except when given as a release of a mortgage by the mortgagee to the mortgagor, in which case it is exempt, but if it contains covenants *may* be subject as an agreement or contract.

Receipts for satisfaction of any mortgage or judgment or decree of any court, exempt

Receipts for any sum of money or debt due, or for a draft or other instrument given for the payment of money, exempt.

Receipts for the delivery of property exempt

Renewal of agreement, contract or charter, by letter or otherwise, same stamp as original instrument.

Sheriff's return on writ or other process, exempt,

Trust deed, made to secure a debt, to be stamped as a mortgage.

Warehouse receipts, exempt,

Warrant of attorney accompanying a bond or note, if the bond or note is stamped, exempt.

Weigher's returns, exempt.

Official documents, instruments, and papers issued by officers of the United States Government, exempt.

Official instruments, documents, and papers issued by the officers of any State, county, town, or other municipal corporation, in the exercise of functions strictly belonging to them in their ordinary governmental or municipal capacity, exempt.

Papers necessary to be used for

Stamp Duty.

the collection from the United States Government of claims by soldiers, or their legal representatives, for pensions, back pay, bounty, or for property lost in the service, exempt.

NOTE.—The last Congress passed an act, " That on and after the first day of October, 1870, the stamp tax imposed in Schedule B, on promissory notes for a less sum than one hundred dollars, and on receipts for any sum of money, or for the payment of any debt, and the stamp tax imposed in Schedule C, on canned and preserved fish, be, and the same are hereby repealed And no stamp shall be required upon the transfer or assignment of a mortgage, where it or the instrument it secures has been once duly stamped."

### CANCELLATION

In all cases where an *adhesive* stamp is used for denoting the stamp duty upon an instrument, the person using or affixing the same must write or imprint thereupon *in ink* the initials of his name, and the date (the year, month, and day) on which the same is attached or used. Each stamp should be separately cancelled When stamps are printed upon checks, &c , so that in filling up the instrument, the face of the stamp is and must necessarily be written across, no other cancellation will be required

All cancellation must be distinct and legible, and except in the case of proprietary stamps from private dies, no method of cancellation which differs from that above described can be recognized as legal and sufficient

### PENALTIES

A penalty of fifty dollars is imposed upon every person who makes, signs, or issues, or who causes to be made, signed, or issued, any paper of any kind or description whatever, or who accepts, negotiates, or pays, or causes to be accepted, negotiated, or paid, any bill of exchange, draft, or order, or promissory note, for the payment of money, without the same being duly stamped, or having thereupon an adhesive stamp for denoting the tax chargeable thereon, cancelled in the manner required by law, with intent to evade the provisions of the revenue act

A penalty of two hundred dollars is imposed upon every person who pays, negotiates, or offers in payment, or receives or takes in payment, any bill of exchange or order for the payment of any sum of money drawn or purporting to be drawn in a foreign country, but payable in the United States, until the proper stamp has been affixed thereto.

A penalty of fifty dollars is imposed upon every person who fraudulently makes use of an adhesive stamp to denote the duty required by the revenue act, without effectually cancelling and obliterating the same in the manner required by law.

O

Attention is particularly called to the following extract from section 155, of the act of June 30 1864, as amended by the act of July 13, 1866 :

"If any person shall wilfully remove or cause to be removed, alter or cause to be altered, the cancelling or defacing marks on any adhesive stamp, with intent to use the same, or to cause the use of the same, after it shall have been used once, or shall knowingly or wilfully sell or buy such washed or restored stamps, or offer the same for sale, or give or expose the same to any person for use, or knowingly use the same or prepare the same with intent for the further use thereof, or if any person shall knowingly and without lawful excuse (the proof whereof shall be on the person accused) have in his possession any washed, restored, or altered stamps, which have been removed from any vellum, parchment, paper, instrument or writing ; then, and in every such case, every person so offending, and every person knowingly and wilfully aiding, abetting, or assisting in committing any such offence as aforesaid, shall, on conviction thereof, * * * be punished by a fine not exceeding one thousand dollars, or by imprisonment and confinement to hard labor not exceeding five years, or both, at the discretion of the court "

It is not lawful to record any instrument, document, or paper required by law to be stamped, or any copy thereof, unless a stamp or stamps of the proper amount have been affixed and cancelled in the manner required by law ; and such instrument or copy and the record thereof are utterly null and void, and cannot be used or admitted as evidence in any court until the defect has been cured as provided in section 158.

All willful violations of the law should be reported to the United States District Attorney within and for the district where they are committed

## GENERAL REMARKS.

Revenue stamps may be used indiscriminately upon any of the matters or things enumerated in Schedule B, except proprietary and playing card stamps, for which a special use has been provided.

Postage stamps cannot be used in payment of the duty chargeable on instruments

The law does not designate which of the parties to an instrument shall furnish the necessary stamp, nor does the Commissioner of Internal Revenue assume to determine that it shall be supplied by one party rather than by another; but if an instrument subject to stamp duty is issued without having the necessary stamps affixed thereto, it cannot be recorded, or admitted, or used in evidence, in any court, until a legal stamp or stamps, denoting the amount of tax. shall have been affixed as prescribed by law, and the person who thus issues it is liable to a penalty, if he omits the stamps with an intent to evade the provisions of the internal revenue act.

The first act imposing a stamp tax upon certain specified instruments took effect, so far as said tax is concerned, October 1, 1862. The impression which seems to prevail to some extent, that no stamps are required upon any instruments issued in the States lately in insurrection, prior to the surrender, or prior to the establishment of collection districts there, is erroneous

Instruments issued in those States since October 1, 1862 are subject to the same taxes as similar ones issued at the same time in the other States

No stamp is necessary upon an instrument executed prior to October 1, 1862, to make it admissible in evidence, or to entitle it to record

*Certificates of loan* in which there shall appear any written or printed evidence of an amount of money to be paid on demand, or at a time designated, are subject to stamp duty as "promissory notes."

When two or more persons join in the execution of an instrument, the stamp to which the instrument is liable under the law, may be affixed and cancelled by either of them ; and "when more than one signature is affixed to the same paper, one or more stamps may be affixed thereto, representing the whole amount of the stamp required for such signatures."

No stamp is required on any warrant of attorney accompanying a bond or note, when such bond or note has affixed thereto the stamp or stamps denoting the duty required, and, whenever any bond or note is secured by mortgage, but one stamp duty is required on such papers—such stamp duty being the highest rate required for such instruments, or either of them In such case a note or memorandum of the value or denomination of the stamp affixed should be made upon the margin or in the acknowledgement of the instrument which is not stamped.

Particular attention is called to the change in section 154, by striking out the words "or used ;" the exemption thereunder is thus restricted to documents, &c , *issued* by the officers therein named Also to the changes in sections 152 and 158, by inserting the words "and cancelled in the manner required by law."

The acceptor or acceptors of any bill of exchange, or order for the payment of any sum of money, drawn or purporting to be drawn in any foreign country, but payable in the United States, must, before paying or accepting the same, place thereupon a stamp indicating the duty

It is only upon conveyances of realty *sold* that conveyance stamps are necessary A deed of real estate made without valuable consideration need not be stamped as a conveyance; but if it contains covenants, such, for instance, as a covenant to warrant and defend the title, it should be stamped as an agreement or contract.

When a deed purporting to be a conveyance of realty sold, and stamped accordingly, is inoperative, a deed of confirmation, made simply to cure the defect, requires no stamp In such case, the second deed should contain a recital of the facts, and should show the reasons for its execution

Partition deeds between tenants in common, need not be stamped as conveyances, inasmuch as there is no sale of realty, but merely a marking out, or a defining, of the boundaries of the part belonging to each but where money or other valuable consideration is paid by one co-tenant to another for equality of partition, there is a sale to the extent of such consideration, and the conveyance, by the party receiving it, should be stamped accordingly.

A conveyance of lands sold for unpaid taxes, issued since August 1, 1866, by the officers of any county, town, or other municipal corporation in the discharge of their strictly official duties, is exempt from stamp tax

A conveyance of realty sold, subject to a mortgage, should be stamped according to the consideration, or the value of the property *unencumbered* The consideration in such case is to be found by adding the amount paid for the equity of redemption to the mortgage debt. The fact that one part of the consideration is paid to the mortgagor and the other part to the mortgagee does not change the liability of the conveyance.

The stamp tax upon a mortgage is based upon the amount it is given to secure. The fact that the value of the property mortgaged is less than that amount, and that consequently the security is only partial, does not change the liability of the instrument. When, therefore, a second mortgage is given to secure the payment of a sum of money partially secured by a prior mortgage upon other property, or when two mortgages upon separate property are given at the same time to secure the payment of the same sum, each should be stamped as though it were the only one

A mortgage given to secure a surety from loss, or given for any purpose whatever, other than as security for the payment of a definite and certain sum of money, is taxable only as an agreement or contract

The stamp duty upon a lease, agreement, memorandum, or contract for the hire, use, or rent of any land, tenement, or portion thereof, is based upon the *annual* rent or rental value of the property leased, and the duty is the same whether the lease be for one year, for a term of years, or for the fractional part of a year only.

An assignment of a lease within the meaning and intent of Schedule B. is an assignment of the *leasehold*, or of some portion thereof, by the *lessee*, or by some person claiming by, from, or under him ; such an assignment as subrogates the assignee to the rights, or some portion of the rights, of the *lessee*, or of the person standing in his place A transfer by the *lessor* of his part of a lease, neither giving nor purporting to give a claim to the leasehold, or to any part thereof, but simply a right to the rents, &c , is subject to stamp tax as a contract or agreement only.

The stamp tax upon a fire insurance policy is based upon the *premium*.

Deposit notes taken by a mutual fire insurance company, not as payment of premium nor as evidence of indebtedness therefor, but to be used simply as a basis upon which to make rateable assessments to meet the losses incurred by the company, should not be reckoned as premium in determining the amount of stamp taxes upon the policies

When a policy of insurance properly stamped has been issued and lost, no stamp is necessary upon another issued by the same company to the same party, covering the same property, time, &c., and designed simply to supply the loss The second policy should recite the loss of the first.

An instrument which operates as the renewal of a policy of insurance, is subject to the same stamp tax as the policy.

When a policy of insurance is issued for a certain time, whether it be for one year only or for a term of years, a receipt for premium, or any other instrument which has the legal effect to continue the contract and extend its operation *beyond that time*, requires the same amount of revenue stamps as the policy itself; but such a receipt as is usually given for the payment of the monthly, quarterly, or annual premium, is not a renewal within the meaning of the statute The payment simply prevents the policy from expiring, by reason of non-performance of its conditions; a receipt given for such a payment requires no stamp When, however, the time of payment has passed, and a tender of the premium is not sufficient to bind the company, but a new policy or a new contract in some form, with the mutuality essential to every contract, becomes necessary between the insurer and the insured, the same amount of stamps should be used as that required upon the original policy.

A permit issued by a life insurance company changing the terms of a policy as to travel, residence, occupation, &c., should be stamped as a contract or agreement

A bill single or a bill obligatory, i e., an instrument in the form of a promissory note, *under seal*, is subject to stamp duty as written or printed evidence of an amount of money to be paid on demand or at a time designated, at the rate of five cents for each one hundred dollars or fractional part thereof.

A waiver of protest, or of demand and notice, written upon negotiable paper and signed by the indorser, is an agreement, and requires a five-cent stamp.

A stamp duty of twenty-five cents is imposed upon the "protest of every note, bill of exchange, check or draft," and upon every marine protest If several notes, bills of exchange, drafts, &c , are protested at the same time and all attached to one and the same certificate, stamps should be affixed to the amount of twenty-five cents for each note, bill, draft, &c , thus protested.

When, as is generally the case, the caption to a deposition contains other certificates in addition to the jurat to the affidavit of the deponent, such as a certificate that the parties were or were not notified, that they did or did not appear, that they did or did not object, &c , it is subject to a stamp duty of five cents

When an attested copy of a writ or other process is used by a sheriff or other person in making personal service, or in attaching property, a five-cent stamp should be affixed to the certificate of attestation

A marriage certificate issued by the officiating clergyman or magistrate, to be returned to any officer of a State, county, city, town, or other municipal corporation, to constitute part of a public record, requires no stamp; but if it is to be retained by the parties, a five-cent stamp should be affixed

The stamp tax upon a bill of sale, by which any ship or vessel, or any part thereof, is conveyed to or vested in any other person or persons, is at the same rate as that imposed upon conveyances of realty sold; a bill of sale of any other personal property should be stamped as a contract or agreement.

An assignment of real or personal property, or of both, for the benefit of creditors, should be stamped as an agreement or contract

Written or printed assignments of agreements; bonds, notes not negotiable, and of all other instruments the assignments of which are not particularly specified in the foregoing schedule, should be stamped as agreements

No stamp is necessary upon the registry of a judgment, even though the registry is such in its legal effect as to create a lien which operates as a mortgage upon the property of the judgment debtor.

When a "power of attorney or proxy for voting at any election for officers of any incorporated company or society, except religious, charitable, or literary societies, or public cemeteries," is signed by several stockholders, owning separate and distinct shares, it is, in its legal effect, the separate instrument of each, and requires stamps to the amount of ten cents for each and every signature, one or more stamps may be used representing the whole amount required

A notice from landlord to tenant to quit possession of premises requires no stamp.

A stamp tax is imposed upon every "manifest for custom-house entry or clearance of the *cargo* of any ship, vessel, or steamer for a foreign port." The amount of this tax in each case depends upon the registered tonnage of the vessel

If a vessel clears in ballast and has no cargo whatever, no stamp is necessary; but if she has any, however small the amount—a stamp should be used.

A bond to convey real estate requires stamps to the amount of twenty-five cents

The stamp duty upon the probate of a will, or upon letters of administration, is based upon the sworn or declared value of all the estate and effects, real, personal, and mixed, undiminished by the debts of the estate for or in respect of which such probate or letters are applied for

When the property belonging to the estate of a person deceased, lies under different jurisdictions and it becomes necessary to take out letters in two or more places, the letters should be stamped according to the value of all the property, real, personal, and mixed, for or in respect of which the particular letters in each case are issued

Letters *de bonis non* should be stamped according to the amount of property remaining to be administered upon thereunder, regardless of the stamps upon the original letters

A mere *copy* of an instrument is not subject to stamp duty unless it is a certified one, in which case a five-cent stamp should be affixed to the certificate of the person attesting it; but when the instrument is executed and issued in duplicate, triplicate, &c., as in the case of a lease of two or more parts, each part has the same legal effect as the other, and each should be stamped as an original.

# POSTAL RATES AND REGULATIONS.

LETTERS.—The law requires postage on all letters (including those to foreign countries when prepaid), excepting those written to the President or Vice President, or members of Congress, or (on official business) to the chiefs of the executive departments of the Government, and the heads of bureaux and chief clerks, and others invested with the franking privilege, to be prepaid by stamps or stamped envelopes, prepayment in money being prohibited.

All drop-letters must be prepaid  The rate of postage on drop-letters, at offices where free delivery by carrier is established, is two cents per half ounce or fraction of a half ounce ; at offices where such free delivery is NOT established the rate is one cent

The single rate of postage on all domestic mail letters throughout the United States, is three cents per half ounce, with an additional rate of three cents for each additional half ounce or fraction of a half ounce  The ten cent (Pacific) rate is abolished.

NEWSPAPERS, ETC.—Letter postage is to be charged on all handbills, circulars, or other printed matter which shall contain any manuscript writing whatever

Daguerreotypes, when sent in the mail, are to be charged with letter postage by weight

Photographs on cards, paper, and other flexible material, (not in cases), can be sent at the same rate as miscellaneous printed matter, viz , two cents for each four ounces or fraction thereof.

Photograph Albums are chargeable with book postage—four cents for each four ounces or fraction thereof.

NEWSPAPER POSTAGE —Postage on daily papers to subscribers when prepaid quarterly or yearly in advance, either at the mailing office or office of delivery, per quarter (three months), 35 cts. ; six times per week, per quarter 30 cts. ; for tri-weekly, per quarter 15 cts. , for semi-weekly, per quarter 10 cts., for weekly, per quarter 5 cents.

Weekly newspapers (one copy only) sent by the publisher to actual subscribers within the county where printed and published, FREE

Postage per quarter (to be paid quarterly or yearly in advance) on newspapers and periodicals issued less frequently than once a week, sent to actual subscribers in any part of the United States  Semi monthly, not over 4 oz , 6 cts , over 4 oz. and not over 8 oz , 12 cts ; over 8 oz and not over 12 oz , 18cts. ; monthly, not over 4 oz , 3 cts ; over 4 oz and not over 8 oz , 6 cts ; over 8 oz and not over 12 oz., 9 cts.; quarterly, not over 4 oz., 1 cent; over 4 oz. and not over 8 oz , 2 cts ; over 8 oz. and not over 12 oz , 3 cts.

TRANSIENT MATTER —Books not over 4 oz in weight, to one address, 4 cts. ; over 4 oz and not over 8 oz , 8 cts , over 8 oz and not over 12 oz , 12 cts ; over 12 oz. and not over 16 oz., 16 cts.

Circulars not exceeding three in number to one address, 2 cts , over 3 and not over 6, 4 cts. ; over 6 and not over 9, 6 cts ; over 9 and not exceeding 12, 8 cts.

On miscellaneous mailable matter, (embracing all pamphlets, occasional publications, transient newspapers, hand-bills and posters, book manuscripts and proof-sheets, whether corrected or not, maps, prints, engravings, sheet music, blanks, flexible patterns, samples, and sample cards, phonographic paper, letter envelopes, postal envelopes or wrappers, cards, paper, plain or ornamental, photographic representations of different types, seeds, cuttings, bulbs, roots and scions,) the postage to be pre-paid by stamps, is on one package, to one address, not over 4 oz in weight, 2 cts , over 4 oz. and not over 8 oz., 4 cts , over 8 oz and not over 12 oz.,6 cts ; over 12 oz  and not over 16 oz., 8 cts  The weight of packages of seeds, cuttings, roots and scions, to be franked, is limited to thirty-two ounces.

Any word or communication, whether by printing, writing, marks or signs, upon the cover or wrapper of a newspaper, pamphlet, magazine, or other printed matter, other than the name or address of the person to whom it is to be sent, and the date when the subscription expires, subjects the package to letter postage.

# Infallible Rules for Detecting Counterfeit or Spurious Bank Notes.

RULE 1st.—Examine the shading of the letters in title of Bank called LATHEWORK, which in genuine notes presents an even, straight, light and silky appearance, generally so fine and smooth as to appear to be all in one solid, pale body. In the counterfeit the lines are coarse and irregular, and in many of the longer lines breaks will be perceived, thus presenting a very inferior finish in comparison to genuine work

2d —Observe the dies, circles and ovals in the genuine; they are composed of a network of lines, which, by crossing each other at certain angles, produce an endless variety of figures; SEE THE ONE CENT STAMP ATTACHED   The fine line alone is the unit which enables you to detect spurious work. In the counterfeit, the REPRESENTED white lines are coarse, irregular, and cross each other in a confused, irregular manner, thus producing blurred and imperfect figures

3d.—Examine the form and features of all human figures on the note. In the genuine, the texture of the skin is represented by fine dots and lines intermixed  In the eyes, the pupil is distinctly visible, and the white clearly seen, the nose, mouth and chin, well formed, natural and expressive; the lips are slightly pouting, and the chin well thrown out; and the delicate shading of the neck perfectly harmonizes with the rest of the figure.  Observe the fingers and toes, they should be clearly and accurately defined.  The hair of the head should show the fine strands and present a natural appearance.  The folds of the drapery of human figures should lay natural and present a fine, finished appearance. In the counterfeit the female figure does not bear the natural prominence in outlines; observe, the eyes and shading surrounding does not present the lifelike appearance it should  The fingers and toes are not properly and proportionately defined, the hair does not bear that soft and finished appearance as in the genuine.

4th —Examine the imprint or engraver's names in the evenness and shape of the fine letters   Counterfeits never bear the imprint perfect  This rule should be strictly observed, as it is infallible in detecting counterfeits.

5th —In the genuine note the landscapes are well finished, trees and shrubs are neatly drawn; the limbs well proportioned, and the foliage presenting a fine natural appearance, clear sky is formed of fine parallel lines, and when clouds or heavy skies appear, they cross each other, and bear a soft, smooth and natural appearance   The perspective, showing a view of the surrounding country, is always clear and distinct.  The small figures in the background are always plainly seen, and their outlines and general character recognized  Ships are well defined and the canvass has a clear texture, railroad cars are very accurately delineated; in examining a train observe carefully the car most distant.  In the counterfeit the landscape is usually poorly executed; the leaves of trees poorly and unnaturally defined.— The lines representing still water are scratchy rather than parallel, the sky is represented generally in like manner, and where rolling clouds are to be seen, the unnatural effect is obvious  Domestic animals are generally poorly executed, particularly the head and limbs; the eyes are seldom clearly defined  Ships are poorly drawn, the texture of the canvass coarse and inferior in style of workmanship, thus giving an artificial appearance. Railroad cars are also poorly executed, the car farthest from the eye is usually the most imperfect  The perspective is always imperfect, the figures in the background can seldom be recognized.

6th —Bills altered from a smaller to a higher denomination, can readily be detected by a close observer, in consequence of the striking difference between the parts which have been extracted and the rest of the note  This difference is readily perceived in the lack of color, body and finish of the dye, we have seen bills where the surrounding shading in altered dies was too dark, but from the back or finish of the white lines you have a sure test　Again observe particularly the words " Five " or " Ten Dollars " as the case may be, denoting the denomination of the note ; the parallel outlines and shading (if any) are coarse and imperfect　Alterations are frequently made by pasting a greater denomination over a smaller, but by holding the bill up to the light, the fraud will be perceived　Another method resorted to is to cut out the figures in the dies as well as the words one dollar, or the words two or three as the case may be, and with a sharp eraser, scrape down the ends and also the edges of the pieces to be inserted; when the pieces thus prepared are affixed they are hardly perceivable, but by passing the note through the hand, so as to feel the die both with the finger and thumb at the same time, the fraud will be detected by the stiffness of the outer edges, " occasioned by the gum or method adopted" in affixing the parts　The letter S should always be examined, as in many alterations it is pasted or stamped at the end of the word " dollar," and even when stamped there, the carrying out of the outlines for its shading will readily show the fraud.　Bills of broken banks are frequently altered by extracting the name of bank, state and town; they may readily be detected by observing first the state, second the title or name of the bank, third the town or location

GENERAL REMARKS IN REFERENCE TO COUNTERFEITS.—The paper on which they are printed is generally of a very inferior quality, with less body, finish and toughness than bank note paper has　The ink generally lacks the rich luster of the genuine; the red letters and figures are generally imperfect, and the ink does not present the vermillion hue as it should.　The printing is generally inferior, usually exhibiting specks of white in the most prominent letters.　The date and filling up, and the President's and Cashier's names are generally written by the same person, although in many instances they present a different appearance　There are bills in circulation bearing either genuine dies or vignettes; but upon close examination you will be enabled to detect any spurious bill, whether counterfeit or altered, by the instructions here given, if persevered in for a short time　We beg to suggest, if time will admit, the learner should examine minutely every bill he receives.　A powerful pocket magnifying glass, which can be purchased for from fifty cents to one dollar at any of the opticians, will greatly enable you to see and comprehend the difference between genuine and spurious work.

---

# HOW TO SUCCEED IN BUSINESS.

What will my readers give to know how to get rich?　Now, I will not vouch that the following rules will enable every person who may read them to acquire wealth ; but this I will answer for, that if ever a man does grow rich by honest means, and retains his wealth for any length of time, he must practice upon the principles laid down in the following essay.　The remarks are not original with me, but I strongly commend them to the attention of every young man, at least as affording the true secret of success in attaining wealth.　A single perusal of such an essay at an impressible moment, has sometimes a very wonderful effect upon the disposition and character.

Fortune, they say, is a fickle dame—full of her freaks and caprices, who blindly distributes her favors without the slightest discrimination　So inconstant, so wavering is she represented, that her most faithful votaries can place no reliance on her promises.　Disappointment, they tell us, is the lot of those who make offerings at her shrine　Now, all this is a vile slander upon the dear blind lady

Although wealth often appears the result of mere accident, or a fortunate concurrence of favorable circumstances without any exertion of skill or foresight, yet any man of sound health and unimpaired mind may become wealthy, if he takes the proper steps.

Foremost in the list of requisites are honesty and strict integrity in every transaction of life.　Let a man have the reputation of being fair and upright in his dealings, and he will possess the confidence of all who know him　Without these qualities every other merit will prove unavailing　Ask concerning a man, " Is he active and capable?"　Yes.　" Industrious, temperate and regular in his habits?"—Oh yes.　" Is he honest?　Is he trustworthy?"　Why, as to that, I am sorry to say that he is not to be trusted; he needs watching; he is a little tricky, and will take an undue advantage, if he can　" Then I will have nothing to do with him," will be the invariable reply Why, then, is honesty the best policy? Because, without it, you will get a bad name, and everybody will shun you

A character for knavery will prove an insurmountable obstacle to success in almost every undertaking. It will be found that the straight line is, in business, as in geometry, the shortest In a word, it is almost impossible for a dishonest man to acquire wealth by a regular process of business, because he is shunned as a depredator upon society.

Needy men are apt to deviate from the rule of integrity, under the plea that necessity knows no law; they might as well add that it knows no shame The course is suicidal, and by destroying all confidence, ever keeps them immured in poverty, although they may posecss every other quality for success in the world

Punctuality, which is said to be the soul of business, is another important element in the art of money getting. The man known to be scrupulously exact in the fulfillment of his engagements, gains the confidence of all, and may command all the means he can use with advantage; whereas, a man careless and regardless of his promises in money matters will have every purse closed against him. Therefore be prompt in your payments.

Next, let us consider the advantages of a cautious circumspection in our intercourse with the world. Slowness of belief and a proper distrust are essential to success The credulous and confiding are ever the dupes of knaves and impostors. Ask those who have lost their property how it happened, and you will find in most cases that it has been owing to misplaced confidence One has lost by endorsing, another by crediting, another by false representations; all of which a little more foresight and a little more distrust would have prevented. In the affairs of this world men are not saved by faith, but by the want of it

Judge of men by what they do, not by what they say Believe in looks rather than words Observe all their movements Ascertain their motives and their ends. Notice what they say or do in their unguarded moments, when under the influence of excitement. The passions have been compared to tortures which force men to reveal their secrets Before trusting a man, before putting it in his power to cause you a loss, possess yourself of every available information relative to him. Learn his history, his habits, inclinations and propensities; his reputation for honor, industry, frugality and punctuality; his prospects, resources, supports, advantages and disadvantages; his intentions and motives of action; who are his friends and enemies, and what are his good or bad qualities. You may learn a man's good qualities and advantages from his friends—his bad qualities and disadvantages from his enemies. Make due allowance for exaggeration in both. Finally, examine carefully before engaging in anything, and act with energy afterwards. Have the hundred eyes of

Argus beforehand, and the hundred hands of Briarius afterwards.

Order and system in the management of business must not be neglected. Nothing contributes more to dispatch Have a place for everything and everything in its place; a time for everything, and everything in its time. Do first what presses most, and having determined what is to be done, and how it is to be done, lose no time in doing it Without this method all is hurry and confusion, little or nothing is accomplished, and business is attended to with neither pleasure nor profit.

A polite, affable deportment is recommended Agreeable manners contribute powerfully to a man's success. Take two men, possessing equal advantages in every other respect, but let one be gentlemanly, kind, obliging and conciliating in his manners; the other harsh, rude and disobliging; and the one will become rich, while the other will starve.

We are now to consider a very important principle in the business of money-getting, namely—Industry—persevering, indefatigable attention to business Persevering diligence is the Philosopher's stone, which turns everything to gold. Constant, regular, habitual and systematic application to business, must in time, if properly directed, produce great results. It must lead to wealth, with the same certainty that poverty follows in the train of idleness and inattention It has been truly remarked that he who follows his amusements instead of his business, will, in a short time, have no business to follow

The art of money-saving is an important part of the art of money-getting. Without frugality no one can become rich; with it, few would be poor Those who consume as fast as they produce, are on the road to ruin As most of the poverty we meet with grows out of idleness and extravagance, so most large fortunes have been the result of habitual industry and frugality The practice of economy is as necessary in the expenditure of time as of money They say if "we take care of the pence the pounds will take care of themselves." So, if we take care of the minutes, the days will take care of themselves

The acquisition of wealth demands as much self-denial, and as many sacrifices of present gratification, as the practice of virtue itself Vice and poverty proceed, in some degree, from the same sources, namely—the disposition to sacrifice the future to the present; the inability to forego a small present pleasure for great future advantages Men fail of fortune in this world, as they fail of happiness in the world to come, simply because they are unwilling to deny themselves momentary enjoyments for the sake of permanent future happiness.

Every large city is filled with persons, who, in order to support the appearance of wealth, constantly live beyond their income, and make up the deficiency by contracting debts which are never paid. Others, there are, the mere drones of society, who pass their days in idleness, and subsist by pirating on the hives of the industrious. Many who run a short-lived career of splendid beggary, could they be but persuaded to adopt a system of rigid economy for a few years, might pass the remainder of their days in affluence. But no! They must keep up appearances, they must live like other folks.

Their debts accumulate; their credit fails, they are harassed by duns, and besieged by constables and sheriff. In this extremity, as a last resort, they submit to a shameful dependance, or engage in criminal practices which entail hopeless wretchedness and infamy on themselves and families.

Stick to the business in which you are regularly employed. Let speculators make thousands in a year or a day; mind your own regular trade, never turning from it to the right hand or to the left. If you are a merchant, a professional man, or a mechanic, never buy lots or stocks, unless you have surplus money which you wish to invest. Your own business you understand as well as other men; but other people's business you do not understand. Let your business be some one which is useful to the community. All such occupations possess the elements of profit in themselves.

---

# How to Secure the Public Lands,

## OR THE ENTRY OF THE SAME UNDER THE PRE-EMPTION AND HOMESTEAD

### LAWS

The following circular gives all necessary information as to the procedure necessary in purchasing and securing the public lands:

DEPARTMENT OF THE INTERIOR,
GEN'L LAND OFFICE, July 19, 1865

Numerous questions having arisen as to the mode of procedure to purchase public lands, or acquire title to the same by bounty land locations, by pre-emptions or by homestead, this circular is communicated for the information of all concerned.

In order to acquire title to public lands the following steps must be taken:

1. Application must be made to the Register of the district land office in which the land desired may be situated.

A list of all the land offices in the United States is furnished by the Department, with the seats of the different offices, where it is the duty of the Register and Receiver to be in attendance, and give proper facilities and information to persons desirous of obtaining lands.

The minimum price of ordinary public lands is $1,25 per acre. The even or reserved sections falling within railroad grants are increased to double the minimum price, being $2,50 per acre.

Lands once offered at public sale, and not afterwards kept out of market by reservation, or otherwise, so as to prevent free competition, may be entered or located

2. By the applicant filing with the Register his written application describing the tract, with its area, the Register will then certify to the receiver whether the land is vacant, with its price; and when found to be so, the applicant must pay that price per acre, or may locate the same with land warrant, and thereafter the Receiver will give him a "duplicate receipt," which he is required to surrender previous to the delivery to him of the patent, which may be had either by application for it to the Register or to the General Land Office.

3. If the tract has not been offered at public sale it is not liable to ordinary private entry, but may be secured by a party legally qualified, upon his compliance with the requirements of the pre-emption laws of 4th September, 1841, and 3d March, 1843, and after such party shall have made actual settlement for such a length of time as will show he designs it for his permanent home, and is acting in good faith, building a house and residing therein, he may proceed to the district land office, establish his pre-emption claim according to law, by proving his actual residence and cultivation, and showing that he is otherwise within the purview of these acts — Then he can enter the land at $1,25, either in cash or with bounty land warrant, unless the premises should be $2,50 acre lands. In that case the whole purchase-money can be paid in cash, or one-half in cash, the residue with a bounty land warrant

4. But if parties legally qualified desire to obtain title under the Homestead Act of 20th May, 1862, they can do so on com-

plying with the Department Circular, dated 30th October, 1862.

5 The law confines Homestead entries to surveyed lands; and although, in certain States and Territories noted in the subjoined list, pre-emptors may go on land before survey, yet they can only establish their claim after return of survey, but must file their pre-emption declaration within three months after receipt of official plat, at the local land-office where the settlement was made before survey Where, however, it was made after survey, the claimant must file within three months after date of settlement; and where actual residence and cultivation have been long enough to show that the claimant has made the land his permanent home, he can establish his claim and pay for the same at any time before the date of the public sale of lands within the range in which his settlement may fall

6 All unoffered surveyed lands not acquired under pre-emption, homestead, or otherwise, under express legal sanction, must be offered at public sale under the President's Proclamation, and struck off to the highest bidder, as required by act of April 24, 1820

J M EDMUNDS,
Commissioner General Land Office.

---

# LAW MAXIMS.

1 A promise of a debtor to give "satisfactory security" for the payment of a portion of his debt, is a sufficient consideration for a release of the residue by his creditor.

2. Administrators are liable to account for interest on funds in their hands, although no profit shall have been made upon them, unless the exigencies of the estate rendered it prudent that they should hold the funds thus uninvested

3 Any person who voluntarily becomes an agent for another, and in that capacity obtains information to which as a stranger he could have had no access, is bound in subsequent dealing with his principal, as purchaser of the property that formed the subject of his agency, to communicate such information

4 When a house is rendered untenantable in consequence of improvements made on the adjoining lot, the owner of such cannot recover damages, because it is presumed that he had knowledge of the approaching danger in time to protect himself from it

5. When a merchant ship is abandoned by order of the master, for the purpose of saving life, and a part of the crew subsequently meet the vessel so abandoned and bring her safe into port, they will be entitled to salvage.

6. A person who has been led to sell goods by means of false pretenses, cannot recover them from one who has purchased them in good faith from the fraudulent vendor.

7. An agreement by the holder of a note to give the principal debtor time for payment, without depriving himself of the right to sue, does not discharge the surety

8. A seller of goods who accepts, at the time of sale, the note of a third party, not endorsed by the buyer, in payment, cannot in case the note is not paid, hold the buyer responsible for the value of the goods.

9 A day-book copied from a "blotter" in which charges are first made, will not be received in evidence as a book of original entries.

10. Common carriers are not liable for extraordinary results of negligence that could not have been foreseen by ordinary skill and foresight.

11 A bidder at a Sheriff's sale may retract his bid at any time before the property is knocked down to him, whatever may be the conditions of the sale.

12 Acknowledgment of debt to a stranger does not preclude the operation of the statute.

13 The fruits and grass on the farm or garden of an intestate descend to the heir

14. Agents are solely liable to their principals.

15 A deposit of money in bank by a husband, in the name of his wife, survives to her

16. Money paid on Sunday contracts may be recovered

17 A debtor may give preference to one creditor over another, unless fraud or special legislation can be proved

18. A court cannot give judgment for a larger sum than that specified in the verdict.

19 Imbecility on the part of either husband or wife, invalidates the marriage

20. An action for malicious prosecution will lie, though nothing further was done than suing out warrants.

21 An agreement not to continue the practice of a profession or business in any specified town, if the party so agreeing has received a consideration for the same, is valid.

22 When A consigns goods to B to sell on commission, and B delivers them to C, in payment of his own antecedent debts, A can recover their value.

23 A finder of property is compelled to make diligent inquiry for the owner thereof, and to restore the same If, on finding such property, he attempts to conceal such fact, he may be prosecuted for larceny

24 A private person may obtain an injunction to prevent a public mischief by which he is affected in common with others.

25 Any person interested may obtain an injunction to restrain the State or a municipal corporation from maintaining a nuisance on its lands.

26. A discharge under the insolvent laws of one State will not discharge the insolvent from a contract made with a citizen of another State.

27. To prosecute a party with any other motive than to bring him to justice, is malicious prosecution, and actionable as such

28 Ministers of the gospel, residing in any incorporated town, are not exempt from jury, military, or fire service.

29 When a person contracts to build a house, and is prevented by sickness from finishing it, he can recover for the part performed, if such part is beneficial to the other party

30. In a suit for enticing away a man's wife, actual proof of the marriage is not necessary Cohabitation, reputation, and the admission of marriage by the parties, are sufficient

31. Permanent erections and fixtures, made by a mortgagor after the execution of the mortgage upon land conveyed by it, become a part of the mortgaged premises

32 When a marriage is denied, and plaintiff has given sufficient evidence to establish it, the defendant cannot examine the wife to disprove the marriage.

33. The amount of an express debt cannot be enlarged by application

34 Contracts for advertisements in Sunday newspapers cannot be enforced.

35 A seller of goods, chattels, or other property, commits no fraud, in law, when he neglects to tell the purchaser of any flaws, defects, or unsoundness in the same.

36 The opinions of witnesses, as to the value of a dog that has been killed, are not admissible in evidence The value of the animal is to be decided by the jury

37 If any person puts a fence on or plows the land of another, he is liable for trespass whether the owner has sustained injury or not

38 If a person, who is unable from illness to sign his will, has his hand guided in making his mark, the signature is valid

39 When land trespassed upon is occupied by a tenant, he alone can bring the action.

40 To say of a person, "If he does not come and make terms with me, I will make a bankrupt of him and ruin him," or any such threatening language, is actionable, without proof of special damage.

41 In an action for slander, the party making the complaint must prove the words alleged, other words of like meaning will not suffice.

42 In a suit of damages for seduction, proof of pregnancy, and the birth of a child, is not essential. It is sufficient if the illness of the girl, whereby she was unable to labor, was produced by shame for the seduction; and this is such a loss of service as will sustain the action.

43 Addressing to a wife a letter containing matter defamatory to the character of her husband is a publication, and renders the writer amenable to damages

44. A parent cannot sustain an action for any wrong done to a child, unless he has incurred some direct pecuniary injury therefrom in consequence of some loss of service or expenses necessarily consequent thereupon.

45 A master is responsible for an injury resulting from the negligence of his servant, whilst driving his cart or carriage, provided the servant is at the time engaged in his master's business, even though the accident happens in a place to which his master's business does not call him, but if the journey of a servant be solely for a purpose of his own, and undertaken without the knowledge and consent of his master, the latter is not responsible

46 An emigrant depot is not a nuisance in law.

47. A railroad track through the streets is not a nuisance in law.

48. If an agreement upon which a party relies be oral only, it must be proved by evidence  But if the contract be reduced to writing, it proves itself; and now no evidence whatever is receivable for the purpose of varying the contract or affecting its obligations  The reasons are obvious. The law prefers written to oral evidence, from its greater precision and certainty, and because it is less open to fraud  And where parties have closed a negotiation and reduced the result to writing, it is presumed that they have written all they intended to agree to, and therefore, that what is omitted was finally rejected by them.—[PARSONS.

49  Delivery of a husband's goods by a wife to her adulterer, he having knowledge that she has taken them without her husband's authority, is sufficient to sustain an indictment for larceny against the adulterer

50.  The fact that the insurer was not informed of the existence of impending litigation, affecting the premises insured, at the time the insurance was effected, does not vitiate the policy.

51  The liability of an innkeeper is not confined to personal baggage, but extends to all the property of the guest that he consents to receive.

52  When a minor executes a contract, and pays money, or delivers property on the same, he cannot afterwards disaffirm such contract and recover the money, or property, unless he restores to the other party the consideration received from him for such money or property.

53  When a person has, by legal inquisition been found an habitual drunkard, he cannot, even in his sober intervals, make contracts to bind himself or his property, until the inquisition is removed.

54  Any person dealing with the representative of a deceased person, is presumed, in law, to be fully apprized of the extent of such representative's authority to act in behalf of such estate.

55  In an action against a railroad company, by a passenger, to recover damages for injuries sustained on the road, it is not compulsory upon the plaintiff to prove actual negligence in the defendants; but it is obligatory on the part of the latter to prove that the injury was not owing to any fault or negligence of theirs.

56.  A guest is a competent witness, in an action between himself and an inn-keeper, to prove the character and value of lost personal baggage  Money in a trunk, not exceeding the amount reasonably required by the traveler to defray the expenses of the journey which he has undertaken, is a part of his baggage; and in case of its loss, while at any inn, the plaintiff may prove its amount by his own testimony.

57  The deed of a minor is not absolutely void  The court is authorized to judge, from the instrument, whether it is void or not, according to its terms being favorable or unfavorable to the interests of the minor.

58.  A married woman can neither sue nor be sued on any contract made by her during her marriage, except in an action relating to her individual property.  The action must be commenced either by or against her husband  It is only when an action is brought on a contract made by her before her marriage, that she is to be joined as a co-plaintiff, or defendant, with her husband.

59  Any contract made with a person judicially declared a lunatic is void

60  Money paid voluntarily in any transaction, with a knowledge of the facts, cannot be recovered.

61  In all cases of special contract for services, except in the case of a minor, the plaintiff can recover only the amount stipulated in the contract.

62  A wife is a competent witness with her husband, to prove the contents of a lost trunk, or when a party.

63.  A wife cannot be convicted of receiving stolen goods when she received them of her husband

64  Insurance against fire, by lightning or otherwise, does not cover loss by lightning when there is no combustion.

65  Failure to prove plea of justification, in a case of slander, aggravates the offence.

66  It is the agreement of the parties to sell by sample that constitutes a sale by sample, not the mere exhibition of a specimen of the goods.

67.  An agent is liable to his principals for loss caused by his misstatements, tho' unintentional.

68  Makers of promissory notes given in advance for premiums on policies of insurance, thereafter to be taken, are liable thereon.

69  An agreement to pay for procuring an appointment to office is void

70  An attorney may plead the statute of limitations, when sued by a client for money which he has collected and failed to pay over

71  Testimony given by a deceased witness on first trial, is not required to be repeated verbatim on the second

72.  A person entitling himself to a reward offered for lost property, has a lien upon the property for the reward, but only when a definite reward is offered.

73.  Confession by a prisoner must be voluntarily made, to constitute evidence against him

74  The defendant in a suit must be served with process; but service of such process upon his wife, even in his absence from the State, is not, in the absence of statutory provisions, sufficient.

75. The measure of damages in trespass for cutting timber, is its value as a chattel on the land where it was felled, and not the market price of the lumber manufactured

76 To support an indictment for malicious mischief in killing an animal, malice towards its owner must be shown, not merely passion excited against the animal itself

77 No action can be maintained against a sheriff for omitting to account for money obtained upon an execution within a reasonable time  He has till the return day to render such account.

78 An interest in the profits of an enterprise, as profits, renders the party holding it a partner in the enterprise, and makes him presumptively liable to share any loss

79 Males can marry at fourteen, and females at twelve years of age.

80 All cattle found at large upon any public road, can be driven by any person to the public pound

81 Any dog chasing, barking, or otherwise threatening a passer-by in any street, lane, road, or other public thoroughfare, may be lawfully killed for the same.

82 A written promise for the payment of such amount as may come into the hands of the promisor, is held to be an instrument in writing for the payment of money

83. The declaration of an agent is not admissible to establish the fact of agency — But when other proper evidence is given, tending to establish the fact of agency, it is not error to admit the declarations of the agent, accompanying acts, though tending to show the capacity in which he acted  When evidence is competent in one respect and incompetent in another, it is the duty of the court to admit it, and control its effects by suitable instructions to the jury.

84 The court has a general power to remove or suspend an attorney for such immoral conduct as rendered him unworthy of confidence in his official capacity.

85 Bankruptcy is pleadable in bar to all actions and in all courts, and this bar may be avoided whenever it is interposed, by showing fraud in the procurement of the discharge, or a violation of any of the provisions of the bankrupt act

86 An instrument in the form of a deed, but limited to take effect at the termination of the grantor's natural life, is held to be a deed, not a will.

87. A sale will not be set aside as fraudulent, simply because the buyer was at the time unable to make the payment agreed upon, and knew his inability, and did not intend to pay.

88. No man is under an obligation to make known his circumstances when he is buying goods.

89. Contracting parties are bound to disclose material facts known to each, but of which either supposes the other to be ignorant, only when they stand in some special relation of trust and confidence in relation to the subject matter of the contract  But neither will be protected if he does anything, however slight, to mislead or deceive the other.

90 A contract negotiated by mail is formed when notice of acceptance of the offer is duly deposited in the post-office, properly addressed.  This rule applies, although the party making the offer expressly requires that if it is accepted, speedy notice of acceptance shall be given him

91. The date of an instrument is so far a material part of it, that an alteration of the date by the holder after execution, makes the instrument void

92 A corporation may maintain an action for libel, for words published of them and relating to its trade or business, by which it has incurred special damages.

93 It is unprofessional for a lawyer who has abandoned his case without trying it, a term or two before trial, to claim a fee conditional upon the success of his client, although his client was successful.

94 Although a party obtaining damages for injuries received through the default of another, was himself guilty of negligence, yet that will not defeat his recovery, unless his negligence contributed to cause the injury.

95. A person may contract to labor for another during life, in consideration of receiving his support, but his creditors have the right to inquire into the intention with which such arrangement is made, and it will be set aside if entered into to deprive them of his future earnings.

96 A grantor may by express terms exclude the bed of a river, or a highway, mentioned as boundary; but if without language of exclusion a line is described as 'along,' or 'upon,' or as 'running to' the highway or river, or as 'by,' or 'running to the bank of' the river; these expressions carry the grantee to the center of the highway or river.

97 The court will take pains to construe the words used in a deed in such a way as to effect the intention of the parties, however unskilfully the instrument may be drawn.  But a court of law cannot exchange an intelligible word plainly employed in a deed for another, however evident it may be that the word used was used by mistake for another.

98. One who has lost his memory and understanding is entitled to legal protection, whether such loss is occasioned by his own misconduct or by an act of Providence

99 When a wife leaves her husband voluntarily, it must be shown, in order to make him liable for necessaries furnished to her, that she could not stay with safety Personal violence, either threatened or inflicted, will be sufficient cause for such separation

100 Necessaries of dress furnished to a discarded wife must correspond with the pecuniary circumstances of the husband, and be such articles as the wife, if prudent, would expect, and the husband should furnish, if the parties lived harmoniously together

101. A fugitive from justice from one of the United States to another, may be arrested and detained in order to his surrender by authority of the latter, without a previous demand for his surrender by the executive of the State whence he fled.

102 A watch will not pass under a bequest of ' wearing apparel," nor of ' household furniture and articles for family use "

103 Money paid for the purpose of settling or compounding a prosecution for a supposed felony, cannot be recovered back by a party paying it

104 An innkeeper is liable for the death of an animal in his possession, but may free himself from liability by showing that the death was not occasioned by negligence on his part

105 Notice to the agent of a company is notice to the company.

106. An employer is not liable to one of his employes for an injury sustained by the latter in consequence of the neglect of others of his employes engaged in the same general business.

107 Where a purchaser at a Sheriff's sale has bid the full price of property under the erroneous belief that the sale would divest the property of all liens, it is the duty of the court to give relief by setting aside the sale

108 When notice of protest is properly sent by mail, it may be sent by the mail of the day of the dishonor; if not, it must be mailed for the mail of the next day; except that if there is none, or it closes at an unseasonably early hour, then notice must be mailed in season for the next possible mail

109 A powder-house located in a populous part of a city, and containing large quantities of gunpowder, is a nuisance

110 When the seller of goods accepts at the time of the sale, the note of a third person, unindorsed by the purchaser, in payment, the presumption is that the payment was intended to be absolute; and though the note should be dishonored, the purchaser will not be liable for the value of the goods

111. A man charged with crime before a committing magistrate, but discharged on his own recognizance, is not privileged from arrest on civil process while returning from the magistrate's office

112 When one has been induced to sell goods by means of false pretences, he cannot recover them from one who has bona fide purchased and obtained possession of them from the fraudulent vendor

113 If the circumstances attendant upon a sale and delivery of personal property are such as usually and naturally accompany such a transaction, it cannot be declared a legal fraud upon creditors.

114 A stamp impressed upon an instrument by way of seal, is good as a seal, if it creates a durable impression in the texture of the paper

115 If a party bound to make a payment use due diligence to make a tender, but through the payee's absence from home is unable to find him or any agent authorized to take payment for him, no forfeiture will be incurred through his failure to make a tender

---

### Government Land Measure.

A township, 36 sections, each a mile square.

A section, 640 acres

A quarter section, half a mile square, 160 acres

An eighth section, half a mile long, north and south, and a quarter of a mile wide, 80 acres

A sixteenth section, a quarter of a mile square, 40 acres.

The sections are numbered from one to thirty-six, commencing at the northeast corner, thus

| 6 | 5 | 4 | 3 | 2 | n w | n e |
|---|---|---|---|---|---|---|
|   |   |   |   |   | s w | s e |
| 7 | 8 | 9 | 10 | 11 | 12 | |
| 18 | 17 | 16 | 15 | 14 | 13 | |
| 19 | 20 | 21 | 22 | 23 | 24 | |
| 30 | 29 | 28 | 27 | 26 | 25 | |
| 31 | 32 | 33 | 34 | 35 | 36 | |

The sections are all divided in quarters, which are named by the cardinal points, as in section one The quarters are divided in the same way. The description of a 40 acre lot would read: The south half of the west half of the southwest quarter of section 1 in township 24, north of range 7 west, or as the case might be, and sometimes will fall short, and sometimes overrun the number of acres it is supposed to contain.

# THE DECIMAL SYSTEM

## OF

# WEIGHTS AND MEASURES.

### As Authorized by Act of Congress--Approved July 28, 1866.

— • • —

## STANDARDS

In every system of Weights and Measures it is necessary to have what are called "*Standards*," as the pound, yard, gallon, &c., to be divided and multiplied into smaller and larger parts and denominations The definition and construction of these Standards involve philosophical and scientific principles of a somewhat abstruse character, and are made and procured by the legislative department of the government The nominal Standards in the new system are the METER, the ARE, the LITER, and the GRAM The only *real* Standard, the one by which all the other standards are measured, and from which the system derives its name of "Metric," is the METER

### THE METER

Is used for all measures of length, distance, breadth, depth, height, &c., and was intended to be, and is very nearly, one ten-millionth of the distance on the earth's surface from the equator to the pole. It is about 39¾ inches, or 3 feet, 3 inches and 3 eighths, and is to be substituted for the yard

### THE ARE

Is a surface whose side is ten Meters, and is equal to 100 square Meters or about 4 square rods

### THE LITER

Is the unit for measuring solids and capacity, and is equal to the contents of a cube whose edge is one-tenth of a meter. It is about equal to 1 quart, and is a standard in cubic, dry and liquid measures

☞ A cubic Meter (or Kiloliter) is called a *stere*, and is also used as a standard in certain cubic measures.

### THE GRAM

Is the Unit of *weight*, and is the weight of a cube of pure water, each edge of the cube being one one-hundredth of a Meter It is about equal to 15¾ grains It is intended as the Standard in *all* weights, and with its divisions and multiples, to supersede the use of what are now called Avoirdupois, Apothecaries and Troy Weights

Each of the foregoing Standards is divided decimally, and larger units are also formed by multiples of 10, 100, &c. The successive subordinate parts are designated by the prefixes Deci, Centi and Milli; the successive multiples by Deka, Hecto, Kilo and Myria; each having its own numerical signification, as will be more clearly seen in the tables hereinafter given

The terms used may, at first sight, have a formidable appearance, seem difficult to pronounce, and to retain in memory, and to be, therefore, objectionable; but with a little attention and use, the apprehended difficulty will be found more apparent than real, as has been abundantly proved by experience The importance, also, of conformity in the use of commercial terms on the part of the United States, with the practice of the many nations in which the system, *with its present nomenclature*, has already been adopted, most greatly overbalance the comparatively slight objection alluded to

# TABLES.

| OLD | MONEY | NEW. |
|---|---|---|
| 4 farthing make 1 penny. | | 10 mills make 1 cent. |
| 12 pence `"` 1 shilling. | | 10 cents `"` 1 dime |
| 20 shillings `"` 1 pound. | | 10 dimes `"` 1 dollar. |

## LONG AND CLOTH MEASURE —New

| 10 | millimeters | make | 1 | centimeter |
|---|---|---|---|---|
| 10 | centimeters | `"` | 1 | decimeter. |
| 10 | decimeters | `"` | 1 | METER |
| 10 | meters | `"` | 1 | dekameter. |
| 10 | dekameters | `"` | 1 | hectometer. |
| 10 | hectometers | `"` | 1 | kilometer |
| 10 | kilometers | `"` | 1 | myriameter |

## SQUARE MEASURE —New

| 100 | square millimeters | make | 1 | square centimeter |
|---|---|---|---|---|
| 100 | square centimeters | `"` | 1 | square decimeter. |
| 100 | square decimeters | `"` | 1 | square meter or CENTARE. |
| 100 | centares | `"` | 1 | ARE. |
| 100 | ares | `"` | 1 | hectare. |

☞ The denominations less than the Are, including the Meter, are used in specifying the contents of surfaces of small extent, the terms *Centare, Are* and *Hectare,* in expressing quantities of land surveyed or measured.

The above table may, however, be continued beyond the Meter, thus:

| 100 | square meters | make | 1 | square dekameter |
|---|---|---|---|---|
| 100 | square dekameters | `"` | 1 | square hectometer. |
| 100 | square hectometers | `"` | 1 | square kilometer |
| 100 | square kilometers | `"` | 1 | square myriameter. |

## CUBIC MEASURE.—New.

### *For Solids.*

| 1000 | cubic millimeters | make | 1 | cubic centimeter. |
|---|---|---|---|---|
| 1000 | cubic centimeters | `"` | 1 | cubic decimeter or liter. |
| 1000 | cubic decimeters | `"` | 1 | cubic meter or stere. |
| 1000 | cubic meters | `"` | 1 | cubic dekameter |
| 1000 | cubic dekameters | `"` | 1 | cubic hectometer. |
| 1000 | cubic hectometers | `"` | 1 | cubic kilometer. |
| 1000 | cubic kilometers | `"` | 1 | cubic myriameter. |

### *For Dry and Liquid Measures*

| 10 | milliliters | make | 1 | centiliter. |
|---|---|---|---|---|
| 10 | centiliters | `"` | 1 | deciliter |
| 10 | deciliters | `"` | 1 | LITER |
| 10 | liters | `"` | 1 | dekaliter. |
| 10 | dekaliters | `"` | 1 | hectoliter. |
| 10 | hectoliters | `"` | 1 | kiloliter |
| 10 | kiloliters | `"` | 1 | myrialiter. |

[☞ A LITER, the standard of Measures of Capacity, usually in a cylindrical form, is equivalent to a cubic *Decimeter*, or the one-thousandth part of a cubic Meter, the contents of which are about one quart ]

The Kiloliter, or STERE, is a cubic Meter, and is used as a unit in measuring firewood and lumber.

| 10 | decisteres | make | 1 | stere. |
|---|---|---|---|---|
| 10 | steres | `"` | 1 | dekastere. |

## ALL WEIGHTS —New

| 10 | milligrams | make | 1 | centigram |
|---|---|---|---|---|
| 10 | centigrams | `"` | 1 | decigram. |
| 10 | decigrams | `"` | 1 | GRAM. |
| 10 | grams | `"` | 1 | dekagram. |
| 10 | dekagrams | `"` | 1 | hectogram. |
| 10 | hectograms | `"` | 1 | kilogram. |
| 10 | kilograms | `"` | 1 | myriagram. |
| 10 | myriagrams | `"` | 1 | quintal |
| 10 | quintals | `"` | 1 | millier or tonnean |

## PRONUNCIATION OF TERMS.

| TERMS. | ENGLISH. | TERMS | ENGLISH. |
|---|---|---|---|
| Meter, | Mee-ter. | Stere, | Stare. |
| Millimeter | Mill-e-mee-ter | Are, | Are. |
| Centimeter, | Sent-e-mee-ter. | Centare, | Sent-are. |
| Decimeter, | Des-e-mee-ter | Hectare, | Hect-are |
| Dekameter, | Dek-a-mee-ter. | Gram, | Gram, |
| Hectometer, | Hec-to-mee-ter | Milligram, | Mill-e-gram |
| Kilometer, | Kill-o-mee-ter. | Centigram, | Sent-e-gram |
| Myriameter, | Mir-e-a-mee-ter. | Decigram, | Des-e-gram. |
| Liter, | Li-ter | Dekagram, | Dek-a-gram. |
| Milliliter, | Mill-e-li-ter | Hectogram, | Hec-to-gram. |
| Centiliter, | Sent e-li-ter. | Kilogram, | Kill-o-gram |
| Deciliter, | Des-e-li-ter | Myriagram, | Mir-e-a-gram. |
| Dekaliter, | Dek-a-li-ter. | Quintal, | Quin-tal |
| Hectoliter, | Hec-to-li-ter | Millier, | Mill-i-er |
| Kiloliter, | Kill-o-li-ter | Tonneau, | Tun-no. |
| Myrialiter, | Mir-e-a-li-ter | | |

---

### Acts and Resolutions of Congress.

#### PUBLIC — No. 183.

AN ACT to authorize the use of the metric system of weights and measures

*Be it enacted by the Senate and House of Representatives of the United States of America in Congress assembled,* That from and after the passage of this act, it shall be lawful throughout the United States of America to employ the weights and measures of the metric system; and no contract or dealing, or pleading in any court, shall be deemed invalid or liable to objection, because the weights or measures expressed or referred to therein are weights or measures of the metric system

Sec 2 *And be it further enacted,* That the tables in the schedule hereto annexed, shall be recognized in the construction of contracts, and in all legal proceedings, as establishing, in terms of the weights and measures now in use in the United States, the equivalents of the weights and measures expressed therein in terms of the metric system, and said tables may be lawfully used for computing, determining and expressing, in customary weights and measures, the weights and measures of the metric system.

---

## MEASURES OF LENGTH

| METRIC DENOMINATIONS AND VALUES. | | EQUIVALENTS IN DENOMINATIONS IN USE. |
|---|---|---|
| Myriamètre, | 10,000 metres, | 6.2137 miles. |
| Kilometre, . . | 1,000 metres, | 0 62137 mile, or 2,280 feet and 10 inches |
| Hectometre, | 100 metres, | 328 feet and one inch. |
| Dekamètre, ..... | 10 metres, | 393 7 inches |
| Metre, . . | 1 metre, | 39.37 inches |
| Decimetre, . | 1-10th of a metre, | 3.937 inches |
| Centimetre, | 1-100th of a metre, | 0 3937inch |
| Millimetre, | 1-1000th of a metre, | 0.0394 inch |

---

## MEASURES OF SURFACE.

| METRIC DENOMINATIONS AND VALUES | | EQUIVALENTS IN DENOMINATIONS IN USE. |
|---|---|---|
| Hectare, . .... .. | 10,000 square metres, | 2 471 acres. |
| Are, ...... | 100 square metres, | 119 6 square yards |
| Centare, | 1 square metre, | 1 550 square inches |

**D**

## MEASURES OF CAPACITY.

| METRIC DENOMINATIONS AND VALUES. | | | EQUIVALENTS IN DENOMINATIONS IN USE. | |
| --- | --- | --- | --- | --- |
| Names. | No of liters | Cubic Measure. | Dry Measure | Liquid or Wine Measure |
| Kilolitre or stere, | 1000 | 1 cubic metre, | 1.308 cubic yard, | 264.17 gallons. |
| Hectolitre, | 100 | .1 of a cubic metre, | 2 bus and 3 35 pecks, | 26 417 gallons |
| Dekalitre, | 10 | 10 cubic decimetres, | 9.08 quarts, | 2 6417 gallons. |
| Litre, | 1 | 1 cubic decimetre, | 0 908 quart, | 1.0567 quart. |
| Decilitre, | 0.1 | .1 of a cubic decimetre, | 6 1022 cubic inches, | 0 845 gill |
| Centilitre, | 0 01 | 10 cubic centimetres, | 0 6102 cubic inch, | 0 338 fluid ounce. |
| Millilitre, | 0 001 | 1 cubic centimetre, | 0 061 cubic inch, | 0 27 fluid drachm |

## WEIGHTS.

| Metric Denominations and Values. | | | Equivalents in Denominations in Use |
|---|---|---|---|
| Names | No of grams. | Weight of what quantity of water at maximum density. | Avoirdupois weight. |
| Millier or tonneau, | 1000000 | 1 cubic metre, | 2204 6 pounds. |
| Quintal, | 100000 | 1 hectolitre, | 220 46 pounds |
| Myriagram, | 10000 | 10 litres, | 22 046 pounds. |
| Kilogram, or kilo, | 1000 | 1 litre, | 2 2046 pounds. |
| Hectogram, | 100 | 1 decilitre, | 3 5274 ounces. |
| Dekagram, | 10 | 10 cubic centimetres, | 0.3527 ounce |
| Gram, | 1 | 1 cubic centimetre, | 15 432 grains. |
| Decigram, | 1-10 | 1 of a cubic centimetre | 0 5432 grain |
| Centigram, | 1-100 | 10 cubic millimetres, | 0 1543 grain |
| Milligram, | 1-1000 | 1 cubic millimetre, | 0 0154 grain |

# INTEREST TABLE

**At Seven per Cent. in Dollars and Cents, from $1 to $10,000.**

| Am'nt | 1 day | 7 days. | 15 days. | 1 mo. | 3 mos | 6 mos | 12 mos |
|---|---|---|---|---|---|---|---|
| $ | $ C. | $ C | $ C. | $ C. | $ C. | $ C. | $ C. |
| 1 | 00 | 00 | 00¼ | 00½ | 01¾ | 03½ | 07 |
| 2 | 00 | 00¼ | 00½ | 01¼ | 03½ | 07 | 14 |
| 3 | 00 | 00½ | 00¾ | 01¾ | 05¼ | 10½ | 21 |
| 4 | 00 | 00½ | 01 | 02⅓ | 07 | 14 | 28 |
| 5 | 00 | 00¾ | 01½ | 03 | 08¾ | 17½ | 35 |
| 6 | 00 | 00¾ | 01¾ | 03½ | 10½ | 21 | 42 |
| 7 | 00 | 01 | 02 | 04 | 12¼ | 24½ | 49 |
| 8 | 00 | 01 | 02¼ | 04⅔ | 14 | 28 | 56 |
| 9 | 00 | 01¼ | 02½ | 05¼ | 15¾ | 31½ | 63 |
| 10 | 00¼ | 01¼ | 03 | 05¾ | 17½ | 35 | 70 |
| 20 | 00⅓ | 02¾ | 06 | 11⅔ | 35 | 70 | 1 40 |
| 30 | 00½ | 04 | 09 | 17½ | 52½ | 1 05 | 2 10 |
| 40 | 00¾ | 05½ | 12 | 23⅓ | 70 | 1 40 | 2 80 |
| 50 | 01 | 06¾ | 15 | 29¼ | 87½ | 1 75 | 3 50 |
| 100 | 02 | 13½ | 29 | 58⅓ | 1 75 | 3 50 | 7 00 |
| 200 | 04 | 27¼ | 58 | 1 16⅔ | 3 50 | 7 00 | 14 00 |
| 300 | 06 | 40¾ | 87½ | 1 75 | 5 25 | 10 50 | 21 00 |
| 400 | 08 | 54½ | 1 17 | 2 33⅓ | 7 00 | 14 00 | 28 00 |
| 500 | 10 | 68 | 1 46 | 2 91⅔ | 8 75 | 17 50 | 35 00 |
| 1000 | 19½ | 1 36 | 2 92 | 5 83⅓ | 17 50 | 35 00 | 70 00 |
| 2000 | 39 | 2 72¼ | 5 83 | 11 66⅔ | 35 00 | 70 00 | 140 00 |
| 3000 | 58 | 4 08¼ | 8 75 | 17 50 | 52 50 | 105 00 | 210 00 |
| 4000 | 78 | 5 44½ | 11 67 | 23 33⅓ | 70 00 | 140 00 | 280 00 |
| 5000 | 97 | 6 80½ | 14 58 | 29 16⅔ | 87 50 | 175 00 | 350 00 |
| 10000 | 1 94 | 13 61 | 29 17 | 58 33 | 175 00 | 350 00 | 700 00 |

## Discount and Premium.

When a person buys an article for $1,00—20 per cent off, (or discount) and sells it again for $1,00, he makes a profit of 25 per cent on his investment  Thus. He pays 80 cents and sells for $1,00—a gain of 20 cents, or 25 per cent of 80 cents  And for any transaction where the sale or purchase of gold, silver, or currency is concerned the following rules will apply in all cases.

RULE 1st.—To find premium when discount is given: Multiply 100 by rate of discount and divide by 100, less rate of discount

RULE 2d —To find discount when premium is given  Multiply the rate of interest by 100, and divide by 100 plus the rate of premium

Suppose A has $140 in currency, which he wishes to exchange for gold, when gold is 27 per cent premium  how much gold should he receive?  In this case the premium is given, consequently we must find the discount on A's currency and subtract it from the $140, as per rule 2d, showing the discount to be a trifle more than 21 per cent and that he should receive $110.60 in gold

| 5 pr ct | Dis allows | †5¼ | pr ct. | Pre | or profit |
|---|---|---|---|---|---|
| 10 " | " | †11 | " | " | " |
| 15 " | " | †17½ | " | " | " |
| 20 " | " | 25 | " | " | " |
| 25 " | " | 33⅓ | " | " | " |
| 30 " | " | *43 | " | " | " |
| 40 " | " | 69¾ | " | " | " |
| 50 " | " | 100 | " | " | " |

☞ A dagger (†) denotes the profits to be a fraction more than specified  A (*) denotes profits to be a fraction less than specified

## Table of Weights of Grain, Seeds, &c.

ACCORDING TO THE LAWS OF NEW YORK.

| Barley weighs . . | . . 48 lb per bushel |
|---|---|
| Beans " .. | 62 " " |
| Buckwheat " | 48 " " |
| Clover Seed . | 60 " " |
| Corn weighs .. . .. | .58 " " |
| Flax Seed* " | . 55 " " |
| Oats " .. | 32 " " |
| Peas " | 60 " " |
| Potatoes " . . | .. 60 " " |
| Rye " . . | . 56 " " |
| Timothy Seed . | .44 " " |
| Wheat .. | 60 " " |

*Flax Seed by cust'm weighs 56 lb. per bush

## Facts on Advertising.

The advertisements in an ordinary number of the London Times exceed 2,500  The annual advertising bills of one London firm are said to amount to $200,000; and three others are mentioned who each annually expend for the purpose $50,000  The expense for advertising the eight editions of the "Encyclopœdia Britannia" is said to have been $15,000

In large cities nothing is more common than to see large business establishments, which seem to have an immense advantage over all competitors, by the wealth, experience, and prestige they have acquired, drop gradually out of public view, and be succeeded by firms of a smaller capital, more energy, and more determined to have the fact that they sell such and such commodities known from one end of the land to the other  In other words, the establishments advertise, the old die of dignity.—The former are ravenous to pass out of obscurity into publicity, the latter believe that their publicity is so obvious that it cannot be obscured  The first understand that they must thrust themselves upon public attention, or be disregarded;  the second, having once obtained public attention, suppose they have arrested it permanently; while, in fact, nothing is more characteristic of the world than the ease with which it forgets.

Stephen Girard, than whom no shrewder business man ever lived, used to say  I have always considered advertising liberally and long to be the great medium of success in business, and the prelude to wealth  And I have made it an invariable rule too, to advertise in the dullest times as well as the busiest, long experience having taught me that money thus spent is well laid out, as by keeping my business continually before the public it has secured me many sales that I would otherwise have lost.

## Capacity of Cisterns or Wells.

Tabular view of the number of gallons contained in the clear, between the brick work for each ten inches of depth ·

| Diameter | | Gallons |
|---|---|---|
| 2 feet equals | | 19 |
| 2½ | " | 30 |
| 3 | " | 44 |
| 3½ | " | 60 |
| 4 | " | 78 |
| 4½ | " | 97 |
| 5 | " | 122 |
| 5½ | " | 148 |
| 6 | " | 176 |
| 6½ | " | 207 |
| 7 | " | 240 |
| 7½ | " | 275 |
| 8 | " | 313 |
| 8½ | " | 353 |
| 9 | " | 396 |
| 9½ | " | 461 |
| 10 | " | 489 |
| 11 | " | 592 |
| 12 | " | 705 |
| 13 | " | 827 |
| 14 | " | 959 |
| 15 | " | 1101 |
| 20 | " | 1958 |
| 25 | " | 3059 |

## Brilliant Whitewash.

Many have heard of the brilliant stucco whitewash on the east end of the President's house at Washington. The following is a recipe for it; it is gleaned from the National Intelligencer, with some additional improvements learned by experiments. Take half a bushel of nice unslacked lime, slack it with boiling water, cover it during the process to keep in the steam. Strain the liquid through a fine sieve or strainer, and add to it a peck of salt, previously well dissolved in warm water; three pounds of ground rice, boiled to a thin paste, and stirred in boiling hot; half a pound of powdered Spanish whiting, and a pound of clean glue, which has been previously dissolved by soaking it well, and then hanging it over a slow fire, in a small kettle within a large one filled with water. Add five gallons of hot water to the mixture, stir it well, and let it stand a few days covered from the dirt.

It should be put on right hot; for this purpose it can be kept in a kettle on a portable furnace. It is said that about a pint of this mixture will cover a square yard upon the outside of a house if properly applied. Brushes more or less small may be used according to the neatness of the job required. It answers as well as oil paint for wood, brick or stone, and is cheaper. It retains its brilliancy for many years. There is nothing of the kind that will compare with it, either for inside or outside walls.

Coloring matter may be put in and made of any shade you like. Spanish brown stirred in will make red pink, more or less deep according to the quantity. A delicate tinge of this is very pretty, for inside walls. Finely pulverized common clay, well mixed with Spanish brown, makes a reddish stone color. Yellow-ochre stirred in makes yellow wash, but chrome goes further, and makes a color generally esteemed prettier. In all these cases the darkness of the shades of course is determined by the quantity of coloring used. It is difficult to make rules, because tastes are different. It would be best to try experiments on a shingle and let it dry. We have been told that green must not be mixed with lime. The lime destroys the color, and the color has an effect on the whitewash, which makes it crack and peel. When walls have been badly smoked, and you wish to have them a clean white, it is well to squeeze indigo plentifully through a bag into the water you use, before it is stirred in the whole mixture. If a larger quantity than five gallons be wanted, the same proportion should be observed.

## How to get a Horse out of a Fire.

The great difficulty of getting horses from a stable where surrounding buildings are in a state of conflagration, is well known. The plan of covering their eyes with a blanket will not always succeed.

A gentleman whose horses have been in great peril from such a cause, having tried in vain to save them, hit upon the expedient of having them harnessed as though going to their usual work, when, to his astonishment, they were led from the stable without difficulty.

## The Chemical Barometer.

Take a long narrow bottle, such as an old-fashioned Eau-de-Cologne bottle, and put into it two and a half drachms of camphor, and eleven drachms of spirits of wine; when the camphor is dissolved, which it will readily do by slight agitation, add the following mixture. Take water, nine drachms; nitrate of potash (saltpetre) thirty-eight grains, and muriate of ammonia (sal ammoniac) thirty-eight grains. Dissolve these salts in the water prior to mixing with the camphorated spirit, then shake the whole well together. Cork the bottle well, and wax the top, but afterwards make a very small aperture in the cork with a red-hot needle. The bottle may then be hung up, or placed in any stationary position. By observing the different appearances which the materials assume, as the weather changes it becomes an excellent prognosticator of a coming storm or of a sunny sky.

## Leech Barometer.

Take an eight ounce phial, and put in it three gills of water, and place in it a healthy leech, changing the water in summer once a week, and in winter once in a fortnight, and it will most accurately prognosticate the weather. If the weather is to be fine, the leech lies motionless at the bottom of the glass and coiled together in a spiral form; if rain may be expected, it will creep up to the top of its lodgings and remain there till the weather is settled; if we are to have wind, it will move through its habitation with amazing swiftness, and seldom goes to rest till it begins to blow hard; if a remarkable storm of thunder and rain is to succeed, it will lodge for some days before almost continually out of the water, and discover great uneasiness in violent throes and convulsive-like motions; in frost as in clear summer-like weather it lies constantly at the bottom; and in snow as in rainy weather it pitches its dwelling in the very mouth of the phial. The top should be covered over with a piece of muslin.

To Measure Grain in a Bin.—Find the number of cubic feet, from which deduct *one-fifth*. The remainder is the number of bushels—allowing, however, one bushel extra to every 224. Thus in a remainder of 224 there would be 225 bushels. In a remainder of 448 there would be 450 bushels, &c.

# VALUABLE RECIPES.

———

[The following recipes are vouched for by several who have tried them and proved their virtues. Many of them have been sold singly for more than the price of this book.—PUB.]

### HORSES.

RING BONE AND SPAVIN.—2 oz. each of Spanish flies and Venice turpentine; 1 oz. each of aqua ammonia and euphorbium; ½ oz. red precipitate; ½ oz. corrosive sublimate; 1½ lbs. lard. When thoroughly pulverized and mixed, heat carefully so as not to burn, and pour off free from sediment.

For ring-bone, rub in thoroughly, after removing hair, once in 48 hours. For spavin, once in 24 hours. Cleanse and press out the matter on each application.

POLL-EVIL.—Gum arabic ½ oz; common potash ½ oz; extract of belladonna ½ dr. Put the gum in just enough water to dissolve it. Pulverize the potash and mix with the dissolved gum, and then put in the extract of belladonna, and it will be ready for use. Use with a syringe after having cleansed with soap suds, and repeat once in two days till a cure is affected.

SCOURS.—Powdered tormentil root, given in milk, from 3 to 5 times daily till cured.

GREASE-HEEL AND SCRATCHES.—Sweet oil 6 ozs.; borax 2 ozs.; sugar of lead 2 ozs. Wash off with dish water, and, after it is dry, apply the mixture twice a day.

CHOLIC IN HORSES.—To ¾ pt. of warm water add 1 oz. laudanum and 3 ozs. spirits of turpentine, and repeat the dose in about ¾ of an hour, adding ½ oz. powdered aloes, if not relieved.

BOTS.—Three doses. 1st. 2 qts milk and 1 of molasses. 2d. 15 minutes after, 2 qts. warm sage tea. 3d. After the expiration of 30 minutes, sufficient lard to physic.—Never fails.

### MISCELLANEOUS.

PILES—PERFECTLY CURED.—Take flour of sulphur 1 oz., rosin 3 ozs., pulverize and mix well together. (Color with carmine or cochineal, if you like.) Dose—What will lie on a five cent piece, night and morning, washing the parts freely in cold water once or twice a day. This is a remedy of great value.

The cure will be materially hastened by taking a table-spoon of sulphur in a half pint of milk, daily, until the cure is affected.

SURE CURE FOR CORNS, WARTS AND CHILBLAINS.—Take of nitric and muriatic acids, blue vitriol and salts of tartar, 1 oz. each. Add the blue vitriol, pulverized, to either of the acids; add the salts of tartar in the same way; when done foaming, add the other acid, and in a few days it will be ready for use. For chilblains and corns apply it very lightly with a swab, and repeat in a day or two until cured. For warts, once a week, until they disappear.

HOOF-AIL IN SHEEP.—Mix 2 ozs. each of butter of antimony and muriatic acid with 1 oz. of pulverized white vitriol, and apply once or twice a week to the bottom of the foot.

COMMON RHEUMATISM.—Kerosene oil 2 ozs.; neats-foot oil 1 oz.; oil of organum ½ oz. Shake when used, and rub and heat in twice daily.

VERY FINE SOAP, QUICKLY AND CHEAPLY MADE.—Fourteen pounds of bar soap in a half a boiler of hot water; cut up fine; add three pounds of sal-soda made thin; one ounce of pulverized rosin; stir it often till all is dissolved; just as you take it off the fire, put in two table-spoonfuls of spirits of turpentine and one of ammonia; pour it in a barrel, and fill up with cold soft water; let it stand three or four days before using. It is an excellent soap for washing clothes, extracting the dirt readily, and not fading colored articles.

**WATER PROOF FOR LEATHER.**—Take linseed oil 1 pint, yellow wax and white turpentine each 2 ozs  Burgundy pitch 1 oz , melt and color with lampblack.

**TO KEEP CIDER SWEET**—Put into each barrel, immediately after making, ½ lb ground mustard, 2 oz  salt and 2 oz  pulverized chalk.  Stir them in a little cider, pour them into the barrel, and shake up well.

**AGUE CURE**—Procure 1½ table-spoons of fresh mandrake root juice, (by pounding) and mix with the same quantity of molasses, and take in three equal doses, 2 hours a part, the whole to be taken 1 hour before the chill comes on   Take a swallow of some good bitters before meals, for a couple of weeks after the chills are broken, and the cure will be permanent.

**CURE FOR SALT RHEUM OR SCURVY.**—Take of the pokeweed, any time in summer; pound it ; press out the juice; strain it into a pewter dish; set it in the sun till it becomes a salve—then put it into an earthen mug; add to it fresh water and bees' wax sufficient to make an ointment of common consistency , simmer the whole over a fire till thoroughly mixed   When cold, rub the part affected   The patient will almost immediately experience its good effects, and the most obstinate cases will be cured in three or four months   Tested —The juice of the ripe berries may be prepared in the same way.

**SUPERIOR PAINT—FOR BRICK HOUSES.**—To lime whitewash, add for a fastener, sulphate of zinc, and shade with any color you choose, as yellow ochre, Venetian red, etc.  It outlasts oil paint

**FELONS.**—Stir 1 oz  of Venice turpentine with ¼ tea-spoonful of water, till it looks like candied honey, and apply by spreading upon cloth and wrapping around the finger.  If not too long delayed will cure in 6 hours   A poke root poultice is also said  to be a sure remedy.

**WATER PROOF BLACKING AND HARNESS POLISH.**—Take two and a half ounces gum shellac and half a pint  of alcohol, and set in a warm place until dissolved , then add two and a half ounces Venice turpentine to neutralize the alcohol ; add a tablespoonful of lampblack   Apply with a fine sponge.  It will give a good polish over oil or grease

**MOSQUITOS**—To get rid of these tormentors, take a few hot coals  on a shovel, or a chafing dish, and burn upon them some brown sugar in your bed-rooms and parlors, and you effectually banish or destroy every mosquito for the night.

**CHEAP OUTSIDE PAINT.**—Take two parts (in bulk) of water lime ground fine, one part (in bulk) of white lead ground in oil   Mix them thoroughly, by adding best boiled linseed oil enough to prepare it to pass through a paint mill, after which temper with oil till it can be applied with a common paint brush   Make any color to suit   It will last three times as long as  lead paint, and cost not one-fourth as much.  IT IS SUPERIOR

**CURE FOR A COUGH.**—A strong decoction of the leaves of the pine, sweetened with loaf sugar.  Take a wine-glass warm on going to bed, and half an  hour before eating three times a day.  The above is sold as a cough syrup, and is doing wonderful cures, and it is sold at a great profit to the manufacturers.

## How to Judge a Horse.

A correspondent, contrary to old maxims, undertakes to judge the character of a horse by outward appearances, and offers the following suggestions, the result of his close observation and long experience:

If the color be light sorrell, or chestnut, his feet, legs and face white, these are marks of kindness.  If he is broad and full between the eyes, he may be depended on as a horse of good sense, and capable of being trained to anything.

As respects such horses, the more kindly you treat them the better you will be treated in return.  Nor will a horse of this description stand a whip, if well fed.

If you want a safe horse, avoid one that is dish-faced   He may be so far gentle as not to scare; but he will have too much go-ahead in him to be safe with everybody.

If you want a fool, but a horse of great bottom, get a deep bay, with not a white hair about him.  If his face is a little dished, so much the worse   Let no man ride such a horse that is not an adept in riding —they are always tricky and unsafe.

If you want one that will never give out, never buy a large, overgrown one

A black horse cannot stand heat, nor a white one cold

If you want a gentle horse, get one with more or less white about the head, the more the better   Many persons suppose the parti-colored horses belonging to the circuses, shows, &c , are selected for their oddity   But the selections thus made are on account of their great docility and gentleness.

## Measurement of Hay in the Mow or Stack.

It is often desirable, where conveniences for weighing are not at hand, to purchase and sell hay by measurement   It is evident that no fixed rule will answer in all cases, as it would require more cubic feet at the top of a mow than at the bottom.  The general rule adopted by those who have tested it, is that a cube, each side of which shall measure eight feet, of *solid* Timothy hay, as taken from mow or bottom of stack will weigh a *ton*.  The rule may be varied for upper part of mow or stack according to pressure.

# Almanac or Calendar for 20 Years.

| C B | A | G | F | E D | C | B | A | G F | E |
|---|---|---|---|---|---|---|---|---|---|
| 1864 | 1865 | 1866 | 1867 | 1868 | 1869 | 1870 | 1871 | 1872 | 1873 |
| D | C | B A | G | F | E | D C | F | •E | D |
| 1874 | 1875 | 1876 | 1877 | 1878 | 1879 | 1880 | 1881 | 1882 | 1883 |

| | | | | | | | |
|---|---|---|---|---|---|---|---|
| 1 8 15 22 29 | Sun. | Sat. | Frid'y. | Thurs. | Wed. | Tues. | Mon. |
| 2 9 16 23 30 | Mon. | Sun. | Sat. | Frid'y. | Thurs. | Wed. | Tues. |
| 3 10 17 24 31 | Tues. | Mon. | Sun. | Sat. | Frid'y. | Thurs. | Wed. |
| 4 11 18 25 .. | Wed. | Tues. | Mon. | Sun. | Sat. | Frid'y. | Thurs. |
| 5 12 19 26 .. | Thurs. | Wed. | Tues. | Mon. | Sun. | Sat. | Frid'y. |
| 6 13 20 27 .. | Frid'y. | Thurs | Wed. | Tues. | Mon. | Sun. | Sat. |
| 7 14 21 28 . | Sat. | Frid'y | Thurs. | Wed. | Tues. | Mon. | Sun. |
| Jan. and Oct. | A | B | C | D | E | F | G |
| May. | B | C | D | E | F | G | A |
| August. | C | D | E | F | G | A | B |
| Feb., Mar., Nov. | D | E | F | G | A | B | C |
| June. | E | F | G | A | B | C | D |
| Sept. & Dec. | F | G | A | B | C | D | E |
| April & July. | G | A | B | C | D | E | F |

EXPLANATION —Find the Year and observe the Letter above it; then look for the Month, and in a line with it find the Letter of the Year, above the Letter find the Day, and the figures on the left, in the same line, are the days of the same name in the month

Leap Years have two letters; the first is used till the end of February, the second during the remainder of the year.

# BROOME COUNTY.

*BROOME COUNTY* was formed from Tioga, March 28, 1806, and named in honor of John Broome of New York, who was then Lieut Gov. of the State, and who acknowledged the compliment by presenting the County with a handsomely executed silver seal, appropriately designed by himself, emblematical of the name. Berkshire and Owego were annexed to Tioga County, March 21, 1822. It is situated near the center of the south border of the State, centrally distant 110 miles from Albany, and contains 706 square miles. Its surface is greatly diversified, consisting of rolling and hilly uplands, broad river intervales and the narrow valleys of small streams. The hills extend from the Pennsylvania line northerly through the County. They are divided into three general ranges by the valleys of the Susquehanna and Chenango rivers. The first range, lying east of the Susquehanna, forms the east border of the County. Its highest summits are 400 to 700 feet above the Delaware, and 1,400 to 1,700 feet above tide. The declivities of the hills are usually steep, and the summits spread out into a broad and hilly upland. This ridge is divided by the deep ravines of a large number of small streams, and in several places it rises into peaks. The second ridge lies in the great bend of the Susquehanna, and is bounded by the valleys of that river and the Chenango. The highest summits are 300 to 500 feet above the Susquehanna, and 1,200 to 1,400 feet above tide. The hills are generally bounded by gradual slopes, and the summits are broad, rolling uplands. The southern portion of this ridge is high above the valleys ; but towards the north the hilly character subsides into that of a fine rolling region. The third ridge lies west of the Chenango and Susquehanna rivers. Its summits are a little less in elevation than those of the second ridge ; and the general characteristics of the two regions are similar. The wide valley of the Susquehanna divides it into two distinct parts, the southern of which is more hilly than the northern. The hills in the central and western parts of the County are rounded and arable to their summits    The narrow valleys that break the continuity of the ridges are usually bordered by gradually sloping hillsides.*

The geological formation of the County is so exceedingly simple that it scarcely received notice in the report of the geological and mineralogical surveying party of the State at an early day.  It possesses little attraction to the scientist.  The principal rock is graywacke, which is found lying in strata, in a nearly horizontal position, in all the hills and in the beds of the largest streams, and which forms the basis of the mountains.  All the rocks are included in the Chemung and Catskill groups.  The former—consisting of slaty sandstone and shales—occupies all the north and west portions of the County ; and the latter—consisting of gray and red sandstone, red shale and slate—crown all the summits in the south and east portions.  Much of the more level portions of the surface is covered to a considerable depth by depositions of sand, gravel, clay and hardpan.  The rocks crop out only upon the declivities and summits of the hills †  The valleys throughout the County give evidence of having been excavated by the action of water, whose currents exerted a force immensely greater than any which seek the ocean through these channels at the present day.  Their origin is referred by geologists to the drift period— a time when the gorgeous hillsides which now afford so many attractive homes, were inundated, and the productive vales pulverized and prepared by the mighty agencies then at work for the occupancy of man.  Weak brine springs were early found, extending for several miles along the valley of Halfway Brook in the north part of the County.‡  Sulphur and other mineral springs are found in various parts of the County. §  Several excavations for coal have been made, but without suc-

---

*French's *Historical and Statistical Gazetteer of New York.*

† "The pebbles found in and near the banks of the Susquehanna and Chenango rivers," says Wilkinson, in the *Annals of Binghamton,* "exhibit an astonishing variety · garnet, tourmaline, quartz, agate, hornstone, porphyry, granite, jasper, feldspar, hornblend, dark blue limestone, and conglomerates of almost every character are occasionally picked up and added to the cabinet of the naturalist."

‡ Several years since a boring was commenced in Lisle, on the site of an old deer lick, and was continued to a depth of more than 400 feet, without any practical result.  More recent attempts have been made to develope the springs in the valley of Halfway Brook, in the town of Barker, a more detailed account of which will be given in the history of that town.

§ A sulphur spring has for some time been developed in the town of Nanticoke , and one was recently discovered at Osborne Hollow, in the town of Colesville, while a shaft was being sunk to ascertain the depth of a vein of lead, traces of which are found there.  A chalybeate spring was recently discovered in Binghamton, in the history of which town a more detailed account of it will be given.

cess, as all the coal measures are above the highest strata of rocks found in the County. It is believed that the County has no valuable minerals, or at least none in sufficient quantity to render them profitable. Traces of copper and nickel are supposed to have been found at Osborne Hollow, but too little is known regarding it to warrant an assertion.

The principal streams are the Susquehanna, Delaware, Chenango, Tioughnioga and Otselic rivers ; Oquaga, Okkanum, Nanticoke, Little Snake, Big and Little Choconut, Castle, Yorkshire, Bradley, Tracy and Kattel creeks ; and Halfway, Page and North brooks.*

* The Susquehanna, having its rise in Otsego Lake, enters the County at Nineveh, on the north line of Colesville, passing in a southerly direction through that town and Windsor, and leaves the County near the south-east corner of the latter town. After forming the *great bend* in Penn it again enters the County on the south line, and runs in a north-westerly direction to the north of Conklin, forming the division between that town and Kirkwood, when it turns and flows nearly due west through the town and city of Binghamton, forming the dividing line between Union and Vestal, and leaves the County on the west border, on the line of these two towns. Passing nearly its entire length through mountainous country, whose prominences are ofttimes abrupt and irregular, it is subjected to frequent changes in its course ; and though this feature detracts from its value for navigable puposes, it adds vastly to the beauty of the country adjacent to its banks. In its upper course through the County its valley is contracted and rendered narrow by the high and steep declivities through which it meanders ; but further west it expands into broad intervales, skirted by gradually sloping hillsides. The usually placid surface of its clear, sparkling waters, the gently receding banks, dotted with the evidences of thrift and industry and mechanical ingenuity, and crowned with the alternating foliage of the forest and cultivated field, combine to present the picture of rare and quiet beauty for which it is so celebrated. This picture is varied at intervals by its more wild and rugged aspects, which develope a romantic beauty, at times approaching the sublime.

In Smith's history of Virginia, the name of this river is written *Sas-que-sa-han-nough* ; and by Mr. Morgan, in the Onondaga dialect, *Ga-wa-no-wa-na-neh.* This last name, says C. P. Avery, in a paper on *The Susquehanna Valley,* which appears in *The Saint Nicholas* of March, 1854, is pronounced as follows : "The first and third *a* pronounced as in the syllable *ah* ; the second one as in *fate* ; the fourth as in *at.*"

The Delaware forms the southern portion of the east boundary of the County, commencing at the village of Deposit, and flowing in a south-east direction, through a deep, rocky valley, bordered by steep and often precipitous hills.

The Chenango enters the County on the north line, a little east and north of Chenango Forks, and pursuing a southerly direction, forming in its course the boundary between the towns of Chenango and Fenton, augments the Susquehanna, with which it unites near the southern limits of the city of Binghamton. In the north part, the valley of this river is hemmed in by high ridges ; but in the south it expands into a broad intervale. It has a uniform descent of five or six feet to the mile, and is free from rapids and sudden turns.

Upon Guy Johnson's map of 1771, this river is named *Ot-si-nin-goo* ; upon DeWitt's map of about the year 1791, *Che-nen-go,* and in Mr. Morgan's work, *O-che-nang.—The Saint Nicholas, March,* 1854, *p.* 412.

The 'Indian name," says French, in his *State Gazetteer,* is "*O-nan-no-gi-is-ka,* Shagbark hickory," the second and fifth syllables in the name being accented.

The soil along the river intervales is generally very fertile, consisting of deep, sandy and gravelly loam, mixed with disintegrated slate and vegetable mold. The narrow valleys of the smaller streams are also fertile. The soil upon the north and west hills consists principally of gravelly loam intermixed with clay and disintegrated shale, and is well adapted to grazing. The declivities of the south and east hills are similar to the last in character, but their summits are generally covered with clay and hardpan. The large proportion of upland and the unevenness of the surface render this County best adapted to pasturage. While all branches of agriculture are pursued,

---

The Tioughnioga enters the County on the north, from Cortland county, and flows in a south-east direction, through the east part of Lisle, the south-west corner of Triangle and diagonally (from north-west to south-east,) across the town of Barker, until it unites with the Chenango at Chenango Forks. Its valley is very narrow, being bordered by high and steep hills.

"This name is formed from Te-ah-hah-hogue, the meeting of roads and waters at the same place."—*Spafford's Gazetteer of New York*, 1813, p 176.

The Otselic also enters the County from the north, and like the Tioughnioga, into which it empties at Whitneys Point, flows through a narrow valley, through the west part of Triangle.

Oquaga Creek enters the County on the north line of Sanford and flows south through the center of that town to McClure Settlement, when it turns east and empties into the Delaware at Deposit.

By the early missionaries this creek was called Onuh-huh-quah-geh, and by the Iroquois, now in Canada, it is so pronounced. Upon an early map it is named O-nogh-qua-gy.—*The Saint Nicholas, March,* 1854, p. 413.

Okkanum Creek, which flows east through the north-west part of Windsor , Nanticoke Creek, which flows south through Lisle, Nanticoke, Maine and Union, nearly to the south-west corner of the latter town ; Little Snake Creek, which rises in the south-east corner of Vestal and flows east through Binghamton and Conklin ; Big and Little Choconut * Creeks, the former of which rises in Penn. and flows north-west through the center of Vestal, and the latter, in the north-west part of Chenango and flows south through the south-east part of Maine, north-east part of Union, crossing in a south westerly direction the north-west corner of Binghamton, and westerly through the south-east corner of Union ; and Tracy Creek, which rises in Penn and flows north through the west part of Vestal, are tributary to the Susquehanna. Castle Creek, which rises in the south-west part of Barker and flows south through Chenango ; Kattel Creek, which rises in the north-east part of Chenango and flows south through that town ; and Page Brook, which enters the County near the center of the north line of Fenton and flows south-west, are tributary to the Chenango. Yorkshire Creek, which enters the County from Cortland County, in the north-west corner of Lisle, and flows south-east through that town ; and Halfway Brook, which also enters this County from Cortland, near the north-east corner of Triangle, and flows south through the east part of that town and to the north-east part of Barker, when it turns west, are tributary to the Tioughnioga. Bradley Creek, rises in the east part of Maine, through which town it flows, in a south-west direction, and empties into Nanticoke Creek a little south of Union Center. North Brook rises in the west central part of Sanford and pursues a south-east course to Oquaga Creek, with which it unites a little south of McClure Settlement.

*Choconut, upon an early map, is written Chugh-nult At the treaty of 1768, it is written the same way, with the exception of the letter I, which is omitted.—THE SAINT NICHOLAS March, 1854, p. 412.

fruit culture, and stock and wool raising, in connection with the products of the dairy, form the leading interests.* Manufacturing is carried on to a limited extent at Binghamton and other places. A stronger disposition to engage in this branch of industry is manifest.

The *County Seat* is located at Binghamton, at the junction of the Susquehanna and Chenango rivers   Previous to the erection of this County, Binghamton (then *Chenango Point*) was a half-shire of Tioga County, and courts were held a part of the time at the house of J. Whitney, until 1802, in which year a court house† was erected.   The County (Tioga) was divided into two jury districts in 1801.   In 1828‡ an act authorizing the erection of a new court house passed the Legislature, and $5,000 were raised in the County for that purpose.§   In 1857 the court house erected in 1828 was superseded by the present elegant structure, which is located at the head of Chenango street, fronting on Court street.‖   The County Clerk's office is a fire-proof building situated on court house square, adjacent to

---

* French's *State Gazetteer*.

† The first court house was located on the north-west corner of Court and Chenango streets, fronting on Court street   In size it was about 36x24 feet, finished in a plain and hasty style, and contained two log jail rooms, a room for the residence of the jailor below, and the court room above.   It was afterwards moved across the road, and stood a little down from the top of Court hill —*Annals of Binghamton*, p. 182.

The first county officers were : Gen. John Patterson of Lisle, *First Judge* ; James Stoddard of Lisle, Amos Patterson of Union, Daniel Hudson of Chenango and Geo. Harper and Mason Wattles of Windsor, *Associate Judges*, (the last named two were added in 1807, the year following that in which the County was erected,) Ashbel Wells of Binghamton, *County Clerk*, and Wm. Woodruff, *Sheriff*.   The first court was held on the second Tuesday in May, 1806, and the first cause tried under the authority of this County was between Amraphael Hotchkiss and Nathan Lane jr. —a civil suit.   The first criminal cause was the people against Ebenezer Centre.

‡ *Annals of Binghamton*, p. 217.   French says the first court house was superseded by the erection of a new one in 1826.

§ Ami Doubleday, Grover Buel and Geo. Wheeler were appointed commissioners to superintend the construction of the work.

‖ This last building is ninety-six feet long and fifty-eight feet wide   The basement is built of stone and the upper stories of brick   A Grecian portico supported by four Ionic pillars, each six feet in diameter and thirty-six feet high, adds beauty and finish to the front.   Its fine dome is surmounted by a statue of justice, whose evenly balanced scales, it is hoped, are a true symbol of the equity meted out in its courts   It contains the usual county offices, the rooms for which are large, convenient and well ventilated.   It was erected at a cost of $32,000.

the court house.*  The jail is on Hawley street a short distance from the court house.†

*The County Poor House* is located on a farm of 130 acres, about three miles north of Binghamton, on the west side of the Chenango River.  Of its management, the committee appointed to inspect it in 1871, say in their report, " that we found the house in excellent order; and everything (apparently) done for the unfortunate inmates, that the liberality of the County and the kind and humane treatment of the keeper and his family could do to make them comfortable."  The children receive instruction at the Susquehanna Valley Home, in the city of Binghamton.‡

---

* This building is to be superseded by one now in process of erection, in the rear of the present one.  The basement of the new building is being constructed of stone, and the upper story will be built of brick, with stone trimmings.  Its front will be forty-six feet and two inches, its length sixty-eight feet and four inches, and its height above ground thirty-one feet and six inches.  The upper story will consist of three commodious rooms, one of which will be used for the office of the clerk, one for that of the recording clerk, and the third as a depository for legal documents.  The basement is designed to be used for storing documents to which reference is seldom made.  It will be a tasty, fire-proof structure, and furnished with modern improvements.  The County appropriated, Dec. 6, 1871, $16,000 for its erection.

The following is an abstract of the first deed recorded in the clerk's office of Broome County .

" THIS INDENTURE made the twenty fourth day of March, in the year of our Lord one thousand eight hundred and six, between James Harvey of the town of Union and county of Tioga, and Catharine, his wife, on the one part, and Lewis Keeler of the town of Chenango and county aforesaid, of the other part, for and in consideration of the sum of Two Hundred Dollars, to them in hand paid, at or before the ensealing and delivery of the presents, by the said party of the second part, the receipt whereof is hereby acknowledged, Have granted, bargained, sold, aliened, remised, released, conveyed, assured, enfeoffed, and confirmed; and, by these presents do fully, freely and absolutely, grant, bargain, sell, alien, remise, release, convey assure, enfeoff, and confirm unto - - - - containing one acre and one hundred square rods of land, more or less, situate - - - ."

The third deed recorded is a conveyance from John and Peter Augustus Jay, esquires, of Bedford, Westchester county, to Garret Williamson, farmer, of the same place, and bears date of Nov 29, 1805  It was recorded May 20, 1806.  By it one hundred acres, a part of sixteen thousand acres granted by letters patent to Jay and Rutherford in 1787, is conveyed.

† The portion of the jail containing the cells was built in 1858, at a cost of $15,000.  In its construction due provisions were made for the safety, health and classification of prisoners —*French's Gazetteer, p.* 179.

‡ From the report of the *Proceedings of the Board of Supervisors in* 1871 we glean the following interesting particulars relative to the poor of the County :  The whole number of paupers relieved or supported during the year ending Dec. 1, 1871, was 1,602, all of whom were County paupers. The number of persons temporarily relieved was 1,375.  The aggregate expense of relieving and supporting paupers was $23,437.48.  Of this sum the amount expended for temporary relief was $10,961.10.  The actual value of the labor of the paupers maintained was $1,200; the estimated amount saved in their support in consequence of their labor was $500; and the sum actually expended independent of the labor and earnings of the paupers, divided by the average number kept during the year, gives $1.54 per week, as the actual expense of keeping each person.  The number of paupers received into the Poor House during the year was 160, two of whom were

The principal works of internal improvement are the Chenango Canal *; the N. Y. & Erie R. R. †; the Syracuse, Bing-

born there. The number who died during the year was five; the number bound out, two; and the number discharged, 141. The number remaining in the Poor House Dec. 1, 1871, was 79, of whom 43 were males and 36, females. Of the males, three were of the age of sixteen years or under, and of the females, two. Of the seventy-nine inmates, twenty-two were foreigners; ten, lunatics; thirteen, idiots; two, mutes; and one was blind. The number of insane paupers, supported by the County, and remaining in Willard Asylum, at Ovid, Dec. 1, 1871, was eleven.

The following table shows the nativity of persons relieved or supported in the County during the year 1871:

| Country. | Male. | Female | Total. |
|---|---|---|---|
| United States... | 397 | 422 | 819 |
| Ireland ......... | 344 | 237 | 581 |
| England . | 22 | 7 | 29 |
| Scotland ... | 4 | 3 | 7 |
| Germany . . | 75 | 56 | 131 |
| France .. | 9 | 4 | 13 |
| Italy ......... | | 8 | 8 |
| Austria .... | 2 | | 2 |
| Russia ........ | 6 | 5 | 11 |
| Denmark ......... | 1 | | 1 |
| Totals............ | 860 | 742 | 1602 |

and the following, the causes of pauperism of persons relieved or supported in the County, during the same year:

| Causes | Male | Female | Total. |
|---|---|---|---|
| Intemperance, direct .. | 94 | 8 | 102 |
| Children having intemperate parents.. | 20 | 40 | 60 |
| Wives having intemperate husbands.............. | | 20 | 20 |
| Debauchery .... | 3 | 22 | 25 |
| Debauchery of parents........ | 5 | 7 | 12 |
| Vagrancy... | 381 | 178 | 559 |
| Idiocy... | 6 | 11 | 17 |
| Lunacy . | 14 | 14 | 28 |
| Blindness.... | 12 | 4 | 16 |
| Lameness | 26 | 8 | 34 |
| Sickness | 66 | 48 | 114 |
| Decrepitude .. | 13 | 7 | 20 |
| Old age ...... | 24 | 26 | 50 |
| Deaf and Dumb ... | 3 | | 3 |
| Indigent and destitute .. | 65 | 125 | 190 |
| Children having destitute parents........ | 80 | 122 | 202 |
| "    "    sick    " | 38 | 60 | 98 |
| Females having sick husbands ... | | 27 | 27 |
| Orphans ... | 8 | 9 | 17 |
| Bastards ......... | 2 | 6 | 8 |
| Totals . ... | 860 | 742 | 1602 |

The first cost of the land and the erections on it was $3,000. The present estimated value of the whole establishment is $30,000.

*This Canal was authorized Feb. 23, 1833, in which year it was begun, and was finished in 1837, at a cost of $1,737,703. It connects the Erie Canal at Utica with the Susquehanna River at Binghamton. It is ninety-seven miles long, exclusive of thirteen and three-fourths miles of feeders, none of which are navigable. It is supplied by the Chenango River and six reservoirs, viz: Madison Brook, Woodmans Pond, Lelands Pond, Bradleys Brook, Hatchs Lake and Eaton Brook reservoirs, all of which are in the south part of Madison County. The Canal extends across to and up the valley of Oriskany Creek to the summit level and down the valley of Chenango River. From Utica to the Summit it rises 706 feet, by 76 locks, and from thence it descends 303 feet, by 38 locks, to the Susquehanna, Of its

† See foot note on following page

hamton & N. Y. R. R.*; the Albany & Susquehanna R. R ‡;

114 locks, two are stone and the remainder composite    Upon the feeders
are twelve road and eighteen farm bridges.   It enters the County on the
north line of Fenton and follows the course of the Chenango, on the east
side
Attempts have been made to effect the extension of this Canal to
Athens, Penn., and large appropriations have been made by the State for
that purpose and considerable work done, but it still remains a huge, unfinished ditch, with little prospect of its being perfected according to the
original design   Efforts, which seem likely to prove successful, are being
made to secure from the State the right of way along this route for the
road-bed of a new railroad

+ *The N. Y. & Erie R. R* was authorized April 24, 1832, and the company organized in July, 1833.   The first preliminary survey was made in
1832, by DeWitt Clinton, Jr., by order of the Government.   In 1834 the
Governor appointed Benj Wright to survey the route; who, assisted by
James Seymour and Chas. Ellett, began the survey May 23d, and finished
it the same year.   In 1845 the Company was reorganized, and forty miles
were put under contract.   Various financial embarrassments, necessitat-
ing State aid and increased private subscriptions, and involving the re-
linquishment by the original stockholders of one-half the amount of stock
held by them, confronted this gigantic enterprise and retarded its accomplishment, so that its final completion to Dunkirk was not effected until
1851   The road was opened to Binghamton Dec 28, 1848, and to Dunkirk
May 14, 1851   It enters the County at Deposit and extends through the
town of Sanford, across the south-east corner of Windsor, when it leaves
the County, passing into Pennsylvania, and enters it again on the east bank
of the Susquehanna, extending along the west line of Kirkwood, through
the north part of the town and city of Binghamton, and the southern part
of Union, leaving the County in the south-west corner of that town
Being the first road opened through the County, it contributed largely to
the latter's growth and development.

* *The Syracuse, Binghamton & N. Y. R. R.* was originally formed July
2, 1851, as the Syracuse and Binghamton R. R    The road was opened
through, Oct 23, 1854   It was sold Oct 13, 1856, on foreclosure of mortgage,
and the name changed to Syracuse & Southern R. R.   Its present name
was assumed under act of March 31, 1857.   In 1858 the company were
authorized to purchase the Union R. R. to the canal at Geddes.   The Delaware, Lackawanna & Western R. R.   company obtained a controling
influence in the road about the first of March, 1869, and still maintain it.
It is 79.33 miles in length.   It enters the county on the north line of Lisle,
and following the west bank of the Tioughnioga to Chenango Forks, it
then follows the general course of the Chenango, making a slight detour to
avoid the bend in that river between the towns of Chenango and Fenton,
passing in its course through Lisle, across the south-west corner of Triangle, through the towns of Barker and Chenango and the north part of
Binghamton to the city of Binghamton   It makes the great salt depot at
Syracuse and, by its connection with Oswego & Syracuse R. R. at the last
named city, the lake and lake ports easily accessible.

‡ *The Albany & Susquehanna R. R.* was organized April 2, 1851, and
opened to Harpersville, in the town of Colesville, Dec. 26, 1867, and to
Binghamton, Jan. 14, 1869.   With its varied connections it brings Binghamton within easy communication with the northern and eastern parts of the
State, and the capital at Albany.   Its length is 142 miles   It enters the
county at Nineveh and runs in a circuitous course through Colesville,
diverging slightly into the east part of Fenton a short distance, through
the south part of Fenton and the north part of Binghamton, connecting
with the Erie R. R. at the city of Binghamton. It is leased to and operated
by the Delaware & Hudson Canal Company.

the Utica, Chenango & Susquehanna Valley R. R.*; the Delaware & Hudson Canal Co.'s R. R. †; and the Delaware, Lackawanna & Western R. R.‡ These routes, which traverse the County in various directions, afford ample facilities for traveling and commercial purposes, and bring the agricultural lands within easy reach of the great eastern markets, and the business and manufacturing centers in close proximity to the coal mines of eastern Pennsylvania. The increasing agricultural and commercial importance of the County may warrant the opening of new avenues in those parts of the County furthest removed from any of the great thoroughfares. The several plank roads which were built at an early day are now mostly abandoned.

There are ten newspapers published in the County; two dailies, one semi-weekly and seven weeklies.

The BINGHAMTON DAILY REPUBLICAN was started as *The Daily Iris*, in 1849, by Wm. Stuart and E. T. Evans. It was soon after changed to its present name and was published by Wm. Stuart alone, until 1864, when he leased it to Messrs. Carl Bros. and J. W. Taylor for five years. They, after publishing it about three years, sold their lease to Malette & Reid. the present publishers, who bought it of Wm. Stuart, April 1, 1867.

THE BROOME REPUBLICAN was established at Binghamton, by Major Augustus Morgan, in 1822. It was published by him until 1824, by Morgan & Canoll until 1828, by Evans & Canoll, until 1835, by Canoll & Cooke until 1839, when it passed into

---

* *The Utica, Chenango & Susquehanna Valley R R* enters the county in the south-east corner of Barker, having its southern terminus at Chenango Forks. It was commenced in 1867, and twelve miles were completed that year.

† *The Delaware & Hudson Canal Co.'s R. R.,* which was recently completed through the County, enters it at Nineveh, and follows the general course of the Susquehanna, which it crosses at Center Village, through the town of Colesville, to the south line of that town, when it deflects from the river and avoids the bend which commences at this point, and again touches the river a little north of Windsor, extending along its valley to the south line of the town of Windsor, where it leaves the County. Large quantities of coal are already shipped over this road from the coal mines in Penn., to which it leads.

‡ *The Delaware, Lackawanna & Western R. R.* was completed to Binghamton in January or February, 1871. It enters the County in the south-east corner of the town of Conklin and runs along the west bank of the Susquehanna to Binghamton, where it connects with the Syracuse, Binghamton & New York R R, and at Syracuse with the Oswego & Syracuse R R, which road is leased to it. This is an important link in the chain of railroads centering at Binghamton, as it brings that city in direct communication with the valuable mines of this company in Penn; and with its connections with the S. B. & N. Y., and O. & S. railroads, which are under its control, this company are enabled to ship direct to their depot in Oswego, and from that point to the northern part of the State, the lake ports and Canada. Vast quantities of coal are shipped over this road, no inconsiderable amount of which is deposited at Syracuse.

E

the hands of Davis & Cooke.  It was continued by Benj. T. Cooke until 1848, and by E. R. Colston until 1849.  It subsequently became the property of Wm. Stuart, who published it until 1864, when he leased it for five years to Messrs. Carl Bros. and J. W. Taylor, who, after about three years, sold their lease to Malette & Reid, the present publishers, by whom the paper was purchased of Wm. Stuart, April 1, 1867, and by whom, in January, 1869, it was consolidated with *The Binghamton Standard*, and printed in connection with that paper as the *Republican & Standard*.  July 4th, 1870, the two papers were disconnected and the original title, *The Broome Republican*, was resumed.  It is published as a weekly.

THE BINGHAMTON STANDARD & SEMI-WEEKLY REPUBLICAN was started as *The Binghamton Standard* in Nov. 1853, by J. R. VanValkenburg, by whom it was sold to G. W. Reynolds, and by the latter to F. N. Chase.  It was afterwards successively purchased by Alvin Sturtevant, M. L. Hawley & P. D. VanVradenburg and, in Jan. 1869, by Malette & Reid, who consolidated it with *The Broome Republican*, and adopted a name embracing that of both papers, the *Republican & Standard*.  July 4, 1870, it was renewed as a separate paper, under its present name.*

The BINGHAMTON DEMOCRAT was started at Binghamton, as the *Broome County Courier*, in 1831, by J. R. Orton, who continued it until 1837, after which it passed successively into the hands of Sheldon & Marble, I. C. Sheldon, E. P. Marble, E. P. & J. W. Marble, and Marble & Johnson.  In 1842 or '3, its name was changed to *The Binghamton Courier & Broome Co. Democrat* and was published by J. & C. Orton.  It passed into the hands of Dr. N. S. Davis, in 1846, into those of J. L. Burtis in 1847, and its name was by him changed to the *Binghamton Courier*.  Mr. Burtis sold it J. T. Brodt, who published it until 1849, when it passed into the hands of Hon. J. R. Dickinson, who changed its name to *The Binghamton Democrat* and published it until 1855, when he took W. S. Lawyer as a partner.  This firm continued its publication until 1857, when Mr. Dickinson sold his interest.  It was published by Messrs. Adams & Lawyer until the death of Mr. Adams in 1861, when it was continued by Mr. Lawyer alone until 1866, at which time his brother, G. L. Lawyer, was admitted to an interest.  It is still published as a weekly by the Lawyer Bros.

The BINGHAMTON DAILY DEMOCRAT was commenced in 1869, by W. S. & G. L. Lawyer, and is still published by them.

*The *Binghamton Daily Republican*, *The Broome Republican* and *The Binghamton Standard & Semi-Weekly Republican* are issued from the same office by Malette & Reid.

THE BINGHAMTON TIMES, weekly, was started by *The Binghamton Times Association*, April 6, 1871, and published by them until April 27, 1872, when it was purchased by A. L. Watson, who, on the first of August of the same year, took as partner Mr. E. H. Purdy and enlarged the paper from a quarto to a folio. It is now published by the firm of Purdy & Watson.

THE DEMOCRATIC LEADER, weekly, was started at Binghamton by A. W. Carl and E. H. Freeman, Sept. 10, 1869. Mr. Carl purchased Mr. Freeman's interest July 1, 1871, and still continues its publication.

THE UNION WEEKLY NEWS was started as *The Union News*, in June 1851, by A. J. Quinlan, who published it until his death, in 1854, when it was purchased of the heirs by R. Bostwick, who continued it a short time and sold it to Cephas Benedict and E. M. Betts, by whom it was published about two years, when Mr. Benedict purchased Mr. Betts' interest and controlled it alone until 1866, at which time he sold it to E. C. & G. W. Mersereau, but continued its editor. Mr. Benedict repurchased it in 1867 and again sold it May 15, 1868, to M. B. Robbins, the present proprietor, who changed its name to that it now bears. It is an independent journal.

THE DEPOSIT COURIER, weekly, was started in the spring of 1848, by M. R. Hulse, who published it five years, when it passed into the hands of his brother, S. D. Hulse, by whom its name was changed to *The Deposit Union Democrat*, and published seven years. In 1860 it passed into the hands of Lucius P. Allen, who changed its name to *The Delaware Courier* and its character to the advocacy of the principles of Republicanism. Mr. Allen published it seven years, when he sold it to Ambrose Blunt and Joshua Smith, who changed the name to that it originally bore, and now bears, and, after about two years, sold it to J. B. Stow. It was subsequently published by Charles N. Stow (son of J. B. Stow) and Adrian L. Watson. In March 1872, Mr. Watson retired and Mr. Stow continues its publication alone.

THE LISLE GLEANER was commenced at Lisle, May 24, 1871, by Gilbert A. Dodge, who sold it, March 7, 1872, to Eugene Davis, the present publisher, by whom it was enlarged from a twenty to a twenty-four column paper. It is a weekly and is independent in politics.*

* The following is a list of obsolete papers published in the County·
*The American Constellation* was started at Union, Nov 23, 1800, by D. Cruger, as is shown by a copy of this paper now in the possession of Mr. Beebe of Owego, which is dated "Union, N. Y., Sept. 12, 1801," and marked "Vol. I, No. 43." It is generally supposed and admitted that this

The first step looking to the settlement of the country adjacent to and partially included within the limits of this County, seems to have been taken in 1785, on the 28th of June of which year a treaty was held at Fort Herkimer between the Governor

paper was printed at "*old* Chenango," then located on the west bank of Chenango River, about one mile above Binghamton, as is asserted in the *Annals of Binghamton*, and, says Dr Charles J Seymour, in a letter dated Binghamton, Aug 9, 1872, it was probably dated to correspond with the postoffice at Union, which, says Dr. Seymour, on the authority of a warrant issued by Postmaster General Habershaw, was established June 23, 1798, (Joshua Whitney being appointed postmaster,) at Binghamton, the station at which place was for several years called Union. French says this paper was published at Union Village, in 1800, but the assertion, as regards location, is believed to be unwarranted. How long this paper was published we have been unable to learn definitely, but there are indications that it was removed to Owego, and its name changed to *The American Farmer*, under which name alone, it is proper to say, Wilkinson refers to it.  He says, after referring to *The Broome County Patriot*, which, he asserts, was the first paper printed in Broome County, "There had a paper circulated here, which was first printed in *old* Chenango, and afterward in Owego, called 'The American Farmer'  While issuing from the former place, it was conducted by Daniel Crugar; and while from the latter, it was conducted by Stephen Mack, afterward Judge of the County," who, it will be seen by referring to the history of *The American Farmer*, in the history of Tioga County, started that paper in Owego, though Stephen B. Leonard, the founder of *The Owego Gazette*, is of the opinion that *The American Farmer* was established and always published in Owego.

*The Broome County Patriot* was commenced in Binghamton in 1812, by Chauncey Morgan.  In 1813 it was transferred to Dr. Elihu Ely and its name changed to

*The Olio*, under which title it was published one year, when it passed into the hands of Dr. Tracy Robinson, who changed its name to the

*Binghamton Phœnix*.  In 1815 Augustus Morgan became partner with Mr. Robinson and it was published by Morgan & Robinson until 1817, when Mr. Robinson's interest was purchased by Anson Howard  The firm then became Morgan & Howard and they published the paper one year, when Mr. Howard purchased Mr. Morgan's interest and continued it until 1819, when it was discontinued.

*The Republican Herald* was commenced in 1818, and successively published by Morgan & Howard and Abraham Bunell and Dorephus Abbey, until 1822

*The Evening Express*, daily, was issued from the Republican office in 1848, by E. R. Colston, and was, after a short time, merged in the *Republican*

*The Iris*, semi-monthly, was started in July, 1839, by C P. Cooke  In July, 1841, it was purchased by Edwin T Evans, who enlarged it and published it weekly until 1853, when it was merged in the *Binghamton Republican.*

*The Binghamton Mercury* was published a short time by Chester Dehart, as a semi-monthly

*The Susquehanna Journal* was started in Oct., 1852, at Binghamton, by Rev Wm H. Pearue, and was merged in the *Broome Republican* in 1855.

*The Broome County American* was started at Binghamton in May, 1855, by Ransom Bostwick, in advocacy of the Know-Nothing principles, and lived but a short time.

*The Binghamton Daily Times* was published by J. R Gould, about 1865 or '6

*The Binghamton Journal* was started about 1870, by John E Williams who published it about six months, when it was discontinued

*The Broome County Gazette* was commenced at Whitney's Point in July, 1858, by G. A. Dodge, by whom it was published several years.

and Commissioners of Indian Affairs in behalf of the State, and the Oneida and Tuscarora Indians, by which the latter for $11,500 ceded all their lands, bounded north by an east and west line from the Chenango to the Unadilla, ten miles above the mouth of the latter, east by the east line of the County,* south by Pennsylvania and west by the Chenango and Susquehanna. At the Hartford convention, in 1786, a tract of 230,400 acres, bounded by the Chenango† and Tioughnioga rivers on the east, Owego Creek‡ on the west, by the north line of the tract previously granted to Daniel Cox and Robert Lettice Hooper on the south, and extending as far north as to include the number of acres specified, was ceded to Massachusetts.§ This tract was sold by the State of Massachusetts to Samuel Brown and fifty-nine others, principally from Berkshire county, in that State, Nov. 7, 1787, for $1,500, and was designated the Boston Ten Townships. These persons were induced by the favorable representations of individuals who had viewed this country while connected with the expedition against the Indians under Gen. Sullivan, in 1779, to make the purchase. The tract, according to the grant made to the company, was to be bounded on the south by the Susquehanna, but when the agents of the company arrived they found that previous grants embraced the valley of that river, consequently its southern boundary was determined by the north line of these grants. The company appointed as commissioners to treat with the Indians, Elijah Brown, Gen. Oringh Stoddard, Gen. Moses Ashley, Capt. Raymond and Col. David Pixley. These gentlemen met the Indians in treaty on the east side of the Chenango, two or three miles above Binghamton, in the forepart of winter, but did not fully complete negotiations, and adjourned to meet at the forks of the Chenango. The second treaty resulted satisfactorily.‖ "The nominal sum paid for this tract is not now known,

* This line was agreed upon at Fort Stanwix, in 1768, and was surveyed by Simon Metcalf the next year. It is designated the "Property Line."

† The Tioughnioga was then termed the west branch of the Chenango and was treated by the surveyors as the main stream.

‡ This creek was then termed the "Owego River" and was identical with what is now generally called the "West Owego Creek," that being treated as the main stream.

§ When this tract was surveyed it was found that its northern limits encroached upon the Military Tract by 17,264 acres, and an amount equivalent to this was granted to the claimants in Junius, Seneca County.

‖ "At this and the former treaty, it is said, the Indians, who were furnished with provisions and liquor at the expense of the company, would get drunk almost to a man, by night, but be sober through the day. While the subjects of the treaty were under discussion from day to day, they would sit in circles upon the ground, and listen with the utmost decorum. Their chiefs, when they spoke, would speak in substance, if not in form, in accordance with parliamentary rule. Captain Dean was their interpreter

but the payment was made, one-half in money, and the other moiety in goods, consisting of rifles, hatchets, ammunition, blankets and woolen cloths.  The last, it is said, the savages, in perfect character with their taste, immediately tore into strings for ornament."  The total cost of the land, including the purchase price, the expense of the treaties and the survey, was about one shilling per acre.  The first sales were uniformly made at twenty-five cents per acre, but after a little they rose to one dollar and even more.*  The deeds of partition were executed in 1789, and were legalized March 3d, of that year, in an act reciting the names of the sixty associates.  The several owners commenced selling and settling their respective allotments. Grants were made in the south and east parts of the County to Hooper, Wilson, Bingham, Cox and others, several of whom resided in Philadelphia.†

The first settlements in the County were made in the valleys of the Susquehanna and Chenango, in 1785, by persons who had traversed the region during the Revolution.  They located while the country was still threatened with Indian hostilities, and before Phelps and Gorham opened the fertile lands of Western New York to immigration.  The early settlement was

and did their business. * * * The land upon the shores of the two rivers, and for some distance back was, even at the time of the purchase, partially cleared, so far as the Indians have their lands cleared.  The under-brush was cleared, having been kept down by burning, and grass growing on the flats.  The Indians uniformly keep down the shrubbery part of their hunting grounds, that they may, with the more facility, discover and pursue their game  Col Rose says that he could see deer upon the mountains immediately back of him for a half mile, so free were they from under-brush.  He observes also, that the woods exhibited a sombre appearance, from their annual burnings.  The large island opposite Judge Stoddard's, was, when the first settlers came, covered with grass and the anacum weed, a tall kind of weed, the roots of which they were in the habit of digging and drying, and then grinding or pounding for bread stuff; or rather its apology, perhaps, when their corn failed them."—*Annals of Binghamton, p.* 50 *and* 51.

* The Indians, in their treaty, reserved to themselves the right to hunt upon the lands sold, for the term of seven years; and also made a reserve of one-half mile square, near the mouth of Castle Creek, in the town of Chenango, as their own possession.  This reserve was known as the "castle farm" and upon it those Indians, who did not remove to New Stockbridge, or Oneida, resided.

The means through which they lost possession of this reserve will be detailed in the history of the town of Chenango.

The remaining Indian titles within the County were extinguished by the treaty of Fort Stanwix in 1788.

†A tract of land containing 49,710 acres, known as "Chenango Township," was granted to A. Hammond and others; another, containing 61,440 acres, known as "Warren Township," to Robert Harper and others; and another, containing 1,000 acres, on both sides of the Susquehanna, was sold to Jacob and John Springstead. Josiah, David and Daniel Stow, David Hotchkiss and Joseph Beebe. Other tracts were sold to Wm. Allison, Jas. Clinton, Isaac Melcher and others.  The islands in the Susquehanna were sold to James Clinton, at four shillings per acre.

retarded by a remarkable ice freshet in 1787—88, which destroyed most of the property of the settler's upon the river intervales. Scarcely less calamitous to life and property was the scarcity that followed in 1789. Oquaga was a noted rendezvous of Tories and Indians during the Revolution.* Most of the invasions into the Schoharie and Mohawk settlements, as well as those upon the frontiers of Ulster and Orange counties were made by way of the Tioga and Susquehanna rivers from Niagara; and this war-path, with its sufferings and cruelties, has been often described in the narratives of returned captives.†

We extract from the *Annals of Binghamton,* by J. B. Wilkinson, the following interesting and amusing particulars relative to the extent to which the early settlers engaged in fishing and hunting, which are illustrative not only of the hardihood and daring of the early settlers, but also of the struggles which many of them so heroically encountered in their efforts to obtain a subsistence.

"In early times, when the country was first settled, and for a long time since, shad ran up the Susquehanna in great numbers as far as Binghamton, and even some to the source of the river. Thousands of them were caught from year to year, in this vicinity, especially at the three great fishing places, at Union, opposite Judge Mersereau's; at Binghamton, opposite the dry bridge, and upon the point of an island at Oquaga. There were two other places of less note; one on the Chenango, opposite Mr Bevier's; the other at the mouth of Snake Creek. [The shad arrived here, and began to be caught generally about the last of April, and the fishing continued through the month of May.] It was made quite a business by some, and after the country was sufficiently filled with inhabitants to create a demand for all that could be caught, the business became a source of considerable profit * * * Several hundred [were] sometimes caught at one draught. Herring also ran up at the same time with the shad; but as it was no object to catch them while a plenty of shad could be caught, their nets were so constructed as to admit them through the meshes

"The nets employed were from sixteen to thirty rods long; [and each employed from six to eight men to manage it.] Their time for sweeping was generally in the night, as the shallowness of the water would not allow them to fish in the day time. Again the shad, in the night, [ran] up on the riffles to sport, which gave to the fishermen another advantage. They [made] their hauls the darkest nights, without lights, either in their boats or on shore. They had their cabins or tents to lodge in, and [were] notified when it was time to haul, by the noise the shoal of fish [made] in sporting at the shallow places.

"The shad seemed never to find either a place or time at which to turn and go back. Even after depositing their eggs, they [continued] to urge their way up stream, until they had exhausted their entire strength, which would, being out of their salt-water element, after a while tail them. The shores, in consequence, [were] strewed with their dead bodies, through the summer, upon which the wild animals [came] down and [fed.] Their

---

*Further mention will be made of this place in the history of the town of Windsor.

†French's *State Gazetteer.*

young fry [passed] down the stream in the fall, having grown to the length of three or four inches, in such numbers as to choke up the eel-weirs

"They have discontinued running up so far as this, for twelve or fifteen years [from 1840, when the *Annals* were published]; consequently none within that time have been caught. The numerous mill-dams and mills on the streams, together with the number of rafts that pass down in the spring, undoubtedly deter them from coming

"As we have spoken of *fishing* in early days, which was so different from what it is at present, so will we speak of the *hunting* of early times

"It is allowed by the old hunters that wild animals were uncommonly plenty here when the country was first settled. Martins were plenty, and caught in dead-falls for their fur. Panthers were frequently met with and shot by hunters Bears were numerous and large. Wild cats were also found. But deer, which may be considered the staple commodity with hunters in a new country, were decidedly numerous. They would be seen sometimes twenty and thirty in a flock Of this species of game great numbers were yearly killed There appear to have been no wild turkies found here when the country was first settled. A solitary flock, some twenty-five or thirty years ago appears to have wandered from its native forests, and was observed in the neighborhood of Oquaga by Deacon Stow, who was at that day a distinguished hunter. He dropped his work in the field, and obtaining a gun from the nearest neighbor, he managed to kill one, before the flock got entirely out of his way. It remained in the neighborhood forest, until the turkies were all shot, except the last one, which was caught in a trap.

"There were several modes of hunting the deer. Besides the ordinary way of pursuing them by day-light with hounds, the hunters [resorted] to the deer licks, of which there were many, and ascertaining, as nearly as they could, where they stood to lap the water, they set their guns so as to take the deer when they came by night to drink. This they [did] before night-fall, and then [remained by their guns and watched] They could hear the deer when in the act of drinking, by the noise they made in lapping the water [This was the signal to discharge their guns, which they often did, several together.] If they heard the deer fall, they went and cut its throat, or their throats, as they sometimes shot more than one at a discharge, and brought them off the ground. They would then set their guns again, and wait for the well-known sound of the lapping to be renewed They would continue their vigilance according to their success; sometimes till twelve and two, and sometimes till the dawn of the next morning. The dressing of the game was ordinarily reserved till the next day.

"Another mode pursued by the hunters was, to take the deer when they came down late in the summer or fall to feed upon the sedge or eel grass which grows in the river Two men would get into a skiff, or boat of any kind that would answer the purpose, [in the forepart of which was a platform covered with turf]; upon this they would kindle a brisk fire, and one would sit in the fore-part, near the fire, with his rifle in his hand; the other would sit in the hinder-part and impel and guide the boat with a single paddle, taking care to make no noise, either in the water or at the side of the boat The deer, at seeing the moving fire, would raise their heads and stamp with their feet, without moving much from their place, even at quite a near approach of the boat. This [enabled] the hunters to come as near to their game as they wished, and to make sure their aim. Sometimes they would take their stand upon the shore and watch by moonlight.

"A story is told of two of the early settlers of Oquaga, one a Dutchman by the name of Hendrickson, the other a Yankee by the name of Merryman. They had been in the habit of going together to a little island in the Susquehanna, called Fish Island, to watch for deer, with the understanding always, that each was to share equally in the game. One fine evening, while the moon was shining in its fullness, it occurred to the Dutchman that he would go down to the island and watch for deer, without letting his brother Yankee know of it. The same thought occurred to the Yankee. They both went down to the island and took their stations *accidentally*, at each end. In the course of the evening while waiting for deer, to their apprehension, two made their appearance and entered the river, and passing by the upper end of the island were fired upon by the *Yankee*, whose station happened to be at that end ; the *deer* bounded, with a mighty splash, down stream ; and passing the *lower* end of the island were fired upon by the *Dutchman*, whose shot took effect and brought *one* down. As the latter went out to drag in his game, the Yankee called out and claimed the *deer*, as he had fired first. The Dutchman muttered some objection, and continued wading. When he came to the weltering and dying animal, to his surprise, instead of a large deer, which he was in full expectation of, behold! he had killed one of his neighbor's young cattle— a two year old heifer ; and which he readily recognized. 'Well, den,' said he to his companion, who was making his way down to him, 'you may have de *deer ;* it is yours, I believe.' The Yankee, when he [also found] what had been done, and feeling they were about equally implicated, proposed that they should send the animal down stream, and say nothing about the matter, as they could not afford to pay for it. The Dutchman—and here we see the characteristic honesty of the one, as well as the characteristic *dishonesty* or disingenuousness of the other—objected ; saying they would take it to the owner, and tell him how they came to shoot it ; and as it would, when dressed, be very good eating, he did not think they should be charged very high for the accident. While they were disputing which course they should pursue, they heard at some little distance, near the shore, or upon it, a noise and difficult breathing, as of an animal dying ; they went to it, and partly hid among weeds and grass, they found, to their further dismay, *another* heifer, belonging to *another* neighbor, in her last struggles, having received a death-wound from the first shot. The Yankee now insisted, with greater importunity, that they should send them both down stream, as they could never think of paying for both. But the Dutchman as strenuously objected, and proposed that the Yankee should go the next morning to the owner of one, and he would go to the owner of the other, and make proposals of restitution on as favorable terms as they could obtain. The Yankee finally acceded, and each went the next morning to his respective man. The Yankee made a reluctant acknowledgement of what had been done the night before, and showed but little disposition to make restitution. The owner was nearly in a rage for the loss of his fine heifer, and was hard in his terms of settlement. While the Dutchman, as if to be rewarded for his honesty, found his neighbor, when he had announced what he had done, and proposed to make satisfactory restitution, as ready to exact no more from him, than to dress the animal, and to take half the meat home for his own use.

"Another distinguished hunter of these early times, and one that was considered pre-eminent above all the others for markmanship and daring feats, was Jotham Curtis, of Windsor. An anecdote or two, related of him, will best express his celebrity.

"He went out [one] afternoon to a *deer-lick*, and having killed a deer, he dressed it and hung the body upon a tree, bringing only the skin home with him. This he threw upon a work-bench in an apartment of the house he used as a shop. In the night he was awakened by a noise which he supposed to proceed from a dog at his deer-skin. He sprung up and opened the door that led into his shop ; and about over the work-bench he beheld the glare of *two eye-balls*, which he knew—so versed was he in the appearance of such animals—to be those of a panther. Without taking his eye from those of the animal, he called to his wife to light a pine stick, and to hand it to him, with his rifle, which she did. With the torch in his left hand, and the gun resting upon the same arm, he took his aim between the eyes, and shot the panther dead upon the bench. It is related to have been a very large one. It had entered the shop through an open window.

"He was one day hunting and came across two cubs. He caught one, and seating himself by a tree, with his back close to it, that he might be sure to *see* the old one when she [came.] He took the young one between his knees and commenced squeezing its head, to make it cry, which he knew would be likely to bring the old one. In a short time she was seen coming with full speed, with her hair turned forward, an indication of rage, and her mouth wide open. He waited deliberately, till she was near enough, and then, with his unerring fire, he brought her to the ground. Some one asked him afterward, what he supposed would have been the consequence had his gun missed fire ? Oh ! he said, he did not *allow* it to miss in such emergencies."

# GAZETTEER OF TOWNS.

*BARKER** was formed from Lisle, April 18, 1831.†   A part of Greene (Chenango Co.) was annexed April 28, 1840.   It lies north-west of the center of the County, and covers an area of 21,147 acres, of which, in 1865, according to the census of that year, 12,081, were improved.   The surface is hilly.   The declivities of the hills are in some instances very steep; but their summits spread out into a broken plateau which renders them capable of tillage.   The highest point, in the north-west part of the town, is about 1,400 feet above tide.·   It is watered by the Tioughnioga river, which flows diagonally through the town, entering it near the north-west corner and leaving it near the south-east corner, where it forms a junction with the Chenango River; Half Way Brook,‡ which flows through the north-east part and empties into the Tioughnioga at about half way in its course through the town; and Castle Creek, which rises, by several branches, in the western part and leaves

---

* Named from John Barker, the first settler, who came from Branford, New Haven Co., Conn., in 1791.

† The first town meeting was held the first Tuesday in March, 1832, and the following named officers were elected: John Stoughton, *Supervisor*, Edward Hebard, *Town Clerk*; Woodruff Barnes, Hugh Cunningham and John Beach, *Assessors*, Wm. Osborn and Orlando Parsons, *Overseers of the Poor*, Lorenzo Parsons, John P. Osborn and Jacob Lowe, *Commissioners of Highways*; John P. Osborn, Harry Seymour and Asa Hubbard, *Inspectors of Common Schools*, Ransford Stevens, Oliver Stiles, Rufus Abbott and Daniel Sweatland, *Justices of the Peace*; David Barker, *Collector*, Rufus Abbott, *Sealer of Weights and Measures*; David Barker, Asa Hubbard, Charles Atwater and Lewis Cook, *Constables.*

‡ In the valley of this brook, springs of weak brine were early discovered and unsuccessful attempts to utilize them and increase the strength of the brine by boring have been made.  A few years since a well was sunk by a stock company to a depth of 700 feet, but operations were suspended in consequence of a broken drill and the difficulty experienced in the efforts made to remove it.  Several subsequent attempts to remove the broken drill and proceed with the boring have proved unavailing.  It is asserted that the brine is equally as strong as that at Onondaga, and the same source is claimed for it, but the faith of those interested does not appear to have been sufficiently strong to induce them to remove the impediment to its practical demonstration.

the town near the center of the south border. The valleys of the river and brooks are narrow, but they furnish a limited intervale of rich and highly fertile land. Upon the hills the soil consists of a clayey loam mixed with disintegrated slate and shale. The people are principally engaged in dairying.

In 1870, the town contained a population of 1,396. During the year ending Sept. 30, 1871, it contained twelve school districts and employed twelve teachers. The number of children of school age was 377; the number attending school, 350; the average attendance, 176; the amount expended for school purposes, $3,055; and the value of school houses and sites, $4,540.

The Syracuse, Binghamton & N. Y. Railroad crosses the town diagonally, following the course of the river.

CHENANGO FORKS (p. v.) is located in three towns—Barker, Chenango and Greene, the latter in Chenango Co.,—but mostly in this town. It is a village of about 600 inhabitants. That part of it lying in this town contains one church, (Congregational) a select school for girls, one hotel, one carriage, three blacksmith and two shoe shops, a saw mill, a grist mill, a drug store, eight other stores and about thirty dwellings. It lies at the forks of the Chenango and Tioughnioga rivers, in the south-east corner of the town, and is a station on the S. B. & N. Y. R. R. and the U. & C. V. R. R., which enters the town at the south-east corner.

HYDE SETTLEMENT in the west part, extending about one and one-half miles on "Hyde Street," is named from the first settlers in that locality, many of whose descendants still reside there. It contains one church (M. E.) a school house and seven houses.

ADAMS SETTLEMENT in the central part, also derives its name from the first settlers there.

BARKER, on the east bank of the Tioughnioga River, north of the center of the town, formerly contained a post office, but it is discontinued.

The first settlement, as previously stated, was commenced in 1791, by John Barker, from Branford, Conn. The next year he was followed by Simeon Rogers, John Allen, Asa Beach and Solomon Rose, all of whom were from Connecticut and settled on the east bank of the Tioughnioga. Barker located at Chenango Forks. He purchased the improvements of Thomas Gallop, whom he found living a hermitage-like life, just west of the Tioughnioga, in the town of Chenango, and with his family, took up his residence in the "treaty house."* Rogers located about one mile from the mouth of the Tioughnioga; and subsequently, in 1792, married the daughter of John Barker. This was the first marriage contracted in the town; and the first birth was that of Chauncey, son of Simeon Rogers, in 1793. A Mr. Lampeer was the first man who ventured any distance up the Tioughnioga. He settled seven miles from its mouth. The first school was taught by Thomas Cartwright, in 1795; the first inn was opened the same year. by Simeon Rogers, who also kept the first store and built the first mill.

There are only two churches in the town, (Congregational and M. E.)

The *Congregational Church* is located at Chenango Forks. It was organized with ten members, but in what year we are not advised. Its Church edifice was erected in 1837, at a cost of $2,000. It will seat 250 persons. Rev. Seth Williston was the first pastor. Rev. Thos Haywood is the present one. The number of members is forty. The Church property is valued at $3,500.

The *Adams Street M. E. Church* was organized with 44 members in Feb., 1871. The Church edifice is now in process of erection and when completed will seat 200 persons, and be worth about $2,000. Rev. A. W. Loomis was the first pastor; Rev. N. S. Dewitt is the present one. The number of members remains the same as when organized.

*The M. E. Church of Barker*, located at the village of Barker, was organized with five members, by Horace Agard, its first pastor, July 15, 1825. The church edifice, which will seat 200 persons, was erected in 1844, at a cost of $1,500. The Church property is valued at $3,000. Rev. N S. DeWitt is the present pastor. The present number of members is twenty.

*BINGHAMTON* was formed from Chenango, Dec. 3, 1855. A part of Vestal was annexed by act of the Supervisors, passed Nov. 24, 1862, and which took effect Dec 15, 1862.† It is one of the south border towns, lying west of the center of the County. Its southern boundary is formed by the Pennsylvania State line, and its northern part lies in the east and west angles formed by the junction of the Chenango with the Sus-

---

*The "treaty house" was a "large double log house," erected for the accommodation of the Indians and Commissioners of the Boston Purchase in the treaty held at this place.

† The part annexed is described as the east part of lot No. 2, in the second tract in Sidney township, containing 250 acres, and being the farm of Wm. Morris.

quehanna. The town contains an area of 20,117¼ acres, of which, in 1865, according to the census of that year, 13,026, were improved. The surface is hilly in the south, but the north part embraces the wide and beautiful intervales extending along the two rivers at and near their junction. The hills are from 300 to 400 feet above the river, and are generally arable to their summits. The soil in the valleys is a deep, rich, alluvial and gravelly loam, and upon the hills it is a fine quality of slaty loam.

The population of the town in 1870 was 14,758.* During the year ending Sept. 30, 1871, it contained nineteen school districts, ten of which were in the city, and employed 44 teachers, thirty-five of whom were employed in the city. The number of children of school age was 2,940, of whom 2,350 (?) were in the city; the number attending school, 2,844, of whom 2,353 were in the city; the average attendance, 1,461, of whom 1,259 were in the city; the amount expended for school purposes, $40,748, of which $37,325 were expended in the city; and the value of school houses and sites, $115,570, those in the city being valued at $105,000.

BINGHAMTON,† the seat of justice‡ of the County, is eligibly situated at the junction of the Susquehanna and Chenango

---

* The population of the town exclusive of the city was 2,066.

† From its location, Binghamton was originally and for a long time known as "Chenango Point." Its present name was given in honor of Wm Bingham, of Philadelphia, who purchased a large tract of land lying on both sides of the Susquehanna, including the site of the city, and to whose beneficence in donating land for the erection of county buildings and a public school, and to the liberal and enlightened exertions of his agent, Gen Whitney, its early prosperity is largely due. Mr. Bingham was a native of England, though he came to this country at an early age. He received a liberal education and graduated at the college of Philadelphia in 1768, at the age of sixteen. He possessed an ample fortune, acquired, it is believed, entirely through his own exertions, and was a shrewd financier. He was agent for this country at Martinique during the Revolution. In 1786 he was a delegate to the Continental Congress from Pennsylvania, and was elected a Senator in Congress in 1795, serving until 1801, and as President *pro tem.* of the Senate during the Fourth Congress. He died at Bath, England, February 7, 1804, aged fifty-two years.

"The first survey of the village was made in 1800, under the direction of Mr. Bingham, at which time the streets were regularly laid out at right-angles. In 1808, a re-survey was made by Roswell Marshall; and in 1835, a full and complete survey was made by Wm. Wentz, of the place. A map was made from this survey by F. B. Tower, in 1836. According to this last survey, the village has an extent of about two miles, measured east and west, and of one mile and a half measured north and south. Upon the east side of the river, where by far most of the village lies, the course of the streets being determined by the course of the two rivers [and] an important bend in the Susquehanna, [are] more short streets, and more that meet and cross at angles somewhat oblique. This defect, if such it should be called, does not, however, mar the beauty of the place generally, [nor] of the streets individually."—*Annals of Binghamton,* 1840.

‡ A description of the County buildings will be found on page 65.

rivers, both as regards the rare, quiet beauty of its surroundings and the valuable commercial facilities it enjoys. It lies north of the center of the town. The Susquehanna enters the corporate limits of the city about the center of the east line and passes in a westerly and slightly southerly direction to near the south-west corner, where it leaves it. It receives the Chenango west of the center of the city. The latter stream flows in a southerly and slightly westerly direction from the center of the north line of the city. The city reposes in the valleys of these streams, encircled by fine hills of considerable elevation. It was incorporated as a village April 2, 1813, and as a city, April 9, 1867. By a charter granted May 3, 1834, its limits were enlarged and its territory was divided into five wards, the number it at present contains.* It is an important station on the Erie R. R., is the southern terminus of the Syracuse, Binghamton & N. Y., and the Albany & Susquehanna railroads, and the northern terminus of the Delaware, Lackawanna & Western R. R. These lines with their numerous connections bring the city within easy communication of all parts of our own State, Pennsylvania and New Jersey. They extend to the valuable salt deposits at Syracuse and the lake ports, via Oswego, on the north, to the extensive coal mines at Pennsylvania on the south, and open to the products of its manufactories and the fine farming section surrounding it the great marts of commerce in the east and west. The city contains eight good hotels, two extensive tanneries and two finishing tanneries, four machine shops, three scale manufactories, one planing mill and two planing mills and sash, door and blind factories combined, six boot and shoe manufactories,† one steam flouring mill, and two flouring mills operated by water, two barrel fac-

---

* WARD BOUNDARIES —*First.*—All that part lying west of Chenango river and north of the Susquehanna, west of its junction with the former stream *Second* —All that part lying between the Chenango and the west side of Collier street to its intersection with Court street, Court street, to its intersection with Chenango street, and the west side of Chenango street. *Third.*—All that part lying east of Chenango street and north of Court street, from its intersection with Chenango street. *Fourth.*—All that part lying east of Collier street, and north of the Susquehanna and south of Court street, from their intersection with Collier street. *Fifth.*— All that part lying south of the Susquehanna.

† The firms engaged in this business are Lester Bros. & Co., Anderson & Tremaine, Meade & Benedict, J M Stone & Co , Benson & Ten Brook and Smith Bros. This business was originally started here in 1852, by Way & Lester. It now employs a capital of about $246,000; gives employment to about 380 persons, including about fifty females; and the annual product amounts to about 364,000 pairs of men's, boy's, women's, misses' and children's boots and shoes, from the coarsest to the finest quality.

tories, one comb manufactory,* one establishment for the

* This business being one of so special a character and requiring in its successful prosecution more than ordinary skill, we deem a brief review of its early and present history as coming legitimately within the scope of this work The business was commenced in this city, in March, 1865, by C. M. Noyes & Co , who are the fourth generation of the family who have engaged in the manufacture of combs and followed it through life Their great-grand-father, Enoch Noyes, is supposed to have been the first one to engage in the business in this country. He learned his trade from a Hessian soldier about the close of the Revolution, and commenced the manufacture of combs in West Newbury, Mass. His son, Ephraim Noyes, continued the business at his death, and Ephraim was succeeded by his son, David E. Noyes, who, in 1846, removed to Newark, N. J , where he pursued the same vocation until his death, in February, 1861, when he in turn was succeeded by his sons, the present proprietors, who, in 1865, moved to this city, where they have since followed the comb business. During Enoch's lifetime the business did not assume much magnitude. The manufacture was carried on entirely by hand-work. David E. Noyes introduced machinery into the manufacture in 1815, and since that time the business has been steadily progressing. Within the last fifteen years it has been so revolutionized by the introduction of machinery that those who first started it would fail to recognize any of the tools now in use as belonging to that business. The new machinery is important, not alone in the manual labor dispensed with and the greater rapidity with which the work is accomplished, but also as an economical agent, by which nearly fifty per cent of the material consumed in the manufacture, and which was heretofore wasted, is utilized. Horns as crumpled as that belonging to the cow, which, as stated in the fable, was milked by a "maiden all forlorn," are, by the ingenious devices employed and the various processes through which they pass, converted into comely combs The horn, which is native stock, is first cut with a circular saw into cross sections, after which it is slit lengthwise. It is then soaked in boiling oil about one minute and is by this means flattened out. This is a very delicate process and requires close observation and an experienced eye. By a series of sawing and planing processes it is reduced to the required size and thickness for cutting the teeth, after which, before the teeth are cut, it is kept in racks for several months to dry and season. After the teeth are cut it passes through a series of processes—about thirty in number—in which the metallic backs are added, before it is ready for market in the shape of combs. The "twinning" machine, or the one with which the teeth are cut, is one of the most ingenious used. It is automatic in its action, making all the changes for cutting the large and small teeth, but is too complicated in its nature for us to attempt a description. It derives its name from the fact that two combs are cut by one operation, from one piece of horn. This principle was introduced in 1812, previous to which time the teeth were cut with hand-saws By an addition to the width of the piece of horn originally used equal to the back of the comb, or the width of the piece extending from the connected end of the teeth to the back edge, two combs are made, and with the addition of about one-third more horn than is required to make a single comb. Here is an important saving in material, which is effected by the use of hollow chisels, or rather by the use of two chisels so constructed with flanges on their edges that, when brought together, a hollow space, corresponding with the shape of the tooth, is left. When cut, the teeth of the two combs interlay each other but are readily pulled apart. The chisels work perpendicularly, and while the small teeth are being cut those which cut the large ones are stationary, and *vice versa*. In the manufacture a comb undergoes about forty operations. In 1864 E M Noyes secured a patent for combining metal with horn, and since that time the business has been confined almost exclusively to the patented article. No others are now made by them. At first this principle was used to combine short pieces of horn which could not otherwise be used The Messrs. Noyes manufacture combs of

manufacture of children's carriages and sleighs,* eight carriage shops, two hub and spoke factories, an oil refinery, a grain elevator, three express offices, (U. S., D. L. & W. and D. & H. Canal Co.,) six banks,† and numerous manufacturing establishments of less magnitude than those enumerated, a fuller description of which will be found in the Directory.   There are ten churches‡—many of them substantial and imposing structures; five public schools, which are so admirably conducted that the several private schools which recently flourished here, or most of them, have become extinct§; one commercial college, four newspaper and one job printing offices,‖ one water cure¶; and it is the seat of the New York State Inebriate Asylum** and the Susquehanna Valley Home.††   The city

various sizes and styles, and use in the manufacture many ingeniously constructed tools, whose advantages and uses are too numerous and complicated to describe here.   They employ a capital of about $50,000; give employment to about thirty persons, including only three or four boys, and manufacture annually about 60,000 dozens of combs, all of which are shipped to Howard, Sanger & Co. of New York, who are connected with them in the manufacture.

* The manufacture of boys' sleighs was commenced by Winton & Doolittle about 1862.   About 1868 the manufacture of children's carriages was added, and in 1871 R. S. Darrow bought Mr Doolittle's interest, when the firm became Winton & Darrow.   They employ about $35,000 capital, give employment to thirty persons and manufacture 18,000 boys' sleighs and from 2,000 to 3,000 children's carriages annually.

† The *Binghamton Savings Bank* was chartered April 18, 1867; the *Chenango Valley Savings Bank* was chartered April 15, 1857, but did not commence business until April 23, 1867; the *City National Bank of Binghamton* was organized in 1852, and was reorganized in 1865, with a capital of $200,000; the *First National Bank of Binghamton* was organized Dec 19, 1863, with a capital of $200,000, the *National Broome County Bank* was organized in 1831, with $100,000 capital; the *Susquehanna Valley Bank* was organized in 1854, with a capital of $100,000   The names of the officers and the locations of the banks will be found in the Directory.

‡ *Christ's Episcopal, First Presbyterian, North Presbyterian, Baptist, Free Methodist, St. Patrick's* (Catholic), *Congregational, Centenary M E., Zion M. E.* (colored), *Bethel M. E.* (colored.)

§ The Seminary building on Chestnut street is now undergoing necessary changes for its occupancy as a Ladies' college, which, it is expected, will commence operations in September, 1872.

‖ A history of the Press will be found on page 69.

¶ The *Binghamton Water Cure*, of which O. V Thayer is proprietor, is beautifully situated on the side of Prospect Hill, facing and overlooking the city, of which it affords a fine view, surrounded by large trees, and supplied with an abundance of pure, soft, spring water, the great essentials for hydropathic purposes.   It was established in Binghamton in 1849, since which time it has treated successfully thousands of invalids.

** This excellent institution is so amply and tersely described in the subjoined article prepared for us under the direction of the Superintendent Daniel G. Dodge, that we deem any further allusion to it unnecessary

"The New York State Inebriate Asylum," at Binghamton, is the oldest and largest establishment of the kind in the world, and may be regarded as the parent of the numer-

†† See foot note on page 87.

F

contains 12,692 inhabitants*; its streets are generally well

ous public and private reformatories and sanataria which are rapidly increasing in number, not alone in the United States and Canada, but also in Great Britain and Australia  The most succinct statement of the purposes for which it was established is embraced in the following declaration of principles put forth by the 'American Association for the Cure of Inebriates,' at its session in New York City in November, 1870

'1  Intemperance is a disease  2  It is curable in the same sense that other diseases are.  3  Its primary cause is a constitutional susceptibility to the alcoholic impression 4  This constitutional tendency may be inherited or acquired '

" The first charter of the Institution was granted by the Legislature, April 23, 1853, and it was designated 'The United States Asylum for the Reformation of the Poor and Destitute Inebriate '  Meetings were held and large subscriptions obtained in the form of shares and stock at $10 each  The charter provided for the election of a board of forty trustees to be chosen from the shareholders, but from the nature of the organization the whole management was practically in the hands of the Superintendent.  This charter was amended and the name of the Institution changed to ' The New York State Inebriate Asylum,' March 27, 1857.

" The corner-stone of the Asylum was laid with masonic ceremonies, by J L Lewis, Grand Master, on the 24th of September, 1858  On this occasion a very large concourse of spectators was present and addresses were delivered by Hon B F Butler, (of New York,) Dr J. W Francis, Rev Dr Bellows, Daniel S. Dickinson and Edward Everett. A poem was also read by Alfred D Street.

" The Asylum, which is two miles east of the city, is built on a beautiful plateau, two hundred and forty feet above the level of the Susquehanna river, and commands picturesque views of the mountains that encircle the Susquehanna and Chenango valleys.  The City of Binghamton donated two hundred and fifty-two acres of the land belonging to the Asylum, to which one hundred and twenty-eight acres were subsequently added by purchase  About $40,000 of private subscriptions having been exhausted and being found entirely inadequate to complete the buildings on the scale of their projection, the property was deeded in trust to the State of New York, in consideration of an appropriation of ten per cent of the excise money for the purpose of completing the Asylum. This per centage amounted to a large sum, but the repeal of the law, after it had been in operation for five years, deprived this institution of this source of revenue  For the last two years the Asylum has received no aid from the State and has had to depend for its support upon the receipts of paying patients.

" The Asylum, which is built of Syracuse limestone, is of the castellated Gothic order of architecture, a very enduring, but expensive and uninviting style for the purpose for which it is built.  The length of the front is 365 feet , the transept is 72 feet deep, with an extension to the rear of nearly 200 feet, and the wings 51 feet in width  It is four stories in height, and besides sleeping rooms for nearly one hundred patients, it has handsomely appointed reception rooms, dining hall, club rooms, lecture room and chapel.

" The north wing was badly injured by an incendiary fire in 1864, and remains in an unfinished state, although a comparatively small appropriation by the Legislature would complete it and double the accommodation for patients.  The eastern extension of the south wing, which contained the dining room, gymnasium, bowling alleys and many needed conveniences, was burned to the ground in 1870

" The building was opened for patients in June, 1864, since which time, with varying fortunes, the Asylum has been in constant operation  The total number of patients admitted has been about eleven hundred  Of these 1,009 have been voluntary and 91 committed patients  The average residence of patients is four months  The proportion of patients cured is about 40 per cent , judging from reliable statistics of the last two years

" The right and title of the property is now vested in the State of New York, and it is under the same control and supervision as other State institutions.  Fifteen Trustees are appointed by the Governor, and the whole management of the Asylum is placed in their hands  The board is subdivided into three committees  Executive, Financial and Management and Discipline.  The officers and Trustees for 1872 are as follows : Dr Willard Parker, President ; Dr. W. C. Wey, Vice-President , Dr. Geo. Burr, 2d Vice-President ; Abel Bennett, Treasurer , Dr. D G, Dodge, Superintendent , Carroll Hyde, Secretary , Rev S. W Bush, Chaplain  Trustees  W. W. Gordon, W. H Bristol, P. S Danforth, Austin Beardsall, P Mundsy, P G Elsworth, A. P Nichols, H. R. Pierson, Dr G A Dayton, Dr J. G Orton, with the President, Vice-Presidents and Treasurer, *ex officio*

" The cost of board, residence and medical attendance is nominally $20 per week, but the Committee on Management and Discipline have the power to reduce this to such an amount as may reasonably come within the means of the patient or his friends,—a right which they exercise with a judicious liberality as is shown by the last annual report, from which it appears that out of a total of 244 patients received in the Asylum in 1871, 30 per cent. paid at the rate of $20 per week ; 25 per cent at the rate of $15 per week , 25 per cent. at from $5 to $10 per week, and 20 per cent. were free patients—or, on the

*See foot note on following page.

shaded and are lighted by gas†; and it is supplied with an abundance of pure, wholesome water.‡ The parts of the

basis of $20 per week, 59 per cent were paying and 41 per cent. free patients. Notwithstanding this large proportion of free patients, however, by judicious management and careful economy, the financial statement showed a balance of $2,039 02 in favor of the Asylum, after all expenses, salaries &c , were paid

"The mode of obtaining admission is by personal application, or letter, setting forth the condition of the patient and the pecuniary ability of himself or his friends This application should be addressed to Dr. D. G. Dodge, Supt. of the Asylum, Binghamton, N Y.

"The people of Binghamton are justly proud of the Inebriate Asylum, which is not only the most important public institution in Broome County, and has been of incalculable benefit to humanity, but it is also the exemplar and inspiration of many other institutions, existing or yet to be established in various parts of the world for the treatment of Inebriation as a disease "

†† The *Susquehanna Valley Home*, located near the west line of the city, was incorporated March 15, 1869. "The design of the institution is to furnish a suitable home for indigent orphan children and such others as the Board of Managers may consider worthy of admission, affording them facilities for acquiring an elementary education and habits of industry and economy, and finally to provide them with permanent homes in families of benevolence and christian principles." From the report of the Board of Managers for the fiscal year ending Sept. 30, 1871, it appears that 123 orphans and destitute children were received, supported and instructed during the fiscal year, thirty of whom were from the Broome County poor house ; and that the average expense per week for support, maintenance and education, independent of all contributions of clothing, provisions, &c., was $2.38.

* Of these 10,350 were native and 2,342 foreign ; 12,382, white, and 310, colored. They were distributed among the several wards as follows:

| WARDS | Native. | Foreign. | White | Colored. | Total |
|---|---|---|---|---|---|
| First Ward . .. ... .. .. | 2702 | 685 | 3326 | 61 | 3387 |
| Second " . .. .. ... | 1488 | 302 | 1756 | 34 | 1790 |
| Third " ..... ..... . .. .. | 2383 | 614 | 2981 | 16 | 2997 |
| Fourth " ... ·. .. .. .. ..... | 2820 | 603 | 3230 | 193 | 3123 |
| Fifth " ..... ... .. .. .... . ...... ...| 957 | 133 | 1089 | 6 | 1095 |

† The *Binghamton Gas Light Co.* was organized Oct. 1, 1853. Its capital is $50,000. The officers are: Chas. McKinney, *president*; C. B. Johnson, *superintendent.*

‡ The *Holley Water Works of Binghamton*, located in the east part of the city, on the north bank of the Susquehanna, were established by special act of the Legislature in 1868. They are owned by the city and controlled by a board of five commissioners, who elect their own officers, and are elected at special elections for a term of five years. The first five commissioners were appointed by the Governor, and were as follows : Wm. P. Pope, Frederick Lewis, Jno. S. Wells, Sabin McKinney and Wm. E. Taylor. Wm. P. Pope was elected president, and Frederick Lewis, treasurer. One commissioner is retired from the board each year, by a vote of the commissioners themselves, and vacancies thus caused are filled by election. Three, viz: Jno. S. Wells, Wm. E Taylor and Frederick Lewis, have been thus retired and elected to the offices to which they were assigned by the Governor. The building is built substantially and tastily of brick, the main part being 40 by 60 feet on the ground, and the boiler room. 40 by 24 feet. The main part is two stories high. The wells are two in number and each is 20 feet deep and 24 in diameter. The water is of a very pure quality and is forced into the pipes by a double engine of 150 horse power, and a pressure of thirty pounds to the inch constantly maintained. Nineteen miles of pipe are laid, by which about seven-eighths of the populated city is supplied with water. Extensions are constantly being made as the requirements of the city demand. Three miles of pipes are to be laid the present summer (1872.) $205,000 have been appropriated by the

city separated by the Chenango are connected by two bridges; the Susquehanna is crossed by the same number within the city limits. There are many magnificent business blocks and a few private residences already constructed and many others are in process of erection or contemplated. Few cities of its size, or even older and larger ones, possess so many elegant buildings. The disposition to construct ornate and elaborate dwellings and buildings seems, from the following extract from the *Annals of Binghamton*, to have been acquired, or rather, perhaps, found opportunity to manifest itself, within the last thirty years. We quote:

"* * * the buildings * * * are neat, convenient, and appear well from the street. There are but few poor houses, remarkable few for the size of the place. Again, it should be remarked, there are but few large and splendid dwellings, or edifices of any kind. A medium appears to have been studied, and much convenience rather than much ornament."

This, it should be remembered, is the description of the city as it appeared in 1840.

It is yet an open question as to whether Binghamton possesses the requisites for making it a great and popular watering place. Certainly the existence of mineral springs in its vicinity is the only thing it *apparently* lacks to constitute it such. But no little excitement was recently created by the discovery of a "*saline-chalybeate*" spring on land near the foot of Mount Prospect, owned by Lewis West. *Cautious capital*, however, and a magnified estimate of the value of the properties of the spring, have thus far prevented its development. Current reports ascribe to it most unusual and valuable qualities, which, if it possesses, must ultimately prove it to be the great *desideratum* of Binghamton. It is claimed to be the only spring of its kind known to exist in the United States, and to resemble very closely the one at Cheltenham, England, which is highly impregnated with salt and iron.* Another spring possessing similar qualities was subsequently found on the property of Thomas A. Sedgwick, adjacent to the former, and the opinion

---

city, and $180,000 of that sum have been expended. The remainder will probably be expended during the summer. Over 2,000 water permits are granted, including railroads and manufacturing establishments, from which the receipts are about $16,000 per annum, or from $3,000 to $4,000 in excess of the expenses. The officers consist of five commissioners, a superintendent and clerk. Three engineers, who are on duty eight hours each, and two firemen, who are on duty twelve hours each, are employed. The quantity of water supplied is ample for fire purposes. The services of the fire engines, in case of fire, are generally unnecessary. Water can be thrown 125 feet high from each of six hydrants at the same time and this pressure maintained. Six streams can with ease be brought to bear upon any fire in the thickly settled part of the city. The protection afforded by the water works has reduced the insurance rates 33 per cent.

* Below we give the result of an analysis of the water from the spring by

is expressed that an indefinite number may be obtained by digging to the level of the source from whence these proceed.

The *Binghamton Normal Music School* was established in this city in the summer of 1871, having began its existence in Florida, Orange county, N. Y., as an experiment the previous summer. Its object is, as its name implies, to perfect teachers in this ennobling accomplishment and fit them to impart instruction to others. Although of recent origin the institution has already acquired an enviable reputation.

The *Binghamton Fire Department* consists of the following named companies:

| | | | |
|---|---|---|---|
| *Excelsior Hook & Ladder Co.* | No. 1,........ | H. E Allen, | Foreman |
| *Crystal Hose Co.* | No 1,........ | A W. Lockwood, | " |
| *Alert Hose Co.* | No 2,....... | A. E. Green, | " |
| *Protection Hose Co.* | No. 3,........ | Daniel Emery, | " |
| *Fountain Hose Co.* | No. 4,... ....  | Jas Lyon, Acting | " |
| *Independent Hose Co* | No. 5, ....... | Robt Crozier, | " |
| *Mechanics Hose Co.* | No. 6,........ | ——— Darrow, | " |

One steamer and two *first-class* hand-engines are connected with the department. An engineer and fireman are employed and paid by the city. The engines are seldom called into requisition, but are always kept in readiness for use in case of an emergency. Reliance is placed principally upon the city water works. No serious fire has occurred since their advent. The companies include 300 active members.

The *Exempt Fire Association* is composed of firemen who have served their time and who band together for mutual protection and benefit. They are not controlled by the chief, but in exigent cases volunteer their services.

W. Stratford, M. D., Professor of Chemistry in the College of the city of New York.

" In an Imperial gallon of 70,000 grains ·

| | |
|---|---|
| Sodium Chloride... . ... . ................... ....... . . | 10 82 grains. |
| Potassium " ......... ............ .. . .... . . | trace |
| Iron Carbonate.. .......... .. . ... . .. ... | 53 12 grains |
| Lime Sulphate....... .- ..... .. . ........ .....6 22 | " |
| " Carbonate - ..... .. ... . ... .. . ... | 32 95 " |
| Magnesia Carbonate ..... ... .. .. .. ...... ..ı | 29 80 " |
| Silica . ... .. .. .. .... ....ı . . | 3 32 " " |

The gases are carbonic acid, sulphurated hydrogen, oxygen and nitrogen; their strength and amount cannot be determined except at the spring

In his letter accompanying the report of the analysis, Prof. Stratford says: "The very large amount of organic matter is unusual and must, I think, have gained access either from leakage of some of the barrels in the vault, from substances left in the jug, or, and it is scarcely possible, from the shale rock itself. However this may be, the *chalybeate properties of the water render it very valuable for medicinal purposes.*" The spring, it is proper to state, was discovered in an excavation made in the side of the hill for a beer vault. The water, it appears, was used in the manufacture of beer, and the peculiar taste it imparted to the latter first led to an examination of its properties.

*The Firemen's Hall* is a fine structure, situated on Collier street, and was finished in 1858, at an expense of about $10,000. Besides an ample depository for the appliances of the fire companies, it supplies a very convenient audience chamber for public meetings, lectures, concerts, and the like.*

Although there are, as yet, no street railroads in operation in Binghamton, projects for the construction of two at least have been and are still in contemplation.† The immediate commencement of work on the Washington, and State Asylum Street R. R. is contemplated.

The *Binghamton Driving Park Association*, " for the improvement of horses and to encourage the breeding of horses," was incorporated by an act passed April 23, 1870. Henry S. Jarvis, John S. Wells, John Rankin, Daniel S. Richards and Wm. E. Taylor were the first directors.

Binghamton was the home of the late distinguished and talented Hon. Daniel S. Dickinson, a son of whom she may well feel proud, whose remains repose in the beautiful *Spring Forest Cemetery*. A monument erected over his sepulcher by the *Bar Association of New York* was unveiled May 31, 1872, in connection with the dedication ceremonies on that day.‡

---

*History of Binghamton,* by Rev Dr. Z. Paddock.

† An act incorporating the Binghamton & Port Dickinson R. R. (horse) was passed May 1, 1868  The route is thus described in the act "commencing at the town line between the towns of Kirkwood and Binghamton, on the north bank of the Susquehauna, near the New York and Erie railroad, in the public highway, and running westerly along said highway, to the corporation line of the city of Binghamton; thence along and through Court street to Main street; thence through and along Main street to the westerly bound of said city; thence along the public highway to the town line of the town of Union, with a branch connecting with said road in Court street at Chenango street, and running thence through and along Chenango street to the northerly bounds of said city, and thence along the public highway leading north up to the Chenango river to Port Dickinson together with all the necessary connections, turnouts and switches for the proper working and accommodation of the tracks on the said route or routes." The act provided that the building of the road should be commenced within one year from the date of its passage, and finished within five years from the date of its commencement  An act was passed April 30, 1869, allowing two additional years in which to commence the building of the road.

‡ Daniel S. Dickinson was born in Goshen, Litchfield Co., Conn., Sept. 11, 1800; he removed with his father to Chenango Co , N. Y., in 1806; received a common school education; and in 1821 he entered upon the duties of a school teacher, and, without the aid of an insructor, mastered the Latin language, and became versed in the higher branches of mathematics and other sciences. He studied law, came to the bar in 1830, and settled in Binghamton, where he long practiced his profession with success. In 1836 he was elected to the State Senate, serving from 1837 to 1840; was Judge of the Court of Errors from 1836 to 1841; from 1842 to 1844 he was President of said Court, Lieutenant Governor, and also President of the Senate; was a Regent of the University of New York in 1843; was a member of the Convention which nominated James K. Polk for President, and a Presidential Elector in 1844; and he was a Senator in Congress from

It is also the home of Prof. Royal E. House, the inventor of House's system of telegraphy.*

HAWLEYTON (p. o.) is a hamlet in the south-west part of the town, on Little Snake Creek. It contains one church, (M. E.) two hotels, two blacksmith shops and one wagon shop. Near it are two saw mills which saw nearly two millions of feet of lumber annually.

PORT DICKINSON (p. o.) is located in the north-east part, three miles north of Binghamton. It lies upon the east bank of the Chenango, and on the Chenango Canal. It contains a store, hotel, whip factory, cotton batting factory, broom factory and about fifty families. The Delaware, Lackawanna & West ern Coal Co. have a depot at this place for the transhipment of coal.†

Previous to the Revolution the country included within the limits of the town of Binghamton is not known to have been trod by the feet of white men, except, perhaps, as prisoners of the Indians, who held undisputed sway of all this region of country, which seems to have been a favorite haunt of theirs. The placid waters of the Susquehanna have carried many a band of warriors on missions of death and rapine to the exposed frontier settlements of the whites. But such pictures are most unhappy retrospects when contrasted with the more pacific ones to which they have given place; hence we leave the Indian in the grandeur of his wildness and barbarity for the more pleasing contemplation of the almost magical transformations which the banks of this beautiful stream have witnessed under the genius of civilization and progress. The first white

New York from 1844 to 1851, serving on important committees, and originating and ably supporting several important measures In 1861 he was elected Attorney-General of the State of New York; was a Delegate to the 'Baltimore Convention' of 1864; and in 1865 he was appointed by President Lincoln, United States District Attorney for the Southern District of New York. He died suddenly in that city, April 12, 1866. Before accepting his last public position he declined several appointments tendered him by the President of the United States and the Governor of New York. His 'Life and Works' were published in 1867, in two volumes."

* Prof. House was born in Vermont, in 1815. He moved to Susquehanna Co., Penn., from there to New York, and to Binghamton, in 1853. He erected a fine residence about one mile south of the city. It stands upon a hill 530 feet above the Susquehanna.

† The Port Dickinson hotel was burned March 23, 1872, and the grist and paper mills formerly at this place, March 29, 1872. Joseph Carman, who built these mills and owned them about ten years, moved to the site of Port Dickinson when nine years old. He worked for Abram Bevier until he was 21 years old, when he purchased the farm he now owns. He was for some time a merchant at this place; had contracts for work on the Erie R. R. amounting to $2,000,000; and has dealt largely in lumber and stock.

visitors to this region came with hostile intent. They were soldiers belonging to a detachment of the American army under the command of General James Clinton, on their way to join another large division of that army, destined against the Indians of this State, under the command of General John Sullivan. They encamped one or two nights upon the site of Binghamton city, where were several Indian wigwams, but no Indians to be seen. Corn, which was growing upon the island, was destroyed. It is quite probable that these troops destroyed an Indian village opposite the site of Port Dickinson, as vestiges of a recent village at that place were visible to the first white settlers.

Eight years later, in 1787, Capt Joseph Leonard, who is believed to have been the first white man to make a permanent settlement in the town, came, with a young wife and two little children, and located on the Chenango, in the vicinity of Port Dickinson. His wife and children were put into a canoe with the goods they brought, and rowed by a hired man; while he came up by land with two horses, keeping the shore and regulating his progress by that of his family. Leonard was originally from Plymouth, Mass., but immediately from Wyoming, Penn., where he owned a farm and lived several years. He was there under arms at the time of the great massacre, though not in the field of action. At the time of the great ice freshet in the Susquehanna, his dwelling, with many others, was carried away by it. This calamity, together with the disputes which existed relative to land titles, induced him to leave and seek more peaceable and secure possessions. He received information from Amos Draper, an Indian trader in this locality, which led him to select this as his home. Two or three weeks subsequent to his arrival came Col. Wm. Rose and his brother, Solomon, the latter of whom settled in Lisle. Col. Rose located a little higher up the river than Capt. Leonard. "It was," says Wilkinson, in the *Annals of Binghamton*, "but a short time after the arrival of the latter, that he, with Amos Draper, invited the Indians of the neighborhood to meet in council, and leased of them, for the term of ninety-nine years, one mile square; for which they were to give a *barrel* of *corn* per year. This lease, however, was invalidated by an act of the Legislature having been previously passed, and without the knowledge of these men, 'that no lands should be leased or purchased of the Indians by private individuals.' But before it was known [by them] that such a law existed, Col. Rose and his brother purchased Mr. Draper's interest in the lease. It embraced where the three had located." Col. Rose and his brother came from Connecticut on foot to Wattle's Ferry,

where they procured a canoe and brought with them stores to
this place.    Parties of Indians on the shore, sitting by their
fires, engaged in their festivities, or skirting the mountains in
pursuit of deer, were often seen by them, but never offered to
molest them.    They designed pushing on to the country
bordering on the Conhocton and settling there; but learning
at Union, from a Mr. Gallop, a temporary settler at that place,
that the country they were seeking was in dispute, that they
could obtain no satisfactory title to their land and that they
would be obliged to fight for their crops, they turned back to
the mouth of the Chenango, whose broad stream and pleasant
banks impressed them favorably as they passed down, and
sought the home before indicated.    Soon after, during the
same year, came Joshua and Wm. Whitney and Henry Green,
from Hillsdale, Columbia county, and settled on the west side
of the Chenango, about two miles above its junction with the
Susquehanna, on what was afterwards called Whitney's Flats.
In this town and in the vicinity of Port Dickinson, it is
probable, was held the first council between the commissioners
representing the proprietors of the Boston Ten-Townships and
the Indians.*    Among the settlers who came the same year,
1787, were —— Lyon, who lived, previous to Leonard's advent
into the town, in a temporary log house, near the site of Col.
Page's ashery; and who afterwards kept for several years the
ferry across the Chenango; Jesse Thayer, who settled where
Christopher Eldredge afterwards lived; Peter and Thomas
Ingersoll, who settled where James Hawley afterwards lived;
Samuel Harding who settled on the Bevier place, on the
east side of the Chenango; Capt. John Sawtell, who settled
opposite the Poor House; —— Butler, who settled
on the river bank, a little below Captain Leonard, and
Solomon Moore, who settled on the site of the city of Binghamton.    The next year about twenty families augmented the little
settlement in this region and received from those who preceded
them, in accordance with the urgency of their needs, the generous hospitality for which the early settlers distinguished
themselves—a hospitality which meant, says Wilkinson, the im-
partial division among the needy settlers of such stores as the
more prosperous had been able to accumulate, and which sorely
taxed them at times to relieve the wants of new comers until
they could create resources of their own.    But this hospitality
proved equal to the severest trial.    The first roads were constructed by following the Indian paths when practicable and
cutting away on either side the fallen logs, underbrush and sap.

* See page 73.

lings until a a sufficient clearing was made to admit the passage
of wagons. A circuit was made to avoid large trees when such
interposed. Roads of this description were, in a few years, built
on both sides of the Chenango, generally where they now run,
and on the north side of the Susquehanna, both above and
below the settlements on it. A sleigh road was opened to Unadilla in 1788. The early settlers had little occasion, however,
to leave home, except to take their grain to mill, which was
done by means of canoes on the river. The nearest mill was
at "Shepherd's Mill," three miles north of Tioga Point, (now
Athens, Penn.,) a distance of forty miles. The journey occupied a week, and sometimes a fortnight. "A considerable portion of their corn, however, was pounded, and thus converted
into samp, by the simple machinery of a stump hollowed out
for a mortar, and a pestle suspended by a sweep." The Indians
raised corn and potatoes, and from them the seed was procured;
but the other seed and the flour, what little was had, was
brought from the Hudson, or up the Susquehanna in canoes
from Wyoming. In 1790 their condition as regards milling
facilities was ameliorated by the erection of a grist mill on Fitch's
Creek, in the town of Kirkwood. John Miller, —— Moore
and —— Luce moved with their families, from New Jersey to
Wyoming, but owing to the unsettled condition of things in
that country they remaind there but a short time and came to
this town the first or second season of its settlement and located
on the east side of the Chenango. Mr. Miller, it appears, was
the first magistrate, he having acted in that capacity in New Jersey. He also first conducted religious exercises, before any regular
minister visited the new settlement. He was a Presbyterian,
and reported to be an eminently pious man. Meetings were
held uniformly at the house of Samuel Harding, and he and
his daughters walked a distance of four miles to attend them.
Rev. Mr. Howe, a Baptist minister, who came in the summer of
1790, officiated in his ministerial capacity and succeeded in
forming a church, consisting of ten or twelve persons, which
was the first Christian society in this region, but which, after
the removal of Mr. Howe, dwindled and became extinct about
1800. A considerable accession was made in the summer of
1789, by persons who settled in the valleys of the Chenango and
Susquehanna. Among these was Daniel Hudson, who settled
between Capt. Leonards' and Col. Rose's. The house erected
on the site of Binghamton, by Solomon Moore, to whom allusion
has before been made, was soon abandoned by him after he
learned that he could not purchase the land, and in consequence
soon dilapidated and disappeared. Thomas Chambers erected
and lived in a log house on the site of the city. Other settle-

ments were made here and a post office established June 23, 1798, with Joshua Whitney as post master. Up to the beginning of the present century, however, little disposition to occupy the site of the city was manifested, the attention of early settlers being diverted to *Chenango village,* a prosperous settlement at that time on the west side of the Chenango, about one mile above Binghamton, and just above the point of Mount Prospect which projects toward and near the river, which boasted of a hotel, a newspaper office, (the *Constellation,* published by Daniel Cruger, to which allusion is made in the history of the press,) a store, a distillery and a doctor's office. In 1800, Joshua Whitney became the agent of Mr. Bingham for the disposal of the latter's lands in this vicinity, and as the whole of the site of the village just alluded to was not embraced in Mr. Bingham's patent, and it had neither the advantage of as eligible a location, nor possessed a sufficiently extensive area for the growth of a village such as might be built up at the junction of the two rivers, Mr. Whitney conceived the idea of diverting attention to the latter place and removing the village there. As a means to this end he took advantage of reports which were circulated to the effect that Lucas Elmendorf of Kingston, Ulster Co., was about to build a bridge across the Chenango on the line of the great western highway which passed through the site of Binghamton, and represented that it must determine the prosperity of settlers in its locality and cause a corresponding decline in the growth of the upper village. He accordingly, in company with several others, who came by appointment, commenced a clearing on both sides of the river at the point, where he represented the bridge was to be located. The ground was surveyed and laid out into streets and lots in village form, the same year. The lots contained three-fourths of an acre and were sold generally for twenty dollars each; the corner lots were held at a higher price. To render the success of his plan more certain, Gen. Whitney purchased a number of buildings in the old village and moved them down to the new one. By this means the nucleus of a village was formed and its prosperity assured. New accessions were rapidly made for a few years and the village soon began to assume size and importance, but the bridge was not built until 1808. It was built by Marshal Lewis and Luther Thurstin, at an expense of $6,000, and was due to the enterprise, perseverance and pecuniary resources of Lucas Elmendorf.* It contributed

* The bridge was rebuilt in 1825, by Col. H. Lewis, as master builder, under the direction of Joshua Whitney, at a cost of over $5,000 On each side of the river, at the ends of this bridge, stood a fine elm tree, and the two were long known as the "twin elms." That on the west side is still

largely to the growth of the village by removing the barrier to highway travel, presented by the Chenango, which had to be crossed at this point. From that time to the present the growth of Binghamton has been gradual but constant. It has suffered neither serious reverse, nor an abnormal inflation. The only important exception, perhaps, to the last part of the previous assertion was manifested by the temporary instability occasioned by the completion or location of the Erie R. R. through the village. That fluctuating tendency, however, gradually subsided into a steady and healthy growth. The advantages which the location of the city presents, if judiciously and liberally seconded or made available by its capitalists, by fostering existing manufacturing enterprises and encouraging new ones, must eventually make Binghamton an important commercial and manufacturing center.*

We purpose now to give a brief history of such of the churches of the town as have given us the necessary information. The first church organized in the town was, as before stated, done through the exertions of Elder Howe, in 1790, or soon thereafter. The Dutch Reformed Church, the second one established, was organized in 1798, by Rev. Mr. Manly, a minister of that persuasion. Meetings were held by the latter society in the chamber of a dwelling house, located about a mile above the village, on the east bank of the Chenango, which was fitted with conveniences for that purpose. Mr. Manly preached alternately at this place and Union, but remained here only a few years. After an interval, during which the society had no minister, the services of Rev. Mr. Palmer were secured, and under his pastoral labors the church was revived and its number augmented. This society, differing so little in the substance of its belief from the faith of the Presbyterians was merged into the latter society, which organized after the establishment of the village.

*Christ Church*, (Episcopal) located at Binghamton, was organized Sept. 19, 1810, by Rev. Daniel Nash, under the title of *St. Ann's Church*. It was dissolved, and reorganized six years later, by Hon. Tracy Robinson. The first edifice was consecrated Nov. 20, 1818, by Bishop Hobart, and named *Christ*

---

standing. The one on the east side fell into the river through the continual wearing away of the bank during a period of fifty years.

* To those who desire a more minute portraiture of the early history of Binghamton, and in fact of the country within a circuit of thirty to fifty miles from it, we would commend them to the *Annals of Binghamton*, a work from which we have made liberal extracts, and in which the early settlements are detailed with greater particularity than is consistent with the scope of this work.

*Church.* In 1822 this building was sold to the Methodists and removed to Henry street, and a new one was erected in that year. In 1854 the present stone edifice was commenced and was opened for worship March 4, 1855. Its cost, including furniture, was about $35,000. It will seat 700 persons. The present value of church property is $75,000. The first pastor was Rev. James Keeler; the present one is Rev. Wm. A. Hitchcock. The present number of communicants is 350.

The *First Presbyterian Church of Binghamton* was organized with twenty members, Nov. 20, 1817, by Revs. Ebenezer Kingsbury and Joseph Wood. The first pastor was Rev. Benjamin A. Niles; at present it is without a pastor. The first house of worship was erected in 1819, and the present one, which occupies its site, was completed April 26, 1863, at a cost of $56,000. It is built of brick, and will seat 1200 persons. There are 637 members. The church property is valued at $75,000.*

The *First Baptist Church of Binghamton* was organized with five members, in 1831, by Rev. M. Frederick, its first pastor.† Their first house of worship was erected in 1831-2; and the present one, which will seat 1400 persons, in 1871-2, at a cost of $75,000. There are 708 members, who are ministered to by Rev. Lyman Wright.* The church property is valued at $110,000.

*St. Patrick's Church* (Roman Catholic) was organized with five members, in 1835, by Rev. Mr. Wainwright. The first house of worship was erected in 1837; and the present one, which is located on LeRoy street, in the city of Binghamton, and will seat 2,000 persons, in 1867, at a cost of $120,000. There are 3,000 members, who enjoy the ministration of Rev. James F. Hourigan, their first and present pastor. The church property is valued at $200,000.‡

The *Congregational Church* was organized Sept. 26, 1836, with nineteen members, by Rev. John Starkweather, its first pastor. The first house of worship was erected in 1837 and dedicated Dec. 22d of that year; the present one, which is located on the

---

*The Presbyterian Church of Castle Creek, and the Congregational Church of Binghamton were formed from this. The former, consisting of 23 members, was organized in 1833; the latter, in 1836.

†Rev. Dr. Paddock, of Binghamton, in his *History of Binghamton*, says this church was organized in May, 1829, with sixteen members—five males and eleven females—and that Elder Michael Frederick was called to preside over the church in 1830. The *data* from which our statement is compiled was furnished by the present pastor.

‡The *Convent of St. Joseph*, under the care of the Sisters of St. Joseph, has 35 boarders and 400 day scholars.
The *St. James School* for boys, numbers 125. D. J. Donaldson is the principal.

corner of Main and Front streets, in the city of Binghamton, and will seat 800 persons, in 1869, at a cost of $50,000. Rev. Edward Taylor, D. D., is the present pastor. The number of members is 310. The value of church property is $75,000.

The *A. M. E. Zion Church* was organized with thirty-six members, in 1836, by Rev. Henry Johnson, its first pastor. Its house of worship, which is located on Whitney street, in the city of Binghamton, was erected in 1840, at a cost of $500. It will seat 125 persons. The present pastor is Rev. Stephen S. Wales; the number of members is 56. The church property is valued at $3,000.

The *A. M. E. Church* (Bethel) was organized with sixty-five members, in 1838, by Rev. Chas. Spicer, its first pastor. The first church edifice was erected in 1838; the present one, which is located on Susquehanna street, in the city of Binghamton, and will seat 250 persons, in 1842, at a cost of $850. The society numbers forty-five. Rev. John Frizbee is the pastor. The value of Church property is $1,500.

The *M. E. Church*, of Hawleyton, was organized with eleven members in 1856, by Rev. —— Blaxey. Their church edifice was erected in 1857. It will seat 250 persons; and cost $2,000. The church property is valued at $3,200. It has fifty-two members. Rev. C. V. Arnold is the pastor.

The *First Free Methodist Church of Binghamton* was organized with ten members, by Rev. B. T. Roberts, in 1862. Rev. D. M. Sinclair was the first pastor; Rev. C. H. Southworth is the present one. Their edifice was erected by the "Protestant Methodists" in or about 1841, and was sold by them, about 1851, to the "Court St. M. E. Society," by whom it was again sold, in March, 1867, to its present occupants, for $3,600. It will seat from five to six hundred. It is located on the corner of Court and Carroll streets. There are sixty members in full connection, and eight probationers. The Church property is valued at $12,500.

The *M. E. Church of Binghamton* was organized by the consolidation of the Henry and Court street M. E. Churches* in 1865, by Rev. D. W. Bristol, D D., its first pastor. It then had

---

* The "Henry Street M. E. Church" was organized by Rev. Ebenezer Doolittle, in 1817, from which time the place was more or less regularly visited by circuit preachers. In 1822 the society provided itself with a house in which to hold meetings by purchasing the one discarded by the Episcopalians, as stated in the history of that Church. The "Court Street M. E. Church" was organized in 1851, under the legal title of *The Second Society of the Methodist Episcopal Church in Binghamton,* and was an offshoot from the "Henry Street Church." The means by which this society acquired its house of worship are stated in the history of the *First Free Methodist Church of Binghamton.*

399 members in full connection, and 30 probationers; it now has 615 members and 58 probationers. Rev. L. C. Floyd is the pastor. The church edifice was commenced in 1866 and completed in 1868, at a cost of $65,000. It is located on the corner of Court and Cedar streets, and will seat 800 persons. The Church property is valued at $70,000. The edifice is known as the Centenary M. E. Church.

The *North Presbyterian Church of Binghamton* was organized with fifty members, April 17, 1870, by Rev. C. Pierpont Coit, its first and present pastor. The church edifice, which will seat 350 persons, was erected in the fall and winter of 1869–70, at a cost of $9,000. It is located on the corner of Chenango and Munsell streets. The society numbers 145 members. The Church property is valued at $12,000.

*CHENANGO** was erected Feb. 16, 1791. It was one of the original towns. Windsor was taken off March 27, 1807; Conklin, March 29, 1824; and Binghamton and Fenton, Dec. 3, 1855. A part of Union was annexed Feb. 26, 1808, and a part of Maine, Nov. 27, 1856. It lies west of the center of the County, its eastern boundary being formed by the Chenango River. Its surface consists of the river intervale, and several ridges which rise to an altitude of from 300 to 600 feet and are separated by the narrow valleys of the streams running parallel with them, north and south, through the town. The principal streams are Castle† and Kattel‡ creeks, which are tributary to Chenango River, and Gilbert Creek, which empties its waters into Kattel Creek. On the north hills the soil consists of a gravelly loam mixed with disintegrated slate and underlaid by hard pan, but further south it becomes a deeper and richer gravelly loam. It is productive, but moist, and for this reason is devoted principally to grazing. Stock raising and dairying form the chief agricultural pursuits. The town covers an area of 21,154 acres, of which, in 1865, according to the census of that year, 14,262 were improved.

In 1870 the population of the town was 1,680. During the year ending Sept. 30, 1871, there were fourteen school districts, and the same number of teachers employed. The number of

---

* "Upon the map of 1771 this is given *Ol-si-nin-goo*. Upon DeWitt's map of about the year 1791, it is written *Che-nen-go*. In Mr. Morgan's work it is given *O-che-nang*."—*The Saint Nicholas for February and March*, 1854, *p*. 412.

† Named from the location of an Indian Castle near its mouth.

‡ Named from a family of early settlers.

children of school age was 761; the number attending school, 679; the average attendance, 281; the amount expended for school purposes, $7,403; and the value of school houses and sites, $8,815.

The Syracuse & Binghamton R. R. enters the town in the north-east corner and follows the course of the Chenango River until it reaches near the center of the east border, when it diverges and crosses the point formed by the bend in the river and leaves the town on the south border, a little east of the mouth of Kattel creek. The Utica & Chenango Valley R. R. just enters the town in the north-east corner. Both these roads are leased and operated by the D. L & W. R. R. Co.

CASTLE CREEK, (p. v) located near the north line, on the creek whose name it bears, contains two churches, (Baptist and M. E.) two stores, one hotel, a steam saw mill, two blacksmith shops, a wagon shop, cooper shop and 180 inhabitants.

KATTELVILLE (p. o.) is in the east part, on Kattel creek, near the S. & B. R. R.

GLEN CASTLE (p. o.) is located about two miles above the mouth of Castle creek.

WEST CHENANGO (p o.) is in the western part.

CHENANGO BRIDGE (p. o.) is located on the S. & B. R. R. at the point where it crosses the Chenango River.

CHENANGO FORKS (p. v.) is partially in this town * That part in this town contains one church, (M. E) two stores, one hotel, a cabinet shop, shoe shop and blacksmith shop.

NIMMONSBURG† is a hamlet in the south part, lying in the valley of the Chenango, three and a-half miles north of Binghamton.

The first settler was Thomas Gallop, who, as previously stated,‡ located at Chenango Forks, in 1787. He is believed to have remained there but a short time. Among the other early settlers were Col. Wm Rose and John Nimmons, who located in the south part Col. Rose settled on the farm now owned and occupied by Wm. R. Nimmons. Jedediah Seward, Wm. Hall, John Jewell, Stephen and Henry Palmer, Josiah Whitney, Jared Page, Nathaniel Bishop, James Temple and Foster Lilly were early settlers. Settlements appear to have been made rapidly and to have assumed some importance, for in 1788, a saw mill, which was owned by Henry French, was built at Glen

---

* For further mention of this village see town of Barker, p 80

+ Named in honor of Burwell Nimmons, who is 83 years old, and is one of the oldest inhabitants in town

‡ See page 80.

Castle. It was the first erected in the county. The Indians from whom the Boston Company purchased their lands, reserved a tract of one-half mile square, which was situated near the mouth of Castle Creek and was known as the "Castle Farm." "Upon this reserve the Indians of the neighborhood who did not remove to New Stockbridge, or Oneida, resided." Their number "is said to have been about twenty families" They cultivated the farm to some extent, but depended chiefly upon hunting and fishing. Wilkinson in speaking of them says : .

"[They] kept up their peculiar mode of dress so long as they remained upon their farm, clothing themselves with their shirt and moccasins, their head bare, except sometimes ornamenting it with feathers, and wearing jewels of silver in their nose and ears Their wigwams were built of logs, locked together at the ends, and sloping up on two sides from the ground to a peak, like the roof of a house.

"Another form of their wigwams was, to erect four stakes, or crotches, two longer and two shorter; upon these to lay two poles, one upon the longer and one upon the shorter crotches Upon these poles they would lay sticks or smaller poles and then barks, with sufficient ingenuity to exclude the rain and weather From the lower crotches to the ground they would tie barks, answering to our weather boarding. They would close up the two ends in the same manner Upon the front side were suspended skins of deer sewed together, from the pole upon the high crotches to the ground, and which they could raise or fall at pleasure Before this their fire was kindled, and the curtain of skins raised by day time, and more or less lowered by night, as the weather might be In some cases they would have their wigwams lined with deer skins. Seldom any floor but the ground Their bed consisted of straw, or skins thrown down When they sat down, it was always upon the ground In eating they sat generally without any order, as they happened to be, upon the ground, with each his piece in his hand. Their adroitness in spearing fish was admired by the whites, in which they displayed as much markmanship as they do with the bow and arrow. They would *throw* the spear at the fish which very seldom failed of transfixing its object, though the distance to which it was thrown should be twenty or thirty feet, the fish moving rapidly at the same time, and the water running swift.

"Their chief was called Squire Antonio This title was given him by the whites on account of his just decisions, his correct judgement, and his sober habits He was very much esteemed by the white people, as well as revered and loved by his own He undoubtedly contributed very materially towards maintaining that peaceful and friendly, or at least orderly, conduct which the Indians have the good name of having observed towards the whites."

But notwithstanding the amicable relations which subsisted between the whites and Indians, and the nominal price at which the latter were induced to sell their vast possessions, there was, in the neighborhood, a person named Patterson, who was sufficiently base, either through his own designs, or as the tool of others, to rob them of the small portion reserved for their own uses, by an appeal to the cupidity of the chief's son, Abraham Antonio.

G

"About 1792 or '3," says Wilkinson, "he went to the Indians at the Castle, and made himself very familiar and sociable with them. He brought with him a silver mounted rifle, which he knew would gain their admiration and excite their cupidity. Abraham Antonio was smitten with a desire for it. He endeavored to purchase it, making such offers as he could afford  But Patterson put him off, telling him he did not wish to sell it; or setting such a price upon it as he knew was beyond the power of Abraham immediately to command  After he had sufficiently prepared the way for himself, he proposed to the young chief, that if he would engage to give him so many bear skins he would  let him have the rifle  This the prince complied with  A note was required on the part of Patterson, with the son and father's name subscribed, that the skins should be delivered against a specified time  Abraham hesitated as to such a course, as he did not understand such a mode of business. He therefore asked his father as to the propriety, who told his son it was a common mode of doing business with the whites.  Patterson then *professedly* wrote a *note*, specifying the number of skins, and read it off to the father and son accordingly, who both signed their names.  But instead of writing a *note*, he wrote a deed for the Castle farm."

For this act of perfidy, however, Patterson is believed to have forfeited his life and that of his family at the hands of Abraham, who either followed him for the purpose to Ohio, whither he moved, or accidentally met him there and summarily revenged the treachery of which he was made the victim.  With the loss of the Castle farm, the Indians appear to have gradually withdrawn from this section, leaving their favorite hunting grounds in undisputed possession of the whites.

Nothing of marked prominence appears in the history of the town until the breaking out of the Rebellion, from which it suffered in common with other sections of the country.  It contributed seventy-one soldiers as its share in the establishment of the supremacy of the Union.

The *First M E Society*, at Chenango Forks, was organized in 1833.  Their house of worship will seat 250 persons.  It was erected in 1863, at a cost of $2,500, which is the present value of Church property.  There are sixty-eight members.  The present pastor is Rev. C. E. Taylor.

The *Castle Creek Baptist Church* was organized in 1844, in which year its first house of worship was erected.  The present one, which will seat 300 persons, was erected in 1870, at a cost of $7,860.75.  There are eighty-seven members.  Rev. A. P. Merrill is pastor.  The Church property is valued at $9,500.

The *M. E Church*, at Castle Creek, was organized with thirty members, in 1847, by Rev. T. D. Wire, its first pastor.  The first Church edifice was erected in 1840; the present one in 1868.  It cost $6,000, and will seat 300 persons.  Rev. N. S. DeWitt is the pastor.  It has eighty members.  The Church property is valued at $7,500.

The *Kattelville M. E. Church* was organized with nine members, by Rev. R. S. Rose, its first pastor, in 1851, in which year was erected the house of worship, at a cost of $1,500. It will seat 225 persons. Rev. C. E. Taylor is the pastor. The number of members is forty-eight. The Church property is valued at $1,600.

The *Glen Castle M. E. Church* erected its house of worship, which will seat 300 persons, in 1851, at a cost of $1,200. Its 39 members are ministered to by Revs. Philo Wilcox and Robert Thomas. The Church property is valued at $2,000.

*COLESVILLE** was formed from Windsor, April 2, 1821.† It lies upon the north border, east of the center of the County. Its surface is broken by an elevated ridge whose summits rise from 400 to 700 feet above the valley of the Susquehanna, by which it is cut in two. The Susquehanna and several small streams tributary to it are the only water-courses. The soil upon the river bottom is a deep, fertile, gravelly loam, while upon the summits of the hills it consists of clay and slate. It is generally much better adapted to pasturage than tillage. The town is traversed by the Albany & Susquehanna and the Delaware & Hudson Canal Co.'s railroads, both of which enter the town on the north line, at Nineveh, and pursue a circuitous course, the former in a general south-west direction and the latter along the valley of the Susquehanna. It covers an area of 47,283¼ acres, of which, in 1865, according to the census of that year, 29,696¼, were improved. The population in 1870 was 3,400. During the year ending Sept. 30, 1871, it contained thirty school districts and employed twenty-nine teachers. The number of children of school age was 1,218; the number attending school, 1,011; the average attendance, 472; the amount expended for school purposes, $6,948; and the value of school houses and sites, $9,090.

HARPERSVILLE (p. v.) is situated north of the center, about one-half mile west of the Susquehanna. It is about one mile

* Named from Nathaniel Cole, one of the first settlers.

† The first town meeting was held on Coles Hill, at the house of Nathaniel Cole, in 1822, and the following named officers were elected: "John W. Harper, *Supervisor;* Daniel Sanford, *Town Clerk*, Ozias Marsh, Harvey Bishop and Gervase Blakeslee, *Assessors;* Nathaniel Cole Jr. and Elisha Humastun, *Overseers of the Poor;* Amos Smith, Alpheus Goodenough and Daniel Sanford, *Commissioners of Highways;* John Wasson and George Wilcox, *Constables;* John Wasson, *Collector;* John W. Harper, Jeremiah Rogers and Harvey Bishop, *Commissioners of Common Schools;* Harvey Martin, Garry Ruggles and Joel K. Noble, *Inspectors of Common Schools;* Geo. Wilcox, Samuel Badger and Samuel Martin, *Trustees of Gospel and School Lands;* Ira Bunnell, *Sealer of Weights and Measures.*"

south-west of the depot on the A. & S. R. R. at Nineveh, and is about one-half mile from the D. & H. Canal Co's R. R., in the same direction. It contains three churches, (Baptist, Episcopal and ——,) two dry goods stores, two drug stores, one grocery, one hardware store and tin shop, two cabinet ware rooms, one saw mill, a furnace and machine shop, a shoe shop, a merchant tailor's store, four blacksmith shops, three carriage shops, one harness shop, one hotel and 320 inhabitants.

CENTER VILLAGE (p. v.) is situated on the Susquehanna and the D. & H. Canal Co.'s R. R., a little east of the center of the town. It contains two dry goods stores, two grist mills, one saw mill, one lath mill, one carriage shop, two blacksmith shops, a tannery, a shoe shop, a harness shop, a wool carding machine, a hotel (now closed) and thirty houses.

NINEVEH (p. v.) is situated on the north line, on the Susquehanna and on the D. & H. Canal Co.'s and A. & S. railroads. It contains two churches, (Presbyterian and ——,) two dry goods stores, two carriage shops, three blacksmith shops, one cooper shop, one harness shop, a shoe shop and about 225 inhabitants.

DORAVILLE (p. o.) is located on the Susquehanna and on the D. & H. Canal Co's R. R. It contains a jewelry store, a grocery, a blacksmith shop, two cooper shops and about a dozen dwellings.

VALLONIA SPRINGS* (p. o.) is located near the north-east corner of the town and on the line of the contemplated branch of the N. Y. & O. Midland R. R.

NEW OHIO, (p. o.) located in the north-west part, near the tunnel† on the A. & S. R. R., on which road it is a station, contains a telegraph office, two groceries, a blacksmith shop, a few dwelling houses and a church (M E.)

NORTH COLESVILLE, (p. o.) located in the north-west corner, contains a grocery, a saw mill, a shoe shop and seventeen dwellings.

OUAQUAGA, (p. o.) situated on the Susquehanna, near the center of the south line, contains one church, (M E.) one store, two blacksmith shops, a carriage shop, two shingle mills,

---

*The waters of this spring have acquired some fame on account of their medicinal properties and are making this a place of considerable resort. They are impregnated with sulphur, magnesia and iron, and are not only efficacious in cutaneous diseases but are highly prophylactic.

†This tunnel is one-half mile long. The rock through which it is constructed was at first hard and compact, but exposure to the atmosphere slacked and dissolved it and rendered it necessary to arch it with stone.

two planing mills, two lath mills, one saw mill, a grist mill and twenty-three dwellings.

OSBORNE HOLLOW,* (p. o.) located in the west part, on the A. & S. R. R., contains one church, one hotel, three groceries, two blacksmith shops, two wagon shops, one steam saw and feed mill and several dwellings.

WEST COLESVILLE, (p. o.) in the south-west part, contains a church, (Baptist,) a blacksmith shop, a shoe shop and a few dwellings.

COLESVILLE (p. o.) is located a little south of the center. It contains a Free Church.

John Lamphere, from Watertown, Conn., made the first settlement in 1785. He was followed by Lemuel and Nathaniel Badger and Casper Spring in 1786; Nathaniel and Vena Cole, Daniel Picket, J. Merchant, Bateman S. Dickinson, —— Wilmot, Daniel Crofoot and Titus Humeston in 1795; John Ruggles and Isaac Tyrrell in 1796; and Eli Osborne and Peter Warn in 1800. The birth of Louisa Badger, which occurred May 28, 1788, was the first one in the town; the death of John Lamphere, which occurred the same year, was the first in the town; and the marriage of Benj. Bird and Mrs. John Lamphere, in 1794, was the first marriage. The first inn was kept by Benj. Bird, in 1794; and the first store, by Bateman S. Dickinson, in 1805. Job Bunnel taught the first school.

Religious services were conducted here by Rev. Joseph Badger as early as 1793, though it does not appear that his ministrations resulted in the formation of a church until 1799, in which year (April 15th) the *St. Luke's Church*, (Episcopal) at Harpersville, was organized.† Their house of worship, which will seat from 300 to 400 persons, was erected in 1828, at a cost of $2,193, and was consecrated Sept. 28th of that year, by Rt. Rev. Jno. Henry Hobart, Bishop of the Protestant Episcopal Church in the State of New York. The first pastor, or missionary was Rev. Philander Chase; the present pastor is Rev. E. Dolloway. There are ninety members. The Church property is valued at $10,000.

---

*There is believed to be a rich vein of lead ore here, and a mining shaft has been (May, 1872,) sunk to the depth of eighty-three feet, nearly to where it is expected to strike the ore bed. Specimens of ore, containing lead, zinc, copper and silver have been taken out.

† The meeting at which the organization was effected, was presided over by Rufus Fancher as chairman, and Rev. Philander Chase (afterwards Bishop) as secretary. At this meeting Titus Humeston and Rufus Fancher were chosen church wardens; and Isaac M. Ruggles, Josiah Stow, Asa Judd, Abel Doolittle, Samuel Fancher, Daniel Merwin, David Way and Wright Knap, vestrymen.

*The First Baptist Church of Colesville,* located at Harpersville, was organized with seven members* in 1811, but their house of worship, which will seat 250 persons, was not erected until 1846. Its cost was $1,600. Elder Levi Holcomb was the first pastor; Rev. T. D. Hammond is the present one. The church property is valued at $2,500. There are 105 members.

The *First Methodist Church,* of New Ohio, was organized by "Billy Way," in 1825, with eight members, and the Church edifice, which will seat 250 persons, was erected in 1844, at a cost of $800. The first pastor was Rev. Morgan Ruger; the present one is Rev. Chas. Shepard. There are twenty-five members. The church property is valued at $1,500.

The *Presbyterian Church* of Nineveh was organized with thirty-five members, by Rev. Mr. Pratt, in 1831. The first Church edifice was erected in 1829; and the present one, which will seat 375 persons, and on which, in 1870, $4,000 was expended in enlargement and repairs, twenty years later, at a cost of $2,000. The first pastor was Rev. Willard M. Hoyt; the present one is Rev. Wm. H. Sawtelle. There are 180 members. The Church property is valued at $8,000.

The *Baptist Church,* at West Colesville, was organized with seven members, in 1846, and their Church edifice, which will seat 150 persons, was erected the following year, at a cost of $600. The present value of church property is $1,000. The first pastor was Elder A. B. Earle; the present one is Rev. Harvey Cornell. It has forty-one members.

The *Ouaquaga M. E. Church* was organized with forty-six members, by Dewitt C. Olmstead, in 1867, and their house of worship, which will seat 300 persons, was erected in 1868, at a cost of $3,000, which is the present value of Church property. Rev. Wm. Round was the first pastor; the present one is Rev. Wm. W. Andrews. There are fifty-two members.

The *Colesville Free Church,* located at Cole's Hill, is composed of twenty members, and is ministered to by Rev. Charles D Shepard. Their house of worship† will seat 125 persons. The Church property is valued at $1,000.

---

*The names of the original members are· Nathaniel J. Gilbert, Stephen and Polly Barker, Silas Moon, Silas Hall, Peter Newton and Lucinda Denny.

†The house was built by the Presbyterians who occupied it several years. It was subsequently used by the Baptists for a term of years; but becoming dilapidated it remained for some time unoccupied. In 1853 it was repaired by the Methodists, who have since occupied it.

*CONKLIN\** was formed from Chenango, March 29, 1824. A part of Windsor was taken off in 1831, and a part of that town was annexed in 1851. Kirkwood was erected from it Nov. 23, 1859. It is one of the southern tier of towns and lies west of the center of the County. Its eastern boundary is formed by the Susquehanna. The surface is generally hilly. The summits of the hills rise from 400 to 600 feet above the valley. Their declivities terminate abruptly on the river. It is watered by several small streams, tributary to the Susquehanna, the principal of which are Big and Little Snake creeks. The former flows through the town in an easterly direction, a little south of the center, and its valley is narrow and bordered by steep hills; while only a small portion of the latter flows (north) through the south-east corner. The soil upon the summits of the hills is a hard clayey and gravelly loam, largely intermixed with fragments of slate.

The Delaware, Lackawanna and Western R. R. enters the town in the north-west corner, and following the course of the Susquehanna, leaves it in the south-east corner.

The town is the smallest in the County. It covers an area of 14,858 acres, of which, in 1865, according to the census of that year, 10,022 were improved. Its population in 1870 was 1,440.

During the year ending Sept. 30, 1871, it contained eight school districts and employed eight teachers. The number of children of school age was 571; the number attending school, 448; the average attendance, 207; the amount expended for school purposes, $2,534; and the value of school houses and sites, $7,670.

CORBETTSVILLE, (p. v.) located in the south-east part, near the line of the D. L. & W. R. R., and the Susquehanna River, contains two stores, two tanneries,† two saw mills,‡ two blacksmith shops, one wagon shop, about twenty-five dwellings and 150 inhabitants. It is surrounded by hills, nearly all of which are covered with forests.

CONKLIN STATION, (p. v.) (formerly known as *Milburn*,) located near the Susquehanna and on the D. L. & W. R. R., contains one church, (Presbyterian) a school house, a store, a

---

\* Named from Judge John Conklin, one of the early settlers.

† The tannery of which Messrs. Parks & Porter are props. and which is located here, is the principal one in the town. It contains sixty-six vats, employs ten persons, consumes one thousand cords of hemlock, and one hundred cords of oak bark, and manufactures from 10,000 to 12,000 sides of "Union Sole Leather" annually.

‡ J. S. Corbett's saw mill, located here, employs from two to six persons and manufactures about 340,000 feet of lumber annually.

wagon shop, a blacksmith shop, the extensive pyroligneous acid works* of A. S. Saxon, thirty-five dwellings and about 140 inhabitants.

CONKLIN CENTER (p. o.) is located about the center of the east border.

There are several other mechanical and industrial institutions in parts of the town which are removed from the business centers.†

The first settlements were made in 1788, by Jonathan Bennett, Ralph Lathrop‡ and Waples Hance,‡ who located at the mouth of Snake Creek. These were followed at an early day by Garret Snedaker, David Bound,§ Daniel Chapman, Peter

---

\* These are the oldest works of the kind in the U. S. They were first started by Turnbull & Co. of Scotland, about 1851  They give employment to ten persons, and annually consume from 1,500 to 2,000 cords of hard wood in the manufacture of acetate lime, sugar lead, red and iron liquor, wood naphtha, charcoal, charcoal facings, &c.

† Among these are:  Ira Corbett's steam saw mill, which is located near the line of the D L & W. R R., about one-half mile south of Conklin Station, and which employs about six men, contains one circular saw and manufactures from 600,000 to 800,000 feet of lumber annually , the *Conklin Grist Mill*, (the only one in town) owned by Levi L. Roe, and located about one and one-fourth miles "below" Conklin Station, which contains three runs of stones for grinding flour, feed and meal; John Jageler's saw mill, (known as "old Major Shaw's Mill,") which is located on the Susquehanna, about two miles from the north line of the town, and which annually saws about 100,000 feet of lumber, principally hemlock and pine; the saw mills of Richard Van Patten and Atwood Vining, both of which are situated on Little Snake Creek, (the latter two and one-half miles from Conklin Station,) and saw about 100,000 feet of lumber per annum, and the latter in addition thereto from 50,000 to 100,000 feet of lath; and Emory Blatchley's grist and saw mill, which is also located on Little Snake Creek and contains two runs of stones.

‡ Wilkinson, in the "Annals of Binghamton," &c., page 134, gives the names of "Ralph Lotrip" and "Waples Hanth;" while French, who also consulted the "Annals of Binghamton," in his Gazetteer of the State of New York, on page 182, spells the names as they are given above.

§ David Bound from New Jersey settled near the mouth of Snake Creek in 1795.  About a year later he was joined by his family, who came with a four horse team, and occupied seventeen days in the journey  Before reaching their destination their provisions were exhausted.  Mr. Bound learned the fact and went to their relief, carrying the provisions nine miles upon his back.  Soon after this, while hunting one day, Mr Bound discovered that the water in the creek was rising rapidly, in consequence of the melting snow.  He hastened home, drove his cattle on a hill and surrounded them with a brush fence to prevent them from straying. When he returned the water was running into his pig pen.  He placed a plank in such a position that the pig was able to walk up it and over the top of the pen, when it was also driven up the hill.  When he returned to the house the water had entered it and put out the fire.  His family had retreated to the chamber, where they had built a fire in a tin pan, and had commenced the removal of their effects.  With the assistance of a Mr. Hance, Mr. Bound built a raft and crossing the stream, procured a large canoe, with which he rescued his family whom he took from the chamber window, and escaped to the hill, where he took refuge in the house of a Mr. Corbett, and where he was obliged to remain about a week until the water subsided sufficiently to admit of his return.

Wentz, Asa Rood, Nathaniel Tagot, Asa Squires, John Bell, Silas Bowker, Joel Lamereaux, Abraham Sneden, David and Joseph Compton, Abraham Miller, Ebenezer Park, Noel Carr, and Thos. Cooper. The latter were followed at a later date by David Bayless, who came from Princeton, N. J., about 1810, and settled near Conklin Station; Edmund Lawrence, who settled on the river road, in the north part of the town, in 1813; Felix McBride, who came from Ireland, in 1820, and settled on the river road, about four miles from Binghamton, and who was followed by his son, Michael, four years later. At that time, says Mr. McBride, there was no regular public highway—only a sled road along the river. He was accustomed to go to mill in the summer with an ox-sled. There were, he says, but three wagons in the town, (which then comprised Kirkwood and a part of Windsor,) most of the carrying business being done in boats on the river.

The first birth was that of Wm. Wentz, Feb. 18, 1795; the first marriage, that of Noel Carr and Sally Tousler in 1803; and the first death that of Silas Bowker. The first school was taught by Geo. Land, in 1801.

The settlers in this vicinity gave early evidence of a deep interest in religious matters. The first religious services were, says French, conducted by Revs. David Dunham and John Leach, Methodist missionaries; but whether the extraordinary zeal displayed by the inhabitants of this locality at an early day was due to their ministrations does not appear, though it is fair to presume they exerted a salutary influence in that direction. The people seem to have been extremely rigorous in the observance of devotional exercises, for in speaking of them, J. B. Wilkinson, in the "Annals of Binghamton," page 140, says, "it is said that in all the families from the mouth of Snake Creek to Harmony, beyond the Bend, [Great Bend in Penn.,] morning and evening prayers were offered; and not one family in this whole distance in which there was not *one* or *more* of the members pious." But what appears more strange is the fact, which we extract from the same work, that "in the course of five and twenty years, instead of nearly *all* the families being pious, not but *two* or *three* were to be found entitled to that sacred epithet." Whether this declension is due to the removal of these early settlers and the influx of an element inimical to their devout practices, or to change in their religious convictions, we have been unable to learn; but the author quoted is inclined to "refer it to the general depravity of men." After the death, in 1814, of Rev. Daniel Buck, the resident minister at Great Bend, infidelity, which had previously manifested itself in a subdued form, was, by many, "openly and publicly avowed;

and its abettors went so far as to hold their meetings on the Sabbath, and to read Paine's 'Age of Reason' to the multitude. They showed their hostility to the Christian religion, by attending meetings for divine worship, and either succeeding with theirs immediately, before the Christian Congregation had dispersed, or they would commence before the stated hour of Christian worship. Meetings then were held in a school house, in which the whole community felt they had an equal right. The magistrate of the place however, who took a part in this demoralizing cause, too active for his own interest or lasting reputation, was in consequence finally deposed from his office." In what the culpability of the so-called infidels, implied in the quotation from Mr. Wilkinson, consisted, does not appear, unless it is found in the persistance of the right to the free exercise of their religious convictions; for the right to the use of the school house for religious purposes remains unquestioned, and his charge does not implicate them in any breach of decorum. But we will draw the mantle of charity over an historic period in which men were sometimes led by blind zeal to unwittingly persecute those who differed with them in matters of religion, and look with intense gratitude at a present which ensures comparative immunity to all from similar persecutions.

The *First Baptist Church of Conklin,* located on the river road, near the east center of the town, was organized in 1855, with forty-three members, by Rev. S. M. Stimson of Binghamton, who was the first pastor. Their house of worship, which will seat 225 persons, was erected in 1856, at a cost of $1,600. There are sixty members. The present pastor is Rev. Edward H. Ashton. The Church property is valued at $4,500.

The *M. E. Church,* located on Little Snake Creek, was organized with sixty members, by Rev. C. N. Arnold, who became and is still its pastor, in February, 1872, in which year their church edifice, which will seat 225 persons, was erected, at a cost of $2,000. The Church property is valued at $2,500. The number of members is 75.

*FENTON** was formed from Chenango, Dec. 3, 1855. It lies upon the east bank of the Chenango River, and borders on

---

* It was formed as Port Crane, (which name it derived from Jayson Crane, one of the engineers on the Chenango canal,) and its name changed to Fenton, March 26, 1867, in honor of Reuben E. Fenton, in consequence of the extreme aversion of a part of the inhabitants to the former name, an aversion which was so potent as to induce some of them to resist the payment of taxes

The names of the officers elected by the Board of Election, (composed of John Bishop, George Hickox, Willet Cross and H. A. Slosson, the latter

the south boundary of Chenango county. Its surface is hilly,
but the hills are broad and the slopes gentle. The steep hills
which border along the Chenango and rise from 500 to 700
feet above it, confine the valley of that river within narrow
limits. Page Brook,* the principal stream, flows in a southerly
direction through the west part, and divides the uplands into
two distinct ridges. Osborn Creek rises near the tunnel on the
A. & S. R. R. in the north part of the town of Colesville, and
entering this town near the south-east corner, flows in an easterly direction to the Chenango, into which it discharges its
waters a little north of Port Crane. Pond Brook is composed
of two ponds over a mile in length and separated from each
other by a sharp ridge, called the "Hog Back," under which
the water from the upper passes into the lower pond. The outlet is but a few rods from the river and as the ponds have a considerable elevation above it, an excellent water power is formed.
This has been and still is a great resort for fishermen. The
ponds are yet stocked with various kinds of fish. The surface
of the country for some distance around is very peculiar. It
consists of plain land interspersed with basins or small valleys,
some of which descend to a great depth below the general level.
These basins have no connection with each other and all present the appearance of having been ponds at some remote
period. The plain was formerly covered with a dense growth
of pine. The soil is well adapted to tillage. On the hills it
consists of a clay and slaty loam underlaid by hardpan, while
in the valleys it is a rich gravelly loam and alluvium. With
the exception of the country bordering the Chenango River
and Page Brook the town is comparatively new. Along these
streams are some fine farms and sightly residences. Among
the latter are the residences of James E. Waite at Port Crane,
Marvin Conniff at North Fenton and Jno. Hull† at the confluence of Page Brook and the Chenango River, which, in point
of architectural beauty, compare favorably with villas of greater
pretensions. The latter is especially attractive. It is situated

about twenty-five rods from the main road, on an elevation of forty feet, covering an area of about two acres. It is approached from the east on an artificial embankment, and is surrounded by trees and shrubbery which give evidence of fine taste in their owner and constitute it a most lovely retreat.

The Chenango Canal extends through the town, following the course of the Chenango river. The Syracuse and Binghamton R. R. crosses the south-west corner, about three-fourths of a mile east of the border. The Albany and Susquehanna R. R. enters the town near the south-east corner and, running in an easterly direction until within about a mile of the south-west border, turns south and runs nearly parallel with the S. & B. R. R., leaving the town on the south border.

The town covers an area of 17,972 acres, of which, in 1865, according to the census of that year, 9,759, were improved. Its population in 1870 was 1,499.

During the year ending Sept. 30, 1871, it contained nine school districts and employed nine teachers. The number of children of school age was 428; the number attending school, 354; the average attendance, 177; the amount expended for school purposes, $2,215; and the value of school houses and sites, $4,260.

PORT CRANE, (p. v.) on the Chenango canal, in the south part, contains two fine, new churches, (Baptist and M. E.) two stores, a hotel and a good school house. It has been for many years a depot for considerable quantities of lumber, and, being a canal village, boat building and repairing has been an important branch of its industry. It is nearly surrounded by hills, although lying on the bank of the Chenango. Formerly, for nearly two miles below, the river washed the base of perpendicular rocks, known as Crocker Mountain, and the inhabitants were obliged to cross this summit to get to Binghamton. But now the canal is cut in its base and is separated from the river by an embankment wide enough for a highway, both of which are protected by a slope wall. A fine view is afforded of the A. & S. R. R. as it winds along the mountain side, far above the level of the canal. Port Crane station on this road is distant from the village about a mile.

NORTH FENTON (p. o.) (also known as Ketchum's Corners) is pleasantly located in the valley of Page Brook, in the north part of the town. It contains a fine church, a store, grocery and a large cheese factory. The people are energetic and enterprising.*

---

* This was the place of residence of the late Rev. Enos Puffer, who, during the Rebellion, invented a bomb-shell charged with inflammable matter.

The first settlement is believed to have been made by Elisha Pease in 1788. Jared Page, —— Vining and Timothy Cross,* were also early settlers. Isaac Page, Garry Williamson,† John F. Miller and Elias Miller settled on Page Brook, in '1807. John F. Miller located one mile below North Fenton, where his son, Robert T. Miller, now resides  He died March 5th,

---

*Mr. Cross is still a resident and is hale and hearty  He is conversant with many of the daring exploits of the early settlers in their encounter with wild beasts  Owing to its peculiar situation Port Crane was for many years a famous sporting field.  It lies outside the arc formed by the bend in the river in its vicinity.  In its rear is a fine circular range of hills, which terminate above and below in perpendicular rocks called the upper and lower rocks, and which is divided nearly midway, by Osborn Creek; while in front are manificent hills filling the arc down to the river's brink.  A hound set after a deer anywhere in the area inclosed by the river and this semi-circle of hills was sure to bring it to the water at one of the points of rocks, and if it escaped those stationed there would cross the stream and take to the opposite mountains.  Deer were numerous and in warm weather, as is their custom, visited the salt licks in large numbers  Mr Cross relates an adventure of Isaac Page, who knew of one of these resorts, and, as was his custom, went one night to watch.  Soon his experienced ear detected signs of the approach of the expected game.  He waited some time, but failing to ascertain their whereabouts, he concluded they had left the vicinity without the usual manifestations, and became convinced that something extraordinary was the matter.  He was not long left in suspense, for his conviction was soon confirmed and his attention riveted to two fire-like balls which gleamed above a log but a few feet in front of him, and from behind which they seemed gradually to rise.  At this critical moment he leveled his trusty rifle, with as much precision as the darkness rendered practicable and fired, and rising, walked deliberately away  In the morning he returned and to his surprise saw that he had shot a large panther  Thus the unaccountable leaving of the deer the previous night was explained

Mr. Cross also relates the following incident of himself: One day he heard hounds on the trail, and as it was evident the deer would cross the lower rocks too soon for him he took his favorite dog in a dug-out and crossed over to the upper point on the other side  As he expected the deer came to the river, crossed and took to the mountains.  The dog, being well trained, crossed likewise and was soon on the trail.  This was as Cross anticipated, and taking his dog in his arms he took his station in the road which runs along the river-bank several feet above the water.  Soon the deer made its appearance in the road and he threw the dog very nearly against it.  Both deer and dog plunged into the river.  The deer came to a bar, on which it was able to maintain a footing, and stood at bay  As the current was swift the deer had the dog at a disadvantage, for as often as the dog swam to it, it was struck under by the fore-paw of the deer, and would come to the surface some distance below.  Cross stood for some time a spectator of the unequal contest, until apprehension for the safety of his dog induced him to wade out to its assistance.  Intent in watching its assailant the deer did not heed his approach until he got within a few feet of it, when it suddenly turned, rose upon its hind feet, and tried to strike him down. In its struggles, the deer struck one foot into Cross's hand.  He immediately grasped it.  At the same time it became so firmly entangled in its horns as to draw its head into the water, where Cross had it entirely at his mercy.  When the dog, which was nearly exhausted, saw its enemy subdued, he took a position on the deer and retained it till its master drew both ashore.

† Garry Williamson's was the third deed recorded in the Broome County Clerk's office.  His son, Garry Willliamson, lives on the old "Homestead."

1869, aged 87 years. His sons (Geo. P., Robert T., Hurd F. and Addison,) are still residents of North Fenton. The birth of Chester Pease, in 1793, was the first in the town; the death of Mrs. Pease, in 1789, was the first death; and the marriage contracted by Gardner Wilson and Polly Rugg, in 1800, was the first marriage. The first saw mill was erected by Elisha Pease in 1797; and the first store was kept by Thomas Cooper, in 1813. Ozias Masch taught the first school in 1800. Rev. John Camp conducted the first religious services in 1798.

As nearly as we have been able to ascertain the number of persons who enlisted during the war of the Rebellion in Port Crane and its immediate vicinity was sixty-four, of whom twelve were killed. Enlistments were made in the 16th N. Y. Artillery, and the 27th, 50th, 89th, 109th, 137th, 149th and 179th Regts. N. Y. Vol. Infty. North Fenton furnished, in addition to the above, twenty-six men, who enlisted in the 8th N. Y. Cavalry and the 79th N. Y. Infty., and of whom six were killed or died from wounds received or disease contracted while in the service.

The *First Baptist Church of Port Crane* was organized with nineteen members, by W. Alibum, in 1860. Their first pastor was Rev. A. P. Menie; the pulpit is at present supplied by Rev. H. H. Mills. Their house of worship, which will seat 350 persons, is a very fine one, and was erected in 1870, at a cost of $5,000. There are thirty-three members. The church property is valued at $6,000.

The *M. E. Church*, at Port Crane, was organized in 1841. Rev. G. A. Burlingame was the first pastor.* Their house of worship, which will seat 250 persons, was erected in 1870, at a cost of $4,700. There are forty-five members. The church property is valued at $5,000.

The *First M. E. Church*, located at North Fenton, was organized in 1832, by Rufus G. Christian, Ebenezer Cole, Charles Elliott, Justin Watrous, Garret Williamson and Claude Hamilton. The first church edifice was erected the same year; the present one, in 1871, at a cost of $2,000. It is a very fine building and will seat 400 persons. The first pastor was Rev. P. S. Worden; the present one is Rev. Thomas Burgess. There are 120 members. The church property is valued at $6,000.

**KIRKWOOD** was formed from Conklin, Nov. 23, 1859. It is one of the southern tier of towns and lies near the center of the County. It is separated from Conklin, on the west, by

---

* Until his death, May 22, 1872, this Society enjoyed the ministrations of Rev Enos Puffer.

the Susquehanna, which, with its several small tributaries, form its waters. The surface is generally hilly, though along the river extends a fine broad intervale, enriched by the fertilizing deposits of the adjacent hills. The hills, which, on the west side of the river, are steep, on the east side have a more gradual descent. On the hills the soil consists of clay and gravel, largely intermixed with slate; while in the valley it is a deep, rich alluvium and gravelly loam. Most of the remaining timber consists of oak and chestnut. The pine, of which there was a considerable quantity, has mostly been cut and sent to market, the stumps being utilized as fences. Various kinds of grain are grown successfully, and dairying is carried on to quite an extent.

The New York and Erie R. R. passes through the town, following the course of the Susquehanna.

The town covers an area of 18,437 acres, of which, in 1865, according to the census of that year, 12,706, were improved. Its population in 1870 was 1,402.

During the year ending Sept. 30, 1871, it contained ten school districts and employed ten teachers. The number of children of school age was 491; the number attending school, 399; the average attendance, 219; the amount expended for school purposes, $2,401; and the value of school houses and sites, $4,360.

KIRKWOOD (p. v.) is located in the south-west part, on the Susquehanna River, and the N. Y. & E. R. R., by which it is distant eleven miles from Binghamton. It contains one church, (M. E.) a school house, three stores, a wagon shop, a harness shop, two blacksmith shops, a shoe shop, a paint shop, forty houses and 155 inhabitants. About one mile south of the village, on the Susquehanna, are the *Kirkwood Mills*, of which M. A. Andrews is prop. They consist of a grist, saw and planing mill. About 100,000 feet of lumber are sawed in the saw mill. Considerable custom grinding is done, and but very little planing.

KIRKWOOD CENTER (p. o.) is situated on the Susquehanna River, and the N. Y. & E. R. R., near the center of the west border. It is distant from Binghamton by rail eight miles.

RIVERSIDE (p. o.) is located in the extreme south part, on the Susquehanna River, and on the N. Y. & E. R. R. It contains one church, (M. E.) one school house, a cooper shop, wagon shop, blacksmith shop, store, twenty-five dwellings and 125 inhabitants.

STANDLEY HOLLOW is located in the north-east part, and contains a school house, blacksmith shop, five or six dwellings and about twenty-five inhabitants.

Ferguson's saw mill, located on the Windsor road, about one mile from the town line, saws about 50,000 feet of lumber annually.

We are unable to give the date of the first settlement of 'this town; but among the early settlers are the following: John and William Jones, who came from near Trenton, N. J., in 1802, and settled on the river about two miles below Kirkwood, at which time the country was new and the forests abounded with all kinds of game; Henry C. Bayless, who, with his father, came from Middlesex Co., N. J., but immediately from Wilkes-barre, Penn., in 1808, and settled on the farm contiguous to the Conklin bridge;* Ely Osborne, who came from Windsor, Conn., about 1812, and located at Standley Hollow, formerly known as "South Osborne Hollow"; Ezra Carrier, who came from Liberty, Sullivan Co., in the autumn of 1814, and located on the river, about five miles from Binghamton, on the farm now occupied by James White; Moses Standley, who came from Bennington, Vt., in 1820, and located in the eastern part of the town, near Osborne Hollow; Thomas M. Carroll, who was one of the first settlers at Standley Hollow; and Arthur Attridge, who located in the north part of the town in 1824, at which time there was only one-house between his and the Chenango River.

The first grist mill† in the County was erected in 1790 at or near the mouth of "Fitch's Creek," about four miles above Binghamton, and it, as well as the creek on which it was located, was named from Jonathan Fitch, to whom it belonged. Mr Fitch was from Wyoming, and settled on the creek to which he gave his name in 1789. He is believed to have been the first representative to the State Legislature from Tioga County, though some confer this honor upon Gen. Patterson, who settled at an early day at Whitney's Point.

* At that time, says Mr Bayless, there were only three families near them, viz · the Berkalews, Bounds and Roods, all of whom lived near Kirkwood, which was then covered by a forest of oak and hickory. The river afforded the principal carrying facilities. Their grists were taken to mill by this means. On one occasion when he and his brother attempted to cross the river at high water, their canoe became unmanageable and ran against a tree, up which they climbed and were obliged to remain some time before they could right their canoe.

† It is probable, that for a few years after this mill was erected, it was the only one within at least eighty miles west of it, for in 1792 we find that the inhabitants of Newark Valley, in Tioga County, and within the limits of what was then known as "Brown's Settlement," carried their grists to this mill, a distance of forty miles.

The *Christian Church*, located at Kirkwood, was organized Oct. 18, 1856, with nineteen members, by Rev. J. G. Noble, its first pastor. Their church edifice, which will seat 250 persons, was erected the following year, at a cost of $1,000. There are forty members; but there is no pastor. The Church property is valued at $900.

The *First M. E. Church of Kirkwood* was organized with twenty-five members, in 1860, in which year their house of worship, which will seat 230 persons, was erected at a cost of $1,500. The first pastor was Rev. J. M. Grimes, the present one is Rev. James N. Lee. There are seventy-five members. The Church property is valued at $4,000.

*LISLE* (named from Lisle in France,) was formed from Union, March 14, 1800. Barker, Nanticoke and Triangle were formed from it April 18, 1831. The line of Berkshire, Tioga Co., was altered in 1812, and a part of Union was taken off in 1827. It is the north-west corner town in the county. Its surface consists of a hilly and broken upland, unequally divided by the valley of Tioughnioga River. The hills have an elevation of from 400 to 700 feet above the river; their declivities are generally steep—too steep to admit of cultivation. Tioughnioga River, which runs through the east part of the town, in a southerly direction, is the principal stream. The other streams are small. They are Yorkshire and Fall creeks The former flows easterly nearly through the center of the town, the latter in the same direction, near the north line; both empty into the Tioughnioga. The head waters of Nanticoke Creek are in the south-west part of the town. The narrow valley of Yorkshire Creek breaks the continuity of the western range of hills Along the valleys the soil is a rich gravelly loam, but on the hills it is characterized by clay and slaty gravel, underlaid by hardpan. The moist clayey loam on the summits of the hills is better adapted to grass than grain culture.

The Syracuse and Binghamton R. R. extends through the town, following the course of the river.

The town covers an area of 25,083½ acres, of which, in 1865, according to the census of that year, 14,560½ were improved. Its population in 1870 was 2,525.

During the year ending Sept. 30, 1871, the town contained twelve school districts, in which fifteen teachers were employed. The number of children of school age was 806; the number attending school, 660; the average attendance, 364; the amount expended for school purposes, $6,396; and the value of school houses and sites, $16,710.

**H**

LISLE (p. v.) is situated on the west bank of the Tiough-nioga, at the junction of Yorkshire Creek with that stream, and is a station on the S. & B. R. R. It is an incorporated village and contains two churches, (Congregational and M. E.) a Union graded school, two dry goods stores, one hardware store and tin shop, a drug store, three harness shops, a carriage shop, three blacksmith shops, one furnace and machine shop, a grist mill, two saw mills, a large tannery for tanning sheep skins, a jewelry store, a variety store, two dental offices, two shoe shops, a clothing and furnishing store, a furniture manufactory, a milliner shop, a tailor shop and about 500 inhabitants.

YORKSHIRE, (Center Lisle p. o.,) situated near the center of the town, on the Creek of the same name, contains three churches, (Baptist, Congregational and M. E.) one hotel, a dry goods store, a grocery, a large tannery* for tanning sheep skins, a steam saw mill and grist mill, a wagon shop, a blacksmith shop, a milliner shop and dressmaker shop.

KILLAWOG, (p. o.) situated in the north-east part, on the S. & B. R. R. and the Tioughnioga River, contains two churches, (Baptist and M. E.) two dry goods stores, a grist mill, a steam saw mill, a blacksmith shop and thirty or forty dwellings.

MILLVILLE, located on the Tioughnioga, near the south-east corner of the town, contains a large tannery, a grist mill and saw mill, a blacksmith shop and several dwellings.

The first settlement is believed to have been made in 1791,† by emigrants from North East, Dutchess Co. Among these and those who subsequently settled at an early day were Eben-ezer Tracy, Eliphalet Parsons, Josiah Patterson, Whittlesey Glea-son, Edward Edwards‡ and David Manning. The last two settled on the Tioughnioga in 1795. The first birth was that of Henry Patterson, in 1793; the first marriage, that of Solomon Owen and Sylvia Cook; and the first death, that of Wright Dudley. Jacob Hill built the first grist mill. Capt. John Johnson from Conn., we are credibly informed, kept the first store and tavern.§

---

*This tannery is 360 feet long, and gives employment to about one hundred men.

†French's State Gazetteer, p. 182.

‡Edwards was grandson of President Edwards of Princeton College, and first cousin to Aaron Burr, who was Vice-President of the United States, in 1801, and was brought up in the family to which Edwards belonged. He was member of the State Legislature in the time of Gov. Jay's administration.
Mr. Edwards is said to have built the first saw mill on the Tioughnioga River.

§Says French, "the first store was kept by Moses Adams and the first tavern by O. Wheaton, in 1799."

Religious services were instituted as early as 1795, by Rev. Seth Williston, who was sent here by the Connecticut Missionary Society at the solicitation of Mr. Edward Edwards. Two years later the labors of Mr. Williston were rewarded by the organization of the *First Congregational Church of Lisle*, whose first pastor he became. At its organization the church consisted of eleven professing members, and five who were not professors. William Osborn was elected to the office of deacon in 1801, but it was not until 1810 that he and Andrew Squires, his colleague, were consecrated. Mr. Williston employed only half his time in pastoral duties in this Society, the residue being occupied in missionary labors in Union, Owego and Oquaga. From 1803, when he was installed pastor of this church, till 1810, when he was dismissed from it, he seems to have devoted all his time within the pastoral limits of this congregation. This church "was the earliest organized, it is believed, of any west of the Catskills and south of Utica."[*] Their first house of worship was not erected until 1822. The present one, which will seat 400 persons, was erected two years later at a cost of $3,000. The present pastor is Rev. R. A. Clark and the number of members, seventy. The Church property is valued at $7,000.

The *M. E. Church*, of Lisle, was organized about 1815, by Rev. Geo. W. Densmore, its first pastor. The first class was organized in 1830 or '31, with P. B. Brooks as leader. Their house of worship, which will seat 250 persons, was erected in 1857, at a cost of $2,000. The present pastor is Rev. A. W. Loomis; the number of members, eighty. The value of Church property is $4,500.

The *Baptist Church* at Center Lisle was organized with seven members, in 1828. Their church edifice, which will seat 400 persons, was erected in 1856, at a cost of $4,400. Rev. Asahel Holcomb was the first pastor; Rev. Gardner Dean is the present one. There are twenty-six members. The value of Church property is $3,000.

The *Congregational Church* at Center Lisle was organized with nineteen members, June 14, 1830, by Rev. Seth Burt. Their first house of worship was erected two years later; and the present one, which will seat 400 persons, in 1855, at a cost of $3,300. Rev. Alvin D. French was the first pastor; at present there is none. The number of members is sixty. The Church property is valued at $6,000.

---

[*] *Annals of Binghamton*, p. 166.

The *Baptist Church* at Killawog was organized with sixty-nine members in 1841. Rev. David Leach was the first pastor. The church edifice occupied by this Society was erected in 1835, and repaired in 1868. It will seat 300 persons. Its original cost was $3,000; its present value, together with all Church property, is $5,000. There are fifty-one members, who are ministered to by Rev. Abner Lull.

The *M. E. Church* at Killawog was organized with thirty members by Rev. Arvine C. Bowdish, its first pastor, in 1867, in which year was erected their church edifice, which will seat 200 persons, at a cost of $3,000, which is the present value of Church property. The present pastor is Rev. Reuben Fox; and the number of members, seventy-five.

The *M. E. Church* at Center Lisle was organized by Rev. D. D. Lindsley, the first pastor, in 1869, in which year their church edifice, which will seat 250 persons, was erected at a cost of $4,500, which is the present value of Church property. Rev. A. W. Loomis is the present pastor.

*MAINE* was formed from Union, March 27, 1848.* A part was annexed to Chenango in 1856. It is located about the center of the west border of the County. Its surface consists of ranges of hills, separated by numerous narrow valleys, the principal of which—the valley of Nanticoke Creek—extends in a north and south direction, a little west of the center of the town. The hills rise from 400 to 600 feet above the valley of Chenango River. The principal streams are Nanticoke, Bradley and Crocker creeks. Bradley Creek rises a little east of the center, and, flowing in a south-west direction, empties into Nanticoke Creek a little south of the south line in Union; Crocker Creek enters the town near the south-west corner, and, flowing in a general south-east direction, discharges its waters into the same stream, about the same distance north of the south line. Several minor tributaries of

---

* The first town meeting was held in the school house in the village of Maine, on the 25th of the following April. At this meeting John C. Curtis, Sands Niles and Louis Gates were the presiding officers, and Nathaniel W. Eastman was clerk. In accordance with the resolutions then adopted the following named officers were elected: Andrew H. Arnold, *Supervisor*: John W. Hunt, *Town Clerk*; Marshall DeLano, *Superintendent of Common Schools*; John T. Davis, *Collector*; Cyrus Gates, John Blanchard and Hanan W. Moores, *Justices of the Peace*; Orange H. Arnold, Thomas Young Jr. and Wm. H. Tuttle, *Assessors*; Hanan Payne and Edward Ward, *Commissioners of Highways*; Dexter Hathaway and Matthew Allen, *Overseers of the Poor*; Eustis Hathaway, John B. Smith, Joel Benson and Ransom T. Gates, *Constables*; Jefferson Ransom, Amasa Durfee and Luke Curtis, *Inspectors of Elections*; James W. Carman, *Sealer of Weights and Measures*; and Lyman Pollard, *Pound Master*.

the Nanticoke spread, fan-like, over the north part, and all pursue a southerly direction. Little Choconut Creek flows almost due south through the south-east corner, entering the town on the north line of the southern angle which projects into the town of Chenango.

The soil is a gravelly loam largely intermixed with the underlying slate. The inhabitants are chiefly engaged in lumbering and dairying. Two "farmers' clubs" have been organized, and periodical meetings are held at the residences of the different members, and the deliberations are participated in by the families of the members. Crops, stock, out-buildings, agricultural implements, &c., are critically examined and commented upon. The subjects discussed at these meetings are designed to embrace all matters of interest to a farming community. Such meetings nurture amicable social relations and afford opportunities for the interchange of ideas, which will tend to stimulate a spirit of generous rivalry and promote the farming interests of the County at large.

The population of the town in 1870 was 2,035. Its area is 27,319¾ acres, of which, in 1865, according to the census of that year, 15,738¾, were improved.

During the year ending Sept. 30, 1871, the town contained thirteen school districts and employed fourteen teachers. The number of children of school age was 634; the number attending school, 556; the average attendance, 283; the amount expended for school purposes, $3,652; and the value of school houses and sites, $5,325.

MAINE (p. v.) is located on the west bank of Nanticoke Creek, west of the center of the town. The principal part of the village is built in the form of a square. Its well laid out and neatly shaded streets present a pleasing aspect. It contains four stores, three churches, (Baptist, Congregational and M. E.) one hotel, a tannery,* a rake factory,† a saw mill, a tin shop, three blacksmith shops, two cooper shops, a wagon shop, two shoe shops, one tailor shop and three hundred inhabitants.

EAST MAINE (p. o.) is located in the east part, south of the center, and contains a cooper shop, wagon shop and blacksmith shop.

BOWERS CORNERS is a hamlet located one mile north of Maine village and contains a store, a shoe shop, blacksmith shop and wagon shop.

---

* The tannery contains 132 vats, employs twenty men, annually consumes 2,500 cords of bark and manufactures 12,000 hides.
† The rake manufactory produces annually an average of from 15,000 to 20,000 rakes in addition to other work of a miscellaneous character.

The two principal saw mills in the town are Pollard's and Baker's. The latter is a steam mill and is capable of saw-ing from 3,000,000 to 4,000,000 feet of lumber annually, though the yearly average does not exceed one and one-half million feet.

The town was principally settled by families from New Hampshire, Connecticut and Massachusetts. Benj. Norton settled about three-fourths of a mile above the site of Maine village, in 1794. He was a native of Stockbridge, Mass. In 1797 Alfred and Russell Gates, two brothers, came from the vicinity of Binghamton, where they had located four years pre-viously, and settled in the north-west part of the town, now known as the Gates settlement. They cut their road through the forest from Centerville, a distance of seven miles. At that period they were in the habit of carrying their dinners to work with them; but they were obliged to be as careful in the selection of food as the most confirmed dyspeptic, as any-thing emitting an agreeable odor was sure to attract to them an escort of wolves, whose number and presence were far from awakening pleasurable emotions. Daniel Howard and Win-throp Roe came the same year. Moses Delano and Nathaniel Slosson are said to have been the first settlers in the vicinity of East Maine. They located there about the beginning of the present century, and were followed by Samuel Stone and Heman Payne in 1816, and by William Hogg in 1836. The latter was joined a few years later by a number of his relatives, who gave the settlement the name of Mount Ettrick, in honor of their uncle.* By industry and intelligent farming they have done much to improve the locality in which they settled. James Ketchum, from Conn., came here from near Binghamton, where he settled about 1790, and located about three miles south-west of Maine village, on lot 155 of the Boston Purchase, in 1802. Timothy Caswell, who appears to have been the first settler in the locality known as the Allen settlement, located there in 1815, and was followed some five or six years later by John Marcau, and in 1836 by Ebenezer and Matthew Allen, from Otsego County. Marsena H. McIntyre, from Otsego County, settled in the north-west corner of the town, in what is known both as North Maine and the McIntyre settlement, on the 7th of May, 1829. The north-east part of the town was the last settled. It is known as "Canada"—a name it owes to the following incident: It was covered with a growth of very fine timber, which persons in its neighborhood were accustomed to appropriate to their own uses. Warrants were

---

* James Hogg, the Scottish poet, who was born in the forest of Ettrick, in Selkirkshire, in 1772, and who in early life followed the occupation of a shepherd, was commonly known as "the Ettrick Shepherd."

frequently issued for the guilty parties, but the inquiries of the officers invariably elicited the reply that those for whom they were searching had gone to Canada.

During the war of the Rebellion this town furnished 190 men, nearly one hundred of whom belonged to the 50th Engineers. Of this number fifteen were killed.

The *Congregational Church*, located at Maine village, was organized with forty members, in 1818, and re-organized in 1833. Its first church edifice was erected in 1824; and the present one, which will seat 260 persons, in 1840, at a cost of $3,000. The first pastor was Rev. Naham Gould; the present one is Rev. William T. Hayward. There are 220 members. The Church property is valued at $7,500.

The *First Baptist Church of Maine* was organized with thirty-one members, by a Council* convened at the Congregational Church, Jan. 21, 1835. The church edifice will seat 300 persons, was erected in 1840, at a cost of $1500, and dedicated in Dec. of that year. Rev. William Gates was the first pastor; Rev. H. R. Dakin is the present one. There are 170 members. The value of Church property is $6,000.

The *M. E. Church*, located near Union Center, was organized with forty-five members, in 1836, and its house of worship, which will seat two hundred persons, was erected the following year. Rev. S. Stocking, was the first pastor; the present one is Rev. Wesley Sartelle.

The *M. E. Church*, located at North Maine, was organized with thirteen members, in 1844, by Marsena H. McIntyre, Orange H. Arnold, Russell Robinson and George M. Hardendorf. Their church edifice was erected in 1870, and dedicated March 8, 1871. It cost $3,000, which is the present value of Church property, and will seat 180 persons. There are thirty-eight members. Rev. Thomas Pitts was the first pastor; Rev. John A. Wood is the present one.

The *M. E. Church*, located at Maine village, was re-organized (the date of its first organization is not known) with forty members in 1866, by Russell Dodds, Clinton Cleveland, Henry Turner, Matthew Allen, James Howard, Daniel Dudley and Henry Van Tuyl. The church edifice, which will seat 150 persons, was erected in 1847 or '8, at a cost of $2,000, which is one-half the present value of Church property. The first pastor

* The Council was composed of the following named delegates: "Revd. J. R. Berdick, Owego, Deacon John Congdon, Binghamton, Revd M M. Everts, Berkshire and Lisle, Deacon B. Eldridge, Barker, Revd. J. J. Miller, 1st Green, Revd. N. Church, 2d Lisle."—*Extract from book in possession of Cyrus Gates.*

was Rev. Edgar Sibley; the present one is Rev. John A. Wood. There are forty members.

The *Abbott Church*, (M. E.) located at Dimmick Hill, (East Maine) was organized with forty members in 1868, in which year the church edifice, which will seat 250 persons, was erected, at a cost of $2,200. The church was dedicated by Rev Daniel W. Bristoe, D. D., Jan. 7, 1869. Rev. —— Abbott was the first pastor; Rev. Edgar Sibley is the present one. There are fifty members. The Church property is valued at $3,000.

A Presbyterian church is now in process of erection in the immediate vicinity of East Maine.

***NANTICOKE**\* was formed from Lisle April 18, 1831. It lies upon the west border, north of the center. The surface consists of an upland broken by a few narrow ravines. The highest summits are from 100 to 300 feet above the Susquehanna, and from 1,200 to 1,400 feet above tide. The town is watered by the two main branches of the Nanticoke and their tributaries. Both these branches flow south, one through the western, and the other through the eastern part. The soil upon the hills is a slaty loam underlaid by hardpan.

The town covers an area of 16,124½ acres, of which, in 1865, according to the census of that year, 7,413½, or less than one-half was improved. The population in 1870 was 1,058.

During the year ending Sept. 30, 1871, the town contained seven school districts and employed seven teachers. The number of children of school age was 399; the number attending school, 323; the average attendance, 161; the amount expended for school purposes, $1,585; and the value of school houses and sites, $2,310.

LAMBS CORNERS, (p. o.) located on Nanticoke Creek, west of the center of the town, contains two churches, (Baptist and M. E.) one store, a wagon shop, a blacksmith shop and two saw mills, one of which (Washington Johnson's) is quite extensive. It is run by steam, and in connection with it are a grist and planing mill. About 300,000 feet of lumber are annually cut, this being done in the spring of the year. The rest of the time is occupied in planing and finishing. The postoffice was established here in 1860 and was removed from Nanticoke Springs.

GLEN AUBREY, (p. o.) (formerly known as Councilman Settlement,) located on the east branch of the Nanticoke,

\* This name is derived from the Indian name of Nanticoke Creek.— *French's State Gazetteer, p. 182.*

near the south line and east of the center, contains two churches, (Christian and M. E.) two stores, three blacksmith shops and one shoe shop. There was formerly a tannery here, but it is burnt down.

NANTICOKE SPRINGS, located on Nanticoke Creek, about one mile south of Lambs Corners and near the south line, derives both its name and importance from the mineral spring located there.

The principal settlements are in the valleys of the streams. They were commenced in 1793 and '4 by John Beachtle, Philip Councilman,* James Stoddard and John Ames, who located on the east Nanticoke. Beachtle was from Luzerne county, Penn., and Stoddard, from Connecticut. The former, and afterwards Ames, occupied the farm now owned by Charles H. and James Stoddard.† Councilman lived by hunting and trapping until he accumulated a sufficient amount to purchase 300 acres of land.

The first settler on the west Nanticoke was Isaac Lamb, who located on the site of the village of Lamb's Corners, in 1804.

The first birth was that of Betsey Stoddard, in 1794, and the first death, that of Miss Bird, sister of Mrs. Stoddard.

The *M. E. Church*, at Lamb's Corners, was organized with twenty members, in 1852, in which year their house of worship, which will seat 200 persons, was erected, at a cost of $1,000, which is two-fifths of the present value of Church property. Rev. John M. Grimes was the first pastor; the present one is Rev. J. N. Lee. There are forty members.

The *Baptist Church*, at Lamb's Corners, was organized with forty members, by Eli Levi Holcomb, in February, 1825, but the church edifice, which will seat 250 persons and was built

---

*The first town meeting was held at Councilman's house the first Tuesday in March, 1832, and was, we are informed, of a stormy nature, as it was introduced by a free fight and several attempts were made to burn the ballot box.—(Statement of Geo. W. Bush and Morgan Spencer.) This meeting resulted in the election of the following named officers Aaron N. Remmele, *Supervisor;* H. B. Stoddard, *Clerk,* Silas Hemingway, H. B Stoddard, David Councilman and Charles Brookens, *Justices,* Samuel Canfield and John Councilman, *Overseers of the Poor;* F. S. Griggs, H. Walter and James Lamb, *Commissioners of Highways,* F. S. Griggs, A. N. Remmele and J. L. Smith, *Commissioners and Inspectors of Schools,* Charles Brookens, Hiram Rogers and Silas Hemingway, *Assessors,* Philip Councilman, 2d *Collector,* Aurora Brayman and Isaac A. Griggs, *Constables;* and Silas Hemingway, *Sealer of Weights and Measures.*

† On this farm is an apple tree which is claimed to be the largest in the State Two feet from the ground the trunk measures eleven feet, six and one-half inches in circumference. One branch is over two feet in diameter, and four others average over thirteen inches each. This tree was planted in 1796, by Miss Polly Beachtle, who brought it from Pennsylvania on horse back.

at a cost of $1,200, was not erected until 1853. Its first pastor was Rev. Granville Gates; the present one is Rev. Geo. W. Bliss. There are forty-five members. The Church property is valued at $3,000.

The *Christian Church*, at Glen Aubrey, was organized with twelve members, in 1857, by Jonathan, Alison and William Stalker. The first pastor was Rev. Edward Tyler; Rev. James Youmans is the present one. The church edifice, which will seat 150 persons, was erected in 1866, at a cost of $1,800. There are thirty members. The Church property is valued at $2,300.

The *M. E. Church*, at Glen Aubrey, was organized with thirty members, but when and by whom we are unable to learn. Their church edifice was erected in 1867. It cost $2,500, and will seat 200 persons. It was dedicated in March, 1868, by Rev. B. I. Ives. Rev. Edgar Sibley was the first pastor; Rev. J. N. Lee is the present one. There are from thirty-five to forty members. The Church property is valued at $3,000.

*SANFORD* was formed from Windsor, April 2, 1821. It is the south-east corner town in the County, and is the largest one in the County. It covers an area of 52,674¾ acres, of which, in 1865, according to the census of that year, 21,024¾, were improved. Its surface consists principally of the high ranges of hills which extend between the Delaware and Susquehanna rivers, and whose summits are from 500 to 900 feet above the valley, and declivities usually steep.* These highlands are separated into two parts by the deep, narrow valley of Oquaga Creek. This valley and that of the Delaware are bounded by almost precipitous mountain declivities. The principal stream is Oquaga Creek, which enters the town near the north-east corner, and, flowing in a south-west direction to a point a little south of the center, turns and runs due east until it empties into the Delaware at Deposit. This creek has numerous falls, which furnish an abundance of excellent water power. It has numerous small tributaries, the principal of which is North Brook. The Delaware forms the east boundary of the town, south of Deposit.

Its geological formation consists in the west part of the Chemung group of the Old Red Sandstone, which terminates on the surface about three miles west of Deposit, where the Catskill group commences. In the former is found a great

*The highest point between the two rivers, by the State Road Survey is 1,688 feet above tide."—*French's State Gazetteer, p. 183.*

number of shells and fossil fish, and in the latter, ferns and other vegetables of enormous size.

In the valleys the soil is a fertile gravelly loam, but upon the hills it is a cold clayey loam, underlaid by hardpan. It is well adapted to dairying purposes, in which the people are largely engaged. The chief wealth of the town consists in its dairy products.

In 1870 the town had a population of 3,249. During the year ending Sept. 30, 1871, it contained twenty-three school districts and employed twenty-four teachers. The number of children of school age was 1,265; the number attending school, 941; the average attendance, 439; the amount expended for school purposes, $7,672; and the value of school houses and sites, $13,064.

DEPOSIT* (p. v.) is situated partly in this town and partly in the town of Tompkins, Delaware county.† It lies on the Delaware, at the mouth of Oquaga Creek. It is the center of a large lumber business, and is an important trading station and wood depot on the Erie R. R. which traverses the southern portion of the town. In addition to the numerous mechanical and other establishments, which are described more minutely in the Directory list for this village, it contains a printing office, (*The Deposit Courier*,) a bank,‡ an academy,§ a library,‖ a carriage factory,¶ and about 1,600 inhabitants.

*It derives its name from having been an important station, or place of *deposit*, for lumber, preparatory to rafting in the spring freshets. It was called by the Indians "*cokeose*," or owls nest, which was corrupted by the English into "Cook house," a name by which it is still designated by the old inhabitants.

The earliest mention of this place is found in *Boudinot's Star in the West*, where it is stated the Indian name was "*O-hoot-ose*," to which name the same meaning is given.

†It was incorporated April 5, 1811, but the original limits of the village were entirely within the town of Tompkins. A part of Sanford was annexed in 1852; and the charter was amended in 1858.

‡ The *Deposit National Bank* was organized February 20, 1854, and was changed to a National Bank July 1, 1854. It has a capital of $125,000. The officers are Charles Knapp, *President*; James G. Clark, *Vice-President*, James H. Knapp, *Cashier*, C. J. Knapp, *Assistant Cashier*; H. W. Knapp, *Teller*.

§The *Deposit Academy* was built in 1866. It has accommodations for 200 boarding students. Connected with it is a library containing 150 volumes, valued at $300; and philosophical and chemical apparatus to the value of $120 The buildings and ground are valued at $7,700 The Principal, R. L Thatcher, A. M., and Preceptress, Mrs. M. E Thatcher, are assiduous in their efforts to promote the mental, moral and physical welfare of those entrusted to their care.

‖The *Deposit Library Association* was organized in 1859. The library contains 575 volumes. T. More is President and A. More, Secretary.

¶The *Deposit Carriage Manufactory*, of which Beardsley & Wall are proprietors, employs about fifteen persons and turns out a large number of wagons, carriages and sleighs.

SANFORD (p. o.) is located on Oquaga Creek, about the center of the town.

NORTH SANFORD (p. o.) is located on Oquaga Creek, near the north-east corner.

GULF SUMMIT, (p. o.) located near the south-west corner, seven miles from Deposit. is a station on the Erie R. R.

McCLURE SETTLEMENT (p. o.) is located at the confluence of Oquaga Creek and North Brook, a little south of the center of the town. The post office was established here in 1865. D. & S. Post's steam saw mill, located here, gives employment to seven men, annually saws four millions of feet of lumber and manufactures 5,000 lath per day.

The first settlement was made in 1787, by Wm. McClure,*

---

*From Mr. M. R. Hulce of Deposit we learn the following interesting particulars relative to McClure. He was born in 1725   His father was a native of Ireland, near Londonderry, and was of Scotch descent.   McClure acquired a good English education—including a knowledge of navigation, surveying and higher mathematics—and some knowledge of Latin   The religious principles imbibed in his boyhood inspired him with a deep reverence for the Deity, and his early training confirmed in him habits of exemplary morality   These, with his proficiency in mathematics, were his chief recommendations to the land-holders, by whom he was employed as surveyor and land-agent   In the Spring of 1787 he started from Orange county, (in which and Dutchess county he had been teaching successfully,) for the *Cookhouse*, in the employ of the owners of the Fisher & Norton Patent in this county, threading the pathless forests with the aid of his faithful mare "Ohio," and followed by assistants who came up the river in a canoe loaded with provisions   On his arrival he built a rude log cabin on Oquaga Creek, about five miles west of Deposit, which he called "Castle William," since known as McClure Settlement.   During the summer and fall he surveyed the greater part of Fisher & Norton Patent into lots one mile square.   His labors were retarded by lack of provisions, caused by the pumpkin flood   As the winter approached he sent his men back and remained in the wilderness with no other companion than a faithful dog.   His Bible, field-book and diary occupied much of his time; while the stream, which abounded with trout, furnished his meat.   The deprivation of society made the time drag heavily; and the want of bread and vegetables was keenly felt by him.   His appetite failed, and toward spring indications of a fever were apparent.   The depth of snow and his weak condition prevented escape.   The nearest human habitation was Hynback's, on the east side of the river, at the "Cookhouse."   His efforts to overcome his increasing weakness were unavailing, and soon he was unable to go to the brook for water and his accustomed supply of fish.   As he lay stretched on his couch of boughs, unable to rise, death seemed the only relief which awaited him.   His dog, which staid with him some days, left one morning, and toward night McClure was greeted by its joyous barking, which heralded the coming of Cornelius Hynback, who soon entered the cabin, with stimulants, which he administered to McClure, whom he found helpless and almost dead   He staid with him until he was sufficiently recovered to render it safe to leave him, when he returned for supplies, which he brought as often as necessary.   Hynback's farm was on elevated ground, so that the flood did not destroy his crops.   The dog had made his way to Hynback's and by his action induced him to suspect that something was wrong at Castle William, and when Hynback started on his journey, the demonstrations of joy made by the dog, which led the way, were of the most extravagant nature. '

from Chester, New Hampshire. Captain Nathan Dean* and family followed him in 1791, and Squire Whitaker† and fami'y in 1797. Among the other early settlers were John Pinney, Anthony West, Luther Hulce, —— Potter, James P. Aplington, John Peters, Simon and Zina Alexander, Alex. Butler, Geo. Plummer, Moses Farnham, Nathan Austin, Jonas Underwood, Silas Seward, (the last three were Revolutionary soldiers) James and Benj. Coburn, Daniel Race, Noah Carpenter, S. P. Green, Joseph Page, Capt. Parker, Isaac Denton and Dexter May.

In 1821 there was not a sufficient number of freeholders in the town to form a jury and a special act was passed constituting any man, a resident, a competent juror. The law is still in force. The 5th of March the following year the first town meeting was held at the house of Wm. McClure.‡

The following spring McClure, having recovered from the prostration produced by his sickness and hibernation, resumed surveying and continued it two or three years during the warm season, after which, more than satisfied with his monastic experience at Castle William, he returned to Orange county and again occupied himself in teaching. While thus engaged he became acquainted with Miss Sarah Farnham, daughter of Capt. Elias Farnham, whom, in the early part of the winter of 1791, he married, and moved to a log house which he erected in November of the previous year, on the site of Castle William, in anticipation of the coming nuptials. Their effects were placed on a light sleigh, to which was hitched his favorite Ohio. McClure had purchased a large tract of land (including the site of Castle William,) with the proceeds of his services in surveying.

His children were William, David, Henry, Walter, Sally, Thomas, Fanny and Prudence. After the death of his first wife he married Lydia Austin of Conn. He died at Castle William in 1826, leaving numerous descendants in its vicinity.

*Nathan Dean located at Deposit in June, 1791, and purchased that part of the village lying in this county. He died in a few years leaving a widow and five children, viz: Nathan L., Joshua, Caleb, Zenas K. and Catharine, (who married James Aplington,) of whom Joshua and Zenas still survive. All had families and their descendants chiefly reside in the town.

†Squire Whitaker came in April, 1797. The same day that he arrived his daughter Elizabeth was married to Conrad Edick. This was the first marriage in the town. The bride was dressed in linsey-woolsey, and the groom in brown-tow and buckskin moccasins, with stocking *au-naturel*. The ceremony was performed by a Baptist missionary named How. Mr. Whitaker and family were at Wyoming at the time of the massacre. He was taken prisoner in Fort Jenkins, but was released and, with his family, fled over the mountains, enduring severe hardships, and reached his former home in Orange Co.

‡At that meeting was elected the following named officers: Wm. McClure, *Supervisor*; Joshua Dean, *Town Clerk*; James P. Aplington, Nathaniel L. Dean and Wm. McClure, *Assessors*; Nathan L. Dean, Alex. Butler and Wm. McClure Jr., *Commissioners of Highways*; John Peters and James P. Aplington, *Overseers of the Poor*; Wm. McClure, Nathan Dean and Alex. Dean, *Commissioners of Common Schools*; Jacob Edick, *Constable and Collector*; Joseph Eddy, *Constable*; Daniel Evans, Ginsham Loomis and Michael Child, *Inspectors of Common Schools*; John Pinney, Eli King and Nathan Austin, *Fence Viewers*. This list of officers includes all the freeholders in the town at that time.

Formerly the streams abounded with fine trout and the forests with wild animals. Until after the Revolution the east line of the town was the division line between the Indians and the King, and was called the "*property line.*" The growth of the town has been gradual but constant, and it is now one of the wealthiest in the County.

The first saw mill was built in 1791 and the first grist mill in 1792, by Capt. Dean, who also opened the first store and kept the first inn in 1794. The first store in Deposit was built by Benj. and Peter Gardner, in 1795, where Vail's brick store now stands, near the Oquaga House. It was stocked with eight sleigh loads of goods which were brought from New York. The men and teams put up at Capt. Dean's. The first death was that of Stephen Whitaker, which occurred Oct. 23, 1793, in which year the first school was taught by Hugh Compton.

The *Deposit Baptist Church* was organized as the *First Baptist Church of Tompkins*, with fourteen members, March 7, 1812. The first house of worship was erected in 1827-8 and was burned down in 1851; the second one was blown down while being repaired in 1866; and the present one, which will seat 450 persons, was erected in 1866-7, at a cost of $9,000. The first pastor was Rev. —— Holcomb; the present one is Rev. J. N. Adams. There are 255 members. The Church property is valued at $13,000.

The *First Presbyterian Church* at Deposit was organized July 21, 1812, by J. T. Benedict and David Harowar, missionaries, with nine members * The first church edifice was erected in 1819 ; the second one, which was consumed by fire in 1855, in 1853, and the present one, which will seat 600 persons, in 1856, at a cost of $6,000. The first pastor was Rev. Elisha Wise; the present one is Rev. Geo. O. Phelps. The present number of members is 255. The value of Church property is $10,000.

The *First Baptist Church of Sanford*, located in the north part of the town, was organized with thirteen members, May 12, 1842, by a council of delegates from the Baptist churches of Coventry, Masonville, Deposit and South Bainbridge. The church edifice was erected in 1846, at a cost of $400. It is still standing, but in consequence of its not being centrally located it has been unoccupied the past three years. The

---

*The church edifice is in Delaware county, but the members reside in both Broome and Delaware counties. The church has a Congregational form of government and is connected with the Presbytery on the "accommodation plan." The three constituent male members at its organization were Wm. McClure, Aaron Stiles and Benj. Hawley.

Society has held meetings regularly at two school houses, alternately. A movement is on foot to secure a site and build a more convenient church. The first pastor was Rev. E. L. Benedict, from Deposit; the present one is Rev. A. H. Hamlin. There are thirty-six members.

*TRIANGLE** was formed from Lisle April 18, 1831. It is situated in the extreme north part of the county, its north line bordering on Cortland county and its eastern, on Chenango county. Its surface consists of a broken upland, divided into ridges by the valleys of Otselic River and Half Way Brook. The hills attain an altitude of from 300 to 500 feet above the valleys. It covers an area of 24,231 acres, of which, in 1865, according to the census of that year, 17,295½, were improved. The soil is generally a gravelly loam, better adapted to grazing than tilling. It is watered by the Tioughnioga River, which flows through the south-west corner; the Otselic River, which flows south through the town, adjacent to the west line, and empties into the Tioughnioga near the south-west corner; and Half Way Brook, which flows south through the town a little east of the center.

The population of this town in 1870 was 1,944. During the year ending Sept. 30, 1871, there were twelve school districts in which were employed seventeen teachers. The number of children of school age was 570; the number attending school, 612; the average attendance, 336; the amount expended for school purposes, $7,673; and the value of school houses and sites, $15,525.

WHITNEYS POINT† (p. v.) is situated near the south-west corner, at the confluence of the Tioughnioga and Otselic rivers, and is a station on the Syracuse & Binghamton R. R., which passes through the south-west corner of the town. It is distant north from Binghamton by rail 20.55 miles, and south from Syracuse 58.78 miles. It was incorporated under the general act of the Legislature passed in 1870, and its boundaries changed by a special act of the Legislature, in April, 1872. It contains one hotel, (another is in process of erection on the site of the one which was recently burned,) five churches, (Grace Prot. Epis., Baptist, Congregational, M. E. and Catholic,) six general stores,

---

* "This name was applied to the tract south of the Military Tract and 'Twenty Towns,' and between the Chenango and Tioughnioga rivers. It was bought by Col Wm. Smith, at three shillings, three pence per acre The Chenango Triangle embraces Smithville and part of Greene in Chenango county, and Triangle and part of Barker in Broome.—*French's State Gazetteer.*

† Named from Thomas Whitney, who owned the bridge and mills at this place and a large landed property in the neighborhood.

two drug stores, a Union School and Academy,\* a jewelry store, two furniture stores, two stove, tin and hardware stores, a steam sash and blind factory,† a steam saw mill, two wagon shops, four blacksmith shops, one harness shop, one brick-yard, two cooper shops, four millinery shops, a photograph gallery, an undertaking establishment, a livery stable, 124 dwellings and about 700 inhabitants.

Messrs. G. C. & J. F. Bishop are about to open a beautiful grove in the south-west part of the village for the accommodation of picnic and pleasure parties. Among its attractions are several ponds which are supplied with water from springs on the ground and which are already stocked with choice fish. In one are some 300 gold fish, in another some 100 yellow perch, while in others are some 2000 trout. From these are now being hatched some 50,000 spawn. A brace of foxes, twenty live mink, a dancing hall 24 by 96 feet, inclosing a collection of stuffed native birds, add to the attractive features of the place.

The grounds of the *Broome County Agricultural Society*, comprising twenty-five acres, are located in the corporation, on the point of land between the Tioughnioga and Otselic rivers. Annual fairs are held there.‡

The factory of *The Stillwater Cheese Manufacturing Co* is located one and one-half miles north of the village. It is a two and one-half story frame building, 35 by 140 feet and is capacitated to use the milk from 1000 cows. Sixty cheeses per week are manufactured.§

UPPER LISLE, (p. v.) located on the Otselic River, near the north line, five miles north of Whitneys Point, contains one hotel, two churches, (Baptist and Universalist,) two stores, a

---

\*The *Whitneys Point Union School and Academy* building, which consists of a two story frame building, forty-five feet square, capable of accommodating 200 pupils, was erected in 1866, at a cost (including the cost of grounds) of $9,000. The library, apparatus for illustrating Philosophy and Chemistry, and musical instruments cost about $2,000 more. T. H. Roberts is the principal.

†Snook, Collins & Co.'s sash and blind factory gives employment to twenty-seven men. The building is a three-story frame structure, 56 by 100 feet. The department comprising the engine room and kiln consists of a two-story building 26 by 40 feet. The motive power is supplied by a fifty horse-power-engine and the building furnished with machinery of the latest and most approved patterns.

‡The Society is officered by the following named gentlemen; Dr E G Crafts, of Binghamton, *President*; C. C. Bennett, of Whitneys Point, *Secretary*; C. S. Olmstead, of Whitneys Point, *Treasurer*.

§Geo W. Hurd is *President*, and J. L Smith, *Secretary*.

tannery,* a saw and planing mill, a blacksmith shop, a wagon shop, a shoe shop, a school house, forty-five dwellings and about 200 inhabitants.

TRIANGLE, (p. v.) located near the south-east corner, on a branch of Half Way Brook, near its junction with that stream, lies in a beautiful and fertile vale, five miles east of Whitneys Point. It contains one hotel, three churches, (Baptist, Congregational and M. E.) a steam saw mill, two stores, two wagon shops, three blacksmith shops, one tannery, a school, forty dwellings and about 180 inhabitants. The farmers in this section are largely engaged in hop raising and dairying.

The first settlement was made in 1791, by Gen. John Patterson, one of the proprietors of the Boston Company, who located at Whitneys Point, precisely where Thos. Whitney subsequently lived. Patterson was a Brigadier General during the Revolutionary war. He possessed a liberal education and refined accomplishments, and though he never became wealthy in this vicinity he was highly revered and an acknowledged leader in public affairs. He was a native of Berkshire county, Mass. The following year David Seymour and family settled on the west bank of the Tioughnioga, a little below Gen. Patterson's. Between 1794 and 1797, Timothy Shepard, who afterwards became a Baptist minister, Asa Rogers, Benjamin and Hendrick J Smith, and John Landers, settled at Upper Lisle. Mrs. Asa Page settled here at an early day and is supposed to be the first white woman who ascended the Otselic. Isaiah Chapman came in 1803 and located on the farm now owned by Joel Rouse & Sons. He was the first physician in the town. He died of cancer in 1812 and was buried on the farm. His bones were exhumed and re-interred in the cemetery at Upper Lisle, in October, 1859. The first death in the town was that of Mrs. Hannah Lee, in 1791. Martha Seymour taught the first school in 1793.†

The military record of the town of Triangle shows that 113 men were furnished for the army during the war of the Rebellion. Of this number two were substitutes. No regular company was organized, but the enlistments were made principally in the 89th, 109th and 137th Infantry regiments. A few enlisted in other regiments, and in Artillery and Cavalry com-

---

* This tannery, of which J. Burghardt & Sons are proprietors, is a two and one half story frame building, 40 by 160 feet, with a leach house 40 by 70 feet. It gives employment to 16 men and tans 20,000 sides of sole leather annually.

† The town records previous to 1840 were destroyed by a fire which consumed the Town Clerk's office; hence we are unable to give a list of the first town officers.

panies.  Ninety-two enlisted for three years, and the others for
different periods.  Only one commissioned officer enlisted; but
two were promoted, one to First Lieut. and the other to Second
Lieut.  Of the whole number enlisted five were killed in battle,
seven died from diseases contracted in the service, four were
captured by the enemy and are supposed to have died in prison.
and three deserted.

The *First Baptist Church of Lisle*, located at Upper Lisle, was
organized March 13, 1802, by Timothy Shepard and others.
Their church edifice, which will seat 500 persons, was erected
in 1840.  The first pastor was Elder Irish; the present one is
Rev. D. T. Ross.  There are twenty members.  The Church
property is valued at $2,000.

The *Universalist Society of Upper Lisle* was organized with
eleven members, July 24, 1819, by Rev. Seth Jones, their first
pastor, but were ministered to as early as 1812, by Rev. Archelaus
Green, and in 1814, by Rev. Udini H. Jacobs, meetings being
held in the school house.  It was reorganized in 1830, and in
1831 their church edifice, which will seat 500 persons, was
erected, and was dedicated in June of that year.  There are 58
members, who are ministered to by Rev. F. B. Peck.  The
Church property is valued at $3,000.

The *Triangle Baptist Church*, located at Triangle, was organized August 30, 1831.  The church edifice, which will seat 500
persons, was erected the following year, at a cost of $1,650.75.
The first pastor was Rev. Asenath Lawton; Rev. H. Cornell is
the present one.  There are forty-five members.  The Church
property is valued at $3,500.

The *M. E. Church*, at Triangle, was organized with ninety-
eight members, in 1838, by E. L. North and Augustus Brown,
who became its pastors.  Their house of worship, which will
seat 350 persons, was erected in 1854, at a cost of $1,300.  There
are sixty members, who enjoy the ministrations of Rev. Alex.
Burrows, who received his Theological education at Drew
Theological Seminary, N. J.  The Church property is valued
at $5,000.

The *M. E. Church*, at Whitneys Point, was organized in 1842,
by Rev. T. D. Wise, its first pastor.  The house of worship,
which will seat 450 persons, was erected in 1841, at a cost
of $3,000 and was remodeled in 1868.  There are seventy-six
members and nineteen probationers.  The present pastor is
Rev. J. W. Hewitt.  The Church property is valued at $8,000.

The *Baptist Church*, at Whitneys Point, was organized with
eleven members, in 1842.  The following year their first house

of worship was erected; the present one, which will seat 250 persons, was erected in 1854, at a cost of $2,500. The present number of members is sixty-seven, and the pastor is Rev. D. T. Ross. The Church property is valued at $6,000.

The *First Congregational Church of Whitneys Point* was organized with thirty-one members, by a council convened for the purpose, Sept. 7, 1854. The church edifice was built by the Lisle Congregational Society, to accommodate those who found it inconvenient to attend the church at Lisle, in 1842, at a cost of about $1,400. It will seat 300 persons. It was purchased by this Society after its organization. This Society is still under the charge of the Presbytery although in name and church discipline it is Congregational. Rev. S. N. Robinson was the first pastor; the present one is Rev. Richard A. Clark. The members number eighty-one. The Church property is valued at $10,000.

The *Grace Church*, (Protestant Episcopal) at Whitneys Point, was organized with eight members, by Rev. J. W. Capen, its first and present pastor, in December, 1870, and its house of worship, which will seat 250 persons, was erected in 1871, at a cost of $5,000, which is five-sixths of the present value of Church property. There are seventeen members.

The *First Baptist Church of Triangle*, located at Hazards Corners, was organized with about fifteen members, by Timothy Shepard, its first pastor, and others, but in what year we were unable to learn. The church edifice, which will seat 150 persons, was erected about 1830. There are twenty members, but there is no pastor. The Church property is valued at $250.

The *Congregational Church*, at Triangle, was organized with fifteen members, by Rev. S. Williston, in 1819. Its house of worship, which will seat 250 persons, was erected in 1825, at a cost of $800. Rev. Henry Ford was the first pastor. At present the pulpit is vacant. There are sixty-two members. The Church property is valued at $2,500.

*UNION* was formed February 16, 1791. Portions were taken off to form the towns of Norwich and Oxford, (Chenango Co) Jan. 19, 1793; Greene, (Chenango Co.) March 15, 1798; Tioga, (Tioga Co.) and Lisle, March 14, 1800; Chenango, in 1808; Vestal, Jan. 22, 1823; and Maine, March 27, 1848. A part was re-annexed from Tioga, (Tioga Co.) April 2, 1810, and from Lisle, April 11, 1827. It is one of the west border towns, lying south of the center of the County. It covers an area of 20,872¼ acres, of which, in 1865, according to the census of that year, 16,510½, were improved.  In the north the surface is hilly and the soil a rich slaty and gravelly loam, while in the south is the intervale of the Susquehanna with its fertile alluvium.  The hills admit of tillage to their summits.  It is watered by the Susquehanna River, which forms the southern boundary, and Nanticoke, Patterson and Little Choconut creeks, all of which are tributary to the Susquehanna.  All the creeks flow in a southerly direction, Nanticoke through the western, Patterson through the central and Little Choconut through the eastern part.

The Erie R. R. extends through the south part, following the general course of the river.

In 1870 the population of the town was 2,538.  During the year ending Sept. 30, 1871, there were fourteen school districts and sixteen teachers employed.  The number of children of school age was 863; the number attending school, 680; the average attendance, 362; the amount expended for school purposes, $6,243; and the value of school houses and sites, $10,737.

UNION, (p. v.) located on the Susquehanna River and the Erie R. R., in the south-west part, is an incorporated village* of about 800 inhabitants.  It is distant eight and one-half miles west of Binghamton, and thirteen and one-half miles east of Owego.  It contains two churches,† (M. E. and Presbyterian,) a Union school, a banking-house,‡ a printing office, (*Union News*) a foundry and machine shop.§ a grain cradle manufactory, a planing mill and sash and blind factory, fourteen stores, four wagon shops, four blacksmith shops, three hotels, a bakery, a harness shop, three shoe shops, two millinery stores, one jewelry store, two cooper shops and a tin and stove store.

UNION CENTER, (p. v.) located near the north line, on Nanticoke Creek, four miles north of Union, contains two churches, (Congregational and M. E.) two stores. a saw mill,‖ a planing

----

* It was incorporated June 16, 1871.  The following named persons constitute the first and present board of officers  F B Smith, *President*, E. C. Moody, *Clerk*, M. C. Rockwell, E. C. Mersereau and T. P. Knapp, *Trustees.*  It was laid out into streets, and lots of three-quarters of an acre in size, in 1836.

† An Episcopal Society was organized about a year ago, (present time April, 1872,) and is preparing to build a church edifice.

‡ Messrs. Chandler & Rockwell's banking-house was established in May, 1866.

§ The *Union Agricultural Works,* of which H. Day & Son are proprietors, are located on Main St., and give employment to six men in the manufacture of agricultural implements, steam engines, grist and saw mills &c.

‖ The *Union Center Steam Saw Mill,* (J C & B. Howard, proprietors,) contains one circular saw, four and one-half feet in diameter, the motive power for which is furnished by a seventy-five-horse power engine, and has a capacity for cutting about 2,000,000 feet of lumber per annum.

mill, a rake factory,* a blacksmith shop, a shoe shop, a cooper shop and about one hundred inhabitants.

HOOPER, (p. o.) (named from Philander Hooper,) located about the center of the south border, on the Erie R. R., two and one-half miles east of Union and six, west of Binghamton, contains a store, a blacksmith shop, a school house and a dozen houses.

CHOCONUT CENTER, (p. o.) located near the north-east corner, on Little Choconut Creek, four and one-half miles north-west of Binghamton, contains one church, (M. E.) a school house, two blacksmith shops, a wagon shop, a steam feed mill and about sixty-five inhabitants.

ASHERY CORNERS, located on the east line, south of the center, contains a school house, a wagon shop, a blacksmith shop, a grocery and harness shop and about twenty houses.†

Permanent settlements were commenced in 1785 by Joseph Draper, who located at Union Village; Nathan Howard, from New London, Conn., and Jabez Winchop, an exhorter, at Hooper, and Bryan Stoddard, near Hooper, who were squatters on the land purchased the next year by Joshua Mersereau; Nehemiah Crawford, a squatter, who settled one mile east of Hooper; Winthrop Roe and —— Fitch, who settled at the mouth of Nanticoke Creek; Gen. Oringh Stoddard, one of the Commissioners appointed by the Boston Company to treat with the Indians, who settled one mile east of Hooper; and Lewis Keeler,‡ from Norwalk, Conn., a tailor by occupation, who lived

* The *Union Center Hand-Rake Manufactory,* (Barzilla Howard, proprietor,) produces about 20,000 rakes per annum.

† In addition to the business interests already noted are the following, which are removed from the business centers: Wells & Brigham's brickyard, located in the east part, uses three machines for pressed and common brick, gives employment to fifty men and manufactures from four million to five million bricks per annum; the *Nanticoke Mill* (custom and flouring) (James E. Harrison, proprietor,) located on Nanticoke Creek, about one mile west of Union Village, has three runs of stones, with a grinding capacity of 400 bushels of grain per day; the *Union Hand-Rake Manufactory,* (Aaron Heath, proprietor,) located about one mile south of Union Center, on Nanticoke Creek, produces from 18,000 to 20,000 rakes per annum; John C. Waterman's circular saw mill, located about one mile south of Union Center, has a capacity for cutting about 400,000 feet of lumber per annum; *Ward's Plaster Mill,* (Luke Ward, proprietor,) located at Nanticoke Creek, about two and one-half miles north of Union, has a capacity for grinding about eleven tons per day—about 300 tons are ground per annum; the *Union Brick Yard,* (A. P. Keeler, proprietor,) located about three miles north of Union, does an extensive business.

‡ It is related of Keeler that, in 1793, he went to Conn. to visit his friends and on his way back, a little west of Deposit, he fell in company with a woman, on horseback, who was going to Lisle to visit her brother and cousin and invest a few hundred dollars she had in lands. They were soon on such good terms that he mounted the horse beside her and before reaching Binghamton they were engaged to be married, and accordingly, the

with Gen. Stoddard. But this locality was perhaps first visited with a view to settlement, by Col. Hooper, the patentee of the tract bearing his name, who was sent by Bingham, Cox, and, it may be, others, to survey the shores of this part of the Susquehanna. He traversed it up and down, in an Indian canoe, managed by a faithful Indian whom he employed. He would lie down in the canoe, with an Indian blanket thrown over him, and take the courses and distances with a pocket compass, in this incumbent position. He took this precaution through fear of being shot by Indians on the shore.* Jeremiah and Benjamin Brown also located near Hooper, in 1785. The following year came Joshua Mersereau,† from

next day, they were married at Binghamton, about one mile above which place they settled  Keeler was afterwards sheriff of Tioga Co.  He built the first house, except the old ferry-house, at Binghamton, and kept the first hotel there.

*Annals of Binghamton,* p  95.

† Joshua Mersereau was a native of France and, in company with his father, fled to this country during the French Persecution, and settled on Staten Island.  He was then a young man, and by occupation a ship carpenter.  During the Revolutionary war he was appointed a Major by Gen. Washington, who, afterwards discovering that he was a better business man than soldier, changed the appointment to Commissary General for the exchange of prisoners and Quartermaster General of the Continental army, which office he filled till the close of the war  He was an intimate friend of Washington's and his house was frequently honored by the presence of the latter.  After the close of the war he was elected member of Assembly, which office he filled till 1784, when he moved to Unadilla (Otsego Co.)  While residing there he was nominated for State Senator in opposition to Judge Wm. Cooper, of Cooperstown, by whom he was defeated by one vote  From there he moved to Union  At that time there were but few settlers in this section of country  There was one house at Binghamton, in which lived a man named Lyons.  Joshua and William Whitney lived a little north of Binghamton; and one or two persons were living at Campville, Tioga county.  Mr. Mersereau was commissioned to survey the Hooper, Wilson and Bingham patents, and received for that service a farm of 300 acres, located at Hooper  He named the County, also the town of Union  He was the first judge of the County and filled the office of *First Judge* till his death in June, 1804.

Statement of Lawrence Mersereau, third son of Joshua Mersereau, who came here with his father, in his fourteenth year.  He is now in his hundredth year.  Lawrence enlisted at the age of fourteen and was commissioned as ensign.  Gov Lewis gave him a Captain's commission  He filled the two offices ten years.  Any soldier, he says, worth $250, was entitled to vote, and in order to enable him to vote for Washington, for the second term to the Presidency, his father gave him five acres of fine land. He enjoyed good health, retained all his mental faculties and transacted all his business until the Thanksgiving of 1870, when he was attacked with a severe fit of sickness, which somewhat impaired his mental faculties. So vigorous was he previous to his sickness that, in 1866, he climbed his apple trees and picked the fruit.  He converses freely and has a retentive memory.  His father and his father's brother, John Mersereau, originated the first line of stages which ran between New York and Philadelphia. Lawrence frequently accompanied them on their trips and he recollects riding in the stage with Washington several times.  He says, at one time Washington was expected to take dinner at the house of his father, who sent him to catch some black fish, of which Washington was particularly fond. He went, as he supposed, according to his father's directions, but returned

Staten Island, who settled at Hooper, Oliver Crocker,* (whose
father was one of the sixty proprietors of the Boston Purchase,
and preceded him a short time,) who came "with his pack upon
his back" and settled about two miles east of Hooper,
on lot 208 of Chenango Township. A Mr. Gallop was a temporary settler at Union as early as 1787, but at what date he
came or how long he remained we have not learned. Walter
Sabin settled at Hooper about 1788, and kept the first school
in the town. John Mersereau, brother of Joshua, came in
1792, and settled first on the south side of the river, in Vestal,
but afterwards moved to the north side. His purchase embraced the site of Union Village. The same year came Abner
Rockwell, who settled near Union Center; Elnathan Norton,
from Stockbridge, Conn., who settled three miles east of Union
Center, where he lived a few years, when he moved to Union
Center and kept a tavern; and Medad Bradley, from Berkshire
Co., Mass., who settled at Union Center. Elisha B. Bradley,
also from Berkshire Co., Mass., came in 1793; Isaac N. Martin,
from Berkshire Co., Mass., came in about this time, perhaps a
little earlier. Henry Richards, from Wyoming Flats, Penn.,
settled soon after. Oliver Crocker, on the farm east of his,
which he bought of Amos Draper. Ezekiel Crocker Jr.,†

without having caught any. His father whipped him, and having again
instructed him where to go, sent him a second time. He returned with
seven fine fish in due time for the feast. Lawrence lived on the old farm
at Hooper until 1837, when he moved to Union Village.

*Crocker was from Richmond, Berkshire Co., Mass. The year previous
to his settling in Union (1785) he worked lands on shares, as a tenant, with
Gen Joshua Whitney, and saved from his summer's earnings $100, with
which he purchased 400 acres of land in this town. He was appointed, by
his father, agent for the sale of lands in New York. He frequently went
to that city, always on foot, and, to make the trip pay, he brought back
with him goods to sell to the settlers. While returning on one occasion
he procured, by permission, from a cider mill in N J., which he passed, a
half bushel of apple seeds, which he stayed there long enough to dry and
pack in his knapsack. A portion of these seeds he planted on his farm
here, and the rest he took to Genoa, (Cayuga Co ) where he had purchased
1250 acres of land, and commenced the second nursery in Cayuga Co. He
built a hotel on his farm here in 1800, where a public house was kept for
many years. It was one of the first kept in the town. "While employed
in clearing his land he lived, he says, for a length of time upon *roots* and
*beech leaves.* He boarded, or rather tarried by night, with William Ed-
minster and his family, who were driven to nearly the same straits. They
were relieved, in some degree, by a scanty supply of cucumbers, and still
later by a deer or two. As young Crocker assisted in shooting the deer,
so he shared in eating them. He says that while reduced to these extrem-
ities for food, he would become so *faint* at his work that he would scarcely be able to swing his ax."

† Mr. Crocker lived here but a short time. His dead body was found in
the Chenango River, into which he is supposed to have fallen from his
canoe. He had lent his own, large canoe to a neighbor to go to mill and
taken in exchange (temporarily) two smaller ones, which he tried to make
answer his purpose. When last seen he was standing with a foot in each
boat.

second son of Ezekiel Crocker, was an early settler near Little Choconut Creek. Amos Patterson was an early settler in the east part of the town, on the Allen farm. Rowland Davis, from Mass., came in in 1794. He worked a farm with Oliver Crocker for two years, after which he bought a farm about one mile north of Hooper, on which he resided till his death, in 1841.

Until 1791, in which year James Ross and Jabez Winchop built the first grist mill, the nearest milling facilities were at Tioga Point, and thither the early settlers carried their grists. It was a common practice among them, however, to grind a portion of their corn by means of a hollowed-out stump and a pestle suspended from a spring-pole, the whole so constructed that when the pestle was borne down upon the corn the pole caused it to recede again when the downward pressure was removed. The first death was that of Mary J. Fisk, June 13, 1789; the first birth that of Joseph Chambers, July 4, 1790. Jabez Winchop opened the first tavern in 1791.

Several Indians had temporary huts near the river, which they occupied more or less for several years after the country was settled. They had a means of obtaining salt which the whites never discovered. They crossed the mountain about opposite Judge Mersereau's, on the south side of the river, and, after an absence of about twelve hours, returned with a kettle of salt, which, immediately on their return, was warm. So cautious were they of revealing the source whence they obtained their supply of salt that all efforts of the early settlers to discover it proved unavailing. John D. Mersereau relates that, when a lad, his father and himself endeavored to follow the Indians when it was known they had set out for salt; but they soon appeared to suspect they were watched and either remained where they were, or turned from their course. Never more than two sat out upon the expedition.*

This town furnished 176 men for the army during the war of the Rebellion.†

---

*Annals of Binghamton*, p. 104

† The following is a list of casualties which occurred among them:
Charles Langdon, private of the 50th Engineers, died of camp fever at Washington, July 2, 1864.
Edwin Kipp, private 50th Eng., died at White House, Va., June 10, 1862.
Judson Balch, private 16th Battery, died of diarrhea, June 10, 1865.
Levi Howard, private 50th Reg. died at Washington, April 10, 1864.
Charles Gardner, private 50th Eng., died in October, 1864.
Huson Gardner, private 50th Eng., died from injury received on the cars, Nov. 10, 1863.
Wm. H. Kipp, private 50th Eng., died of diphtheria, April 10th, 1864.
Lewis Howard, 51st Infty., died at Covington, Ky., Aug. 30, 1863.
James Fredenberg, 16th Battery, died at Andersonville prison, Aug. 22, 1864.

The first Church (Ref. Prot. D.) was organized in 1789, at Union village, and the first settled preacher was Rev. John Manley.

The *First Presbyterian Church of Union,* located at Union village, was organized with fourteen members, July 17, 1822, by Rev. Benjamin Niles, Horatio Lombard and Marcus Ford. The first church edifice was erected in 1820; the present one, which will seat 600 persons, in 1871–2, at a cost of $15,000. Rev. John Whiton was the first pastor; Rev. C. Otis Thacher is the present one. There are 138 members. The Church property is valued at $20,000.

The *Union Center Congregational Church* was organized with seventy-three members, Nov. 2, 1841, by Rev. Nathaniel Pine, its first pastor. Their house of worship, which will seat 300 persons, was erected in 1840, at a cost of $1,500, and was rebuilt in 1870. Rev. Charles W. Burt is the present pastor. There are 103 members. The Church property is valued at $6,000

The *M. E. Church of Union,* located at Union village, on the corner of Union and Nanticoke streets, was organized by Rev. Charles Burlingame, its first pastor, March 4, 1842. The first house of worship was erected in 1848; the present one,

Jasper Waterman, private 16th Battery, is supposed to have died at Philadelphia, Pa.

Benj. Whittemore, private 109th Infty, killed in battle of Spotsylvania, May 12, 1864.

Austin R. Barney, 137th Infty., killed at battle of Lookout Mountain, Oct. 30, 1863.

Benj. F. Dunning, 89th Inf., died at Fort Schuyler, N. Y., April 16, 1864.

John J. Englesfield, private 89th Infty , was killed at the battle of Antietam, Sept. 17, 1862.

John Cannine, private 137th Infty., was killed at the Battle of Gettysburg, July 3d, 1863.

Ezra Cleveland, private 89th Infty., died from wounds, Dec. 7, 1864.

Lewis Kipp, private 76th Infty , died of chronic diarrhea at Rappahannock Station, Va., Nov. 18th, 1863.

Manton C. Angell, Capt. 16th Infty., was killed in the battle of Antietam, Sept. 17, 1862.

David Millen, corporal 109th Infty., was killed while leading his company in battle of Petersburgh, Va , July 30, 1864.

Wm J Millen, private 61st Infty., was killed in battle, May 8, 1864.

Squire D. Gager, corporal 109th Infty, died of small pox at Washington, Feb. 14, 1864.

Friend Pratt, private 89th Infty., died from a wound in the fall of 1864.

Henry H. Pulsipher, 16th Heavy Artillery, when last heard from was in Andersonville prison, where he is reported to have died

Benj. F. Mason, corporal 137th Infty., killed in battle of Lookout Mt., Nov. 24, 1863

Frederick Miller, private 50th Eng., died in hospital at Washington, D. C., Sept. 1, 1864.

James F. Marble, private 21st Cavalry, is reported dead.

Franklin Dunning, private 89 Infty , died of disease at Washington, D. C.—[*Town Records.*

which will seat 450 persons, in 1871–2, at a cost of $12,000. The present number of members is 120, and the present pastor, Rev. A. J. Van Cleft. The value of Church property is $18,000.

The *Grace Church of Union,* (Episcopal) located at Union village, was organized with five members, in February, 1871, and the following April Rev. J. E. Battie became its first pastor, though services were conducted by Rev. Wm. A. Hitch-cŏck, rector of Christ Church, Binghamton, in Nov. 1870, and are still continued by him one each week, in the absence of any settled pastor. A church edifice, which, when completed, is to cost about $4,000, is now in process of erection. The Society numbers eighteen communicants.

*VESTAL* was formed from Union, January 22, 1823.* It is the south-west corner town of the County, and covers an area of 22,982 acres, of which, in 1865, according to the census of that year, 12,746, were improved. The surface formation resembles that of Union, though the relative position of hills and vales is reversed. The south is hilly, while the north part is covered by the intervale of the Susquehanna. The soil is of a good quality. The fine slaty loam on the hills, which are cultivated to their summits, and the deep rich alluvium of the valleys adapt it both to grain culture and grazing. It is watered principally by the Big Choconut and Tracy creeks, which flow north, the former through the central and the latter through the western part of the town, and empty into the Susquehanna River, which forms the north border of the town.

In 1870 the population of the town was 2,221. During the year ending Sept. 30, 1871, there were seventeen school districts and the same number of teachers employed. The number of children of school age was 774; the number attending school, 629; the average attendance, 303; the amount expended for school purposes, $3,899; and the value of school houses and sites, $6,490.

VESTAL, (p. v.) situated near to and east of the mouth of Big Choconut Creek, contains one church, one store, a wagon shop and about twenty-five houses.

VESTAL CENTER (p. v.) is situated on the Big Choconut Creek, a little south of the center of the town, and four miles east of Tracy Creek village.

---

*The first town meeting was held at the house of J. Rounds, Feb. 11, 1823, and the following named officers were elected. Samuel Murdock, *Supervisor*, David Merserau, *Town Clerk*, Daniel Mersereau, James Brewster and Nathan Barney, *Assessors and Commissioners;* John Layton and Elias Morse, *Poormasters*, Nathaniel Benjamin, *Collector*, Nathaniel Benjamin and Ephraim Potts, *Constables.*

# VESTAL.

143

TRACY CREEK, (p. v.) situated on the creek whose name it bears, west of the center of the town, and six miles south-west of Vestal, is a thriving village containing one church, (M. E.) and another (R. M.) which is in process of erection, a saw mill,* a planing mill, a wagon shop, a cooper shop, two blacksmith shops, one harness shop, two shoe shops, a tannery, a store and about thirty houses.

The tannery of which Messrs. J. & W. Clark are proprietors, located in this town, about two miles south of Union village, contains thirty-six vats and four leaches, consumes six hundred cords of hemlock bark, gives employment to thirteen men and has facilities for tanning one hundred thousand sheep skins. The motive power is furnished by a thirty-five-horse power engine.

This section of country is not known to have been trod by the foot of a white man previous to Gen. Sullivan's expedition against the Indians of this State in 1779.† It remained in its pristine wildness until 1785, in which year the settlement of the town was commenced by Col. Samuel Seymour, who located in the extreme north-west corner, and Daniel Seymour, his brother. Major David Barney came down the river from Cooperstown, in a canoe, with a large family of children. The canoe upset while they were on the way, but the children were saved. Daniel Price and Ruggles Winchel settled about four miles back from the main road. Two years later, in 1787, Col. Asa Camp, an emigrant from Columbia county, settled on the LaGrange homestead, where he lived several years. Col. Camp served during the Revolution, in the capacity of Sergeant, with bravery and distinction, though the military title by which he was known was acquired in after life. He witnessed the execu-

* The *Tracy Creek Steam Saw Mill* was erected in 1869, by the present proprietors, Messrs. Noyes & Bullock. It gives employment to six men and is capacitated to cut 8,000 feet of lumber per day.

† Skirmishes occurred in this vicinity between the Indians and a detachment of Gen. Sullivan's forces, composed of Gen. Clinton's troops, which were moving to form a junction with Sullivan's, and a small portion of Sullivan's, which had been detached to ascertain the whereabouts of Clinton's forces, and were returning with the latter to join the main body at Tioga Point. Cannon balls, supposed to have been thrown from their cannon, have been found south of the river, a little east of Hooper; and on the farm of John D Mersereau, north of the river, (in Union) and east of Union village, were, at a recent date, to be seen traces of an Indian fort, which, according to tradition, was thrown up at that time. Evident marks of musket shot upon the trees near the shore here were visible when the country was first settled. The most considerable skirmish occurred on what is called Round Hill, which lies at the south-west corner of the corporation of Union village, where, it appears, the Indians collected in considerable numbers, encouraged, no doubt, by the small detachment of Sullivan's troops which were observed to pass up the river to meet those under Clinton. The large force which returned soon caused the Indians to make a precipitate retreat.

tion of the ill-starred Maj. Andre, whose grave he helped to dig. John Mersereau settled about three-fourths of a mile above the bridge at Union in 1792, but soon moved across the river into Union, as stated in the history of that town. John LaGrange settled at an early day, though the precise date is not known. He came, when quite young, from Elizabethtown, N. J., and purchased lands of his uncle, Judge Mersereau, opposite to whom he settled.* John Fairbrother came in 1796, and settled about a mile south of Vestal Center. That part of the country, says his son, who is now in his 78th year, was wild and inhabited only by Indians and wild beasts. Choconut Creek abounded with panthers. Mr. Fairbrother dug the first cellar in Binghamton. He was from England and his son, our informant, was born on the ocean, he being two years old when his father came here. Stephen Platt settled near Vestal in 1800. Wm. Potts settled near the bridge at Union in 1803; and Wm. Garrison the first settler on Tracy Creek, settled about two miles below Tracy Creek village.

The first inn was kept by Samuel Coe, in 1791; the first grist mill was built by R. Winchell, in 1786; and the first school was taught by John Boutch, in 1793.

The Methodist at Vestal was the first Church organization in the town.

The *First Reformed Methodist Church*, located near Tracy Creek village, was organized with twenty members, about 1820, by Rev. Winthrop Collins, its first pastor. Previous to its organization meetings were held by Elder Buckley of Apalachin Creek, Tioga Co., and others of this denomination, which resulted in the formation of this Society. The church edifice, which will seat 400 persons, was erected in 1832, at a cost of $1,000, which is one-half the present value of Church property. It has been several times repaired. There are sixty-eight members, who are ministered to by Rev. Henry Cole.

The *Baptist Church* at Vestal Center was organized with twenty-one members, by Rev. James Clark, Dec. 16, 1834. The first pastor was Rev Charles G. Swan; the present one is Rev. John Phelps. The number of members is fifty-nine. The house of worship was erected in 1853, at a cost of $2,000. It will seat 200 persons. The Church property is valued at $5,000.

---

* "When he came," says Wilkinson, in the *Annals of Binghamton*, "he was unacquainted with a wooden country, and even with farming. So that his partial success for a length of time, and his frequent irritations, from want of more experience, as well as the unpropitious aspect of a newly settled country, induced him many times to wish that he had stayed where the elements around him were less at variance with his knowledge and habits. His wife, however, would bear up his courage, or pleasantly ridicule his little vexations."

The *First Reformed Methodist Church*, at Tracy Creek, was organized with thirteen members, by Joseph Chidester, in 1841, in which year the first church edifice, with a capacity to seat 200 persons, was erected at a cost of $500. The first pastor was Elder Lake; the present one is Elder Cole. There are 100 members. The Church property is valued at $200.

The *Reformed Methodist Church*, at Tracy Creek, was organized Dec. 30, 1860, by Rev. Daniel D. Brown, its first pastor. The first house of worship was erected in 1870. A new one is in process of erection, which is to be completed in October, 1872. There are forty-eight members. The pastor is Rev. Henry Cole.

The *M. E. Church of Tracy Creek* was organized with twenty-five members in March, 1871, and its house of worship, which will seat 200 persons, was completed in December of the same year, at a cost of $2,500, which is the present value of Church property. Rev. S. W. Lindsley was the first pastor; Rev. J. D. Bloodgood is the present one. The number of members has not increased.

*WINDSOR* was formed from Chenango, March 27, 1807. Colesville and Sanford were taken off April 2, 1821, and a part of Conklin, in 1851. A part of Conklin was annexed April 18, 1831. It is one of the southern tier towns, lying east of the center of the County. It covers an area of 51,997 acres, of which, in 1865, according to the census of that year, 23,790, were improved. The surface consists principally of two elevated ridges, which are separated by the narrow valley of the Susquehanna. The hills in the eastern range attain an altitude of from 400 to 800 feet above the valley, and terminate in several sharp ridges; while those in the western range, though being generally less elevated rise in some instances to an equal height. Oquaga Hill, in the north-east part, is one of the highest peaks in town. The declivities of the hills are generally quite abrupt. About two-thirds of the town—the western and central portions—lie within the great bend of the Susquehanna, by which river and its tributaries (Okkanum, Red and Tuscarora creeks) it is watered. The soil in the valleys of these streams is a deep, rich, gravelly loam; and on the hills it consists of a gravelly loam underlaid by clay and hard-pan. The Delaware & Hudson Canal Co.'s railroad passes through the town following the general course of the river; and the Erie R. R. crosses the south-east corner. These, with the river, furnish ample facilities for the transportation of the products of the farm, dairy and mill.

In 1870 the town had a population of 2,958. During the year ending Sept. 30, 1871, it contained twenty-two school districts and employed twenty-three teachers. The number of children of school age was 1,010; the number attending school, 911; the average attendance, 451; the amount expended for school purposes, $6,113; and the value of school houses and sites, $8,525.

WINDSOR, (p. v.) located on the west bank of the Susquehanna, a little east of the center of the town, contains four churches, (Free Methodist, Episcopal, M. E. and Presbyterian,) five dry goods stores, one hardware store, two hotels, a foundry and machine shop, one harness, three wagon, four blacksmith, one cabinet, three shoe and one milliner shops, an undertaker's establishment, one whip and two spoke manufactories, one planing, one grist and one saw mills, a spring-bed bottom manufactory and 600 inhabitants. It is a thriving village, surrounded by a good farming country and a wealthy farming community, and enjoys the ready transit of the river and the D. & H. Canal Co.'s R. R. The Susquehanna is spanned here by a free bridge, 700 feet long.*

CASCADE VALLEY, (p. o.) located near the south-east corner, on the Erie R. R., is simply a post station, and derives its name from the two falls on the creek on which it is located, each of which is one hundred feet in height. The surrounding country presents a wild aspect.

RANDOLPH CENTER, (p. o.) located west of the center, and so named from its being the center of Randolph's patent, contains one church, (Baptist) a wagon and blacksmith shop and eight or ten houses. It is a fine dairy country.

HAZARDVILLE, located in the south-west part, contains one church, (Wesleyan) a school house, a blacksmith shop, a grocery, four saw mills,† one of which is operated by steam and

---

* About 1846 a high school was established here and continued until 1849, when an application was made for its conversion into an academy and a charter was granted for that purpose. Grover Buel, B H. Russell, Oliver T. Bundy, Jeremiah Hull, Enoch Copley, Elisha Hall, George Dusenbury, James Y. Brown, Seymour Butts, Henry L. Sleeper, Hiram W. Gilbert and Adam Craig were appointed trustees of the academy, which was known as the *Windsor Academy.* After several years it was changed to a graded school, with an academical department.

† Uri E. Blatchley's steam saw mill, located near Hazardville, is operated by an engine of thirty-horse power, gives employment to seven persons and is capacitated to saw 12,000 feet of lumber daily.

three by water, one grist mill and twenty-six houses. It is surrounded by a good grazing country.*

STILLSON HOLLOW (West Windsor p. o) is located in the north-west part, contains one church, (Union) a store, a blacksmith shop and a wagon shop.

BARTONVILLE is located south of the center. Stannard & Son's saw mill, situated near here, has a capacity for cutting 200,000 feet of lumber per annum.

For a long time anterior to its settlement by the whites the country embraced within the limits of this town was the home of the red man. Windsor,† says Wilkinson, "appears to have been a half-way resting place for the 'Six Nations,' as they passed south to Wyoming or its neighborhood; or for the tribes of the Wyoming valley as they passed north. Their path over the Oquago mountain, and also over a mountain this side, nearer the village, [Binghamton] was worn very deep, and is still plainly visible." The mountain referred to in the quotation, extends on both sides of the river, towards which, on either side, it has a gentle slope, and incloses a beautiful vale from three to four miles in length and from one to one and one-half miles in width. The route pursued by the Indians was also the one followed by many of the early New England settlers to reach their western homes. "That portion of Gen. Clinton's army, not embarked in the boats, at the time of his inroad against the Iroquois of [this] valley in 1779, took the same course from river to river; and in 1785 a portion of James

* The place derives its name from a family named Hazard, five brothers of whom (Hiram, Edward, John B., O. P. and S H.) settled there at an early day. Families named Phillips, Trowbridge, Vergason and Blatchley were among the first settlers. Samuel and Reuben Stephens erected the first saw mill, and Dyer Vergason built the first grist mill.
Fifteen persons from this School District entered the army during the war of the Rebellion, only seven of whom returned.

† Windsor was formerly known as Oquaga. The latter name is variously written, but the orthography here given is that generally accepted by modern writers. In a letter from Rev. John Ogilvie, a missionary to the Indians at this place, to Sir Wm. Johnson, dated Albany, May 14, 1756, as appears in Doc. Hist. Vol. IV, page 302, it is written "Onogquaga;" in a letter from Rev. Dr. Wheelock, also to Johnson, dated at Lebanon, Oct. 24, 1764, on page 342 of the work before quoted, it is written "Onoquagee," and in an editorial foot note on the same page of the same work, "Onohoghquage;" in the report of Rev. Gideon Hawley's journey to this place in 1753, Doc. Hist. Vol. III, page 1033, it is written "Onohoghgwage;" and says C. P. Avery, in an article on *The Susquehanna Valley* which appears in *The Saint Nicholas* for March, 1854, it was written by the early missionaries "Onuh-huh-guah-geh," and is so pronounced by some of the Iroquois now in Canada, and, he says, "upon the early map," it appears as "O-nogh-qua-gy." Officially, at the present day, the name of the post-office at Oquaga, in the south part of the town of Colesville, from which this is sometimes distinguished by the prefix *old*, is spelled "Ouaquaga."

McMaster's pioneer company from the Mohawk crossed from that point over the same ground which their Indian predecessors with their intimate knowledge of the geographical features of the country, had so long before, with intuitive woodland sagacity, pronounced feasible."* "The evidence we have," says Wilkinson, in the *Annals of Binghamton,* "of its great antiquity, and of its distinction at some date or other, is from the numerous and valuable trinkets that were found by the whites when they came to dig and plow upon its plains. The apple trees also found growing there, of great size, and of apparently great age; their number, too, and the variety and richness of the fruit; all indicated the antiquity and importance of the place. A great number of human bones from various depths below the surface, were thrown up from time to time. Some of these were of peculiar formation. A scull was found with the lower jaw attached to it, which had an entire *double row* of teeth; a *single* row above, but *all* double teeth." Remains of a fort, constructed to meet the enemy from the river, were discernible to the first settlers; and as they presented indications of its recent construction the impression prevailed that it was built when Gen. Clinton passed down the river. This, however, seems improbable, since the Indians did not offer any resistance to him or even show themselves. It is highly probable, (in view of the fact that traces of its existence would, at that early day, require much more time for their obliteration, than under the attrition of the present comparatively thickly populated country in its vicinity,) that it was constructed at a much earlier day, and quite possibly during the French and Indian war, as we find mention of a fort which it was then contemplated to erect at this place, and expressions of fear that opposition would be made to the project which would render it difficult to procure workmen for that service, in a letter addressed by Rev. John Ogilvie to Sir Wm. Johnson under date of May 14, 1756.† The object of erecting this fort was doubtless to afford protection to and extend the missionary labors in this section, which were instituted about the middle of the last century. The Indians of Oquaga were religiously disposed and were among the first to avail themselves of the advantages of the Indian School instituted at Stockbridge at a very early day. They are supposed for this reason to have belonged to the Iroquois, who were distinguished for their deep interest in religious matters. A large number of them went to Stockbridge while Jonathan

* *The Saint Nicholas,* March, 1854.

† Doc. Hist. Vol IV, 302.

Edwards,* who was afterwards president of Princeton College, was a missionary there, and were commended to him by the sachems of the Mohawks, in council, as being worthy of peculiar tenderness and care, since, as they ingenuously admitted, the Oquagas "much excelled their own tribe in religion and virtue." Accordingly Mr. Edwards interested himself in their behalf and secured for them a missionary in the person of Rev. Gideon Hawley, who, in company with Timothy Woodbridge and Mr. and Mrs. Benjamin Ashley,† the latter of whom went in the capacity of interpreter, visited Oquaga in 1753, and Hawley remained there until the breaking out of the French war, when he was admonished that it was unsafe to remain longer, his companions having previously returned.

Mr. Hawley thus describes his reception at Oquaga.

"June 4th. [1753] In the afternoon appeared at a distance Onohoghgwage mountain, and shewed us the end of our journey and the object of our wishes  It rained  Wet and fatigued, we arrived near night  The Indians flocked around us, and made us welcome.  Our hopes were raised by favorable appearances  But our accommodations, considering our fatigues, were not very comfortable.  Our lodgings were bad, being both dirty and hard, and our clothes wet.

"June 5th  To-day there were many the worse for the rum that came with us  One of our horses hurt an Indian boy, and this raised and enraged such a party against us, as Ashley, his wife the interpreter, and the Indians at whose house we lodged, hid themselves, and would have me and Mr Woodbridge get out of sight, but we did not think proper to discover the least symptoms of fear, although they threatened us in the most provoking and insulting manner  In the afternoon came the chiefs of the Onohoghgwages, and assured us that those insulting and ill-behaved

---

* About one year previous to Mr. Hawley's visit to Oquaga Mr. Edwards sent his son, Jonathan, there to learn the Indian language, with a view to preparing him for the Indian missionary service.  He was then nine years old.  At the commencement of the French war, the Indian, to whose special care he was entrusted, conveyed him safely to his father, carrying him at intervals upon his back.  This lad subsequently became president of Union College, Schenectady, succeeding Rev. John Blair Smith, its first President, in 1799, and held the office until his death in August, 1801.

† The services of Mr. Ashley, it appears, were not needed, and, in the opinion of Mr Hawley, had better been dispensed with, since, he says, "he was a fanatick, and on that account unfit to be employed in the mission." The services of Mrs Ashley, who, says Mr Hawley, "was a very good sort of woman, and an extraordinary interpreter of the Iroquois language," were indispensable, and as they could not be obtained without the employment of her husband, the mission were obliged to accept the unwelcome alternative.  Writing of Mrs. Ashley, Mr. Hawley says.  "Rebecca, my interpreter, laid her bones at Onohoghgwage in August 1757  She was much lamented by the Indians.  Her Indian name was *Wausaunia.*"— *Doc. Hist. Vol. III* 1037-8.

J

Indians did not belong to them,[*] but were foreigners. We pointed out to them the ill effects of intemperance, and remonstrated against their permitting rum to be brought among them; and that it was necessary in future it should be prohibited, or the dispensing of it regulated, in case we founded a mission and planted Christianity among them. In short, we now opened a treaty with them upon the affairs of our advent, and the importance of our business in every view. Having shewn our credentials, Mr. Woodbridge addressed himself in a well adapted speech of considerable length, to an assembly who were collected upon the occasion. "It affected them, and they appeared to be religiously moved, convicted and even converted."

The war with all its pernicious influences does not seem to have eradicated from the minds of these aborigines their religious predilections.

Oquaga was also a noted rendezvous of Tories and Indians during the Revolution.

John Doolittle, who settled on the west side of the Susquehanna, about four miles above the bridge, in 1786, is believed to be the first white man to make a permanent settlement in this town. In 1787 came David Hotchkiss and his two sons, Amraphael and Cyrus. They settled on the west of the river, a little below the bridge. Hotchkiss took up a large tract of land, on both sides of the river, purchasing only the possession of a Mr. Swift, who came the same year. This was a little before the land was patented, or at least before the patentees were known to the settlers. John Gurnsey, who also came in 1787, took up a patent of 1,000 acres, next south of Hotchkiss' tract. This he left to his sons, of whom there were many, and all of whom left it. North of this, on the river, was the Ellis patent, which embraced the land taken by Mr. Hotchkiss. It consisted of seventeen lots of two hundred acres each, of which Mr. Hotchkiss took ten. Mr. Hotchkiss was the first magistrate appointed in the place. It is related of him that he was very generous and that often, in times of scarcity, he refused to sell his grain to those who had money, preferring rather to supply those who had none. Settlements were made in considerable numbers during the succeeding years, principally by persons from Connecticut. Among these was Major Josiah Stow, from Danbury, Conn., on whose lands were a large number of the ancient apple trees previously mentioned. It was the opinion of the first settlers that they were one hundred years

---

[*] "This was partly the case."
This statement seems confirmed and the general good character of these Indians substantiated by an address delivered by them to Mr Woodbridge, to be, by him, submitted to Col. Wm. Johnson, which in substance implored the latter gentleman to intercede for them with "the great men of Albany, Skenectetee and Skoharry," and implore them not to send them any more rum, which, they said, "has undone us."— *See Doc. Hist. Vol. II. 627.*

old at the time of their settlement. Some of the apples, says Wilkinson, were large enough to weigh a pound. The trees stood irregularly and their trunks ran up very high, with few or no limbs for some distance from the ground, thus indicating that they grew in a forest. The large number of human bones plowed up in after years beneath these trees led to the supposition that this was the place of sepulcher for the Indian dead.*

Samuel Stow came in 1793. In August, about the year 1794, occurred the "pumpkin freshet." The water in the Susquehanna rose much above its usual height and swept away in its torrent the products of the fields along its banks. A great scarcity of provisions was the natural consequence. During this period the characteristic generosity and hardihood of Major Stow manifested itself. He shouldered a bushel of wheat, in which the whole neighborhood had a share, and with it started to Bennett's mills, via Wattles ferry, a distance of more than forty miles, to get it ground. He performed the journey on foot, and returned in the same manner. During the journey he purchased a quarter of a pound of tea, a luxury to which those early settlers were then entirely unaccustomed, to supplement the feast which his return was to inaugurate. On the Major's arrival the company assembled at his house and active preparations were soon begun to complete the arrangements for a sumptuous feast, in which all were to participate. A short-cake was made from the flour, and as no lard was to be had, the Major bethought himself of some bear's grease he had in the house, which was used as a substitute therefor. As tea was a new article in their bill of fare they did not possess the usual conveniences for preparing and serving it. A small kettle was procured and made to serve the purposes of both tea-kettle and

---

*Since the Indians are known to have shown a respect, amounting almost to reverence, for the resting places of their dead, the following incident, the substance of which we extract from the *Annals of Binghamton*, lends credibility to the supposition.

In the early part of his residence here Maj. Stow, one evening, observed an Indian girdling one of these trees with a hatchet. He remonstrated with him, but as the Indian's reply was made in his own dialect, the Major could only glean from it the word "Sullivan," which the Indian repeated several times. As the savage continued his onslaught upon the tree, Mr. Stow commanded him to desist, but as his command was disregarded he reiterated it and threatened to shoot him with the rifle he held in his hand unless he relinquished his project of destroying the tree. The Indian seemed aware of the unwavering purpose of the Major and glanced furtively at his own rifle which lay near him upon the ground; but evidently deeming his chances in the event of a collision unequal, he sullenly and reluctantly repaired to his canoe and pursued his way down the river Undoubtedly the Indian had come with the intention of girdling the trees of whose fruit his own tribe had, perhaps, eaten for half a century or more, but which had fallen into the possession of strangers and enemies, who, he imagined, desecrated by their presence the resting-place of his fathers.

tea-pot. Instead of tea-cups and saucers a wooden bowl was filled with the savory beverage and passed around in a cosmopolitan, if inelegant way. But who shall contrast with disparagement to the former the social cheer which prevailed at that feast, with that which is evoked by similar gatherings in modern times.

Until 1797, when Nathan Lane built the first grist mill in the town, the settlers were obliged, at first, to go more than forty miles with their grists to mill, but somewhat later, and previous to the erection of Lane's mill, one was built about ten miles east of Deposit, which lessened the distance about one-half. Shortly previous, or soon after, (which the memory of old residents does not satisfactorily determine,) the erection of the saw mill by Mr. Lane, the same year in which his grist mill was built, a saw mill was built by Mr. Doolittle Amraphael Hotchkiss built the first mills upon the Susquehanna.* David Hotchkiss built the first frame barn.

Frederick Goodell was an early settler. He came from Conn., in 1787, and settled about three miles above Windsor, on the river. In 1798 he moved to that part of the town known as Randolph, which was then a wilderness, and cleared a farm and raised a family, some of whom still reside in the town. Lyman and Henry Beebe came with their father from Wilkesbarre, Penn., May 9, 1803, and settled on the Susquehanna about one mile north of the State line. Lyman Beebe was five years old the day on which he moved into the town. He has since resided within a mile of his present residence. Luman Blatchley came with his son, Neri, and two daughters from Conn., in 1806, and located at Randolph. Soon after his brother, Daniel Blatchley Jr., settled at Hazardville. Jehiel Woodruff was one of the first settlers in the west part of the town. He came with a family of six children, (three of whom still live in the town,) from Long Island, in 1811. On the Randolph hills, around Oquaga, were extensive groves of locusts, so valuable in ship building. Great quantities of this timber were carried to Deposit and thence conveyed in rafts down the Delaware to Philadelphia. The Randolph hills locust had a high reputation, and was found in many of the principal sea-ports east of Philadelphia.†

The first birth in the town was that of David Doolittle, Dec. 27, 1786; the first marriage, that of Capt. Andrew English and Miss Rachel Moore; and the first death, that of Mrs. Ashley, the interpreter accompanying Rev. Mr. Hawley in his

* Annals of Binghamton, p. 152
† Spafford's Gazetteer of New York, in 1812, page 330-1.

mission to Oquaga, in August, 1757, as before stated. The first death among the permanent settlers was probably that of Mrs. Rhoda Goodell, wife of Frederick Goodell, in 1803.* Josiah Stow opened the first inn and store, in 1788; and Stephen Seymour taught the first school in 1789.

The first settlement at Randolph Center was made by Capt. Samuel Rexford, and family, in 1782. He settled on one hundred acres of land given him as an inducement to locate there. He built a log house and covered it with bark, and grappled manfully with the hardships and privations incident to the opening of a new country. Joseph Brown settled there in 1812, and still resides there.

Windsor may point with just pride to the record of her participation in the war of the Rebellion. She did her duty nobly. The town furnished 237 men for the army, and, as far as we have been able to ascertain, they were distributed as follows:

In Company G † 89th Regt. N. Y. S Vols ................ . ......97
    "    "    B  137th  "     "    . .. ............ .. 41
    "    "    F. 137th  "     "    .. ... . .. ... 16
    " other Co.'s of 137th  "     "    . ............... ...... 16
    ." other regiments  ........ .. ... .... .. ..... .. .. .....67
Of this number thirty-five are reported killed, wounded or missing

The first church (Cong.) was organized by Rev. Mr. Judd, Aug. 15. 1793.

The *Union Chapel* (M. E.) society, located at East Randolph, was organized with six members, in 1803, by J. Herron, Samuel

---

*Statement of E. Goodell of this town.

† We have been furnished the following interesting particulars relative to this company: It was organized in the fall of 1861, by Capt. Seymour L. Judd,‡ its commandant, and mustered in for three years. It left Elmira with the regiment, Dec. 5, 1861, for Washington, and one month later, having been assigned to the Burnside Expedition to North Carolina, was out on the ocean. In August, 1862, it came north to re-inforce McClellan after his defeat near Richmond. It participated, and suffered severely, in the battles of South Mountain and Antietam. At Fredericksburgh, in Dec., 1862, it was among the first to cross the river and captured the sharp shooters who prevented the laying of the pontoons. At Suffolk the 89th crossed the Nansemond and captured a rebel fort, with all its cannon and men. The regiment was with Gen Dix on the "blackberry raid" at the time of the battle of Gettysburg. It next went to the assistance of Gen. Gilmore, who soon after took Fort Waggoner and battered down Sumter. The next spring it returned north and formed a part of Gen Butler's James River expedition At Bermuda Hundreds those whose term of service expired were mustered out, while those who re-enlisted in this company, remained with the regiment until it was mustered out. The dead of this company sleep at Hatteras, Roanoke Island, South Mountain, Antietam, Fredericksburg, Suffolk, Folly Island, Bermuda Hundreds, in front of Petersburg and at Chapins Farm.

‡ Capt Judd's rank dated from Oct 31, 1861, and his commission, Dec 18, 1861 He resigned Oct 1, 1862, and was re-commissioned Nov. 7, 1862 He died at Fortress Monroe, Aug 27, 1864, of wounds received in action before Petersburg, June 15, 1864

Budd and John P. Weaver. Its first pastors were Revs. Dunham and Leach; the present pastor is Rev. L. F. Ketchum. Their church edifice, which will seat 250 persons, was erected in 1865, at a cost of $500. There are forty-two members. The Church property is valued at $600.

The *M. E. Church*, at East Windsor, was organized with seven members, in 1812, by Revs Nathaniel Reader and Nathan Dodson, its first pastors. Their house of worship was erected in 1852, at a cost of $600. It will seat 200 persons. The present number of members is twenty-five; the present pastor, Rev. C. D. Shepard. The Church property is valued at $1,000.

The *Windsor Baptist Church*, at Randolph Center, was organized with twenty-eight members, by a council composed of representatives from the churches of Chenango, Colesville and Great Bend, Sept. 20, 1838. Their first house of worship was purchased in 1850, and sold in 1866; the present one, which will seat 275 persons, was erected in 1867, at a cost of $1,500. There are fifty-seven members, and though there is at present no settled pastor the pulpit is regularly supplied each Sabbath. The Church property is valued at $2,000. The first pastor was Rev. Abiah P. Worden.

The *Zion Episcopal Church*, at Windsor, was organized with five members, by Rev. Dr. Van Ingan, in 1842. The church edifice, which will seat 150 persons, was erected in 1863, at a cost of $1,600. The first pastor was Rev. James Keeler; the present one is Rev. Wm Roberts. There are thirty-five members. The value of Church property is $5,000.

The *First Wesleyan Church of Windsor*, located at Hazardville, was organized with eight members, in 1843, by Rev. D. E. Baker, its first pastor. The church edifice was erected in 1860. It cost $800, and will seat 250 persons. It has a membership of twenty-seven. Rev. Seth Burgess is the present pastor. The Church property is valued at $1,400.

The *East Randolph Wesleyan M. E. Church* was organized with sixteen members, by Rev. D. E Baker, its first pastor, in 1844. The church edifice, which was erected in 1865, and is designated *Union Chapel*, will seat 250 persons. It cost $500. The present value of Church property is $600. Rev. Seth Burgess is the pastor; and the number of members, thirty-seven.

The *Christian Advent Church*, located at Wilmot Settlement, was organized with ten members, in 1867, by Rev. C. F. Sweet, its first pastor. The church will seat 100 persons. It was erected in 1868, at a cost of $1,000. The present value of Church property is $1,200. There are twenty members. The pulpit is supplied by Rev. E. C. Cowles and J. W. Taylor.

The *First Free M. E. Church,* located at Windsor, was organized with ten members, in 1867, by Rev. Wm. Gould, its first pastor. The house of worship was purchased from the Baptist Society in 1866, for $2,000. It will seat 300 persons. Rev. Wm. Jones is the pastor. The number of members is thirty-six. The Church property is valued at $3,500.

# TIOGA COUNTY.

*TIOGA\* COUNTY* was formed from Montgomery, Feb. 16, 1791. Broome was taken off March 28, 1806; Chemung, March 29, 1836; a part of Chenango, March 15, 1798; and a part of Tompkins, March 22, 1822. A part of Broome was re-annexed in 1822. It lies a little west of the center of the south border of the State, centrally distant 135 miles from Albany, and contains 542 square miles. Its surface is broken by the prolongation of the Allegany Mountains, which extend in a series of ridges northerly through the county, and whose summits attain a nearly uniform elevation of 1,200 to 1,400 feet above tide. These ridges are cut diagonally by the valley of the Susquehanna, and are separated by numerous lateral valleys which extend in a north and south direction and give a great

---

\* Tioga is written in Mr. Morgan's work, *The League of the Iroquois,* in the Oneida dialect, *Te-ah-o-ge,* the Mohawk, *Te-yo-ge-ga;* the Cayuga, *Da-a-o-ga;* and Seneca, *Da-ya-o-geh,* meaning "at the forks." In the text of his work it is written, *Ta-ya-o-ga,* the first *a* having the broad sound as in *fall.* Upon Guy Johnson's map of 1771, it is written *Ti-a-o-ga.* The eloquent Red Jacket pronounced it *Tah-hiho-gah,* discarding the suffix, "Point," which has been universally added when applied to the locality now called Athens, saying that the Indian word carried the full meaning—"the point of land at the confluence of two streams," or "the meeting of the waters."

variety of feature to the surface. The width of these valleys varies from a few rods to a mile and sometimes more. They are generally defined by steep acclivities which rise from 250 to 400 feet above them, and whose summits are commonly broad and rolling, though occasionally broken and rocky.

The rocks of the County belong to the Chemung and Catskill groups. All the rocks cropping out upon the surface north of the river, and those underlying the hills south of it, may be classed in the former group; and those crowning the summits of the hills south of the river, with the latter. Except the sandstone of the Chemung group, which is quarried for flagging; the red sandstone of the Catskill group, some of which is sufficiently compact to make good building stone; and limestone, from which lime is manufactured and which is found along the Pennsylvania border, there are no important minerals. A deep drift, consisting of sand, clay and gravel, lies in the valleys and covers the adjoining hills. This deposit near Factoryville is eighty feet deep, and a wide belt of it seems to extend north, in an almost unbroken line, from that place to Cayuga Lake.

The principal streams are Susquehanna* River, and Owego,† Catatunk, Cayuta, Pipe and Apalachin creeks, with their branches. These streams have, generally, rapid currents, though few waterfalls; and they furnish all necessary water power for local purposes. Their valleys are generally narrow and rocky in their upper courses, but toward the Susquehanna they expand into broad and beautiful level intervales.

The *Susquehanna* enters the county a little south of the center of the east border of the town of Owego and extends in a south-westerly direction through the south part of the County,

---

* See page 63 for origin of name.

† Owego was pronounced by the Indians who frequented this section, *Ah-wah-gah*, with the accent on the second syllable. In "Morgan's League" it is spelled *Ah-wa-ga*, the *a* in the second syllable being pronounced as in the word *fate* Upon Guy Johnson's map of 1771, it is written *O-we-gy*; it is also so written on the map accompanying the treaty of 1768, at Fort Stanwix; but in the deed of cession, drawn at the same time, it is spelled *Os-we-gy*, showing conclusive inaccuracy, probably, in both.
By the early settlers it was pronounced *O-wa-go*, the *a* being pronounced as in *fate*. In a document of 1791, and letters written in 1799, 1801, and as late as 1805, it is so written. Mrs. Whitaker, who was acquainted with the locality of Owego village during her captivity with the Indians, and became a resident in its immediate vicinity previous to, or about the time of the extinguishment of the Indian claim, has given sanction to the last orthography It signifies—"Where the valley widens." The narrows, below and above upon the river, and also upon the creek, about two miles from its mouth, to which this name was also given, render that meaning peculiarly significant as applied to this extended valley or basin, the outlet to which, on all sides, is through narrow gorges or passes.—*The Saint Nicholas, March*, 1854, *p*. 411.

passing in its course through the town and village of Owego, forming the boundary between the towns of Nichols and Tioga on the north, and Barton on the west, and leaves the County on the south line, between Barton and Nichols.

*Owego Creek* takes its rise by its east branch in Virgil, Cortland Co., and, its west branch in Dryden, Tompkins Co. The east and west branches flow south, the former centrally through the towns of Richford, (on the north line of which it enters the county) Berkshire and Newark Valley, and across the northwest corner of the town of Owego, to its confluence with the west branch, which enters the county on the north line of Richford, and forms the boundary between that town, Berkshire, Newark Valley and a small portion of Owego on the east, and Candor and Caroline (Tompkins Co.) on the west. They unite about five miles north of Owego village, and form the boundary, below their junction, between the town of Owego to the north line of Owego village and of Owego village to the Susquehanna, (into which they empty) on the east and the town of Tioga and a part of the town of Candor, on the west.

*Catatunk Creek* rises in the south part of Tompkins county, enters this county on the north line of Spencer and flows in a south-east direction through that town, Candor, and across the north-east corner of the town of Tioga. It empties into Owego Creek from the west about equi-distant from the mouth of the latter stream and the confluence of its two branches.

*Cayuta Creek* rises in Cayuta Lake (Schuyler Co.) and enters this county from Chemung county in the north-west corner of the town of Barton, forming, for a short distance, the boundary between that town and Van Etten, in the latter county, and flowing in a southerly direction through the west part of Barton it leaves the county on the south line of that town a little east of Waverly.

*Pipe Creek* rises in Barton and flowing diagonally across Tioga empties into the Susquehanna at Tioga Center.

*Apalachin Creek* rises in the town of Apalachin, Susquehanna Co., Penn., and flows north through the south-east part of the town of Owego, near the south-east corner of which it enters the county, and empties into the Susquehanna a little southeast of Apalachin Corners.

The soil along the valleys is a deep, rich, gravelly loam, with an occasional intermixture of clay and sand. The intervales along the Susquehanna are especially noted for their fertility. The uplands are gravelly and sandy and moderately fertile. Upon the summits the soil is hard and unproductive, and in many places the rocks are entirely bare. A considerable portion of the uplands is still covered with forests. Since the removal of the most valuable timber and the consequent decline of the lumber and tanning business, the attention of the people is mainly directed to agricultural pursuits and a good degree of success is exhibited in its various branches. The cereals and root crops are mostly cultivated on the lowlands, or valleys of the streams, and the uplands are devoted to stock raising, wool growing and dairying. The opening of the railroads has developed considerable commercial interest, and a stronger disposition to engage in manufacturing enterprises is manifested along the line of these thoroughfares.

*The County Seat* is located at Owego, where, since the erection of Chemung county in 1836, the courts have been held. By the organic act of 1791, Tioga was constituted a half-shire county, and it was provided that courts should be held alternately at "Chenango" (now Binghamton) and "Newtown Point" (now Elmira.) Upon the organization of Broome County in 1806, the half-shire was abolished, and in 1811–12 the court house was removed from Elmira to Spencer village, in conformity with the decision of a committee* appointed Feb. 17, 1810, to select a site for a new court house and superintend the erection of the building. The County was divided into two jury districts June 8, 1812, and the courts were held at Elmira and Spencer.† In 1821 the court house at Spencer was burned, and in 1822, by an act of the Legislature, the half-shire system was re-established and Elmira and Owego were made the half-shire towns. In 1836 Chemung county was erected from Tioga, and Elmira then became the county seat of the former county, and Owego, of the latter.‡ The court house, a wooden structure, was erected about fifty-two years since, at a cost of $8,000, on ground donated for a public square by James McMaster, the patentee. The jail, jailor's house and barn, all of brick, were built in 1851, at a cost of about $6.000. The jail contains eight double cells. The clerk's office is a fire-proof building, and was erected in 1855, at a cost of $2,200. All these buildings occupy a square in

---

* This committee consisted of Nathaniel Locke, Anson Cary and Samuel Campbell.

†The East Jury District embraced the towns of Berkshire, Candor, Caroline, Danby, (the two latter now in Tompkins Co.) Owego, Spencer and Tioga; and the West, those of Cayuta, Catharine, Chemung and Elmira, the two former being now in Schuyler county, and the latter two, in Chemung.

‡The first county officers were Abram Miller, *First Judge;* Wm. Stuart, *District Attorney*, Thomas Nicholson, *County Clerk;* James McMaster, *Sheriff;* and John Mersereau, *Surrogate.*

the center of the village. The present court house and clerk's office being deemed inadequate to satisfactorily meet the requirements of the business transacted in them, at a special session of the Board of Supervisors in 1870–71 it was resolved to erect a new court house and clerk's office, on grounds deeded to the County for that purpose by the village of Owego, Feb. 1, 1871, and an appropriation of $30,000 was made for that purpose March 21, 1871.*

*The County Poor House,* a stone building, is located three miles from Owego, upon a farm of sixty-five acres. The number of persons relieved and supported in 1871 was 194, at an average expense per week of $1.64¼. The present (July, 1872,) number of inmates is forty. The average number is about fifty.

The principal works of internal improvement are the N. Y. & Erie R. R.,† which extends through the south part of the County, along the north bank of the Susquehanna, and passes through the towns of Owego, Tioga and Barton; the Cayuga Division of the Delaware, Lackawanna & Western R. R.,‡ which

---

* The building committee consisted of D. M. Pitcher, John J. Taylor and Lucien Horton. H. A. Beebe was subsequently substituted for Mr. Taylor. The plans submitted by Miles F. Howes, architect of Owego, were adopted Feb. 3, 1871, and the bid of Messrs. Keeler & Houk, of Owego, for the construction of the building, was accepted March 21, 1871. The latter gentlemen contracted to erect the building according to the original plans and specifications for $55,700.
The building is located in the center of the public square. It is built of brick, trimmed with cut Onondaga limestone, in a style of architecture combining the Grecian and modern styles It is 70 by 90 feet on the ground The height of the main building is 46 feet. It is inclosed with Mansard roof. There are four towers, two of which are 120 feet in height, and the other two, 100 feet. It has two main fronts, ornamented with beautiful cut stone porticos, one on Main, and the other on Front street. On the lower floor, on the west side of the main hall, are the offices of the District Attorney and Sheriff and the grand jury room; and on the east side, are the Surrogate's and County Clerk's offices, the latter being fire-proof. Up stairs are the court room, (48 by 56 feet) ladies' witness room, library and two jury rooms. The contract provides for the completion of the work by Nov. 1, 1872. When finished the building will cost about $65,000, and will be an ornament to the village and a credit to those having its construction in charge.

† A further description of this road will be found on page 68.

‡ This road was originally known as the Ithaca & Owego R. R , and was chartered Jan. 28, 1828—the second railroad charter granted in the State. The road was opened in April, 1834. At Ithaca was an inclined plane with a rise of one foot in every 4 28-100 feet, up which the cars were drawn by means of a stationary steam engine. Above this was another inclined plane, which rose one foot in twenty-one feet, on which horse power was used. The road was subsequently sold by the Comptroller on stock issued by the State, on which the company failed to pay interest A new company was organized and the name of Cayuga & Susquehanna R. R. was assumed April 18, 1843. The road was reconstructed, the inclined planes being done away with. In 1852 it was sold for $4,500, the sum of $500,000 having been expended in its construction. Jan 1, 1855, it was leased to the

has its northern terminus at Ithaca pier, and enters this County from Tompkins, on the north line of Candor, passing through that town and Tioga to Owego village, where it connects with the Erie road; the Southern Central R. R., which has its northern terminus at Fair Haven, (Little Sodus) on the shore of Lake Ontario, enters this county from Cortland, on the north line of Richford, and extends along the valley of the east branch of Owego Creek, passing through Richford, Berkshire, Newark Valley and Owego, to Owego Village, when it diverges to the west, and, following the course of the Susquehanna, passes through Tioga and Barton, and thence into Pennsylvania; and the Ithaca & Athens R. R., whose name indicates its termini, which enters the county from Tompkins, on the north line of Spencer, and runs south to a little south of Spencer village, where it deflects to the west, and passes into Chemung county, where it again turns south and enters the county at the north-west corner of Barton, passing through that town along the valley of Cayuta Creek, and leaving the county on the south line of that town, at Factoryville. Few counties in the State possess railroad facilities superior, or even equal to those enjoyed by this county. Every town in the county except Nichols is traversed by one or more railroads, and that town is in such close proximity to the Erie and Southern Central roads, from which it is separated by the Susquehanna, that the absence of any road is measurably compensated thereby. These roads afford ample facilities for the transportation of the products of the farm and manufactory, and open an inviting field for the prosecution of mechanical enterprises.

There are seven newspapers published in the County, all weeklies.

THE OWEGO GAZETTE was commenced by Judge Stephen Mack, in 1803,[*] at Owego, as *The American Farmer*, the first paper published in Tioga County, and was published on the north side of Front street, near Church. In 1813 it was purchased by Hon. Stephen B. Leonard,[†] who changed its name to that it now bears, and the place of publication to the the north side of Front street, near Paige. Mr. Leonard subsequently admitted J. B. Shurtleff as a partner, but in what

---

Delaware, Lackawanna & Western R R Co., by whom it is still operated as the Cayuga Division This is an important route from the coal mines of Pennsylvania and coal forms the principal item of business.

[*] Dr. C. J. Seymour of Binghamton has in his possession a copy dated Wednesday, March 18, 1807, (No. 188, or Vol. IV., No. 31) which shows the above date to be correct.

[†] Mr. Leonard was originally from New York, from which place he went to Albany, where he worked two years as a journeyman printer, when he removed to Owego, where he still resides, aged over eighty years.

year we have been unable to ascertain,* and it was published by
Leonard & Shurtleff. In 1835 Mr. Shurtleff purchased Mr.
Leonard's interest. At this time it was published on the south
side of Front street, in the second story of the first building
above the bridge crossing the Susquehanna River. In 1841,
the office was burned and the paper was soon after continued
by Edward P. Marble, "in the second story of Judge Drake's
new building, corner of Lake and Front streets." In 1842 it was
sold to Thomas Woods, who, in 1843, sold it to Hiram A. Beebe,
by whom it was again sold in 1845 to Thomas Pearsall, and by Mr.
Pearsall, in 1846, to David Wallis & Son, who kept it one
year, when it was again, in 1847, purchased by Mr. Beebe. The
office was again burned in September, 1849, when Mr. Beebe
removed the paper to the west side of Ithaca Street, (now North
Avenue,) opposite the Tioga House (since demolished.) The
premises on Front street were rebuilt by Isaac Lillie, and Mr.
Beebe returned to his old location in July, 1850, and remained
until May, 1853, when he moved to the third story of the building on the west side of Lake street, owned by T. P. Patch. In
January, 1867, Mr. Beebe completed a three-story brick building on the opposite side of the street, (now known as "Gazette
Block,") into which he moved and where the paper is now
published   August 1, 1871, L. W Kingman purchased a half
interest in the paper, which is now published by the firm of
Beebe & Kingman. It is a weekly and in politics has always
been Democratic, and generally, as at the present time, has been
the only Democratic paper in the county.

THE OWEGO TIMES, weekly, was started as *The Owego Advertiser* in 1835, by Andrew H. Calhoun, who published it until
1853, when he sold it to an association of some twelve persons
of Owego, (of whom the present proprietor was one) by whom
it was leased for one year to Powell & Barnes, and its name was
changed by the latter gentlemen to *The Owego Southern Tier
Times*. In 1854 Wm. Smyth purchased the interest of the other
parties comprising the association and changed the name to
that it now bears, under which name he conducted it alone
until May, 1872, when his son, Wm A Smyth, became a partner, since which time it has been published under the firm name
of Wm. Smyth & Son.

The TIOGA COUNTY RECORD, weekly, was started at Owego,
by C. H. Keeler, March 18, 1871, and is still published by him.

---

* The present publishers have copies dated Oct 23, 1827, and Nov. 13, 1827,
published by Leonard & Shurtleff, showing that the latter's connection
with the paper dates as early as 1827.

The AHWAGA CHIEF, weekly, was started at Owego, by Horace A. Brooks, Feb. 23, 1872, and is still published by him.

The WAVERLY ADVOCATE, weekly, was started as the *Waverly Luminary*, in 1859, by Thomas Messenger, who published it about two years, when it was discontinued by foreclosure of mortgage. It was resuscitated in 1852, by F. H. Baldwin, who changed its name to the *Waverly Advocate* and published it one year, when he sold it to M. H. Bailey, who continued it about one year and sold it to Wm. Polleys. F. H. Baldwin purchased an interest with Mr. Polleys, and it was published by Baldwin & Polleys until Dec. 1, 1869, when O. H. P. Kinney purchased Mr. Baldwin's interest, and the firm became Polleys & Kinney, who still continue its publication.

The WAVERLY ENTERPRISE, weekly, was started as a semi-monthly, in 1866, by F. T. Scudder, who still continues its publication. Jan 1, 1870, it was changed from a semi-monthly to a weekly.

The CANDOR FREE PRESS was established in 1867.*

The first settlements were made soon after the Revolution, by emigrants from New England, principally from Connecticut and Massachusetts, in the east part of the County, upon the fertile intervales of the Susquehanna and Owego Creek, under the inspiration of the Boston Company. All that part of the County lying east of the west branch of Owego Creek and north of Coxe's Patent, which extended west of Owego, is embraced in the "Boston Ten Townships."† While settlements were being made in the east part by persons coming directly from

---

* We have been furnished with no data from which to compile a history of this paper

The following is a list of defunct publications which have been issued in this County:

*The Republican* was commenced at Owego in 1833, by —— Chatterton, who published it one year.

*The Saint Nicholas*, a monthly literary magazine, was commenced at Owego in 1853, and published at the *Gazette* office about one year.

*The Tioga and Bradford Democrat* was started at Waverly, by F H Baldwin, in 1864, and was published by him about one year, when he removed it to Corry, Penn

*The Waverly and Athens Democrat* was started at Waverly, in 1867, by S C Clizbe, who, after publishing it about six months, sold it to D. P. Shultz, by whom it was published two years and then discontinued.

*The Owego Trade Reporter* was started at Owego in March, 1868, by C. H Keeler, who published it until March, 1871. It was a monthly issue devoted to advertising and news.

† For further particulars relative to the "Massachusetts Purchase" we refer the reader to page 73. The early history of this County is so intimately connected with that of Broome, which was formerly embraced within its limits, that, to avoid repetition, the reader is referred to the history of the latter County for information relevant to both, especially as regards the settlement of this purchase

New England, the western part was being settled by the same class of people, who had previously settled in the beautiful and inviting, but ill-starred valley of the Wyoming, which they reluctantly left in consequence of the troubles growing out of the Indian hostilities and the conflicting claims of the Connecticut and Pennsylvania governments for the territory it embraced, by which the tenure of their lands was rendered uncertain and their occupation unsafe. They fled with dismay and disappointment from the accumulating perils of the home of their choice to accept the little less inviting ones offered by old Tioga, where at least they were free from the perplexities in which the controversies in regard to titles involved their former homes.

The following extract from an article written by C. P. Avery, entitled *The Susquehanna Valley,* and which appeared in *The Saint Nicholas* for March, 1854, well illustrates the uncommon ties by which these hardy and heroic pioneers were bound to the Wyoming country.

"The 'farewell' to Wyoming must have been painful indeed. She had been not only redeemed from the wilderness by the honest industry of their fathers, brothers, relatives and neighbors from Connecticut, but enriched by their blood which had flowed freely upon many sanguinary fields. They had stood as a frontier breastwork during the whole of the Revolutionary war against the incursions of the common enemy ; and in that grand carnival of slaughter, of July, 1778, Wyoming became a valley of death, and the chivalrous spirits who relinquished all to serve the Republic, and whose memories the storied monument now perpetuates— thanks to the noble hearted ladies of the valley by whose energy it was reared—were the near relatives or intimate friends of the exiles. The 'farewell' to Wyoming must have been painful indeed."

Wyoming's loss was Tioga's substantial gain. These settlers, undaunted by former reverses, entered with commendable zeal into the transformation of the wilderness into which their lot was cast into broad and fertile farms, assimilating those so recently abandoned by them. They have left the impress of their works upon the soil their energy and industry have consecrated, and of their characters upon the lives of those who succeed them. In the sons are discernible the evidences of hardy toil and habits of frugality in which the fathers were nurtured ; and no better legacy could be transmitted by parent to child.

Evidences of the occupancy of the country comprised within the limits of this County, by the Indians, prior to its settlement by the whites, either as favorite hunting grounds, or for long continued residence, are found in the many articles of handicraft and use belonging to them, which have been discovered by the plow and other means of excavating. A tree was found by the early settlers at Newark Valley upon the blaze of which were painted certain pictures, which were supposed to be a means by which the aborigines communicated their ideas, and to belong to their system of picture writing. "One of these figures," says C. P. Avery, " well remembered by several now living, was an accurate representation of an Indian in full costume for war, facing southerly with tomahawk uplifted. It was put on in durable black paint, continuing for many years after the valley was first settled. It dated back quite probably to the Revolutionary era, and as was customary with parties upon the war-path, was placed there, not unlikely, to indicate to other bands who might follow, the course which the one in advance pursued. There were other painted marks and figures upon the same tree which have not been accurately remembered, but very likely elucidated some important facts connected with the expedition, as to the strength, tribe and destination of the party. A specimen of emblematic or picture writing was also found at an early day upon a tree at Chocomut, somewhat similar in character, but much more complex and enigmatical. Its meaning, even by conjecture, has never yet transpired "

On the river plain between Owego and Athens lived a number of Indians for a length of time after its settlement by the whites, who demanded from the latter, for their land, for three or four years after the first settlement, a yearly rent, which they expected to be paid in corn. Their chief was designated Captain John. They maintained a semblance of amity toward the whites, being pleased to have them eat with them and appearing offended with a refusal. When they begged something to eat, instead of expressing their wishes in words, they placed their hand first on their stomach and then to their mouth. It was their custom when attended with ill success to eat a root which created sickness and vomiting, and which, they supposed, was efficacious in restoring them to more auspicious circumstances.

A few years after the country was first settled an extensive and serious famine prevailed which was felt most severely in the region of country lying between Owego and Elmira. For six weeks or more the inhabitants were entirely without bread or its kind. The famine occurred immediately before harvest time and was supposed to result from the unusual large number of new settlers, and the great scarcity which prevailed in Wyoming that season. During its prevalency the "people were languid in their movements, irresolute and feeble in what they undertook, emaciated and gaunt in their appearance." Wild beans, which were found in considerable quantities, and the most nutritious roots were substituted for more substantial food. "As soon as their rye was in the milk, it was seized upon, and by drying it over a moderate fire, until the grain acquired some consistency, they were enabled to pound it into a sort of meal, out of which they made *mush*. This was a very great relief, although the process was tedious, and attended with much waste of grain. In the early part of the scarcity, while there was a possibility of finding grain or flour of any kind abroad, instances were not unfrequent of families tearing up their feather beds and sending away the feathers in exchange for bread. Instances also of individuals riding a whole day and not obtaining a *half* of a loaf [are cited.]" Though none died of hunger during this trying period, two young men died in consequence of eating to excess of green rye.*

From this time the section of Susquehanna's beautiful valley embraced within the limits of Tioga attracted many sturdy and active emigrants from the comparative luxury of their eastern homes to grapple with the temporary hardships and privations incident to the settlement of a new country. A steady and healthy growth has been maintained; and though Tioga cannot point to any gigantic commercial or mechanical enterprise within her borders, she can, with just pride, refer the stranger to the no less gratifying evidences of wealth, prosperity and contentment exhibited by the tillers of the soil, who have supplemented nature by improving an already beautiful country and transformed it from its pristine wildness to the productive and attractive farm lands which adorn its gentle slopes. If we do not hear the busy hum of mechanical industry as it greets us in large and populous cities and villages, neither do we see nor deplore the disparaging contrasts between affluence and poverty which the latter picture invariably presents. Here all are producers, and the wealth of the country is more uniformly distributed. While few have an excessive abundance of this world's goods, few also are driven to a position of dependency. Founded on this substantial basis of prosperity Tioga's future progress is assured.

The excessive stringency of pioneer life was gradually ameliorated by the introduction of public improvements as the influx of settlers rendered them necessary and possible. Public roads were opened, bridges erected and better means of conveyance than the early rough state of the country rendered serviceable were introduced. Mills were erected by private capital and individual enterprise. These improvements not only vastly mitigated the severities experienced by the early settlers in reclaiming this wilderness to the uses of civilization; but

*Annals of Binghamton.*
K

tended also to attract to it others who were looking for eligible homes in the west, as this country was then considered.

The issuing of the first commission to lay out the road leading from Catskill Landing on the Hudson to the town of Catharines, in Tompkins county, but then in Tioga, in 1797, may be considered the first effort at internal improvement directly benefiting this locality. This, with the projection of other avenues of travel by the construction at various times of highways and railroads, opened up new sections of the county to immigration.

Previous to 1793, in which year Col. Pixley erected his mill at Owego, there was no grist mill in the county. The early settlers of Owego, in 1788, found no mill nearer than Wilkesbarre, Penn.,[*] and thither they conveyed their grain in canoes down the Susquehanna, until 1790, in which year Jonathan Fitch built his grist mill.[†] In 1792 Mr. Fitch established a grist mill at Nanticoke, (Broome Co.) and until 1793, the settlers carried their grists to that point. What a striking contrast is presented between that time and the present! The laborious process of conveying the products of the farm to the mill or market by means of canoes, or over roads, whose passage at the present day would be pronounced impracticable, is now unknown. The agents which the genius of man has made subservient to his use do the work in less time than was formerly necessary to make preparation for the journey, which occupied, not unfrequently, two or more weeks.

A good index of comparative values is found in the prices of real estate at certain periods, and as this indicates with a good degree of certainty, the degree of prosperity which any particular locality has enjoyed, we append the following copy of the first deed recorded in the Clerk's office of Tioga county, believing that, although the tract to which it refers is not now in this county, since it was embraced in its original limits, and is, perhaps, equally pertinent to the idea we wish to illustrate it will be both interesting and instructive.

"MEMO'D　　　　　　Annis & Warren
"THIS INDENTURE made this twenty second day of June in the year of our Lord one thousand seven hundred and ninety one, and in the fifteenth year of the Independence of the United States of America, WITNESSETH that I Charles Annis of the county of Tioga and State of New York Yeoman have bargained sold and do by these presents Bargain and sell unto Enoch Warren, James Warren & Bessie Warren of the county and State aforesaid, for and in consideration of two hundred and thirty pounds to me in hand paid, the receipt whereof I do acknowledge to have received to my full satisfaction and contentment, all that Santain Lot of Land sit-

[*] *The Saint Nicholas*, March 1854.
[†] See page 116 for further mention of Fitch's mill.

uate in the township of Chemung and State and county aforesaid, No 9 Beginning at a large swamp white oak tree marked with three notches, and a blaze on three sides and the letter F. on the north side standing on the north side of the Tioga river, above Chemung narrows so-called being the corner of three Lots and thence runs north one hundred Chains to a small white oak tree marked standing about one Rod north of a brook thence West thirty seven chains to a stake with stones round it, thence South one hundred and six chains, to a Large Black walnut tree marked, standing on the Bank of the said river, thence down the river its several courses to the place of beginning, Containing three hundred and seventy acres· Together with all and singular the rights hereditaments and appurtenances to the same belonging or in any wise appertaining, excepting and reserving to the State aforesaid all Gold and Silver mines, and five acres of every hundred acres of the said tract of Land for Highways

"To have and to hold the above described and bargained premises unto the said Enoch Warren, James Warren and Bessey Warren, their heirs and assigns as a good and indefeasible estate of inheritance forever, and I do by these presents for myself my heirs executors or administrators Warrant and defend the above described premises unto the foresaid Enoch Warren, James Warren & Betse Warren their heirs & assigns for ever, as their Lawful purchased property; in confirmation of which and in Testimony whereof, I have hereunto set my hand and seal day and year above written.

"Signed sealed and Delivered in presents of us Witnesses Enoch Warren Junr. Elijah Buck"

"Charles Anis
"Sarah ⋈ Anis"
   her
   mark

"TIOGA COUNTY S. S. BE IT REMEMBERED, that on this Twenty eighth day of June, 1791, personally appeared before me Brinton Paine Esqr one of the Judges of the Court of Common Pleas for the said County of Tioga, Elijah Buck one of the subscribing Witnesses to the within Indenture, and being by me duly sworn, deposeth and saith, that he saw the within named Charles Annis, and Sarah his wife, sign seal and deliver the within Indenture of Release as their Voluntara act and Deed, for the purposes therein mentioned ; and that he this Deponent, together with Enoch Warren Junr. the other witness signed the same as Witnesses in the presence of each other —I having examined the same, and therein finding no material erasures, or interlineations do therefore allow it to be recorded
Brinton Paine

"Entered in this Register July 9, 1791."

As allusion has been made both in the history of this and Broome county to the Indian Expedition under Gen. Sullivan, it may not be inappropriate, in view of the importance its success bore upon the country embraced within the original limits of Tioga county, to briefly outline its salient features before proceeding with a somewhat minute description of the early settlements under the heads of the several towns.

The country comprised within the original limits of Tioga county may be considered the geographical center of the home of the Iroquois, which lay chiefly in this State and embraced a small portion of Pennsylvania. The territory over which they held lordly sway has been figuratively described as a fan, with the handle, or pivotal point resting at Athens, (formerly Tioga Point) and the radiating arms representing the network of trails which converged at that point—the confluence of the Chemung and Susquehanna rivers—the right extreme resting upon the Hudson, the left, on Lake Erie. From its earliest known history to the time of Sullivan's incursion, the United Confederacy of the Six Nations had successfully resisted every hostile invasion into the Iroquois territory, and in 1688, "carried its victorious arms to the walls of Montreal, in the face of the flower of the French army, whose prowess and chivalry many a battle field of Europe had witnessed." It will be seen then that Sullivan had a powerful, proud and valorous foe to contend with; and it will not appear so surprising that the idea of a large body of men thridding the fastnesses of the wilderness and reducing a stronghold which repeated failures to enter led them to consider impregnable should provoke laughter in these not altogether uncouth savages

At the commencement of the Revolutionary struggle the Six Nations solemnly promised the Colonies to preserve neutrality, but unfortunately for them their accomplished, sagacious though somewhat unscrupulous chief—Brant—listened and yielded to the seductive wiles of the English Baronet, Sir Wm. Johnson, and espoused the cause of the mother country. Anticipating a blow from this formidable enemy upon the exposed western frontier, the Colonial Government contemplated an invasion of the Iroquois territory in the early part of 1778, previous to the Wyoming massacre. Had this measure been acted upon that calamity would have been avoided, but unfortunately other counsels prevailed and the project was deferred. In October of the same year, the public mind having been aroused by that horrible intervening event, strenuous efforts were again made in this direction; but the season for active operations being so far advanced, and circumstances rendering delay unavoidable, it was put off till 1779. The army of Gen. Sullivan, to whom the execution of this project was entrusted, consisted of three divisions: one from New Jersey, under command of Gen. Maxwell; another from New England, under command of Gen. Hand; and the third from New York, under command of Gen. Clinton. The New Jersey and New England divisions marched from Elizabethtown, N. J., via Easton, thence to Wyoming, and up the Susquehanna to Athens. These two divisions, under command of Sullivan, left Wyoming, July 31, 1779, and moved up the east side of the river. They numbered 3,500 men. In transporting the baggage and stores 120 boats and 2,000 horses were employed. The boats were propelled up the stream by soldiers with setting-poles, and were guarded by troops. The provisions for the daily subsistence of the troops were carried by horses, which threaded the narrow Indian path in single file and formed a line about six miles in length. Indians in considerable numbers had collected at Athens on the arrival of the army there, but being apparently awed and dismayed by its formidable appearance they yielded their stronghold with only a few inconsiderable skirmishes. Upon the 22d of August, a few days after the arrival of Sullivan's forces at Athens, they were augmented by those under Clinton, 1,500 in number, making a combined force of 5,000. Clinton collected his forces at Canajoharie, and endeavored to induce the Oneidas and Onondagas, who had not taken an active part against the colonies, to join the expedition. His efforts would doubtless have proved successful, as he at first supposed they were, but for an address, written in the Iroquois language, and sent them by Gen. Haldemand, then Governor of the Canadas, which discouraged all but a few of the Oneidas from sharing in it. Bateaux to the number of 220, which had been constructed the previous winter and spring at Schenectady, were taken up the Mohawk to the place of rendezvous, and from thence were transported by land to Otsego Lake, a distance of twenty miles. Each bateau was of such size that in its transit from the river to the lake four strong horses were required to draw it, and, when placed in the water, was capable of holding from ten to twelve soldiers. About the first of July, Clinton proceeded with his troops to the southern extremity of the lake, and there awaited orders from Gen. Sullivan. In the meantime he constructed a dam across the outlet, in order to make the passage of the river feasible and rapid. He waited through the whole of July for orders from Sullivan, who immediately upon his arrival at Athens dispatched a force of 800 men under Gen. Poor to form a junction with Clinton and with him re-join the main army at that place, but not until the 9th of August was the dam torn away and the flotilla committed to the bosom of the river thus suddenly swollen, and which afforded a current not only sufficiently deep to float the bateaux, but at Oquaga and other places overflowed the river flats, and destroyed many fields of corn belonging to the Indians. The detachment of Sullivan's forces met the troops under Clinton near the mouth of the Choconut, about thirty-five miles from Athens, and returned with them to Athens. What emotions must have swelled the swarthy bosoms of the Iroquois at the sight of this formidable hostile array, which portended to them the devastation of their loved homes and the breaking of the scepter by which they had so long held the supremacy of this vast territory, and coming too in a dry season, on the bosom of a river swollen much beyond its ordinary dimensions, can be better imagined than described. So much was it invested in mystery that little resistance was offered to the advancing foe. The Indians fled from their homes and cultivated fields, in many of which, it is remembered by those who participated in the expedition, corn was growing in abundance and great perfection, or cautiously watched their progress from the neighboring hills. Their consternation was doubtless increased and a spirit of revenge aroused by the sight of the treacherous Oneidas who were induced to join the expedition and act as guides

After the junction between Sullivan's and Clinton's forces was effected the whole army proceeded up the Chemung River *
In the vicinity of Elmira, (authorities differ as to the exact locality) where the Indians under their trusty leader, Brant, had concentrated, a battle was fought, and its issue was hotly contested.† The Indians and Tories (the latter commanded by Col. John Butler, a British officer) combined, numbered 1,500.‡
The field of battle was well and maturely selected by the Mohawk warrior, and evinced the sagacity and military tact with which he is credited. Upon this contest the Indians staked their all. Their success or defeat was to determine whether the invaders should encroach further upon the Iroquois territory or be hurled back with such disaster as they considered their temerity justly merited. Hence they fought with desperation. Driven from the heights they first occupied the Indians made another stand about one and one-half miles further up the river ; but the choice of position could not compensate them for the fearful odds against which they contended. Their valor only served to delay the completion of the bloody contest. At the Narrows, ten or twelve miles above Elmira, they made a final and determinate stand. Thither the victorious army pursued them and though they fought with the desperation of despair they were compelled to make a precipitous retreat. Their loss in killed and wounded was great, while our army lost five or six killed and forty to fifty wounded. Thoroughly defeated and dispirited the Indian and Tory allies did not again invite a general

---

* The crossing of the Susquehanna by those who came by way of Wyoming, and the mouth of the Chemung was effected by fording. At the latter place the water was nearly up to the soldiers' arm-pits, and each was ordered to keep hold of his file-leader's shoulder, that the current might not break their order.—*Annals of Binghamton.*

† Stone, in his *Life of Brant*, says the battle occurred at Elmira. Wilkinson, in his *Annals of Binghamton*, fixes it at a distance of six miles below that place and nearly opposite Wellsburgh. The latter opinion is the one most generally credited by modern writers.

‡ *The Saint Nicholas.* Wilkinson says the forces opposed to Sullivan consisted of 800 Indians and 200 Tories.

engagement, and Sullivan, with little hindrance, penetrated to the Genesee country, destroying in his course villages, orchards and crops  The intrepid Brant did not, however, lose sight of his powerful enemy from the time his warriors sustained their disastrous defeat to the time when the Colonial army retraced its steps, leaving behind it a scene of desolation and woe.  He hovered around it and harassed it by making sudden descents upon its advanced guards and small detatched parties, but kept a safe distance from the main army.  Sad, indeed, must have been the feelings of the defeated savages to witness the destruction of their homes and yet be powerless to prevent it.

The successful completion of the expedition and its happy results to the frontier inhabitants elicited for Sullivan and his army a vote of thanks which was tendered them by Congress.

The following winter, 1779–80, was one of unexampled rigor and was distinguished by the name of *hard winter.*  It must have borne with extreme severity upon the unfortunate Indians whose houses and crops were destroyed.

# GAZETTEER OF TOWNS.

**BARTON** was formed from Tioga, March 23, 1824.  It is the south-west corner town of the County and contains 32,698 acres, of which, according to the census of 1865, 19,894, were improved.  The surface is generally hilly, though a small portion of level land lies along the south border.  The highlands on the west rise abruptly from the valley of Cayuta Creek, and are divided into two ridges by the valley of Ellis Creek.  Their summits are broad and rolling and to some extent covered with forests.  The highest points are 400 to 600 feet above the river. The soil is a rich alluvium in the valleys and a sandy and gravelly loam upon the hills.  A sulphur spring is found on Ellis Creek near the center of the town.

The principal streams are Cayuta and Ellis creeks, both of which are tributary to the Susquehanna, which forms the south part of the east border and divides this town from Nichols. Cayuta Creek enters the town in the north-west corner and runs south through the west part; and Ellis Creek rises in the north part of the town, near North Barton village, and flows south through the center. The Chemung River forms a very small portion of the west border, in the south part.

The Erie R. R. extends through the town near the south border, passing through Barton, Factoryville and Waverly; the Ithaca & Athens R. R., near the west line, along the valley of Cayuta Creek, and connects with the Lehigh Valley road; and the Southern Central runs close to the Erie track to a point a little east of Factoryville, when it turns south into Pennsylvania. These roads cross each other at right angles and afford a ready transit for passengers and goods to points north, south, east and west.

The population of the town in 1870 was 5,087; of whom 4,697 were natives and 390, foreigners; 5,030, white and 57, colored.*

During the year ending Sept. 30, 1871, the town contained nineteen school districts and employed twenty-three teachers. The number of children of school age was 1,518; the number attending school, 1,025; the average attendance, 428; the amount expended for school purposes, $9,501; and the value of school houses and sites, $17,161.

WAVERLY, (p. v.) located in the south-west corner, on the east bank of Chemung River, partly in this State and partly in Pennsylvania, is a station of considerable importance on the Erie and Lehigh Valley railroads, and is distant one mile west of the Ithaca & Athens R. R., with which it is connected by hacks connecting with the trains.† It was incorporated in 1854, and had a population in 1870, of 2,239.‡ It contains six churches, (M. E., Presbyterian, Episcopal, Baptist, Old School Baptist and Catholic) one Union school,§ (public) four hotels,‖

* In 1850 there was only one colored person in the town; in 1860 there were 67.

† A very large freight business is done at this station. For the week ending Aug 20, 1872, there were transferred from the Erie to the Lehigh Valley road 214 cars, or 2,105 tons of freight, and from the latter road to the former 1,185 cars, or 15,047 tons  The total number of cars transferred was 1,399, and the tons of freight 17,152.

‡ Of this number 2,008 were natives and 231, foreigners; 2,192, white and 47, colored.

§ The Union graded school system was adopted in 1871, at which time the academy which formerly existed here was merged into it and is now the academic department of the Union school

‖ A very fine hotel is now in process of erection and will be ready for occupancy in the spring of 1873.

two banks,* (one national and one private) two weekly news-papers, (*Waverly Advocate* and *Waverly Enterprise*) two sash, door and blind factories, one of which manufactures all the parts (wood) needed in the erection of a house, one foundry, two cigar manufactories, a manufactory of mouldings and cornices from plaster paris, one express office, (U. S.) and three public halls, one of which is an opera house. A building is now in process of erection, nearly completed, for the manufacture of boots and shoes on a large scale; and the Cayuta Car Wheel Manufacturing Co. are erecting works south-east of the village for the manufacture of car wheels, and expect to commence operations in the fall of 1872.

FACTORYVILLE, (p. v.) located in the south-west corner and bordering on the east line of Waverly is a station on the Ithaca & Athens railroad. Cayuta Creek runs through the village. It is a very pleasant village of 318 inhabitants.† It contains one church, (Baptist) one dry goods store, two groceries, one hotel, one tannery, one grist mill, one paper mill, two carriage shops, two blacksmith shops, two shoe shops and a sarsaparilla and soda manufactory.

BARTON CITY (Barton p. o.) is situated near the south-east corner, on the Erie and Southern Central railroads, and on the north bank of the Susquehanna, and contains one church, (M. E.) one school, one hotel, five stores, one saw and grist mill and about 160 inhabitants.

BARTON CENTER (p. o.) is, as its name implies, located in the center of the town, and contains one school, one saw mill and about six houses.

NORTH BARTON, (p. o.) located in the north part, near the head waters of Ellis Creek, contains one church, (Union) and one school. It is a hamlet.

BINGHAMS MILLS, (p. o.) named from the father of J. & G. W. Bingham of Waverly, is located a little north of the center of the west border, on Cayuta Creek, and the Ithaca & Athens R. R., and contains one store, one shoe shop, two saw mills, one grist mill and one plaster mill.

---

* The *First National Bank of Waverly* was incorporated Feb. 13, 1864, with a capital of $50,000. The officers are, Howard Elmer, *President*, R. A. Elmer, *Cashier*, O. E. Hart, *Teller*.

The *Waverly Bank* (private) was organized April 1, 1872. The officers are H. T. Herrick, *President*; Geo. Herrick, *Cashier*, H. T. Sawyer, *Teller*.

† Of this number 289 are natives and 29, foreigners; 313, white and 5, colored.—*Census Reports*, 1870.

HALSEY VALLEY (p. o.) is located near the north of the east line, in the town of Tioga, in the history of which a description of it will be found.*

The first settlement was made in 1791, by Ebenezer Ellis and Stephen Mills, near the mouth of Ellis Creek. Both had previously settled in Nichols, the former having come there from Wyoming in 1787. Nearly, if not quite contemporaneous with them was a man named Aikens, who located near Barton City, upon a tract of nine hundred acres which was afterwards purchased by Gilbert Smith. Ezekiel Williams, an early settler, located, on what was subsequently known as the Williams lot; and a family named Curry lived in this town at an early day, but soon removed to Pennsylvania. John Hanna, William Bensley, Luke Saunders and James Swartwood came here at an early day, the former from Wyoming, about 1795. He lived to the age of 101 years. Charles Bingham, Layton Newell, Lyon C. Hedges, Philip Crans, Justus Lyons, John Manhart and —— Reed were pioneers upon Cayuta Creek; and Silas Woolcott, upon Ellis Creek. Geo. W. Buttson settled at Barton City, on the creek which passes through that village and bears his name, and erected there the first saw mill in the town. Gilbert Smith, who formerly lived in Nichols, made a permanent settlement here after his purchase from Aikens, and his name is intimately associated with the early history of the town from the transaction of business connected with extensive land agencies and otherwise.

The *Tioga & Barton Baptist Church*, located near Halsey Valley, was organized with nine members, Feb. 20, 1796, by a delegation, consisting of a portion of its own original members and of the members of the Baptist Church at Chemung, appointed for that purpose. It was organized as the *Baptist Church of*

---

* *The Barton City Steam Saw Mill* is capable of sawing 6,000 feet of lumber per hour; *Barton Center Saw Mill*, 5,000, in the same time; Bingham's Mills (saw and grist) are capable of sawing 6,000 feet of lumber per day, (the grist mill contains three runs of stones,) *Lott's Mills*, (G. W. Lott, prop.,) located on Cayuta Creek and the I & A R R., three and one-half miles south of VanEttenville, is capable of sawing 1,000 feet of lumber per hour; *Reniff & Sons' Saw Mill*, situated on the I. & A. R. R., about eight miles north of Waverly, is capable of sawing 10,000 feet of lumber per day, connected with it is a shingle and lath machine which manufactures from six to seven thousand shingles and from six to ten thousand lath per day, and adjacent to it is a stone quarry owned by the same persons, A. B. Reniff & Sons; *Dean Creek Steam Saw Mill*, located on Dean Creek, about nine miles north of Waverly, contains one circular saw fourteen feet in circumference and is capable of sawing 20,000 feet of lumber per day of twenty-four hours, connected with it is a planing and matching machine which is capable of turning out 11,000 feet of matched and planed stuff in the same length of time; and *Manning's Mill*, situated on the I. & A. R. R. about six miles north of Waverly, is capable of sawing 6,000 feet of lumber per day.

*New Bedford*, but the name of *Tioga* was after substituted for that of *New Bedford*, and in 1847, the name was again changed to that it now bears, to correspond with its location. The first pastor was Rev. David Jayne; at present there is no pastor, the pulpit is supplied by Rev. Ira Thomas. The society worshiped in dwelling and school houses until 1848, in which year the church edifice was erected, at a cost of $800. It has since been repaired and somewhat altered. It will seat 300 persons. There are fifty members. The Church property is valued at $3,500.

The *North Barton M. E. Church* was organized with eighteen members, in 1869. The following year the church edifice, which will seat 160 persons, was erected at a cost of $1,565. The first pastor was Rev. Wm. H. Gavit; the present one is Rev. John B. Davis. The number of members is eighteen. The Church property is valued at $2,000.

The *First Presbyterian Church of Waverly* was organized with twenty-two members, June 8th, 1847, by Revs. Messrs. Thurston, Carr and Bachus, a committee from the Chemung Presbytery. Their house of worship was erected in 1849 and rebuilt in 1860.* Its original cost was $1,500. The present building will seat 400 persons. Rev. Nathaniel Elmer was the first pastor; Rev. W. H. Bates is the present one. There are 170 members. The Church property is valued at $10,000.

**BERKSHIRE** was formed from Tioga, Feb. 12, 1808.† Newark Valley was taken off April 12, 1823, and Richford, April 18, 1831. It lies upon the east border, north of the center of the County, and covers an area of 17,434¼ acres, of which, in 1865, according to the census of that year, 11,125, were improved. The surface is broken by hills, which have a mean elevation of from 1,200 to 1,400 feet above tide; the highest lies east of the center and its declivities are steep. The streams are the east and west branches of Owego Creek, and their tributaries. The former flows south through the center of the town, and the latter forms the west boundary, dividing the town from Candor, and Caroline (Tompkins county.) In the valleys the soil is a sandy and gravelly loam; upon the hills it is a tough clay and hardpan.

---

* This Society contemplates the erection of a new church worth $30,000.

† At the first town meeting held March 1, 1808, the following named officers were elected: John Brown, *Supervisor*; Artemas Ward, *Town Clerk*; Esbon Slosson and Ebenezer Cook, *Assessors*; Henry Moore and Elijah Belcher, *Poormasters*; Noah Lyman, Hart Newell and Leonard Haight, *Commissioners*, Peter Wilson, *Collector* and *Poundmaster*, Jesse Gleason and Adolphus Dwight, *Constables*, Asa Berment, Nathaniel Ford, Asa Leonard, John Berment, Lyman Rawson and Elisha Jenks, *Fence Viewers*; and Joseph Waldo, *Sealer of Weights and Measures.*

In 1870 the town had a population of 1,240.* During the year ending Sept. 30, 1871, it contained six school districts and employed seven teachers. The number of children of school age was 418; the number attending school, 361; the average attendance, 207; the amount expended for school purposes, $2,955; and the value of school houses and sites, $3,450.

The Southern Central R. R. crosses the town, following the general course of the East Branch of Owego Creek, which stream it crosses near the center of the town. This road opens an easy communication with Owego, the County seat, and the Erie R. R., with which it connects at that point, on the south, and Auburn and intermediate places and the N. Y. C. R. R. on the north.

BERKSHIRE (p. v.) is centrally located on the west bank of the East Branch of Owego Creek, and on the S. C. R. R. It contains two churches, (Presbyterian and M. E.) one hotel, one school, four stores, one grist mill, one saw mill, one tannery, an ax factory, a rake factory, two blacksmith shops, one carriage shop and about 125 inhabitants.

EAST BERKSHIRE (p. o.) lies in the east part, a little north of the center, and contains three houses, in one of which the postoffice is kept.

WILSON CREEK (p. o.) lies in the south part, east of the center, three miles south-west of East Berkshire. There is no considerable settlement, the houses being about eighty rods apart. The postoffice is kept in a private house.

*Brookside Seminary*, located about one mile north of Berkshire, was founded by Rev. Wm. Bradford of the *New York Evangelist*. No school has been kept here since the Rebellion.

The first settlers were Daniel Ball and Isaac Brown, who, in company with Elisha Wilson and others, emigrated from Stockbridge, Mass., in 1791. Wilson settled in Newark Valley.† Ball settled on the farm subsequently occupied by Barnabas Manning; and Brown about two miles south of Berkshire, where his son, Isaac Brown, Jr., is now living. Mr. Ball lived but a short time to enjoy the fruits of his toil. He died before the beginning of the present century. Stephen Ball came here in 1793 and settled upon the lot he subsequently occupied; Samuel, his brother, and Peter Wilson, brother of Elisha, the pioneer, came in company from Stockbridge upon foot, carry-

---

* Of this number 1104 were natives and 46, foreigners; 1237, white and 3, colored.

† Fuller and more interesting particulars relative to the journey of those men will be given in the history of the town of Newark Valley.

ing upon their backs their valuables and the supplies which
were to sustain them upon the journey. They pursued the
route taken by Elisha Wilson to Wattles Ferry, and from that
point crossed direct to the Chenango, through "Jones Settlement," striking that river some distance above Binghamton.
They followed a line of marked trees and emerged from the
forest in sight of Elisha Wilson's cabin, where they were wel-
comed as only "brothers and schoolmates" could be "after
such an eventful separation, and under such circumstances,
upon this extreme frontier—then one of the outposts in the
march of civilization." Josiah Ball, one of the Boston proprietors, and father of the Messrs. Ball before named, came with
his family from Stockbridge, Mass.. by means of two sleds
drawn by horses and one by a team of oxen, in the winter of
1794, and settled upon the farm upon which he resided until his
death at the age of 68 years. Judge John Brown, Capt. Asa
Leonard, Ebenezer Cook, Daniel Carpenter, Consider Lawrence,
Judge David Williams, Ransom Williams, Judge Joseph Waldo,
who came in October, 1800, Nathaniel Ford, Abel, Azel and
Nathaniel Hovey, Jeremiah Campbell, Samuel Collins, who
came in 1805, and Caleb and Jesse Gleazen, all from Berkshire county, Mass., were early settlers in this town. The
last two moved to Richford, within whose present limits they
were quite early residents. Judge David Williams, who was
from Richmond, Mass, moved to Tioga in June, 1800. Speaking of Judge Williams, C. P. Avery, in *The Saint Nicholas* for
March, 1854, says of him:

"The discharge of many important official duties, and trusts has de-
volved upon Judge Williams in the course of his long and useful career
He served upon the Bench of the Court of Common Pleas of Broome
county, as one of the Associate Judges, from the year 1815 to * * * 1822,
and with the exception of one year, he held the position continuously,
from the first day of his service until 1826, having been transferred to
the Bench of the Tioga Common Pleas, by appointment, after the change
of boundaries. For three years while his town was within the limits of
Broome, and for six years after it had been surrendered to Tioga, he was
its Supervisor; and for many years, commencing at an early date, he discharged the duties of many minor offices, with exactness, good judgement
and ability.

"In 1827 and 1831, Judge Williams represented his county in the Legislature, and from the various posts which he has been called upon to fill.
he has always retired with the increased regard and respect of his consti-
tuents

"Methodical in his habit of thought, firm in his adherence to what he
has deemed rules of right, and of uncompromising integrity—he will leave
to those who are to follow him, an example of moral worth, and an im-
pressive illustration of what may be achieved by fixed purpose, steady
effort and well regulated life."

Joseph Waldo built the first house in town. It is now standing about one mile south of the village of Berkshire. He was the first physician who settled in this vicinity. Ichabod Braineid made the first clearing at East Berkshire, near where Jeremiah Jones now resides. The first death was that of Isaac Brown.* W. H. Moore kept the first inn and store, and David Wilhams erected the first mill † The first male teacher was Rev. Gaylord Judd, and the first female teacher, Miss Lydia Belcher.‡

On the farm now owned by Lyman Aikens, in the west part of the town is a sulphur spring which, in early times, was a noted deer lick. Here the early settlers were accustomed to lie in ambush to shoot the deer which congregated at the spring. On one occasion a hunter, whose name we failed to learn, was concealed beneath a heap of bushes, and was suddenly alarmed by an object which leaped upon the bushes and commenced tearing them away. He drew his large hunting knife and struck at random. The object bounded off into the bushes and after a few struggles, all was quiet. By the aid of a light he discovered a very large panther which a fortunate blow of his knife—entering its heart—had killed. The skin was stuffed and was, for many years, on exhibition at the fur store of Mr. Ackley in Ithaca. Wild animals were quite numerous at an early day, and extreme vigilance and the enactment of bounty laws were necessary to rid the country of them and afford protection to domestic animals. Isaac Brown, who was the second child born in the town, who was born on the farm on which he now resides, and occupies the first barn erected in the town, had a flock of fifty sheep killed by wolves and panthers.

The first religious services were conducted by Rev. Seth Williston, a Congregational missionary from the east.

The *M. E Church*, located at Berkshire, was organized with fifteen members, about 1825. The church edifice was erected in 1828, at a cost of about $1,500. It has since been repaired, and will seat 300 persons. The first pastor was Rev. Gaylord Judd; the present one is Rev N. S Reynolds. The number of members is about one hundred. The Church property is valued at $6,000

---

*Statement of Deacon Royce of Berkshire.

† French's State Gazetteer.

‡ Statements of F. H. and Isaac Brown   French says Miss T. Moore taught the first school

*CANDOR* was formed from Spencer, Feb. 22, 1811.* It lies in the center of the north border of the County, and is the second largest town in the County. It contains 51,750½ acres, of which, in 1865, according to the census of that year, 31,384, were improved. Its surface consists of high, broad rolling uplands, divided into ridges by the narrow valleys of streams flowing in a southerly direction. The declivities of the hills are generally abrupt, and their summits are to a considerable extent covered with forests. Its streams are Catatunk and Doolittle creeks; the former enters the town about the center of the west line and flows east to Candor village, when it turns and flows south-east, leaving the town at the village of Catatunk; the latter rises in the north-east part of the town and, flowing in a south-east direction, discharges its waters, at the village of Weltonville, into the west branch of Owego Creek, which forms the east boundary of the town. In the valleys the soil is a very fertile gravelly loam, and upon the hills it is moderately so.

The Cayuga Branch of the Delaware, Lackawanna & Western R. R. passes through the town along the valley of Catatunk Creek and its northern branch, passing through the villages of Willseyville, Gridleyville, Candor, South Candor and Catatunk.

The population of the town in 1870 was 4,250, of whom 4,105 were natives and 145, foreigners; 4,233 white, 10, colored and 7, Indians.

During the year ending Sept. 30, 1871, the town contained twenty-three school districts and employed twenty-six teachers The number of children of school age was 1,444; the number attending school, 1,182; the average attendance, 613; the amount expended for school purposes, $8,234; and the value of school houses and sites, $15,504.

CANDOR, (p. v.) centrally located on Catatunk Creek and on the Cayuga Branch of the D. L. & W. R. R., contains four churches, (Baptist, Congregational, Episcopal and M. E.,) a

*The first town meeting was held March 5, 1811, at the house of Capt. Abel Hart, and the following named officers were elected: Joel Smith, *Supervisor*, Asa North, *Town Clerk*; Wm. Scott, Orange Booth and Samuel Smith, *Assessors*, Nathaniel Sackett, Seth Bacon and Charles Taylor, *Commissioners of Highways*, Truman Woodford, *Constable and Collector*; Abel Hart and Asa North, *Overseers of the Poor*; Edward Picket and Daniel R Parks, *Constables*, Joseph Delind, Charles Taylor, Eli Bacon and Joh Judd, *Fence Viewers and Damage Appraisers*; Wm Taylor, Joseph Schoonhover, Thomas Baerd, Daniel H. Bacon, Joseph Kellsey, Jacob Clark, Alex. Scott, Jacob Herrington, Seth Bacon, Oziru Woodford, Geo. Allen, Daniel Cowles and Reuben Hatch, *Overseers of Highways*, and Thos. Parks, James McMaster and Ezra Smith, *Pound Masters*.

Union school,* one bank,† three hotels, a woolen factory,‡ two flouring mills,§ two blacksmith shops, a tannery,‖ two wagon-repair shops, a foundry, several stores of various kinds, and a population, in the limits of the proposed corporation,¶ of 1,050.

WILLSEYVILLE, (p. v.) named from Hon. Jacob Willsey, is situated on the north branch of Catatunk Creek and on the Cayuga Division of the D. L. & W. R. R., in the north-west part. It contains one church, two stores, one shoe shop, two blacksmith shops, two saw mills, a dental office, thirty dwellings and about 120 inhabitants.

CATATUNK, (p. v.) located on the south line, on the Catatunk Creek and the Cayuga Division of the D. L. & W. R. R., contains one tannery,** (G. Truman & Co.'s) one blacksmith shop and two saw mills, (Beer's and Sackett's.) Most of the houses are occupied by the tannery employes.

EAST CANDOR is located in the east part on Doolittle Creek.

WELTONVILLE (p. o.) is located on the east line, on the West Branch of Owego Creek, seven miles above Owego. It was formerly a thriving village, but its business has declined and it now manifests little or no enterprise.

WEST CANDOR (p. o.) is located on the west line, a little south of the center, four miles west of Candor. It contains a hotel and tin shop.

<hr/>

*The *Candor Union School and Free Academy*, of which Prof. L D. Vose is principal, was established in 1868 The building was erected that year, and, with the grounds, cost $9,000. It has accommodations for 250 pupils, and has at present an average daily attendance of 180 Four teachers are employed. A normal class is taught during the fall of each year. The school has a library containing nearly four thousand volumes, and philosophical apparatus, to both of which yearly additions are made. It is under the supervision of the Regents of the University.

† The *First National Bank of Candor* was organized in 1864, with a capital of $50,000, and the privilege of increasing it to $100,000. It is located at the corner of Kinney avenue and Main street. Jerome Thompson is cashier

‡ *Candor Woolen Mills* are situated on Catatunk Creek They give employment to ten persons and are capable of manufacturing 30,000 yards of cloth per annum. Wm. Ward is proprietor.

§ *Sackett Flouring Mill*, leased by U P. Spaulding, contains four runs of stones and is capable of grinding 300 bushels of wheat per day.

‖ *Humbolt Tannery*, owned by E S. Esty, of Ithaca, and Hoyt Bros., of New York, gives employment to thirty men, consumes 4,000 cords of bark and is capable of manufacturing 40,000 sides of leather per annum.

¶ Efforts are being made the present year (1872) to effect the incorporation of the village.

** *Catatunk Tannery* was built by Sackett & Foreman in 1852. In 1864 it was purchased by the present proprietors, G Truman & Co. It gives employment to about thirty-five persons, annually consumes 3,000 cords of bark and tans 40,000 sides of sole leather. It is located on Catatunk Creek, four and one-half miles above Owego.

GRIDLEYVILLE is a hamlet on Catatunk Creek and Cayuga Division of the D. L. & W. R. R., about one mile above Candor.

PERRYVILLE is a hamlet in the north-west part, on Shandaken Creek, about one mile south of Willseyville.*

On the farm of Isaac D. Van Scoy, in the north-east part of the town, a subterranean lake was discovered a few years since, while an excavation was being made for a well. At a depth of twenty-two feet a layer of rock was met with, which, when perforated, allowed the drill to drop down as far as its size would admit. Subsequent investigation proved the existence under this layer of rock, of a strong current of water, of unknown depth. All attempts to fathom it have thus far proved futile, but whether from its supposed great profundity or the velocity of the current we are unable to state. At certain seasons the water is of a milky color, and that of about one hundred springs which are supposed to originate from this source presents a similar appearance. The excavation is made on high ground.

The first settlement in the town was made by Thomas Hollister, Elijah Smith, Collings Luddington and Job Judd, from Connecticut, in 1793. Joel Smith, brother of Elijah, came the following spring and settled on the Catatunk, on the farm now owned by Jared Smith. Elijah Smith was a well known and accomplished surveyor, and many plots surveyed by him at an early day are not unfrequently referred to at the present time to establish boundary lines and settle disputes relative thereto. Job Judd was a Revolutionary soldier, and had in his possession articles and accouterments used by him during that war. Israel Mead, a Revolutionary soldier, came from Bennington Co., Vermont, March 17, 1795, and settled near West Candor, on the farm now owned by Wm. Gridley. Abel Hart came from Stockbridge, Mass., in December, 1796, and located on the farm known as his homestead. Four or five years previously he visited some of his old townsmen who had emigrated to the "Brown Settlement," and seems to have been so well pleased with the country that two years subsequently, in the mouth of

---

*Strait's circular saw mill, located on the Ithaca & Owego turnpike and Cayuga Division of the D. L & W. R. R, three miles north-west of Candor, operates one saw five feet in diameter and four smaller ones, employs about twenty persons and is capable of sawing 5,000,000 feet of lumber and the same quantity of lath per annum. A planing machine and bark grinder is attached to it.

Booth's saw mill situated on Catatunk Creek, "about two miles from Candor Corners," is owned by Lorin Booth. It contains one large circular saw, a "mully" saw, a lath saw, a cross-cut saw and one for cutting siding, and is capable of sawing 1,000,000 feet of lumber per annum. It has a planing and matching machine attached.

Three mills have been erected on this site; the first was built in 1829, by Orange F. Booth and Chas. Gridley, the present one, by Lorin Booth.

L

February, he came with sleds drawn by oxen to make a permanent settlement. He did not however come immediately to this town. He first settled about five miles below Binghamton, not far from Gen. Stoddard's In 1797 he went to Ithaca, to supply himself with a barrel of salt, which he brought from that place on a cart, run on two low wagon wheels, and drawn by oxen. The road was located upon an Indian trail all the way from the Susquehanna to Cayuga Lake. Ithaca then contained but one frame house, and between that point and his residence there were but few log cabins. Mr. Hart was preceded in his settlement by families named Collins, Sheldon, Marsh, Wm. Bates, (who settled on what was subsequently the homestead of John B. Dean) and Richard Ellis, (who then occupied the premises afterwards occupied by Ebenezer Woodbridge.) Capt. Daniel R. Park settled in the south-east corner of the town, on the farm he now owns, May 3, 1797. He was a soldier in the war of 1812, and is now eighty-eight years old. Hiram Williams came here the same year (1797) and settled on the " Ford Location." He was one of the first to locate in that part of the town. Seth and Capt. Eli Bacon were early residents of the town in the latter part of the last century. The father of Russel Gridley came with his family, from Hartford Co., Conn., in May, 1803. The Messrs. Booth and Caleb Hubbard were also early settlers, the latter in 1805. Jacob Clark also became a resident in 1805. He came from Orange county. He was the father of eleven children, eight of whom are now living, but only two in the town—Hiram Clark and Rachel Lake. Elias Williams, who was a Revolutionary soldier, and Alexander Graham, who was a noted hunter and trapper, came about 1806.

Among other early settlers were Moses Grimes, who came from Washington county in 1811 and settled on the farm now owned by his son, J. M. Grimes, was one of the first members of the Presbyterian Church in Owego, held several public offices and whose life of usefulness exerted an influence which is still felt; Hon. Jacob Willsey, who came from Fairfield (Herkimer Co.) and settled in the north part of the town in 1815, who held the office of County Judge eight years and filled other responsible positions for many years, and who gave his name to the village on whose site he located; John Whitley, who came from Vermont about 1816 and settled in the north part of the town, on the farm now owned by Andrew J. Whitley;* Joel Robinson, who settled on the farm he now occupies,

*Mr. Whitley was pressed into the British army in 1778 and after serving four and one-half years, during which time he participated in the battle of St. Augustine, he effected his escape while the English were on Long Island.

near Candor village, in 1816, who built the first Methodist church in the town and the grist mill near his place, now owned by U. P. Spaulding, and who is now in his eighty-seventh year; and Israel Barnum, who was one of the first settlers in the north-east part of the town, in 1822. Bissell Woodford, a Revolutionary soldier, resided here during the last years of his life.

"It is said that Wm. Goodwin, who afterwards lived at Ludlowville, made the first journey with a team, from Owego to Ithaca, over a road then first widened from the Indian trail."

When Mr. Hart commenced his residence here, on the lot where Thomas Gridley, a Revolutionary soldier, formerly resided and near the site of the mills of John J. Sackett, was a fort which was said to have been used by the Indians as a fort or prison for captives. It was overgrown with moss, but, with the exception of the roof, was in a fair state of preservation.

C. P. Avery, in *The Saint Nicholas*, 1854, says of it:

"It stood in the midst of a thick hemlock grove, almost impenetrable to light, the dark and sombre character of which is well remembered by some of the pioneers yet living

"It is handed down by tradition, and in some degree confirmed, that here lived for several years, in an Indian family, a young white girl, who had been captured in the vicinity of Wyoming She is represented to have been singularly beautiful; her costume rich and ornamented with broaches of silver; and to have so much aroused the sympathy of the first white settlers upon the Susquehanna, that, among others, Amos Draper endeavored to procure her release. It was not, however, effected, the reason having been, according to one account, that her captors declined acceding to any terms which were offered for her redemption; while, it is otherwise stated, that the want of success was attributable to her own unwillingness to leave. She probably shared the fate of her captors, and removed with them to Canada. Many Indian relics have here been found Indications of *caches* still exist. hatchets, arrow-heads, maize-pounders, a pipe of handsome workmanship, and all the usual evidences of Indian occupancy, have been disclosed upon the surface, from time to time, by the plough and in excavations."*

Elisha Forsyth and Thomas Parks were early settlers in the east part of the town, near Owego Creek. The father of Forsyth was a settler in the Wyoming Valley under a title derived from Connecticut. In the massacre of July, 1778, he lost everything in the shape of property, valuable documents, deeds, &c., but fortunately escaped with the lives of himself and family. He subsequently returned to Wyoming and passed through the perils of a residence there until peace was declared; soon after that happy event he moved to Towanda, and from there to Choconut, then the name of a locality a little

* Deacon Jonathan Hart, who resides about one mile west of the village of Candor, has a valuable collection of curiosities, which embraces relics of this locality.

above the village of Union, previous to Elisha's settlement here. At the time of his removal from Towanda, (prior to 1787) there was living at Tioga Point, by which he passed, but one white man, whose name was Patterson. Capt. Thomas Parks achieved a reputation for great energy and prowess upon the sea, during the Revolutionary war; and, under letters of marque and reprisal, brought in numerous prizes.

The first inn was kept by Thomas Hollister; the first store, by Philip Case; the first grist mill was erected by Elijah Hart, and the first school was taught by Joel Smith, in a log house near where his brother lived. The nearest postoffice was Owego.

The first preacher was Rev. Seth Williston, who came to this locality as early as 1797-8 Rev. Jeremiah Osborne was the first settled minister; and the name of the first church organization was the *Farmington Society.**

*West Owego Creek Baptist Church*, located at Weltonville, was organized with ten members.† in 1802. Rev Levi Baldwin was the first pastor; Rev. R. A. Washburn is the present one. The church edifice, which will seat 300 persons was erected in 1842, at a cost of $2,000. The present number of members is fifty-eight. The church property is valued at $3,500  *The Fairfield Union Church* was partially composed of members from this church; also the *Newark Valley Baptist Church.*

The *Congregational Church*, at Candor, was organized with nine members, in 1808, by Rev. Seth Williston. The first church edifice was erected in 1818; the second, in 1825; and the present one, which will seat 700 persons, in 1867, at a cost of $4,000. Previous to 1818 meetings were held in barns and other places in which it was most convenient to congregate. The first pastor was Rev. Daniel Loring; the present one is Rev. Geo. A. Pelton. There are 223 members  The Church property is valued at $16,000.

*St. Mark's Church*, (Episcopal) at Candor Village, was organized April 23, 1832, by Rev. Lucius Carter, its first pastor. The number of communicants at its organization was three. The church edifice was erected in 1836, at a cost of $1,500; and was altered and repaired in 1868. It will seat 200 persons  The present number of communicants is thirty; the present pastor is Rev. A. Rumph. The Church property is valued at $4,500.

---

* *The Saint Nicholas,* 1854.  French's State Gazetteer says, Rev. Daniel Loring was the first preacher.

† The following are the names of the original members  Louis Mead, Lovina Mead, Jasper Taylor, Catharine Taylor, John Bunnell, George Lane, Sarah Lane, Abram Everett, Deborah Everett and Hannah Bunnell.

*Candor Village Baptist Church* was organized with twenty-five members, in 1855, in which year their house of worship, which will seat 300 persons, was erected, at a cost of $5 000. The society numbers 120 members, who are under the pastoral care of Rev. I. A. Taylor. The value of Church property is $8,000.

*Fairfield Union Church*, at East Candor, was organized about Dec. 7, 1858, by Baptists, Methodists and "Christians." Their house of worship, which was erected in 1854, at a cost of $1,500, and repaired in 1870, will seat 200 persons. The society is composed of about eighty members. The Church property is valued at $1,500.

The *Anderson Hill M. E. Church* erected its house of worship in 1860, at a cost of $750. It will seat 150 persons. The first pastor was —— Burgess; the present one is Rev. J. K. Peck. There are about thirty members. The Church property is valued at $1,000.

*NEWARK VALLEY** was formed from Berkshire, April 12, 1823.† It lies upon the center of the east border of the County, and covers an area of 29,382 acres, of which, in 1865, according to the census of that year, 18,116½, were improved. Its surface is broken by hilly uplands, which attain a mean elevation of about 1,200 feet above tide, and which are traversed by the narrow valleys of small streams tributary to Owego Creek, the east and west branches of which creek form its principal streams. The east branch of Owego Creek runs in a southerly direction, west of the center; the west branch, forms the west boundary of the town.‡ The soil in the valleys consists of a fine gravelly loam, which is fertile and yields abundant returns for the labor bestowed on it; on the hills it consists largely of an unproductive hardpan. Dairying and

* It was formed as *Westville*. Its name was changed to *Newark*, March 24, 1824, and to *Newark Valley*, April 17, 1862.

† At the first town meeting, which was held at the house of Otis Lincoln, March 2, 1824, the following named officers were elected: Solomon Williams, *Supervisor*; Beriah Wells, *Town Clerk*; Francis Armstrong, Ebenezer Pierce and Benj. Walter, *Assessors*, Anson Higbe, Abram Brown and Reuben Chittenden, *Commissioners of Highways*; Wm Slosson, *Collector*, Lyman Legg, *Constable*, Henry Williams, Wm Richardson and Otis Lincoln, *Commissioners of Common Schools*; Benj. Walter, Wm. B. Bennett and Geo Williams, *Inspectors of Common Schools*, Peter Wilson and Ebenezer Robbins, *Overseers of the Poor*, Joseph Benjamin, *Sealer of Weights and Measures*.

‡ The streams, says Wm. W. Ball, who was the first white child born in this section, in his recollection, abounded with fish and the forests which then adjoined them, with game. He has, he says, shot many a deer near his present residence. He was born Sept. 8, 1794, and is now residing in the north part of the town.

lumbering are the chief pursuits of the people. Butter is the chief product of the dairy; it is packed in pails and shipped daily to New York. The lumbering interests, which are now important, are increasing with the increased facilities for reaching a market which are afforded by the Southern Central R. R.,* which traverses the town along the valley of the east branch of Owego Creek. The timber is principally hemlock.

The town, in 1870, had a population of 2,321. During the year ending Sept. 30, 1871, it contained thirteen school districts and employed fifteen teachers. The number of children of school age was 796; the number attending school, 633; the average attendance, 343; the amount expended for school purposes, $4,729; and the value of school houses and sites, $5,900.†

NEWARK VALLEY (p. v) is located west of the center of the town, on the west bank of the east branch of Owego Creek, and on the S. C. R. R., ten miles north of Owego. It contains three churches, (Baptist, Congregational and M. E.) two hotels, three stores, a telegraph office, a U. S. express office, two saw mills, a grist mill, a tannery‡ and several other minor shops and offices incident to a village of its size.' It is a pleasant and thriving village, containing many fine residences and about 700 inhabitants.

The *Newark Valley Trout Ponds and Picnic Grounds,* designed to accommodate picnic and pleasure parties, are a new and promise to be an attractive feature §

The *Cemetery Association of Newark Valley* was formed Aug. 28, 1867, under the rural cemetery laws of the State. A por-

---

*The town is bonded in aid of this railroad to the amount of $45,600. The bonds were issued in 1867, '8 and '9, and draw seven per cent. annual interest. They are exempt from taxation for ten years from date of issue. The first bonds become due in 1877, and the last in 1887, one-tenth maturing each year after '77

† Oct. 12, 1870, a Union free school district was organized from districts Nos 2 and 14, and is now known as district No 2  It is designed to form a graded school, but as yet there are no suitable buildings erected.

‡ This tannery is owned by Davidge, Landfield & Co. It employs thirty-five persons, contains 130 vats and 12 leaches, uses spent tan for fuel and manufactures from 36,000 to 40,000 sides of sole leather per annum  The motive power is supplied by a forty-five-horse power engine. It was established about 1845; and was burned and rebuilt in 1857.
Belonging to the same company is a steam circular saw mill, which runs a five feet saw, operated by a sixty-five-horse power engine, and is capacitated to saw 3,000,000 feet of lumber per annum.
The saw mill of Moore, Cargill & Co., also located here, gives employment to ten persons, uses a circular saw four and one-half feet in diameter, which is run by a forty-horse-power engine, and has a capacity for cutting about 2,000,000 feet of lumber per annum.

§ These grounds were opened to the public June 6, 1872.  N. K. Waring and John Davidge are the proprietors

tion of the enclosure has been occupied since 1820, as a public burying ground.* The association is composed of the owners of lots.

The *Newark Valley Lodge No. 614, F. & A. M.,* organized June 28, 1866, with eight members, and Geo. H. Alison as first *Worshipful Master,* now numbers sixty members.

KETCHUMVILLE, (p. v.) located in the north-east corner, contains one church, (Reformed Methodist) one hotel, one store, a blacksmith and wagon shop and about 100 inhabitants.

JENKSVILLE, (p. o.) situated in the north-west corner, on the west branch of Owego Creek, contains one church, (M. E ) one store, a saw mill, a grist mill, a blacksmith shop, a creamery and cheese factory† and about fifty inhabitants.

WEST NEWARK (p. o.) is a hamlet on the west branch of Owego Creek, two miles south of Jenksville. The post office is kept in a private house. It contains one church (Congregational.)

The settlement of the town was commenced in 1791, by Elisha Wilson,‡ from Stockbridge, Berkshire Co., Mass., who, on the 23d of February in that year, in company with Daniel Ball,§ son of Josiah B. Ball, one of the patentees of the Boston Purchase, Abram and Isaac Brown,‖ grandsons of Samuel B. Brown, the leading proprietor, John Carpenter, Daniel Carpenter, who came in the employ of the Browns, —— Dean and —— Norton, all of whom were from the same county, left the cultured associations of his native town to accept the hardships and perplexities of a frontier life, in an unbroken wilderness. Most of

---

* The first burial was made Aug. 24, 1820. The remains of Mrs. Rachel Williams, Jacob Everett and Linus Gaylord were the first interments.

† This factory, of which Wm. H. Armstrong is proprietor, was built in 1867, and manufactures into butter and cheese the milk received from between 300 and 400 cows. The milk is set in coolers and skimmed before it sours. The cream is churned in dash churns by the aid of steam power. The milk after being skimmed is made into cheese in the ordinary way. In 1871 about 500,000 lbs. of milk were received, and from it about 15,000 lbs. of butter and 27,000 lbs of cheese were made. The average price of butter at the factory was 32 cents per pound, and of cheese 7 cents.

‡ Wilson purchased land of Elisha Blin, one of the sixty proprietors, who then resided at great Barrington, Mass., in 1790, on lot 184, after having visited, with a party of surveyors, the tract included in the Boston Purchase, for the purpose of examining it and correcting errors in an original plot.

§ Ball settled in Berkshire, on the farm subsequently occupied by Barnabas Manning.

‖ Isaac Brown settled in Berkshire, on the farm on which his son of the same name subsequently resided.

these settled in the valley of Owego Creek.   The journey occupied thirty-seven days *

In 1793, Enoch Slosson and his son Esbon, with their families, also from Stockbridge, settled at what was then and for
some time afterward known as Brown's Settlement.  Esbon
came the year previous to make prepations for settlement.  He
built the first frame house and kept the first inn and store in
town, in 1800.  A portion of the house forms a part of the
hotel now kept by Edward B. Lincoln.  Asa Bement Jr., one of
the sixty proprietors, settled in 1794.  "He was a man of substantial worth of character, and contributed much, together with
the other settlers from Berkshire county, to give to the region
in which he settled, the good name and character it has ever
since enjoyed."

The first settlers upon the west branch of Owego Creek
were Michael, Laban and Elisha Jenks, Jonas Muzzy,† Captain

---

* Their means of conveyance was two sleds drawn by yokes of oxen.
Their route was direct from their homes to the Hudson at Coxsackie,
thence through Durham, across the Catskills, through the old towns of
Harpersfield and Franklin to the Susquehanna, at the mouth of the Ou-
le-out, and down the Susquehanna to Oquaga  Thus the tedium of the
journey—mostly through a wilderness and over a road not deserving the
name of highway--was relieved only by the sight of log cabins at intervals
varying from ten to twenty miles  At Oquaga they crossed the river, taking with them only such of the stores and movables as were indispensable,
and pursued their journey across the highlands which separate the Susquehanna and Chenango rivers, to avoid the circuitous route by the Great
Bend  They reached the Chenaugo about one mile above its mouth, but
for several days were unable to cross it, owing to the unsafe condition
of the ice  When the ice broke up canoes were procured and the whole
party, except Mr. Wilson, embarked and proceeded towards Owego, where
they, (except young Dean and Norton, who parted company at Choconut
to make a permanent settlement there,) again joined Wilson, who remained
to care for the oxen and sleds, which he left for safe keeping, until they
could be conveniently sent for, with Gen. Stoddard, a short distance below, and proceeded to Owego by land.   After enjoying the hospitalities of
Owego, which then numbered six families, they commenced the laborious
task of cutting a road from there, through the forest, to a point about three
miles above Newark Valley, where they arrived the first day of April.
The season being favorable, Mr. Wilson and his three companions made
the necessary preparations for making sugar, and notwithstanding the
limited facilities, were very successful.  Their camp was established upon
the homestead of John Harmon, now deceased  Within three days after
their arrival three of the party started back for the goods left at Oquaga
and the teams and sleds left at Gen Stoddard's.  The journey there and
back occupied eleven days, and on their return Mr Wilson regaled them
with the sight of 150 pounds of sugar, as one of the fruits of his labors during their absence.

Wilson kept bachelor's hall until 1797, when he was joined by his mother
and sister, and having no one to share with him the fruits of his labor he
did not sow wheat the first year.  The Messrs. Brown made the first clearing for wheat, and on the new ground the yield was abundant ; twenty to
forty bushels per acre was an ordinary harvest.  In December, 1799, Mr.
Wilson married Electa Slosson, daughter of Enoch Slosson.

† From the statement of Calvin Jenks of Berkshire we learn that Mr.
Muzzy was the first to settle on the West Branch.  Mr. Muzzy was from
Spencer, Mass.

Scott and Thos. Baird. Michael Jenks built a saw mill on the West Branch, about 1803, and a grist mill on the same stream in 1814. These were the first mills erected on that creek and were located at Jenksville.

The first school was taught by David Master, part of the time in this town and part of the time in Berkshire.* The whole was then included in the town of Union.

The record of the part taken by this town in the suppression of the Rebellion is a very creditable one and will be referred to with just pride by the descendants of those who were residents of the town during that eventful period. About 125 men were furnished for the army, and the enlistments were made principally in the 50th Engineers and 109th and 137th regiments of Infantry. Of this number about twenty-five were killed or died from wounds and diseases contracted while in the service. Capt. Oscar Williams was the first to enlist. He joined the 44th Infantry, the celebrated "Elsworth's Avengers," as private. He was taken sick while in the field and returned home, where, after regaining his health, he took an active part in raising a new company, of which he was elected captain. It was designated Co. G. of the 137th Infantry. He was instantly killed at the battle of Gettysburg, July 3, 1863. The town raised $5,000 by the issue of town bonds, and always filled its quotas promptly †

The *First Congregational Church*, of Newark Valley, was organized Nov. 17, 1803,‡ by Rev. Seth Williston, with six members. It was the first church in Tioga county. The first house of worship was erected in 1804; the present one, which will seat 500 persons, was erected in 1868, at a cost of $13,000. The first pastor was Rev. Jeremiah Osborn; the present one is Rev. Jay Clisbe. The Church property is valued at $15,000.

The *Congregational Church of West Newark* was organized with twelve members, Sept. 16, 1823, by Rev. Zenas Riggs, its first pastor. The house of worship, which will seat 250 persons, was erected in 1847, at a cost of $1,500, which is one-half

*Statement of D. Williams Patterson, the distinguished genealogist of Newark Valley, who has kindly furnished us with much information pertaining to this town and vicinity.

†This information was obtained by our agent while canvassing the town. He exercised great care, but the correct figures may vary from those here given.

‡French says, in his State Gazetteer, that it was organized in 1798, by Rev. Seth Williston, a missionary from Connecticut. Our informant is D. W. Patterson, to whom we have previously acknowledged our indebtedness.

There is little doubt that Williston officiated in the capacity of missionary prior to 1803, as we are otherwise informed that he held the first religious exercises in the barn of Wm. W. Ball.

the present value of Church property. Previous to the erection of the church edifice, meetings were held in the barn of Wm. Richardson, until the erection of a commodious school house, when that was used. The church was formed under the Presbyterian form of government, but was changed to Congregational in 1842. The present number of members is twenty-four; the present pastor is Rev. Wm. Macnab.

The *First M. E. Church* of Newark Valley, was organized Dec. 3, 1830, with eighteen members, by Rev. Moses Adams. The house of worship was erected in 1832; and was rebuilt and enlarged in 1857. It will seat 300 persons, and was erected at a cost of $2,000. The present value of Church property is $5,000. The present pastor is Earles S. Alexander; the number of members, 234.*

The *Reformed Methodist Church* at Ketchumville, was organized with nine members, in 1837, by Seneca Ketchum, at the instigation of Ephraim M. Turner. The house of worship, which will seat 250 persons, was erected in 1852, at a cost of $1,000. There are fifty-five members. Rev. S. L. Dimmick is the pastor.

The *Alpha Church* (M. E.) at Jenksville, was organized with about twenty-five members, by Rev. —— Salisbury, the first pastor, in 1852, in which year the house of worship, which will seat 350 persons, was erected at a cost of $1,500, which is the present value of Church property. There are twenty-five members. Rev. S. Lindsley is the pastor.†

The *Newark Valley Baptist Church,* at Newark Valley, was organized with twenty-six members, Oct. 27, 1857, by Rev. L. Ramsted. Meetings were held for a short time in the Congregational church, until about 1858 or '9, when a building was procured and remodeled, and was used for religious services until the present edifice was built in 1869. It will seat 450 persons, and was erected at a cost of about $10,000. Rev. D. F. Leach was the first pastor; the present one is Rev. Russell H. Spafford. There are 115 members. The Church property is valued at $11,000.

*NICHOLS* was formed from Tioga, March 23, 1824. It lies upon the south bank of the Susquehanna, near the center of the south border of the County, and contains 19,850 acres,

---

* Two and one-half miles east, at what is known as East Settlement, is a church, an offshoot of this, under the same pastoral care. The building is worth about $2,000.

† This church is a part of the Speedsville (Tompkins county) charge and is under the same pastoral care.

of which, in 1865, according to the census of that year, 13,402, were improved. It had a larger per centage of improved land than any other town in the County. The surface is a broken upland, which terminates in steep declivities upon the river. The summits of the hills are broad and attain an elevation of from 300 to 500 feet above the river. A productive gravelly loam forms the soil of the valleys, and a moderately fertile gravelly and clayey loam, underlaid by red sandstone, the hills.

The only important stream in the town is Wappasening Creek, which enters the town from Pennsylvania at the village of Wappasening and flows north into the Susquehanna. That river forms the north and west boundaries of the town.

The population of the town in 1870 was 1,663. Of this number 1,637 were natives and 26, foreigners; 1,645, white and 18, colored.

During the year ending Sept. 30, 1871, the town contained twelve school districts and employed the same number of teachers. The number of children of school age was 527; the number attending school, 421; the average attendance, 219: the amount expended for school purposes, $4,477; and the value of school houses and sites, $6,320.

NICHOLS,* (p. v.) situated near the center of the north border, on the south bank of the Susquehanna, near the mouth of Wappasening Creek, contains two churches, (Presbyterian and the "Free Meeting House," which is occupied by the Methodists,) a fine school, five general stores, one drug store, one hardware store, one boot and shoe store, two hotels, two wagon shops, one blacksmith shop, one cooper shop, one shoe shop and a grist and saw mill. It is about two miles distant from Smithsboro station on the Erie R. R., and is nine miles below Owego. Its population in 1870 was 281.†

---

* Nichols was formerly known as "Rushville," which name was given it by Dr. Gamaliel H Barstow, in honor of Dr. Rush, of Philadelphia; but when it was ascertained that there was another village of the same name in the State, (Yates county) its name was changed to that it now bears in honor of Col. Nichols, the patentee of Nichols Patent. In return for the compliment Col Nichols directed his agent, Judge Emanuel Coryell, to give $200 toward the erection of some public building, and this sum was applied to the erection of the "Free Meeting House," the one now occupied by the Methodists and which was the first church built in the village A meeting was held Feb 20, 1829, at the house of Peter Joslin, and a Free Church was organized. The following trustees were appointed, viz.: Emanuel Coryell, Nehemiah Platt, Gamaliel H Barstow, Peter Joslin, Jonathan Hunt, Wright Dunham, Daniel Furgeson, John Petts, John Cassel, Sylvester Knapp, Ezra Canfield, Edwin Ripley, Cyrus Field, Justus Brown and James Thurston. The church was built in 1829-30, by Hezekiah Dunham, contractor.

† Of the inhabitants of Nichols in 1870, 275 were natives and 6, foreigners; 280, white and 1, colored.

HOOPERS VALLEY, (p. v.) named in honor of Robert Lettice Hooper, patentee of Hooper's Patent, is situated on the south bank of the Susquehanna, opposite Smithsboro, on the Erie R. R., with which it is connected by a bridge crossing the Susquehanna. It contains one wagon shop, two blacksmith shops and about twenty houses.

EAST NICHOLS (p o ) is located in the south-east corner, six miles south of Owego.

WAPPASENING is a hamlet situated on Wappasening Creek, near the State line, about one and one-half miles above Nichols village, and contains a blacksmith shop, a saw mill, a grist mill, a turning shop, twenty houses and about seventy-five inhabitants.

CANFIELD CORNERS is situated in the north-east part, on the east bank of the Susquehanna.

The first settlement in the town was made by John and Frederick Evelin, (the descendants of the family now spell the name *Eveland*,) A Vangorder and two sons (Leonard and Benjamin) and a man named Sullivan, all of whom lived near Canfield Corners.* The families of Ebenezer Ellis, Pelatiah Pierce and Stephen Mills settled in the town at a very early day, as early as 1787, and probably prior to that time, as Daniel Pierce and Daniel Mills, sons of Pelatiah Pierce and Stephen Mills, were born in the town, the former in 1787 and the latter in 1788. Alex. Ellis, of Barton, son of Ebenezer Ellis, was born in Barton, in October, 1788, to which town Messrs. Ellis and Mills soon removed. Geo. Walker purchased the premises of Mr. Ellis and occupied them. James Cole settled here about the same time as those previously mentioned, on the farm where Emanuel Coryell subsequently resided, and when Judge Coryell and Robert Lettice Hooper visited the valley on their exploring and surveying tour, they were entertained at his house. The settlers in the town thus far claimed but a possessory interest in the land they occupied, having, as yet, received no title from the patentees. Judge Emanuel Coryell came, with his family, from Coryell's Ferry, on the Delaware, N. J., in 1791.† Families by the name of Jones, (Isaiah) Bass

* Statement of John W. Lanning, (son of Daniel Lanning, one of the first permanent settlers,) who was born in this town and is now nearly eighty years of age.
French says Ebenezer Ellis, Pelatiah Pierce, Stephen Mills and James Cole made the first settlement in 1787.
† Judge Coryell had been in the valley of the Susquehanna, at this and other points above, two or three years previous, in company with Robert Lettice Hooper, exploring and surveying lands, in which the latter had an interest as patentee. He became the agent of Mr. Hooper and of those

and Emmons lived at an early day upon the Moughantowano Flats, and the latter is credited with having raised the first crop of wheat in the town. Caleb Wright occupied the farm upon which the village of Nichols now stands at an early day, and Stephen Dodd resided next below him. Major Jonathan Platt and his father, also named Jonathan, came with their families from Bedford, Westchester county, in 1793, and settled upon what was known for many years as their homestead. The elder Mr. Platt died two or three years afterwards from the effects of an injury received while preparing a field for wheat. His son, the Major, held among other offices of trust, that of sheriff, for several years. At his house the first town meeting was held. Col. Richard Sackett was a contemporary pioneer with Major Platt. Miles Forman, a Revolutionary soldier and pensioner, well known at an early day as sheriff Forman, also came from Westchester county in 1794-5. Major John Smyth, a Revolutionary soldier, came from Monroe county, Penn., in 1794. He was accompanied by his sons General John, Gilbert and Nathan Smyth. Gilbert became a resident of Barton. John, after his marriage with the daughter of Benjamin Goodwin, of Tompkins county, in 1797, became a resident of Ithaca, and

who subsequently acquired the title to the patents originally vested in that gentleman.

He served in the Commissary Department during the Revolutionary war, and was granted a pension of $240 per annum, under the act of 1832.

His journey, with his family, to Nichols was made by crossing directly from the Delaware to Wilkesbarre, and thence ascending the river in a Durham boat, by the aid of men employed at the latter place. The journey upon the river occupied two weeks.

Owing to the reasonable prices at which the lands for which he was agent were held, and the liberal inducements offered those who were seeking homes in the west, this section of the county was more rapidly settled than others, and even than the Boston Ten Townships, where the lands were held at prices which were deemed unwarranted.

Mr. Coryell served, for many years, with rare ability and dignity, as First Judge of the Court of Common Pleas of the widely-extended county of Tioga; and was, for several years, elected Member of Assembly from this county, in which position he wielded an extensive influence, and by his affability, acquired a strong personal popularity. He was the first Supervisor of the town. Says C. P. Avery, in *The Saint Nicholas:*

" His house was the center of good cheer for the vicinity in which he lived, and, bred among gentlemen of the old school, who were models of hospitality—he knew well how to cheer the coming and brighten the heart of the parting guest.

" From early youth he suffered from a physical infirmity, which interfered much with his walking, and caused him great inconvenience, yet his natural flow of good spirits and his usefulness were not materially affected by it; a constitutional cheerfulness saved him from anything like gloomy and morose feelings. With great kindness of heart and a hand open to charity, he was at the same time tenacious of his personal honor and prompt to resent an intentional insult or injury, by whomsoever and under whatsoever circumstances it might be offered.

" * * * His political views, like all his other principles of action were openly and freely avowed, and, as an ardent admirer of General Hamilton and of the school of policy and doctrines of which he was recognized at the time as the exponent, Mr. Coryell, with characteristic frankness, was not lukewarm in identifying himself with the politicians and statesmen of that party."

Mr. Coryell died in January, 1835, at the age of 82.

owned a tract of land upon which a portion of that village
stands. Nathan, who was noted for his practical benevolence,
died on the farm on which he resided for sixty-three years previous to that event, May 15, 1857. The following statement
made by him previous to his death, describing the manner in
which the early settlers lived, was furnished us by his nephew,
Hon. Washington Smith. He says:

"Many of the settlers brought plenty of clothing with them  As that
was used up *domestic manufacture* was the popular doctrine of the Valley
—wool, flax and deer skins being the *raw material* for the manufacture of
clothes for male and female

"Buckskin was much worn; some men dressed in buckskin from head
to foot  As for food, there was an abundance of deer, and the river
afforded shad and other fish plentifully, corn and wheat were soon raised
in sufficient quantities to supply the inhabitants  But the difficulty of getting the grain to a mill was such that much of it was prepared for food by
pounding it in Indian mortars.  Wheat was sometimes boiled and eat with
milk.  Soon there were two or three tub mills built, one at Shepard's
and one at Owego.  Caleb Wright built the first mill in what is now the
town of Nichols.  The Indian mortars were generally constructed in the
top of hardwood stumps, and the grain cracked by means of a stone pestle
made for the purpose and attached to a bent sapling as a sweep."

Lewis Brown, from Westchester county, Benjamin Lounsbury, Ziba Evans, Jonathan Hunt, Richard Sarles and Asahel
Prichard, a soldier of the Revolution, were early settlers. Messrs.
Prichard and Sarles afterward removed to Owego, where they
died at advanced ages.  Daniel Shoemaker, a Revolutionary
hero, and native of Ulster county, came here from Monroe
county, Penn., in 1801 or '2 and settled upon the Maughan-
towano plain, on land purchased by him of Robert L Hooper,
in 1792, and which is now occupied by H. W. Hooper, his
grandson.  Jonathan Pettis, Joseph and John Annibal, Joseph
Morey and David Briggs, of Briggs settlement, Wm. Thatcher,
Daniel Laning and John Russell were early settlers.  The latter
served in the war of the Revolution, and moved from Litchfield, Conn., in 1801, to Orwell, Bradford Co., Penn., relying
upon the title of the State from which he emigrated, and, finding it invalidated, removed to this town the year following,
and subsequently to Windham, Penn.  Isaac Sharp, an early
settler in this town, served with distinguished bravery during
the Revolution.  An incident which appears in *The Saint Nicholas*, for March, 1854, will serve to illustrate the devotion with
which he entered into that struggle.

"Upon one occasion, at an early period of the war, the Colonel of his
regiment desired a detachment of picked men for an expedition then
planned and which required men of nerve and prowess  Among other
volunteers for the enterprise, Sharp stepped forward, although destitute
of shoes. The officer in immediate command drew the attention of the

superior officer to the condition of his feet, remarking that they required men with shoes. Sharp promptly convinced them, in his own ready way, that his feet, although unprotected, were as sound as his courage."

Judge Gamaliel H. Barstow emigrated to this town from Sharon, Conn., in 1812. "No gentleman within the limits of the County," says C. P. Avery, "has shared more largely in public confidence, and none whose political influence at home and throughout the State, has been more marked and distinguished." In 1815 he was elected Member of Assembly and filled the position three successive years. In 1818 he was elected State Senator from the Western District, which then comprised nearly half the territory of the State, and in the same year was appointed First Judge of the Court of Common Pleas of his county. In 1823 he was again elected to the Assembly. He was Treasurer of the State of New York in 1825. In 1826 he was elected to the Assembly, and in 1830 he was elected to Congress, serving one term. In 1838 he was made Treasurer. He filled other minor offices with marked ability; and his whole political career is pronounced singularly free from corruption. The first frame house erected in the village of Nichols was built by him. He died at Nichols, in April, 1865, aged eighty years.

The first birth in the town was that of Daniel Pierce in 1787.

C. P. Avery, in speaking of the early occupancy of the town by Indians, says:

"For many years after this town was first settled, many Indian families lived upon the plain, near the mouth of the Wappasening. That portion of this town and the river flats generally, have furnished many articles of Indian handicraft and use, which have been brought to light by excavations and the plough, as well as by the washings of the streams. The Maughantowauo plain was a favorite corn-ground of the natives, and while it continues still unimpaired in its aboriginal distinction, it is of no little fertility and historic value, in the vestiges of our Indian predecessors, which are thrown upon its surface from time to time, and have already enriched many cabinets. From events of stirring interest, which have there occurred, * * * it is emphatically 'storied ground.'"

The first grist and saw mill built in the County was erected in this town, by Caleb Wright; and the first steam saw mill in the County was also built in this town, by George Kirby, in 1833 or '4.

*Asbury M. E. Church,* located on the river road in the northwest part of the town, was organized in 1817, with four members,* by Rev. John Griffin, its first pastor. The church edifice, which will seat 250 persons, was erected in 1822, at a cost of $2,000, or one-half its present value. It was the first church

---

* The four original members were Elijah Shoemaker and Phebe, his wife, and Daniel McDowell Shoemaker and Anna, his wife.

built between Owego and Elmira. Rev. George Comfort is the present pastor. The number of members is thirty-eight.

The *M. E. Church,* located at Nichols village, was organized in 1829 The Society worships in the "Free Meeting House," (of which previous mention has been made,) which was repaired and rededicated by it in 1872. The original cost of the building was $2,000. It will seat 400 persons Although repaired and occupied by the Methodists it is still a *free* (²) church—"open to all orthodox denominations." The present number of members is 149; the present pastor, Rev. George Comfort. The Church property is valued at $8,000.

The *First Presbyterian Church of Nichols* was organized with thirteen members, in 1859, and their house of worship, which will seat 300 persons was erected in 1865, at a cost of $3.000. Rev. G. M. Life was the first pastor; Rev. A McMaster is the present one. There are eighty-five members. The Church property is valued at $10,000.

*OWEGO* was organized Feb. 16, 1791. Spencer was erected from it Feb. 28, 1806 It is the south-east corner town in the County. It is the largest town in the County, and covers an area of 53,650¼ acres, of which, in 1865, according to the census of that year, 34,985½, were improved. The surface consists mostly of uplands, which are cut in two by the Susquehanna, and broken by the valleys of small streams. Their summits are broad and rolling, and rise from 300 to 500 feet above the river. The river intervale presents, in some places, an unbroken flat of more than a mile in width. The declivities bordering on the streams are generally very steep. The soil in the valleys is a deep, rich, gravelly loam; upon the hills it consists of a less productive gravelly loam, underlaid by hardpan. The principal streams are Susquehanna River and Owego, Apalachin and Nanticoke creeks. The Susquehanna flows west through the central part; Owego Creek flows south to the Susquehanna, through a broad and beautiful valley, its two branches uniting in the north-west part, and forms the west boundary of the town north of its recipient; Apalachin Creek flows north, through the south-east part, to the Susquehanna, and Nanticoke Creek, which rises in the north part, flows south through the center, to the Susquehanna Numerous small streams are tributary to these

Traces of valuable minerals have been found in the town, but they have not been sufficiently developed to determine whether they exist in sufficient quantity to render them profitable. On the farm of Henry McCormick, about one mile south of Owego village, have been found traces of gold, zinc, lead and

# F. M. SNOOK,

# DENTIST!

## Filling Teeth and locating Diseases of the Mouth made a Specialty.

### PLATE WORK OF ALL KINDS
#### DONE AT HIS OFFICE.

*Tooth Powder and Brushes of the best quality always on hand.*

*OFFICE IN SHIPMAN BLOCK,*

### COR. BROAD AND WAVERLY STREETS,
### WAVERLY, N. Y.

# G. F. STRAIT,

MANUFACTURER AND DEALER IN

## PINE, HEMLOCK AND HARD-WOOD

LUMBER, LATH,

### GROUND HEMLOCK BARK, &c.,
### CANDOR, - TIOGA CO., N. Y.

Constantly on hand and for sale, Seasoned PINE, CHESTNUT, HEMLOCK AND HARDWOOD LUMBER AND LATH.  Also HEMLOCK BARK.

L2

silver. A company has been formed and drilling is now in progress to determine the value of the underlying strata. One and three-fourths miles south of the village of Apalachin is a salt well, from which flows about forty barrels of brine per day.

The N. Y. & Erie R. R. extends through the town, along the north bank of the Susquehanna. The Southern Central R. R. enters the town on the north line and extends along the valley of Owego Creek to Owego. The Cayuga Division of the D. L. & W. R. R. enters the town at Owego.

In 1870 the town had a population of 9,442. Of this number 8,622 were natives and 820, foreigners; 9,250, white and 192, colored.

During the year ending Sept. 30, 1871, the town contained 37 school districts and employed 50 teachers. The number of children of school age was 3,180; the number attending school, 2,285; the average attendance, 1,283; the amount expended for school purposes, $22,267; and the value of school houses and sites, $23,175.

OWEGO,* (p. v.) the County Seat,† is finely situated at the confluence of Susquehanna River and Owego Creek. The former stream flows through the southern part of the village, and the latter forms its western boundary. It was incorporated April 4, 1827. The population of the village in 1870 was 4,756.‡ It contains seven churches, (Episcopal, (St. Paul's) Presbyterian, Congregational, Baptist, M. E., African M. E. (Bethel) and Catholic) six graded public schools,§ six hotels, two boot manufactories,‖ the Bristol Iron Works,¶ Erie R. R. Bridge shop,

---

*Owego is named from the creek at whose mouth it is located, and means, says Wilkinson, "*swift or swift river.*" Further mention is made of this creek on page 157.
On Guy Johnson's map of the *Frontiers of the Northern Colonies,* in 1768, it is spelled Owegy.

† A description of the County buildings will be found on page 159.

‡ The population included 4,174 natives and 582, foreigners; 4,594, whites and 162, colored.

§ The charter of incorporation of the *Owego Academy* bears date of April 17, 1828 The trustees of the academy were, James Pumpelly, Aaron Putnam, Joseph Castle, Anson Camp, Eleazer Dana, Charles Pumpelly, Joel S. Paige, Latham A Burrows, Gurdon Hewitt, Jonathan Platt, B Leonard, Jno. R. Drake and Amos Martin. Aug. 1, 1829, Thomas Farrington was elected a trustee to fill the vacancy occasioned by the resignation of Joseph Castle. Aug. 18, 1869, the academy was merged in the Union Schools of Owego, as the *Academical Department of the Union School District of Owego.*

‖ This business is conducted by L. N Chamberlin and J. H. Clapp & Co. The former commenced about twenty years ago, and the latter in 1868 The business uses $37,000 capital, gives employment to forty-eight persons and produces 23,600 pairs of boots per annum—valued at about $100,000.

¶ The *Bristol Iron Works* (Hon. W. H. Bristol, Chas F. Johnson Jr., Edwin Ellis and Geo. W Bristol, proprietors,) were established in 1866.
L2

four large tanneries, three planing mills, the Southern Central
R. R. shops, (now in process of erection) three saw mills, two sash,
door and blind factories, one foundry, one steam grist mill, one
flouring mill, operated by water, two carriage factories,* Haywood & Toomb's marble factory, one silver ware manufactory,
one soap and candle factory, one piano factory, one spoke factory, a half-mile trotting course, four weekly newspapers,†
(*Owego Gazette, Owego Times, Tioga County Record* and *Ahwaga
Chief*) three banks ‡ (two National and one private) one express
office (U. S.) and two telegraph offices, both of which belong to
the Western Union Telegraph Co.§ The village is lighted by
gas, but has no general water supply. Its streets are generally well
shaded, paved and provided with clean and substantial walks.
It is the commercial center of a large and productive agricultural region.  Its eligible location and railroad facilities constitute it one of the most important villages in the southern
tier of counties.  It is an important station on the Erie and
Southern Central railroads, and the southern terminus of the
D. L. & W. R. R.  Owego Creek is crossed by two bridges within
the limits of the village, and the Susquehanna, by one.‖

All kinds of machinery and agricultural implements are manufactured,
but a specialty is made of the "Champion Grain Drill," of which about
400 are made per annum   About six stationary steam engines are manufactured in the same length of time   This company have the contract for
manufacturing "Haywood & Tomb's Marble Derrick and Polisher," of
which they make from 65 to 100 per annum.  A capital of $60,000 is used in
the business; and sixty-five men are employed.

* Moore & Ross commenced the manufacture of carriages and sleighs
April 1, 1859.  Hill & Barry commenced the same business, but confined
principally to light work, Aug 26, 1863.  In May, 1866, Mr Hill sold his
interest to Scott Harris, when the firm became Harris & Barry.  Jan 1,
1868, Mr. Barry purchased Mr. Harris' interest, and since then has conducted the business alone.
The business uses a capital of $50,000, and gives employment to 38 men.
The value of annual manufactures is about $40,000.

† A history of the press appears on pages 160-2.

‡ The *Tioga National Bank* was organized in 1865   The officers are T
C. Platt, *President*, F. E Platt, *Cashier*; E. W. Stone, *Teller*
*Platt & Jones' Bank* (private,) was organized Sept. 1, 1868, as the Platt,
Jones & Co.'s Bank   H. R. Wells retired from the firm July 1, 1872
The *First National Bank* was organized in 1864.  Capital $100,000   The
officers are Lyman Truman, *President*, John B. Brush, *Cashier*; C. A.
Thompson, *Teller*.

§ Messrs. Bayette Bros. of Richford, have purchased a three story brick
building on Main street, in this village, and will soon remove their cigar
manufactory there   They have hitherto employed 25 men, but, when
established in their new quarters, will largely increase that number.

‖ The *Owego Bridge Co.* was incorporated in 1827 or '28   The first stock
was issued May 7, 1828   The first bridge in the village, the one crossing the
Susquehanna, was finished and opened to the public Jan. 1, 1828.  It was
carried away by floods, March 15, 1868, and was replaced by the present
one, which was opened for use in November, 1868   The cost of the present bridge was $54,550.01.  The superstructure is 920 feet long.  The road

Glen Mary, situated on Owego Creek, was for several years the residence of N. P. Willis. It was here that his matchless *Rural Letters* were written.

APALACHIN (p. v.) is situated on the left bank of the Susquehanna, eight miles east of Owego and about one and one-half miles south of Campville station on the opposite side of the river. It contains two hotels, four general stores, one drug store, two shoe shops, two grist and two saw mills, one rake factory, two wagon shops, two blacksmith shops, three churches, (Presbyterian, Baptist and Wesleyan Methodist) one harness shop and one meat market. In 1870 it had a population of 300.*

FLEMINGVILLE, (p. v.) situated in the north-west part, on the Southern Central R. R. and near the junction of the east and west branches of Owego Creek, is four and one-half miles north of Owego, and contains one church, (Methodist) two hotels, a cooper shop, a blacksmith shop, and in 1870, had a population of 91, all of whom were natives.† The village derives its name from David Fleming.

CAMPVILLE, (p. v.) situated on the right bank of the Susquehanna, seven miles east of Owego, is a station on the Erie R. R. and contains one church, (Methodist) a hotel, store, grist mill, plaster mill, blacksmith shop, saw mill and about twenty houses. The village was named from Asa Camp.

GASKILL CORNERS,‡ (p. o.) situated on Little Nanticoke Creek, about five miles north-east of Owego, a little north of the center of the town, contains one store, two saw mills, a cheese factory and creamery,§ two blacksmith shops, a wagon shop, a

---

bed is 32 feet above low water mark. It consists of nine spans. The officers are Wm. Pumpelly, *President;* F. L. Jones, *Secretary and Treasurer*, and Wm. Pumpelly, Geo. J. Pumpelly, A. P. Storrs, Thomas C. Platt and F. L. Jones, *Directors.*

The following are the rates of toll:

| | |
|---|---|
| One vehicle drawn by four animals . .. . . ..... .. . ... .. | 50 cents |
| " " " two " .. . ... .. ..... .. | 20 " |
| " " " " one animal ..... . ....... .. .. ... | 15 " |
| " animal and rider .... . ......... .. . ..... ... . . ... .. | 10 " |
| " footman . . . . .......... .. . .. . . 3 | " |

Although the charter allows them to charge this fare both ways it is demanded only one way

*Of this number 295 were natives and 5, foreigners; 299, white and 1, colored.

†The number includes 87 white, and 4 colored persons.

‡Named from Joseph Gaskill, who moved into the town from Richmond, Cheshire county, N. H., his native place, March 20, 1789, and to Gaskill Corners, about 1824. He was born in 1780, and died June 19, 1866.

§The factory was built by a stock company at an expense of over $5,000. The milk from 300 to 500 cows is used.

carpenter and turning shop (now being built) and about twenty houses.

SOUTH OWEGO (p. o.) is located on the Owego & Montrose turnpike, near the Pennsylvania line, about seven and one-half miles south-east of Owego. The *South Owego M. E. Church* is located about one mile north of the postoffice.

GIBSON CORNERS is a hamlet in the west part, about four and three-fourths miles south of Owego, containing a school house, a blacksmith shop and half a dozen houses.

SOUTH APALACHIN is situated in the south-east part, on Apalachin Creek. Efforts are being made to establish a post-office here.*

The first settlements in the town, it is believed, were made on the site of Owego village, in 1786,† by Wm. and Robert McMaster, Wm. Taylor, John Nealy and Wm. Wood, who came from the east by way of Otsego Lake and the Susquehanna, and made a clearing and sowed grain on an Indian improvement, embraced in the West Half-Township purchased a few years previous by James McMaster and John McQuigg, the original patentees. This purchase, says Wilkinson, was made previous to that of the Boston company and was embraced within its limits, but as it was conducted legally and had the advantage of priority that company relinquished any claim they might have been supposed to possess by reason of the provisions of their title, which extended their patent to the west branch of Owego Creek. In 1787 Amos Draper, an Indian agent and trader, moved his family to the site of Owego to a house built by him the previous year, while residing temporarily at Smithboro, to which place he came from the Wyoming country, in 1786. The house erected by him was the first one in the town. The following year (1788) McMaster and McQuigg, the patentees of the West Half-Township, moved their families to the site of Owego. They came from New England. Other early settlers were —— Yates, who came from Mass. in 1791, and settled at

---

* D R. Garrison's steam saw mill, located on Apalachin Creek, about three-fourths of a mile from the Pennsylvania line, is capable of sawing about 7,000 feet of lumber per day.

*The Owego Upper Leather Tannery* (Samuel Archibald. prop.,) is located at the south end of the bridge crossing the Susquehanna in the village of Owego. It contains 75 vats and 3 leaches, gives employment to ten men, consumes annually about 1,000 cords of bark and is capable of tanning from 8,000 to 10,000 hides per year.

Sherwood, Cornell & Co's steam saw mill, located in the north-east part, was erected in 1871. It contains one circular saw four and one-half feet in diameter, and is capable of cutting 30,000 feet of lumber per day

† Wilkinson fixes this date in 1785, and Spafford in 1787; but French and Stephen Dexter, who was one of the oldest residents of the county, agree upon this mean.

the mouth of Apalachin Creek; Caleb and Simeon Nichols, Isaac Harris and Abel and John Bills, all of whom settled in 1792; Hicks Horton, who settled about the same time; Henry Billings, who came in 1798–9; Asa and Sylvester Camp, in 1800. The Nichols were from R. I., and settled near Apalachin. Both were Revolutionary soldiers. Wm. Nichols, son of Simeon, says when they came there were but two houses at Owego. There were two tribes of Indians living at the mouth of Owego Creek, one on each side of the creek. The nearest grist mill was at Wilkesbarre; and when they first came they constructed a canoe from a tree, and with it went to mill, the trip occupying fourteen days. Hicks Horton was from R. I. and settled about two miles below Campville soon after the Messrs. Nichols came. Isaac Harris, also from R. I., located about one and one-half miles east of Apalachin. John Bills and his nephew, Abel Bills, came from New Lebanon, Columbia Co., and were the first settlers at Apalachin. Henry Billings settled at Apalachin, and kept the first tavern there. Asa Camp moved here from the town of Vestal, Broome county, about 1792, having moved into that town from Chatham, Columbia county, in 1787. He located first near Apalachin, on what is known as the "Catlin farm," and in 1800 he crossed the river and settled at Campville, where he built the first hotel at that place, which was kept by his son Roswell Camp, who is still residing in the town, aged eighty-eight years. Campville was named from Asa Camp, who kept the first post office there. Col. David Pixley came, with his wife and three children (David, Amos and Mary) from Stockbridge, Mass., at an early day* and settled about one mile west of Owego, in the town of Tioga, on a beautiful plateau of 3,000 acres, which was known at an early day as "Campbell's Location" In 1802 he disposed of this property to Judge Noah and Eliakim Goodrich, and removed to Owego, where he continued to reside until his death in 1807. Col. Pixley was one of the leading proprietors of the Boston Purchase and was one of the commissioners appointed by the Boston Company to treat with the Indians. He was a man of enterprise and estimable repute, and did much to properly mold the character of his associates. Previous to his settlement he visited the country on one or more tours of exploration. He was an active participant in the Revolutionary struggle and early evinced his devotion to the cause of liberty by accepting a commission in the Colonial army, issued July 1, 1775, by order of the Congress of the United Colonies, and bearing the bold and characteristic signature of John Hancock, President. Col. Pixley familiar-

---

* C. P. Avery, in *The Saint Nicholas*, fixes the date as 1791

ized himself with the Indian language and became popular with and doubtless exercised a strong and salutary influence over the tribes who settled in and visited this locality. "Mrs. Pixley," says Wilkinson, "was eminently pious, and made her house a *home* for strangers, and especially for the missionaries and ministers of that early day."

"The following inscription was copied from a monument in the [Owego] village grave yard.

"'In memory of Col. David Pixley, who departed this life Aug 25, 1807, in the 67th year of his age —He was an officer of the revolution at the siege of Quebec in 1775, under Gen Montgomery, was the first settler of Owego in 1790, and continued its father and friend until his death.' "*

The date of Col Pixley's settlement, if reference is made to the village of Owego, as seems quite apparent, and the assertion that he was the first settler in either the village or town, the latter of which, it will be remembered, at that date included the purchase on which he located, are palpably incorrect.

Reuben Holbrook and David Barney were early settlers in this town. The former was a Revolutionary soldier; the latter built the first house upon Apalachin Creek. Capt Elisha Ely, from Saybrook, Conn., another Revolutionary hero, settled at Owego in 1799. Many of his descendants still reside there. He died in 1801. Joseph Gaskill, to whom reference has previously been made,† settled here in 1789. Daniel Ferguson, who died near Flemingville many years since, was an early settler in that locality. During the early progress of the Revolutionary war, in which, though quite a young man, he was a soldier, he was captured on the Delaware, by the Indians, and detained on the site of Owego village during the winter and for a large portion of the year. He was adopted into an Indian family who occupied a bark lodge near where Paige street intersects River street. Upon his settlement in the town he was able to designate its precise locality, from its proximity to the rounded Indian burial mound, upon or near the homestead premises of the late Eleazar Dana, which retained its peculiar shape long after the village was settled. Although he admitted the considerate kindness of his captors, their mode of life possessed little charm for him ; and while on a hunting expedition on the Delaware in company with the Indian by whom he was adopted, he escaped by an ingenious stratagem during the night, and made his way to· Port Jervis, Orange county, where his friends resided previous to his capture.

Jesse McQuigg, one of the sons of the pioneer, John McQuigg, was accustomed to relate that the Iroquois, exclusive

---

* *Barber's Historical Collections of New York, p.* 551.

† See page 196-E.

of the Mohawks, who had removed to Canada, when on their way to attend the council held at Tioga Point, shortly previous to the defeat of Gen. St. Clair in the Miami country, in September, 1791, to conciliate the Iroquois and dissuade them from participating against us in the war then threatening our exposed north-western frontier, and represented on the part of our government by the distinguished Indian negotiator, Thomas Pickering, and Robert Morris, son of the talented and able financier of the Revolutionary crisis, and on the part of the Indians, among others, by Farmer's Brother and the gifted orator, Red Jacket, disembarked near his father's house, and prepared and eat their breakfast upon the open plain. They extended, so numerous were they, from the house of his father to that of James McMaster. Several hundred natives of both sexes attended this council from the head waters of the Susquehanna and its tributaries. They presented an imposing display as they approached the site of the village of Owego, in bark canoes, arranged in compact order and moving with regularity and uniformity. "In stature they were above the medium size, and with their head-dresses, glittering broaches and flowing blankets, they presented a spectacle, not novel at that period, but after this lapse of time, invested, in its contemplation, with a romantic interest, like that which attaches to a legend rather than to actual history."

Emanuel Duel, a Revolutionary soldier, settled, with his family, in the north part of the village, in 1790.* A family by the name of Talheimer, from the Mohawk, settled here at an early day, and was followed by several other families of Dutch and Irish extraction. Judge Stephen Mack became a resident of Owego village in 1799. As the pioneer printer in Tioga county,† his history, as well as that of Stephen B. Leonard, who early engaged in the same profession, is intimately connected with that of this town. Judge Mack held for many years the position of Justice of the Peace, and, at a later day that of First Judge of the Court of Common Pleas of Broome County. "In

---

* At an early period in the settlement of Owego, when no flour could be obtained at any point less distant than Wilkesbarre, Mr. Duel started in his boat for that place to obtain a supply, leaving his family with but slender means of subsistence. The unexpected prolongation of his stay rendered their situation critical; but at this juncture the timely assistance of an Indian, called by the whites, Captain Cornelius, (who entered the house, and perceiving their situation, departed and returned in a few hours with a supply of venison,) relieved them from want for many days. He also shared with them his "corn flour" which had been prepared in the usual Indian mode, by the maize-pounder

This Indian was shot down about the time of the holding of the council The cause assigned is jealousy of his friendship for the whites. The name by which he was designated by his own people was *Kanuukwis.*

† See pages 71 and 160.

all his official positions," says C. P Avery, he "brought to the
discharge of his duties unimpeached integrity of character,
and strong native powers of discrimination, improved by a good
education." His social qualities evinced no less marked excellence. Stephen B. Leonard came to Owego, when young, in
company with his father, a Revolutionary soldier, and a native
of Berkshire county, Mass., in 1806, having previously lived in
New York, his place of birth, and began at the age of fourteen
to learn the printing business, in the office of Judge Mack.
At the expiration of his term of apprenticeship he visited New
York and Albany and remained two years at the latter place to
perfect himself in his business. He returned to Owego and in
1813 purchased *The American Farmer* from Judge Mack, and
changed the name of the paper to *The Owego Gazette,* which he
continued to publish for about twenty-two consecutive years,
though during much of that time he was associated with J. B.
Shurtleff, to whom he subsequently sold the paper.* He was a
Representative in Congress from 1835 to 1837, and from 1839
to 1841. He performed the arduous duties devolving upon him
in that capacity with fidelity and ability. He still, after a life
of active usefulness, resides in Owego, having reached the ripe
old age of eighty years.

In 1791 there were six families living on the site of Owego
village, the number having doubled since 1788.

Wm. Williamson made the first settlement at Flemingville in
1820. He came from Scipio, Cayuga county, and has resided on
the farm on which he located till the present time. He is 73
years of age. At the time of his settlement the country in his
vicinity was a wilderness, and his nearest neighbor was three
miles distant. John Giles, who came in 1832, was the first doctor that lived at Apalachin. He was drowned while crossing
the river to visit a patient, by stepping into an air-hole in the
ice.

The first white child born in the town was Electa Draper,
daughter of Amos Draper, the pioneer and Indian agent. She
became the wife of Stephen Williams Jr., and moved to Newark
Valley, where she died. She was born June 19, 1788. The first
school was taught by ——— Kelly, in 1792; the first store and
hotel were kept by Wm. Bates, at Owego, on the lot where the
Ahwaga now stands; the first post office was located on the
bank of the river, above the Ahwaga House, and was kept by
Stephen Mack, who was postmaster at different times for several
years; the first grist mill was built by Col. Pixley on Owego
Creek, in 1793, previous to which time and until the erection

of Fitch's mill, four miles above Binghamton, in 1790, the early settlers in this locality were obliged to go to Wilkesbarre, Penn., with their grain, by means of canoes on the Susquehanna, a journey which usually occupied about two weeks; the first saw mill was built by Amos Stafford; the first tannery was started by Lemuel Brown.

Speaking of Owego in 1813, Spafford, in his *Gazetteer of New York*, says, "The lands are held in fee, and the inhabitants manufacture their own clothing in their own houses, from the growth of their own farms."

For many years the postoffice at Owego was one of the four distributing offices of the State. The growth of that village was greatly enhanced by the salt, plaster, lumber and wheat shipped for the Pennsylvania and Maryland markets. A very destructive fire occurred Sept. 7, 1849, in Owego, by which seventy-five dwellings were consumed.

The first religious services were conducted by Rev. S. Williston, the pioneer preacher in the Susquehanna Valley.

The *First Free Will Baptist Church of Owego*, located at South Apalachin, was organized with fourteen members, in October, 1816, by Rev John Gould, its first pastor. The first Church edifice was erected in 1844, and was burned in 1859; the present one, which will seat 200 persons, in 1865, at a cost of $1,500. Rev. Hiram S. Ball is the present pastor; the number of members is fifty-five. The Church property is valued at $3,500.*

The *First Presbyterian Church*, of Owego, was organized with eleven members, July 24, 1817, by Revs. Hezekiah May, Jeremiah Osborne and William Wisner, the former being its first pastor. The first house of worship was erected in 1820; and the present one which will seat 700 persons, in 1854, at a cost of $13,000. The Society numbers about 400, and is under the pastoral care of Rev. Samuel T. Clarke. The Church property is valued at $25,000.

The *First Baptist Church*, of Owego, was organized with thirty members, (twelve males and eighteen females.) Aug. 2, 1831. The first house of worship was erected in 1835; the present one which will seat 700 persons, in 1858, at a cost of $4,000. It was greatly enlarged and improved in 1870. The first pastor was Rev. Samuel Ford; the present one is Rev. W. H. King. There are 787 members. The value of Church property is $70,000.

*St. Paul's Church* (Protestant Episcopal,) was organized in 1834, and its house of worship was erected in 1839. It will seat

---

*The Church was originally organized at Little Meadows, in the town of Apalachin, Penn , (then the town of Choconut, Penn.,) the Society embracing two neighborhoods, one at Little Meadows and the other at South Apalachin, where meetings were held alternately.

350 persons. The building is located on the south side of Main street, near McMaster street, in the village of Owego. Rev. John Bailey was the first pastor; Rev. J. H. Kidder is the present one. There are about 120 communicants connected with the Society.

*St. Patrick's Church* (Catholic) was organized with twelve members, in 1840. Their house of worship, located on Main street, in the village of Owego, was erected in 1840, at a cost of $1,200, and was enlarged in 1860. It will seat 500 persons. Rev. Father O'Riley was the first pastor; Rev J. Rogers is the present one. There are 2,000 members. The Church property is valued at $20,000. Connected with it are a free school and the Convent of the Sisters of Mercy.

The *Congregational Church* was organized with forty-six members, Feb. 19, 1850. Their house of worship is located on Park street in the village of Owego It was finished Feb. 10, 1852, and cost $5,000. It will seat 500 persons. The first pastor was Rev. S. C. Wilcox; the present one is Dwight W. Marsh. The number of members is 227. The value of Church property is $20,000. The church is out of debt.

The *First Wesleyan Methodist Church*, at Apalachin, was organized with thirteen members, by Rev. Matthew Dearstine, the first pastor, Feb. 25, 1850. Their house of worship was erected in 1871, at a cost of about $1,500, and was dedicated Dec. 11th of that year. It will seat 200 persons. The Society numbers forty-eight members. The pulpit is vacant in consequence of the death of their pastor in February, 1872. The Church property is valued at $2,000.

The *Presbyterian Church*, at Apalachin, was organized with five members in 1855, through the efforts of Mrs. Margaret Camp and Rev. O. N. Benton,* its first pastor. The church edifice was erected in the spring of 1856, at a cost of $2,600, and will seat 250 persons. There are twenty-five members; but the pulpit is vacant at present. The Church property is valued at $3,000.

The *M. E. Church of South Owego*, was organized May 20, 1856, though a class was formed in 1830. Their house of worship was erected in 1856, at a cost of $1,200, and will seat 200 persons. Rev. Joseph Whitham was the first pastor after the erection of the church edifice, though Rev. John Griffin was the first to preach to them prior to that time. The pulpit is

---

* Mr. Benton was chaplain of the 51st Regt. N. Y. Vol Infty during the war of the Rebellion, and was killed at the battle of Newbern, N. C., March 14, 1864. His remains are interred at Owego.

now supplied by Rev. W. Keatley, of Little Meadows, Penn. The number of members is about thirty-five. The Church property is valued at $3,000.*

The *Free Will Baptist Church of Apalachin* was organized in 1869, by Rev. H. S. Ball, its first pastor. The church edifice is now in process of erection and will cost $3,000 and seat 250 persons. The Society numbers thirty-six. Rev. John Swank is the pastor.

The *M. E. Church of Owego* erected its first house of worship in 1822, and the present one, which is located in the village of Owego, in 1871-2, at a cost of $42,000. It will seat 1,100 persons. The date of its organization and the name of its first pastor are unknown, the record being lost. The church was dedicated by Revs. Jesse T. Peck (now Bishop Peck) and B I. Ives. Its 384 members are under the pastoral care of Rev. William Bixby. The Church property is valued at $50,000.

*RICHFORD* was formed from Berkshire, as *Arlington*, April 18, 1831, and its name changed April 9, 1832.† It lies in the extreme north-east corner of the County, and is bounded on the north by Cortland and Tompkins counties, on the east by Broome county, on the west by Tompkins county, and on the south by the town of Berkshire. It covers an area of 18,457¼ acres, of which, in 1865, according to the census of that year, 10,462, were improved. The surface is broken and very hilly. Its hills are the highest in the County, being estimated at 1,400 to 1,600 feet above tide. The roads, where practicable, follow the valleys. It is watered by the east and west branches of Owego Creek (both of which flow south, the former through the center of the town, and the latter separates it from Tomp-

---

*The first trustees were Ezra Tallmadge, Caleb Lamb, Clark Beecher, Russel D. Gifford, Smith Gould, H. B Gifford and Wm G. Knights.
*Rural Cemetery Association of South Owego*, was organized in 1864. The grounds are located about one-fourth mile south of the church and contain ninety square rods. They are regularly laid out and beautifully shaded with spruce and maple trees. The first officers of the Association were Ezra Tallmadge, *President*, Chester Graves, *Treasurer*, and Milton Slawson, *Clerk*.

† The first town meeting was held at the house of Simeon M Crandall, Tuesday, March 6, 1832, and the following named officers were elected — Wm. Dunham, *Supervisor*, John C. Stedman, *Town Clerk;* Wm Belden, George P. Simmons and Jesse Moore. *Assessors;* Lorrain Curtis, Hubbard F Wells and Heman Daniels, *Commissioners of Highways,* Jacob Burgett, Elijah Powell and Tower Whiton, *Commissioners of Common Schools;* Simeon R. Griffin, Israel Wells and Edward W Surdam, *School Inspectors;* Nathaniel Johnson and Wm. G. Raymond, *Overseers of the Poor*, Obediah L. Livermore, *Collector*, Hiram N. Tyler and Henry Talmage, *Constables*, Seth B. Torrey, *Sealer of Weights and Measures*, Platt F Grow, Eri Osborn and David C. Garrison, *Justices of the Peace.*

kins county,) and several small tributaries to them. The soil in the valleys is generally fertile and the hills are susceptible of cultivation to their summits. The town is covered to a considerable extent with forests and lumbering is carried on to a limited extent.

The old Catskill turnpike extends through the town in a westerly direction. This road is much traveled.

The Southern Central R. R. extends through the town along the valley of the east branch of Owego Creek *

In 1870 the town had a population of 1,434 Of this number 1,403 were natives and 31, foreigners; 1,415, white and 19, colored.

During the year ending Sept. 30, 1871, the town contained nine school districts and employed ten teachers. The number of children of school age was 516; the number attending school, 433; the average attendance, 225; the amount expended for school purposes, $3,324; and the value of school houses and sites, $6,004.

RICHFORD (p. o.) is located south of the Center on the east branch of Owego Creek and on the S. C. R. R., and contains one church, (Congregational,) a school house, a hotel, store, grocery, drug store, billiard saloon, cigar manufactory,† tin shop, shoe shop, two blacksmith shops, one harness shop, a wagon repair shop, a saw mill,‡ an express office, (U. S.) and 150 inhabitants. This is the only postoffice in the town.

*Valley Lodge No. 463, I. O of G. T.* located here was instituted Dec. 11, 1867, with 23 members. The present (June 1, 1872,) number of members is 78.

EAST RICHFORD is a hamlet east of the Center. There is a Free Will Baptist Church here.

<hr>

* The town gave bonds to the amount of $45,000 in aid of this road The bonds are issued in denominations of $100 and $500 and bear 7 per cent annual interest. They are exempt from taxation ten years from date of issue They mature at the times and in the amounts specified below. Bonds due in 1875, $3,000; in '76, $3,000; in '77, $4,500; in '78, $5,000; in '79, $5,000; in '80, $6,000; in '81, $6,000; in '82, $6,000; in '83, $6,500.

†The cigar manufactory of Bayette Bros. was established in 1847, by their father, who commenced business on a small scale, employing but few outside of his own family. The business now requires $25,000 capital and gives employment to twenty-five persons, who manufacture annually about one and one-half million cigars. The Bayette Bros. have purchased a building in Owego with a view to removing their establishment to that village. See page 196-D.

‡*The Richford Steam Mills*, located here, (H. S. & C. W. Finch, proprietors,) have a circular saw five feet in diameter, which is operated by a fifty horse power engine, give employment to about fifteen persons, and are capable of sawing 3,000,000 feet of lumber annually. A large quantity of lath is also made.

WEST RICHFORD is a hamlet in the north-west part, near the west branch of Owego Creek. There is a Christian Church here.

At the point where the Catskill turnpike intersects the west branch of Owego Creek is the neighborhood known for miles around, since the early settlement of the country, as "Padlock," for the reason that the early settlers in that locality were so suspicious of each other that they secured all their buildings with padlocks.*

In the north-west corner of the town is a neighborhood known as "De Maraudeville Hollow," named from the first settlers, from which the inhabitants can reach the center by public highway only by passing into Tompkins or Cortland counties.

The date of the first settlement is unknown, but it is believed to be about the beginning of the present century. Among those who settled at an early day were Evan Harris, who located at the village of Richford, on the lot upon which the Congregational church stands; Samuel Smith, Samuel Gleason, Nathaniel Johnson, —— Stevens, Jeremiah Campbell, Caleb and Jesse Gleason, Ezekiel Rich and William Dunham, many of whom came from the adjoining town of Berkshire. Samuel Smith and Samuel Gleason are said to have been the first settlers.

"One of the communications from the Susquehanna to the 'council fire' of the Iroquois at Onondaga, was located upon the east branch of Owego Creek * * *. The trail followed the bank of the creek to a point not far from its source, where it divided into two branches, one passing over by a short cut to a tributary of the Tioughnioga, and up the latter to its headwaters in Onondaga; the other crossed to the headwaters of what is now called Fall Creek, and thence to the head of Cayuga Lake. These trails were observable to the early surveyors of the 'military tract,' and explorers for several years."†

The first marriage was contracted by Ezekiel Dewey and Lucy Johnson, in 1817.

This town took a noble part in aiding to suppress the Rebellion. She furnished 118 men, who enlisted from and were credited to the town; and fourteen, who went from other towns. Of the enlisted men 11 went with Capt. Catlin; 31 with Capt. Powell, who was the only commissioned officer from the town and who raised a company in the early part of the war; 19, with Capt. Hyde; 20, with Capt. Williams of Newark Valley;

---

*Statement of S. M. Allen, a resident in the town for fifty years.
† *The Saint Nicholas.*

and 36 with other companies.   In the draft of 1863, thirty-three were drawn.   Three of these entered the army as drafted men; thirteen paid $300 commutation; one sent a substitute; and one enlisted, but subsequently deserted and went to Canada. The town raised $2,800 for bounties.   Her quotas were always promptly filled, and although her representatives passed through some of the hardest fought battles of the war, the loss was light compared with other localities.*

It is a fact worthy of honorable mention, and one, perhaps, without parallel in the history of the war, that from the family of a widow lady named Lacy, (who subsequently became Mrs. Deacon Hart of Richford,) consisting of nine sons and one son-in-law, the latter and seven of the former enlisted, (the remaining two were not old enough )   Three joined the 3d, and two 137th Infantry, and two, in company with the three who joined the 3d Infantry and subsequently re-enlisted, the 50th Engineers.   The son-in-law entered the 109th Infantry.   All served their time faithfully and returned home without having sustained the least injury from the weapons of war †

The *First Congregational Church of Richford*, at Richford village, was organized with forty-one members, Jan. 14, 1823, by Rev. Seth Burt, its first pastor, as a Presbyterian church, and was changed to Congregational in 1827, though it retained its connection with the Presbytery until 1868.   Their first church edifice was erected in 1823, mostly by contributions of labor by the people living in the neighborhood.   The present house was erected in 1854, and will seat 300 persons.   There are seventy-eight members.   Their pastor is Rev. A. L. Green.   The Church property is valued at $2,500.   Mrs. Rich is the only one of the original members now living

The *Christian Church of West Richford* was organized with thirty members, in 1851, by Elder Wm. Grimes, its first pastor; and until the erection of the house of worship in 1861, meetings were held in the school house, the woods and barns.   It was first organized as a branch of the South Harford (Cortland county) church.   The church edifice cost $1,000, and will seat 300 persons.   There has been no regular pastor since 1867; and, owing to the death and removal of some of the leading members the Society has gradually become disorganized.

The *First Free Will Baptist Church*, at East Richford, was organized as a branch of the Dryden *Free Will Baptist Church* by Simeon P. Willsey and others, in 1863, and as a separate church, with seven members, by Rev. J. N. Hills, in 1864.

---

* From statement of J. H. Deming, Supervisor.
† From statement of Grant W. Barnes of Richford.

Their house of worship, which was erected in 1868, at a cost of $1,000, will seat 300 persons. There are thirty members. The first pastor was Rev. S. B. Culver; the present one is Rev. Oscar D. Moore. The Church property is valued at $1,500.

*SPENCER* was formed from Owego, Feb. 28, 1806.* Candor in this county and Caroline, Danby and Newfield in Tompkins county were erected from it Feb. 22, 1811. Cayuta in Schuyler county was erected from it March 20, 1824. It lies in the north-west corner of the county, and covers an area of 29,136¾ acres, of which, in 1865, according to the census of that year, 16,313¾, were improved. The surface is an upland, broken by the valleys of several small streams. The ridges extend in a general north and south direction. Their declivities are generally steep and their summits broad and broken. The north-west portion forms the watershed between Susquehanna River and Cayuga Lake. Catatunk, or *Catetant* Creek, as it was called at an early day, flows east through the center of the town and cuts these ridges at nearly right angles, forming a deep and narrow valley. This is the principal stream, though it is supplemented by numerous small tributaries. The soil in the valleys is a gravelly loam, and upon the hills it is a hard shaly loam.

The Ithaca & Athens R. R. enters the town on the north line, near the north-west corner, and extends through the north-west part to a point a little west of Spencer village, where it turns to the west and leaves the town on the west line, a little south of the center.

In 1870 the town had a population of 1,863, of whom 1,819 were natives and 44, foreigners; 1,832, white and 31, colored.

During the year ending Sept 30, 1871, the town contained thirteen school districts and employed the same number of teachers. The number of children of school age was 627; the number attending school, 536; the average attendance, 279; the amount expended for school purposes, $3,539; and the value of school houses and sites, $2,972.

SPENCER, (p. v.) located west of the center, on Catatunk Creek, is a station on the I. & A. R. R., and is on the line of

*The first town meeting was held at the house of Jacobus Shenichs, Tuesday, April 1, 1806, and the following named officers were elected:—Joel Smith, *Supervisor*, Jacobus Ferris, *Town Clerk*, Edmund Hobart, Daniel H. Bacon and Levi Slater, *Assessors*, Moses Read, Benjamin Jennings and Joseph Barker, *Commissioners of Highways*, Lewis Beers and Samuel Westbrook, *Overseers of the Poor*, Isaiah Chambers, *Collector*; John Shoemaker, Nathan Beers, Wm. Curran, John Murphy and Isaiah Chambers, *Constables*, John F Bacon, John McQuigg, John Mulks and Jacob Swartwood, *Pound Masters*, John I. Speed, John English, Joseph L. Horton, Jacob Herrington, Alex Ennis and Lewis Beardsley, *Fence Viewers*.

the U. & E. R. R.* It contains three churches, (Baptist, Congregational and M. E,) one Union school, one steam saw and grist mill, one sash and blind factory, eight stores, four blacksmith shops, two wagon shops, two cabinet shops, one hotel, a livery stable, two milliner shops, one dental and two doctor's offices, an undertaking establishment, photographing establishment, three shoe shops, two tailor shops, a meat market, a paint shop, a water-power saw mill,† two harness shops and about 100 dwellings and 500 inhabitants. It was named from Judge Spencer of New York.

*Spencer Camp Ground* is located in a very pleasant grove, near the village, and but a few rods from the depot on the I. & A. R. R. It has been used for this purpose several years, and the accommodations are ample and good.

SPENCER SPRINGS, (p. o ) located in the north-east part, is named from and noted for the springs located here, which make it a popular place of resort during the summer months. The water is impregnated with iron and sulphur and possesses valuable medicinal properties. There is a hotel here with ample accommodations for visitors, and surrounded by picturesque scenery. It is three and one-half miles north-east of Spencer village.

NORTH SPENCER, (p. o.) located in the north-west part, on the I. & A. R R., about three and one-half miles north of Spencer, contains one church, (Union) a school house, a store and about fifteen dwellings and seventy-five inhabitants.

COWELLS CORNERS (named from Joshua Cowell, an early settler,) is a hamlet located on Catatunk Creek, about one and one-fourth miles east of Spencer, and contains a school house, a shoe shop, two cooper shops, nine dwellings and about thirty-three inhabitants.

There are several industrial and mechanical enterprises in various parts of the town, removed from the business centers ‡

---

*The *Utica & Elmira R R*, now in process of construction, will pass through this town, near the center, from east to west, following the valley of Catatunk Creek. Grading for it was recently commenced in this town.

† The water-power by which this mill is operated is said to be the best in the town The mill is located in the north part of the village and saws about 100,000 feet of lumber per annum John Hallock is the proprietor

‡ John A Nichols' steam saw mill, located one mile south-west of Spencer village, is operated by a forty-horse-power engine, gives employment to twelve persons and is capable of sawing 1,000 feet of lumber per hour. Connected with it is a lath mill, which manufactures large quantities of lath and pickets.

A Seeley & Bro.'s steam saw, lath and shingle mill, is operated by a forty-horse-power engine, gives employment to ten persons, and saws about 9,000 feet of lumber, a large quantity of lath and some shingles per

The first settlement was made in 1795, by the families of Benj. Drake and John Barker. Mr. Drake settled on the site of the village of Spencer, which he owned. He erected the first frame building there, which was afterwards known as the "Purdy house." He commenced in this wilderness in a very primitive way. It is interestingly stated by Gen. George Fisher that Mr. Drake "dug out a trough," one end of which he occupied as a sleeping apartment and the other as a kitchen. One day while he was working some distance off his rude habitation caught fire and was entirely consumed—a loss he doubtless mourned sincerely. Phineas Spaulding,* Joseph Barker and Edmund Ho-

day. This company contemplate erecting a grist mill the present year (1872) which will contain three or four runs of stones.

Bangs & Bro.'s saw mill, planer and lath and cider mill, located on Catatunk Creek, gives employment to four persons and manufactures annually one million feet of lumber, one-half million feet of lath, 500 cords of wood and about 1,500 barrels of cider, and planes 300,000 feet of lumber.

The Dean saw mill, owned by John D. Vannatta, and located on Dean Creek, in the south-west part of the town, is a small water-power mill and manufactures about 15,000 feet of lumber annually.

Sabin's saw mill, in the north part, on a branch of Catatunk Creek, is a small water-power mill. The water-power is not constant; hence the quantity manufactured varies with the varying supply of water

Signer's saw mill, in the north part, on a branch of Catatunk Creek, contains an upright and a circular saw, which are operated by water-power, and manufactures about 300,000 feet of pine and hemlock lumber and a considerable quantity of lath per annum.

The saw mill owned by J. VanMarter and J. S. Smith, located on the south branch of Catatunk Creek, about five miles south-east of Spencer village, contains three circular saws which are operated by water, and saws about 400,000 feet of lumber per annum The proprietors intend converting it into a steam mill this season.

Hug & Mowers' saw mill, located in the north-west part, gives employment to fifteen men and annually manufactures about one million feet of lumber and a large quantity of stove wood from the slabs The lumber is shipped principally to Ithaca.

Dodge's grist and saw mill, located at the foot of "Huggtown Pond," contains three runs of stones, does a large amount of custom grinding and is capable of sawing one million feet of lumber per annum. It is now operated by water-power, but the proprietors intend to convert it into a steam power mill this season.

Hulburt's saw mill, located at Dry Brook, in the north-west part, is capable of sawing a large quantity of lumber, though it is in operation but a small portion of the time.

The Cook saw mill, located on the Catatunk Creek, is operated by water and is capable of doing a large amount of business, but is not run to its fullest capacity. It saws from 50,000 to 100,000 feet of lumber per annum.

James C. Emery's saw mill, located near Spencer Springs, saws about 300,000 feet of lumber annually.

*While hunting one day Mr. Spaulding shot a panther in a tree and broke its under jaw. When it reached the ground it was attacked by his dog, but was not so much disabled as to be unable to defend itself from its attack. Seeing that his dog was likely to come to grief Mr Spaulding went to its assistance and was in turn attacked by the panther. He jammed the butt end of his gun into its mouth and before the panther could disengage itself he cut its throat.

At another time during the early settlement of the town, Mr Spaulding, in company with Levi English, another early settler, followed a bear track

L3

bart, it is believed settled the same year, soon after Mr. Drake. Spaulding was from New Hampshire and located in the north part of the town. Joseph Barker came from Wyoming, Penn., and settled on the site of Spencer village. He taught the first school in his own house. He filled the office of Justice of the Peace for twenty-eight years. He raised a large family of children, most of whom are now dead. Edmund Hobart located a short distance north of Spencer village where Benj. Hull now lives. Rodney Hobart emigrated from Conn. and took up his residence at Spencer village in 1796.

John and George K. Hall, brothers, came from Westchester county in 1798, and settled where John McQnigg now lives. They moved their families here in 1806. John McQuigg,* —— McLane and —— Case settled in the town previous to 1800, and those named are believed to be all who settled previous to the present century.

---

made in the snow which fell the previous night  The course pursued by the bear lay across the site of the village of Spencer, and they followed it about three miles, when they treed the bear.  Mr. Spaulding shot at it five times but failed to bring it down, and as he had but one ball left they concluded to cut down the tree, which they did  When the tree fell the bear was attacked by three dogs the hunters had with them.  One of the dogs was killed and the other two driven off, when Mr English went to their assistance with an ax.  He in turn became the object of attack and was pressed so closely that he jumped over the fallen tree, and was immediately followed by the bear  Whichever side of the log English felt constrained to occupy temporarily the unpleasant proximity of the bear on the same soon rendered the opposite side most inviting; and the bear, doubtless relying upon the superior judgment of English, invariably manifested the same partiality as was apparent in the latter, for he changed his position to opposite sides of the log as often as did English, and exhibited his preference with so much alacrity that the latter found it impossible to apprise it of his evident antipathy for its companionship in the way he wished.  English jumped over the log and back again several times all the while imploring Spaulding to fire which the latter had been preparing to do with all possible haste.  The former, however, was in too imminent peril, or was too solicitous for the welfare of the bear, to accurately note the lapse of time, and the length necessary to load a gun seemed to him exceedingly great  In due time Mr. Spaulding put an end to his intense anxiety by delivering a well directed shot through the head of the bear, which killed it

* The following, copied from a paper printed at the time the incident occurred, in 1803, explains itself

"LOST CHILD"

"DISTRESSING EVENT.—On Saturday last the eldest son of John M. McQuigg of the town of Owego, [which then included the town of Spencer,] a boy about seven years old, went into the woods to hunt the cows and has not been heard of since, notwithstanding the vigilance and exertions of the inhabitants generally throughout the country, who have been collected together in parties, and who have been in continual pursuit of him.  It is supposed that a dog belonging to Mr McQuigg followed the boy and still remains with him  What a heart-rending thought! a little infant only seven years old wandering through the wilderness to be devoured by beasts of prey or perish of hunger!  We understand that not less than 400 people are this day in pursuit of him  From their exertions we hope he may yet be found to console his afflicted parents and relations
"Since writing the above we have had the pleasure to learn that the boy was found in perfect health, with his faithful dog, about six or seven miles from home"

Wm. Hugg and his son, William, came from Connecticut, in 1800, and settled on the west branch of Catatunk Creek, two and one-half miles north of Spencer village. Mr. Hugg brought his family and effects all the way on a single sled drawn by an ox team. Game was plentiful and beasts of prey were too numerous for the peace of mind of the early settlers. The howl of the wolf might be heard every night for twenty years after the first settlements were made. Mr. Hugg recollects to have seen as many as seventeen deer in one herd. Isaac Hugg came in 1801 and located near Wm. Hugg. David McQuigg, an early settler, purchased 100 acres of land of Benj. Drake, the pioneer settler, at $5 per acre, and paid the whole amount with venison and furs.

George Watson, from Canaan, Litchfield county, Conn., came in 1804, and settled on the north limit of Spencer village, on land called the "Watson tract," named from his father, a Revolutionary soldier. Mr. Watson married the daughter of Joseph Barker, one of the pioneers. He had fourteen children, ten of whom are now living. He died at the age of eighty-eight, not having known sickness until that which resulted in his death.

Judge Henry Miller and Andrew Purdy came in company from Westchester county in 1805. The former was a member of the Court of Common Pleas of his county and both were highly esteemed. Elizabeth Miller, the widow of Judge Miller, is still a resident of the town, having reached the ripe old age of ninety-nine Caleb Valentine and John and Leonard Jones came also from Westchester county the same year and settled on the Catatunk, in the east part of the town. They were the first settlers in that locality Richard Ferris and his son Daniel came from the same county the following year and settled on the Catatunk, east of Spencer village. Thomas Mosher, from Westchester county, became a resident in 1805.

Benjamin Cowell came with his family from Connecticut in 1807 and settled near North Spencer. He met with a painful death from the accidental discharge of his gun, which he carried, as was his custom, while looking after the cows.

Gen. George Fisher came from New York in 1810 and settled on the site of Spencer village when, he says, there was only one house there, and no road. He has taken a lively interest in the progress of the village and surrounding country, and still lives at the venerable age of ninety to enjoy the fruits of his early arduous labors. His brother, Thomas, preceded him in his settlement one year. Solomon Mead settled about the same year as Gen. Fisher, near "Huggtown Pond." His son John Mead, who came with him, still resides where they first located. Hartman Lotze, from Salisbury, Litchfield county, Conn., came

about 1811.   He still resides here and is eighty-three years of
age.   Joshua H. Ferris came about 1812.   His father, Judge
Joshua Ferris, who was a gentleman of intelligence and worth,
a member of the Court of Common Pleas, a land agent and accurate surveyor, became a resident about 1800.   Micah Penin,
from Conn., came about 1817 and settled four miles north of
Spencer village.   Joseph Cole came about the same time.   Nathan Martin and three of his sons settled about one and one-
half miles north of Spencer village in 1817.   Ira Martin,
another son, joined them the following year.   Alvin Benton
settled in the north-west part of the town in 1819.   Cyrus
Woodford settled on the Catatunk about two and one-half miles
east of Spencer village about 1822 ; and S. D. Bliven became a
resident at Spencer village in 1829.   A Mr. Cramer, who was
an early settler, and built a log-house near the stream which
was afterwards called Cramer Creek, was one day at the house
of Benj. Drake, the pioneer.   The latter had killed a deer and
gave Cramer a portion to take home, which he started to do after
dark, carrying a pine torch to light his way.   He had not gone
far before he heard wolves following him.   He hurried on, but
they came so near that he was obliged to climb a stump.   He
swung his torch to frighten them, but they pressed him so close
that he threw his meat as far as he could, and while the ravenous ferocity of the wolves was thus temporarily appeased he got
down from the stump and by making good use of his legs arrived home safe.   Thomas Andrews was an early settler at
North Spencer.

The first birth was that of Deborah, daughter of Benj. Drake ;
the first death was that of Prescott Hobart, who was buried on
the farm now owned and occupied by James B. Hull & Son and
who was re-interred in the village (Spencer) cemetery.   The
first wheat raised in the town was on this same farm ; and the
first clover which grew there, on the farm now owned by Jas
Nelson.   The latter grew from seed dropped by a horse hitched
thereon the previous year by a man from Owego.   The first
marriage was contracted by John B. Underwood and Polly
Spaulding.   The first inn was kept by Andrew Purdy ; and the
first store by Samuel Doolittle.   The first grist mill was built by
Benj. Drake; and the first saw mill, by Edmund Hobart, on the
site of Cook's saw mill.

Spencer village was the county seat of Tioga county from
1812 to 1821.   Tioga county then included Chemung county.
At the burning of the Court house the last named year the
county seat was removed to Owego.

The first religious meeting was held by and at the house of P. Spaulding, and the first religious association (Baptist) was organized by Elder David Jayne.

The *Union Church*, at North Spencer, was organized with thirty members in 1870, and its church edifice, which will seat 275 persons, was erected the same year, at a cost of $1,500. It has no regular pastor, its pulpit being supplied from Spencer village. The Church property is valued at $1,700.

*TIOGA** was formed from Union, (Broome Co.,) March 14, 1800. Berkshire was taken off Feb. 12, 1808, a part of Union, April 2, 1810, and Barton and Nichols, March 23, 1824. It is an interior town, the only one in the county which is not partially bounded by territory lying outside the county. It lies upon the north bank of the Susquehanna, which separates it from Nichols. Its eastern boundary is formed by Owego Creek, its northern, by the towns of Candor and Spencer, and its western, by the town of Barton. It covers an area of 33,344½ acres, of which, in 1865, according to the census of that year, 20,940½, were improved. Its surface consists principally of uplands, which terminate in bluffs along the river intervale. Its streams are Catatunk and Pipe creeks, and numerous small streams tributary to them and the Susquehanna. Catatunk Creek enters the town on the north line, near the east border, and flowing in a south-east direction, discharges its waters into Owego Creek, near the center of the east border; Pipe Creek enters the town on the west line, near the north-west corner, and flowing in a south-east direction, empties into the Susquehanna, near Tioga Center. The soil is a fine dark loam in the valleys and gravelly upon the hills.

The N. Y. and Erie and Southern Central railroads extend through the south part of the town, along the valley of the Susquehanna, and the Cayuga Division of the Delaware, Lackawanna & Western R. R. crosses the north-east corner, following the course of Catatunk Creek.

In 1870 the town had a population of 3,272, of whom 2,995 were natives and 277, foreigners; 2,244, white and 28, colored.

During the year ending Sept, 30, 1871, the town contained twenty school districts and employed twenty-one teachers. The number of children of school age was 930; the number attending school, 848; the average attendance, 422; the amount expended for school purposes, $5,504; and the value of school houses and sites $7,741.

* For definition and origin of name see p 155.

SMITHBORO (p. o.) is located near the south-west corner on the bank of the Susquehanna, which is crossed at this point by a bridge. It is on the N. Y. & Erie and Southern Central railroads and is distant nine and three-fourths miles west from Owego It contains one church, (Methodist) three hotels, four stores, two groceries, one drug store, two wagon shops, two blacksmith shops, two harness shops, a shoe shop, a creamery,* and, in 1870, had 304 inhabitants.†

TIOGA CENTER (p. v.) is located about the center of the south border, near the mouth of Pipe Creek, and is a station on the N. Y. & Erie and S. C. railroads It is distant five and one-fourth miles west of Owego and four and one-half, east of Smithboro. It contains two churches, (Baptist and Methodist, the latter is now being built,) one hotel, tannery,‡ shoe shop, three stores, a grist mill, three saw mills,§ (one of which is operated by water and two by steam,) a blacksmith shop, about thirty buildings and had, in 1870, 304 inhabitants.‖

HALSEY VALLEY (p. v.) is located in the north-west part, on the line of Barton, and contains two churches, (Christian and Methodist,) two general stores, a grocery, a saw mill,¶ blacksmith shop, wagon shop, two cooper shops, a shoe shop, about thirty dwellings and had, in 1870, 103 inhabitants.**

STRAITS CORNERS is a hamlet located near the north line, on a branch of Pipe Creek, and contains a grocery, saw mill and a few dwellings.††

---

* Smithboro creamery was built in 1866 by Ketchum, Smith & Co., and is now owned by Joseph Winters It is capable of using the milk from 200 cows, though it is at present receiving it from only 75 It produces from 12,000 to 13,000 lbs of butter per annum

† The number of inhabitants comprised 277 natives and 27 foreigners, and were all white.

‡ Quirn's tannery was erected in 1871, the old one built by Wm Ransom having been burned It gives employment to 45 men and annually tans 175,000 calf-skins, all of which are imported.

§ Hoff & Thayer's steam saw mill was built in 1867, by the present owners. Smith's steam saw mill was built in 1851, by R. & J. G. Smith and was operated by water until May, 1872, when steam was introduced as the motor. It saws one million feet of lumber annually.

‖ The number of inhabitants comprised 268 natives and 36 foreigners; 300 whites and 4 colored persons.

¶ Taylor's steam saw mill was built for a shingle mill in 1868, and in 1871 was remodeled and machinery adapted to a saw mill introduced. It saws 5,000 feet of lumber per day.

** All its inhabitants were natives and all except one were whites.

†† It was named after David Strait, the first and present postmaster. The postoffice was established here in 1853 and two mails are received per week—Tuesdays and Saturdays

Among other manufacturing establishments in this town are. Giles' steam saw mill, which is located on the line of Barton, and manufactures

Settlements were commenced in this town as early as 1785. Enos Canfield, according to the statement of his son, Amos, came about that year and settled in the south part, on the farm on which Amos Canfield is now living. The latter was born in the town He says there were but few settlers scattered along the river when his father came. Samuel and William Ransom, —— Primer and Andrew Alden came up the Susquehanna from Wyoming Valley the same year and settled on Pipe Creek. Wm. Ransom and Andrew Alden located near the mouth of that creek, on the site of the village of Tioga Center. Wm. Ransom subsequently married the daughter of James Brooks, (Rachel) who came with his family two years later, and raised a family of nine children, some of whom are still living on the old homestead. Col. Wm Ransom, son of the pioneer by the same name, was born in April, 1801, and still resides at Tioga Center. Col. David Pixley from Massachusetts and Abner Turner from New Hampshire came in 1791, both having previously visited the country on one or more exploring tours. Col. Pixley moved to Owego in 1802, as is stated in the history of that town. Mr. Turner settled near the east line, upon the homestead where he afterwards lived and died. Joel Farnham settled in the east part in 1794–5. Jeremiah White from Wyoming settled at a very early day on the river, a short distance below Owego, on premises subsequently occupied by Abel Stafford, Elizur Wright and, in 1803, by Samuel Giles. Hugh E. Fiddis was an early settler adjacent to Joel Farnham. John Hill from Waterford, Berkshire county, Mass., a Revolutionary soldier, settled near the river bank, below Mr. White, in 1792. Wm. Taylor, who accompanied James McMaster to Owego in 1785, settled subsequently a little lower down the river. Nathaniel Catlin, one of the survivors of the sanguinary battle of Minisink, purchased Mr. Taylor's farm in 1800. Daniel Mersereau from Staten Island settled here the latter year on property purchased from Cornelius Taylor, who came shortly previous from Plymouth, in the Wyoming Valley. He continued his residence there until his death. Judge Noah and Eliakim Goodrich from Glastenbury, Conn., settled on property purchased of Col. David Pixley in 1802, on the latter's removal to Owego. Both died in the town at advanced ages. John

---

lumber and shingles. The first mill on this site was built in 1854, by Wm. W. Giles. It was burned in 1864 and rebuilt the same year. In 1871 the boilers exploded and did damage which required eleven weeks to repair.

Grove Steam Mill, located two miles east of Halsey Valley, was built by its present owner, L. B. Ferbush, in 1871. It saws about 7,000 feet of lumber per day and 500,000 shingles annually.

Beaver Meadows steam saw mill, located about four miles from Tioga Center, was erected in 1870 on the site of a water mill, and is owned by Nichols & Ross. It is capable of sawing 1,000 feet of lumber per hour.

Smith was an early settler in this town.   Jas. Schoonover settled
further down the river in 1794 and left numerous descendants
in the county.   Families by the name of Taylor and Hungerford settled in the same locality.   Francis Gragg, Nathaniel
Goodspeed, Lodowick Light, Jesse Ziba and Amos Miller, (the
last four from Westchester county,) families named Fountain
and Lyon, (who settled at the Ferry, a short distance above
Smithboro,) and Ezra Smith, (who settled at Smithboro, and
from whom that village was named,) were all early settlers.
Mr. Smith held letters patent from the State, covering a large
tract of land in that vicinity, and, in company with Mr. Light,
and others, moved from Westchester county in 1791.   Beniah
Mundy, who located in the south part, was one of the first to
settle in this town.   He came about 1787.

Asa Severn from Tompkins county was an early settler in the
north-west part of the town, when it was a wilderness.   He
erected a log house and made a clearing.   Stephen Rider from
Blenheim, Schoharie County, settled in the south part of the
town in April, 1816.   At the time he came, Mr. Rider says the
town along the river was settled to some extent, but the north
part was a wilderness, without roads, and infested by wild beasts
which frequently preyed upon the sheep belonging to the settlers.   Peter Lott settled with his family at Halsey Valley about
1801, and he and his daughter were accustomed to walk to Factoryville, a distance of fourteen miles, to attend church.

Upon the brow of the cliff on the west bank of Owego
Creek in this town was an Indian burying ground, which, from
the remains found there, appears to have been extensively used.
Many Indian graves were also found near the bank of the river
a short distance below Cassel's Cove.   The remains here were
found in the usual posture, surrounded by the customary implements of the chase and ornaments such as were usually deposited with the body which they had contributed to support
and adorn in life.

About forty years since, the east part of the town, at the west
end of the "Glen Mary," owned by George J. Pumpelly, a large
brass kettle, filled with articles of various kinds, of ancient
appearance and manufacture, was disclosed by the plow.   Among
the contents was a copper tea kettle, which inclosed a pewter
vessel filled with untrimmed rifle balls, just as they came from
the mould.   Other articles were an old-fashioned and peculiarly
shaped hammer; a parcel of pewter plates of two sizes, the
smaller ones showing no marks of use, being bright and un-
dimmed by corrosion, and bearing the impress of the word
"London"; and a peculiarly shaped iron or steel instrument,
six or eight inches in length, pointed and like the head of an

arrow or spear, except that it had a single barb about two inches long, on one side only, and at its other end was a socket, apparently intended for a handle. Other articles of similar value were inclosed by the kettle, and are supposed to have been presents made to the Iroquois by the English agents during our Colonial history to cement the bonds of friendship between them, and to have been deposited where found by some member of that tribe on the approach of Gen. Sullivan's army, to prevent their falling into the hands of the invaders. Death or the fortunes of war, or forgetfulness of the precise spot where they were secreted may have prevented a resumption of the possession on the retirement of the army.

The *Christian Church* at Halsey Valley was organized in 1847, and erected a house of worship in 1856. It cost $1,200, and will seat 200 persons. The Society now numbers seventy members Its first pastor was Rev. A. J. Welton; the present one is Rev. Alfred Saxton. The church property is valued at $1,600.

*Tioga Center Baptist Church* was organized in 1849, by members from North Barton and Owego, and its church edifice, which will seat 250 persons, was erected in 1850, at a cost of $2,000. Rev. Nathaniel Ripley was the first pastor; Rev. Geo. Brown is the present one. There are fifty members, and the Church property is valued at $3,000.

The *Christian Church* at Straits Corners was organized with seventeen members in 1850, by Rev. B. R. Hurd, its first pastor. Its house of worship will seat 200 persons. It was erected in 1855, at a cost of $950. The present number of members is twenty. The present pastor is Rev. Alfred Saxton. The Church property is valued at $2,000.

The *M. E. Church* was organized with thirty-six members in November, in 1870, and its house of worship, which is located in the north part of the town and will seat 300 persons, was erected the same year, at a cost of $3,000. Its first pastor was Rev. —— Eckert; its present one is Rev. S. B. Keeney. The number of members remains the same as at its organization. The value of Church property is $3,050.

The *M. E. Church* at Halsey Valley erected its house of worship, which will seat 400 persons, in 1854. The pulpit is filled by Rev. J. B. Santee of Barton. There are twenty members. The Church property is valued at $2,500.

The *M. E. Church* at Smithboro erected its house of worship in 1867. It will seat 250 persons. Services are conducted by Rev. J. B. Santee of Barton. The Church property is valued at $5,000.

M

# BROOME COUNTY
# BUSINESS DIRECTORY.

————◆————

## EXPLANATIONS TO DIRECTORY.

Directory is arranged as follows: 1. Name of individual or firm   2. Post office address in parenthesis   3 Business or occupation

A Star (*) placed before a name, indicates an advertiser in this work   For such advertisement see Index.

Figures placed after the occupation of *farmers*, indicate the number of acres of land owned or leased by the parties.

Names set in CAPITALS indicate subscribers to this work.

The word *Street* is implied as regards directory for the City of Binghamton and villages.

**For additions and corrections see Errata, following the Introduction.**

## BARKER.

### (Post Office Addresses in Parentheses.)

Adams, Amos, (Castle Creek,) lot 198, farmer 270

Adams, Asa 2d, (Whitney's Point,) lot 242, farmer leases of Asa K , 400.

Alderman, Talcot, (Castle Creek,) lot 164, farmer 85.

Alexander, Levi, (Chenango Forks,) lot 52, carpenter and farmer 50.

Alexander, Rufus, (Chenango Forks,) lot 52, farmer 60.

Allen, John, (Whitney's Point,) sawyer and farmer.

Allen, John N., (Whitney's Point,) lot 70, farmer 80.

Atwater, Chester, (Whitney's Point,) lot 48, assessor and farmer 184

Bacon, Manly, (Chenango Forks,) lot 240, farmer leases of Violetta Rummer, 46.

Barr, James, (Chenango Forks,) lot 62, farmer leases 194.

Beach, Abel W., (Whitney's Point,) lot 281, justice of the peace and farmer 107

BEACH, ASA, (Whitney's Point,) (*with Franklin*,) lot 47, farmer 230

Beach, Charles B., (Whitney's Point,) (*with Franklin*,) farmer.

BEACH, FRANKLIN, (Whitney's Point,) (*with Asa*,) lot 47, farmer 230.

Beach, John M., (Whitney's Point,) lot 281, farmer 147.

BEACH, WILLIAM, (Whitney's Point,) lot 47, farmer 160.

Baals, Wm. H., (Whitney's Point,) lot 244, farmer 280.

Bedell, Ira, (Whitney's Point,) lot 239, farmer 124.

Blair, EH, (Chenango Forks,) lot 159, farmer 150

Bliss, Burt, (Chenango Forks,) lot 201, constable and farmer 100

Bliss, Perry, (Chenango Forks,) lot 40, farmer 105.

Bolster, Giles, (Castle Creek,) lot 165, carpenter and farmer 80

Boughton, David, (Triangle,) lot 35, justice of the peace and farmer 115.

Boughton, George, (Triangle,) lot 37, farmer leases of John W. Rich, 50

Brazee, Betsy Ann Mrs , (Chenango Forks,) lot 163, farmer 80

Brewer, Milton, (Whitney's Point,) lot 49, farmer 85.

M

Brockett, Willis, (Triangle,) lot 21, farmer 60.

Brown, Parley M., (Whitney's Point,) lot 73, farmer 190

Bughardt, Chas. M, (Whitney's Point,) lot 361, farmer 135

Burroughs, Benj, (Chenango Forks,) egg and produce dealer, and farmer

BURROUGHS, BENJAMIN J, (Chenango Forks,) (*Porter & Burroughs*)

Burroughs, Harvey L, (Chenango Forks,) lot 239, farmer 227.

Caton, Hugh, (Whitney's Point,) lot 70, farmer leases 315

Clark, Elijah M, (Castle Creek,) lot 238, drover and farmer 160

Cole, John, (Chenango Forks,) lot 200, butcher and farmer 100

Combe, Rufus, (Chenango Forks,) lot 64, farmer 100.

Cook, Chester, (Whitney's Point,) lot 322, carpenter and farmer 10

Cook, Squire D., (Chenango Forks,) lot 63, farmer 135

Copeland, Lorenzo D., (Chenango Forks,) carriage maker

Courtney, Henry, (Whitney's Point,) lot 320, farmer leases of Chester Atwater, 114

Coy Cyrus J (Whitney's Point,) lot 237, farmer 240.

Crowell, Alfred, (Castle Creek,) lot 204, farmer leases of Philo Landers, 75.

Crowell, Hamilton L, (Chenango Forks,) (*Harrington & Crowell*)

Cunningham, Asa, (Chenango Forks,) lot 202, farmer 40

Davis, Walter W. (Whitney's Point,) lot 244, farmer 94.

Decker, A. B., (Chenango Forks,) lot 198, farmer leases of Lyman Lyon, 196.

Dickinson, Frances M, (Whitney's Point,) lot 361, farmer 39.

Dickinson, Henry B., (Whitney's Point,) lot 322, farmer 60.

Dunham, Alex M Mrs, (Whitney's Point,) lot 284, farmer 64.

Dunham, Elias, (Glen Aubrey,) lot 205, farmer 50.

Dunham, Hiram, (Whitney's Point,) lot 282, farmer 150.

Dunham, Leonard W., (Castle Creek,) lot 167, farmer 55

Dunham, Nelson, (Castle Creek,) lot 157, butcher, drover and farmer 100.

Eldridge, Benedict, (Whitney's Point,) lot 280, farmer 100

Eldridge, Geo. W, (Whitney's Point,) lot 242, farmer 100.

Eldridge, John B, (Whitney's Point,) lot 321, farmer 120

Ellerson, Hamilton, (Whitney's Point,) lot 360, farmer 120

Ellerson, Ruth Mrs., (Whitney's Point,) lot 360, farmer 40.

ELLIOTT, JOSEPH, (Chenango Forks,) lot 66, farmer 100

English, David, (Whitney's Point,) lot 48, farmer leases of Nathaniel Newell, 314

English, Jonathan, (Chenango Forks,) lot 49, farmer 100

English, Mary Mrs., (Chenango Forks,) lot 39, farmer 50

Ferguson, O. Clark, (Whitney's Point,) lot 202, farmer 100.

Filkins, George, (Chenango Forks,) farmer

Filkins, Jane Miss, (Chenango Forks,) toll collector

Foote, John M., (Whitney's Point,) lot 284, farmer 72.

Foote, Wm, (Castle Creek,) lot 204, carpenter and farmer 131.

Ford, Nathan, (Whitney's Point,) lot 319, farmer 175

Fuller, Orlando C, (Whitney's Point,) lot 49, farmer 215

Galloway, G W., (Castle Creek,) lot 165, farmer 120

Gaylord, Aaron, (Castle Creek,) lot 165, farmer 150

Gaylord, Calvin H., (Whitney's Point,) lot 283, farmer 71

Gaylord, Chas., (Whitney's Point,) lot 244, farmer 80.

Gaylord, Elias, (Whitney's Point,) lot 244, farmer 180

Gaylord, Osborne, (Whitney's Point,) lot 282, farmer 280

Graves, Edward, (Castle Creek,) lot 204, farmer 190.

Gray, Albert, (Chenango Forks,) lot 199, farmer 58

Gray, Ambrose, (Castle Creek,) lot 157, farmer 200.

Gray, Harriet Mrs., (Castle Creek,) lot 164, farmer 73

Gray, Harvey, (Castle Creek,) lot 195, farmer 120.

Gray, Hiram, (Whitney's Point,) lot 278, farmer 10

Gray, John, (Chenango Forks,) lot 200, farmer 95

Gray, Richard, (Chenango Forks,) lot 168, farmer 130.

Green, Luke E., (Chenango Forks,) lot 40, farmer 165

Guernsey, Milo M, (Whitney's Point,) lot 361, sawyer and farmer 12

Hagaman, John, (Chenango Forks,) (*with Maurice*,) farmer, in Fenton, 72.

Hagaman, Maurice, (Chenango Forks,) (*with John*,) farmer, in Fenton, 73

Hagaman, M & Son, (Chenango Forks,) general merchants.

HALL, DAVID, (Chenango Forks,) lot 160, farmer 260

HANES, ROBERT T., (Chenango Forks,) horse shoeing and carriage ironing

Hanes, Willhelmus M., (Chenango Forks,) blacksmith

Harrington & Crowell, (Chenango Forks,) (*Hamilton L. Crowell and Franklin Harrington*,) groceries, crockery and hardware

Harrington, Franklin, (Chenango Forks,) (*Harrington & Crowell*)

HARRINGTON, RUSSELL, (Whitney's Point,) lot 320, farmer 300.

HARRINGTON, SALPHRONIUS H., A. B., M. D, (Chenango Forks,) druggist, physician and surgeon, and farmer 10.

HATFIELD, WM., (Chenango Forks,) lot 201, farmer 230.

Hayes, Augustin, (Castle Creek,) lot 204, farmer 50

Hayes & Beach, (Whitney's Point,) (*Elias Hayes and —— Beach*,) lot 279, farmer 70.

Hayes, Elias, (Whitney's Point,) (*Hayes & Beach*)

Hayes, Harriet Mrs., (Castle Creek,) lot 164, farmer 70

Hayes, Jacob, (Castle Creek,) lot 164, farmer 135

Heath, Wm.,(Whitney's Point,) lot 279, farmer 15

HAYWOOD, THOMAS Rev., (Chenango Forks,) lot 67, pastor of Congregational Church

Hill, John A, (Chenango Forks,) proprietor of Tioughnioga House

Hoadley, George, (Chenango Forks,) general merchant

Hoag, John, (Triangle,) lot 38, farmer leases 140

Holder, William, (Chenango Forks,) lot 67, constable and carpenter.

Holland, Elijah D., (Chenango Forks,) lot 240, farmer 74.

Holland, Elmira Mrs., (Whitney's Point,) lot 362, farmer 25

Holland, John, (Chenango Forks,) lot 162, farmer leases of Lot Brown, 60.

Holland, Silas W., (Chenango Forks,) lot 241, farmer 100.

Holmes, Wm. H (Castle Creek,) lot 195, farmer 153

Howard, Henry & Son, (Castle Creek,) (*Ira,*) lot 166 farmer 70

Howard Ira, (Castle Creek,) (*Henry Howard & Son*)

Hulslander, Samuel, (Whitney's Point,) lot 283, farmer leases of Edwin F Hyde, 150

Hurlbut, Chas. (Chenango Forks,) lot 203, farmer leases of Harry Lyon, 250.

Hurlbut, Chauncy L ,(Whitney's Point,) lot 74, farmer 420.

Hurlbut, Homer, (Chenango Forks,) lot 50, farmer leases of Chauncy L , 120

Hyde, Chas. Jr., (Whitney's Point,) lot 277, farmer 85

Hyde, Chas. Sen , (Whitney's Point,) lot 283, farmer 220.

Hyde, Geo (Whitney's Point,) lot 277, farmer 260.

Jackson, William, (Chenango Forks,) lot 67, agent for patent medicines and toll collector.

Johnson, Theodore, (Chenango Forks,) lot 54, farmer leases of Simon, 130.

King, Harry, (Chenango Forks,) lot 202, assessor and farmer 70

KINYON, JOHN W (Chenango Forks,) town assessor, hardware, crockery and tin ware

Kinyon, Jonathan, (Whitney's Point,) lot 73, farmer 136

Kinyon, Milo, (Chenango Forks,) lot 54, farmer leases 226

Kinyon, Nathaniel Sen., (Chenango Forks,) lot 49, farmer 70.

Kinyon, Thurston, (Chenango Forks,) lot 40 farmer 93.

Kirby, Wm., (Whitney's Point,) lot 361, farmer 72.

Knapp, Asa, (Chenango Forks,) lot 163, farmer 140.

Knapp, E. C., (Chenango Forks,) lot 199, farmer leases 147

Knapp, John, (Whitney's Point,) lot 322, farmer 75.

Knapp, Richard, (Chenango Forks,) farmer 20

Knapp, Warren, (Chenango Forks,) lot 199, farmer 147.

Lakey, Thomas R., (Chenango Forks,) grocer

Lamb, Darius N., (Castle Creek,) lot 166, farmer 125

Leach, Parley Mrs , (Whitney's Point,) lot 280, farmer 200.

Lincoln, Jed D , (Chenango Forks,) lot 162, farmer leases of H. L Burroughs, 125.

LIVERMORE, BURR, (Chenango Forks,) lot 67, boot and shoe maker.

Lord, Lyman, (Chenango Forks,) shoe maker.

Lowell, Daniel, (Chenango Forks,) general merchant.

Lull, Daniel, (Whitney's Point,) lot 238, farmer leases of Asa Beach, 140

Madison, Lewis, (Chenango Forks,) lot 281, farmer leases of Mrs. Chester Eldridge, 100.

Marsh, Henry and Sarah, estate of, (Triangle,) lot 21, 110 acres.

Masten, James R , (Chenango Forks,) lot 62, farmer 108

Meade, Alexander, (Whitney's Point,) lot 69, farmer 100

Merrill, Almeron P. Rev., (Castle Creek,) lot 238, Baptist clergyman and farmer 130.

Mix, Geo . (Chenango Forks,) lot 162, farmer 100

Morse, John S., (Triangle,) lot 36, farmer 150

Murphy, Thos , (Whitney's Point,) lot 236, farmer 70

Morphy, Wm., (Whitney's Point,) lot 236, farmer 50.

Murray, James, (Whitney's Point,) lot 360, farmer 110.

Myrick, John, (Castle Creek,) lot 166, farmer 50.

Newman, Isaac, (Whitney's Point,) lot 43, farmer 250

Ockerman, John W , (Chenango Forks,) lot 65, farmer 100.

Owen, Daniel, (Chenango Forks,) lot 64, farmer 72

Page, Enos, (Whitney's Point,) lot 320, farmer 120

Palmer, Jenkins, (Chenango Forks,) blacksmith and, in Fenton, farmer 90.

Parsons, Alvah, (Chenango Forks,) (*with Benjamin B ,*) farmer.

Parsons, Benjamin B , (Chenango Forks,) (*with Alvah,*) farmer.

Parsons, Chauncy, (Chenango Forks,) lot 160, farmer 150.

Parsons, Horace W., (Whitney's Point,) lot 359, farmer 330

Parsons, Joseph S., (Whitney's Point,) lot 360, supervisor, lumberman and farmer 250.

PEASE, ALONZO, (Whitney's Point,) (*Wm. Pease & Son,*) lot 361, justice of the peace and farmer 17.

Pease, Newell, (Whitney's Point,) lot 319, farmer 200.

PEASE, WM., (Whitney's Point,) (*Wm. Pease & Son,*) lot 322, farmer 149.

PEASE, WM. & SON. (Whitney's Point,) (*Alonzo,*) lumbermen.

Phelps, Baruch, (Triangle,) lot 37, carpenter and farmer 70

Phelps, Orsemus, (Whitney's Point,) lot 284, farmer 66.

Phelps, Seth, (Triangle,) lot 21, farmer 80.

PORTER & BURROUGHS, (Chenango Forks,) (*Erastus B Porter and Benjamin J Burroughs,*) produce commission merchants and grocers

PORTER, ERASTUS B., (Chenango Forks,) (*Porter & Burroughs.*)

Porter, James H , (Chenango Forks,) merchant tailor.

Potter, Eugene, (Chenango Forks,) lot 49, farmer 100

Prince, David, (Chenango Forks,) lot 40, farmer 106.

Prince, Samuel, (Chenango Forks,) lot 39, farmer 76

Puffer, Moses, (Castle Creek,) lot 164, farmer 40 and leases 73.

Purdy, William E., (Chenango Forks,) lot 62, road commissioner and farmer 69.

Read, Thomas P , (Chenango Forks,) lot 60, farmer leases of Niles Kinyon, 160

Relyea, Selah O., (Chenango Forks,) lot 200, farmer 70

Remmelee. John J., (Whitney's Point,) local M E preacher.

Reynolds, Peter, (Chenango Forks,) lot 53, farmer 85

Rich, John W , (Triangle,) farmer leases 450.

Rich, John W. Mrs., (Triangle,) lot 37, farmer 150

Rogers, Charles, (Whitney's Point,) lot 38, farmer 134.

Rogers, George, (Chenango Forks,) lot 87, farmer 200.

ROGERS, HENRY A., (Chenango Forks,) postmaster and prop. of refreshment room

Rogers, John, (Chenango Forks,) (*with Simeon B ,*) lot 67, farmer 75.

ROGERS JOHN B , (Chenango Forks,) (*J. B. Rogers & Co.,*) (*Rogers & Wheeler*)

ROGERS, J. B. & CO , (Chenango Forks,) dealers in and shippers of all kinds of produce

Rogers, Simeon B , (Chenango Forks,) (*with John,*) lot 67, farmer 75

Root, Myron S. (Whitney's Point,) lot 281, farmer 100

Rummer, Henry, (Castle Creek,) lot 196, sawyer and farmer 30,

Shandley, Michael, (Whitney's Point,) lot 236, marble cutter and farmer 60.

Shattuck, David, (Chenango Forks,) lot 54, farmer 140

Sherwood, Isaac, (Chenango Forks,) lot 51, farmer leases of Simon Strickland, 125,

Shevalier, Solomon, (Whitney's Point,) lot 236, farmer 74.

Shipman, Lawson, (Whitney's Point,) lot 320, justice of the peace and farmer 98,

Smith, Darius M , (Whitney's Point,) lot 284, farmer 70.

Smith, John, (Chenango Forks,) lot 63, farmer 60

Sparling, Henry, (Whitney's Point,) farmer 3.

Spendley, Zina A., (Chenango Forks,) allo physician.

Stickney, Franklin (Whitney's Point,) lot 48, bridge builder and farmer 100,

Stiles, Simeon, (Whitney's Point,) lot 244, farmer 100

Stoddard, Angeline, (widow,) (Chenango Forks,) lot 67, agent for sewing machines and musical instruments

Stoddard, Ebenezer, (Chenango Forks,) lot 162, farmer 25.

STODDARD, ISAAC T.,(Chenango Forks,) town clerk, notary public, general insurance agent, &c

Stoddard, Thomas, (Chenango Forks,) grocer and farmer 10.

Stoughton, Garritt V. H., (Whitney's Point,) (*G. V. H. Stoughton & Son,*) lot 279, farmer 50

Stoughton, Geo., (Whitney's Point,) (*G. V. H. Stoughton & Son* )

Stoughton, G V H & Son, (Whitney's Point,) (*Garritt V. H. and Geo.,*) lot 279, farmer 160.

Stoughton, John, (Whitney's Point,) lot 279, farmer 73.

Stowell, Isaac R , (Triangle,) lot 21, farmer leases of Asa D Leonard, 150

Stowell, Oscar, (Castle Creek,) lot 166, poor master and farmer 100

Stowell, Sherman, (Triangle,) lot 22, carpenter and farmer 36

Strickland, Uriah, (Chenango Forks,) lot 63, carpenter and farmer 140

SWEETLAND, ALVAN, (Triangle,) lot 22, farmer 200

Terwilliger, Harman B , (Triangle,) lot 21, farmer 88

Terwilliger, Harmon S., (Chenango Forks,) lot 62, farmer 50

Terwilliger. Nelson, (Chenango Forks,) lot 85, farmer 95.

Terwilliger, William, (Whitney's Point,) lot 74, farmer leases 140

Thompson, Anson B., (Chenango Forks,) lot 160, farmer 40

Thurston, Ransom, (Whitney's Point,) lot 300, farmer 80

Thurston, Thomas, (Chenango Forks,) lot 51, farmer 50.

Torry, A Rev , (Chenango Forks,) lot 6, farmer 285.

Walter, A. B , (Whitney's Point,) lot 284, farmer 218

Walter, Philo G., (Whitney's Point,) lot 858, farmer 121.

Weller, James E., (Chenango Forks,) lot 67, harness maker.

Wentworth, David F., (Whitney's Point,) lot 320, farmer 15.

Westover, Dorus, (Whitney's Point,) lot 71, constable and farmer 187.

Whaley, Thomas, (Chenango Forks,) lot 67, farmer 10.

Wheeler, Cyrus, (Chenango Forks,) lot 67, saw and grist mills

White, Henry M', (Castle Creek,) lot 237, sawyer, school teacher and farmer 60

Wooster, James K , (Whitney's Point,) (*with Moses,*) lot 318, farmer 136

Wooster, Moses, (Whitney's Point,) (*with James K ,*) lot 318, farmer 136.

Wright, Reuben W., (Castle Creek,) lot 196, farmer leases of John Foote, 20.

# BINGHAMTON. (Town.)

### (Post Office Addresses in Parentheses.)

### *For Directory of Binghamton City, see Index to Business Directory.*

ABBREVIATIONS.—B P., Bingham's Patent; H. T., Hornby Tract; S. T, Sidney Tract; C. P., Cooper's Patent; S Ts., Sidney Township.

Aldrich, Henry, (Hawleyton,) lot 19, farmer

Aldrich, Solomon, (Binghamton,) lot 3, builder and farmer 300. /

Andrews, Peleg, (Binghamton,) carpenter, Main

Andrus, E. F., (Binghamton,) insurance agent.

ARNOLD, C V Rev., (Hawleyton,) pastor of M E Church.

Bacon, J. J, (Binghamton,) lot 3, farmer 20

Badger, F. F., (Binghamton,) farmer 7, Main

Bailey, Oliver, (Binghamton,) lot 32, B. P, farmer 150.

Baird, Lewis, (Binghamton,) lot 17, B. P., farmer leases 121.

Baird, Lorenzo, (Binghamton,) lot 17, B. P, carpenter and farmer 2.

BAKER, H. N., (Binghamton,) lot 2, inventor of printing telegraph, electric lamp, magneto and electric machines, silver plater, gilder and farmer 78.

Balcom, George, (Hawleyton,) teacher.

Barnum, Zenus Jr, (Binghamton,) lot 27, B P, farmer 92.

Beach, David, (Binghamton,) lot 206, farmer 85

Beaty, Napoleon, (Port Dickinson,) miller

Bedell, Ira, (Binghamton,) lot 198, farmer 7.

BEDELL, MARCUS, (Binghamton,) lot 80, C. P, farmer 32½.

Bedell, Seneca, (Binghamton,) lot 198, farmer 5

BEEBE, J. E., (Binghamton,) lot 10, B. P., farmer 166

Bevier, C, (Port Dickinson,) broom manuf and carpenter.

Blair, Franklin, (Binghamton,) lot 198, farmer 6.

Blanding, P. M. Mrs., (Hawleyton,) school teacher.

Blanding, William, (Hawleyton,) lot 19, cheese maker.

Bouran, Andrew, (Hawleyton,) lot 65, C. P, pump and block maker and farmer 150.

Bowley, Henry, (Binghamton,) lot 180, farmer 80

Bradley, Dan E, (Hawleyton,) lot 58, C. P., farmer 50.

Brady, Bartholomew, (Hawleyton,) lot 55, C. P., farmer 50

Brady, Michael, (Hawleyton,) lot 63, farmer 50.

Bronson, Samuel, (Binghamton,) lot 12, B. P., farmer 1.

Broome Co Alms House, (Binghamton,) lot 28, B. P., farm 130, M. B. Payne, keeper

Brown, L. H, (Binghamton,) gardener and farmer

Brown, Levi J., (Binghamton,) lot 29, B P, farmer leases 100

BROWN, P. M., (Binghamton,) farmer 40

Brown, Sallie Mrs, (Binghamton,) lot 3. B. P., farmer 70.

Bump, Roswell, (Binghamton,) lot 2, B P., gardener, dealer in plants and farmer 16.

Burbank, Geo W, (Binghamton,) lot 33, B. P, farmer 75.

Burlingame, Pardon T., (Binghamton,) lot 5, H. T., farmer 55.

Bush, S. W., (Binghamton,) chaplain of New York State Inebriate Asylum.

Butler, Lewis, (Hawleyton,) lot 36, C. P, farmer leases 25.

Cadden, Philip, (Hawleyton,) prop of Union Hotel and farmer 243.

CADDIN, MICHAEL, (Hawleyton,) lot 57, C. P, farmer leases 142.

Cafferty, Josiah, (Binghamton,) lot 3, farmer

Callan, Christie, (Hawleyton,) lot 19, farmer 100.

Carman, Cornelius, (Binghamton,) lot 8, S. Ts, farmer 50.

CARMAN, ISAAC W., (Binghamton,) lot 5, farmer 30 and leases of Thomas R Carman, 55

CARMAN, JOSEPH. (Port Dickinson,) lot 31, town assessor, milk dealer, gardener and farmer 270.

Carman, Stephen, (Binghamton,) lot 5, farmer 200.

Carman, S. N., (Port Dickinson,) lot 31, clerk for McKinney & Phelps and farmer 150.

Carman, Thomas V, (Binghamton,) lot 36, C. P, farmer leases 25

CARR, A L., (Binghamton,) (*T. E Carr & Co.*)

CARR, T E & CO , (Binghamton,) (*A. L. Carr,*) butchers, residence Clinton St., market 2 Main

CARVER, JAMES, (Binghamton,) lot 12, B P , farmer 805; Mr. Carver has several farms for sale in the vicinity of Binghamton, those wishing to purchase will do well to call.

Cary, Sturges, (Binghamton,) retired farmer 30.

Cash, Stephan, (Binghamton,) lot 32, B P., stone mason and farmer 5½.

Castle, George, (Binghamton,) lot 21, farmer 200.

Champlin, P , (Port Dickinson,) lot 6, B. P., painter.

Chapine, R C., (Binghamton,) lot 17, B. P , farmer.

Chapman, John, (Hawleyton,) lot 24, farmer 100.

Chase, Franklin N , (Binghamton,) lot 32, B P., painter and farmer 6.

Clapp, C. S (Binghamton,) lot 11, B P , farmer 136.

CLARK, CHAS A , (Binghamton,) lot 2, carpenter and builder

Clark, Otis, (Binghamton,) lot 3, farmer leases 7

CLINE, DANFORD B , (Hawleyton,) lot 68, C. P., farmer leases of P. J. S. Coon, 111

Cline, D N. (Hawleyton,) lot 71, C. P., carpenter and farmer 38

Cline, Daniel N (Hawleyton,) lot 71, C. P., farmer 40

Cline. James L , (Hawleyton,) lot 54, C P , farmer 200

Cline, Wm. M., (Hawleyton,) lot 54, C. P., farmer.

COCKS, DAVID, (Binghamton,) lot 32, B. P , gardener and farmer 37.

Congdon, Ezra, (Port Dickinson,) miller

Congdon, Joel G., (Binghamton,) lot 201, farmer 50.

CONKLIN, ELIAS, (Port Dickinson,) canal collector and (*with Wm M. Temple,*) wagon ironing and jobbing

CONKLIN, E W , (Binghamton,) lot 81, B P , drover, jobber in seeds &c. and farmer 152.

Conklin, Horace, (Binghamton,) lot 32, B. P , farmer 50

Connerty, Thomas, (Hawleyton,) lot 61, C P , farmer 163

Coon, Asa, (Hawleyton,) lot 20, farmer 130

Coon, Datus J W., (Hawleyton,) lot 59, C. P , farmer 100.

COON, PETER J. S., (Hawleyton,) lot 19, justice of the peace, notary public, carpenter and farmer 246.

COONRAD, WILLIAM A , (Binghamton,) farmer 1.

Curran, James, (Binghamton,) shoe maker

Curtis, Watson, (Binghamton,) lot 201, milk dealer and farmer 142.

Cutler, J. W. (Binghamton,) lot 30, B P , ice dealer and farmer 270.

Cutler, Philander, (Binghamton,) (*with Wm*) lot 31, B P , ice dealer

Cutler P E , (Binghamton,) lot 32, B. P., ice dealer.

Cutler. Wm., (Binghamton,) (*with Philander,*) lot 31, B P , ice dealer

Danforth, William, (Binghamton,) lot 3, toll gate keeper and farmer 67

Davis, Abram A , (Binghamton,) lot 200, farmer 100

Davis, Cornelius, (Binghamton,) (*with Jas Q ,*) farmer leases 100

Davis, Isaac A., (Binghamton,) lot 179, farmer 100

Davis, James Q , (Binghamton,) (*with Cornelius,*) farmer leases 100.

Dean Levi F , (Binghamton,) bridge builder and gardener, Main

Denison, B. A., (Binghamton,) farmer 6.

Dewey, Augustus T., (Binghamton,) lot 10, S Ts , town assessor and farmer 136

DICKINSON, EDGAR, (Port Dickinson,) (*Dickinson & Hunt* )

DICKINSON & HUNT, (Port Dickinson,) (*Edgar Dickinson and Amos O. Hunt,*) manufa of all kinds of whips

Dickson, Luke, (Binghamton,) lot 3, B. P., farmer 30.

Didrick, Daniel, (Binghamton,) lot 199, farmer 200.

Dings, John A , (Binghamton,) lot 8, farmer 16.

Disbrow, Samuel, (Hawleyton,) lot 77, C. P., farmer 20.

Dodge, D G Dr , (Binghamton,) supt. of New York State Inebriate Asylum.

Dolan, Bernard, (Binghamton,) lot 15, C. P , farmer 84

DOONEN, CHARLES, (Hawleyton,) lot 36, C P , farmer 125

Drake, Cornelius, (Binghamton,) lot 36, C. P., farmer 50

Drake, Elijah, (Hawleyton,) lot 51, farmer 80

DRAKE, MORGAN, (Hawleyton,) lot 19, farmer 108.

Drake, William T., (Hawleyton,) lot 51, C. P . farmer 50.

Dutcher, George, (Binghamton,) engineer

Edgcomb, Samuel A , (Binghamton ) lot 7, farmer 144

Edgcomb, Thomas, (Binghamton,) lot 30, C. P., farmer 70.

Edgcomb, William H , (Binghamton,) lot 30, C P , farmer 117.

Ellis, Levi, (Binghamton,) lot 14, farmer 105

ELY, JOSEPH E. Hon , (Binghamton,) farmer 80

Ely, Marietta B. Mrs , (Binghamton,) Sunny Side, farmer 70.

EVANS, ELIZABETH A Mrs , (Binghamton,) lot 10, B. P., farmer 40

Everetts, R., (Hawleyton,) lot 77, C. P , farmer 20

FAIRCHILD, HENRY W., (Binghamton,) gardener and farmer 7, Main

Fairchild, Wm., (Binghamton,) gardener.

Finney, I. A., (Binghamton,) farmer 12, Clinton St

Finney, Richard, (Binghamton,) carpenter, Clinton St

FLEMING, LEONARD, (Binghamton,) lot 11, B. P., farmer leases 136

Folmsbee, James, (Binghamton,) lot 1, S Ts, farmer 2.

Fonaby, James, (Binghamton,) lot 3, farmer 2½

Fosburgh, Henry, (Hawleyton,) lot 52, C. P , farmer 4

Fosburgh, Luman, (Hawleyton,) lot 52, C. P., farmer 24.

FRANK, CHARLES, (Binghamton,) lot 32, B P, farmer leases of H. F. Bronson, 20.

French, Oliver, (Binghamton,) lot 15, farmer 62.

GAFFNEY, JOHN, (Binghamton,) lot 23, C P., farmer 50

Gaffney, Martin, (Binghamton,) lot 32, B. P., farmer leases of Lewis Seymore, 120

Gage, Asa, (Hawleyton,) lot 55, C. P., farmer 60.

Gage, Asa, (Hawleyton,) carpenter

Gage, Benjamin S, (Hawleyton,) retired farmer.

GAGE, EDWARD H., (Hawleyton,) lot 19, sawyer.

Gage, Isaac G., (Hawleyton,) lot 20, farmer.

Gage, Jesse, (Hawleyton,) lot 20, farmer 200

Gage, Moses, (Binghamton,) lot 29, C P., farmer 90

GAGE, STEPHEN, (Hawleyton,) lot 53, C P, farmer leases of E A. Meeker, 57

GAGE, THEODORE H., (Hawleyton,) lot 19, postmaster, hop raiser and farmer 120

Gahagan, Thomas, (Hawleyton,) lot 24, farmer 150

GAIGE, ANSEL H. (Binghamton,) lot 32, B P, gardener, fruit raiser and farmer 5

Gale, A C (Binghamton,) lot 32, B. P., mechanic and farmer 8.

Gale, John, (Binghamton,) lot 15, C. P., farmer 53.

GARRISON, WARREN, (Binghamton,) lot 2, farmer.

Germon, Wm., (Port Dickinson,) carpenter.

Giblin, John, (Hawleyton,) lot 56, C. P., farm estate of P Giblin, 100

Graves, Wm., (Binghamton,) lot 34, B. P., farmer 20

Green, Charles, (Binghamton,) lot 2, B. P., gardener.

GREEN, WILLIAM, (Port Dickinson,) farmer

HALLSTEAD, W. B., (Binghamton,) overseer of D. L. & W. R Binghamton Bridge

HAMILTON, AUGUSTUS, (Binghamton,) lot 11, C. P., farmer 200

Harder, Jacob, (Binghamton,) lot 198, farmer 12.

Harding, A W., (Hawleyton,) lot 20, blacksmith and farmer 26.

Harmon, O, (Binghamton,) surveyor and carpenter, Brown.

HASKINS, HENRY, (Binghamton,) gardener, fruit dealer and farmer 30.

Hanver, Wm A. Mrs. (Binghamton,) lot 27, B. P., farmer 62.

Hematrought, Leonard, (Binghamton,) farmer leases 80.

Hoadley, Jerry N, (Binghamton,) lot 32, B. P., farmer 12.

Holmes, Frederick A, (Binghamton,) lot 9, B. P., farmer 90

Holmes, Seth, (Binghamton,) (*Ogden & Holmes.*)

Holmes, W. S., (Binghamton,) lot 2, B P, gardener.

HOLT, J. N, (Port Dickinson,) butcher and farmer 36

Holt, Walter M., (Binghamton,) lot 3, B P, butcher

Hooper, A, (Binghamton,) lot 33, B. P., farmer 52.

House, Royal E. Prof (Binghamton,) inventor of printing telegraph and farmer 92.

Howard, Samuel, (Binghamton,) lot 17, B. P, farmer 200

Howell, Walter, (Binghamton,) lot 8, S Ts., farmer leases 109.

Hulbert, Newton M., (Binghamton,) lot 32, B P., farmer 40.

Humphrey, Joseph, (Binghamton,) lot 3, farmer 53 and leases of John Lockwood, 90

HUNT, AMOS C, (Port Dickinson,) (*Dickinson & Hunt.*)

Hurlbut, LeRoy, (Binghamton,) lot 32, B. P., farmer 30.

Jarvis, Wm A, (Binghamton,) lot 14, C. P., farmer 63.

Jaycox, Ebenezer, (Hawleyton,) lot 20, farmer 25.

Jaycox, Henry L., (Hawleyton,) lot 19, farmer 50.

Jaycox, Henry W, (Hawleyton,) lot 20, apiarian, hop raiser and farmer 50.

JEWELL, G A., (Port Dickinson,) (*C. P. Jewell & Son,*) postmaster, town clerk and agent for Paloubt, Pelton & Co's standard organs

JEWELL, C. P & SON, (Port Dickinson,) (*G A.,*) dry goods, groceries, boots, shoes, &c., also props. of National Hotel.

JONES, M. L., (Port Dickinson,) school teacher and clerk for canal collector

Keator, George N., (Hawleyton,) prop. of Six Mile House

Kelley, Wm. H., (Binghamton,) captain of whaling vessel.

Kent, A. F., (Port Dickinson,) milk peddler.

KIRBY, HENRY M, (Binghamton,) farmer leases of Mrs. Charlotte Moeller, 200.

Langdon, Calvin, (Port Dickinson,) lot 6, B P., farmer 7.

Lawrence, Benjamin, (Binghamton,) (*Lawrence & Waldron.*)

Lawrence & Waldron, (Binghamton,) (*Benjamin Lawrence and Jacob V A. Waldron,*) lot 10, S. Ts., lumber manufs and dealers, and farmers 220.

Layton, Smith, (Binghamton,) lot 8, farmer leases of O H Chalker, 22.

Lee, Edwin, (Port Dickinson,) boatman

Lee, Josiah, (Port Dickinson,) speculator

Livermore, I. B, (Binghamton,) lot 32, B. P., farmer 35.

Lockland, Thomas, (Binghamton,) lot 8, S. Ts., farmer 165.

Matthews, A. C (Binghamton,) farmer 85.

Matthews, E. F., (Binghamton,) farmer 70

McCarty, Patrick, (Binghamton,) lot 2, B. P., farmer.

McCloud, Ralph, (Binghamton,) lot 30, C. P., farmer leases 100.

McGRAW, D. C., (Binghamton,) (*Mills & McGraw.*)
McIvor, Wm. C, (Binghamton,) mason, Main
McKeeby, George, (Binghamton,) farmer leases 25.
McKeeby, Martha Mrs., (Binghamton,) farmer 25.
MEAKER, ANDREW, (Hawleyton,) lot 70, C. P., farmer 6 and leases 68.
Meeker, Alphens, (Hawleyton,) lot 71, C. P., farmer 80
Meeker, Andrew, (Hawleyton,) lot 77, C P., farmer 50.
MEEKER, CHARLES J., (Binghamton,) C P., farmer 128.
MEEKER, ELI S., (Hawleyton,) lot 19, carpenter, lumber manuf and farmer 64
MEEKER, LORENZO D., (Hawleyton,) lot 20, farmer 75.
MEEKER, SAMUEL, (Hawleyton,) lot 70, C P., farmer 63.
MERRILL, H. E., (Binghamton,) lot 2, farmer leases of I. L. Bartlett, 110.
Milk, Benjamin B., (Hawleyton,) lot 20, wool carder and farmer 50.
Milk, David, (Hawleyton,) lot 24, farmer 50.
*MILLS & McGRAW, (Binghamton,) (*M. H. Mills and D C. McGraw,*) props. River Side Gardens, half a mile east of water works, producers and dealers in choice flowers, and vegetable seeds, also greenhouse plants, ornamental shrubbery and trees, fruit trees and small fruits.
MILLS, M. H., (Binghamton,) (*Mills & McGraw.*)
Moore, Charles F., (Binghamton,) lot 17, B P., farmer 1 and leases of John Moore, 200
Morey, Giles, (Binghamton,) lot 8, S. Te., farmer 100.
Morris, John, (Binghamton,) lot 8, S. Ta., stone quarry and farmer 15.
MOSES, JOHN, (Hawleyton,) lot 19, sawyer and farmer 108¼.
Mosher, Henry, (Hawleyton,)wagon maker.
Murphy, Michael, (Binghamton,) farmer 40.
Nash, A. B., (Port Dickinson,) carpenter
Nash, D., (Port Dickinson,) lot 6, B. P., carpenter.
NATIONAL HOTEL, (Port Dickinson,) C. P. Jewell & Son, props.
New York State Inebriate Asylum, (Binghamton,) Dr. D. G. Dodge, supt ; Carrol Hyde, secretary; S. W. Bush, chaplain.
NORTON, ELIHU, (Binghamton,) stock dealer and builder.
O'BRIEN, JAMES, (Binghamton,) canal grocery.
Ogden, Charles, (Binghamton,) overseer of Port Dickinson Paper Mill,
Ogden, Henry B., (Binghamton,) (*Ogden & Holmes.*)
Ogden & Holmes, (Binghamton,) (*Henry B. Ogden and Seth Holmes,*) brick manufs.
Olds, Erastus H., (Binghamton,) lot 27, B. P., farmer leases 62.
Ostrander, Jared, (Hawleyton,) lot 20, farmer leases of Lorenzo D. Meeker, 75.

Page, Henry, (Binghamton,) lot 33, B. P., farmer 35.
Parker, Uriah, (Binghamton,) lot 32, B, P., farmer 40.
Parsons, Charles N., (Hawleyton,) lot 19, farmer
Parsons, Samuel W., (Hawleyton,) lot 19, farmer 75
Payne, A. R, (Binghamton,) supt. Susquehanna Valley Home
Payne, A. R. Mrs, (Binghamton,) matron Susquehanna Valley Home.
Payne, John F, (Binghamton,) lot 12, B. P., farmer 20.
Payne, L. J., (Binghamton,) agent and farmer 9.
PAYNE, M. B, (Binghamton,) lot 28, B. P., keeper of Broome Co Alms House
Place, Andrew, (Binghamton,) lot 8, farmer 50.
PLATT, ANDREW, (Hawleyton,) (*with Henry,*) lot 37, C. P., farmer leases of Frank Pierce, 63
PLATT, HENRY, (Hawleyton,) (*with Andrew,*) lot 37, C. P, farmer leases of Frank Pierce, 63.
PRENTICE, ELIAS, (Hawleyton,) lot 19, teamster and farmer 5
PRENTICE, HARVEY L., (Hawleyton,) lot 19, farmer 11¼.
Prentice, Wm M, (Binghamton,) lot 8, farmer 53.
Presson, Joseph G, (Binghamton,) lot 12, C. P., farmer 74.
Richards, Ezra, (Binghamton,) farmer 175
Rider, L, (Binghamton,) teamster and farmer 25.
*RIVER SIDE GARDENS, (Binghamton,) half a mile east of water works, Mills & McGraw, props., producers and dealers in choice flowers and vegetable seeds, also greenhouse plants, ornamental shrubbery and trees, fruit trees and small fruits.
ROBERTS, E. W, (Port Dickinson,) lot 6, farmer and, (*with Wm. H. and John W.,*) owns trout pond.
ROBERTS, JOHN W., (Port Dickinson,) (*with Wm. H. and E. W.,*) owns trout pond.
ROBERTS, WM H, (Port Dickinson,) lot 6, farmer 2½ and, (*with E. W. and John W.,*) owns trout pond.
ROCKWELL, M. C., (Binghamton,) director of Washington and Asylum Street Rail Road and farmer 42.
Ronk, C., (Binghamton,) lot 13, C. P., farmer 75.
Ross, L A, (Binghamton,) carpenter.
Rosencrance, Charles, (Binghamton,) lot 28, C. P., farmer leases 50
Rowley, Nathaniel, (Hawleyton,) lot 89, farmer 200.
Rowley, Timothy T., (Hawleyton,) lot 20, farmer 110
Rozell, Joshua, (Binghamton,) lot 181, farmer 150.
Rulofson, John W., (Hawleyton,) lot 77, O. P., farmer 70.
Sanford, Dudley, (Hawleyton,) (*with Frederick,*) lot 53, farmer 200
Sanford, Frederick, (Hawleyton,) lot 53, (*with Dudley,*) farmer 200.

Sanlsbury, George, (Hawleyton,) lot 67, C P , farmer leases of Wesley Cline, 15.

Scoville, Henry, (Port Dickinson,) lot 3, B. P , farmer.

Settle, Andrew, (Binghamton,) mason, Main

Shear, Jacob D , (Binghamton,) lot 198, carpenter and farmer 33.

Sherman, David, (Hawleyton,) lot 19, farmer 27

Sherwood, George, (Binghamton,) lot 1, S Ts , farmer 118

Shippey, Daniel, (Binghamton,) lot 15, farmer 98.

SMITH, ERASTUS W , (Binghamton,) lot 35, B P., farmer 180

Smith, Wm , (Binghamton,) lot 8, S. Ts., farmer leases of Mrs. Jane Sester, 115

Smithers, Michael, (Binghamton,) shoemaker, foot of Clinton

Soule, Caleb N , (Hawleyton,) lot 58, C. P., farmer 60.

Spafford, Charles, (Hawleyton,) lot 70, C P., farmer 28.

SPRAGUE, CHARLES R., (Binghamton,) lot 27, B P , milk dealer and farmer 140.

STAGE, CHAUNCEY T , (Binghamton,) gardener and dealer in vegetables, plants, trees &c., Cary.

Stephens, Daniel, (Binghamton,) lot 27, O P , farmer 105

Stephens, John, (Binghamton,) lot 12, S. Ts , farmer 2.

Sternbergh, E., (Binghamton,) lot 4, farmer 50.

Stever, H . (Port Dickinson,) stage driver

Stiger, Joseph, (Binghamton,) lot 10, B. P , farmer leases 40

Stone, Archibald, (Binghamton,) lot 3, S. T , farmer 25

STONE. FREDERICK W , (Binghamton,) lot 2, commissioner of highways and farmer 8½.

STONE, W S , (Binghamton,) lot 3, S. T., farmer 200, leases of Archibald Stone, 25 and of Jas Munsel, 140.

Stow, E S , (Port Dickinson,) whip manuf.

Stow, George, (Port Dickinson,) lot 3, B. P , stock dealer and farmer 250.

Stow, Nelson, (Port Dickinson,) real estate dealer.

Strait, Samuel, (Hawleyton,) lot 19, shingle manuf.

Stringham, Smith, (Port Dickinson,) shoe maker.

Stroughtenborg, Oscar, (Binghamton,) carpenter

Susquehanna Valley Home, (Binghamton,) A. R. Payne, supt. ; Mrs. A. R Payne, matron

Swan, George P., (Binghamton,) farmer 17

TAMKINS, JAMES, (Binghamton,) lot 2, carpenter and joiner.

Taylor, Allen, (Binghamton,) cooper and farmer

TEMPLE, WM. M., (Port Dickinson,) (*with Elias Conklin.*) wagon ironing and jobbing.

Thompson, W. A , (Binghamton,) lot 12, B. P., farmer 200.

TIERS, JOHN, (Binghamton,) wagon maker and repairer, and justice of the peace.

Townsend, George, (Binghamton,) lot 181, farmer 10.

Tripp, Ablal, (Hawleyton,) lot 64, C. P., (*with James H ,*) farmer 100.

TRIPP, JAMES H., (Hawleyton,) lot 64, C. P., (*with Abial,*) farmer 100.

Tripp, Solomon, (Hawleyton,) lot 62, C P., farmer 41.

TRUESDELL, EMORY. (Binghamton,) real estate dealer and farmer 50.

Unkenbolz, Frederick, (Binghamton,) lot 17, B P., farmer leases 50

Van Valkenburg, James, (Binghamton,) lot 32, B P , farmer 75.

VAN WAGONER, EDWARD, (Binghamton,) groceries, provisions &c , foot of Clinton

Van Wagoner, Wm., (Binghamton,) farmer 3, end Clinton.

VERGASON, HIRAM K., (Hawleyton,) lot 19, millwright, lumber manuf and farmer 73

Wagner, Philip, (Binghamton,) lot 3, farmer 84.

Wagoner, Andrew, (Binghamton,) teamster

Waldron, Jacob, V A., (Binghamton,) (*Lawrence & Waldron*)

Warner, J D., (Binghamton,) farmer 1

Webb, David, (Hawleyton,) lot 19, farmer leases 250.

Wells, John J (Binghamton,) lot 32, B. P., gardener and farmer 10.

Whalen, Michael, (Binghamton,) lot 8, farmer 25.

Whitaker, Sylvester S., (Binghamton,) lot 5, H T , milk dealer and farmer 270½

WHITFORD, CHESTER G., (Binghamton,) grocer and harness maker at Ashery Corners, 2¾ miles north-west of city.

Whitmore, James, (Binghamton,) butcher, foot of Clinton.

Whitney, Henry J.,(Binghamton,) gymnast.

WHITNEY, RUFUS P . (Binghamton,) lot 33, B P , farmer leases 100.

Whitney, Washington, (Binghamton,) lot 33, B P , farmer 100

WHITNEY, WILLIAM, (Binghamton,) lot 13, town supervisor and farmer 120.

WIDERMAN, M H , (Binghamton,) lot 2, B P., farmer leases of John A Collier, 100.

Wilbur, Abram T., (Hawleyton,) lot 67, C. P , farmer 50.

Wilbur, Hiram L , (Hawleyton,) lot 60, C. P., farmer leases 152

Wilbur, Joseph, (Hawleyton,) lot 75, C P., farmer 35.

Wilcox, P. Rev (Port Dickinson,) pastor M. E Church.

Williams, J. O., (Hawleyton,) blacksmith

Wilson, Daniel, (Binghamton,) milk dealer and farmer 17.

Wilson, Wm. Y , (Binghamton,) cartman.

Woolsey, Edgar, (Binghamton,) lot 4, painter and farmer 70.

Wright, Erastus, (Binghamton,) lot 8, farmer 70.

Yagar, Adam, (Binghamton,) farmer 4.

Youngs, Wm., (Binghamton,) boatman.

# CHENANGO.

## (Post Office Addresses in Parentheses.)

ABBREVIATIONS.—G D B P, Grand Division of the Boston Purchase; S D B P, Small Division of the Boston Purchase.

Aitchison, John, (Binghamton,) lot 121, S. D. B. P., farmer 100.

Aitchison, Thos , (Binghamton,) lot 121, S D. B. P., (*with John*,) farmer 100

Aitchison, Thos. W., (Binghamton,) lot 162, S. D. B. P , farmer 50

Alderman, Bradley J., (Castle Creek,) lot 117, G D. B. P., farmer 90.

Alderman, Israel P (Castle Creek,) lot 77, G D B P, lumberman and farmer 152.

ALLEN, LEWIS, (Castle Creek,) (*Judd & Allen*)

ALLEN, SOLOMON P, (Castle Creek,) allo. physician and surgeon

Bacon, Almira Mrs., (Chenango Bridge,) lot 35, S. D B P., tailoress.

Bacon, Norman, (Port Crane,) lot 9, S. D. B. P, constable and peddler.

Bacon, Willard, (Glen Castle,) lot 4, G. D. B P., farmer 14

Barton, Bradford, (Castle Creek,) lot 118, G. D B P, farmer 16.

Bartoo, Edward B., (Castle Creek,) prop Temperance Hotel.

BISHOP, HENRY T., (Kattelville,) lot 40, S. D. B. P, (*with Samuel H* ,) farmer.

BISHOP, SAMUEL H, (Kattelville,) lot 40, S D. B. P., farmer 68

Black, Ransom, (Binghamton,) lot 23, S. D. B P., stock broker and wool dealer.

Blair, A Edson, (Castle Creek,) lot 123, G. D. B. P., town assessor and farmer 155.

Blair, Willis A., (Castle Creek,) lot 44, G. D. B. P., carpenter and farmer 60.

Booth, Larry D., (Chenango Bridge,) lot 16, S D. B. P, wagon maker and farmer 53.

Booth, Sylvester, (Glen Castle,) lot 104, S. D B P., cooper and farmer 60

Bowen, Geo. S., (Castle Creek,) lot 124, G D B. P, carpenter and farmer 16

Bowen, Julius D., (Castle Creek,) lot 124, G. D. B. P., (*with Geo. S.*,) farmer 16.

Brigham, Nathan W , (Castle Creek,) lot 76, G. D. B. P. farmer 150.

Bristol, James, (Castle Creek,) (*J. Bristol & Son*,) postmaster.

Bristol, J. & Son, (Castle Creek,) (*James and Wm. H.*,) general merchants and lumber dealers.

Bristol, Wm. H., (Castle Creek,) (*J. Bristol & Son*,) farmer 50

BROOKS, ALFRED, (Castle Creek,) lot 75, G. D. B. P., farmer 70

BROOKS, ALFRED W., (Kattelville,) (*Brooks & Palmer*,) lot 3, G. D. B. P., farmer 62

Brooks, Franklin, (Castle Creek,) lot 77, G D. B P, school teacher, carpenter and farmer 23

Brooks, Geo. M , (West Chenango,) lot 36, G. D. B P, constable and farmer 6¼.

Brooks, Norman H , (Glen Castle,) lot 36, G. D. B. P., farmer 50.

BROOKS & PALMER, (Kattelville,) (*Alfred W. Brooks and Lockwood E Palmer*,) general agents Nixon's Double Shovel Plow

Brooks, Samuel D., (Castle Creek,) lot 75, G D B. P., farmer 70

Brown, Chas (Chenango Bridge ) lot 10, S. D B P farmer 40.

BROWN, JAMES, (Chenango Forks,) drover and farmer

Bullock, Joseph, (Kattelville,) lot 40, S D. B. P., farmer 15.

BULLOCK, MARTIN H., M D., (Kattelville,) physician and surgeon

Burr, Almond, (Castle Creek,) lot 85, G. D B P, farmer 34

Burroughs, Jacob, (Castle Creek,) carpenter and farmer 2

Byers, Robert W., (Binghamton,) lot 165, S. D. B. P., farmer 135.

Callan, Patrick, (Binghamton,) lot 107, S D B. P., farmer 100

Carroll John, (Kattelville,) lot 38, S D B P , farmer 51.

Cary, Walter, (Glen Castle,) lot 64, S D B P , supervisor and farmer 96

CLARK BROS., (Kattelville,) (*Corydon, Sydney L , Philo A., Oscar E. and Ira O.*,) lot 5, S. D B. P., farmer 152

CLARK, CORYDON, (Kattelville,) (*Clark Bros* )

CLARK, IRA O., (Kattelville,) (*Clark Bros* )

CLARK, OSCAR E, (Kattelville,) (*Clark Bros.*)

CLARK, PHILO A , (Kattelville,) (*Clark Bros.*)

CLARK, SYDNEY L., (Kattelville,) (*Clark Bros* )

Cloyes, Orren M., (Glen Castle ) lot 96, S. D. B. P., saw and grist mills

COLE, JESSE, (Kattelville,) lot 72, S D B. P., farmer 120.

COLE, JOHN, (Chenango Forks,) butcher.

Cole, Samuel C., (Chenango Forks,) lot 122, G D B P , farmer 75

Collins, Adelbert, (Binghamton,) lot 128, S. D. B P , (*with Chas* ,) farmer.

Collins. Chas , (Binghamton,) lot 128, S. D
B P. breeder of Hambletonian stock
and farmer 95

Congdon, Nathanial, (Castle Creek,) retired farmer.

Conklin, Azariah, (Chenango Forks,) lot
119, G D B P , farmer 62

Cook, Daniel, (Castle Creek,) (J D. Cook
& Bros.)

Cook, John D , (Castle Creek,) (J D. Cook
& Bros )

Cook, J D & Bros , (Castle Creek,) (John
D . Titus D. and Daniel,) lot 87, G. D
B P , farmer 186.

Cook, Titus D , (Castle Creek,) (J. D. Cook
& Bros )

Cooley, Daniel O., (Binghamton,) lot 21, S.
D B P , lumberman and farmer 100

Cooley, Wm , (Binghamton,) lot 20, S D.
B. P , lumberman and farmer 278.

Cowan, Thos. L , (Chenango Bridge,) lot 7,
S. D B. P., farmer 50.

Cunningham, John, (Castle Creek,) lot 44,
G D B P , fruit grower and farmer 19

DAYTON, MARCUS M., (Castle Creek,)
prop stage route between Castle Creek
and Binghamton, constable, town col
lector and farmer 12.

Dawey, Wallace P , (Castle Creek,) lot 118,
G D B P., farmer 57.

DeWitt, Henry, (Chenango Bridge,) lot 13,
S. D B P., farmer 60

DeWitt, Noah S Rev (Castle Creek,) pastor M E Church

Dimmick, Smith S , (Chenango Bridge,)
lot 16 S. D B P., farmer 1

Dorman, Jerome, (Glen Castle,) lot 95, S.
D B P., butcher.

Dutcher, Aaron, (Chenango Bridge,) lot 16,
S. D B P., farmer leasee of Mrs. Parsons, 50.

Eaton, Samuel B., (Castle Creek,) lot 115,
G D. B P , farmer 2.

Ellison, DeWitt, Chenango Forks, (with
Wm ,) lot 119, G D B P . farmer

Ellison Wm (Chenango Forks,) lot 119, G.
D. B P , farmer 127

EMENS, ISAAC, (Castle Creek,) breeder of
fine dairy stock, dairy and farmer 227.

English Geo , (Chenango Forks,) blacksmith

EVERETT, GEO. A , (Glen Castle,) lot
96, S D B.P , postmaster, butcher and
farmer 2½.

Everett, Henry C., (Castle Creek,) blacksmith

EVERETT, NEWTON F., (Chenango
Bridge,) lot 12, S D B P., town assessor and farmer 125.

Fitzgerald, Richard, (Kattelville,) lot 8, G.
D B. P., farmer 35,

French, Carson, (Glen Castle,) lot 124, S.
D B P , (with Ebenezer S ) farmer.

French, Ebenezer S , (Glen Castle,) lot 124,
S D. B. P., farmer 165.

French, Franklin, (Glen Castle,) lot 103, S.
D. B. P., farmer 61.

French, Ira, (Castle Creek,) lot 44, G. D. B.
P., farmer 110.

Frier, Phœbe A. Mrs., (Chenango Bridge,)
lot 73, S D B. P., farmer 130.

Frier, Washington, (Chenango Bridge,) lot
66, S D B P., farmer 106

Gates, Adln V , (Glen Castle,) lot 94, S D
B. P., farmer leasee of W & B Nimmons, 106

GAYLORD, JAMES, (Castle Creek,) lot
84, G D B P., farmer 148

Gibson. Montillo H , (Glen Castle,) lot 77,
S. D B. P , farmer 92.

Gilmore, John L , (Kattelville,) lot 70, S.
D B. P., farmer 2.

GOODSPEED, OLIVER M , (Castle
Creek,) carriage maker, carpenter and
joiner

GOODSPEED, PHILARMAN, (Castle
Creek,) lot 117, G D. B. P., farmer 100.

GOTHIC HOUSE, (Chenango Forks,) Norman S. Kinyon, prop.

Gray, Eli, (Chenango Forks,) lot 80, G. D.
B., farmer leasee of Geo. Port.

Gray, Richard C , (Castle Creek,) lot 124,
G. D. B. P., farmer 20.

Greengard, Isaac, (Kattelville,) grocer.

Haight, Lewis, (Glen Castle,) lot 37, G D.
B P , farmer 91.

Hall, A Martin, (West Chenango,) lot 35,
G. D. B. P., postmaster and farmer 62

Hall, Henry, (Chenango Bridge,) lot 98, S.
D. B. P., (with James,) farmer 93.

Hall, James, (Chenango Bridge,) lot 98, S.
D B P., farmer 93

HALL, SETH S., (West Chenango,) lot 86,
G D. B. P., carpenter and joiner, and
farmer leasee of A. Palmer, 125

Haud, Newton B , (West Chenango,) lot 75,
G. D. B P , farmer 60

Handy, Asher, (Kattelville,) (with Joseph,)
farmer

Handy, Joseph, (Kattelville,) lot 70, S D.
B., farmer 81.

Harper, Pheoa Mrs , (Chenango Bridge,)
lot 16, S. D. B. P., farmer 44

Harris, Lyman, (Binghamton,) lot 24, S D.
B., farmer 19.

Harvey, Newman, (Chenango Bridge,) lot
35, S. D B P , farmer 108.

Hasbrouck, Deyo, (Binghamton,) lot 28, S.
D B F., farmer 2.

Hatch, Sylvanus, (Kattelville,) lot 99, S. D.
B. P., farmer 72.

Kanver, Jeremiah, (Binghamton,) lot 24,
S. D. B. P., farmer 18.

HAWKES, DEXTER, (Glen Castle,) lot 93,
S. D. B P.

Hawks, Elihu S., (Castle Creek,) lot 84, G.
D. B. P., farmer 200.

Heath, Chas A., (Kattelville,) lot 1, G. D.
B P , (with Edward,) farmer 80

Heath, Edward, (Kattelville,) lot 1, G D.
B P., farmer 80.

Heath, Frederick M , (Kattelville,) lot 40,
G. D. B P., farmer 1½

Heller, Calvin B., (Castle Creek,) lot 45, G.
D. B P , town assessor and farmer 195.

Hinman, Chas , (Chenango Bridge,) lot 19,
S. D. B. P , farmer 409.

Hodges, Joseph, (Chenango Bridge,) lot
14, S. D. B. P., farmer 118.

Holt, David, (Kattelville,) lot 66, S D. B.
P , farmer 8.

Howard, Isaac, (Glen Castle,) lot 5, G D.
B. P., farmer 150.

Ingraham, Anstin S., (Chenango Forks,)
lot 82, G. D. B. P., farmer leasee of
Mrs. Robert Collins, 155

Jewell, Chas. H. Rev. (Chenango Bridge,) postmaster.

Jewell, Walter, (Chenango Bridge,) lot 16, S. D. B. P., overseer of the poor and farmer 105.,

Johnson, Chas. H., (Binghamton,) lot 23, S. D B P, (*with Orville D.*,) farmer

Johnson, Ezra, (Glen Castle,) lot 95, S. D B P, farmer 40.

Johnson, Geo , (Binghamton,) lot 26, S. D B P., farmer 240.

Johnson, Hermon, (Binghamton,) lot 26, S. D. B. P , (*with Geo.*,) farmer.

Johnson Joseph, (West Chenango,) lot 36, G. D B P., saw mill and farmer 68.

Johnson, Joseph P., (Chenango Forks,) grocer.

Johnson, Leonard. (Glen Castle,) (*Belcher & Johnson,*) lot 5, G. D. B P , farmer 228.

Johnson, Orville D , (Binghamton,) lot 23, S. D. B P., farmer 96.

Johnson, Samuel, (Glen Castle,) lot 5, G D B P , threshing machine and farmer 50.

Johnson, Wm. B., (Binghamton,) lot 23, S D. B. P., (*with Orville D ,*) mechanic and farmer

JUDD & ALLEN, (Castle Creek,) (*Samuel E. Judd and Lewis Allen,*) props. steam saw mill and dealers in all kinds of lumber.

JUDD, SAMUEL E., (Castle Creek,) (*Judd & Allen* )

**JUDD, SAMUEL H.,** (Castle Creek,) lot 43, S. D. B. P., (*with Sylvanus*,) farmer.

**JUDD, SYLVANUS,** (Castle Creek,) lot 43, S. D. B. P., salesman of live stock in New York City, real estate broker and farmer 250.

KATTELL, ALONZO E , (Kattelville,) lot 1, G. D. B P., post master and farmer 215.

KEELER, DAVID T., (Chenango Bridge,) (*Sprague & Keeler.*)

Keeler, Herod M., (Chenango Bridge,) lot 9, S D. B P , farmer 50

Keeler, Revilo, (Chenango Bridge,) lot 13, S D B. P., farmer 215.

KEELER, SAMUEL M., (Chenango Bridge,) dealer in general merchandise

King, Geo R., (Chenango Forks,) (*H. King & Son.*)

King, Hiram, (Chenango Forks,) (*H King & Son,*) justice of the peace

King, H. & Son, (Chenango Forks,) (*Hiram and Geo. R ,*) general merchants and dealers in hides, skins &c.

KINYON, NORMAN S., (Chenango Forks,) prop. Gothic House.

Knapp, John S , (Castle Creek,) lot 4, G. D. B. P., farmer 150.

Kolb, John G , (Binghamton,) lot 6, G. D. B P., farmer 50.

Lake, Joseph, (Kattelville,) lot 40, S. D. B. P., farmer leases of Milton Holt, 85.

Leamans, Oliver W., (Castle Creek,) stone mason.

Lee, Alonzo S., (Glen Castle,) lot 77, S. D. B. P., carpenter and farmer 40

Lee, Daniel D., (Glen Castle,) lot 95, S. D. B P , farmer 115

Lee, Samuel, (Chenango Forks,) lot 120, G. D. B. P., farmer 96.

Lee, Stephen B., (Kattelville,) lot 68, S. D. B. P., farmer 55.

Lee, Wm A., (Kattelville,) lot 68, S D B. P., carpenter and farmer 8

**LEWIS, JABEZ J.,** (Castle Creek,) (*Williamson & Lewis.*)

Lewis, Joshua, (Kattelville,) lot 39, S. D. B P , carpenter and farmer 9½

**LEWIS, JULIUS C.,** (Kattelville,) lot 89, S D. B P., farmer 12

LEWIS, POLLY MRS., (Kattelville,) tailoress.

Lewis, Rachel, (Chenango Bridge,) farmer, in Union, 50.

Lilly, Jonathan, (Binghamton,) lot 43, G D B. P., inventor of well curb and wagon jack, saw mill and farmer 34

Lilly, Oreamos, (Castle Creek,) lot 37, G. D. B P , farmer 100.

Loomis, Chester, (Port Crane,) lot 9, S. D B P , market gardener and farmer 53.

Lown, A Jackson, (Glen Castle,) lot 95, S D B P., carpenter, wagon maker and farmer.

Lum, Samuel, (Castle Creek,) farmer 39.

Malkin, John, (Chenango Bridge,) lot 16, S. D. B. P., farmer 5½.

Martin, Jodson, (Kattelville,) lot 39, G D. B P , farmer 156.

Marvin, Wm , (West Chenango,) lot 6, G. D B P., blacksmith and farmer 50.

May, James, (Castle Creek,) lot 44, G. D. B. P., shoemaker and farmer 9

McNary, Chas., (Castle Creek,) lot 116, G D B. P , farmer 70.

Megher, John, (Kattelville,) lot 43, G. D. B. P., farmer 73.

Miller, Wallace A , (Kattelville,) lot 1, G D. B P , farmer 128

Mills, Horace R , (Castle Creek,) lot 117, G. D. B P , (*with Sylvester W ,*) butcher and farmer.

Mills, Rufus A , (Castle Creek,) lot 117, G. D. B. P., farmer 18.

Mills, Sylvester W., (Castle Creek,) lot 117, G. D. B. P., butcher and farmer 98

Mix, Bradley, (Chenango Forks,) lot 122, G. D. B. P , farmer 75

Mix, Courtland, (Chenango Forks,) shoemaker.

Mix, Eli, (Chenango Forks,) lot 122, G D. B. P., farmer 100

Monroe, Richard, (Glen Castle,) lot 96, S. D. B. P., blacksmith and farmer 100.

Moran, Michael, (Kattelville,) lot 68, S D. B P , farmer 4.

Munsell, John, (Chenango Bridge,) lot 16, S D B. P., farmer 50

Munsell, John Jr., (Castle Creek,) allo. physician and surgeon.

Myres, Rhoda Mrs., (Glen Castle ) (*with Mrs Mary E Webster,*) lot 43, S. D. B. P , tailoress and farmer 8

Newman, Elias, (Kattelville,) lot 39, S D. B P., farmer 50

Newman, Geo. W., (Kattelville,) (*G. H & G. W. Newman* )

Newman, G. H. & G. W., (Kattelville,) (*Gilbert H and Geo. W.,*) lot 41, S. D. B. P , farmer 106.

Newman, Gilbert H., (Kattelville,) (*G. H. & G. W. Newman* )

Nimmons, Burwell, (Binghamton,) lot 22, S. D B P, farmer 50.

Nimmons, Burwell Jr., (Binghamton,) lot 22, S D. B. P , market gardener and farmer 75

Nimmons, John, (Glen Castle,) lot 103, S D B. P., farmer 2

NIMMONS, WM R , (Binghamton,) lot 25, S. D B P, farmer 91

NIMMONSBURG HOTEL, (Binghamton,) James Rockenstyre, prop.

Norton, Dallas, (Kattelville,) lot 1, G D B P , farmer 13

Norton, John, (Kattelville,) assistant post-master and notary public

Norton, Sylvester, (Kattelville,) lot 1, S. D. B P., farmer 15.

Nowlan, John G., (Kattelville,) lot 3, S D B P , farmer leases of Luther Crocker, 82.

Oakley, Tobias G , (Glen Castle,) lot 75, S D B P , farmer 85

Ockerman, Lawrence, (Chenango Forks,) lot 120, G. D B P., farmer 130.

Page, Emery J., (Chenango Forks,) lot 3, G D B P., farmer leases of Mrs. Hatch, 75

Page, John, (Glen Castle,) lot 43, S. D. B P farmer 52.

Palmer, Andrew, (Castle Creek,) lot 85, G. D B P farmer 260

Palmer, Ashbell, (Kattelville,) lot 41, G. D B P., farmer 44.

Palmer, Caleb M., (Kattelville,) lot 3, G. D B P , (with Lockwood E.,) farmer 226

Palmer, Henry, (Chenango Bridge,) lot 16, S D B P , farmer 90

Palmer, Horatio N , (Kattelville,) lot 1, G. D B P., farmer 2

Palmer, Ira, (Kattelville,) lot 41, G D B. P , (with Ashbell,) farmer 41.

Palmer, Isaac S., (Kattelville,) lot 3, G D. B P. (with Lockwood E ,) farmer 226

PALMER, LOCKWOOD E., (Kattelville,) (Brooks & Palmer,) lot 3, G. D. B P., farmer 226.

Palmer, Philip H , (Kattelville,) lot 1, G D B P. farmer 3

Palmer, Reuben, (Kattelville,) lot 69, S. D. B. P. farmer 50

Palmer, Reuben 2d, (Castle Creek,) lot 43, G D B P., farmer 34.

Palmer, Sherwood, (Kattelville,) lot 69, S D B P., (with Reuben,) farmer 50.

Palmer, Warren D., (Castle Creek,) lot 35, G D B P (with Andrew,) farmer.

Palmer, Westall W., (Kattelville,) lot 1, G. D B P , farmer 50.

Palmer, Zina, (Kattelville,) lot 70, S D. B P , farmer 37

Parker, Geo W , (Chenango Bridge,) lot 16, S D. B. P., section foreman S & B. R R , and farmer 3

Parker, Hial W., (Chenango Bridge,) lot 16, S D B P, justice of the peace, coal dealer and shoemaker.

Parker, Richard H , (Castle Creek,) lot 43, G. D B P., farmer 74.

Phelps, Apollos N., (Castle Creek,) lot 84, G D. B. P., farmer 183.

Pierce, Geo F , (Castle Creek,) lot 117, G D B. P farmer 1

POET, JESSE, (Chenango Forks,) lot 70, G. D. B P., farmer 213

Port, John, (Kattelville,) lot 89, G. D B. P, farmer 190

Prentice, Jonas, (Chenango Bridge,) lot 16, S D B P., stock broker and farmer 170

Prentice, Wm , (Kattelville,) lot 67, S D. B. P , farmer 120

Quinn, Wm., (Binghamton,) lot 120, S. D. B P , farmer 150.

Redfield, Joseph E., (Binghamton,) lot 163, S. D. B. P., farmer 50

Reid, Elwyn S , (Kattelville,) lot 101, S. D. B P , carpenter and farmer 3

*RILEY, JOHN, (Castle Creek,) general merchant.

Ritenburg, John, (Kattelville ) lot 37, S D B. P , farmer leases of Marvin Freer, 40.

Roach, Patrick, (Binghamton,) lot 79, S. D. B. P , farmer 95

Robinson, Aaron H , (Binghamton,) lot 129, S D. B. P., hop grower and farmer 175

Robinson, Nathaniel, (Kattelville,) lot 37, S D B P , blacksmith and farmer 65.

ROCKENSTYRE, JAMES, (Binghamton,) prop. Nimmonsburg Hotel and farmer 6

Ross, Geo M , (Castle Creek,) lot 44, G. D B. P., farmer 98.

Ross, Wm , (Castle Creek,) lot 78, G. D. B P , farmer 116.

Rummer, Bennett, (Kattelville,) lot 1, S. D B P , farmer 75

Rummer, Daniel, (Kattelville,) lot 1, S D. B P , (with Bennett,) farmer 75.

Sanford, Geo L , (Castle Creek,) lot 86, G. D. B P , farmer

Satchwell, Truman, (Castle Creek,) lot 83, G D B P , fish dealer and farmer 85.

Schermerhorn, Abram P., (Castle Creek,) lot 118. G D B P , farmer leases of Anson Dewey, 110.

SCOFIELD, J L., (Chenango Bridge,) lot 102, S D B P, prop cider mill, tobacco grower and farmer 60

Seeber, James D., (Chenango Forks,) cabinet maker and undertaker

Siver, Henry, (Glen Castle,) lot 64, S D. B. P , carpenter and farmer 20

Siver, James H., (Glen Castle,) lot 104, S D. B. P., farmer leases of W. Cary, 52.

Slattery, Wm., (Castle Creek,) shoemaker.

SMETHURST, JOSEPH, (Chenango Bridge,) lot 15, S. D B. P , farmer 50.

Smith, James, (Kattelville,) lot 2, G D. B. P., farmer 14

Smith, John, (Binghamton,) lot 24, S. D B. P , farmer 47.

Smith, Patrick, (Kattelville,) (with Wm.,) lot 65, S D B P , farmer 130

Smith, Robert, (Binghamton,) lot 163, S D. B P , farmer 150.

Smith, Thos , (Kattelville,) lot 65, S D. B P., farmer 50.

Smith, Wm., (Kattelville,) (with Patrick,) lot 65, S. D. B P , farmer 130.

Spencer, Chas. Z , (Castle Creek,) lot 73, G D B. P , farmer 113

Spencer, Philander B., (Castle Creek,) lot 116, G. D. B P , farmer 200

SPRAGUE, ALBERT J., (Chenango Bridge,) (Sprague & Keeler,) manuf. and dealer in lumber and lath, flour, meal and feed, and farmer 100

Sprague, Barney, (Chenango Bridge,) lot 16, S. D. B. P., farmer 120.

SPRAGUE & KEELER, (Chenango Bridge,) (Albert J. Sprague and David T Keeler,) props. Sprague's Mills

SPRAGUE'S MILLS, (Chenango Bridge,) Sprague & Keeler, props

St. John, Moses, (Castle Creek,) lot 46, G D B P, farmer 90.

St John, Sylvester, (Castle Creek,) lot 46, G. D. B. P., farmer 75

Stone, Aaron, (Chenango Bridge,) lot 102, S D. B P., farmer 58

Strickland, B. T., (Chenango Forks,) ticket agent S. & B. R. R. and D. L. & W. R. R

Strickland, Jonathan, (Chenango Forks,) (J Strickland & Son.)

Strickland, J. & Son, (Chenango Forks,) (Jonathan and Simon T.,) commission merchants, dealers in butter, cheese &c

Strickland, Simon T., (Chenango Forks,) (J. Strickland & Son,) billiard and eating saloon, and farmer 126.

Strickland, S. T. Mrs., (Chenango Forks,) (with Miss J Terwilliger,) millinery

Swimmer, Frank, (Castle Creek,) lot 115, G D B P, farmer 70.

Taber, David B., (West Chenango,) (with James C.,) lot 46, G. D. B. P., farmer 186.

Taber, James C., (West Chenango,) lot 46, G. D. B. P, farmer 186

Taber, John C., (West Chenango,) lot 46, G. D. B. P., (with James C.,) farmer

Taft, Amos F., (Kattelville,) lot 37, S. D B. P, farmer 40.

TERRY, BRADFORD W., (Port Crane,) lot 10, S. D B. P, (with Lewis C.),

TERRY, LEWIS C, (Port Crane,) lot 10, S D B. P., general agent Reynolds Patent Churn Lid Screen, for State of Pennsylvania and all of New York except 13 north eastern counties, and farmer 40.

Terwilliger, Jasper, (Chenango Fork,) lot 122, G D B P, farmer 89.

Terwilliger, J. Miss, (Chenango Forks,) (with Mrs S. T Strickland,) millinery

Terwilliger, Peter D, (Kattelville,) lot 101, S. D B P, farmer 60

Terwilliger, Silas B., (Castle Creek,) lot 118, G. D B P., farmer 75

Terwilliger, Thos H., (Kattelville,) lot 86, S D B. P., farmer 56.

THOMAS, GEO. H., (Chenango Bridge,) lot 16, S D B P, commissioner of highways and farmer 24

Thomas, Wm W., (Chenango Bridge,) lot 125, S. D. B. P., farmer 146

Tompkins, Chas A , (Castle Creek,) lot 75, S D. B. P., town clerk, agent for agricultural implements and farmer 98.

Trafford, Chas , (Castle Creek,) justice of the peace and cooper

Treadwell, Horace, (Glen Castle,) lot 85, G. D B P, justice of the peace and farmer 100.

VanKEUREN, JONATHAN C., (Kattelville,) lot 101, S. D B P., carpenter and joiner, and farmer 26

West, Geo. N., (Glen Castle,) lot 45, G D. B. P., (with Hiram,) farmer 33

Westfall, Harvey, (Castle Creek,) lot 38, G D B P, farmer 84

Whitney, Oliver C., (Kattelville,) lot 59, S D B P, farmer 48.

Wilcox, Amos, (Glen Castle,) lot 4, G D. B P, farmer 59

Wilcox, John B., (Kattelville,) lot 2, S D B. P., farmer leases of Mrs. Frazer, 84.

Wilcox, Martin L , (Chenango Forks,) lot 42, G D B P, farmer leases 75.

WILLIAMSON, CHAS., (Castle Creek,) (Williamson & Lewis )

WILLIAMSON & LEWIS, (Castle Creek,) (Chas Williamson and Jabez J Lewis,) carriage makers and general blacksmiths.

Wilson, James, (Binghamton,) lot 147, S. D. B. P., farmer 75

Wilson, Thos., (Binghamton,) lot 105, S D. B P , farmer 85

Winfield, John, (Binghamton,) lot 60, S D. B P , farmer 50

Witherwax, Adam, (Binghamton,) lot 6, G. D. B. P., farmer 140

Wood, Chas. A., (Castle Creek,) lot 115, G. D. B. P, dealer in lumber, bark and wood, and farmer 50,

Wooster, Mary E Mrs , (Glen Castle,) (with Mrs Rhoda Myres,) lot 43, S. D. B P , tailoress and farmer 8.

Wright, Morton C., (Chenango Bridge,) station agent, telegraph operator and assistant postmaster

Writenburg, Alvah, (Kattelville,) lot 1, G D. B. P., butcher and farmer 10.

Young, Hugh, (Castle Creek,) lot 124, G. D. B P , farmer 115

Young, John W , (Castle Creek,) lot 43, G. D. B. P., farmer 63.

# COLESVILLE.

## (Post Office Addresses in Parentheses )

ABBREVIATIONS.—H. P, Harper's Patent; S P., Smith's Patent, Ham. P., Hammon's Patent, W P, Watts' Patent, D., District.

ABBOTT, HENRY M., (Center Village,) farmer 200
Ackert, Stephen, (West Colesville,) lot 51, W. P., farmer 68
Adams, Josiah, (Doraville,) cooper and farmer 18
ADKINS, POMEROY H., (Harpersville,) lot 80, S P , farmer 70
Allen, Goodlo H., (Center Village,) farmer 1¾
Allen, John B , (Harpersville,) lot 16, Ham. P , farmer 95.
Andrews, Sarah Mrs., (Center Village,) lot 10, farmer 51
Apley, Henry, (Harpersville,) lot 18, Ham. P , farmer 40
APPLEY, JAMES, (Ouaquaga,) (*Butler & Appley*)
Archer, John, (Vallonia Springs,) farmer 6
ARMLIN, GEORGE, (Osborne Hollow,) lot 5, W. P., farmer 50.
Arnts, Daniel, (Ouaquaga,) lot 16, H. P., farmer 168.
Attridge, Mary A Mrs , (West Colesville,) lot 33, Ham P.. farmer 12¾.
AUSTIN, ASA, (Center Village,) engineer in tannery.
AUSTIN, IRA E , (Center Village ) foreman in tannery of Edward P. Northrop
Austin, Lydia Miss, (Center Village,) farmer 2½.
Austin, Reuben, (North Colesville,) lot 87, S P , farmer 200
AVERELL, ADAM G., (Vallonia Springs,) farmer 41
Baker, Calvin, (Colesville,) lot 35, Ham. P., farmer 75
Baker, Charles N., (West Colesville,) lot 54, W P., farmer 80
Baker, Christopher, (West Colesville,) lot 34, Ham. P , farmer 140
BAKER, EGBERT A , (Belden,) lot 96, S. P , farmer 100.
BAKER, JEROME, (Osborne Hollow,) lot 21, W. P., blacksmith, carriage maker and farmer 1
Baker, Smith, (Center Village,) lot 40, farmer 140
BAKER, WALTER G , (Center Village,) butcher, dealer in patent rights, farmer 75 and, in Sanford, 60.
Ball, Adam, (West Colesville,) lot 42, W. P., farmer 111.

N

Bancroft, Geo. W., (Harpersville,) farmer 1.
Barnes, George B , (Harpersville,) lot 6, H P , farmer 116.
BARNES, GERMAN B , (Harpersville,) carpenter and joiner.
BARNES HOTEL, (Harpersville,) Wm. Hars, prop
Barnes, Judson H., (Harpersville,) lot 15, Ham. P farmer 175.
Barnum, Enoch, (Osborne Hollow,) lot 15, W. P , farmer 250
Barnum, Samuel, (West Colesville,) lot 43, W. P., carpenter.
Bates, Henry M , (Harpersville,) lot 93, S P., farmer 115.
BATES, MARTIN, (Center Village,) millwright
BATY, ALONZO B , (Harpersville,) manuf. of bedsteads and furniture dealer.
BAXTER, MOSES, (New Ohio,) lot 92, S. P , carpenter and joiner, and farmer 2.
Beale, Joshua R., (Belden,) lot 90, S P , farmer 100.
BEARDSLEY, EPHRAIM G., (Harpersville,) lot 99, farmer 150.
Beardsley, Harvey F., (New Ohio,) lot 85, also physician, grocer, postmaster and farmer 15
Becker, Abraham, (Center Village,) lot 17, H P., farmer 118¾
Becker, Hiram, (West Colesville,) lot 34, W. P , farmer 53.
Bedlent, Edgar L , (Harpersville,) hardware, stoves and tinware
Bedurfey, Attheus, (New Ohio,) lot 97, S. P , farmer 50
BEHRENDT, JOHN, (Center Village,) lot 19, H P , farmer 42.
Beman, Aaron G , (New Ohio,) lot 86, S P , farmer 160
Beman, Ackley, (New Ohio,) lot 86, S P , farmer 108.
BEMAN, REUBEN G , (New Ohio,) lot 86, S. P., house painter and farmer 1.
Benn, Aaron, (Ouaquaga,) lot 15, H P , farmer 3
Bennet, John, (Nineveh,) farmer 8.
Bennett, John D., (Harpersville,) lot 2, H P., farmer 321.
Bennett, Joseph, (Harpersville,) lot 84, S. P., farmer 138

Berray, Addis E., (Osborne Hollow,) lot 5, W. P., farmer 190

Beuman, Henry, (Center Village,) lot 19, H P., farmer 110.

BEVIERS, WILLIAM, (Center Village,) lot 22, H P., farmer 50

Birch, Snel W., (Vallonia Springs,) farmer 50

Birdsell, George W. Mrs., (Nineveh,) milliner

BISHOP, ESTHER S Mrs., (Onaquaga,) lot 53, Ham P., farmer 82

Bishop, John F., (Harpersville,) carriage maker and blacksmith, prop of public hall and farmer 2

Blachley, Charles, (West Colesville,) lot 35, W P., carriage maker and farmer 53

BLACHLEY, WILLIAM H, (West Colesville,) carriage maker.

Blake, Andrew P, (Harpersville,) (with Benj. B,) lot 93, S. P., farmer 138

Blake, Benjamin B., (Harpersville,) (with Andrew P,) lot 93 S P., farmer 138

BLAKESLEE, EDWARD C., (Center Village,) lot 18, H. P., farmer 102¾

BLANCHARD, JAMES C, (Belden,) lot 94, farmer 56.

BLANCHARD JOHN, (Harpersville,) lot 94, S P., farmer 24

BLULER, RODOLPH, (Onaquaga,) lot 39, Ham P., farmer 50

BOOTH, EBENEZER H, (West Colesville,) blacksmith

Booth, John W., (West Colesville,) allo physician

Boyes, Edwin R, (Belden,) lot 90, S P, blacksmith and farmer 4

Brainard, Joel G, (New Ohio,) lot 86, S P, farmer 75

Brant, Frank F, (Nineveh,) farmer 10.

Bristol, James E, (Harpersville,) druggist

BRIZZEE WILLIAM, (Center Village,) farmer 97.

BROWN, BERNARD H., (Osborne Hollow,) engineer

Brown, David C., (Center Village,) harness maker.

BROWN, JEFFERSON R., (Nineveh,) boot and shoe shop

BROWN, JESSE (Harpersville,) general merchant and dealer in ready-made clothing.

Brown, Mary A. Mrs., (Harpersville,) farmer 6.

Brown, Samuel C., (Harpersville,) blacksmith and farmer 49

Brownson, Porter H, (Onaquaga,) lot 45, Ham. P., farmer 68.

Bump, Ezra, (Osborne Hollow,) lot 100, S. P., farmer 77.

Bump, Jedadiah, (Osborne Hollow,) lot 20, W P, farmer 100

Bunker, James, (Doraville,) lot 28, H. P., farmer 5

BURROWS, JOHN H, (Harpersville,) lot 6, H P., farmer leases of Judson T. Blakeslee, Binghamton, 210

Bush, Henry P, (Nineveh,) farmer 150

BUSH, RILEY, (Nineveh,) farmer 10¼.

BUTLER, ANDREW, (Onaquaga,) (Butler & Appley,) farmer 1.

BUTLER & APPLEY. (Onaquaga,) (Andrew Butler and James Appley,) eclectic physicians.

Butler, Stephen W., (Onaquaga,) lot 55, Ham P., farmer 30

Button, Lamer E., (Osborne Hollow,) lot 5, W P., farmer 205.

Cane, James, (New Ohio,) lot 92, S P., farmer 70.

Caniff, Benjamin, (Binghamton,) lot 50, W P., farmer 63

CANIFF, JOHN E, (West Colesville,) lot 53, W P., farmer 43

CARL ISAAC (Center Village,) lot 20, H. P., farmer 55.

Carnegie, Norris, (North Colesville,) lot 82, S. P., farmer 11

Carpenter, William A., (Harpersville,) lot 14, Ham P., farmer 150

Carrol, Harrison H., (West Colesville,) post master

Carrol, Mathew, (West Colesville,) lot 43, W P., farmer 3.

Cary, Harriet Mrs, (New Ohio,) lot 81, S P., farmer 69

CASE, GAYLORD, (New Ohio,) lot 92, S P., farmer 46.

CASE, JOHN, (New Ohio,) laborer

CASS, EDWIN H., (Osborne Hollow,) (Cass & Sornborger)

CASS & SORNBORGER, (Osborne Hollow,) (Edwin H Cass and Edward M Sornborger,) steam saw mill

Casson, Myron H., (New Ohio,) lot 92, S P. farmer 42

CASTLE, MARY L Mrs, (Center Village,) lot 19, H P, farmer 27

CHADDEN, GARRET T, (Center Village,) deputy sheriff and farmer 1

Chafee, Franklin D, (Harpersville,) lot 11, H. P., farmer 56.

Chafee, James A, (Harpersville,) lot 11, H. P., farmer 64

Chase, William W., (West Colesville,) lot 86, W. P, saw mill and farmer 5.

Chattock, Homer, (Colesville,) lot 35, Ham. P., farmer 32.

Christian, Eli, (Colesville,) lot 37, Ham P., farmer leases 87.

Churchill, Stoddard S., (Osborne Hollow,) lot 14, W. P., farmer 140.

Cole, Henry, (Center Village,) farmer 38.

Cole, James H, (Colesville,) lot 28, Ham P., farmer 160

Collar, Isaac, (Osborne Hollow,) lot 97, S. P., farmer 80

COLLAR, LEVI B, (Center Village,) boot and shoe maker.

COLLER, DANIEL B, (Osborne Hollow,) lot 100, S P, farmer 34.

Coller, Dorcas Mrs., (Osborne Hollow,) lot 100, S P, farmer 46.

COMSTOCK, JAMES R., (Center Village,) farmer 100

COOK, NATHANIEL, (Harpersville,) lot 80, S. P, farmer 150

Cook William T., (Center Village,) miller for Lewis Northrup

Coomba, George A, (Center Village,) lot 11, H P, farmer 65.

Cox, John E, (West Colesville,) lot 42, W. P, farmer 74

Crary, Nathan, (Doraville,) lot 18, H P, farmer 100.

Craver, Alexander, (West Colesville,) lot 34, W. P., farmer 54.

Craver, Isaac, (Osborne Hollow,) lot 21, W P., general merchant, postmaster and farmer 135.

Craver, Marshall, (Osborne Hollow,) lot 19, W P., farmer 100.

Cresson, Rufus, (Ouaquaga,) lot 48, Ham P., farmer 40.

CROFFUT, FRANKLIN R, (Harpersville,) lot 5, Ham. P., farmer 166.

CROFFUT, JOEL B, (Colesville,) lot 29, Ham P., farmer 80

Crofut, Egbert J., (West Colesville,) lot 45, W P., carpenter and farmer 53.

Crofut, William, (Harpersville,) lot 18, Ham. P., farmer 72.

CROSBY, MARVIN J, (Center Village,) leather finisher and farmer 7

Crosett, Eric, (Harpersville,) stone mason.

Currin, James, (Center Village,) farmer 1.

DANN, SAMANTHA Mrs , (Belden,) lot 96, S P., farmer 100

DARLING, CHARLES E., (West Colesville,) laborer

Darling, George, (West Colesville,) lot 53, W P , farmer 65

Dashaw, John, (West Colesville,) lot 33, W. P , farmer 50.

Davenport, John, (Doraville,) lot 23, H. P , farmer 200.

Davis, Asher M , (Center Village,) farmer 8

Davis, Frederick, (Harpersville,) cattle broker.

Davis, Lewis H., (New Ohio,) blacksmith.

Davis, Oliver, (Vallonia Springs,) farmer 59.

Davison, James, (West Colesville,) lot 40, W P , farmer 106

Dean, Jonathao, (West Colesville,) lot 35, W. P , farmer 125.

Debble, Alonzo, (Harpersville,) lot 17, Ham P , farmer 152.

Demeree, James W , (Doraville,) lot 20, farmer 102 and, in Sanford, 50.

Dewilleger, Henry N., (Vallonia Springs,) farmer 2½

DIBBLE, A S., (Center Village,) lot 13, eclectic physician, saw mill and farmer 8

DICKINSON, ALONZO, (Nineveh,) cooper

DIMORIER, GEORGE O., (Center Village,) sawyer and farmer 45

Dolloway, Edward Rev, (Harpersville,) pastor of Episcopal Church

Doolittle, Alanson, (Center Village,) lot 17, H P , farmer 54

DOOLITTLE, BURTON, (Ouaquaga,) lot 48, Ham P , farmer 150.

DOOLITTLE, CHARLES B., (Doraville,) lot 18, postmaster and farmer 95.

Doolittle, Edgar, (Ouaquaga,) lot 40, Ham. P , farmer 80.

Doolittle, Egbert, (Doraville,) lot 18, farmer 57

Doolittle, Frank, (West Colesville,) (*with Marcus*) lot 45, Ham P , farmer 78.

DOOLITTLE, FRANKLIN, (Ouaquaga,) lot 21, H. P., farmer 112.

Doolittle, Garret, (Ouaquaga,) lot 55, Ham. P , farmer 115.

Doolittle, German, (Doraville,) lot 24, farmer 110

Doolittle, Marcus, (West Colesville,) (*with Frank*,) lot 45, Ham. P., farmer 78.

DOOLITTLE, NELSON E., (Ouaquaga,) lot 63, Ham P., farmer 56.

Doolittle, Terris H., (Ouaquaga,) lot 54, Ham. P., farmer 140.

Doolittle, Warren, (Ouaquaga,) lot 54, Ham P , farmer 80 and, in Windsor, 22.

Dort, David, (Osborne Hollow,) lot 24, W P., farmer 109.

Doud, Leander H , (West Colesville,) lot 53, W P , farmer 96.

Draper, Edward A., (Harpersville,) lot 79, S. P , farmer 72

DYE & HIGLEY, (Osborne Hollow,) (*John P. Dye and Henry Higley*,) saw mill.

DYE, JOHN P., (Osborne Hollow,) (*Dye & Higley*,) lot 8, W P , farmer 254

Dykeman, George, (Center Village ) cooper

Dykeman, Peter, (Doraville,) lot 20, farmer 50.

DYKMAN, NANCY L. Mrs., (Center Village,) farmer 51.

Eaton, Clark, (West Colesville,) lot 41, W P., farmer 135.

Eaton, Llewellyn, (Harpersville,) homeo. physician.

Edgerton, Franklin, (Nineveh,) postmaster, general merchant, druggist and farmer 2.

Edmonds, Charles, (Harpersville,) lot 81, farmer leases of Mrs H. J. Lull, 80

EDSON, AVERY, (West Colesville,) lot 51, W P , farmer 60.

EDSON, HIRAM E., (West Colesville,) lot 43, W. P , farmer 53

Edson, John J., (Harpersville,) lot 93, S. P., farmer 75.

EDSON, LEROY, (West Colesville,) lot 42, W. P., farmer 106

Edwards, Luther, estate of, (West Colesville,) lot 52, W. P , 106 acres

Edwards, Wm., (West Colesville,) lot 51, W. P., farmer 3.

ELDORADO HOUSE, (Harpersville,) Simon J. Groat, prop

Eldred, Alexander, (Harpersville,) lot 11, H P., farmer 2

Eldred, John B , (Center Village,) farmer 102.

Eldred, Mervin P., (New Ohio,) lot 81, S. P , farmer 80.

Ellis, Elias, (West Colesville,) lot 40, W. P., farmer 34.

Estes, Shervin F., (Center Village,) farmer 55.

Fairchild, Benajah, (Ouaquaga,) general merchant.

Fairchild, Frederick, (North Colesville,) cooper

FARRINGTON, EUGENE, (Osborne Hollow,) blacksmith and carriage maker.

Farrington, Luke, (Osborne Hollow,) lot 12, W P , farmer 131

FELLOWS, EDWARD R., (Harpersville,) lot 93, S. P , farmer 130.

FERGUSON, ALONZO, (Doraville,) lot 15, H. P., farmer 142.

FERRIS, DARIUS, (Osborne Hollow,) lot 15, W. P , farmer 142

Finch, John M., (Belden,) (*with Bennett Hart*,) lot 89, farmer 72.

Finn, Martin, (New Ohio,) lot 96, farmer leases of Mrs. A. Kedder, 50.

# HOBBS BROS.,

## Nineveh,

*Broome County, N. Y.*

MANUFACTURERS OF

# Fine Carriages,

AND DEALERS IN

## Carriage Goods.

GEO. W. HOBBS        C. H. HOBBS.

# CHARLES KILMER,

DEALER IN

# STOVES,

AND MANUFACTURER OF

## Tin, Sheet Iron and Copper Ware.

Peddlers supplied at the lowest rates    All Peddlers ware made by me bears my trade mark, and is warranted as represented

*Crosby Block,    -    39 Hawley Street,*

## Binghamton, N. Y.

DON'T ARREST HIM!
LET HIM GO TO
**G. G. KNIBB'S,**
13 Lewis Street,
**BINGHAMTON, N. Y.**
And get a Pair.
They almost give them
away there!!

# BOOTS AND SHOES

*Made to order from the best quality of Stock and by experienced workmen.*

# Repairing Neatly and Promptly Done.

Flagg, John A., (Center Village,) wool carder and farmer 1.

Flansburgh, John W., (Center Village,) lot 12, H. P., farmer 104½

FLINT, MICAH C., (West Colesville,) peddler

Foreyth, James, (Belden,) lot 96, S P., farmer 76

FOSTER, ASA, (Belden,) (*with Martin*,) lot 91, farmer 65

FOSTER, MARTIN, (Belden,) (*with Asa*,) lot 91, farmer 65.

Francia, Robert, (Ouaquaga,) lot 63, Ham P., farmer 107.

FRASIER, JAMES B., (Harpersville,) cabinet maker, undertaker and prop of saw mill

Freeland, Orin M., (Harpersville,) lot 18, Ham. P., farmer 100

Freeman, George, (Ouaquaga,) lot 63, Ham. P., farmer 45

FULLER, JAMES, (Center Village,) saw mill and farmer 184.

Ganow, Isaac, (Osborne Hollow,) lot 18, W P., farmer 185.

Ganow, Isaac J., (Osborne Hollow,) (*with John W*.) lot 18, farmer 106

Ganow, John W., (Osborne Hollow,) (*with Isaac J*.,) lot 18, farmer 106

Ganow, Margaret Mrs., (Osborne Hollow,) lot 18, W. P., farmer 93.

Gardner, Jonathan, (Osborne Hollow,) (*with Orlando*,) lot 25, W. P., farmer 120

Gardner, Orlando, (Osborne Hollow,) (*with Jonathan*,) lot 25, W P., farmer 120

Gillett, Joel, (Vallonia Springs,) farmer 60

Givings, Frances Mrs., (Harpersville,) lot 11, H. P., farmer 1.

Godfrey Daniel, (Osborne Hollow,) lot 21, W. P., farmer 47½

Goodsell, David B., (Belden,) lot 96, S P., farmer 24.

GOODSELL, EUGENE A., (Belden,) laborer

GOSS, CHARLES P., (West Colesville,) boot and shoe maker

Green, William H.,(Ouaquaga,) lot 54, Ham. P., farmer 150

GROAT, SIMON J., (Harpersville,) prop. of Eldorado House and farmer 22.

Guernsey, David B., (Ouaquaga,) post master and grocer.

Guy, Ezekiel, (Harpersville,) allo. physician and farmer 80.

Guy, Hammon, (Harpersville,) lot 20, Ham P., farmer 127

Guy, Timothy, (Nineveh,) allo. physician

Haight, John, (Center Village,) farmer 112.

HAKES, CARLES A., (Harpersville,) carriage maker.

Hakes, George W., (Harpersville,) blacksmith and farmer 4

HALLOCK, GEORGE A., (Doraville,) lot 4, farmer 68 and, in Windsor, 53

Hammond, Timothy D Rev., (Center Village,) lot 19, H P., pastor Baptist Church and farmer 50

Harding, Isaac S, (West Colesville,) lot 43, W. P., farmer 110

Hare, Charles, (Harpersville,) farmer 1.

HARE, CHARLES W., (Harpersville,) (*Thompson & Hare*.)

HARE, WILLIAM, (Harpersville,) prop of Barnes Hotel and farmer 1

Harrington, Chancey W., (New Ohio,) lot 81. S P., farmer 80

Harper, Roswell, (Harpersville,) lot 16, H. P., farmer 50.

Harper, Simeon, (Doraville,) lot 24, H. P., farmer 50

HARPER, WILLIAM W., (Doraville,) lot 24 saw mill and farmer 100

HARPUR, EDWARD, (Harpersville,) land surveyor, general agent for mowing machines and farmer 90

HARPUR, ROBERT,(Harpersville,) farmer 250

HARPUR, ROBERT G., (Harpersville,) farmer 52.

Hart, Bennett, (Belden,) (*with John M Finch*,) lot 89, farmer 72

HASKELL, BENJAMIN F., (Port Crane,) lot 4, W. P., farmer leases 45

Hastings, Peter, (Harpersville,) lot 18, Ham P., farmer 110.

Hathaway, Geo E Rev., (Harpersville,) pastor of M E Church

Havens, Bradford H, (North Colesville,) lot 81, S P., farmer 40

HAVENS, FREDERICK L., (Harpersville,) (*with Orville G*,) lot 84, S P, farmer 112½.

HAVENS, ORVILLE G, (Harpersville,) dealer in musical instruments and (*with Frederick L*,) lot 84, S. P., farmer 112½.

Hayes, John H, (North Colesville,) blacksmith

Haynes, Archelaus, (New Ohio,) lot 91, S. P., farmer 165.

Heath, Asa, (Ouaquaga,) lot 54, Ham. P., shingle, planing and lath mills, turning lathe and farmer 2

Heath, Stephen W, (West Colesville,) lot 44, W P, farmer 106

HENDRICKSON, EDWIN E., (Doraville,) farmer leases of Simon, 37.

Hendrickson, Isaac, (North Colesville,) cooper.

HENDRICKSON, LEVI, (Doraville,) lot 20, H P., farmer 27½.

HENDRICKSON, MARCUS, (Doraville,) blacksmith.

Hendrickson, S. Mrs., estate of, (Doraville,) lot 19, H. P., 26 acres.

Hess, Albert, (Center Village,) lot 17, H. P., farmer leases 105

HICKOX, GEORGE, (Harpersville,) lot 98, S. P., farmer 33

Hickox, Louisa Mrs., (Harpersville,) lot 93, S P, farmer 60.

Hicks, Enos, (West Colesville,) lot 35, W P., farmer 76

HICKS, RALZEY, (Osborne Hollow,) lot 100, S. P, farmer 15

HIGLEY, HENRY, (Osborne Hollow,) (*Dys & Higley*,) lot 8, W P, farmer 150

Hill, Benjamin, (Belden,) lot 90, S P, farmer 80.

Hill, Franklin, (Belden,) lot 90, S P, saw mill and farmer 25.

Hilton, Willis B, (Osborne Hollow,) lot 23, W P., farmer 53.

Hinkley, Eliza L Mrs, (Osborne Hollow,) lot 12, W. P, farmer 95.

HITCHCOCK, EUGENE, (West Colesville,) lot 43, W P , farmer 10½
*HOBBS BROS., (Nineveh,) manufs of fine carriages and dealers in carriage goods
Hobbs, Joseph W., (Nineveh,) notary public.
Holcom, Imrl, (New Ohio,) lot 87, S. P, farmer 120
Holcomb, Alvin, (Belden,) lot 95, S P , farmer 91.
Holcomb, David, (Belden ) lot 96, S P , (with Milo,) farmer 200.
Holcomb, Edwin S., (New Ohio,) lot 86, S P , farmer 153
Holcomb, George A , (New Ohio,) lot 92, farmer 75
Holcomb, Harriet Mrs., (New Ohio,) lot 97, S. P., farmer 25
Holcomb, Homer, (New Ohio,) lot 87, hotel keeper and farmer 120
Holcomb, Milo, (Belden,) lot 96, S P., (with David,) farmer 200.
Holcomb, Orswin, (New Ohio,) lot 92, farmer 26
Holcomb, Rollin M , (Osborne Hollow,) lot 21, W P , farmer 150.
Homaston, Lewis, (Harpersville,) carpenter.
Hoskins, Daniel S., (Harpersville,) lot 24, Ham P , farmer 66
Houghtaling, John, (New Ohio,) lot 96, S P , farmer 40
HUBBARD, DAVID, (Doraville,) lot 18, farmer 24
HUBBARD, ERASTUS, (Colesville,) lot 35, Ham P., farmer leases 341.
HUMASTON, RUSSELL, (Belden ) lot 96, S P., farmer 106.
HUMASTON, WILLIAM S., (Center Village,) (H Martin & Co )
Humiston, Charles, (Harpersville,) lot 84, S P , farmer 73
HUMISTON, SIDNEY G , (Osborne Hollow,) lot 14, W P., farmer 200
Humphrey, Nelson C , (Center Village,) carriage maker, blacksmith, carding machine and planing mill
Hungerford, Elisha G , (Binghamton,) lot 50, W P., farmer 50.
HUNT, HENRY, (New Ohio,) lot 91, S. P., farmer 87
Huntley, Lewis, (Harpersville,) lot 85, S. P , farmer 99
Hurd, Griffin S , (Belden,) lot 90, S P , farmer 100
Hurd, Johnson, (Harpersville,) lot 84, S. P., farmer 106
Hurd, Stephen, (Belden,) lot 89, S P , farmer 13
Hurlbert, George, (Center Village,) farmer leases of John Hurlbert, 225.
Hurlbert, Edmond A., (Harpersville,) lot 88 S P , farmer 100.
HURLBURT, ISAAC A , (Harpersville,) lot 84, S P , farmer 167
Hurlburt, Isaac A , (Belden,) lot 84, farmer leases of Malcomb D. Hurlburt, 250
Hurlburt, Maria Mrs , (Harpersville,) lot 98, S P., farmer 227.
HURLBURT, URI, (Harpersville,) lot 11, Ham. P., farmer 188
Hurlburt, William, (Harpersville,) lot 11, H. P., farmer 100.

HUSTON, ROBERT, (Center Village,) farmer 44.
JENKINS, ALBERT, (Harpersville,) lot 31, Ham P , cooper and farmer 80.
Jenkins, Thomas, (Osborne Hollow,) lot 23, W P , farmer 136.
Jewel, James E , (Colesville,) lot 45, Ham. P., post master and farmer 10
Johnson, Henry, (Afton, Chenango Co ,) lives in town of Afton, farmer 103
JOHNSON, IRA W , (Center Village,) farmer leases 47
Johnson, Isaac S., (Doraville,) lot 19, H P , farmer 75
Johnson, Martha Mrs , (Doraville,) lot 20, H P , farmer 36
Johnson, Thomas, (Center Village,) farmer 31.
Jones, George W , (Harpersville,) mason.
JONES, JOHN, (Harpersville,) railroad laborer
Jones, John K , (Harpersville,) lot 6, H P , farmer leases of Judson T. Blakeslee, Binghamton, 180.
Joslin, Thomas, (New Ohio,) lot 81, S P., farmer 152
Judd, Ama A Mrs , (Harpersville,) lot 11, H P , farmer 59
Judd, John, (Doraville,) lot 19, H. P., farmer 35
Judd Peter, (Doraville,) lot 19, H P . farmer 25
Kasson, Elisha, (New Ohio,) lot 82, farmer 50
Kasson, Theodore C., (New Ohio,) lot 82, farmer 170
Keech, George A , (West Colesville,) lot 33, Ham P , farmer 45
Keech, Henry D , (West Colesville,) lot 50, W P., farmer 41 and, in Windsor, 15
KEECH, WILLIAM (Colesville,) lot 45, Ham P , boot and shoemaker, farmer 205 and, in Windsor, 25.
KEECH, WILLIAM W , (West Colesville,) lot 45, W P , farmer 72
Keenan, Patrick, (Osborne Hollow,) lot 100, S P , farmer 174
Kelley, Nelson E., (Harpersville,) lot 93, S. P , farmer 185
KETCHAM, JAMES, (Belden,) lot 96, farmer leases 53
KETCHUM, ELIZA ANN MRS , (Onaquaga,) lot 54, Ham. P., farmer 50
KETCHUM, JOSEPH F , (Ouaqnaga,) lot 38, Ham. P., farmer 52
Kipp, Aaron V , (West Colesville,) lot 33, W P , farmer 54.
Kipp, Alfred, (Osborne Hollow,) lot 33, W. P , farmer 44
Knowlton, Miles, (Onaquaga,) lot 52, Ham. P., farmer 50.
Knox, Caleb, (Center Village,) lot 18, H. P , farmer 107
Knox, E Stratton, (Onaquaga,) lot 16, H. P., farmer 44.
Lackey, George F., (Center Village,) lot 17, H P , carpenter and farmer 5
LANDON, AMBROSE, (Harpersville,) laborer.
Landon, Fennetta Mrs , (Harpersville,) lot 20, Ham P., farmer 86.
Lason, James W , (West Colesville,) lot 45, Ham. P , farmer 185.

LAUGHLIN, WILLIAM L., (West Coles-
ville,) lot 51, W P , farmer 186.
Lawton, Erwin, (Nineveh,) harness maker.
LECOUVER, WILLIAM H., (Center Vil-
lage,) rents grist mill of Barnes & Stow
LEE, EDWARD, (Osborne Hollow,) la-
borer
Lee, John H , (Vallonia Springs,) farmer 7.
Livingston, Isaac R., (Osborne Hollow,)
lot 9, W P , farmer 100
Look, Henry, (Osborne Hollow,) lot 9, W
P , farmer 64
Loope, Altana Mrs , (Harpersville,) lot 11,
H P., farmer 1
LORD, ALFRED A , (Harpersville,) boot
and shoe maker.
Lovejoy, Henry F , (Nineveh,) farmer 87
Lovejoy, Miles, (Harpersville,) lot 93 S. P.,
saw mill and farmer leases of Henry
Pratt, 30.
Lovejoy, Reuben, (Nineveh,) farmer 53.
Lynk, Charles O., (Harpersville,) tele-
graph operator.
LYON, ABIJAH, (Harpersville,) lot 80, S
P , farmer 107
Lyon, George C., (Center Village,) farmer
leases 270
MAIN, GEORGE, (Nineveh,) carriage
maker.
Manville, Henry, (Belden,) lot 90, S. P.,
saw mill and farmer 100
Manville, Isaac, (Center Village,) farmer 6.
Manville, Levi, (Harpersville,) lot 8, Ham
P., saw and planing mills, and farmer
204
Marble, Mary J Mrs , (Osborne Hollow,)
lot 21, W. P., farmer 2¾.
MARSH, FRANCIS J., (Belden,) lot 89, S.
P , farmer 50.
Marsh, Osias M , (Harpersville,) lot 12,
Ham P , farmer 80
MARSHALL, JAMES M., (Center Village,)
carpenter.
MARTIN, HARRY, (Center Village,) (*H
Martin & Co.*)
MARTIN, H. & CO., (Center Village,)
(*Harry Martin and William S Humas-
ton,*) general merchants
Martin, Lucius E,, (Harpersville,) lot 12,
Ham P , farmer 264
Martin, Warren E., (Harpersville,) farmer
3
Mason, Alonzo F., (Nineveh,) farmer 106
Mason, Charles A , (Center Village,) far-
mer leases of George Collington 200
MASON, CHARLES H , (Center Village,)
(*with Sarah A.,*) farmer 126
MASON, SARAH A , (Center Village,)
(*with Charles H ,*) farmer 126
May, William S., (Harpersville,) lot 6,
Ham P , farmer 90.
McCall, Thomas D , (Nineveh,) prop of
Nineveh House and farmer 1½
McCuller, James M., (North Colesville,)
house painter.
McCullor, Charles L., (New Ohio,) lot 86,
S P , farmer 225
McCumber, Ezra, (West Colesville,) lot 54,
W. P , farmer 12
McIntosh, Robert, (Center Village,) far-
mer 56.
Merrell, Ransom P., (Belden,) lot 89, S. P.,
farmer 105.
Merrill, Shubel, (Nineveh,) farmer 95.

Merrills, Horace, (Harpersville,) lot 11, H.
P., farmer 240.
Merrit, Hannah Mrs , (Vallonia Springs,)
farmer 1.
Merritt, Sarah Mrs., heirs of, (Center Vil-
lage,) lot 13, farmers 47.
MERWIN, MATSON S , (Harpersville,)
blacksmith and farmer 1¼.
Miller, Christopher S , (New Ohio,) lot 86,
S. P., farmer 30
Miller, Harvey, (New Ohio,) lot 86, S P ,
mason and farmer 1
MILLER, JACOB, (New Ohio,) lot 91,
S P., carpenter and joiner, and farmer
45
Miller, William A , (Harpersville,) lot 23,
Ham P., farmer 97.
MONROE, GEORGE W , (New Ohio,) ex-
press agent and telegraph operator.
MONROE, SAMUEL B , (New Ohio,) lot
92, ticket agent and farmer 2¼
MONROE, SAMUEL E., (Harpersville,)
ticket, freight and express agent, and
farmer 20
Montgomery, Eugene E., (Harpersville,)
lot 85, farmer 43.
Montgomery, Isabell Mrs , (Harpersville,)
milliner.
Montgomery, Medad, (Onaquaga,) lot 21,
H P , farmer leases of George M. Doo-
little, 143
Moon, John, (Nineveh,) farmer 1¼
Moore, George T , (Onaquaga,) lot 46, Ham
P., farmer 63.
MOOT, JOHN I , (New Ohio,) lot 95, S P ,
farmer 68
Moot, John M., (New Ohio,) lot 96, S P ,
farmer 50
Moot, Nicholas, (New Ohio,) lot 97, S P ,
farmer 70
Moot, Thomas, (Onaquaga,) lot 54, Ham. P.,
farmer 51.
MORRISON, PETER D , (Center Village,)
lot 18, H P., farmer 87¼
MORSE, JEROME J , (Harpersville,) pat-
ent right dealer and farmer 31¼.
Mott, Warren H , (Onaquaga,) lot 63, Ham
P , farmer 35.
Mudge, William L , (Harpersville,) general
insurance agent and farmer 154
Mull, Abram, (Harpersville,) lot 1, Ham P ,
farmer 80 and (*with Sayer Utter,*) 120
Mumford, Orville, (Belden,) lot 95, S. P ,
farmer 160.
Munger, John, (Harpersville,) lot 81, S. P.,
farmer 65.
MYRICK, HORACE E , (Onaquaga,) lot 56,
Ham P , farmer 52.
Nash, William O., (Harpersville,) lot 84,
S. P , farmer 189¼.
Neal, William, (Center Village,) farmer 22.
Newell, William, (Harpersville,) lot 24,
Ham P., farmer 130
Nineveh House, (Nineveh,) Thomas D
McCall, prop.
Niven, Daniel, (Nineveh,) general mer-
chant.
Noble, Elbon, (Colesville,) lot 30, Ham
P., farmer 140
NOBLE, RODERICK J., (West Colesville,)
lot 51, W P., farmer 50
NORTHRUP, EDWARD P , (Center Vil-
lage,) tannery and farmer 232.
Northrup, Edwin, (Harpersville,) farmer 70

A lso Agents for **HERRING'S SAFES, BINGHAMTON, N. Y.** See
advertisement on Map.

Northrup, Lewis, (Center Village,) grist, saw and lath mills, and farmer 5

Northrup, Lewis and Edward P., (Center Village,) farmers 159 and, in Sanford, 317

Oakley, Isaiah, (West Colesville,) lot 54, W P., farmer 50

O'Brien, Patrick, (Harpersville,) lot 79, S P., farmer 75.

ODELL, ENOS H, (Osborne Hollow,) lot 21, W. P., hotel keeper, grocer and farmer 50

Olendorf, Henry A., (Harpersville,) general merchant.

Olmstead, Madison N., (Doraville,) lot 23, farmer 90

Osborn, Orris, (Binghamton,) lot 40, W P., farmer 75

Osgood, William, (Center Village,) lot 12, H. P., farmer 60

Ostrom, Elijah, (West Colesville,) lot 54, W P., farmer 60

Packard, Larkin D, (Harpersville,) lot 81, S P., farmer 40.

Paddleford, Hanford, (North Colesville,) (Watrous & Paddleford)

Paddleford, Newel S, (North Colesville,) lot 82, postmaster and farmer 23.

Pangmon, Daniel, (Center Village,) farmer 32

Parker, Lydia D. Miss, (Nineveh,) dress maker

PARSONS, CHARLES E, (Center Village,) farmer 1½

Parsons, Edward, (Belden,) lot 94, farmer 31

Parsons, Edwin, (West Colesville,) lot 51, W P., farmer leases of William Burton, Binghamton, 60

Parsons, Harvey W, (Center Village,) lot 7, farmer 37½

Parsons, Sylvester, (Center Village,) farmer 132

Parsons, Sylvester, (Harpersville,) (Parsons & Welton.)

Parsons & Welton, (Harpersville,) (Sylvester Parsons and Brundage H Welton,) insurance agents

PEARSALL, DARIUS W, (Harpersville,) postmaster, dealer in groceries, boots and shoes

Peckham, Joseph, (Center Village,) lot 12, H. P., farmer 115

Penny, John, (Doraville,) lot 13, H. P., cooper.

Philips, Wilber F, (Harpersville,) lot 14, Ham P, farmer 100.

Phillips, John W, (Colesville,) lot 35, Ham P, farmer 14½.

Pierce, Curtis, (Doraville,) lot 23, farmer 46.

Pierce, Henry, (West Colesville,) lot 29, Ham P, cooper

PIERCE, ROBERT E., (Doraville,) farmer.

PIKE, GORDON H, (Harpersville,) lot 80, S. P, farmer 26

Pike, William C, (Harpersville,) lot 79, farmer leases 50

Pine, George W., (Ouaquaga,) lot 46, Ham. P., farmer 63

PINE, PETER, (Ouaquaga,) lot 63, Ham. P, blacksmith and farmer 63

Poole, Samuel J., (Center Village,) farmer 112.

PORTER, MARVIN B, (Center Village,) laborer.

Porter, Sibel Mrs., (Center Village,) lot 11, H P, farmer 45.

Pratt, Eleanor Mrs, (North Colesville,) lot 82, farmer 8

PRATT, GEORGE H, (Harpersville,) lot 1, farmer 60

Pratt, Hannah Mrs, (Harpersville,) lot 93, farmer 22.

Pratt, Levi, (Belden,) lot 89, S. P, farmer 28

Pratt, Samuel, (Harpersville,) lot 94, S P., farmer 75

PRENTICE, JAMES, (West Colesville,) lot 34, W P, farmer 106½

Puffer Smith C, (Harpersville,) blacksmith

Pulver, Nelson, (New Ohio,) lot 92, S P, farmer 83½.

Putman, David, (Doraville,) farmer 27

Quin, Thomas, (Port Crane,) lot 3, W. P, farmer 100

Randal, Norman S, (Binghamton,) lot 50, W P, farmer 80

Randall, Augustus B, (North Colesville,) shoemaker

Randall, James, (West Colesville,) lot 54, W P, farmer 137

Rector, William H., (Center Village,) farmer 50

Reynolds, Augustus, (Osborne Hollow,) lot 25, W P, farmer 110.

Reynolds, Austin, (Osborne Hollow,) lot 24, W P, farmer 104.

REYNOLDS, CORNELIUS, (Osborne Hollow,) lot 32, W P, ticket, freight and express agent, and farmer 106

Reynolds, Ira, (Osborne Hollow,) lot 26, W P, farmer 126.

Richards, Charles M., (Harpersville,) (C. M & G Richards)

Richards, C. M. & G, (Harpersville,) (Charles M and George,) furnace and machine shop, and farmers 14

Richards, George, (Harpersville,) (C M. & G Richards)

Riley, Robert, (New Ohio,) lot 92, S P, general merchant, farmer 1 and, in Chenango, 130

ROACH, JEREMIAH Jr, (West Colesville,) lot 36, W P, farmer 48.

Robinson, David, (Center Village,) farmer 66.

Robinson, George, (Vallonia Springs,) blacksmith and farmer 85.

Robinson, Lewis, (Belden,) lot 95, S P., farmer 100.

Ross, Andrew, (West Colesville,) lot 51, W P, farmer 43.

Rounk, George, (Port Crane,) lot 3, W P., farmer 150

Rowe, Deloss, (Vallonia Springs,) farmer 100.

ROWE, SEYMOUR, (Center Village,) farmer 83.

Ruggles, Alva, (West Colesville,) lot 83, Ham P, farmer 30

Russell, Eunice A Mrs., (Osborne Hollow,) lot 21, W P, farmer 53¾

Russell, Ira, (West Colesville,) lot 43, W. P, farmer 45

Russell, John, (Osborne Hollow,) lot 21, W P., farmer 2¾.

COLESVILLE. 221

Sabin, Isaac E., (Vallonia Springs,) farmer leases of William C. Poyer, Binghamton, 200.
Sandell, James, (Harpersville,) lot 89, S. P., farmer 40.
Sanders, Shepard L, (Vallonia Springs,) farmer 33.
SANDS, ANDREW J., (Vallonia Springs,) prop. Vallonia Springs House, physician, postmaster and farmer 24.
Sawtelle, William H. Rev., (Nineveh,) pastor of Presbyterian Church
Schouten, William 2d, (Harpersville,) lot 94, S P., farmer 50
Schughten, William, (Harpersville,) lot 88, S P., farmer 86
Scudder, Aaron, (West Colesville,) lot 88, Ham. P, cooper and farmer 20.
Scudder, Corbin A., (Osborne Hollow,) lot 17, Ham P, farmer 95
Searles, Emily M. Mrs., (Center Village,) lot 10, farmer 75.
Searles, Harry G., (Afton, Chenango Co.,) farmer 100.
Seward, Chloe Mrs., (Vallonia Springs,) farmer 95.
Seward, Daniel S., (Center Village,) blacksmith, farmer 80 and, in Sanford, 40.
Seward, Henry D, (Doraville,) lot 24, H. P., farmer 61
Seward, Levi, (Vallonia Springs,) farmer 250
Shay, William, (Belden,) lot 99, S. P., farmer 90
Shepard, Charles D Rev., (Harpersville,) pastor of M E Church
Shores, Alanson F., (North Colesville,) cooper
SKINNER, CARLTON J, (Center Village,) farm laborer.
Skinner, Stanley J, (Center Village,) farmer 160.
SMITH, CARLOW K., (Doraville,) farmer 250
Smith, Emily Mrs, (Nineveh,) lot 13, farmer 100.
Smith, Harvey, (Nineveh,) farmer 125.
SMITH, HIRAM, (West Colesville,) lot 41, W. P., farmer 84.
Smith, Howard Z., (Doraville,) farmer.
Smith, Martha Mrs., (Doraville,) lot 23, farmer 84¾.
Smith, Nathan, (Center Village,) farmer 9
SMITH, NATHANIEL, (Nineveh,) carriage ironer, blacksmith and farmer 3.
Smith, Robert W, (Doraville,) lot 18, H P, farmer 87
Snitchler, William, (Doraville,) lot 24, farmer leases 61.
Snyder, Solomon, (Belden,) lot 99, S. P., farmer 1.
SORNBORGER, EDWARD M., (Osborne Hollow,) (Cass & Sornborger,) farmer 130.
SONBORGER, SIDNEY, (Harpersville,) farmer 63.
Soule, Charles, (Onaquaga,) rents grist mill of Peter.
SPENCER, AMBROSE, (Afton, Chenango Co.,) farmer 80
Spencer, Benjamin F., (New Ohio,) lot 86, farmer 100.
Spencer, Hiram E, (Center Village,) blacksmith.

Spencer, Nelson H., (New Ohio,) lot 94, S. P, farmer 110
SPRINGSTEEN, GEORGE R, (Doraville,) lot 8, H. P., farmer 118 and, in Windsor, 110.
SQUIRE, DANIEL W, (Onaquaga,) lot 22, H P, farmer, in Windsor, 100 and leases of Mrs S. E. Whitney, Binghamton, 550
STAATS, ROENA Mrs., (Harpersville,) farmer 1
Stephens, David L, (Harpersville,) lot 89, S. P., farmer 180
Stephens, Marcus, (Onaquaga,) lot 58, Ham. P., farmer 83.
Stephens, Peter, estate of, (Harpersville,) lot 83, S P, 135 acres.
Stephens, Willard, (Onaquaga,) carpenter.
Stephens, Wm, (Onaquaga,) carpenter
STEVENS, CHARLES P., (Harpersville,) carpenter and joiner
STEVENS, REUBEN Rev, (Onaquaga,) lot 62, Ham. P., pastor M E Church and farmer 53
Stilson, Avery, (Center Village,) lot 20, H P., farmer 32½.
Stow, Levi, (Onaquaga,) lot 21, H. P., farmer 23 and, in Windsor, 25.
Stow, Robert, (Harpersville,) druggist and grocer
Stringham, Charles H, (Doraville,) (with John W) lot 23, H P, farmer 240
STRINGHAM, JAMES W., (Doraville,) lot 23 H P, farmer 131
Stringham, John W, (Doraville,) (with Chas. H) lot 23, H. P., farmer 240
STRINGHAM, WALTER, (Onaquaga,) lot 16, H. P., farmer 70.
Swagart, Richard C (Onaquaga,) lot 64, Ham. P., farmer 30.
Taggart, Calvin R., (Center Village,) lot 10, farmer 70
Teller, Jacob, (Center Village,) lot 17, H P., farmer 40
Terry, John O Jr, (Vallonia Springs,) farmer 58.
Thompson, Curtis, estate of, (Harpersville,) lot 88, S. P, 73 acres
THOMPSON & HARE, (Harpersville,) (John G Thompson and Charles W Hare,) harness makers
Thompson, John, (Belden,) lot 94, S. P., farmer 70
THOMPSON, JOHN G, (Harpersville,) (Thompson & Hare)
Thompson, Sylvester, (Harpersville,) lot 94, S. P., farmer 46
Thorn, James W, (Center Village,) lot 20, H. P., farmer 97½.
Throop, Benjamin, (Center Village,) farmer 71.
THROOP, BENJAMIN F., (Center Village,) laborer
THROOP, JOSEPH D, (Doraville,) lot 18, H P, farmer 47
Throop, Josiah, (Center Village,) farmer 254
Thurber, Ansel M., (West Colesville,) lot 42, Ham. P, saw mill and farmer 95
THURBER, EGBERT A, (West Colesville,) lot 85, W. P., farmer 50.
Thurber, Jeremiah, (Binghamton,) lot 50, W. P, farmer 63.

TICE & WEEKS, (Center Village,) (*William Tice and Solomon Weeks*,) general merchants

TICE WILLIAM, (Center Village,) (*Tice & Weeks*,) postmaster

Tompkins, George M., (Doraville,) jeweler and grocer.

Topping, John, (Harpersville,) merchant tailor.

Truesdale, Elisha, (Harpersville,) lot 15, Ham P., farmer 100.

TRUESDELL, HARVEY, (Harpersville,) lot 93, S. P., brick maker and farmer 80

TRUESDELL, JOHN, (Harpersville,) lot 80, S P, saw mill and farmer 130

Truesdell, Robert, (Belden,) lot 99, S. P., farmer 60.

TRUESDELL, WILLARD B, (Harpersville,) lot 80, S P., farmer 78.

TUBBS, ANNA Mrs, (widow,) (Nineveh,) resident

Turner, James J., (Harpersville,) lot 16, H P., farmer 10.

Tylor, Joseph, (Osborne Hollow,) lot 15, W P., farmer 24.

TYRRELL, BARTHOLOMEW, (Harpersville,) lot 93, S P, farmer 97¾

TYRRELL, HIRAM E, (Harpersville,) general coal agent and farmer 13.

Tyrrell, Leroy A, (Harpersville,) lot 20, Ham P, farmer 90

TYRRELL, LEWIS H., (Ouaquaga,) lot 21, H. P, farmer 140.

Tyrrell, Milton, (West Colesville,) lot 33, Ham. P., farmer 69.

Underwood, Isaac E, (Harpersville,) lot 16, H P, farmer 50.

Utter, Henry, (Harpersville,) lot 89, Ham P, farmer 80.

UTTER, SAMUEL, (Harpersville,) lot 11, Ham P, farmer 125

Utter, Sayer, (Harpersville,) lot 1, Ham. P., (with *Abram Mull*,) farmer 120.

Utter, Stephen, (Belden,) lot 99, S P, farmer 126.

UTTER, STEPHEN D, (Harpersville,) lot 39, Ham P., cooper and farmer 2

Utter, William, (New Ohio,) lot 91, S P, grocer, farmer 48 and, in Sanford, 106

VALLONIA SPRINGS HOUSE, (Vallonia Springs,) Andrew J. Sands, prop

Vancott, John, (Harpersville,) lot 83, S. P., farmer 75.

Vanderburgh, Clarence F, (Center Village,) farmer 113

Vaness, John W., (Center Village,) D. 10, farmer leases 102

VANNESS, RANSLER, (Belden,) lot 94, S. P, farmer 110.

VANZILE, GEORGE A, (Osborne Hollow,) lot 21, W P, steam saw mill, lath, feed and corn mills and farmer 3.

Viney, John, (Harpersville,) manuf. of cigars.

VOSBURY, HENRY O., (Doraville,) carpenter and joiner, and farmer 1½

VOSBURY, LUCY M. Mrs., (Doraville,) lot 23, H. P, farmer 90.

Wakeman, John S., (Harpersville,) lot 93, S P, farmer 44.

WALDORF, NICHOLAS, (New Ohio,) lot 91, S P, farmer 53

WALLACE, NATHANIEL S., (Belden,) lot 89, grocer, post master and farmer 1.

Wallace, Reuben, (Osborne Hollow,) lot 32, W P, farmer 25

Walling, A. Judson, (New Ohio,) lot 91, S. P, farmer 100.

Waltruss, Selden, (Ouaquaga,) carriage maker.

Warner John, (North Colesville,) lot 83, S P., farmer 188 and, in Fenton, 166

Warner, Noel, (Osborne Hollow,) lot 4, W P, farmer 60

Wasson, Stephen, (Center Village,) farmer 132

Waterman, Lyman, (Belden,) lot 2, Ham. P., farmer 76.

Watrous, Dewitt, (North Colesville,) lot 82, S. P, farmer 166.

Watrous, Eli E, (Ouaquaga,) blacksmith.

Watrous, Hubert, (North Colesville,) (*Watrous & Paddleford*.)

Watrous, John W, (North Colesville,) lot 82, grocer, farmer 450 and, in Fenton, 310

Watrous, Lyman, (North Colesville,) lot 82, farmer 40

Watrous & Paddleford, (North Colesville,) (*Hubert Watrous and Hanford Paddleford*,) saw mill

WATROUS, WILLIAM, (Ouaquaga,) lot 16, H P, cooper and farmer 50.

Watrouss, Nelson, (North Colesville,) lot 83, S. P., farmer 180.

WAY, LORENZO E, (Harpersville,) lot 83, S P, farmer 125

Wayman, Ambrose, (Osborne Hollow,) lot 5, W P., farmer 25

Webster, Alva, (New Ohio,) lot 86, S P., farmer 60.

Webster, Henry J, (Belden,) lot 89, S P, carpenter and farmer 11

Wedg, Amos, (Colesville,) lot 35, Ham. P., farmer 214.

Wedg, Joseph, (Colesville,) lot 27, Ham. P, farmer 82¾

Wedge, Alanson, (Vallonia Springs,) farmer 64.

WEDGE, EDGAR P, (Harpersville,) lot 88, S P, farmer 136

Weed, Orin, (Osborne Hollow,) grocer

Weeks, Lucius G., (Harpersville,) carpenter and farmer 2

WEEKS, SOLOMON, (Center Village,) (*Tice & Weeks*,) farmer 1½

Welton, Brundage H, (Harpersville,) (*Parsons & Welton*)

Welton, Emeline E. Miss, (Doraville,) lot 1, H. P, farmer 1¼.

Welton, George W., (Ouaquaga,) lot 16, H. P, cooper and farmer 5.

Welton, Joel S., (Harpersville,) lot 16, H P, mason and farmer 25

Welton, Susan Mrs., (Center Village,) farmer 53.

Wenn, Almond, (West Colesville,) lot 38, W. P., farmer 50.

WEST, PHILO, (Harpersville,) lot 31, Ham. P, farmer 80.

West, Phœbe Mrs., (West Colesville,) lot 43, W P., farmer leases of George Wilcox, Binghamton, 60.

Whitaker, Clark, estate of, (Belden,) lot 89, S P, 86 acres

Whitaker, John, (Belden,) lot 86, S P., farmer 43.

Whitaker, Leroy. (Belden,) lives in Pa., lot 85, farmer 185

Whitaker, Seth, (New Ohio,) lot 85, S. P., farmer 200.

Whitaker, Seth P B., (New Ohio,) lot 90, S P., farmer 79

White, Sanford, (West Colesville,) lot 45, Ham P, farmer 25.

Whitham, William, (Osborne Hollow,) lot 20, W. P, farmer 105.

Whitmore, Sarah Mrs, (Osborne Hollow,) lot 25, W P., farmer 45.

Wight, Jane Mrs., (West Colesville,) lot 41, W P , farmer 10.

Wilber, Ferris, (Vallonia Springs,) farmer 73.

Wilder, Addison S., (Center Village,) farmer 125

Wilder, Henry, (Center Village,) D. 10, farmer 25.

Wilder, Perry, (Center Village,) D. 10, carpenter and farmer 50.

WILES, CHRISTOPHER, (West Colesville,) lot 36, W.P., farmer 110.

Williams, George L Rev , (Osborne Hollow,) pastor M. E. Church.

WILLIAMS, NATHAN K , (West Colesville,) brick and stone mason

WINN, HENRY J , (West Colesville,) lot 44, W. P , farmer 40

WOOD, HIRAM D., (Afton, Chenango Co.,) farmer 26.

Wood, Levi, (Onaquaga,) lot 38, Ham. P., farmer leases of Charles Law, 63

Woodworth, Mary Mrs , (Vallonia Springs,) farmer 91.

Wright, Henry, (Onaquaga,) lot 36, Ham. P , farmer 123.

WYLIE, JOHN, (North Colesville,) lot 82, S P., farmer 320.

Yager, Adam, (Belden,) lot 94, S. P , farmer 128

Yager, John, (Belden,) lot 84, S P , farmer 20.

Yager, John N , (Belden,) lot 94, S. P , bridge carpenter and farmer.

YALE, EDGAR A , (Onaquaga,) laborer

Yale, Philetus, (Nineveh,) (*with Thomas*,) farmer 70.

Yale, Stanley, (Onaquaga,) lot 21, H. P , farmer 90.

Yale, Thomas, (Nineveh,) (*with Philetus*,) farmer 70

Yeoman, Peter, (Onaquaga,) lot 38, Ham P , farmer 88

Youmans, Henry M., (Onaquaga,) lot 48, Ham P , farmer 18.

Young, David W., (Osborne Hollow,) lot 22, W P., farmer 83

Youngs, Catharine Mrs , (Harpersville,) lot 1, farmer 8.

Youngs, Williams, (West Colesville,) lot 54, W. P , farmer 50

---

# CONKLIN.

### (Post Office Addresses in Parentheses.)

Adams, Charles J., (Conklin Station,) lot 19, farmer 80

Allen, Irania, (Conklin Station,) lot 1, farmer 50

BADGER, FREDERICK P , (Conklin Station,) lot 27, station agent, D. L. & W. R R.

Badger, Lemuel W., (Conklin Station,) lot 27, farmer 26.

Bagley, Alfred, (Conklin Center,) lot 2, carpenter and farmer 30.

Bagley, Church, (Binghamton,) lot 8, farmer 47

BANTA, JACOB, (Corbettsville,) lot 7, farmer 125

Barlow, Franklin, (Conklin Station,) lot 7, farmer 16

Barlow, Jacob, (Binghamton,) lot 8, farmer 106

Barlow, Morgan, (Conklin Station,) lot 7, shingle maker and farmer 8

BARLOW, WALKER, (Binghamton,) lot 8, farmer 40

Bayless, Burtis J , (Conklin Station,) lot 27, postmaster, grocer and town clerk

Bayless, Daniel, (Conklin Station,) carpenter.

BAYLESS, JOHN L., (Conklin Station ) lot 22, farmer 150.

Beadle, Abram, (Conklin Center,) lot 1, farmer leases 60

Beecher, Bartholomew, (Brookdale, Susquehanna Co , Pa ,) lot 2, farmer 100.

Bell, Arthur W., (Hawleyton,) lot 11, farmer 118

Benson, Michael, (Binghamton,) lot 7, farmer 100.

BISHOP, ELIZABETH A Mrs , (widow,) (Binghamton,) lot 14, farmer 47

Bishop, Isaac, (Binghamton,) lot 25, assessor and farmer 94

Bishop, James H., (Conklin Station,) carpenter

Bishop, Josiah, (Binghamton,) lot 28, farmer 145

Blatchley, Emory, (Conklin Station,) lot 8, grist and saw mills, millwright and farmer 20.

Bostwick, John F., (Binghamton,) lot 5, farmer 6.

Boyle, Thomas, (Corbettsville,) section foreman D. L & W. R. R.

BRADLEY, ARTHUR, (Corbettsville,) lawyer

Brant, John A., (Conklin Station,) lot 9, farmer 105.

Brant, Jonas, (Conklin Center,) lot 33, farmer 50

Brooks, Hiram K., (Conklin Station,) lot 16, farmer 64.

Brooks, Horatio D , (Binghamton,) lot 5, carpenter and farmer leases 22

BROWNELL, J A , (Binghamton,) lot 20, millwright

BULL, JEREMIAH, (Conklin Station,) retired

Bonta, Jacob, (Conklin Station,) lot 19, farmer leases 90

Bunts, Jacob, (Conklin Station,) teamster.

BURGETT, ISAIAH Jr., (Binghamton,) lot 34, farmer 130.

Butler, Joel, (Conklin Station,) lot 8, hunter and farmer 10.

Campbell, John O., (Conklin Station,) lot 26, farmer 54

Carlin, Cornelius, (Binghamton,) lot 41, farmer 45.

Carlin, Edward B , (Conklin Center,) lot 37, farmer leases 80

Chalker, Alanson, (Corbettsville,) lot 35, lumberman and farmer 140

Clark, Seth, (Conklin Station,) lot 27, millwright.

Clement, Samuel, (Binghamton,) lot 5, farmer 200

CONKLIN GRIST MILL, (Conklin Station,) Levi L. Roe, prop.

Conroy, George, (Binghamton,) lot 4, farmer 50.

Coon, Anna and Marian Misses, (Binghamton,) lot 4, farmers 51

Coons, Hiram, (Binghamton,) lot 3, farmer 57

Corbett, Ira, (Conklin Station,) lot 26, general merchant, prop saw mill and farmer 225

Corbett, Julius S , (Corbettsville,) lot 32, assessor, prop. of saw mill and 370 acres of lumber land

CORBETT, WILLIAM S , (Conklin Station,) clerk in I. Corbett's store.

Cruser, John, (Corbettsville,) lot 6, lumberman and farmer 52.

Cruser, John L , (Corbettsville,) farm laborer.

Curran, William, (Conklin Center,) lot 8, farmer 25.

Davis, James, (Corbettsville,) lot 33, farmer 98.

Decker, David, (Conklin Station,) teamster and peddler.

Dedrick, George W., (Conklin Station,) lot 5, farmer 100

DEWITT, AMOS T , (Conklin Station,) lot 21, farmer leases 150.

Dickerson, Robert B., (Binghamton,) lot 4, farmer 40.

Dillon, Hamlet, (Conklin Station,) lot 27, retired

Dings, Stephen A , (Binghamton,) lot 7, confectionery peddler and farmer 62

Disbrow, Alexander, (Conklin Station,) lot 6, farmer leases 117.

Driscoll, Jane A Mrs , (Conklin Station,) lot 27, resident.

Emerson, Charles, (Binghamton,) lot 6, farmer 70

Engelbert, Edward, (Conklin Station,) lot 27, farmer leases 117

Farrell, James, (Binghamton,) lot 40, farmer 55

FERRIS, JONATHAN, (Conklin Station,) lot 22, tanner and farmer 5.

Finch Aaron, (Binghamton,) lot 2, jobber

FINCH, DUDLEY T , (Conklin Station,) lot 23, farmer 130.

Finch, Ezekiel J , (Binghamton,) lot 3, blacksmith and farmer 20.

Finch, Nathaniel I , (Conklin Station,) lot 7, mason and farmer 50

Finch, Sylvester M., (Conklin Station,) lot 6, mason and farmer 70

FINCH, THOMAS J , (Conklin Station,) lot 14, farmer 180.

FISH. JOHN C , (Corbettsville,) lot 36, lawyer and farmer 190.

Franklin, Jacob, (Conklin Station,) farmer 3½.

Fuller, Charles E , (Conklin Station,) (with *Joseph,*) lot 23, farmer 100

FULLER, GEORGE, (Corbettsville,) lot 37, farmer 150

Fuller, Joseph, (Conklin Station,) lot 23, carpenter and (with *Charles E.*) farmer 100.

Fuller, Lucius E , (Conklin Station,) lot 23, farmer 26.

Gardner, Ira, (Conklin Station,) lot 25, farmer 208

Gill, Charles, (Binghamton,) lot 7, farmer leases 20

GILLIENS, THOMAS, (Conklin Station,) lot 27, lumberman

Golan, William, (Binghamton,) lot 18, farmer 50

GRAY, JONATHAN, (Conklin Station,) lot 26, carpenter and joiner

Gregory, Harvey, (Conklin Station,) lot 27, carpenter

Halbert, Edgar, (Binghamton,) lot 8, farmer 43.

Halpin, Patrick, (Binghamton,) lot 7, farmer 80.

Hardey, George, (Conklin Center,) lot 43, farmer 20.

HARDEY, GEORGE W , (Conklin Center,) lot 43, farmer 20

Hopkins, George, (Binghamton,) lot 17, farmer 15.

Horton, Arnold E , (Binghamton,) lot 7, farmer 68

Horton, Benjamin D., (Conklin Station,) lot 7, carpenter and farmer 12.

Humiston, John S., (Conklin Station,) lot 9, farmer leases 89

Humphrey, John Q., (Conklin Station,) lot 3, lumber manuf. and owns 100 acres lumber land

Hupman, Charles H., (Corbettsville,) lot 31, blacksmith.

Ives, Reuben N., (Corbettsville,) lot 31, farmer 86

Ives, Sheldon S., (Corbettsville,) wagon maker.

JAGELER, JOHN, (Binghamton,) prop. of saw mill and manuf of lumber.

Jenks, Charles, (Corbettaville,) lot 38, farmer 24

Johnson, Brewater C , (Conklin Center,) lot 2 postmaster and farmer 60.

Jones, Jesse, (Binghamton,) lot 7, farmer 68

Ketchum, George L , (Corbettaville,) lot 32, farmer and R. R. laborer

Ketchum, Luther, (Corbettaville,) sawyer

KNIGHT, STEPHEN L , (Conklin Station,) prop of Milburn Cemetry, sexton of Presbyterian Church and shoemaker.

Lamoreaux, Samuel, (Binghamton,) lot 7, farmer 110.

LATHROP, FRANK A., (Binghamton,) farmer.

Lathrop, Marvin R , (Binghamton,) lot 4, justice of the peace and farmer 51.

Lawrence, Benjamin W , (Binghamton,) (*Lawrence & Waldron,*) lot 5, supervisor, lumberman and farmer 130.

Lawrence, Edwin, (Binghamton,) lot 5, farmer 90.

Lawrence, Mortimer, (Binghamton,) lot 5, farmer 37.

Layton Robert, (Binghamton,) lot 7, farmer 33.

Layton, Samuel F , (Conklin Center,) lot 7, farmer leases 15.

LEACH & RUSSELL, (Conklin Station,) (*Winslow C Leach and Leverett Russell* ) wagon manufs. and dealers in bent stuff for carriages

LEACH, WINSLOW C., (Conklin Station,) (*Leach & Russell* )

Lebarnon, Benjamin C., (Binghamton,) carpenter

Leeve, William D , (Binghamton,) lot 1, farmer 170.

Levee, Jacob, (Binghamton,) lot 25, farmer 75

LIGHT, GILBERT, (Binghamton,) laborer.

Lobdell, Gideon, (Binghamton,) lot 8, farmer 160

LOCKWOOD, DANIEL C , (Conklin Station,) lot 16, farmer 78

Loveless, Joseph B , (Corbettaville,) farm laborer

Lowe, George, (Conklin Station,) lot 8, farmer 104

Lnee, Asa C , (Conklin Station,) retired.

Maine, Lodic L , (Conklin Station,) lot 18, farmer leases 87

Malkin, William R , (Binghamton,) lot 8, farmer 44½.

MANWARREN, JAMES J , (Binghamton,) lot 3. farmer leases 195.

MARKHAM, WILLIAM O , (Conklin Center,) engineer

Martin, Joseph P., (Conklin Station,) lot 27, carpenter and justice of the peace.

McBride, Michael, (Binghamton,) lot 6, assessor and farmer 100.

McDongall, Benjamin, (Binghamton,) lot 7, carpenter and farmer 75

McLaory, Henry W , (Corbettaville,) farmer leases

MEAD, ARTHUR G , (Conklin Station,) (*G. W. & A G Mead* )

MEAD, GEORGE W., (Conklin Station,) (*G. W. & A. G. Mead,*) lot 24, farmer 100.

MEAD, G W & A G., (Conklin Station,) (*George W and Arthur G ,*) groceries, meat and hides

Mead, John, (Conklin Station,) retired

Miller, George H , (Conklin Center,) lot 3, farmer 55.

MINKLER, CHARLES, (Corbettaville,) lot 31, carpenter, justice of the peace and farmer 25.

Mosher, Edwin, (Conklin Station,) lot 13, farmer 89¼.

MURPHY DANIEL J , (Corbettaville,) lot 31, general merchant, postmaster, cattle dealer and farmer 94

Murphy, Peter, (Binghamton,) lot 28, farmer 104.

Newton, James D , (Binghamton,) lot 21, carpenter

Niver, Charles S , (Conklin Station,) lot 21, farmer 200.

Northrup, Alvin, (Conklin Station,) lot 13, farmer 70.

Ostrander, James C , (Binghamton,) lot 13, farmer 75

Ostrander, John W , (Conklin Center,) farmer 2

Owen, Amos, (Corbettsville,) lot 32, farmer 15.

PALMER THEODORE H , (Conklin Station,) teamster and farm laborer

Pardee, Samuel, (Conklin Station,) lot 27, retired.

PARKS, JOHN T., (Corbettaville,) (*Parks & Porter* )

PARKS & PORTER, (Corbettaville,) (*John T Parks and John O Porter,*) manufs of sole leather.

PARSONS, ASA B , (Binghamton,) lot 27, farmer 55.

Parsons, Leroy M , (Conklin Station,) lot 27, harness maker.

PATERSON, DUNCAN S , (Conklin Station,) blacksmith.

Paterson, John, (Conklin Station,) lot 10, farmer 110.

PENCIL, JOHN, (Conklin Station ) lot 24, farm laborer.

Pethcal, Jacob, (Conklin Center,) lot 1, farmer 110

PIERSON, MILTON, (Binghamton,) lot 7, farmer 25

Pink, George, (Binghamton,) lot 4, farmer 40

PORTER, JOHN O ,(Corbettaville,) (*Parks & Porter.*)

PRENTICE, ANCIEL R., (Conklin Station,) lot 17, farmer 140

PRICE, GEORGE S , (Binghamton,) lot 26, farmer leases 105.

Redfield, George S., (Conklin Station,) allo. physician

Redfield, John, (Conklin Station,) lot 27, farmer 17

ROE, LEVI L., (Conklin Station,) lot 23, prop of Conklin Grist Mill and farmer 6.

Roe, William T , (Conklin Station,) miller.

Rogers, Jesse L., (Conklin Center,) lot 7, farmer 200

Rose, Charles P , (Corbettsville,) sawyer

Ross Erastos, (Binghamton,) lot 1, farmer 124.

Ross, Orlando J., (Binghamton,) lot 20, farmer 110.

RULISON, FRANCIS, (Hawleyton,) lot 12, farmer 40

RUSSELL, LEVERETT, (Conklin Station,) (*Leach & Russell*)

Rutherford, Christopher,(Conklin Station,) lot 27, farmer 25 and, in Union, 80.

Ryan, James, (Binghamton,) lot 27, farmer 150.

SAXON, ABRAM S, (Conklin Station,) (*J A Emmons & Co.,*) prop. of Milburn Acid Works.

Scofield, William W, (Conklin Station,) lot 11, farmer 25½

Severson, Christopher, (Conklin Center,) lot 32, farmer 124.

SHAVALIER, WILLIAM J., (Conklin Center,) lot 43, farmer 10.

Shepard, Joseph, (Binghamton,) lot 8, dealer in meat and farmer 86

Shepard, Reuben, (Binghamton,) lot 8, farmer leases 81

Shufelt, Frederick P.,(Conklin Station,) lot 14, farmer 43

Shufelt, James M, (Binghamton,) carpenter

Simmons, Peter, (Binghamton,) lot 8, farmer 40.

Simpson, Michael, (Binghamton,) lot 39, farmer 85

Smith, Eliza J Mrs, (widow,) (Binghamton,) lot 2, farmer 60.

Smith, John, (Binghamton,) lot 8, farm laborer

Snedaker, Henry P, (Corbettsville,) lot 38, carpenter and farmer 44.

Snedaker, Sanders, (Conklin Station,) lot 27, carpenter

Spafard, Albert P., (Hawleyton,) lot 11, farmer 57

Sprague, George H, (Conklin Center,) lot 32, farmer 50

STALKER, WILLIAM H, (Binghamton,) lot 2, shingle maker and farmer 33.

Standley, Hiram, (Binghamton,) lot 41, farmer 7.

Standley, Sanford, (Binghamton,) lot 41, teamster and farmer 40.

STERLING, CHARLES J, (Conklin Station,) telegraph operator.

Stone, Ashbell F, (Binghamton,) lot 85, blacksmith and farmer 108

Stuart, John A, (Conklin Station,) lot 12, farmer 85

Sullivan, James, (Conklin Station,) lot 15, farmer 100

TAMKINS, CHARLES H, (Conklin Station,) lot 24, carpenter and farmer 48.

TAMKINS, JOHN, (Conklin Station,) lot 24, dealer in meat and farmer 75

Tarbox, John, (Conklin Station,) lot 20, farmer 50.

Teany, Ephraim B., (Binghamton,) lot 8, farmer 90

Tompkins, Edward C, (Conklin Station,) lot 24, dealer in meat and inspector of elections.

Townsend, Jackson S, (Binghamton,) lot 34, farmer 118.

Treadwell, Charles H, (Binghamton,) lot 7, farmer 152

TRIPP, ADELBERT D, (Conklin Station,) lot 11, farmer leases of Ephraim D, 35.

TRIPP, GEORGE S., (Conklin Station,) lot 3, farmer 40.

Tripp, James W, (Binghamton,) lot 9, farmer 50.

Tripp, Joseph F, (Brackney, Susquehanna Co, Pa,) lot 18, farmer 40.

Tripp, William H, (Conklin Station,) lot 9, farmer 4

TRIPP, WILLIAM J., (Conklin Station,) lot 5, wall builder and farmer 3¼.

Tyler, Perry, (Binghamton,) lot 2, farmer 50.

Tyler, William D., (Binghamton,) lot 1, farmer 116

TYLER, WILLIAM W., (Binghamton,) farmer

Van Patten, Richard, (Binghamton,) saw mill and farmer 170.

Van Wormer, Aaron, (Conklin Station,) lot 22, farmer 50.

VAN WORMER, AARON, Jr, (Conklin Station,) lot 22, farmer 100

Van Wormer, John, (Conklin Station,) lot 22, farmer leases 50.

VINING, ATWOOD P, (Conklin Station,) prop. of saw and lath mill, and millwright

VINING, NEWEL J, (Conklin Station,) lot 16, farmer 35.

Vosbury, Levi E, (Conklin Station,) lot 23, farmer 60

VOSBURY, RICHARD C, (Conklin Station,) lot 23, farmer 40.

VOSBURY, SAMUEL S., (Conklin Station,) lot 24, farmer 6

WALDRON, CORNELIUS J, (Conklin Center,) lot 3, farmer 90.

WALKER, JOHN H, (Binghamton,) jobber at clearing land

Walsh, James, (Corbettsville,) lot 37, blacksmith.

Waltermire, John, (Conklin Station,) carpenter

Waterman, George P, (Binghamton,) lot 4, farmer 100

Watrous, Henry N., (Conklin Station,) lot 25, farmer 96 and 100 acres of lumber land

WEBB, DAVID P, (Binghamton,) lot 43, carpenter and farmer 10

WELTON, CHAUNCEY, (Binghamton,) lot 14, farmer 70.

WHALON, MARTIN, (Binghamton,) lot 14, farmer 68

Whitney, Charles, (Conklin Center,) lot 2, professor of elocution and farmer 160.

Whitney, James E, (Conklin Center,) lot 2, farmer 40.

Whitney, John B, (Conklin Center,) lot 55, farmer, in Fenton 96.

Wilber, Daniel, (Binghamton,) lot 8, farmer 25.

Wilber, Hiram, (Binghamton,) shingle maker

WILBUR, ELIAS, (Binghamton,) lot 21, justice of the peace and farmer 185.

Wilbur, Hiram, (Conklin Station,) lot 27, blacksmith, collector, constable and farmer 5.

Wilson, John, (Binghamton,) lot 15, farmer 23.

WINANS, CORNELIUS, (Corbettsville,) prop of tannery and shoe shop

Woodside, James (Conklin Station,) foreman in A. S. Saxon's acid works.

WOODSIDE, JOHN M , (Conklin Station,) lot 27, farmer 40
Woodworth, W J , (Binghamton,) lot 6, farmer leases 79.

Worden, Abiah P. Rev., (Conklin Station,) lot 10, Baptist minister, and farmer 89

# DEPOSIT VILLAGE.

Adams, J. N. Rev., pastor of Baptist Church, Pine.
ALDERSON, JAMES, (Alderson & Watkins )
ALDERSON, JAMES W., mason and brick layer.
ALDERSON & WATKINS, (James Alderson and Willis Watkins.) contractors, jobbers and builders, dealers in lime, plaster and cement, Front
Babcock, Aaron, carpenter, Pine.
BABCOCK, EDWARD A., carpenter and builder, Pine.
Babcock, Giles M , harness maker
BALL, I C., (Demander & Ball,) farmer 27.
Bean. Egbert, horse trainer and doctor, prop. of livery.
Beardsley, E , (Beardsley & Wall,) horse shoeing &c
Beardsley & Wall, (E. Beardsley and John Wall,) carriage makers
Behrle. L., lawyer and saloon keeper, Church
Belknap, D. K., general agent, E. R. R.
Bixby, Henry W , hardware and groceries, Front.
Bixby, T. M., cabinet maker and undertaker, Church
Borrill & Croft, grocers, Front.
Boyd, E. T , (Wickwire, Russell & Co )
Brant, S. M. Miss, music teacher, Deposit Academy
Brown, Charles K., druggist and bookseller, Front
Buel, Louise, assistant teacher, Deposit Academy
Buell, M P., general insurance agent, Main.
BUNDY, O. T , physician and surgeon, U. S examining surgeon for pensioners, Cottage.
BUNDY, OLIVER T. JR , physician and surgeon, Cottage.
Burch, L. Miss, milliner, Front.
Burrows & Edick, (James T. Burrows and Charles T. Edick,) general merchants, corner Broad and Main.
Burrows, Henry, (H Burrows & Son.)
Burrows, H. & Son, (Henry and Wm. H.,) boots and shoes, Front.
Burrows, James T , (Burrows & Edick.)
Burrows, Wm. H., (H. Burrows & Son )

Carpenter, J B & Co., (J. K Reeve,) books, stationery &c.
Carpenter S R , Allen
Caswell, A. G., blacksmith.
CLARK, J Q , (Mapes, Clark & Co )
Clark, ——, (Debereux & Clark.)
Conrow, G , saloon, Main
Corcoran, John, physician
Croft, ——, (Borrill & Croft )
Cummings, Alex , attorney and insurance agent, Front
Dailey, James, (Gallaher & Dailey )
Dann, G W , grocer, liveryman and constable.
Davis, A R , gunsmith, machinist &c , Main.
Dean, A B , farmer 25, Front
Dean, John P., assessor and farmer 250, Front
Dean, Patterson, engineer, E R R
DEAN, S. O , general merchant, Front, residence Cottage
DEAN, ZENAS K., farmer 150.
Debereux & Clark, props Deposit Tannery
DEMANDER & BALL, (George Demander and I C. Ball,) manufa. of wagons, carriages and sleighs.
DEMANDER, GEORGE, (Demander & Ball,) general blacksmith and farmer 22.
Demonay, D L , agent for Singer Sewing Machine, Main.
Deposit Chapter, No 187, R A M , James Knapp, M. E. H. P.; John T. More, E K. , Josiah Sims, E. S ; Andrew Wickwire, treas.; Chas T. Edick, secretary, Oliver T. Bundy Jr., C of H , Chas. P. Stiles, P. S ; Daniel N. Walling, R. A C ; L R Brown, M of 3d V , Philip Alexander, M of 2d V , I C. Ball, M. of 1st V ; Rev. L. H. Lighthipe, chaplain ; Elliott Evans, tiler, regular communications 2d and 4th Saturdays of each month
*DEPOSIT COURIER, office Main, Chas. N Stow, editor and proprietor.
Deposit Lodge, No. 396, F & A M , meets 1st and 3d Monday evenings in each month.
DeSilva, Dwight, blacksmith, E R R
Dickinson, Gilbert, shoemaker, Front.
Dickinson, Hiram, prop Sherwood House, corner Front and Allen.

# Conner & Orr,
## GENERAL BLACKSMITHS
### AND

# Horse Shoers,
### Corner South Main and DeRussey Sts.,
## Binghamton, Broome County, N. Y.

Quarter Cracks, Split Feet, and all diseases of the Hoof made a Specialty  **Conner's Celebrated Hoof Ointment** constantly on hand    Orders from a distance promptly attended to.    None genuine without the written signature of JOHN H CONNER

# Nelson Bowker,
# BUILDER,
## Shop in J. S. Wells' Old Stand,
*First Door West of the Congregational Church,*
## MAIN STREET,
# BINGHAMTON, N. Y.

### Jobbing Promptly Attended to.

# J. S. FREAR,
# Furnishing Undertaker!

*Coffin Ware Room,*
## No. 6 Court Street,
## Binghamton, N. Y.

**Ready-Made Coffins, Masonic, Odd-Fellows** and **Fire Department EMBLEMS, BURIAL ROBES** and **SHROUDS,** always on hand, or furnished to order on short notice.

Doolittle, S. S. & Co., (*Wm. D. Lewis,*) general insurance agents, Front.

Dunn, L. S., expressman, Allen.

Edick, Charles T , (*Burrows & Edick* )

Evans, Henry, lumberman and farmer 1,000.

Flemming, Michael, fireman, E R R.

Ford, A. P., (*Ford & Stetson.*)

Ford & Perry, (*Wm L Ford and John B. Perry,*) general merchants.

Ford & Stetson, (*A P Ford & —— Stetson,*) lumbermen, brokers, and own Sherwood House

Ford, Wm L., (*Ford & Perry.*)

FOURNIER, M J, REV., pastor St. Joseph's Church, (Cath.)

Freeman, L T , lawyer, Main.

Freeman, Wm. J., cabinet maker and undertaker

FULLER, HIRAM B., carpenter and builder, Center.

Gallaher & Dailey, (*Thomas Gallaher and James Dailey,*) general merchants and farmers 700, Front.

Gallaher, Thomas, (*Gallaher & Dailey.*)

Gilbert, M E , milliner, Front

Ginavan, George W., engineer on Erie R R , Allen

Goodrich, Seely, carpenter and painter.

Govejoy, George, carpenter and builder, Church

Green, T J , blacksmith and wagon maker, Division

Gregory, Harrison, physician and surgeon.

Groat, Nicholas, shoemaker, Allen.

Hadley, B E., merchant and lumberman.

Halpin, Michael, (*T & M Halpin.*)

Halpin, Thomas, (*T. & M. Halpin.*)

Halpin, T & M , (*Thomas and Michael,*) general merchants and own 28 acres

HATHAWAY, C M , (*Hathaway & Simpson* )

HATHAWAY & SIMPSON, (*C. M Hathaway and Henry Simpson,*) hardware, stoves and tinware, Front

Hayes Bryan, (*Hayes & Studdert.*)

Hayes & Studdert, (*Bryan Hayes and John Studdert,*) general merchants

HERR, J. M., (*Mapes, Clark & Co.*)

Herring, Jacob, cabinet maker.

HICKEY, JAMES E , manuf of wagons, carriages and sleighs, Pine

Higgins, S. D., allo. physician and surgeon, Main.

HOLMES, G W , groceries and provisions, justice of the peace, Front.

HUGUINER, PHOEBE J , prop of Western Hotel, opposite Depot.

HULCE, M R , surveyor, engineer, notary public, local historian and farmer

Hyde, Sheldon, carpenter and farmer 75.

Joslin, ——, carpenter, Pine

Kingsbury, Wm., carpenter, Pine

Knapp, Charles, ticket agent, E R R

Knapp, H W , teller Deposit National Bank, Cottage

KNAPP, JOHN E , (*Radeker & Knapp,*) town supervisor.

Knapp, J. H , cashier Deposit National Bank, Cottage

Lewis, Wm. D., (*S. S. Doolittle & Co* )

Loomis, Albert, prop. of stage line to Afton and Bainbridge.

Lovejoy, George, carpenter and builder.

Lyons, James, section foreman, E. R. R.

MALE, CHARLES, (*Wm. Male & Son* )

MALE WM & SON, (*Charles,*) shoemakers, Church.

MAPES, CLARK & CO., (*R. H Mapes, J. Q. Clark and J. M. Herr,*) planing mill, sash, blinds, doors, moldings, brackets &c , Front.

MAPES, R. H , (*Mapes, Clark & Co.*)

MARSHALL, JAMES W , supt. sub. div. 2, E. R. R.

Marshall, John, shoemaker.

Marvin, Lewis B , paper hanger and ornamental painter

McCLURE, GILBERT, wagon maker, Allen.

McCLURE, WILLIAM, surveyor and farmer 200, Second.

McCoy, —— Mrs , boarding house.

McHenry, William, resident, Allen.

McNaught, James, engineer, Allen

Meley, Edward, grocer, Front

Miller, George, shoemaker

MINOR, A P (*Minor & Smith* )

Minor, J S , (*Putnam & Minor* )

Minor, J. S , (*S F Whitaker & Co* )

MINOR & SMITH, (*A P Minor and J. M. Smith,*) general house builders' and mechanics' hardware, stoves, tin, carriage makers' materials, harness trimmings, agricultural implements &c

Minturn William, merchant tailor, Front.

Moore, Eli, western ticket agent

MORE, ARTHUR, (*T. & A More,*) town clerk.

More, T. & A., attorneys.

Morehouse, S. R , real estate dealer

MOSES, A C , attorney and counselor at law, Front.

MOSHER, WESSON, owns 174 acres.

Ogden, Chas Mrs., resident, Front.

OQUAGA HOUSE, Main, S W Smith, prop

Parks, Wm., watches and jewelry, Front.

Perry, John B , (*Ford & Perry*)

Phelps, G. O Rev , pastor of First Presbyterian Church, corner Pine and Cottage

PIERCE, WILDER, carpenter and builder, Orchard.

Putnam, C. M , (*Putnam & Minor,*) (*S F Whitaker & Co* )

Putnam & Minor, (*C. M. Putnam and J S. Minor,*) dry goods, carpets, boots, shoes, hats, caps &c.

QUINN, MICHAEL, manuf of firkins, tubs, churns, pails, buckets, lager beer kegs, pork barrels, pounding barrels, meat casks &c

RADEKER, BOLIVER, (*Radeker & Knapp.*)

RADEKER & KNAPP, (*Boliver Radeker and John E. Knapp,*) general merchants and agents for A. B. Howe Sewing Machine, corner Church and Front.

Ray, George, farmer 70.

Reeve, J K , (*J. B Carpenter & Co.*)

Revoyre, John A , baker, Dean.

Russ, W S , general merchant

Russell, M. C , (*Wickwire, Russell & Co* )

SCUDDER, A L & CO , (*John L. Wager,*) watches, clocks, jewelry and musical instruments, Front

Simmons, Wm., livery.

# BOUCK'S HOTEL,

## D. I. BOUCK, - Proprietor,

### BINGHAMTON, N. Y.

This new house is located in the pleasantest part of the city, on Chenango Street, corner of Pearne, within a short distance of the Erie Depot. The rooms are airy and pleasant, and are newly furnished throughout. Table at all times supplied with the delicacies of the season.

## Good Horses and Carriages Furnished.

## ☞ *CHARGES ALWAYS REASONABLE.*
## GOOD STABLING ATTACHED.

# THE DEPOSIT COURIER

## Newspaper & Job Printing Establishment,

### CHARLES N. STOW,

### Editor & Proprietor.

### Office over the Post Office.

*The Courier stands No. 1 as a LOCAL PAPER, giving all news of interest in both Broome and Delaware Counties, in each of which it circulates free.*

### The Courier Job Office,

is the best appointed office in the County, and turns out beautiful work at city prices. Orders by mail promptly attended to.

**Carrington & Porter,** Dealers in first-class Cook and Parlor Stoves, Tinware, &c.

SIMPSON, HENRY, (*Hathaway & Simpson*)
SIMS, JOSIAH Rev., pastor of M. E. Church, Front.
Sinsabaugh, David, engineer, E. R. R.
Sinsabaugh, Frank, fireman, E R R
Smith, Charles R., livery, office Oquaga House.
Smith, H. T., flour, feed, grain and provisions, Allen corner 2nd.
SMITH, J. M., (*Minor & Smith.*)
SMITH, S W., prop of Oquaga House and Oquaga Hall, Main
Stetson, ——, (*Ford & Stetson.*)
*STOW, CHARLES N., editor and prop. of *Deposit Courier*, and practical job printer, Main
Stow, J. B., postmaster, dealer in hats, caps, furs, notions &c
Street, Joseph S., groceries.
Studdert, John, (*Hayes & Studdert*)
Sturdevant, Frank, physician and surgeon
Thatcher, M. E. Mrs., preceptress, Deposit Academy.
Thatcher, R. L., principal of Deposit Academy.
Thurman, C. F., watchmaker.
Tiffany, John, carpenter
Tinkler, John, shoemaker, River.
TUTTEL, WILLIAM, mason.
Vail, A. A., real estate broker
*VAIL, ALBERT R, dry goods, carpets &c
VAIL, JAMES A., druggist, liquor dealer and tobacconist, wholesale and retail.
Valentine, Hannah, dressmaker, Allen.
WAGER, JOHN L, (*A. L Scudder & Co.,*) dentist and physician, Front, residence Allen.

Wall, John, (*Beardsley & Wall.*)
Walley, Samuel J , prop of Deposit House, corner River and Pine.
Walling, Alexander, prop. of Deposit Marble Works
Walling, D N , foreman of Deposit Marble Works.
Walling, J. H., agent for Deposit Marble Works
Warriner, E. R., teacher and farmer 5.
WATKINS, WILLIS, (*Alderson & Watkins.*)
Watkins, Willis, carpenter and builder, Allen.
Watson. Jas. L , shoemaker, Front
WESTERN HOTEL, Phœbe J. Huguiner, prop , opposite Depot
Wheeler, Nelson K., farmer 40 in corporation, 200 in Delaware Co. and, in Sanford, 360.
Whitaker, S. F. & Co., (*J. S. Minor and C. M. Putnam,*) millers and coal dealers.
White, Adolph, merchant tailor, gents' furnishing goods, &c
WHITE, JOSEPH A., barber.
White, Peter, barber.
Whitney, A. B., milliner and dress maker, Front
Whitney, —— Mrs., milliner and dress maker.
Wickwire, A. E., (*Wickwire, Russell & Co*)
Wickwire, Russell & Co., (*A. E Wickwire, M. C. Russell and E. T. Boyd,*) tinware, stoves and hardware, corner Front and Dean.
Wilcox, H. W , meat market, Front
Worth, Silk, physician, corner Allen and Church.

---

# FENTON.

### (Post Office Addresses in Parentheses.)

Ackley, George, (Chenango Forks,) lot 3, farmer leases 56.
Allen, James, (North Fenton,) lot 33, farmer 5.
Allerton, Isaac, (Port Crane,) lot 44, builder and architect.
Amsbury, Israel, (Port Dickinson,) lot 34, farmer 100
Amsbury, James H., (Binghamton,) lot 33, farmer 27
Andrews, Stephen P , (Port Dickinson,) lot 34, farmer 14
Ashcroft, William R., (Port Crane,) hotel keeper and farmer 2
Aylesworth, Roswell R., (North Fenton,) lot 33, farmer leases 42.
Baird, Benjamin, (Osborne Hollow,) lot 94, farmer 200
Baker, Charles M., (North Fenton,) lot 61, farmer 15.

Baldwin, Norman, (North Fenton,) lot 21, farmer 50.
Baldwin, Samuel I., (North Fenton,) lot 51, farmer 100
Barnes, James J., (Port Crane,) lot 97, farmer 152.
Barnum, Ebenezer, (Port Crane,) lot 18, farmer 53.
BEARDSLEY, MARCUS D., (North Fenton,) lot 58, farmer 200.
Beckwith, George, (Binghamton,) lot 33, farmer 30
Bennett, Rufus B., (North Fenton,) lot 61, farmer 60.
Bentley, George W., (Osborne Hollow,) lot 19, farmer 1.
Bevier, Warren, (Binghamton,) lot 32, farmer 45
Bickel, Joseph, (North Fenton,) lot 18, farmer 25.

Bixby, Jerry, (Chenango Forks,) lot 12, farmer 40

Blanchard, Charles, (Port Crane,) lot 17, farmer 117.

Bogart, John, (Port Crane,) lot 1, farmer 15

Brady, James, (Binghamton,) lot 37, farmer 34

Brainerd, Selden L., (Port Crane,) lot 36, farmer 51.

Brissee, Miller Mrs , (Port Crane,) lot 45, farmer 50

Brown, Joseph D., (Port Dickinson,) carpenter and farmer 5

Brown, Patrick E , (Port Crane,) lot 26, farmer 81.

Bolfinch, Warren, (Port Crane,) lot 14, farmer 67

Bunnel, Elmore C , (Port Crane,) lot 47, farmer 65

Bunnel, Nenemiah, (Port Crane,) lot 47, farmer 17

Bunsay, Ira, (Osborne Hollow,) lot 104, farmer 70

Burgess, Thomas Rev , (North Fenton,) pastor M E Church

Burrows, Edward, (North Fenton,) lot 60, farmer 50

Burrows, Elisha, (North Fenton,) lot 60, farmer 50

Butler, John H , (Port Dickinson,) lot 41, farmer 54

Canniff, Marvin, (North Fenton,) lot 33, carpenter and jobber

Canniff, Ransom, (North Fenton,) shoe maker.

Carman, Robert, (Port Crane,) farmer 3

Chapman, Charles H., (Port Crane,) farmer 2

Christian, George W , (North Fenton,) lot 34, mason and farmer 50

Christian, Henry W , (North Fenton,) lot 33, mason and farmer 40

Christian, Hosea, (North Fenton,) lot 15, farmer 56

Christian, Rufus G., (North Fenton,) resident.

Cole, Albert, (Port Crane,) lot 2, farmer 140

Cole, Ambrose, (Port Crane,) lot 99, farmer 100

Cole, Chauncey R , (Port Crane,) farmer

Cole, Edmund, (Port Crane,) lot 6, farmer 140

Cole, Tompkins, (Port Crane,) lot 47, farmer 6

Collins, Sally Mrs , (Port Crane,) lot 44, farmer 4

Cook, Bristol, (North Fenton,) lot 57, farmer 90

Cook, John, (Port Crane,) lot 5, farmer 28

Cook, Mathew, (North Fenton,) lot 34, farmer 280

Corey, Rufus, (North Fenton,) lot 10, farmer 50.

Cornell, John C , (Port Crane,) carriage maker and undertaker.

Crocker, Ebenezer, (Binghamton,) lot 87, farmer 35.

Cross, Timothy, (Port Crane,) gardener 1

Crouze, Marcus, (Binghamton,) lot 88, farmer leases 107

Cunningham, James, (Port Dickinson,) shoemaker

Davidson, Chauncey, (North Fenton,) carriage maker and farmer 15

Davis, Ambrose, (Port Crane,) lot 98, farmer 94

Davis, Daniel D. T., (Port Crane,) lot 49, farmer 85.

Davis, Levi A., (Port Crane,) dealer in real estate.

Dean, Amos, (Binghamton,) lot 41, farmer 50

Demanstoy, Lewis N , (North Fenton,) lot 31, farmer 12

Dickinson, Edgar, (Port Dickinson,) whip maker and farmer 2

Dodge, Daniel, (Port Crane,) carpenter and farmer 3½

Duel, — , (Port Crane,) lot 2, farmer 20

Dutcher, James, (Port Dickinson,) gardener 4

English, Jerry, (Chenango Forks,) lot 12, farmer 66

English, Nathaniel, (Osborne Hollow,) lot 18, farmer 180

Esell, James M., (Port Crane,) town clerk

Ferris, Alexander, (Chenango Forks,) lot 4, farmer 71

Ferris, Almira, (North Fenton,) lot 15, farmer 20

Ferris, Nathaniel, (North Fenton,) lot 22, farmer 50.

Finch, Andrew, (North Fenton,) lot 41, farmer 130.

Finch, Sidney, (North Fenton,) lot 41, farmer 25

Foster, George W , (North Fenton,) lot 33, farmer 42

Freeman, Wilder, (North Fenton,) lot 49, farmer 50

Frier, Lorenzo, (Binghamton,) lot 35, farmer 55

Frier, Tracy M., (Binghamton,) lot 35, farmer 5

Gage, Joel S , (Port Crane,) lot 45, farmer 42

Gannung, David, (North Fenton,) lot 39, farmer 100

Gates, Joseph E., (Port Dickinson,) lot 35, farmer 80

Gee, Thomas, (Port Crane,) lot 26, farmer 100

Greene, James D., (Port Crane,) lot 53, farmer 50

Hageman, ———, (Port Crane,) lot 54, farmer leases 115

Haight, David L , (North Fenton,) farmer leases.

Hall, George W., (Chenango Forks,) lot 13, farmer 60.

Harper, John M , (Port Crane,) lot 39, farmer 62

Harwood, Ezra B , (Port Crane,) farmer 4

Hatch, Oliver W , (North Fenton,) lot 31, farmer 109.

Hawkins, Elijah, (North Fenton,) lot 54, farmer 40

Hawkins, Jonathan, (Chenango Forks,) lot 4, farmer 17

Hays, Harvey, (New Ohio,) lot 90, farmer 100.

Hickox, Robert, (Port Crane,) lumberman.

Hicks, Thomas, (North Fenton,) farmer 100.

Hill, Henry, (Port Crane,) lot 97, farmer 90

Hinds, Marvin, (Port Dickinson,) lot 84, farmer 20

Hinde, Wing, (Port Dickinson,) lot 84, farmer 40.

Hobbs, George W , (Osborne Hollow,) carpenter.

Hofftail, David, (Port Crane,) lot 1, farmer 50.

Holcomb, Edgar, (New Ohio,) lot 67, farmer 87.

Holcomb, Marcena, (North Fenton,) lot 49, farmer 118.

Holcomb, Vicknew, (North Fenton,) lot 49, farmer 80.

Holt, Jefferson W , (North Fenton,) lot 21, farmer 172.

Horton, Nathan T., (Port Crane,) farmer 1

Horton, William H., (Port Crane,) lot 41, farmer leases of Reuben Finch, 50

Hotaling, Hiram, (New, Ohio,) lot 93, farmer 50.

Hotaling, Jacob, (New Ohio,) lot 55, farmer 50.

Hotchkiss, Henry, (Port Dickinson,) farmer 25

Hubbard, Amos, (Port Crane,) lot 18, farmer 80

Hughston, William J. Jr., (Port Crane,) station agent

Hull, Charles, (Port Crane,) lot 44, manuf tobacco and cigars, and farmer 60.

Hull, John, (Port Crane,) lot 4, contractor and farmer 175.

Hungerford, Peter G , (Port Crane,) cigar maker.

Hunt, Henry S., (Osborne Hollow,) lot 105, farmer 85.

Hunt, James D., (Osborne Hollow,) lot 105, farmer 260

Hord, Stephen H., (Port Crane,) lot 43, farmer 144.

Ingraham, John, (Chenango Forks,) lot 4, farmer leases of Polly Hall, 56.

Ingraham, Sylvester, (Chenango Forks,) lot 13, farmer 15

Ingraham, West A., (Chenango Forks,) lot 13, farmer 45.

Jeffreys, Leverett, (Port Dickinson,) lot 84, farmer 30.

Jewel, Phebe, (Port Crane,) gardener 5

Jone, Silas, (Port Crane,) lot 47, farmer 80.

Kark, Abram, (Osborne Hollow,) lot 105, carpenter and farmer 60.

Kark, Henry, (Port Crane,) carpenter.

KEECH, HENRY, (West Colesville.)

Keeler, Job H., (Port Crane,) merchant.

Kells, Henry, (Osborne Hollow,) lot 109, farmer 150

Kells, John, (New Ohio,) lot 91, farmer 100

Ketchum, John, (Chenango Forks,) lot 14, farmer 8.

Lawton, William, (North Fenton,) grocer and farrier.

Lewis, Ellis, (North Fenton,) lot 25, farmer 20.

LEWIS, J. Mrs., (North Fenton,) lot 32, farmer 75.

Lewis, Robert, (Port Crane,) lot 6, farmer 50.

Lewis, William, (Port Crane,) lot 6, farmer 90

Lockwood, Valentine, (Port Dickinson,) lot 84, farmer 70.

Lounsbury, Polly, (Chenango Forks,) lot 11, farmer 125.

Lounsbury, Simmons J., (Chenango Forks,) lot 11, farmer 130.

Lowe, David, (Chenango Forks,) lot 15, farmer 70

Lown, Henry H , (Port Crane,) lot 47, farmer 45

Lown, Thompson, (Port Crane,) lumberman and farmer 1.

Macomber, Eugene L , (North Fenton,) lot 61, carpenter and farmer 42

MACOMBER, MELVIN A , (North Fenton,) merchant and postmaster.

Marsh, Rufus, (North Fenton,) lot 62, farmer 15

Marshman, Peter, (Chenango Forks,) lot 13, farmer 17

Martin, Daniel, (Port Crane,) lot 17, farmer 150

Martin, James, (Binghamton,) lot 41, farmer 24

Mason, James H., (North Fenton,) lot 62, farmer 75

Mayhne, George B., (Port Crane,) blacksmith

McDaniel, Hiram, (Port Crane,) lot 47, farmer 8

McDaniel, Hiram G., (Port Crane,) carpenter

McDonald, Alvin, (North Fenton,) lot 10, farmer 50.

McDonald, Asa H., (North Fenton,) lot 35, farmer 180.

McDonald, John, (North Fenton,) carpenter.

McGowan, Peter, (Chenango Forks,) lot 25, farmer 100

McHugh, Francis, (North Fenton,) lot 22, farmer 130

Merrill, Ira, (New Ohio,) lot 109, farmer 60.

Merrills, John W., (North Fenton,) lot 68, farmer 75

Merriman, Levi, (North Colesville,) lot 74, farmer 60.

Merritt, Esther Mrs., (North Fenton,) farmer 1

Merritt, Gilbert, (North Fenton,) boatman

Miller, Addison, (North Fenton,) lot 33, justice of the peace and farmer 33

Miller, George P , (North Fenton,) lot 80, farmer 150.

Miller, Hurd L., (North Fenton,) blacksmith

Miller, James H., (North Fenton,) (*Miller & Son,*) lot 47, farmer 105

Miller, Robert R., (North Fenton,) lot 19, farmer 121

Miller, Samuel, (North Fenton,) lot 47, farmer 118

Miller & Son, (North Fenton,) saw mill

Mooney, Alexander, (Port Crane,) lot 100, farmer 48

Mooney, John, (Port Crane,) lot 100, farmer 45.

Mott, Philo, (Binghamton,) lot 32, farmer 2.

Nowland, James, (Port Crane,) lot 41, farmer 40.

Nowland, Thos. Mrs , (Binghamton,) lot 37, farmer 1.

Ogden, Ambrose, (Binghamton,) lot 33, farmer 25

Ogden, William, (Binghamton,) lot 33, farmer 35

Orton, Frederick, (New Ohio,) lot 68, farmer 50.

Paddleford, Nelson, (North Fenton,) lot 75, farmer 75

Paddleford, Roswell J , (New Ohio,) lot 67, farmer 93.

Page, William, (North Fenton,) lot 62, farmer 31

Palmer, Alonzo, (Port Crane,) lot 6, farmer 100.

Palmer, Ammi, (North Fenton,) lot 54, farmer 50.

Palmer, Horatio, (North Fenton,) lot 11, farmer 50

Palmer, Ira, (Chenango Forks,) grocer and farmer 150.

Palmer, Jenkins, (Chenango Forks,) lot 7, farmer 80.

Palmer, R. R., (Binghamton,) lot 37, farmer 16

Palmer, William R , (Port Crane,) lot 5, farmer 44.*

Pangburn, William E , (North Fenton,) lot 37, farmer 75.

Parker, Obadiah, (Port Crane,) lot 40, farmer 50

Parsons, Albert, (North Fenton,) lot 25, farmer 8

Pierson, Charles O , (Port Crane,) harness maker

Porter, Emmet, (Osborne Hollow,) lot 104, farmer 104.

Potter, Benjamin A., (Port Crane,) lot 53, farmer 115.

Pratt, Lewis J , (New Ohio,) lot 91, farmer 71

Prentice, Benajah, (Port Crane,) lot 40, farmer 40

Prentice, David, (Port Crane,) lot 39, farmer 90

Prentice, Hiram, (Port Dickinson,) carpenter and farmer 5

Prentice, Hiram, (Port Crane,) lot 39, farmer 16.

Prentice, Ira, (Binghamton,) lot 38, farmer 20

Prentice, Joseph, (Port Crane,) lot 47, farmer 60.

Prentice, Joseph, (North Fenton,) farmer leases.

Prentice, Luther, (Port Crane,) lot 39, farmer 70.

Prentice, Moses, (Port Crane,) lot 36, farmer 87.

Puffer, Harry, (Port Crane,) blacksmith

Randall, Freeman, (Port Crane,) lot 47, farmer 41

Randall, Myron, (Port Crane ) boatman.

Reynolds, Francis, (North Fenton,) lot 1, farmer leases 350.

Richards, Halsey, (Chenango Forks,) lot 12, farmer 50

Rider, James, (Port Crane,) lot 99, farmer 186.

Roberts, Chester A., (Port Crane,) lot 44, lumberman

Roberts, Lorenzo P., (Port Crane,) eclectic physician.

Robinson, Mill, (Chenango Forks,) lot 2, farmer 50

Root, William R , (North Fenton,) lot 33, farmer 42.

Sawyer, Simon P., (Osborne Hollow,) lot 108, farmer 57

Scott, Garry B., (North Fenton,) lot 36, farmer 175.

Scott, Marcus W., (North Fenton,) teacher.

Scott, Thomas, (North Fenton,) lot 33, farmer 100.

Shaw, Horace, (Port Crane,) boat owner

Shaw, Jerome, (Port Crane,) boat owner.

Shaw, John, (Port Crane,) lot 40, farmer 26

Shaw, Peter, (Port Crane,) lot 40, farmer 12

Shaw, Richard, (Port Crane,) boatman

Shear, Eseck & Son, (Port Crane,) (*William C ,*) lumber and plaster dealers

Shear, Henry, (Port Crane,) lot 48, farmer 200.

Shear, William C., (Port Crane,) (*Eseck Shear & Son.*)

Shed, Ira, (North Fenton,) farmer 30

Shepardson, Jesse C , (Port Crane,) lot 2, farmer leases of Mrs. Sally Collins, 70.

Sherwood, Reuben, (Port Crane,) farmer 96

Shufelt, Peter, (Port Crane,) lot 97, farmer 78.

Slosson, Newell M., (Port Crane,) lot 103, farmer leases of Lee Davis, 87.

Slosson, Rowland H , (Port Crane,) lot 97, farmer 100

Slosson, William, (Port Crane,) lot 35, farmer 88.

Smith, Henry, (New Ohio,) farmer leases 176.

Smith, James, (Binghamton,) lot 37, farmer 15.

Smith, James Jr , (Osborne Hollow,) lot 92, farmer leases 70.

Southworth, Truman A , (North Fenton,) lot 37, farmer leases 270

Spencer, Harrison, (North Fenton,) farmer 50

Spendly, William, (Port Dickinson,) gardener

Steed, Michael, (North Fenton,) lot 11, farmer 50

Stone Alvin, (North Fenton,) lot 34, carpenter and farmer 50.

Strickland, Martin S , (North Fenton,) blacksmith

Surdam, Charles, (Chenango Forks,) lot 6, farmer 65

Sweet, Ambrose, (Port Dickinson,) gardener 1.

Taber, Thomas S., (Chenango Forks,) lot 3, farmer 50.

Tammany, Charles, (North Fenton,) lot 10, farmer 50.

Taylor, Anson B , (Port Crane,) lot 3, farmer 88

Taylor, Crocker, (North Fenton,) lot 41, farmer 25 and leases 117.

Tracy, Andrew, (Chenango Forks,) lot 5, farmer 66

Travis, John W., (North Fenton,) lot 33, carpenter and builder

Tumath, Robert, (Port Crane,) lot 26, farmer 81.

Turner, Theodore, (North Fenton,) lot 34, farmer leases 40.

Tuttle, William I , (Osborne Hollow,) lot 94, farmer 109

Vanemburgh, Gilbert, (Port Crane,) boat builder.

Vanemburgh, Henry T., (Port Crane,) boat owner.

Vanemburgh, John, (Port Crane,) boat builder and farmer 6.

Vanemburgh, Truman, (Port Crane,) lumberman

Vincent, Daniel, (North Fenton,) lot 54, farmer 25.

Waite, Herman V., (Port Crane,) lot 44, saw mill, lumber dealer and farmer 105

Waite, James E., (Port Crane,) postmaster, lumber manuf and farmer 300

Walker, Sarah Mrs., (Chenango Forks,) lot 16, farmer 170.

Warner, Bela, (North Fenton,) lot 34, farmer 50.

Warner, Hoyt, (North Fenton,) lot 54, farmer 10.

Warner, Jeremiah S., (Binghamton,) lot 37, farmer 20.

Warner, Samuel, (North Fenton,) lot 54, farmer 50.

Watrous, Samuel, (New Ohio,) lot 78, farmer 120.

Wells, Josiah D., (Binghamton,) lot 41, farmer 63.

Wenn, Obadiah, (Port Crane,) lot 44, farmer 50.

Weyman, Jacob, (Port Crane,) lot 102, farmer leases 100.

Weyman, Moses, (New Ohio,) lot 55, farmer 25.

White, Linus, (Osborne Hollow,) lot 105, farmer 40.

Willard, Oliver, (Chenango Forks,) lot 16, farmer 40

Williams, Hamilton, (North Fenton,) mason.

Williams, Samuel, (North Fenton,) lot 32, farmer 100.

Williamson, William, (North Fenton,) lot 31, farmer 175

Wilmot, Oscar B., (Port Dickinson,) lot 35, farmer 55

Wilson, Aaron W., (Port Crane,) cooper

Wilson, Orrin J., (Port Crane,) lot 44, cigar manuf

Winn, David D., (Port Crane,) lot 44, apiarian.

Winn, Isaac, (Port Crane,) lot 102, farmer 50.

Winston, Daniel, (North Fenton,) lot 50, farmer 50

Wright, Edward G., (Port Dickinson,) lot 41, farmer leases 50

Youngs, Gregory B., (Port Crane,) lot 47, farmer 15

Youngs, John, (Port Crane,) lot 102, farmer 160.

Youngs, Sylvester A., (Osborne Hollow,) lot 19, farmer 1.

---

# KIRKWOOD.

### (Post Office Addresses in Parentheses.)

##### ABBREVIATIONS.—B. P., Bingham's Patent.

Adams, James, (Binghamton,) lot 29, farmer 140

Akerly, Jeremiah, (Kirkwood Center,) lot 10, farmer leases of M. A Sheak, Binghamton, 125.

Alden, Henry P., (Kirkwood,) lot 4, farmer 100.

Andrews, Daniel C., (Kirkwood,) lot 17, farmer 90

Andrews, George J., heirs of, (West Windsor,) lot 17, farmer 60.

ANDREWS, MILES A., (Kirkwood,) lot 17, prop. of grist, saw and planing mills, dealer in flour, grain, meal, feed &c.

Andrews, Orlando L., (West Windsor,) lot 16, insurance agent and farmer 60

Andrews, Thomas J., (West Windsor,) lot 21, farmer leases of Reuben Sherwood, 18

Attridge, Arthur, (Binghamton,) lot 39, farmer 123.

Baker, Edmund, (Binghamton,) constable.

Ball, John, (Binghamton,) lot 26, carpenter and farmer 25.

Ball, Sylvanus B., (Port Dickinson,) carpenter.

Barlow, Edmund W., (Binghamton,) lot 19, town clerk and (*with Roswell,*) farmer 200

Barlow, Roswell, (Binghamton,) (*with Edmund W.,*) lot 19, farmer 200.

Barnes, Sylvester, (Riverside,) lot 5, farmer 80

Bayless, Henry C., (Binghamton,) lot 20, farmer 50.

Bayless, Samuel, (Binghamton,) lot 21, farmer 200.

Benn, Henry, (Binghamton,) lot 11, farmer 70.

Benn, Julius, (West Windsor,) lot 25, farmer 50

Bennett, William W., (Kirkwood,) mason.

Berkslew, Abraham, (Kirkwood,) lot 11, cider mill, carpenter and farmer 48.

Berkalew, Jahiel W , (Kirkwood,) lot 9, farmer 150.

Bird, Isaac, (Kirkwood,) lot 3, B. P , farmer 72

Bonnell, John A , (Kirkwood,) painter and grainer

Bonnell, Lewis, (Kirkwood,) lot 12, retired.

Bortlett, Joseph, (Binghamton,) lot 22, lumberman and farmer 168

Bound, George W , (Kirkwood,) lot 15, farmer 55

Bound, Isaac, (Kirkwood,) lot 15, justice of the peace and farmer 50.

Bound, James, (Kirkwood,) lot 12, shoemaker

Bound, Martin, (Kirkwood,) toll collector at Conklin Bridge

Boyce, Henry O., (West Windsor,) teacher.

Brink, Charles P , (Kirkwood,) lot 6, commissioner of highways and farmer 215

Brink, Thomas M., (Riverside,) lot 2, farmer leases 50

Brown, Enoch, (Kirkwood,) lot 11, laborer.

BROWN, JOEL, (Riverside,) lot 4, farmer leases of Ira Brown, Binghamton, 300.

Brown, Joseph C., (Kirkwood,) R. R. laborer

Brown, Joseph C , (Kirkwood,) lot 11, conductor of freight train N Y & E R R.

Brown, William, (Riverside,) lot 2, farmer 50.

Brownell, Jacob, (Binghamton,) lot 12, overseer of the poor and farmer 50

BROWNELL, JULIUS D , (Binghamton,) carpenter and joiner.

Bump, Heman A., (Binghamton,) (with Jedediah Jr ,) lot 22, meat dealer and farmer 39.

BUMP, JEDEDIAH Jr , (Binghamton,) (with Heman A ,) lot 22, meat dealer and farmer 39.

Burt, Henry, (Kirkwood,) lot 3, farmer 47

Burt, John, (Kirkwood,) farmer works 47

Button, Charles, (Binghamton,) lot 9, farmer leases of Michael A Sheak, Binghamton, 200

BUTTON, HENRY A., (Binghamton,) farm laborer

CARROLL, THOMAS, (Binghamton,) lot 48, farmer 98.

Casper, Daniel, (Binghamton,) lot 18, blacksmith and owns 3 acres

Casterton, Thomas, (Kirkwood,) lot 4, farmer 235

Chase, Silas P , (Kirkwood,) lot 3, farmer 100

CHURCH, JOHN, (Kirkwood,) lot 12, teamster and farmer.

Clark, Harriet Mrs , (widow,) (Binghamton,) lot 9, farmer 7¾

CLEARY, FRANK, (Kirkwood,) jobber

CLEARY, MICHAEL, (Kirkwood,) lot 1, farmer 147.

CLINE, JOHN, (Riverside,) lot 1, farmer 60.

COLEMAN, FRANK E., (Binghamton,) lot 56, blacksmith

COLLIER, HERMAN, (Kirkwood Center,) lumberman

Collier, Isaac I., (Kirkwood Center,) lot 6, farmer 110

Collier, John I., (Kirkwood,) lot 8, farmer 60.

CONKLIN, CHARLES M., (Kirkwood,) lot 7, farmer 70

Conklin, Elias, (Kirkwood,) retired.

CONKLIN, FRANCIS D., (Kirkwood,) lot 7, farmer 30.

CONKLIN, JOHN E , (Kirkwood,) lot 7, farmer 30

CONKLIN SOLON, (Kirkwood,) (Murry & Conklin.)

CONKLIN, THOMAS J , (Riverside,) lot 2, merchant and assistant postmaster

Connor, John, (Kirkwood,) lot 6, farmer 130

Cook, John, (Kirkwood Center,) lot 26, farmer 72½

Coon, Ichabod, (Binghamton,) lot 33, farmer 80

CROFT, OBADIAH, (Binghamton,) lot 20, farmer 95.

Day, Dennis O , (Binghamton,) lot 14, farmer 70

Dickinson, Lester E , (Binghamton,) lot 19, farmer leases 100.

DIVINE, EBER S , (Binghamton,) lot 25, carpenter and school teacher, and farmer 2

Donvan, James, (Kirkwood,) lot 8, farmer 67

Doolittle, Marcus, (Binghamton,) lot 22, farmer 43, in Colesville 40 acres wood land and in Penn , 690

Doubleday, John H , (Kirkwood,) lot 14, postmaster and farmer 208

DOWNING, RICHARD, (Binghamton,) lot 7, farmer leases of Alvah Wood, 170

Duell, Henry, (Binghamton,) lot 23, farmer 100

Dwight, Chester, (Kirkwood,) lot 4, farmer 157.

DWIGHT, HORACE, (Kirkwood,) lot 2, B P , farmer 78

Edson, Albert, (Binghamton,) lot 27, farmer 108

Ellis, Henry, (Binghamton,) lot 9, farmer 154

ELWELL, EDGAR R , (Binghamton,) lot 26, farmer 100.

EMMONS, GEORGE W Jr., (Kirkwood,) farmer 3 and leases 180.

Emmons, John A., (Kirkwood,) (J. A. Emmons & Co ,) agent Erie R. R.

Emmons, J A & Co., (Kirkwood,) (John A Emmons and A S Saxon,) manufacturing chemists.

Emmons, Nicholas E., (Kirkwood,) lot 12, resident.

EVERTS, ELY O., (Binghamton,) lot 43, inspector of elections and farmer 145

Everts, William, (Binghamton,) lot 55, farmer 80.

Fagan, James, (Binghamton,) lot 19, farmer 105.

Ferguson, Ozias S , (West Windsor,) lot 22, saw mill, assessor and farmer 20

Finch, Julius M , (Binghamton,) lot 2, farmer, works farm of Ruff.

Finch, Ruff, (Binghamton,) lot 20, justice of the peace and sessions, and farmer 50.

Finn, James M., (Riverside,) lot 1, farmer 125.

Fox, James, (Binghamton,) lot 23, farmer 50

FOX, JOHN, (Binghamton,) farm laborer.

FULLER, NICHOLAS D , (Osborne Hollow,) lot 29, farmer leases of George Craver, Binghamton, 150

Fuller, Peter J , (West Windsor,) lot 3, thrashing machine and farmer 2.

GAIGE, LEONARD, (Binghamton,) lot 12, justice of the peace, assessor and farmer 150

GORMAN, JOHN, (Kirkwood,) lot 6, farmer 64.

Grace, Jeremiah, (Kirkwood,) lot 6, farmer 90.

Grace, Sarah Mrs., (widow,) (Kirkwood,) lot 7, farmer 106

Greene, Frederick E., (Binghamton,) carpenter

Greene, Loring S., (Binghamton,) carpenter.

Griffith, William, (Binghamton,) lot 20, farmer 40

Guernsey, Henry N., (Binghamton,) lot 29, farmer 43

Gurnsey, Jacob, (Riverside,) lot 3, farmer 50

Hadley, John F , (Binghamton,) lot 7, farmer 50

Hagerty, Michael, (Kirkwood,) lot 6, farmer 170

Halpin, John, (Binghamton,) lot 64, farmer 70 and leases of Michael Quilty, Binghamton, 124.

Haskins, Charles, (Binghamton,) lot 23, farmer leases 60.

Hastings, Edward, (West Windsor,) lot 23, farmer 145.

HAWKINS, GILBERT, (Kirkwood,) lot 15, carpenter and joiner

Hays, Adam, (Kirkwood,) lot 16, farmer 158

Hays, John B , (Kirkwood,) lot 11, farmer 48

Hoadley, Edward, (West Windsor,) lot 23, farmer 63

Hogoboon, Richard, (Binghamton,) overseer of Asylum farm

Hotchkiss, Melvin W., (Riverside,) lot 2, farmer 16

Hunt, Alfred, (Riverside,) (*with John M. and Uriah*,) lot 3, farmer 100.

Hunt, John M., (Riverside,) lot 3, conductor of coal train, S. & B. R R , also (*with Alfred and Uriah*,) farmer 100.

Hunt, Uriah, (Riverside,) (*with John M and Alfred*,) lot 3, farmer 100.

Hunter, George W., (Binghamton,) lot 19, farmer 55

Hunter, Thomas, (Binghamton,) lot 33, mason and farmer 58.

Ingraham, John C., (Kirkwood Center,) lot 6, farmer 50

Jackson, Charles, (Binghamton,) lot 7, farmer 45

Jackson, Jacob M., (Kirkwood,) lot 5, farmer 48.

JONES, CHARLES D., (Kirkwood,) lot 12, general merchant

Jones, Cotez P., (Kirkwood,) lot 3, farmer 113.

Jones, Daniel M., (Kirkwood,) lot 1, farmer 100

JONES, LEWIS, (Kirkwood,) lot 12, farmer 80.

Jones, Richard W , (Kirkwood,) lot 1, farmer 340.

Jones, Samuel, (Kirkwood,) lot 19, farmer 200

June, David, (Binghamton,) lot 49, farmer 80

Keyes, Stalham, (West Windsor,) lot 26, farmer 1 and leases of heirs of Israel Keyes, 116

Langdon, Calvin, (Port Dickinson,) farmer 7.

Langdon, David, (West Windsor,) lot 23, farmer 170.

LANGDON, MYRON, (Kirkwood,) lot 3, B. P., farmer 230.

Lawrence, Isaiah S , (Binghamton,) lot 17, farmer 101

Layton, Byron, (Binghamton,) lot 20, farmer 50.

LAYTON, GEORGE W., (Binghamton,) lot 13, farmer leases 107

Layton, Morris D , (Kirkwood Center,) lot 7, farmer leases of Byron Layton, 30

Leamre, George, (Kirkwood Center,) carpenter

Lea, James N Rev., (Kirkwood,) pastor of M E. Church.

Lewis, Lydia, (Kirkwood,) lot 12, resident.

Lewis, William B., (Kirkwood,) lot 12, blacksmith.

McCracken, Edward J , (Binghamton,) lot 7, boat builder and farmer 18.

McNamaro, Michael, (Binghamton,) lot 14, farmer 240.

McPHERSON, JOHN, (Binghamton,) lot 15, farmer leases of John A. Collier, Binghamton, 580.

Moore, Anthony R , (Kirkwood,) lot 16, conductor of gravel train, N. Y. & E. R. R., and farmer 7.

Moore, John B., (Kirkwood,) lot 19, farmer 50.

Moore, Seely P., (Kirkwood,) lot 1, farmer 115

Mosher, James H , (Kirkwood,) lot 6, farmer leases 100

Murphy, John, (Binghamton,) lot 37, farmer 50

Murphy, Thomas H , (Binghamton,) lot 13, farmer 100.

Murphy, William, (Binghamton,) lot 13, farmer 115.

MURRY & CONKLIN, (Kirkwood,) (*Jessie H Murry and Solon Conklin*,) manufs. of Murry's Combined Washer and Wringer

MURRY, JESSIE H., (Kirkwood,) (*Murry & Conklin*.)

NEWBERRY, DAVID S , (Kirkwood,) lot 6, supervisor of town and farmer 107.

NEWTON, GEORGE E , (Kirkwood,) jour harness maker

Ogden, Alexander N., (Kirkwood,) lot 11, carpenter

Ogden, Charles W , (Kirkwood,) brakeman and carpenter

O'Loughlin, Bryan, (Binghamton,) lot 14, farmer 65.

O'Loughlin, John, (Binghamton,) lot 15, farmer 45.

O'LOUGHLIN, PATRICK, (Binghamton,) lot 11, farmer 145.

O'Neil, Michael, (Binghamton,) lot 63, farmer 100.

O'NEILL, ARTHUR, (Binghamton,) lot 17, farmer 133.

O'Neill, David, (Binghamton,) lot 14, farmer 70

O'Shea, Henry, (Binghamton,) let 22, R. R. laborer

O'Shea, Thomas, (Binghamton,) lot 14, farmer 52

Park, Abram L, (Binghamton,) (*with Edward*,) lot 16, farmer 200

Park, Edward, (Binghamton,) (*with Abram L.*,) lot 16, farmer 200.

Parke, William A , (Kirkwood,) lot 3, justice of the peace and farmer 100.

PARSONS, JOHN C , (Kirkwood,) lot 12, harness maker, deputy sheriff, inspector of elections and saloon keeper

Patch, Jerome B., (Kirkwood,) general merchant.

Pease, Chas. A., (Kirkwood,) lot 16, farmer 32½.

Pease, George, (Kirkwood,) lot 16, farmer 65

Pease, Lewis S , (Kirkwood,) lot 1, carpenter and farmer 50.

Persooeus, David Rev., (Kirkwood,) pastor M E Church

PETTIT EMORY, (Binghamton,) lot 9, farmer 75

Pharson, William, (Riverside,) lot 2, blacksmith and farmer 56

Pierce, James E , (Binghamton,) butcher.

Pierson, George E., (Kirkwood,) allo. physician

Pitts, Paul R., (Binghamton,) lot 7, auctioneer and farmer 171

Quain, John, (Binghamton,) lot 14, farmer 100

Randall, Hiram, (Binghamton,) lot 56, farmer 150

Randall, James L., (Binghamton,) lot 55, farmer 63

RANDALL, JEROME, (Binghamton,) farm laborer.

Ray, Aaron, (Binghamton,) lot 22, farmer 50

Rider, Gambia, (Kirkwood,) lot 3, farmer 80

Ritter, Robert R , (Riverside,) lot 3, farmer 140 and, in Windsor, 60 acres wood land

Robbins, Francis, (Kirkwood Center,) lot 8, farmer 96.

Roberts, Edwin, (Riverside,) lot 1, farmer 150.

SANDERS, HENRY, (Binghamton,) lot 11, farmer leases of R. S. Bortlett, Binghamton, 220.

Sanders, John, (Binghamton,) lot 16, farmer 31

Sanders, Reuben, (Binghamton,) lot 16, farmer 31

Saxon, A S., (Kirkwood,) (*J. A. Emmons & Co.*)

Severson, Cornelius B., (Binghamton,) lot 38, farmer 75

Shear, George,(Binghamton,) lot 28, farmer 50.

Shear, Ira, (Binghamton,) lot 18, farmer 145.

Shear, John W , (Binghamton,) lot 8, farmer 40.

Sherwood, Barney W , (West Windsor,) lot 21, farmer 57

Smith, Harvey, (West Windsor,) lot 16, farmer 91

SMITH, HIRAM, (Binghamton,) lot 25, farmer 125

SMITH, JACOB M , (Binghamton,) lot 37, farmer 78.

Smith, John, (West Windsor,) lot 3, farmer 180.

Smith, Luke, (Kirkwood,) lot 1, B P., farmer 140

Smith, Whitman, (Binghamton,) inspector of elections and farmer

Snedaker, George, (Riverside,) lot 1, farmer

SOUTHEE MATTHEW, (Binghamton,) lot 10, farmer 303.

Springer, Anna Mrs , (widow) (Binghamton,) lot 49, farmer 140.

SPRINGER, TERRY A., (Binghamton,) farmer

Standley, Benajah B , (Binghamton,) lot 57, farmer 9

Standley, Isaac, (Binghamton,) lot 57, farmer 119

Standley, John, (Binghamton,) lot 57, farmer 50.

Standley, Mary Ann Mrs , (widow,) (Binghamton,) lot 57, farmer 100

Standley, William, (Binghamton,) lot 49, farmer 77.

Stewart, Richard, (Kirkwood Center,) lot 24, farmer 93

Stiner, Ambrosia Mrs., (widow,) (Binghamton,) lot 21, farmer 15.

Stiner, John E , (Binghamton,) lot 18, collector, constable and farmer 40

STOWE, FRANKLIN, (Binghamton,) lot 22, farmer 70.

Sullivan, John, (Kirkwood,) lot 6, farmer 125.

Sullivan, Mary Mrs., (Kirkwood,) lot 15, farmer 84

Swarts, Boltia, (Kirkwood,) lot 12, grocer.

SWEET, JOHN H , (Binghamton,) lot 25, farmer 70

Taber, L Chandler, (Kirkwood,) lot 12, farmer leases of T. R. Morgan, Binghamton, 203

Tewksbury, Benjamin P., (Riverside,) cooper and constable.

THURBER, ADELBERT D., (Binghamton,) farm laborer.

Thurber, Jeremiah L , (Binghamton,) carpenter and farmer 15.

VAIL, TRACY G., (Kirkwood,) lot 1, farmer 281

VAIL, WILLIAM B , (Kirkwood,) lot 12, inspector of elections

Van Auken, John V , (Riverside,) inspector of elections.

VanBuran, Tobias, (Riverside,) lot 2, wagon shop, postmaster and farmer 15.

VanWagoner, John, (Binghamton,) lot 28, farmer 65.

VanWinkle, Henry, (Kirkwood,) lot 11, farmer 120

VanWinkle, Peter R., (Kirkwood,) lot 11, laborer.

Walker, Willard, (Kirkwood,) lot 12, retired.

WATROUS, ELI W., (Kirkwood Center,) lot 7, postmaster and farmer 280.

Watrous, John H , (Kirkwood Center,) (*with Smith B.*,) lot 7, farmer leases 280.

Watrous, Smith B., (Kirkwood Center,) (*with John H*,) lot 7, farmer leases 280.

Weed, Hiram N., (Kirkwood,) lot 3, farmer 40

Welton, Ransom W., (West Windsor,) lot 16, farmer 23.

West, William, (West Windsor,) lot 21, farmer 26.

White, James, (Binghamton,) lot 17, farmer 400

Whitlog, George S., (Kirkwood,) lot 12, wagon maker

Wilcox, Charles E., (Riverside,) lot 4, farmer leases of Elijah Castle, Binghamton 270.

WILCOX, DANIEL, (Port Crane,) lot 25, farmer 95

WILCOX, PHILO B, (Binghamton,) lot 27, local preacher M E. Church and farmer 160.

Wildey, Alanson, (Binghamton,) lot 16, farmer 240

Wildey, Alanson, (Kirkwood,) lot 16, farmer 47

Williams, John, (Binghamton,) lot 26, farmer 62.

WILSEY, SIMON K., (Riverside,) carpenter and joiner

WILSON, JOHN J., (Riverside,) lot 2, farmer 58

Wilson, Wm J., (Kirkwood,) laborer

Wood, Alvah, (Kirkwood,) lot 8, assessor and farmer 165.

YOUNG, PETER M, (Binghamton,) lot 24, farmer 74.

YOUNGS, JAMES E., (Binghamton,) lot 14, farm laborer.

---

# LISLE.

## (Post Office Addresses in Parentheses.)

Adams, Charles J., (Killawog,) (*with Garrett Penoyer*.) lot 4, farmer 164

ARNOLD, JACKSON, (Center Lisle,) lot 393, farmer 144

Arnold, Stephen, (Center Lisle,) lot 409, farmer 99¼.

Arnold, Warren, (Center Lisle,) carpenter.

Atwood, Charles, (Killawog,) lot 521, farmer 300

Atwood, George, (Killawog,) lot 8, farmer 65

Atwood, Linus, (Killawog,) lot 8, carpenter and farmer 40.

Atwood, William, (Killawog,) lot 560, farmer 127

Babcock, Elisha, (Center Lisle,) lot 474, farmer 45¼

Babcock, Henry C., (Lisle,) lot 2, farmer 10.

Babcock, Nelson, (Killawog,) lot 562, farmer 60.

Baker, Leonard, (Center Lisle,) lot 370, farmer 210.

Baker, William H., (Lisle,) lot 478, gunsmith and farmer 17.

Balch, Austin, (Killawog,) lot 7, farmer 50.

BARROWS, EDSON, (Center Lisle,) (*Pinkney & Barrows*.)

BARROWS, IRAM, (Killawog,) lot 563, farmer 136

Barrows, Seth, (Center Lisle,) lot 434, farmer 187.

Bassett, George, (Lisle,) furnace and machine shop, manuf. of agricultural implements.

Benedict, Nathan O., (Center Lisle,) lot 445, farmer 15.

Bishop, Catharine Mrs., (Center Lisle,) lot 527, farmer 212.

BLANCHARD, REUBEN S, (Lisle,) sawyer.

Bouton, Thomas S., (Lisle,) harness maker.

Bowen, Charles W., (Center Lisle,) allo physician

Boynton, Polly Mrs., (Whitney's Point,) lot 399, farmer 5.

BRAMAN, JOHN, (Lisle,) lot 367, farmer 84 and, in Nanticoke, 8.

Briggs, Andrew, (Center Lisle,) lot 438, farmer 75.

Brockway, Henry, (Killawog,) (*Brockway & Hitt*.)

Brockway & Hitt, (Killawog,) (*Henry Brockway and Irving Hitt*,) saw mill

Brooks, Samuel, (Killawog,) carpenter

BROWN, FANNIE S Mrs., (Lisle,) lot 3, farmer 90.

Brown, Hiram, (Center Lisle,) lot 526, shingle mill and farmer 350

Brown, Jeremiah, (Killawog,) lot 568, farmer 40

Brown, Mary A. Mrs., (Killawog,) lot 565, farmer 130

BURGHARDT, CLINTON P, (Lisle,) R. R. ticket and express agent, dealer in coal, stone and water lime, brick, plaster, Ashton and barrel salt. grain, flour, feed, meal, shorts, ships &c

Burghardt, Erastus, (Lisle,) butcher and meat market

Burghardt, Franklin, (Center Lisle,) lot 474, farmer 117.

Burt, Asa, (Center Lisle,) lot 517, farmer 110

Burt, John, (Center Lisle,) lot 485, farmer 110.

Burt, Warren C., (Center Lisle,) lot 485, farmer 83

Butterfield, George, (Hunt's Corners, Cortland Co ,) lot 565, farmer 92

Canfield, John, (Lisle,) lot 479, farmer 10

CAPRON, WILLIAM, (Lisle,) lot 480, brick and stone mason, and farmer 30

Carley, Ebenezer, (Lisle,) lot 480, farmer 120.

Carley, Orin, (Lisle,) lot 443, farmer 44.

Carley, Orin Jr., (Center Lisle,) lot 444, farmer 122

Chatterton, Fred. H., (Lisle,) drugs, groceries, books and stationery.

CHRISTIANA, ABRAM H., (Lisle,) rents grist and saw mill.

Church, George W., (Lisle,) lot 479, farmer 10.

Clark, Charles L , (Lisle,) lot 2, farmer 85

Clark, Joshua, (Center Lisle,) *(with Wilmot,)* lot 435, farmer 215.

Clark, Rufus G , (Lisle,) lot 368, farmer 144

Clark, Spencer, (Center Lisle,) lot 445, shoemaker and farmer 1¼.

Clark, Wilmot, (Center Lisle,) *(with Joshua,)* lot 435, farmer 215

Coggshall, Alfred, (Killawog,) *(Coggshall & Brother )*

Coggshall & Brother, (Killawog,) *(Alfred and William B ,)* lot 559, tannery and 8 acres

Coggshall, William B., (Killawog,) *(Coggshall & Brother )*

Cole, Louisa Mrs , (Lisle,) milliner and dressmaker

Colluar, Norris, (Lisle,) lot 441, farmer 175

COLLINS, ALONZO, (Whitney's Point,) *(Perry & Collins )*

Cook, Caleb M., (Center Lisle,) lot 446, shoemaker and farmer 1

Cook, George H., (Center Lisle,) *(with William W.,)* lot 436, farmer 158

COOK, IRA S , (Center Lisle,) lot 475, farmer 52½

Cook, Oscar F , (Whitney's Point,) lot 399, farmer 23½.

Cook, William W., (Center Lisle,) *(with George H.,)* lot 436, farmer 158.

Cooper, George, (Hunt's Corners, Cortland County,) lot 568, farmer 100.

Cooper, William H , (Whitney's Point,) lot 399, farmer 69.

Couch, George W , (Center Lisle,) lot 524, farmer 82½.

Councilman, Polly Mrs., (Lisle,) lot 354, farmer 74.

COX, GEORGE W , (Center Lisle,) *(with Orlando,)* lot 407, farmer 98

COX, ORLANDO, (Center Lisle,) *(with George W ,)* lot 407, farmer 98

Cox, William, (Center Lisle,) lot 435, farmer 50.

Coy, Cyrus, (Lisle,) lot 479, farmer 18.

CRANDALL, ROBERT H., (Killawog,) lot 561, farmer 100.

Crane, Hezekiah, (Killawog,) lot 8, farmer 1½

Crary, Abram, (Lisle,) lot 439, farmer leases of Henry Smith, 200

Culver, Dan, (Center Lisle,) lot 446, shoemaker and farmer 3.

CULVER, LEWIS J., (Center Lisle,) farm laborer

*DAVIS, EUGENE, (Lisle,) book and job printer, and publisher of the *Lisle Gleaner.*

Davis, John C , (Killawog,) lot 560, farmer 3.

DAY, LEWIS A., (Lisle,) lot 478, wood and feed mill and farmer 105.

Dean, Gardner Rev , (Center Lisle,) pastor Baptist Church.

Dexter, Barzillia, (Killawog,) lot 7, farmer 22

Dickinson, Dewitt, (Center Lisle,) lot 475, carpenter and farmer 4

Dickinson, Ira, (Center Lisle,) stage prop from Center Lisle to Lisle

Dickinson, Orin, (Center Lisle,) lot 485, saw mill and farmer 48

Dimmick, Marvin, (Lisle,) *(Vanvalen & Dimmick )*

Douglass, Charles, (Center Lisle,) lot 444, farmer 5

Dyer, John, (Whitney's Point,) lot 399, farmer 171

Earle, William, (Center Lisle,) lot 473, farmer 32.

Edmister, Amos, (Lisle,) lot 520, farmer 27½.

Edmister, Edwin, (Lisle,) lot 441, farmer 75.

Edmister, Pierce, (Lisle,) lot 478, farmer leases 47

EDMISTER, PHILOTUS, (Lisle,) lot 44, postmaster, dealer in ready-made clothing, hats, caps, books, stationery &c , deputy sheriff and farmer 5.

Edwards, Emily Mrs., (Center Lisle,) lot 445, farmer 12

EDWARDS, FRANKLIN B., (Lisle,) *(F. B & H. Edwards )*

EDWARDS, F B. & H , (Lisle,) *(Franklin B and Hamilton,)* lot 441, saw mill and farmer 385

EDWARDS, HAMILTON, (Lisle,) *(F. B. & H Edwards )*

Edwards, William, estate of, (Lisle,) lot 442, 50 acres

Edy, Charles, (Lisle,) lot 354, farmer 180 and, in Nanticoke, 40

ELLIS, EDMUND, (Killawog,) lot 7, grist mill and farmer 1½.

Ensign, Datus W , (Hunt's Corners, Cortland Co ,) lot 568, saw mill and farmer 200.

Fairbanks, Amanda Mrs , (Lisle,) lot 408, farmer 11

Fenner, Allen, (Center Lisle,) lot 352, farmer 50

Fenner, Frank, (Center Lisle,) lot 369, farmer 100

FENNER, FREDERICK, (Lisle,) dentist

Fenner, Jeremiah, (Lisle,) *(Whitney, Fenner & Co )*

FENNER, JERRY B., (Lisle,) photographer and dealer in French goods and toys

Fenner, John, (Center Lisle,) lot 352, farmer 20.

Fenner, William, (Center Lisle,) lot 392, farmer 50

Finch, William, (Center Lisle,) lot 393, farmer 75

FORBES, ROBERT, (Center Lisle,) lot 489, farmer 100½

Fox, John F , (Lisle,) lot 478, farmer.

Fox, Nicholas, (Center Lisle,) lot 405, farmer 90.

Franklin, Charles R , (Center Lisle,) lot 408 farmer 210.

Freelove, Joseph, (Lisle,) lot 396, farmer 18¾.

FREER, JACOB, (Whitney's Point,) miller.

French, Dwight, (Lisle,) furniture manuf

French, Salpronius H., (Lisle,) lot 441, retired physician, farmer 180 and, in Nanticoke, 70.

French, Seward, (Killawog,) carpenter

Fulmer, Frederick, (Center Lisle,) lot 485, farmer 100

Ganung, Thomas, (Center Lisle,) lot 449, farmer 186.

GEE, WARREN R ,(Berkshire, Tioga Co ,) engineer in steam saw mill.

GLEZEN, FRANK E , (Center Lisle,) works in tannery.

GLEZEN, JOHN C., (Center Lisle,) lot 475, farmer 120

GLEZEN, LEVI W., (Center Lisle,) lot 446, farmer 1¼

Glezen, Marshal M., (Center Lisle,) lot 446, farmer leases of Chas A , 30

Glezen, Solomon, (Center Lisle,) lot 444, planing mill and farmer 1

Gonong, Dewitt, (Center Lisle,) lot 893, farmer 73

Greaves, Susan D. Mrs., (Center Lisle,) lot 409, farmer 167

GUERNSEY, AAI, (Lisle,) (*Smith & Guernsey* )

HALL, HENRY C., (Lisle,) allo. physician

HAND, RUFUS A , (Lisle,) carpenter and joiner

Harman, Norman G., (Killawog,) lot 6, farmer leases of Joseph B Richardson, 120.

Harris, Isaac, (Lisle,) tailor.

HASKINS, JAMES, (Center Lisle,) prop. of Haskins House

Hill, Edward B , (Killawog,) lot 620, farmer 100

Hill, Ferris, (Killawog,) lot 621, farmer 185

Hill, James W., (Killawog,) lot 559, farmer 14

Hitt, Irving, (Killawog,) (*Brockway & Hitt.*)

Hoard, Braddock, (Center Lisle,) lot 488, farmer 160.

Hodskin, Albert A , (Lisle,) lot 2, farmer 4.

Hollenbeck, L. Mrs., (Center Lisle,) lot 478, farmer 12

Hollister, Russel L , (Lisle,) (*Marsh & Hollister* )

Hotaling, Seth M., (Center Lisle,) lot 627, farmer 268

Houghtaling, John, (Center Lisle,) lot 486, farmer 300

Houghtaling, Samuel, (Center Lisle,) lot 654, farmer 330.

Howland, Barnabas, (Center Lisle,) lot 432, farmer 65

Howland, Charles, (Center Lisle,) blacksmith.

Howland, Daniel W , (Center Lisle,) lot 448, farmer 102 and, in Richford, Tioga Co , 44

Howland, George, (Center Lisle,) lot 892, farmer 70

Howland, Horace O , (Center Lisle,) lot 448, farmer 200.

Howland, Isaac , (Lisle ) lot 479, farmer 70

Howland, Isaac, (Center Lisle,) lot 473, farmer 66

HOWLAND, MARY Mrs., (widow,) (Center Lisle,) lot 449, farmer 35

Howland, Melvin, (Center Lisle,) (*with Warren*,) lot 474, farmer 265

HOWLAND, MORGAN, (Center Lisle,) lot 432, farmer, in town of Richford, Tioga Co , 53

Howland, Orson, (Center Lisle,) lot 432, farmer 230

Howland, Pardon, (Lisle,) lot 443, farmer 150.

Howland, Warren, (Center Lisle,) (*with Melvin*,) lot 474, farmer 265

Howland, ——, (Center Lisle,) (*Maning & Howland* )

Hoyt, Chester, (Killawog,) lot 660, farmer 10

Huntley, Wallace, (Killawog,) lot 8, farmer 27.

Japhet, Andrew, (Lisle,) lot 477, farmer 68

Japhet, Ellen J Mrs , (Center Lisle,) milliner

Jennings, Dan. R , (Killawog,) lot 564, farmer 245

Jennings, George W., (Killawog,) lot 564, farmer 260.

Johnson, Erastus, (Killawog,) lot 560, farmer 244

Johnson, Franklin N , (Lisle,) lot 2, farmer 50

JOHNSON, HENRY B., (Lisle,) lot 2, farmer 105.

JOHNSON, NANCY M. Mrs., (Lisle,) farmer

Johnson, Oscar (Lisle,) lot 2, farmer 1.

JOHNSON, SALINA, (Lisle,) lot 2, farmer 60

Johnson, Vincent, (Lisle,) lot 2, farmer 75

Johnson, Wheeler A., (Lisle,) lot 2, farmer 43.

Johnson, William H., (Killawog,) lot 561, farmer 34

Kane, Patrick, (Killawog,) lot 568, farmer 45

Keller, Adam, (Killawog,) cheese factory.

Ketchum, Robert J., (Lisle,) lot 440, farmer 80.

Knapp, Nathan, (Lisle,) lot 480, farmer 20.

Lander, Gideon, (Center Lisle,) grocer.

Lawrence, William H , (Lisle,) jeweler and watch repairer

Lee, Betsey Mrs , (Lisle,) lot 483, farmer 20

Lee, George, (Lisle,) lot 397, farmer 102

Leesk, Samuel R , (Center Lisle,) carpenter and repairer of wagons and sleighs

Leet, Isaac N . (Center Lisle,) lot 517, carpenter and farmer 90

Lewis, Alonzo, (Lisle,) (*A. Lewis & Son* )

Lewis, Alonzo P., (Lisle,) (*A. Lewis & Son.*)

Lewis, A , & Son, (Lisle,) (*Alonzo and Alonzo P ,*) hardware and tinware

Lewis, George W., (Lisle,) (*J. C Lewis & Brother.*)

Lewis, James, (Whitney's Point,) carpenter

Lewis, John C , (Lisle,) (*J. C. Lewis & Brother*)

Lewis, J C & Brother, (Lisle,) (*John C and George W ,*) general merchants

Lewis, Marquis H., (Center Lisle,) lot 472, farmer 47½

Lincoln, Randall, (Center Lisle,) lot 391, farmer 50 and, in Berkshire, Tioga Co , 50

*LISLE GLEANER, (Lisle,) Eugene Davis, publisher

Livermore, Asa A., (Center Lisle,) lot 352, farmer 60

Livermore, Brigham, (Center Lisle,) lot 369, farmer 30.

Livermore, Byron, (Center Lisle,) lot 352, farmer 54.

Livermore, Charles H , (Center Lisle,) lot 474, farmer 113

Livermore, Charles T , (Lisle,) lot 438, farmer 97.

Livermore, George, (Center Lisle,) lot 445, farmer 20

Livermore, George W., (Center Lisle,) lot 408, farmer 115.

Livermore, Joseph W , (Center Lisle,) carpenter and farmer 2½

Livermore, Lorin, (Center Lisle,) lot 408, farmer 130.

Lloyd, George, (Whitney's Point,) millwright.

LOBDELL, JAMES E , (Center Lisle,) patent right dealer and inventor.

LOBDELL, ROSANDER F., (Center Lisle,) carpenter and joiner, and repairer of machinery

LOBDELL, ZIMRI, (Lisle,) carpenter and joiner

Loomis, A. W. Rev , (Lisle,) pastor M. E. Church.

Love & Smith, (Lisle,) livery.

Luce, Warren, (Center Lisle,) lot 369, farmer 90.

LUSK, CORNELIUS M., (Center Lisle,) lot 445, carpenter and joiner, and farmer 99

LUSK, DANIEL D , (Center Lisle,) farmer 65 and, in Richford, 14

LUSK, DENNIS, (Center Lisle,) lot 433, farmer 80

Lusk, Hubbard, (Center Lisle,) lot 446, farmer 160.

Lusk, Jason C , (Center Lisle,) lot 435, farmer 47½

Lusk, Pomeroy H., (Center Lisle,) lot 489, farmer 100 and, in Richford, 12

Lusk, Simon J , (Center Lisle,) lot 434, farmer 89

Lusk, William C , (Center Lisle,) farmer, in Richford, 30

LUSK, WILLIAM J., (Center Lisle,) carpenter and joiner

Lynde, Oliver W., (Killawog,) lot 5, farmer 118.

Lynde, William, (Killawog,) lot 5, farmer 11.

Maning & Howland, (Center Lisle,) steam saw mill, grocers and farmers 468

Manning, George J., (Center Lisle,) lot 444, farmer 179.

MARKS, BENONI, (Lisle,) lot 356, farmer 45

MARKS, CHARLES E., (Lisle,) lot 396, farmer 106

MARKS, THOMAS O., (Center Lisle,) lot 395, farmer 46

MARKS, WILLIAM H., (Center Lisle,) lot 395, farmer 50

Marsh, George R , (Lisle,) (*Marsh & Hollister.*)

Marsh & Hollister, (Lisle,) (*George R. Marsh and Russel L. Hollister,*) saw mill and farmers 5.

Mathewson, James D., (Lisle,) lot 397, farmer 56

MATHEWSON, MORGAN L , (Lisle,) lot 396, farmer 57½

Maynard, Winslow J., (Killawog,) lot 560, farmer 54.

McDowell, Alexander, (Lisle,) lawyer

McHenry, Michael, (Killawog,) lot 561, farmer leases of Polly Underwood, 45.

McNiel, Elias, (Center Lisle,) lot 475, farmer 73

Millen, David H., (Center Lisle,) lot 485, farmer 183

Millen, Joel, (Center Lisle,) lot 478, farmer 67.

Morenus, Hannah Mrs., (Center Lisle,) lot 527, farmer 49

Morenus, John, (Center Lisle,) lot 627, farmer 25

Morenus, Maria Mrs., (Center Lisle,) lot 627, farmer 30

Morenus, Peter, (Center Lisle,) lot 472, farmer 64 and, in Richford, 31

Muckey, Harmon, (Killawog,) lot 7, farmer 80

Newton, Herod, (Killawog,) lot 560, farmer 10

Nickels, George L , (Center Lisle,) lot 393, farmer 82¼

Northrop, William Mrs., (Lisle,) dressmaker

NUSUM, ROBERT W., (Lisle,) lot 440, farmer 68¾.

Nutting, Jonathan E., (Lisle,) dentist

O'Connel, Patrick, (Lisle,) lot 408, farmer 119.

Oliver, Henry W., (Center Lisle,) lot 394, farmer 70

Oliver, John, estate of, (Center Lisle,) lot 405, 40 acres.

Oliver, Orville B., (Center Lisle,) lot 406, farmer 40

Oliver, Orville T., (Lisle,) lot 403, farmer 60.

Orton, Charles D., (Lisle,) lot 440, farmer 35.

Orton, Darius, (Center Lisle,) lot 488, farmer 49.

Orton, Henry, (Center Lisle,) lot 370, farmer 50.

Orton, Lambert, (Center Lisle,) lot 478, farmer 60

Orton, William J., (Lisle,) allo. physician.

Osborn, Robert S., (Lisle,) general merchant

Ostrander, Lorenzo S., (Center Lisle,) lot 448, farmer 61.

Parker, George, (Killawog,) lot 562, farmer 18.

Payne, Louisa Mrs., (Center Lisle,) dressmaker

Peck, Walter L., (Lisle,) lot 401, farmer 100

Pendell, Elkanah D., (Lisle,) lot 481, farmer 74¾

Pendell, James M., (Lisle,) lot 437, farmer 169.

Penoyer, Garret, (Killawog,) (*with Charles J Adams,*) lot 4, farmer 104.

Perce, Daniel H., (Lisle,) lot 479, farmer 105.

Perce, J W., (Center Lisle,) lot 484, farmer 130

Perce, Martin, (Center Lisle,) lot 436, farmer 200

Perce, Riley J., (Center Lisle,) lot 477, farmer 142.

PERRY & COLLINS, (Whitney's Point,) (*Fred H Perry and Alonzo Collins,*) props of tannery, grist and saw mills and blacksmith shop, farmers 387, in Nanticoke, 573 and, in Barker, 352.

PERRY, FRED. H., (Whitney's Point,) (*Perry & Collins*)

Pettis, Ralph, (Center Lisle,) shoemaker

Phelps, Alexander, (Killawog,) lot 562, farmer 60.

Phelps, Charles H., (Killawog,) lot 559, farmer 135

Phelps, Samuel H., (Killawog,) carpenter.

Phetteplace, Israel, (Killawog,) lot 560, general merchant and farmer 5.

PHILLIPS, LEWIS P., (Center Lisle,) photographer.

Pierce, Elkanah, (Lisle,) lot 478, farmer 110.

Pierce, Hermon, (Lisle,) shoemaker.

Pierce, John, (Lisle,) lot 483, farmer 150.

Pierce, Levi, (Lisle,) lot 481, farmer 60.

Pierce, Truman L., (Center Lisle,) lot 477, furniture manuf and farmer 13

Pike, Joseph, (Killawog,) lot 10, farmer 100

PINKNEY & BARROWS, (Center Lisle,) (*Oscar F. Pinkney and Edson Barrows,*) lot 477, saw and lath mills, and farmers 12

PINKNEY, OSCAR F., (Center Lisle,) (*Pinkney & Barrows.*)

Piteley, Dennis L, (Lisle,) lot 443, farmer 51¼

Pollard, Bennett, (Hunt's Corners, Cortland Co ,) lot 555, farmer 58

Potter, Lester W., (Center Lisle,) lot 515, farmer 120.

Pratt, Stephen D, (Killawog,) lot 560, farmer 10.

Preston, John S., (Killawog,) blacksmith

Randall, Allen J., (Whitney's Point,) lot 401, farmer 100

Randall, George W, (Whitney's Point,) lot 401, farmer 90

REED, ALMON L,, (Center Lisle,) lot 409, farmer 149½

Reed, Solomon, (Center Lisle,) lot 432, farmer 70 and leases of Isaiah, 70.

Richards, Jonathan H , (Center Lisle,) lot 444, farmer 5.

Richardson, Joseph B , (Killawog,) lot 9, farmer 22.

RICHARDSON, LYSANDER, (Lisle,) lot 396, farmer 32¼.

RICHARDSON, WILLIAM A., (Lisle,) laborer.

RINDGE, EDWIN R., (Killawog,) lot 560, ticket, express, freight and coal agent, and farmer 10¼.

ROBISON, EUGENE A., (Center Lisle,) lot 433, farmer 100

Rood, Leander W., (Center Lisle,) lot 446, carriage maker and farmer 170.

Rood, Lucy Mrs., (Center Lisle,) lot 445, farmer 108

ROOD, REUBEN, (Center Lisle,) lot 445, farmer 125

Root, Hiram C., (Center Lisle,) lot 447, farmer leases 250

Root, William, (Center Lisle,) lot 448, farmer 30.

Rose Eber W., (Killawog,) lot 7, farmer 101

Runyan, David B., (Hunt's Corners, Cortland Co.,) lot 558, saw and planing mills, and farmer 70.

Salesbury, Noyes, (Killawog,) mason

Salisbury, Loren, (Killawog,) general merchant.

Sanford, Philo N., (Center Lisle,) lot 444, farmer 50.

Saxton, Philander, (Lisle,) carpenter.

SCHERMERHORN, GEORGE C., (Killawog,) lot 9, farmer 264.

Selem, James, (Center Lisle,) lot 395, farmer 50.

Scott, Elon, (Center Lisle,) lot 392, farmer 60.

Sessions, Archimedes, (Killawog,) lot 563, farmer 144.

SESSIONS, CELESTIA Mrs., (Killawog,) lot 563, farmer 209

SESSIONS, JOHN L , (Killawog,) lot 163, farmer 193.

Shelden, Anson S., (Center Lisle,) lot 352, farmer 45

SLITER, JONAS C., (Lisle,) lot 397, farmer 226.

Smith, George H., (Lisle,) lot 479, farmer works 3

SMITH & GUERNSEY, (Lisle,) (*James E Smith and Aai Guernsey,*) saw mill and farmers 7.

SMITH, JAMES E , (Lisle,) (*Smith & Guernsey*)

Smith, John W., (Lisle,) (*Whitney, Fenner & Co*)

Smith, J. Wesley, (Lisle,) carriage ironer

SMITH, LEROY H., (Center Lisle,) (*L. S. Smith & Son.*)

Smith, Lewis S., (Center Lisle,) lot 445, post master, general merchant, tanner of sheep skins, grist, saw and lath mills, and farmer 360¼.

SMITH, LEWIS S., (Center Lisle,) (*L S. Smith & Son*)

SMITH, L. S. & SON, (Center Lisle,) (*Lewis S and Leroy H.,*) lumbermen and meat market

Smith, Philo, (Lisle,) blacksmith

Smith, Renny, (Lisle,) lot 443, farmer 150

Smith, ——, (Lisle,) (*Love & Smith*)

Sparrow, Joseph, (Lisle,) lot 440, farmer 38

SPARROW, THOMAS J., (Lisle,) lot 440, livery, teamster and farmer 13

SPENCER, JIRAH P., (Center Lisle,) lot 352, farmer 210 and, in Nanticoke, 95

Spicer, Leander, (Lisle,) lot 403 farmer 5.

Squire, Thomas, (Lisle,) lot 440, farmer 100.

Squires, William H , (Lisle,) lot 441, farmer 5

STALKER, WILLIAM H , (Lisle,) sawyer.

STANFORD, HENRY M., (Lisle,) carpenter and joiner

Steel, Mary A. Mrs., (Lisle,) lot 441, resident.

Stoddard, George W., (Lisle,) lot 440, farmer 85.

Stoddard, William H., (Lisle,) lot 441, farmer 160

Stone, Lee C., (Whitney's Point,) blacksmith

STORRS, MADISON M., (Center Lisle,) lot 525, farmer leases of Mrs. Ellen Japhet, 53¾

Snllivan, Dennis, (Lisle,) lot 440, farmer 25.

Snllivan, Richard, (Lisle,) lot 401, farmer 85

SWIFT, GEORGE M , (Lisle,) lot 354, farmer 115.

Taber, Isaac W., (Center Lisle,) lot 475, blacksmith and farmer 45.

Taber, Pardon Jr , (Center Lisle,) carpenter and cooper.

Talbot, Alfreder Miss, (Hunt's Corners, Cortland Co ,) lot 568, farmer 1½

Talbot, John Q , (Hunt's Corners, Cortland Co ,) lot 568, farmer 93

Talbot, Joseph, (Hunt's Corners, Cortland Co.,) lot 568, farmer 5.

Tarble, Samuel B., (Killawog,) lot 560, farmer 68.

Tarbox, Carrie Mrs., (Center Lisle ) lot 445, farmer 2

Terrel, Isaac, (Lisle,) basket maker.

THELEMAN, WALLACE, (Lisle,) lot 353, farmer 178

Thomas, James A., (Center Lisle,) lot 473, farmer 47½.

Thurstin, David, (Lisle,) lot 478, farmer leases of Theodore G Gurney, 75.

Todd, George W , (Killawog,) lot 560, farmer 37

Tompkins, Henry M., (Whitney's Point,) lot 399, farmer leases of John Sullivan, 56

Tmver, Henry, (Lisle ) saloon

TRAVIS, HENRY G , (Lisle,) lot 367, farmer 256.

Turner, Ephraim M , (Killawog,) lot 660, shoemaker and farmer 4½

TURNER, JOHN A., (Killawog,) lot 562, farmer 57

Tuttle, Theodore F., (Lisle,) harness maker

Twiss, Alanson (Lisle,) lot 483, farmer 6.

Twiss, Albert A , (Lisle,) lot 480, lawyer and farmer 12

Tyler, Oliver, (Lisle,) lot 369, farmer 40 and leases of E. Tyler, 46

Ukin, William, (Lisle,) shoe maker.

Underwood, Asa, (Center Lisle,) lot 393, farmer 164½.

Underwood, Richard, (Center Lisle,) lot 436, farmer 21½

Upham, Damon Y , (Killawog,) lot 6, farmer 112.

Vanvalen & Dimmick, (Lisle,) (*Oliver B. Vanvalen and Marvin Dimmick,*) harness makers

Vanvalen, Oliver B , (Lisle,) (*Vanvalen & Dimmick )*

Waterman, Url, (Killawog,) lot 520, farmer 100.

Watkins, Carlos, (Center Lisle,) boarding house

Wattles, Harry J , (Hunt's Corners, Cortland Co ,) (*with Herbert,*) lot 568, farmer 460

Wattles Herbert, (Hunt's Corners, Cortland Co ,) (*with Harry J.,*) lot 568, farmer 460.

Wells, Edwin L., (Whitney's Point,) lot 401, farmer 68.

Wells, William H , (Lisle,) lot 366, farmer 65

Whalen, James, (Lisle,) lot 481, farmer 47

Wheaton, Calvin J , (Killawog,) lot 7, farmer 131

Wheaton, Frank M , (Killawog,) lot 6, farmer 100.

WHEATON, JOHN C , (Killawog,) lot 8, farmer 8

Wheaton, John J., (Killawog,) lot 6, postmaster and farmer 18

White, Lester L., (Killawog,) lot 6, farmer 100

Whitney, Fenner & Co , (Lisle,) (*Hiram N Whitney, Jeremiah Fenner and John W. Smith,*) carriage manuls

Whitney, Hiram N , (Lisle,) (*Whitney, Fenner & Co.)*

Wilcox, Stephen S., (Center Lisle,) lot 445, farmer 30.

WILLIAMS, ASHLEY, (Killawog,) carpenter and joiner

WILLIAMS, JOHN J., (Center Lisle,) engineer in tannery

WILLIS, JUDSON, (Lisle,) foreman of tannery.

Witty, John, (Killawog,) lot 561, farmer 6½

Witty, Thomas, (Killawog,) lot 621, farmer 20

WOOD, DAVID, (Lisle,) lot 481, farmer 150.

Wood, Thomas, (Lisle,) lot 437, cooper and farmer leases of Mrs Jane Pittsley, 16

Wright, Thomas S , (Lisle,) lot 441, carpenter and farmer 20.

Yarington, Lewis R , (Killawog,) house painter.

YARRINGTON, FREDERICK U., (Killawog,) house painter.

P

# MAINE.

## (Post Office Addresses in Parentheses.)

Adams, Thomas, (Union Center,) lot 14, N T, farmer 44.

AKER, HENRY (East Maine,) (*with William*,) lot 83, C T, farmer 204

Aker, James E, (Maine,) lot 86 N T, farmer 50

Aker, Samuel, (East Maine,) lot 83, C T, resident.

AKER, WILLIAM (East Maine,) (*with Henry*,) lot 83, C. T., farmer 204

Allen, Belden, (Maine,) lot 152 G D, farmer 57.

Allen, Ebenezer B, (Maine,) (*with John J.,*) lot 152, G D farmer 240

Allen, John J., (Maine,) (*with Ebenezer B*,) lot 152, G. D., farmer 240.

Allen, Matthew, (Maine,) lot 129, G D farmer 118.

Allison & Sherwood, (Maine,) tannery.

Anderson Ezekiel, (East Maine,) lot 9, G D, farmer 40

Andrews, Brooke, (West Chenango,) lot 34, G D, farmer 68½.

Andrews, Frederick N, (Union Center,) lot 13, N T, farmer 54

Andrews, William, (West Chenango,) lot 34, G D, farmer 40

Ashley, William H., (Maine,) lot 190, G. D, farmer 50

Atwater, Garret S, (Maine,) lot 169, G. D, farmer 52

Atwater, John J., (Maine,) lot 111, G. D, farmer 121

Bailey, James W., (Union Center,) lot 76, N T, farmer 40

Baker, Charles H, (Maine,) lot 130, G D, farmer occupies 20.

BAKER, HENRY (Maine,) lot 111, G D, prop. of steam saw mill and farmer 855

Baker, Richard D., (Union Center,) lot 177, N T, farmer 27

BANCROFT, LEONARD F, (Union Center,) lot 98, N T, farmer 3

Barlow, John, (Maine,) lot 92, G D., farmer 50

Barlow, Samuel A., (Maine,) lot 129, G D., carpenter, builder and farmer 12

Barnes, Jacob C, (Maine,) lot 172, G. D, farmer 120

Barnum, Henry, (Maine,) lot 10, G D, farmer 50

Baxter, Charles H, (Castle Creek,) lot 114, G. D., farmer 45

BEAN, WM F., (Maine,) blacksmith and carriage ironer

Belcher, Yelles, (Binghamton,) lot 80, C. T, saw and grist mills, and farmer 24

Benjamin, Asahel, (Maine,) lot 90, G D, farmer 28

Benjamin, Bela E, (Glen Aubrey,) lot 192, G D, farmer 30

Benjamin, Edwin, (Maine,) lot 90, G D, farmer 23

Benton, John W, (Maine,) lot 110, G. D, carpenter, millwright and farmer 90

Berry, David, (West Chenango,) lot 6, G D, farmer 50

Blair, Lorenzo, (Maine,) lot 95, N T, farmer 80

Bliss, Eleanor Mrs, (widow,) (Maine,) lot 23, N T, farmer 14

Bliss, Mary J Mrs, (widow,) (Maine,) lot 23, N T, farmer 64

Bostwick, Samuel A, (Union Center,) lot 15 N T, farmer 121.

Boughton, Benjamin W, (East Maine,) lot 83, N T farmer 82

Bowers, C G & L M., (Maine,) clothing, boots, shoes, notions and furniture

Bowers, Gardner S, (Maine,) lot 51, G D, farmer 60

BRADLEY, TRUMAN W, (Maine,) lot 11, G. D, cooper

BRANDAY, MARK D, (Maine,) lot 191, G D, school teacher and farmer 40

Briggs, Justice W, (Maine,) lot 191, G D, farmer 21

Bronk, Jacob W, (East Maine,) lot 8, G D farmer 52.

Bronk, Joel, (East Maine,) lot 73, G. D., farmer 50

Brooker, Jacob, (Maine,) lot 96, N T, local preacher and farmer 13

BROOKS, EUGENE, (West Chenango,) (*with John,*) lot 74, G D, farmer 50

Brooks, Harvey, (Maine,) lot 94, N T, farmer 120

BROOKS, JAMES M, (West Chenango,) lot 47, G D, farmer 95.

BROOKS, JOHN, (West Chenango,) (*with Eugene,*) lot 74, G D, farmer 50.

Brooks, John H, (Lamb's Corners,) lot 210, G D., farmer 30.

BROOKS, MARCUS, (West Chenango,) farmer.

Brooks, W R, (Maine,) lot 191, G. D, carpenter and farmer 40

Brougham, Joseph H, (Union Center,) lot 163, N. T., farmer 34

Brougham, Sarah Mrs, (widow,) (Union Center,) lot 162, N. T., farmer 318.

Brown, Caleb F., (Maine,) lot 70, G. D, farmer 60.

Brown, Judson T , (Union Center ) lot 24, N. T , farmer 78.

Brown, Mary Mrs., (widow,) (Maine,) lot 30 G. D., resident.

Brown, Norman P , (Maine,) (*Hull & Brown.*)

Brown, Samuel, (Maine,) lot 9, G. D., farmer 75.

Budd, Elijah P., (Union Center,) lot 97, N. T., farmer 4

Bunsey, Jacob, (Union Center,) lot 74, N T , farmer 64

Burell, David, (West Chenango,) lot 130, C T , farmer 30

BURGESS, JOSEPH, (Maine,) lot 129, G D , painter, grainer and paper hanger

Burns, James, (Binghamton,) lot 7, G D , farmer 74

Bush, David M , (Maine,) lot 211, G. D , farmer 30

Bush, Lorenzo D , (Maine,) lot 212, G. D., grocer

Butler, William, (Maine,) physician and surgeon.

Canneff Mercy D Mrs., (widow,) (Maine,) lot 70, G. D., farmer 10

Carman & Green, (Maine,) lot 70, G. D., grist and flouring mill.

Carman, James W., (Maine,) lot 96, N. T., grist mill

Carpenter, John, (East Maine,) lot 84, C. T , farmer 70

Casey, John, (Binghamton,) lot 57, C. T., farmer 100

Casey, John 2nd, (Binghamton,) lot 119, C. T , farmer 85

Casey, Richard, (East Maine,) lot 7, G. D farmer 66

Casey, William, (Binghamton,) lot 49, C. T , farmer 68.

Catlin, Charles M., (Union Center,) lot 155, N T , saw mill and farmer 240.

Chauncey, Israel, (Hooper,) lot 70, N. T., farmer 130.

Chauncey, Russell F., (East Maine,) lot 8, G. D , postmaster and farmer leases 78

Chauncey, Russell L , (East Maine,) lot 8, G D , wagon maker, blacksmith and farmer 103

Church, Adoniram J., (Maine,) lot 212, G D , farmer 102.

Church, Andrew, (Maine,) (*Church & Sherwood*)

Church, Delos, (Maine,) (*Church & Sherwood*)

Church & Sherwood, (Maine,) (*Delos and Andrew Church and William H Sherwood,*) general merchants.

CLARK, ALBERT D., (Binghamton,) lot 111, C T , farmer 15

Clark, Cyrus N., (Maine,) lot 70, G D , farmer 20.

Clark, Fannie L. Mrs., (widow,) (East Maine,) lot 8, G D , farmer 25

Clark, Jeremiah, (Binghamton,) lot 11, C. T., farmer 18

Clark, Jesse W., (Binghamton,) lot 112, C T , carpenter and builder, and farmer 60

Cleveland, George, (East Maine,) lot 85, C. T , farmer 45.

Clyde, Alfred, (Maine,) lot 23, N. T., farmer 35.

Clyde, Steuben, (Maine,) lot 85, N. T., farmer 64

Coe, Frank, (Union Center,) lot 74, N. T., farmer 71

Congdon, James, (Binghamton,) lot 7, G. D , farmer 50.

CONGDON, SMITH T , (Maine,) lot 111, G. D., farmer 200

Cook, Francis, (Binghamton,) lot 117, C. T , farmer 57.

Cooper Elizabeth Mrs , (widow,) (East Maine,) lot 8, G D , farmer 40

Copley, Benjamin P., (Maine,) lot 29, G. D , auctioneer and farmer 11.

Cornell, David, (Union Center,) lot 155, N. T., sawyer and farmer 54

Councilman, Ezra J , (Maine,) lot 169, G. D., farmer 96

Councilman, John W., (Maine,) sawyer and farmer 54

Conse, Moses W , (Glen Aubrey,) lot 169, G D , farmer 52.

Crafts, Edgar G , (Maine,) lot 88, G. D., physician and farmer 350

Crane, Robert W., (Maine,) lot 10, G. D., farmer leases of Warren Moorce, 66

Crawford, Absalom, (Union Center,) lot 176, N T , farmer leases of Leonard F. Bancroft, 180.

Crawford, Ezra, (Union Center,) lot 156, N. T., farmer leases 12 ).

Crawford, Martin F., (Union Center,) lot 75, N. T., farmer 56.

Cronk, Smith H., (Union Center,) lot 24, N. T., farmer 64.

Crysler, Elias (Union Center,) lot 19, N T , farmer 60

Crysler, Evert, (Union Center,) lot 157, N. T., farmer 80.

Cummings, Frederick A , (Maine,) lot 51, G. D., shoe maker.

Cummings, Manly L., (Maine,) lot 210, G D., farmer 52.

Cummings, May G., (Maine,) lot 70, G. D , pump maker

Cummings, Warren F , (Maine,) lot 149, G D , commissioner of highways and farmer leases 48

Cunningham, Emory, (Union Center,) lot 17, N T , farmer 100

Curlhair, Freeman C , (Maine,) town clerk and harness maker.

Curtis, Abel, (Maine,) lot 92, N T , farmer 50

Curtis, Asa U , (Maine,) lot 90, N T , farmer 300

Curtis, Cyrus M., (Maine,) lot 91, N. T., farmer 112

Curtis, John C , (Maine,) lot 91, N. T., farmer 4

Curtis, Luke, (Maine,) lot 90, N. T., produce commission merchant

Curtis, Warner, (Maine,) lot 92, N. T , farmer 90.

DANIELS, ORMANDO R., (Maine,) farmer 64

Davey, George W., (Maine,) lot 112, G D , farmer leases of heirs of Joseph Mareac, 90

Davis, Dewitt, (Maine,) lot 110, G. D., farmer 85

Davis. George S., (Maine,) lot 212, G. D , farmer 45

DAVIS, JOHN T., (Maine,) lot 130, G. D , farmer 12.

Dayton, Albert D., (Maine,) lot 51, G. D., farmer 50.

Dayton, Henry H , (Maine,) lot 70, G D , farmer leases of F H Marean, 30

DeLano, Aaron, (Maine ) lot 90, G. D., blacksmith and farmer 27.

DELANO, MARSHAL, (Maine,) lot 71, G. D , farmer 55.

DeLano, Moses, (Maine,) lot 71, G. D., farmer 33

Dikenbeck, Solomon, (Maine,) lot 210, G D , farmer 50.

Donovan, Malachi, (East Maine,) lot 51, N T , farmer 87.

DOWNS, WILLIAM, (Choconut Center,) lot 100, C. T , farmer 50

Dudley, Daniel, (Maine,) lot 11, G D., farmer 80

Dudley, Dwight, (Maine,) physician and surgeon.

Dudley, J., (Maine,) lot 92, N. T., farmer 98.

Duncan, Truman J., (Maine,) lot 171, G D., carpenter and farmer 21.

Durfee, Amasa, (Maine,) lot 90, N T., carpenter and farmer 100.

Durfee, Marsden A , (Maine,) lot 90, G D., farmer 38

Dyer, William E , (Maine,) cooper.

Eckerson, James, (Maine,) lot 212, G D., farmer 100

Ellis, Michael H , (Maine,) lot 111, G D , farmer 25

Emerson James M., (Maine,) lot 72, G. D., farmer 38.

ENGLE, CHARLES, (Binghamton,) lot 134, C T., farmer 100

Fairfield, John, (Maine,) lot 11, G. D , farmer 132

Fairfield, Smith, (Maine,) lot 11, G. D., carpenter and farmer 2.

Finch, Joseph C., (Binghamton,) lot 133, C. T , farmer 50.

Fisher, John, (Maine,) lot 50, G. D., farmer 147

Fitzgibbons, Garret, (Choconut Center,) lot 81, C T , refused information.

Flint, Abner, (Castle Creek,) lot 114, G. D., farmer 100

Flint, William J., (Maine,) lot 50, G D., undertaker and farmer 38

Foster, Henry A , (Maine,) lot 190, G D., farmer 56.

Freeman, Albert, (Maine,) lot 212, G. D., farmer 100

Frost, Looma Mrs , (widow,) (Maine,) lot 72, G. D., farmer 40

Fuller, Otis, (West Chenango,) lot 73, G. D , farmer 110

Fuller, Philander, (Maine,) (*with Prentice,*) lot 212, G. D., farmer 106

Fuller, Prentice, (Maine,) (*with Philander,*) lot 212, G. D., farmer 106

Gallup, Seth, (East Maine,) lot 54, C. T., farmer 70.

Gardner, Julia M , (widow,) (Maine,) lot 97, N. T., farmer 5.

Gaskill, George S , (East Maine,) lot 112, C. T., farmer 24.

Gates, Alfred A., (Maine,) lot 190, G. D , farmer 82

Gates, Byron C., (Maine,) (*with Eugene O ,*) lot 191, G D , farmer 110

Gates, Cyrus, (Maine ) lot 191, G D , surveyor and insurance agent

Gates, Elizabeth Mrs., (widow,) (Maine ) lot 151, G D , saw mill and farmer 200

Gates, Eugene O , (Maine,) (*with Byron C ,*) lot 191. G. D., farmer 110

Gates, Livingston T , (Maine,) lot 171, G D., farmer 150

Gates, Louis, (Maine,) resident.

Green Rathbun, (Maine,) lot 149, G D., farmer 50.

Green, ——, (Maine,) (*Carman & Green* )

Greene, Job, (Maine,) lot 51, G. D , hop raiser and farmer 29

GUY, CLEMENT N., (Maine,) homeo. physician

HARDENDORF, GIFFORD, (Maine,) lot 189, G D , carpenter and joiner.

Hardy, John A., (Maine,) lot 72, G. D., farmer 42.

Harold, Martha Mrs , (widow,) (East Maine,) lot 8, G. D., farmer 40.

Harper, Edgar G , (Binghamton,) lot 132, C. T , farmer 125.

Harris Levi R , (Maine,) lot 130, G D , farmer leases of John Chase. 18.

Harvey, John M , (Maine,) blacksmith

Haskin, Joshua, (Maine,) lot 81, N. T , farmer 92.

Hatfield, Horatio, (East Maine,) lot 73, G. D., farmer 84.

Hathaway, David, (Maine,) resident.

HATHAWAY, GEORGE J , (Maine,) lot 51, G. D., farmer 87

Hathaway, Horace E , (Maine,) hotel keeper

Hayes, Michael, (East Maine,) lot 8, G. D., farmer 150.

Hayes, Patrick, (Maine,) lot 38, G. D , farmer 80

Hayes Roger, (East Maine,) lot 7, G. D , farmer 84

Hayes, William, (Binghamton,) lot 108, C T., farmer 65

Haywood W T Rev , (Maine,) pastor Congregational Church

Heath, Alva, (Union Center,) lot 73, N T , farmer 36

*HEATH & NORTON, (Maine,) rake factory, manufa fork, hoe and broom handles, wood turning, planing &c.

Hennessey, John, (East Maine,) lot 58, C T , farmer 50.

Highee, Chancellor L., (Hooper,) lot 71, N. T , farmer 140

Higby, Edward, (Hooper,) lot 83, N T . farmer 50

Hinman, Asaph M., (Maine,) lot 79, N T., farmer 152

HOGG, JAMES 2ND, (East Maine,) lot 47, G D., farmer 62.

HOGG, JAMES G (West Chenango,) lot 47, G D., farmer leases of James, 80

Hogg, Robert, (East Maine,) lot 48, G D , carpenter and farmer 27

Hogg, Robert 2nd, (East Maine,) lot 74, G D , farmer 130.

Hogg, Robert 3rd, (East Maine,) lot 74, G. D , farmer 61.

HOGG, WILLIAM, (East Maine,) lot 47, G D , justice of the peace and farmer 96

HOGG, WILLIAM 2ND, (East Maine,) lot 48, G. D , farmer 95.

Holbrook William, (Maine,) lot 171, G D , farmer 100.

Holden, Oren, (Maine,) lot 12, G D , music teacher and farmer leases of Horatio Stevens, 150

Holdrege, Charles H , (East Maine,) lot 9, G D shoemaker.

Howard, Benjamin, (Hooper,) lot 72, N T , farmer leases of Youngs Van Wormer, 188

HOWARD. JAMES M., (Maine,) lot 22, N. T , farmer 123

HOWARD, SAMUEL S , (West Chenango,) lot 87, G D., farmer 103

Howard, Stephen S , (Union Center,) lot 98, N. T , wagon maker and farmer 83.

Hughson Joel, (Maine,) lot 80, N T , farmer 95.

Hull & Brown, (Maine,) (Douglas W Hull and Norman P. Brown,) hardware, stoves, tinware &c

Hull, Douglas W (Maine,) (Hull & Brown )

Hullander, William H., (Maine,) lot 70, G. D., wagon maker

Hydin, Henry, (Maine,) lot 190, G D., farmer 63.

Hydin, John H , (Lamb's Corners,) lot 211, G D , farmer 30

Ingerson Lewis H., (East Maine ) lot 84, N T , farmer 48.

Jackson, Jonathan C., (East Maine,) lot 54, C T , farmer 64.

Johnson, Amasa, (West Chenango,) lot 34, G D , farmer 68

Johnson, George W , (Maine,) shoemaker.

Johnson, Jared T., (Maine,) lot 92, G D., farmer 50

Johnson, Watson A., (West Chenango,) lot 34, G D farmer 68½

Johnson, William R , (West Chenango,) lot 6, G D., farmer 124

Keeler, Hiram K , (Union Center,) lot 98 N T , farmer 15.

Kelley, George W , (Maine,) lot 10, G D., farmer 55.

Kelly, Daniel. (East Maine,) lot 82, C T , farmer 139

KELSEY, SYLVESTER, (Maine,) night watchman at tannery.

*KETCHUM, EPHRAIM, (Maine,) prop of Ketchum's Hotel and horse dealer

Ketchum, Lewis, (Union Center,) lot 155, N. T., farmer 300.

Kinitick John, (Binghamton,) lot 108, C T., farmer 48

Knapp Joseph E , (Union Center,) lot 98, N T , farmer 15.

Knapp, Peter, (West Chenango ) lot 127, G D , farmer 870

Knapp, William M , (Union Center ) lot 97, N T , farmer 68.

Laehier, Aaron, (Maine,) lot 23, N. T , farmer 40.

LAYTON, JOHN, (West Chenango,) lot 113, G D , farmer 118

Layton, Shedrick, (Lamb's Corners,) lot 211, G D , farmer leases of Enos Norton, 109

Leadbetter, Mortimer, (East Maine,) lot 78, N. T , farmer 85

LEADBETTER WILLIAM L , (East Maine,) lot 78, N. T , shingle maker and farmer 114

LeBarron, Sylvester, (Union Center,) lot 75, farmer 64

LeBarron, William, (Union Center,) lot 15, N. T., farmer 7.

Lee, James N Rev , (Maine,) pastor M E. Church

Lewis, Benjamin F , (Maine,) lot 30, N T., farmer 110

Lewis, Charles, (Maine,) lot 69, G. D., farmer 81

Lewis, Eliza Mrs , (widow ) (Maine,) lot 52, G D., farmer 175

Lewis, Judson, (Maine,) lot 111, farmer 120.

Lincoln, William & Son, (Maine,) general merchants

Livingston, John R , (Maine,) lot 89, N T., farmer 18

LIVINGSTON, WM , (Campville, Tioga Co.,) auctioneer and farmer

Loomis, Anson, (Maine,) lot 171, G D , farmer 125

LOOMIS, GEORGE A., (Maine,) lot 150, G D farmer 46

Lotton, George, (Maine,) lot 31, G D , farmer 185

LOTTON, THEODORE T , (Maine,) lot 31, G. D , farmer 163

Malane, David, (Binghamton,) lot 183, C T. farmer 50.

Malone, Martin, (East Maine,) lot 81, C T , farmer 50.

Maples, Alexander, (Maine,) lot 91, N T , farmer 90

Maples Daniel, (Maine,) lot 50, G. D., farmer 80

Marean, Chester, (Maine,) lot 71, G D., farmer 100.

Marean, Francis H , (Maine,) (F H. Marean & Son,) postmaster

Marean, F H & Son, (Maine,) general merchants

Marean, Jason, (Maine,) lot 11, G. D., farmer 48

Marean, Thomas, (Maine,) lot 50, G D , farmer 90

Marean, William A , (Maine,) lot 152, G D farmer 102

Matterson, Atwell, (East Maine,) lot 8, G D., cooper

McGowan, John, (East Maine,) lot 78, N. T., farmer 94

McGregor, James B., (Maine,) mason and farmer 4

McIntyre Franklin F , (Maine,) lot 189, G. D farmer 147

McINTYRE MART H., (Maine,) lot 212, G D., prop. of saw mill and farmer 3

Meeker, Joseph L., (Union Center,) lot 155, N T , farmer 50

Merrick, George W , (Maine,) lot 171, G. D., farmer 50

MERRILL, PHILANDER, (Maine,) lot 212, G. D., farmer 46.

Mersereau, David, (Maine,) lot 16, N T., farmer 65.

MILLER, DAVID W , (Maine,) lot 29, G D , prop. of wagon shop and farmer 30.

Moak, Baltis H , (Maine,) lot 72, G. D , farmer 47

MOAK, JOHN, (East Maine,) lot 52, C T, carpenter and farmer 7
MOOERS, EDWARD N., (Maine,) lot 30, G. D, farmer 41.
MOORES, JUSTICE E., (Maine,) lot 10, G D., mason, carpenter and farmer 120
Moore, Haman W., (Union Center,) lot 97, N. T, blacksmith and farmer 11
Morgan, Dennis, (Maine,) lot 212, G D, butcher and farmer 6.
Murtch, Joshua, (East Maine,) lot 9, G. D., farmer 50
Newton, Aaron D., (Maine,) lot 93, N. T., farmer 43
NOOSBICKEL, JACOB, (Maine,) lot 128, G. D., farmer 68.
North, Arthur, (East Maine,) lot 33, G D, farmer 50.
NORTH ARTHUR W, (East Maine,) lot 55, C. T, farmer 140
NORTON, D. C., (Maine,) (*Heath & Norton*)
Norton. Eliza, (widow,) (Union Center,) lot 51, N. T., farmer 30.
Norton, Geo E, (Maine,) lot 51, G D, carriage maker.
O'Brien, Patrick, (Binghamton,) lot 50, C T, farmer 44
OLIVER, WILLIAM, (Maine,) lot 212, G D, farmer 26
OLIVER, WILLIAM N, (Union Center,) lot 176, N T, farmer leases of Mrs. L Smith, 60.
Omans, William R, (Maine,) lot 211, G. D, farmer 125
PACKARD, IRA B, (Binghamton,) lot 114, C. T., farmer 65.
Paisely, William, (West Chenango,) lot 74, G D., farmer 72.
PAISLEY, FRANK, (West Chenango,) lot 87, G. D, farmer 80.
Parker, Lester, (East Maine,) lot 52, C. T., farmer 100.
Parsons, Timothy, (Maine,) lot 22, N T, farmer 128.
Parsons, Walter L., (Maine,) lot 22, N T, farmer occupies 128
Payne, Almon R, (East Maine,) lot 53, C. T, farmer 100.
Payne, Chancey, (Maine,) shoemaker.
Pender, Daniel, (Binghamton,) lot 91, C T, farmer 100.
PERRY, DAVID B., (West Chenango,) lot 87, G D, farmer 52
Perry, Sylvanus, (West Chenango,) lot 87, G. D, farmer 90
Phillips, Milton, (Maine,) lot 52, G. D., farmer leases of G. Councilman, 60
Phipps, Levi, (Maine,) lot 110, G. D., farmer 160
Phipps, Samuel, (Maine,) lot 149, G D, farmer 48.
Pier, James M., (Maine,) lot 132, G. D., saw mill and farmer 57.
Pier, John, (Maine,) lot 132, G. D., farmer 128
PIERSON, LEWIS M, (West Chenango,) lot 74, G D, farmer 19
Pitcher, Elias, (Maine,) lot 31, G D, farmer 70.
Pitcher, Jeremiah, (Maine,) lot 92, G D, farmer 270.
Pitkin, Frederick, (Union Center,) lot 19, N. T., farmer 100

Pitkin, Nathan U, (Union Center,) lot 16, N T, farmer 100
PITKIN, WILBER, (Union Center,) lot 75, N. T, farmer 50
Pitkin, William A, (Union Center,) lot 20, N. T., farmer 64
Place, Richard, (Maine,) lot 12, G. D, farmer 124
Pollard L & Son, (Maine,) saw mill
POLLARD, WILLIAM C., (Maine,) lumberman.
Pope, Edgar, (Maine,) lot 151, G. D., constable and farmer occupies 128.
POPE, SAMUEL, (Maine,) lot 151, G. D., farmer 128
Pulsipher, Araunah, (Union Center,) lot 98, N. T, farmer 3
Ransom, Jefferson, (Maine,) wagon maker
Rhodes, George, (East Maine,) lot 9, G. D, farmer 74.
RIDDELL, JAMES, (Maine,) lot 48, G D, farmer 75
Riley, George W, (Maine,) lot 72, G. D, carpenter and farmer 68
RING, JOHN N., (Maine,) justice of the peace, notary public and conveyancer.
Robins, Daniel, (Maine,) lot 16, N. T, farmer 20.
Robinson, Darius, (Union Center,) lot 98, N. T, farmer 23
Robinson, Ebenezer, (Maine,) lot 112, G. D, farmer 100
Robinson, Harley, (Union Center,) lot 98, N T, farmer 65
Robinson, John, (Union Center,) lot 74, N T., farmer 38.
Robinson, John A., (Union Center,) lot 98, N T, carpenter.
Rockwell, George C., (Union Center,) lot 25, N T, farmer 64.
Rockwell, Timothy, (Maine,) lot 82, N. T., farmer 66
Ross, Alexander, (Maine,) lot 210, G D, tannery and farmer 9.
Rozell, Charles F., (Maine,) lot 130, G. D., farmer 80
Rozell, Henry, (Maine,) farmer 100
RUSSELL, BENJAMIN R, (Union Center,) lot 76, N. T., farmer 10.
Russell, Charles, (Union Center,) lot 73, N. T., farmer 32.
Russell, Oliver, (Hooper,) lot 76, N. T., farmer 44.
Sayrles, Luke, (Maine,) lot 171, G. D., saw mill and farmer 4
Schermerhorn, Simon, (Binghamton,) lot 133, C T, farmer 50
Seabury, Job, (East Maine,) lot 53, C. T., farmer 48
Searles, Nelson, (Lamb's Corners,) lot 211, G D, farmer 54
Shafer, Charles, (Binghamton,) lot 111, C T, farmer 64
SHAFER, GEORGE W., (East Maine,) lot 112, C T, farmer 29
Shafer, Peter C., (East Maine,) lot 88, C T., supervisor and farmer 160.
Sherwood, William H., (Maine,) (*Church & Sherwood*)
Sherwood, —, (Maine,) (*Allison & Sherwood*)
SHIPPEY, ISAAC C., (Maine,) lot 51, G D, dealer in dry goods, groceries &c.

SLADE, FRANK M., (Maine,) lot 51, G D., practical horse shoer and farrier

Slosson, Giles, (Maine,) (*with Henry W.,*) lot 172 G D, farmer 122.

Slosson, Henry W, (Maine,) (*with Giles,*) lot 172, G D, farmer 122

Slosson, Silas B., (Choconut Center,) lot 119, C T., farmer 75

Smith, Burr H, (Maine,) lot 95, N. T, farmer 64.

Smith, Charles C, (Maine,) lot 171, G D, farmer 170.

Smith, George B., (Maine,) lot 94, N T., farmer 113.

Smith, Isaac J, (Castle Creek,) lot 114, G D, farmer 39

Snediker, Rachel Mrs, (widow,) (Union Center) lot 25, N T, farmer 54

Soper, Clarissa Mrs, (widow,) (West Chenango,) lot 58, C T, farmer

Southerland, Henry N., (Maine,) lot 174, N T, farmer 124

Stalker, Alsom, (Glen Aubrey,) lot 169, G D., farmer 70

Stevenson, Sanford, (Maine) blacksmith

Swift, Alonzo, (Castle Creek,) lot 114, G D, farmer 50

Swift, Solomon, (Maine) (*with John E. Van Tuyl,*) lot 52, G D, farmer 64.

Taylor Bros, (Maine,) (*R. D and B L,*) general merchants

Taylor, B L, (Maine,) (*Taylor Bros*)

Taylor, James, (Maine,) lot 149, G D., cattle dealer and farmer 50.

Taylor, R D, (Maine,) (*Taylor Bros*)

Taylor, Zarah S Mrs (widow,) (Maine,) lot 91, G D, farmer 120

Thorn, Franklin, (Maine,) lot 51, G. D., farmer 85

Toby, James D., (Union Center) lot 163, N. T, farmer 32

Totten, George, (Maine,) lot 11, G D, farmer 4

Totten, Walter, (Maine) lot 191, G D, farmer 37

Tracy, Levi, (West Chenango,) lot 47, G. D., farmer 15.

Travers, Adonijah, (Binghamton,) lot 116, C T, farmer 100.

TRIPP, GEORGE H, (Maine,) lot 12, G. D., stone mason, builder and farmer 8

Tripp, James A, (Union Center,) lot 167, N T, millwright and farmer 32.

Turner, George, (Union Center,) lot 161, N. T, farmer 9

Twining, William F, (Binghamton,) lot 87. C. T, farmer 54

Updegrove, Franklin, (East Maine,) lot 8, G D., wagon maker

Van Tuyl, Henry, (Maine,) lot 70, G D., farmer 66.

Van Tuyl, John E, (Maine,) (*with Solomon Swift,*) lot 52, G. D., farmer 64.

Van Tuyl, Marvin A, (Maine,) lot 129, G D, farmer 83

Walter, Alvin, (Maine,) lot 21, N T, farmer 91

Walter, Horace, (Glen Aubrey,) lot 192, G D, farmer 165.

Walter, Mark, (Maine,) lot 21, N T., farmer 54

Ward, Francis E, (Maine,) wheelwright

Webb, David B., (West Chenango,) lot 80, C. T, basket maker and farmer 3.

Webb, Geo W, (Maine,) lot 190, G D, farmer leases 53

Wescoat, David, (Union Center,) lot 155, N T, farmer leases 120

Wescott, David, (Union Center,) farmer 128

Westcott, Nicholas, (Union Center) lot 150, N. T, saw mill and farmer 128

Wheat, Mahlon, (Maine,) lot 191, G D, carpenter and farmer 9

WHEELER, HARMAN L, (Hooper,) lot 77, N. T., farmer 50

Wheton Calvin, (Binghamton,) lot 110, C T, farmer 50

Wiles, David, (Maine,) lot 90, G D, mechanic and farmer 16

Willis, Abner, (Union Center,) lot 14, N T., farmer 68

Wilson, Barlow, (Maine,) lot 109, G. D., farmer 100

Wilson, John, (Maine,) lot 110, G D, farmer 78

Wilson, Joseph B., (Maine,) lot 72, G D, farmer 135

Wintfield, Tyrus, (West Chenango,) lot 87, G D, farmer 6.

WOOD, JOHN A Rev, (Maine,) pastor of M E Church.

Woodward, William W., (Maine,) lot 189, G. D., farmer 100

Wooster, Jasper, (Union Center,) lot 13, N T, farmer 100

Worrick, David A, (Union Center,) lot 98, N T, farmer 50

WRIGHT, ADDISON, (Binghamton,) lot 135, C T, farmer 150

Wright, Harvey, (Maine,) lot 90, N T, farmer 70

Wright, Norman W., (Maine,) lot 91, G D, farmer 156.

Wright, William, (East Maine,) lot 113, C T, farmer 107

Youmans, James T. Rev., (Glen Aubrey,) lot 192, G D, clergyman

Younger, Elias, (Union Center,) lot 163, N T, saw mill and farmer 80

Zhe, Charles A, (Maine,) lot 132, G D, farmer leases of George Congdon, 52

ZHE, NICHOLAS, (Maine,) lot 189, G D, farmer 65.

# NANTICOKE.

(Post Office Addresses in Parentheses.)

Adams. Elijah R , (Lamb's Corners,) lot 287, farmer 100.

Adams, Mason, (Glen Aubrey,) lot 314, farmer 253

Adriance, James Edward, (Glen Aubrey,) lot 193, saw and turning mills, and farmer 12

Adriance, John W., (Glen Aubrey,) lot 193, farmer 110

ADRIANCE, STEPHEN H , (Glen Aubrey,) lot 234, general blacksmith and farmer 88

Adriance, Thomas Jefferson,(Glen Aubrey,) lot 206, farmer 30

Ahern, Patrick M , (Whitney's Point,) lot 357, farmer 120.

Ames. John, (Glen Aubrey,) lot 285, farmer 50

Ames, Sidney, (Glen Aubrey,) lot 208, retired farmer

Andrews, Henry. (Lamb's Corners,) lot 271, farmer 6

Arnold, Jerry, (Ketchumville, Tioga Co ,) lot 291, farmer 112

Balch, James B., (Lamb's Corners,) lot 231, farmer 220.

Baldwin, Levi, (Lamb's Corners,) lot 289, farmer 140.

Baldwin, Levi H., (Lamb's Corners,) lot 289, farmer 98

Ballard, Daniel, (Lamb's Corners,) lot 329, farmer leases 100.

Ballard, Gardner, (Lamb's Corners,) lot 329. saw mill and farmer 207

BARNHARDT, GEORGE, (Glen Aubrey,) lot 208, farmer 83

Barnhardt, Philip V , (Glen Aubrey,) lot 208, farmer occupies 83.

Barns, Nathan, (Whitney's Point,) lot 315, farmer 194

Bauder, Edward S., (Lamb's Corners,) lot 271, deputy sheriff.

Bauder, Maryett, (widow,) (Lamb's Corners,) lot 271, farmer 6

BAUDER, MICHAEL, (Lamb's Corners,) lot 271, coroner and general blacksmith.

BROOKS, L LAROY, (Lamb's Corners,) lot 271, general merchant, shipper of all kinds of produce, justice of the peace, notary public and post master.

BROWN, CLARISSA, (widow,) (Whitney's Point,) lot 285, farmer 40

Brown, Daniel, (Whitney's Point,) lot 324, farmer 80

BROWN, EDWARD, (Lisle,) lot 365, farmer 92.

Burdick, Lewis, (Glen Aubrey,) farmer leases.

Burke, Patrick, (Whitney's Point,) lot 317, farmer 71.

Bush, George C., (Lamb's Corners,) lot 250, farmer 56

BUSH, GEORGE W., (Lamb's Corners,) lot 314, farmer 52

Cady. Corelli, (Lamb's Corners,) lot 271, farmer 131.

Cady, Dwight T., (Ketchumville, Tioga Co. ) lot 270, farmer 115

Cady, Jariel J., (Glen Aubrey,) lot 235, farmer 100

Cary, Thomas, (Lamb's Corners,) lot 271, farmer 10

Cavanaugh, Edward, (Glen Aubrey ) lot 233, farmer 37

Collard, Horace B., (Lamb's Corners,) lot 314, farmer 52.

Coassart, James L , (Glen Aubrey,) lot 208, blacksmith and farmer 4

COUNCILMAN, GEORGE, (Glen Aubrey,) lot 246, farmer 70

Councilman, James C., (Glen Aubrey,) lot 234, farmer 79.

Councilman, Nathan J., (Lamb's Corners,) lot 271, farmer 70

Councilman, Silas T., (Lamb's Corners,) lot 326, farmer 74.

Couse, John C., (Glen Aubrey,) lot 208, farmer 65

COUSE, ORVILLE E , (Glen Aubrey,) lot 208, dealer in groceries, dry goods, notions &c , and notary public

Davern, James, (Lamb's Corners,) lot 270, farmer 60

Dent, Samuel, (Glen Aubrey,) lot 247, farmer 83

Dodge, Lovel P., (Glen Aubrey,) lot 247, farmer 16.

Driscoll, Cornelius, (Whitney's Point,) lot 364, farmer 76

Driscoll, Cornelius Jr , (Whitney's Point,) lot 316, farmer 80

Driscoll, Jeremiah, (Whitney's Point,) lot 317, farmer 142

Driscoll, Michael, (Whitney's Point,) lot 316, farmer 80.

Dunham, Albert H., (Glen Aubrey,) lot 194, farmer 65

Dunham Amy, (widow,) (Glen Aubrey,) lot 167, farmer 150.

Dunham, Charles F., (Glen Aubrey,) lot 167, farmer 4

Dunham George M , (Glen Aubrey,) lot 167, farmer 32.

Dunham, George W., (Glen Aubrey,) lot 194, farmer 260.

Dunham, Theron W ,(Glen Aubrey,) lot 208, justice of the peace, mason and mechanic

Dunham, Willis W , (Glen Aubrey,) lot 167, mechanic and farmer 51.

Dyer, Alexander, (Glen Aubrey,) lot 287, shingle maker and farmer occupies 50

Dyer, Dexter, (Glen Aubrey,) lot 208, mason.

DYER, GEORGE, (Lamb's Corners,) lot 273 farmer 110

Dyer, Jackson, (Glen Aubrey,) lot 206, farmer 30

Dyer, Peter, (Glen Aubrey,) lot 286, farmer leases 86.

EDWARDS, DeRONDA, (Lamb's Corners,) lot 327, commissioner of highways and farmer 92.

Elliott, Horace, (Lamb's Corners,) lot 327, farmer leases 68

English, Eli, (Whitney's Point,) lot 315, farmer leases of Alonzo Collins, 250

EVERETT, DANIEL T ,(Whitney's Point,) lot 285, farmer 123

Everetts, Egbert N , (Whitney's Point,) lot 285, farmer 50.

French, Jonathan D , (Whitney's Point,) lot 286, farmer 14

Fuller, Orlando R., (Lamb's Corners,) lot 288, farmer 128

Gates, Lewis, (Ketchumville, Tioga Co.,) lot 230, cooper and farmer 8.

Gaylord, David, (Glen Aubrey,) lot 208, farmer 22

GAYLORD, HENRY, (Glen Aubrey,) lot 207, farmer 60.

Gaylord, John, (Glen Aubrey,) lot 234, farmer 22.

Green, Abraham H , (Maine,) lot 154, grist mill and farmer 210

Green, John H., (Maine,) lot 154, farmer 50

Griggs, Frederick S , (Whitney's Point,) lot 356, farmer 270

Griggs, Reuben C , (Lamb's Corners,) lot 327, farmer 180

Hall, James G , (Lamb's Corners,) lot 270, physician and farmer 75.

Harris, Luther R , (Glen Aubrey,) lot 153, farmer 81.

Hartwell, Albert, (Lamb's Corners,) lot 271, carpenter

Hartwell, Archibauld, (Lamb's Corners,) lot 271, farmer 50

Hawver, Abraham P., (Glen Aubrey,) lot 208, justice of the peace, carpenter and farmer 114

Hawver, Peter A , (Glen Aubrey,) lot 287, farmer 70

Hicks, Spencer, (Glen Aubrey,) lot 234, farmer 37.

Hinman, David D , (Glen Aubrey,) lot 235, farmer 50.

Hinman, Solomon, (Glen Aubrey,) lot 285, farmer 3

HODGES, HENRY, (Glen Aubrey,) lot 274, farmer 120

HOLDEN, DALLAS, (Lamb's Corners,) lot 271, wagon maker

Horton, Edgar F., (Lisle,) lot 365, farmer 76.

Houghtaling, John C , (Glen Aubrey,) lot 234, carpenter and farmer 6

Howard, Chauncey K , (Glen Aubrey,) lot 208, farmer 3.

Ingraham, Hiram O , (Glen Aubrey,) lot 274, farmer 30.

Jay, Theda, (widow,) (Glen Aubrey,) lot 153, farmer 41

JOHNSON, WASHINGTON, (Lamb's Corners,) lot 250, prop of saw, planing and grist mills, and farmer 30

Kenyon, Joseph, (Glen Aubrey,) lot 248, farmer 137.

Kenyon, Samuel, (Glen Aubrey,) lot 234, farmer 43

Ketchum, Riley, (Lamb's Corners,) lot 329, carpenter

King, Jewitt, (Glen Aubrey,) lot 207, farmer 35.

Lamb, Isaac T., (Lamb's Corners,) lot 272, farmer 82.

Leonard, Charles R , (Lamb's Corners,) lot 272, carpenter and farmer 48

Lewis, Gilbert, (Ketchumville, Tioga Co ,) lot 230, carpenter and farmer 100.

Loomis, Burton, (Ketchumville, Tioga Co.,) lot 270, farmer 77

Maloney, Patrick, (Glen Aubrey,) lot 285, farmer 31

Manwaring, Charles B , (Lamb's Corners,) lot 327, farmer 70.

Manwaring, Edgar C , (Lamb's Corners,) lot 313, farmer 80

Marean, Vincent, (Glen Aubrey,) lot 168, farmer 100

Marks, James A., (Lisle,) lot 365, farmer 72.

McConnell, John, (Ketchumville, Tioga Co.,) *(with William,)* lot 310, farmer 40.

McConnell, William, (Ketchumville, Tioga Co ,) *(with John,)* lot 310, farmer 40

MONROE, ERASTUS, (Lamb's Corners,) lot 288, farmer 96

Monroe, Harrison, (Lamb's Corners,) farmer leases of Florence Potter, 120.

Monroe, Samuel E , (Lamb's Corners,) lot 271, saw mill, carpenter and farmer 16

Morgan, Elisa H , (Lamb's Corners,) lot 288, farmer leases 197

Morgan, George W., (Lamb's Corners,) lot 271, carpenter and farmer 16.

Morgan, Merca C , (widow,) (Lamb's Corners,) lot 288, farmer 197.

Morgan, Roswell, (Lamb's Corners,) lot 250, farmer 36.

Morgan, Waldo, (Lamb's Corners,) lot 250, farmer 20.

Morgan, William B., (Lamb's Corners,) lot 288, constable and farmer occupies 197.

Murray, Murty, (Lamb's Corners,) lot 290, farmer 83

O'Neill, Patrick, (Whitney's Point,) lot 324, farmer 110.

Pendell, Warren, (Whitney's Point,) lot 358, farmer 100.

Perkins, Addison, (Lamb's Corners,) lot 271, farmer 50.

Perry, George, (Whitney's Point,) lot 286, farmer 165.

Phillips, Charles, (Lamb's Corners,) lot 271, farmer 200

Phillips, Waterman R., (Lamb's Corners,) lot 372, farmer 43

Pierce, Sherman, (Glen Aubrey,) lot 275, farmer leases of James E. Vanderburgh, 25.

Pierce, William H., (Glen Aubrey,) lot 275, farmer 84.

Pollard, Nosh, (Lamb's Corners,) lot 271, farmer 60.

Pollard, Timothy, (Lamb's Corners,) lot 329 farmer 200

POTTER, FLORENCE A., (Lamb's Corners,) lot 288, farmer 120

Preston, James S., (Glen Aubrey,) lot 247, farmer 58

QUICK ABRAHAM H, (Glen Aubrey,) lot 208, general blacksmith and farmer 13.

Quinliven, James, (Lamb's Corners,) lot 290, farmer 77.

Quinliven, Patrick, (Ketchumville, Tioga Co.,) lot 290, farmer 57.

Reardon, Jeremiah, (Whitney's Point,) lot 364, farmer 120

Remmele, Hariet, (Whitney's Point,) lot 274, farmer 61

Reynolds, Jesse W., (Lamb's Corners,) lot 311, farmer 62

Reynolds, LeRoy, (Lamb's Corners,) lot 339, farmer leases 21

RICHARDS, LOYAL, (Glen Aubrey,) lot 286, farmer 125

Richards, Nathan, (Glen Aubrey,) lot 286, farmer 71

Richards, William, (Whitney's Point,) lot 286, farmer 130

Rigby, Marcus E., (Lamb's Corners,) lot 250, farmer 133.

RILEY, WILLIAM H, (Glen Aubrey,) lot 208, supervisor of town, postmaster, dealer in groceries, dry goods, boots, shoes &c.

Ryan, Matthew, (Ketchumville, Tioga Co.,) lot 230, farmer 80

Ryan, William, (Lamb's Corners,) lot 270, farmer 60

Sanford, John, (Glen Aubrey,) lot 153, farmer 41.

Sarringar, Albert M., (Lamb's Corners,) lot 213, dentist and farmer 48.

Sciam, Naomi, (widow,) (Glen Aubrey,) lot 273, farmer 50.

Shanley, John, (Glen Aubrey,) lot 233, farmer 85

Simkins, Nelson A., (Glen Aubrey,) lot 247, farmer 31

Slack, Delilah, (widow,) (Whitney's Point,) lot 247 farmer 200.

SLACK. HIRAM W, (Whitney's Point,) lot 324, prop. of saw mill and farmer 160

Slack, Nathan, (Whitney's Point,) lot 285, farmer 25

Slack, Samantha, (widow,) (Glen Aubrey,) lot 208, farmer 43

Sly, George, (Glen Aubrey,) lot 208, shoemaker and farmer 25

Smith, Benjamin F., (Glen Aubrey,) lot 273, farmer 68

Smith, Charles, (Glen Aubrey,) lot 207, farmer 110.

Smith, Charles, (Lamb's Corners,) lot 231, farmer 114

Smith, Chester M., (Glen Aubrey,) lot 247, farmer 54.

Smith, Elijah, (Glen Aubrey,) lot 206, farmer 70.

Smith, George A., (Glen Aubrey,) lot 233, farmer 57

Smith, Henry, (Lamb's Corners,) lot 271, farmer 250

Smith, John L, (Lamb's Corners,) lot 311, farmer 50

SMITH, THOMAS, (Glen Aubrey,) lot 233, farmer 77

Snyder, William H, (Lamb's Corners,) lot 327, farmer 31.

Spencer, Enoch, (Lamb's Corners,) lot 311, farmer 162

Spencer, Morgan, (Lamb's Corners,) lot 313, farmer 70

SPORE, GEORGE E, (Whitney's Point,) lot 363, farmer 4.

STALKER, ADAM R., (Whitney's Point,) lot 363, carpenter and joiner

Stalker, Charles, (Whitney's Point,) lot 363, carpenter and farmer 11.

Stevens, Emeline, (widow,) (Lamb's Corners,) lot 271, farmer 10

STODDARD, CHARLES H, (Glen Aubrey,) (*with James B.,*) lot 208, farmer 140.

STODDARD, JAMES B, (Glen Aubrey,) (*with Charles H,*) lot 208, farmer 140

STRAIT, WILLIAM, (Whitney's Point,) lot 323, farmer leases of John Hazelton, 117.

Sutphen, Christian, (widow,) (Lamb's Corners,) lot 287, farmer 72,

Sutphen, Phelon E, (Lamb's Corners,) lot 287, town clerk and farmer occupies 72

Swan, Charles, (Glen Aubrey,) lot 275, farmer 25.

Swan, John, (Glen Aubrey,) lot 246, farmer 12.

SWAN, WILLIAM, (Glen Aubrey,) lot 275, farmer 25.

Sweeney, Edmund, (Lamb's Corners,) lot 290, farmer 50

Tanner, Lorenzo D, (Glen Aubrey,) lot 208, retired merchant and farmer 8

Taylor, Charles R, (Ketchumville, Tioga Co.,) lot 311, farmer 97

Tompkins, Chloe, (widow,) (Whitney's Point,) lot 365, farmer 70

Tompkins, Oryin F., (Whitney's Point,) lot 365, farmer 50

Torpy, John, (Glen Aubrey,) lot 249, farmer 75

Toll, Nehemiah, (Glen Aubrey,) lot 275, farmer 25

TYLER, SHERMAN D., (Lisle,) lot 326, farmer 98.

Vandeburgh, George W, (Glen Aubrey,) lot 246, farmer 71

VANDEBURGH, STEPHEN P, (Glen Aubrey,) lot 246, farmer 146

WALTER, BENJAMIN F, (Whitney's Point,) lot 363, farmer 184

WALTER, CHARLES J, (Whitney's Point,) lot 357, town assessor and farmer 205

Walters, James P., (Whitney's Point,) (*with William W,*) lot 363, farmer 166.

Walters, William W., (Whitney's Point,) (*with James P,*) lot 363, farmer 166

Warner, Joshua L, (Glen Aubrey,) lot 286, saw mill and farmer 2

Wilson, Albert A, (Lisle,) lot 365, farmer 50.

Wilson, Eliza M., (widow,) (Lisle,) lot 365, farmer 49.

Woods, James, (Glen Aubrey,) lot 233, farmer 135

Youngs, William, (Lamb's Corners,) lot 289, farmer 51.

# SANFORD.

(Post Office Addresses in Parentheses.)

ABBREVIATIONS—D T , Delaware Tract; W P , Wate Patent, W T , Watson Tract; E. T., Edgar Tract. C L , Carpenter Location, F & N T , Fisher & Norton Tract R T , Randolph Township ; L T 1, Livingston Tract. No. 1 ; L T 2, Livingston Tract, No 2 , L T 3, Livingston Tract, No 3 ; M. T , McClure Tract; L T , N. P.. Lane Tract. Nichols Patent ; N T , Norton Tract; S L , State Lands; G & S L . Gospel and School Lot ; L L , Literature Lot , Sub , Subdivision

*For Directory of Deposit Village, see page 227.*

Ahrens, John, (Sanford,) great lot 16, F & N T , farmer 140
Alexander, George, (McClure Settlement,) farmer occupies 87.
Alexander, Philip, (Deposit,) farmer 75½
Alexander, Sydney B , (Hale's Eddy. Delaware Co.,) sub, 1, D. T., farmer 67.
Allen, Elbert (Gulf Summit,) great lot 13, F & N T , farmer leases of Abram Mattice 87
Ames, Marcus (Sanford ) farmer 106
Aplington, Nathan, (Vallonia Springs,) lot 13, L T & justice of the peace. farmer 60 and (with James Hawkins) 186
ATWELL, EDWARD, (Gulf Summit,) L T , N P , prop of circular saw mill and farmer 173
ATWELL, RUMMER H., (Gulf Summit,) L T, N P, farmer 86
Austin Estate, (Deposit ) (Chas and Geo. Austin and Geo. Ray,) great lot 20, F. & N T , farmer 226
Austin, E L , (Deposit,) great lot 17, F. & N. T , farmer 600.
Austin, Geo , (Deposit,) farmer 60
Austin, G L , (Deposit,) great lot 17, F & N. T , farmer 112
BAGLEY, GEO W , (Sanford,) great lot 6, F & N T , farmer 82.½
Bailey, Nathan, (Sanford,) farmer 50.
Baker, D J , (Sanford,) lot 81, L. T 1, farmer 117.
Baker, Geo , (Sanford,) lot 22, L T 2, farmer 173
Baker, Geo D , (Sanford,) farmer 73
BAKER J W , (Hale's Eddy, Delaware Co ,) C L., farmer 100.
BARNETT, LEWIS E , (Center Village,) G & S L , farmer 81
Barringer, Myron, (Hale's Eddy, Delaware Co ,) sub 5, D T , farmer 30
Baskerville, William, (Deposit,) farmer 102.
Bathrich, N S , (Sanford,) great lot 11, F. & N T., farmer 40
Baughan, John, (Deposit,) nightwatch on E R R and farmer 50
Beadle, Abram, (North Sanford,) sub 41, L T 2, farmer 60.
Beers, N G , (Deposit,) cabinet maker, painter and farmer 25.

Bice, Henry, (Deposit,) great lot 24, F. & N T , farmer 75
BILBY, G H , (Deposit,) great lot 21, F & N. T., farmer 350.
BILBY, SAMUEL, (Sanford,) great lot 11. F & N T , commissioner of highways and farmer leases of J. Bragg, 404
Biley, Daniel, (Sanford,) lot 40, L T 1, farmer 175
Bishop, Jacob, (Gulf Summit,) lot 14, W. P., farmer 42
Bishop, W.. (Gulf Summit,) lot 13, W. P, farmer 42
Bixby Brothers, (North Sanford,) (Francis M and Geo W ,) general merchants
Bixby, Francis M , (North Sanford,) (Bixby Brothers,) shoemaker
Bixby, Geo W., (North Sanford,) (Bixby Brothers,) postmaster
Blish, H M , (Gulf Summit,) lot 17, R T., carpenter and farmer 40.
Blowers, Hiram, (North Sanford,) L T 2, farmer 137½
Bodley W. E., (North Sanford,) shoemaker.
BOOTH BOUTON, (Gulf Summit,) lot 24, R T , farmer 165.
Brazie, Cornelius E , (Sanford,) farmer 113.
Bresee Herman, (Deposit,) lot 26, R T., farmer 80
Brewer, James, (Gulf Summit,) farmer 48.
BROAD, OSCAR E , (North Sanford,) lot 41, L T 3, farmer 84
Broad, Porter W., (North Sanford,) lot 54, L. T 3, farmer 115.
Brown, A , (Gulf Summit,) lot 16, W. P., farmer 84.
Brown, Franklin, (Deposit,) sub 10, D T , farmer 160.
Brown, G W , (Deposit,) lot 5, W. P., farmer 99½.
Buchanan, W , (Gulf Summit,) lot 14, W. P , farmer 44
Burke, John, (Deposit,) farmer 130
Burlingame, Lewis, (North Sanford,) lot 26, L T. 2, farmer 100
Burns, Michael, (Deposit,) lot 28, R T., farmer 50
Burrows, Daniel E , (Deposit,) lot W. and D , farmer 19.

BURROWS, ELISHA, (Deposit,) retired carpenter
Burrows, Stephen, (Deposit,) farmer 110
Campbell, A , (North Sanford,) lot 8, L. T. 2 farmer 200
CAMPBELL, DENSMORE, (North Sanford,) lot 38, L T 3, farmer 200
Carawford, Hugh, (Vallonia Springs,) lot 4, L T 2, mechanic and farmer 50.
CASS, E , (Vallonia Springs,) lot 1, L. T 2, owns saw mill and farmer 145
Cass Nahum, (Vallonia Springs,) lot 2, L. T 3, farmer 7.
CASS, VALLMORE, (Vallonia Springs,) (with Nahum,) farmer.
Cheesman, George, (Gulf Summit,) farmer 175
Childs, Henry F , (Sanford,) great lot 15, F & N T , farmer leases 200
CLARK, B F , (Vallonia Springs,) lot 7, L. T. 3, farmer 51¼.
Clark, Benjamin J , (Deposit,) great lot 18, F. & N T., farmer leases of N. K Wheeler, 371
Clark, James H , (McClure Settlement,) farmer 105.
CLENDENING, DAVID H , (Deposit,) great lot 23, F & N T., farmer 60.
Colwell, Benjamin A , (Sanford,) great lot 21 F & N T., farmer 100
COLWELL, LAUREN H., (Sanford ) sub 21, L. T. 1, farmer 94 and leases 93
Colwell, Patrick Thomas, (Sanford,) physician
CONKLIN, N J., (Gulf Summit,) lot 16, R T , farmer leases of Thomas Powell, 122
Conrow, Almeon, (Deposit,) farmer 80 and leases 101.
Conrow, Alpheus, (Hale's Eddy, Delaware Co ,) sub 5, D. T , farmer 83
Conrow, S , (Deposit,) farmer occupies 50
Cornell, F., (Deposit,) lot 28, R T , farmer 25
CORWIN, ALFRED, (Gulf Summit,) lot 25, R T., farmer 35
Corwin, David, (Gulf Summit,) lot 24, R T , farmer 16
Crandall Mark E , (Sanford,) lot 17, L. T. 1 saw mill and farmer 60
CRANE, JOEL, (Sanford,) L. T. 2, farmer 87
CRANE, NELSON, (Sanford,) sub. 50, L T 1, surveyor and farmer 227
Cross, Willard, (North Sanford,) farmer 12
Crumb, C W , (Hale's Eddy, Delaware Co ,) lot 7, E. T . farmer 108½
Crumb, Sylvester, (Deposit,) farmer 53.
CULVER, THOMAS, (Sanford,) grocer and farmer 40.
Cumming, Adelia Miss, (North Sanford,) (with Sabrina and Caroline,) sub 41, L T 2, farmer 103
Cumming, Caroline Miss, (North Sanford,) (with Adelia and Sabrina,) sub. 41, L T 2. farmer 103
Cumming, Sabrina Miss (North Sanford,) (with Adelia and Caroline,) sub 41, L T 2, farmer 103
Cunningham, Simon, (Deposit,) lot 18, R T , farmer 80
Daniels, Chas A , (Deposit,) farmer 165
Darling, Charles, (Deposit,) farmer 80

Darling, H J , (Gulf Summit,) carpenter and builder
Darling, Jeremiah, (Hale s Eddy, Delaware Co ,) sub. 4, D. T. farmer 80.
Dan, Isaac, (Deposit,) lot 2, W P., farmer 75
DEARSTYNE, GEO , (Deposit ) farmer 64
Dearstyne, Henry, (Gulf Summit,) (Decker & Dearstyne )
Dearstyne, Sanford, (Gulf Summit,) lot 23, R T farmer 80.
Decker & Dearstyne, (Gulf Summit,) (Ezra Decker and Henry Dearstyne,) lumbermen and own saw mill
Decker, Ezra, (Gulf Summit,) (Decker & Dearstyne )
Decker, Ezra, (Deposit ) farmer 140
DELANEY, JOHN, (Deposit,) lot 28, R. T, farmer 110
Demeree, Albert, (Vallonia Springs,) lot 23, L T 2, farmer 86
Demeree, Jno, (Sanford,) lot 13, L T 1, farmer 50
Demoney, Duane, (Deposit,) (with Geo D Wheeler,) M T., farmer 320.
Demoney, Henry, (Deposit,) farmer 90.
Denton, Hirum, (North Sanford,) lot 31 L T. 2 farmer 84.
Deyo, Stephen, (Deposit,) great lot 4, F. & N. T , farmer 40
Dibble, Henry, (Gulf Summit,) farmer 40
Dibble, J. A , (Vallonia Springs,) farmer 40
DIMORIER CHARLES, (Sanford,) farmer leases of Mrs Huggins, 212.
Donadson, Samuel, (Sanford,) lot 33, L. T. 2, farmer 350.
Donaldson, James, (Afton, Chenango Co ,) farmer 150
DRESSER, ELIJAH S., (McClure Settlement ) farmer 200.
Dresser, Eugene S , (McClure Settlement,) carpenter and farmer 76
Driggs, Elisha, (Deposit,) lot 28, R T , farmer 50
Dunning, Daniel (McClure Settlement,) carpenter and farmer
DUNNING, MARY H , (McClure Settlement ) lumbering, stone cutting and farmer 200.
Dyson, Henry, (Sanford,) farmer
Edwards, Silas, (McClure Settlement,) farmer leases 54.
Faucher, Smith, (Sanford,) great lot 20, F. & N. T , farmer 44
FANNING, FORD, (Deposit,) farmer 84
FARNHAM, GEO W , (McClure Settlement,) lumberman and farmer 84
FAULKNER, CHAS G , (Deposit,) farmer 80
FERGUSON, HEMAN, (Center Village,) G & S L , farmer 175
Fink, Eli, (North Sanford,) (with J. B. Miller,) farmer.
FINK, MARTIN, (Sanford,) carpenter, lumberman, leases mill of B. F. Wheeler.
Flint, M C , (McClure Settlement,) great lot 7, F & N T , farmer 8
Foley, John, (Deposit ) farmer 32½
FORTNER, LEANDER (McClure Settlement,) great lot 7, F & N. T., farmer 25
FRANK, NICHOLAS, (Deposit ) great lot 19, F and N. T., farmer 70

Freeman, Wm B , (Deposit,) farmer 284.

French, Emerson, (North Sanford,) farmer 100

French, John H , (North Sanford,) farmer

FRENCH, NELSON (North Sanford,) L T 3, dairyman, 40 cows, and farmer 400

French, T A , (McClure Settlement,) carpenter and farmer

French, Thomas H., (McClure Settlement,) farmer 63

Fritts, John W., (Deposit,) farmer leasee of E B McClure, 80.

Fuller, Lydia, (North Sanford,) lot 41, L. T 3, farmer 100.

Gardinier, Abbie, (Deposit,) W T , farmer 225

GARLICK, T H , (Sanford,) lot 28, L. T. 1, farmer 182

Gennings, Geo., (Vallonia Springs,) farmer 40

Gifford, William, (Bennettsville, Chenango Co ,) lot 52, L T 3, farmer 103

Goodenough, Benjamin, (Sanford,) great lot 15, F and N T , farmer 70

Goodrich, Wallace, (Gulf Summit,) lot 17, R T , farmer 29

GRAVES, EDWIN, (Gulf Summit,) lot 17, R. T., farmer 54

Green, G C , (Vallonia Springs,) lot 4, L T 3 farmer 50

Gregory, William, (McClure Settlement,) great lot 13, F & N T , farmer 105

Gregory, W. S., (Deposit,) W P , farmer 50

Hall Harrison, (Gulf Summit,) farmer 9½

HALL, JOEL M , (Gulf Summit,) lot 24, R T , lumberman and farmer 600.

HAMLIN, A E , (North Sanford,) sub 14, L T, 1, farmer 316

HAMLIN A J., (Deposit ) great lot 24, F & N T , farmer 112

Hamlin, A. K Rev , (North Sanford,) Baptist clergyman

HAMLIN GIDEON, (North Sanford,) sub 9, L. T 1, farmer 165.

Hamlin, Wm H., (North Sanford,) L T , farmer 330

Hammond D , (Sanford ) farmer 60.

Hawkins, Giles, (Vallonia Springs,) farmer 40

Hawkins, Heman, (Vallonia Springs,) lot 19, S T 2, supt of poor and farmer 80

HAWKINS, IRA, (McClure Settlement,) great lot 4, F & N T , farmer 210

HAWKINS, JAMES (Vallonia Springs,) lot 18, L T 3, constable, mason and (with Nathan Aplington,) farmer 186.

Hempstead, Prudence, (Gulf Summit,) lot 17, R T farmer 68

Hewitt, Walter, (McClure Settlement,) blacksmith and postmaster

Hill, Chancey L., (Deposit,) farmer 50.

Hill Morris, (Windsor,) L. T., N P., farmer 100

Hitt, Geo , (North Sanford,) sub 28, L T 2, farmer 96

Hitt Geo. A., (North Sanford,) farmer 96

HORTON, JOSEPH T., (Afton, Chenango Co ,) (with William H ,) lot 15, L T 3, farmer 100

HORTON WILLIAM H , (Afton, Chenango Co ,) (with Joseph T.,) lot 15, L T 3, farmer 100

Honae, Wm., (McClure Settlement,) lot 13, N. T , farmer 254

Howe, Alvin R , (Sanford,) (with Israel,) farmer.

Howe Israel, (Sanford,) lot 25, L T 1, surveyor and farmer 155.

Howe, Philo P , (Sanford,) (with Israel,) farmer

Hugaboom, L Mrs , (Deposit,) lot 25, R. T , farmer 10

Huggins, Andrew, (Sanford,) (with James and Charles,) farmer 118

Huggins, Charles, (Sanford,) (with James and Andrew,) farmer 118.

Huggins, James, (Sanford,) (with Charles and Andrew,) farmer 118

Huggins John, (Sanford,) lot 27, L T. 1, farmer 110

HUYCK, ANDREW J., (Deposit,) great lot 23, F & N T , farmer 102

Huyck, E , (Deposit,) great lot 23, F & N T , farmer 218

Huyck, Henry, (Deposit,) great lot 23, F. & N T , farmer 100.

Huyck, Lorenzo L , (Sanford,) great lot 6, F & N T , farmer 57

Jackson, Andrew, (Deposit,) harness maker and farmer 6.

Jaycox, Zina, (Deposit,) lot 28, R. T., farmer leasee 256.

Jennings, Stephen, (Vallonia Springs,) farmer 1

JOHNSON, JAMES, (Deposit,) lot 19, R T farmer 125

JOHNSTON, NAPOLEON B., (Sanford,) lot 24, F. & N T., farmer 123

KEDZIE, ANDREW, (Sanford,) blacksmith

KEDZIE, A. A., (Gulf Summit,) lot 24, R. T , supt of poor and farmer 100.

Kenyon, Theodore, (Deposit ) lot 26, R. T., mason and farmer 115.

Keyes, Elizabeth, (Sanford,) farmer 2

KING, ADDISON, (North Sanford,) lot 52, L T 3, farmer 250

Kinney, James, (Deposit,) lot 28, R. T., farmer 100

Kinney, John, (Deposit,) (with James,) farmer

KINYON, SAMUEL, (Deposit,) lot 25, R T, farmer 221

Knapp, John, (Deposit,) farmer 40.

KNISKERN, LEWIS, (Sanford,) lot 42, L. T 1, farmer 110.

Kniskern, Wesley, (Sanford,) (with Lewis,) farmer

Konkright, Charles, (Sanford,) L. L , farmer 60

Konkright, John, (Sanford,) L L., farmer leasee 60

KROFT, GEO., (Deposit,) lot 26, R T , farmer 80

Kroft, William, (Deposit,) farmer.

Lamore, Hiram, (Vallonia Springs,) lot 4, L T 3, farmer 96

Landers, Geo. W., (Vallonia Springs,) lot 21, L T 2, farmer 100

Lathan, John, (Sanford,) sub 20, L T. 1, farmer

Lee, Cornelius, (Gulf Summit,) farmer 70.

Lee, Edwin, (Deposit,) sub 12, E. T , farmer 70

Lee, George, (Deposit,) farmer occupies 126

Lee, Joseph, (Gulf Summit,) lot 9, W. P., farmer 47.

Lee, Wm., (Deposit,) sub. 12, E T., farmer 48.

Light, A , (Sanford,) lumberman and farmer 200

Light, Joshua, (Sanford,) farmer 150.

Lobdell, Abram, (Sanford,) farmer 50.

Lobdell, Britton, (Afton, Chenango Co.,) lot 32 L. T 8, farmer 220

Lobdell, Geo , (Sanford,) farmer 50.

Lobdell, Jason, (Sanford,) farmer 70

Lobdell, John, (Sanford,) farmer 69

Lord, Asa, (Vallonia Springs,) lot 3, L T. 2, farmer 24

Lord, Asa A , (Vallonia Springs,) mason and farmer 3.

Lord, David, (Hale's Eddy, Delaware Co.,) farmer leases

Lord, James, (Vallonia Springs,) farmer 61

Lord, O , (Vallonia Springs,) carpenter.

LORD, RUFUS, (Vallonia Springs,) carpenter

Love, Albert, (Deposit,) saw mill and farmer 7

Love, Albert, (Deposit,) farmer 5.

Lovelace, M. W , (Hale's Eddy, Delaware Co ,) millwright and farmer 2

LUSCOMB, AUSTIN, (Gulf Summit,) farmer 60

Luscomb, John, (McClure Settlement,) lot 17, R T , lumberman and farmer 320.

LYONS, JAMES, (Gulf Summit,) lot 24, R T., farmer 80.

Maley, Michael, (Deposit,) lot 18, D. T , farmer 45

MARTIN, CHAS. S., (Deposit,) (with John,) farmer

Martin, Gideon G , (Gulf Summit,) lot 28, R T , farmer 25

Martin, John, (Sanford,) farmer 104

MARVIN, URIAH, (Deposit,) painter, paper hanger and farmer 25

MATTHEWS, JOHN P , (Deposit,) great lot 24, F & N T , farmer 75

Mattice, John, (Sanford,) tin peddler and farmer 108

Mayo, Hiram, (Hale's Eddy, Delaware Co.,) C L , farmer 114

McCarter, Joseph, (Deposit,) farmer 53.

McCarthy, Joseph, (Deposit,) farmer 188

McClane, James, (Deposit,) great lot 13, F. & N T , farmer 50.

McClane, Wm , (Vallonia Springs,) lot 21, L T 2. farmer 63

McClure, Edgar, (Gulf Summit,) farmer 130.

McClure, Hannah, (Gulf Summit,) great lot 4, F & N T , farmer 40.

McCLURE, HENRY, (McClure Settlement,) lumberman and farmer 20.

McClure, W. E , (Deposit,) great lot 7, F. & N T , farmer 53½.

McColley, Elizabeth, (North Sanford,) lot 25, L T 3, farmer, McColley Estate

McCULLEY, THOMAS, (Afton, Chenango Co ,) lot 16, L T. 3, farmer leases 130.

McDonald, George, (Sanford,) farmer 100

McGill, Thomas, (Deposit,) farmer 2

McLaury, Martin, (Deposit,) farmer 40

McLaury, Richard, (Deposit,) farmer 120

McLAURY, THOMAS, (Deposit,) farmer 50

McMahon, Bryan, (Gulf Summit,) lot 19, S. L., farmer 90

MEEK, ALEXANDER, (North Sanford,) lot 36, L. T. 3, farmer 260

Merrill, Asa J., (Deposit,) great lot 24, F. & N T., farmer 125.

Merrill, John, (Sanford,) great lot 11, F & N. T., farmer 104.

Merrill, John R., (Sanford,) great lot 12, F. & N T., miller, inspector of elections and farmer 100

Miller, E. M , (McClure Settlement,) great lot 13, F, & N. T., farmer 130.

Miller, John B., (North Sanford,) sub 9, L. T. 1, farmer 60

Moore, Star B., (Gulf Summit,) farmer 55

Morse, C. B , (McClure Settlement,) lot 14, N. T., farmer 64.

Morse, Edward, (Deposit,) sub. 10, D. T., farmer 25.

MOSHER, A T., (North Sanford,) sub. 12, L T 2, dairyman and farmer 500.

Mosher, W H , (North Sanford,) farmer

Mulford, George, (Deposit,) farmer 234

Munger, B C , (McClure Settlement,) farmer 65.

Myrick, Thomas, (Deposit,) farmer 40

Newby estate, heirs of, (Vallonia Springs,) farmers 72.

NEWBY, STANLEY W , (Vallonia Springs,) teacher and farmer

Newby, Wm W , (Vallonia Springs,) lot 5, L T 3, farmer leases 139

NORRIS, H M., (Sanford,) lot 23, L. T. 2, farmer 80.

O'Brien, John, (Sanford,) farmer 100.

O'Brien, P , (Deposit,) great lot 22, F. & N T., farmer 156

Olendorf, John, (North Sanford,) lot 34, L. T 8, farmer leases 112.

ORWEN, JOHN P , (North Sanford,) lot 46, L T 3, farmer 190.

ORWIN, R J P., (North Sanford,) sub 51, L T 3, town assessor and farmer 86.

Owen, Myron L , (North Sanford,) sub. 27, L. T. 2, farmer 71

Owen, Stephen, (McClure Settlement,) great lot 9, F. & N T , farmer 166

Padget, L , (Afton, Chenango Co ,) farmer occupies 40.

Page, James, (Sanford,) farmer 40

Page, Jeremiah, (Vallonia Springs,) lot 9, L T 3, farmer 30.

Page, John, (Sanford,) lot 23, L. T. 2, farmer 40

Page, Luther, (Sanford,) farmer 125.

Page, Nelson, (Sanford,) lot 47, L T 1, farmer 100

Page, T. W , (McClure Settlement,) lot 12, N T , carpenter and farmer 27

Page, Wm , (Vallonia Springs,) lot 3, L T 8, farmer 180

Parish, W S., (Sanford,) lot 35, L. T. 1, farmer 120.

PECK, HENRY E., (Sanford,) great lot 21, F. & N T., farmer 101.

PECK, LEVI Rev , (Sanford,) retired Baptist minister

Peters, Henry, (Deposit,) L T., N. P., farmer 370

Peters, John, (Deposit,) farmer leases of Henry, 370

PHILLEY, A L., (Sanford,) shoemaker and farmer 27

PHILLEY. ALANSON L , (Sanford,) shoe-maker
PHILLEY, D SMITH, (Sanford,) tanner, tans upper leather, harness leather and calf skins, also farmer 34.
Pinney, Elezur, (Sanford,) great lot 11, F & N T , farmer 120
Pinney Grover, (Sanford,) great lot 11, F & N T lumberman and farmer 200
POST, DANIEL, (McClure Settlement,) (D & S. Post & Co.)
POST, DAVID, (McClure Settlement,) (D & S Post & Co )
POST, D & S & CO., (McClure Settlement,) (Daniel, Stephen and David Post ) lumbermen and farmers 1,200
POST, STEPHEN, (McClure Settlement,) (D & S Post & Co )
Post, Stephen Sen , (McClure Settlement,) farmer
PRENTICE, SAMUEL G , (Afton, Chenango Co ,) prop of saw mill and mechanic
Preston, Wm , (Vallonia Springs,) farmer 139.
Quick, Peter, (Hale's Eddy, Delaware Co.,) C L , farmer 100
Quirk, Dennis, (Gulf Summit,) lot 23, R T farmer 82.
Ray Charles, (Sanford,) great lot 15, F & N T , farmer 103
RECTOR, EDWARD, (McClure Settlement ) lot 18, R T , farmer 35.
Rector, Edward, (Gulf Summit,) farmer 35
Rector, Leonard, (McClure Settlement,) farmer 40
REICHARD, HENRY, (Deposit,) great lot 7, F & N T , farmer 250
Reymond, S. E , (Gulf Summit,) farmer 200
Reynolds, Holman, (Gulf Summit,) L. T., N P , farmer 58
RICKS, ALEXANDER, (Deposit,) sub 10, E T , farmer 96.
Rikard, Hiram, (McClure Settlement,) F & N T , farmer 75
RIVENBURGH, JONAS, (Deposit,) sub. 8, E T , mechanic and farmer 130
Roberts, Charles, (Sanford,) lot 40, L T. 1, farmer 75
Roberts, Henry E., (Sanford,) farmer 80
Roberts, James E , (Sanford,) lot 34, L. T. 1 carpenter and farmer 140
Roberts, J W , (Sanford,) great lot 16, F & N T , farmer 220
Robins, Job, (Bennetteville, Chenango Co ,) L T 3, farmer 80
ROBINS, SOLOMON, (Afton, Chenango Co ,) farmer 137
Reeney John (Deposit,) great lot 22, F. & N T , farmer 50
Rosencrants, Ziba (North Sanford,) carpenter and builder.
Rowe, Hanford D., (Vallonia Springs,) lot 14, L T 3, farmer 100
Rowe, Henry, (North Sanford,) lot 20, L. T. 3 farmer 165.
Rowe, John, (Vallonia Springs,) lot 1, L. T 3 farmer 30.
RUSSELL, L L , (Afton, Chenango Co ) lot 22, L T 3 justice of the peace and farmer 215
SALISBURY ALBERT, (Sanford,) L L , farmer 130

Salisbury, Wm , (Sanford,) L. L., farmer 214
Sampson, Hiram, (Deposit,) farmer 40 and occupies 40
Sanders, Elisha, (Vallonia Springs,) mason and farmer 40
Sanders, Simeon J , (Afton, Chenango Co ,) farmer.
Schriver, Jeremiah, (Hale's Eddy, Delaware Co ,) sub. 8, D. T , farmer leases 74½
Scofield, Egbert, (Deposit,) great lot 23, F & N T , farmer 50.
Scott, James H , (Deposit,) sub. 8, E T , farmer 98
Scott, William (Deposit,) farmer 63
Scutt, George W., (Deposit,) farmer
Scutt, William, (Deposit,) great lot 14, F & N T , farmer 264.
Scutt, Wilson P , (Deposit,) farmer.
Sears, F , (Sanford,) cooper
Seley, E P., (Sanford,) great lot 6, F & N. T , farmer 82
Seward, Henry D , (McClure Settlement,) great lot 9, F & N T , farmer 60
Seward, Luman P , (McClure Settlement,) great lot 14, F. & N T., farmer 135
Seward, Sanford, (McClure Settlement,) great lot 13. F & N T , farmer 222
Seward, Silas, (McClure Settlement,) butcher and farmer 45
SEXMITH, LEVI, (North Sanford,) lot 42, L T. 3, farmer 106
Shaffer, Frederick, (Deposit,) great lot 20, F & N T., farmer 290.
Shaffer. R. W., (Deposit,) farmer.
Shaw, Philetus, (Vallonia Springs,) lot 8, L T 3. farmer 98
Shelden, John W , (Deposit,) great lot 7, F. & N T , farmer 179
Shelden, Sydney, (Deposit,) great lot 4, F. & N T , farmer 202
SHERLOCK, JOHN, (Deposit,) farmer 50.
Sherman, John D , (Sanford,) lot 16, L T 1. peddler and farmer 76
SHINER, JOHN, (Deposit,) great lot 14, F. & N T , farmer 120
Silvernail, Joseph, (Gulf Summit,) lot 17, R T , farmer 80
SIMMONS, PETER L., (Deposit,) lot 19, R T., farmer 125
Slatery, Patrick, (Gulf Summit ) lot 24, R T , farmer 80
SMITH, HENRY, (North Sanford,) lot 39, L T 3, farmer 68.
Smith, Henry T , (Deposit,) poor master and farmer 127
SMITH, ISAAC, (Gulf Summit,) L T , N. P., carpenter and farmer 84½
Smith, John, (North Sanford,) carpenter and farmer 51
SMITH, JOHN JR , (North Sanford,) lot 37, L T 3, farmer 51½
Smith, Wm., (Deposit,) great lot 19, F. & N T , farmer 102.
Smith, Zachariah, (North Sanford ) L. T. 1. farmer 25.
SPAFFORD, L D , (Hale's Eddy, Delaware Co ,) sawyer for F B Whitaker.
Speers. Ellen, (Deposit,) lot 19, R T , farmer 110
Springer, Barton, (North Sanford,) farmer 2
Squares, Miles, (Deposit,) W T , farmer leases of Jacob Gardinier, 240

Squares, Orange, (Hale's Eddy, Delaware Co.,) lot 7, D. T., farmer 80.

STEWART, JAMES, (Deposit,) lot 18, R T., farmer 437.

Stewart, James, (Gulf Summit,) lot 11, W P., farmer 480.

STILES, B T., (Deposit,) lot 25, R T., farmer 165 •

STILES, CHAS H., (Deposit,) lot W & D., farmer 120.

Stoddart, John, (Sanford,) farmer

Swait, David, (Deposit,) great lot 24, F & N. T., farmer 90

Switzler, Daniel, (Center Village,) G & S L., farmer 20

TARBOX, CHAS. A., (McClure Settlement,) great lot 2, F & N T., farmer 287

TARBOX, GEO., (McClure Settlement,) lot 13, N T., farmer 103.

Tarbox, Malvin, (McClure Settlement,) great lot 2 F & N T., farmer 107

TERREL, ELIAS G., (Deposit,) lot 26, R T., farmer 80

Thater, Wm., (Sanford,) farmer leases of Sarah Luscomb, 109

Thomas, James, (Deposit,) lot 4, W P., farmer 40

Thompson, John, (Deposit,) farmer 60.

Thompson, Henry, (Sanford,) L. L., mason and farmer 105.

THOMSON, JOHN N., (Sanford,) L. L., mason and farmer 58

Thomson, Robert, (Deposit,) mason and farmer 136¼

Thorn, Stephen, (Sanford,) lot 45, L. T 1, farmer 160.

THURSTON, W. S., (Sanford,) great lot 16, F & N T., mason and farmer 135

TILLOTSON, JEROME, (Sanford,) great lot 12, F. & N. T., farmer 325.

Titus, Celey R., (Deposit,) farmer 100.

Titus, John C., (Afton, Chenango Co.,) farmer 88.

Tompkins, Albert, (Sanford,) great lot 6, F & N T., farmer 109

Townel, I P. Rev., (McClure Settlement,) M E clergyman

TRYON, ELAM R., (Afton, Chenango Co.,) lot 13, L. T 3, farmer 50

Turner, Sarah Mrs., (Deposit,) lot 3, E. T., farmer 33.

TUTTEL, WILLIAM W., (Deposit,) great lot 18, F. & N. T., farmer 75.

Udell, Daniel, (Vallonia Springs,) lot 4, L T 2, farmer 43

Underwood, George, (Hale's Eddy, Delaware Co.,) C L., farmer 100.

Underwood, Jonas, (Deposit,) farmer 180.

Underwood, P. D., (Deposit,) lot 18, R T., farmer 118

Valentine, M. G. G., (Deposit,) great lot 21, F & N T., farmer 155.

VanCUREN, MATHEW, (Deposit,) great lot 19, F & N T., farmer 111.

VanDeuwarker, Henry, (Sanford,) lot 14, L T 1, farmer occupies 119.

Vanderhule, Samuel, (North Sanford,) sub. 11, L. T. 2, farmer leases of W. Mosher, 180.

VanDUSEN, J W., (Sanford,) great lot 6, F & N. T., farmer 92

VanHorne, Hubbard, (Sanford,) carpenter and builder.

VanTassel, C., (Deposit,) sub. 10, D. T., farmer

Varrin, Isaac F., (Deposit,) farmer 30.

Vaughn, John, (Deposit,) lot 19, R T., farmer 56

Vincent, Butler, (Deposit,) lot 6, W. P., farmer 200

Vincent, David, (Deposit,) lot 27, R T., farmer 40

VOSBURGH, THOMAS, (Sanford,) mason and farmer 6¾ •

Wakeman, Silas, (North Sanford,) lot 25, L. T. 2, farmer 203

WAKEMAN, S B., (North Sanford,) (with Selas Wakeman,) farmer.

Walker, David, (Deposit,) great lot 24, F. & N T., farmer 150

Walker, Joseph, (Afton, Chenango Co.,) refused information

Waterman, John, (Vallonia Springs,) lot 9, L. T 3, farmer 50.

Waterman, William, (Afton, Chenango Co.,) farmer 263.

Watterman, Henry, (Afton, Chenango Co.,) lot 27, L T 3, farmer 50

Waymon, Thomas, (Deposit,) farmer 64

WEED, ALFRED, (Center Village,) G & S L., farmer leases of Mrs Graves, 200.

Weed, Joel, (McClure Settlement,) farmer 136.

Weeks, James W., (North Sanford,) farmer 139.

Whaley, G A. & Son, (Vallonia Springs,) lot 7, L T 3, farmer 51.

Wheaton, Cyrus A., (Deposit,) great lot 24, F & N T., farmer 137

WHEELER, BENJAMIN T., (Sanford,) lot 39, L T. 1, constable and farmer 110

Wheeler, E F., (Sanford,) constable and farmer 114.

Wheeler, Geo D., (Deposit,) M T., farmer 115 and (with Duane Demoney,) 320

Whitaker, D. W., (Deposit,) lumberman and farmer

Whitaker, F R., (Hale's Eddy, Delaware Co.,) C L., saw mill

White, John C., (Deposit,) great lot 24, F. & N T., farmer 168. •

Whitman, Jesse, (Bennettaville, Chenango Co.,) lot 55, L. T. 3, farmer 190.

Whitney, Jacob, (Sanford,) great lot 16, F & N T., inspector of elections, mason and farmer 280.

Whitney, Samuel, (Sanford,) post master and farmer 135

Wickham, Jeremiah, (Deposit,) farmer 25.

WICKHAM, REUBEN, (Deposit,) great lot 24, F. & N. T., farmer 75.

WICKHAM, SELAH (Deposit,) great lot 24, F. & N. T., farmer 83

Widman, Adron, (Gulf Summit,) farmer 40.

WILCOX, J. C., (Deposit,) lot 2, W P., blacksmith and farmer 30.

Williams, Andrew, (Sanford,) farmer leases

Williams, E. A., (Afton, Chenango Co.,) lot 11, L T. 3, farmer leases 130.

WILLIAMS, G. S., (Gulf Summit,) merchant, postmaster, justice of the peace, station agent E R R, and farmer 32.

Wood, Henry, (Sanford,) farmer 17

Woodford, C L., (Deposit,) farmer 40

Woodford, Harrison, (Deposit,) (with O B,) farmer.

Q

Woodford, Orange B., (Deposit,) lot 2, E T., farmer 188.
Yaple, Henry C., (Afton, Chenango Co.,) lot 17, L. T. 8, farmer 121.

Yaples, Cornelius B., (Afton Chenango Co.,) lot 9, L. T. 8, farmer 100.

# TRIANGLE.

### (Post Office Addresses in Parentheses.)

Adams, Frank, (Upper Lisle,) lumbering.
Adams, Horace, (Triangle,) lot 32, farmer 140.
Adams, Perry, (Whitney's Point,) cooper.
Aikin, Caroline Mrs., (Triangle,) lot 67, farmer 67
Alexander, Stephen, (Triangle,) farmer
Ames, Jesse P., (Whitney's Point,) lot 86, farmer 305.
Andrews, J J, (Whitney's Point,) oyster saloon.
Arnold, R B., (Whitney's Point,) lot 39, carpenter and farmer 80.
ASHLEY, C. P., (Whitney's Point,) lot 5, blacksmith and farmer leases 96
Ashley, Geo., (Upper Lisle,) farmer leases 155
ASHLEY, HARRY, (Upper Lisle,) lot 24, farmer 168
Austin, A, (Upper Lisle,) general merchant and postmaster
Badger, Orrin W., (Whitney's Point,) lot 42, farmer 150.
Baker, Cyrus, (Whitney's Point,) lot 33, farmer 150.
BAKER, GIDEON, (Upper Lisle,) (Gideon Baker & Son)
BAKER, GIDEON & SON, (Whitney's Point,) (Wm W) lot 32, farmer 140
BAKER, GUY E, (Triangle,) farmer 226.
BAKER, WM. W, (Whitney's Point,) (Gideon Baker & Son)
Baldwin, W. S., (Whitney's Point,) farmer 135.
Ballard, Dwight, (Upper Lisle,) lot 42, farmer 160
Ballard, H S, (Upper Lisle,) lot 42, secretary Triangle Cheese Co. and farmer 140
BEACH, ASA, (Whitney's Point,) (Collins & Beach,) (F & A Beach.)
Beardslee, Pernet, (Whitney's Point,) lot 39, farmer 75
Beckwith, John F., (Smithville Flats, Chenango Co.,) lot 26, farmer 142
Beeman, Ansel, (Triangle,) lot 61, farmer 150.
Bennett, C. C., (Whitney's Point,) lot 27, secretary Broome Co. Agricultural Society and farmer 119.
Bennett, Wm. G., (Upper Lisle,) lot 23, farmer 164

Benson, Wm., (Triangle,) lot 54, farmer 130.
Bigsby, John, (Whitney's Point,) horse dealer.
Birdsall & Davis, (Whitney's Point,) (S. H Birdsall and D B. Davis,) general merchants, Main
Birdsall, S E, (Whitney's Point,) clothing, boots and shoes, hats and caps, Main
Birdsall, S. H., (Whitney's Point,) (Birdsall & Davis)
BISHOP, GEO C, (Whitney's Point,) (G C Bishop & Son,) undertaker and furniture dealer, Collins
BISHOP, G C & SON, (Whitney's Point,) (George C and Junius F.,) grove and fish ponds, 3½ acres
BISHOP, JUNIUS F, (Whitney's Point,) (G C. Bishop & Son)
Blancher, Geo, (Upper Lisle,) lot 25, wagon maker, prop. thrashing machine and farmer 14½.
Blancher, Luther, (Upper Lisle,) lot 32, farmer 60
Bliss, F, (Whitney's Point,) lot 59, farmer 150
Boardman, Eli, (Triangle,) lot 1, farmer 50
Brawer, Byron, (Whitney's Point,) (Brewer & Seymour)
BREWER, EUGENE L, (Triangle,) farmer 106
Brewer, John, (Triangle,) lot 67, farmer 300
Brewer & Seymour, (Whitney's Point,) (Byron Brewer and G. W. Seymour,) brick makers.
Brown, David, (Whitney's Point,) lot 58, farmer 110.
Brown, Gardeon H, (Smithville Flats, Chenango Co.,) lot 27, veterinary surgeon and farmer 237
Brown, John, (Whitney's Point,) farmer 10.
Burghardt, Henry, (Upper Lisle,) lot 14, farmer 181
Burghardt, Jacob, (Whitney's Point,) lot 38, farmer 225
BURGHARDT, JOHN Jr, (Upper Lisle,) (J. Burghardt & Sons.)
BURGHARDT, JOHN Sen, (Upper Lisle,) (J Burghardt & Sons.)
BURGHARDT, J. & SONS, (Upper Lisle,) (John Sen., John Jr. and Robert,) lot 12, tanners, props. saw and planing mills, and farmers 800

BURGHARDT, ROBERT, (Upper Lisle,) (*J Burghardt & Sons,*) lot 13, farmer

BURGHARDT, R M., (Upper Lisle,) lot 13, farmer 170.

Burlingame, Chas , (Whitney's Point,) carpenter

BURROWS, ALEX. REV., (Triangle,) pastor M E. Church.

BUTTS, DANIEL D , (Whitney's Point,) (*Butts & Gardner.*)

BUTTS & GARDNER, (Whitney's Point,) (*Daniel D. Butts and Wm. Gardner,*) house and sign painters, grainers and paper hangers

Cady, J H , (Whitney's Point,) (*R. A. & J H. Cady.*)

Cady, R A & J H., (Whitney's Point,) lot 45, farmer 50.

Cahar, James. (Whitney's Point,) (*with Philip,*) farmer leases of Isaiah J. Dings, 100.

Cahar, Philip, (Whitney's Point,) (*with James,*) farmer leases of Isaiah J Dings, 100

CAMPBELL, ORRIN B , (Upper Lisle,) boot and shoe manuf

Canfield, Asa, (Upper Lisle,) lot 16, farmer 224

Carter, Henry, (Upper Lisle,) lot 18, farmer 57

CARTWRIGHT, EARL, (Whitney's Point,) lot 63, supervisor and farmer 177

Cartwright, Samuel, (Triangle,) farmer 25

Chubb, Abraham, (Upper Lisle,) lot 22, farmer 56

Clark, Cynthia Mrs , (Upper Lisle,) lot 20, farmer 150

Clark, Richard A Rev , (Whitney's Point,) pastor First Congregational Church.

Clough, Francis B (Upper Lisle,) lot 21, drover and farmer 460

Clough, Barry, (Upper Lisle,) lot 21, salesman Triangle Cheese Co. and farmer 110

COLLINS, ALONZO, (Whitney's Point,) (*Collins, Perry & Co.,*) (*Perry & Collins,*) (*Snook, Collins & Co ,*) (*Collins & Beach,*) farmer 700.

COLLINS & BEACH, (Whitney's Point,) (*Alonzo Collins and Asa Beach,*) dealers in farm produce, Main.

COLLINS, PERRY & CO , (Whitney's Point,) general merchants, Main.

COLLINS, WM. W , (Whitney's Point,) (*Collins, Perry & Co.*)

Conrad, John, (Upper Lisle,) blacksmith.

Conro, L , (Triangle,) lot 61, farmer 100

Cook, Chas. A., (Whitney's Point,) (*C. A. & C. M. Cook*)

Cook, C A. & C M , (Whitney's Point,) (*Chas A. and Chas. M ,*) farmers 175.

Cook, Chas. M , (Whitney's Point ) (*C. A & C. M. Cook,*) surveyor and lumberman.

Cook, Wm. W , (Whitney's Point,) farmer 127.

Cooler, Daniel A., (Whitney's Point,) tailor, Main.

Corbin, John P , (Whitney's Point,) dealer in Eureka Butter Workers

Cornell, H Rev , (Triangle,) pastor Baptist Church.

Crane, Nathaniel M , (Whitney's Point,) (*Merchant & Crane*)

Currier, John H , (Upper Lisle,) lot 80, farmer leases 250.

Daniels, G H . (Whitney's Point,) watches, jewelry &c.

Davis, D B , (Whitney's Point,) (*Birdsall & Davis*)

DAY, GEO A., (Upper Lisle,) (*Newell & Day,*) justice of the peace

Day, Geo. W , (Whitney's Point,) lot 82, farmer 50.

Dewey, John, (Upper Lisle,) lot 24, farmer leases of John T Landers, 175.

Dewey, Levi, (Upper Lisle,) lot 11, farmer 100.

Dickinson, Cyrus, (Whitney's Point,) lot 43, farmer 57

Dickinson, Seth, (Whitney's Point,) lot 43, farmer 79.

Dillenbeck, Hiram N., (Upper Lisle,) lot 21, farmer 100.

Dillenbeck, Jacob, (Upper Lisle,) lot 24, farmer 112

Dimmick, ——, (Whitney's Point,) (*Hanford & Dimmick*)

Dings, Isaiah J , (Whitney's Point,) carriage maker, justice of the peace and farmer 110.

Dodge, Avery B , (Whitney's Point,) lot 39, dealer in patent medicines and farmer 15.

Dorchester, Walter, (Whitney's Point,) lot 41, (*W M. & W. Dorchester*)

Dorchester, Wm , (Whitney's Point,) lot 39, (*W M. & W. Dorchester*)

Dorchester, W. M. & W , (Whitney's Point,) (*Wm and Walter,*) farmers 300.

Dornburgh, Abram, (Triangle,) lot 57, farmer leases 100

Dunckel, Geo , (Triangle ) wagon maker and farmer 9½.

Dunham, E., (Whitney's Point,) expressman

Dunham, Griffin & Co , (Whitney's Point,) (*Lewis Dunham, Chas Z. and J P. Griffin,*) butchers, Main.

Dunham, Lewis, (Whitney's Point,) (*Dunham, Griffin & Co.*)

Edwards, Hiram M , (Triangle,) lot 59, farmer 100.

Egbertson, John H., (Upper Lisle,) lot 25, constable and dealer in hides, pelts &c.

Eggleston, Chas. W., (Triangle,) lot 2, farmer 100.

Eggleston, Dorcy H , (Triangle,) farmer 2

Eggleston, Frederick, (Triangle,) lot 54, farmer 260.

Eggleston, Frederick C , (Triangle,) lot 54, farmer 113

Eggleston, Joseph. (Triangle,) lot 61, grain thresher and farmer 64.

Eggleston, J. D., (Triangle,) farmer leases 116.

Eggleston, Maria Mrs , (Triangle,) lot 72, farmer 119½.

Eggleston, Orlando, (Triangle,) lot 20, farmer 24

EGGLESTON, ORTHELLO, (Triangle,) lot 74, farmer 110.

Eggleston, Sylvester H , (Triangle,) lot 2, carpenter and farmer 62

EGLESTON, ROCITER, (Triangle,) lot 62, farmer 30.

ELDREDGE & HYDE, (Whitney's Point,) (*Milo B Eldredge and Edwin F Hyde*,) dealers in coal, lime, salt, plaster &c.

ELDREDGE, MILO B, (Whitney's Point,) (*Eldredge & Hyde*) station agent D L & W R R

Elliott, Delatus, (Upper Lisle,) lot 26, farmer 90

Elliott, L B, (Upper Lisle,) prop Upper Lisle Hotel

English, Benj., (Triangle,) lot 63, farmer 128

English, Sidney, (Triangle,) lot 64, farmer leases 158

Failing, Abraham, (Whitney's Point,) cheese maker

Fuller, Abram, (Smithville Flats, Chenango Co.,) farmer.

Fuller, Orlo B, (Smithville Flats, Chenango Co.,) lot 25, farmer 217

Gardner, Mary C Miss, (Whitney's Point,) milliner, Collins

GARDNER, WM, (Whitney's Point,) (*Butts & Gardner*)

Gates, Albert, (Triangle,) lot 20, farmer

Goutchens, John D, (Upper Lisle,) lot 25, farmer 192

Goodrich, Allen, (Whitney's Point) (*Goodrich & VanDerson.*)

Goodrich & VanDerson, (Whitney's Point,) (*Allen Goodrich and Isaac VanDerson,*) blacksmiths, Main

GRAY, ORIN D., (Triangle,) lot 55, farmer 231

Green, F W., (Whitney's Point,) saw and planing mills and farmer 5

Green, J. G., (Whitney's Point,) lot 39, estate of Eben Green, farmer 154.

GRIDLEY, F D, (Whitney's Point,) (*Snook, Collins & Co,*) eclectic physician, surgeon and farmer 10

Griffin Bros, (Whitney's Point,) (*J P and Chas Z,*) general merchants Collins

Griffin, Chas Z, (Whitney's Point,) (*Dunham, Griffin & Co*)

Griffin, J. P., (Whitney's Point,) (*Griffin Bros,*) (*Dunham, Griffin & Co*)

Gross, Hannah Mrs, (Triangle,) lot 18, farmer 87

Gross, Nelson I., (Triangle,) lot 18, farmer leases of Peter Bates, 30

Guier, Peter, (Whitney's Point,) musician and farmer 3

HALL, CHAS S, (Triangle,) assessor and farmer 270.

HALL, EUGENE V, (Triangle,) lot 52, farmer 125

Hall, Theresa Mrs, (Whitney's Point,) lot 50, farmer 230

Hand, Andrew, (Upper Lisle,) lot 20, farmer leases 150.

Hanford & Dimmick, (Whitney's Point,) harness makers, Main.

Hanford, M L, (Whitney's Point,) (*Hanford & Dimmick*)

Hawley, F E, (Whitney's Point,) barber, Main

HAYES, LEVI (Triangle,) farmer 128

Hayes, Nathaniel, (Triangle,) tanner and farmer 2½

Hayes, Sabin, (Triangle,) lot 59, farmer 357

Hazard, Franklin C., (Whitney's Point,) lot 32, farmer 198

Hazard, John E., (Smithville Flats, Chenango Co.,) lot 27, farmer 225

Hemingway, E B, (Whitney's Point,) (*H. Hemingway & Son.*)

Hemingway, H, (Whitney's Point,) (*H Hemingway & Son,*) farmer 270.

Hemingway, H & Son, (Whitney's Point,) (*E B,*) clothing, boots and shoes, drugs, paints and oils, Main

Hemingway, Vincent W, (Whitney's Point,) farmer leases of Dr. Hemingway, 248

Hewitt, J W, Rev., (Whitney's Point,) pastor M E Church

Hibbard, Delosa, (Upper Lisle,) lot 20, mechanic and farmer 38

Hibbard, Henry K., (Upper Lisle,) lot 20, farmer 60

Hoag, Chas F., (Upper Lisle,) (*N. D Hoag & Son*)

Hoag, Franklin, (Upper Lisle,) blacksmith and farmer 1½.

Hoag, N D & Son, (Upper Lisle,) (*Nehemiah D. and Chas. F.,*) general merchants.

Hoag, Nehemiah D, (Upper Lisle,) (*N. D. Hoag & Son*)

HODGES, ALEX, (Whitney's Point,) lot 39, assessor and farmer 300.

Hopkins, John, (Whitney's Point,) (*Johnson & Hopkins*)

Howland, Edgar, (Whitney's Point,) lot 37, farmer leases 275.

Howland, Frank, (Whitney's Point,) egg dealer.

Howland, Minor, (Whitney's Point,) lot 37, farmer 275.

HOWLAND, RANSOM, (Whitney's Point,) lawyer, president of village and farmer 2.

Hurd, Geo. W, (Whitney's Point,) lot 5, farmer leases 335

HYDE, EDWIN F., (Whitney's Point,) (*Eldredge & Hyde,*) farmer 75

Ingraham, Andrew W, (Whitney's Point,) lot 38, farmer 7 and leases 225

Jackson, Chas W, (Triangle,) farmer 2½.

Jackson, Henry, (Triangle,) lot 41, farmer leases of Job Taft, 92½

Jackson, Nelson R, (Triangle,) lot 2, thresher and farmer leases of Geo. English, 117

Jeffords, Allen C, (Upper Lisle,) lot 22, farmer 160

JEFFORDS, URIAH A, (Upper Lisle,) lot 22, farmer 60

Jenks, S H, (Upper Lisle,) lot 11, farmer 25

Johnson, Chas, (Whitney's Point,) lot 58, farmer 139

Johnson, Geo C, (Whitney's Point,) lot 33, farmer 109

Johnson & Hopkins, (Whitney's Point,) (*John Johnson and John Hopkins,*) hardware, tinware and stoves, Collins.

Johnson, Jabez, (Whitney's Point,) flour and feed dealer and farmer 15

Johnson, John, (Whitney's Point,) (*Johnson & Hopkins*)

Johnson, Justin L, (Upper Lisle,) lot 16, justice of the peace, carpenter and farmer 40.

Johnson, Lucius A., (Whitney's Point,) farmer 29

Johnson, Peter, (Triangle,) lot 3, farmer 212

Kells, Margaret Mrs., (Whitney's Point,) lot 36, farmer 60

Kelly, Dewitt B., (Upper Lisle,) lot 25, farmer 83

King, H., (Whitney's Point,) expressman

KINYON, BENJ, (Triangle,) allo physician and surgeon, and farmer 2

KNICKERBOCKER, W. E., (Whitney's Point,) cooper.

Ladd, C H Mrs., (Whitney's Point,) photograph artist, Collins.

Landers, Betsy M Mrs., (Upper Lisle,) lot 11, farmer 87¾

Landers, Eben, (Upper Lisle,) farmer 6.

LANDERS, JOHN T., (Upper Lisle,) lot 24, farmer 175.

Landers, Philo, (Upper Lisle,) farmer 55

Lewis, Asa, (Whitney's Point,) lot 51, farmer 128

Lewis, Henry W., (Whitney's Point,) lot 52, farmer 80

Livermore, Nathan, (Whitney's Point,) (*Livermore & Terpening*)

Livermore & Terpening, (Whitney's Point,) (*Nathan Livermore and Truman Terpening,*) carriage makers

Longbothum, J. E., (Whitney's Point,) stencil cutter.

Loomis, J. F., (Whitney's Point,) machinist

Love, Chas., (Triangle,) blacksmith

Love, Geo., (Whitney's Point,) blacksmith

Love, Moses, (Whitney's Point,) blacksmith.

Low, C. A. Mrs., (Triangle,) dress maker

Mack, Chas M., (Triangle,) lot 44, farmer 118¾

MATTHEWSON, AUGUSTUS M., (Upper Lisle,) lot 27, justice of the peace and farmer leases of Chauncy C Bennett, 64

Matthewson, Edmund, (Upper Lisle,) lot 27, surveyor and farmer 64

McFarland, A. C., (Upper Lisle,) lot 13, cabinet maker and farmer 3

McGee, Albert, (Triangle,) lot 61, farmer 100

Merchant & Crane, (Whitney's Point,) lot 2, farmer 300

Meyers, J., (Upper Lisle,) lot 19, farmer 60

Meyers, Levi, (Upper Lisle,) lot 19, carpenter and farmer 60.

Mitchell, Geo W., (Whitney's Point,) lot 56, farmer 355.

Mitchell, Smith, (Whitney's Point,) lot 66, farmer leases of Mrs Green, 36

Mitchell, Wm G., (Whitney's Point,) farmer leases 40.

Mowry, Andrew, (Triangle,) lot 41, farmer 125½.

Mowry, George R., (Triangle,) lot 41, shoe maker and farmer 4

Mowry, Henry D., (Triangle,) lot 60, mason and farmer 10

Mowry, Morris, (Upper Lisle,) lot 22, farmer leases of R Thurston, 40

NEWELL & DAY, (Upper Lisle,) (*Nathaniel Newell and Geo. A Day,*) lot 14, farmers 183

NEWELL, NATHANIEL, (Upper Lisle,) (*Newell & Day,*) lot 25, farmer 125.

Nosom, R. C Mrs., (Triangle,) lot 1, farmer 46

Olmstead, Chandler, (Triangle,) groceries, crockery &c

OLMSTEAD, CHARLES S., (Whitney's Point,) dealer in groceries, stationery, boots, shoes &c, postmaster, town clerk, village clerk, treasurer Broome Co. Agricultural Society and treasurer Union Free School.

Osborn, Frederick I., (Whitney's Point,) farmer 80

PAGE, CYRUS, (Whitney's Point,) lot 60, farmer 200.

Page, John O., (Whitney's Point,) lot 34, agent for wagons and farmer 75

Page, Lander, (Triangle,) lot 74, farmer 170.

Page, Luther, (Whitney's Point,) lot 34, farmer 170.

Page, Orlan T., (Whitney's Point,) lot 34, farmer 170

Page, R D., (Whitney's Point,) lot 40, egg dealer and farmer 196

Page, Sherman, (Upper Lisle,) lot 5, farmer 85

PAGE, SHERMAN C., (Triangle,) lot 58, farmer 200

Park, Edwin, (Whitney's Point,) farmer 160

Park, Rufus, (Whitney's Point,) carpenter and farmer 11

Parker, Bion, (Triangle,) lot 44, farmer 52.

Parker, Thos., (Triangle,) lot 41, farmer 156.

Pearsall, Egbert, (Triangle,) lot 20, farmer 166

Peck, Andrew L., (Whitney's Point,) lot 43, farmer 76.

Peck, John D., (Whitney's Point,) farmer 55.

PERKINS F L., (Whitney's Point,) (*Perkins & Whitcomb*)

Perkins, Randall, (Whitney's Point,) sawyer, lumberman and farmer 8

PERKINS & WHITCOMB, (Whitney's Point,) (*F. L. Perkins and G C. Whitcomb,*) dealers in groceries, crockery ware, wall paper and general merchandise, also dealers in wool, hides and tallow, Collins.

Perry, W. H Mrs., (Whitney's Point,) milliner, Main.

Perry, ——, (Whitney's Point,) (*Collins, Perry & Co.*)

Pike, Fred R Mrs., (Upper Lisle,) lot 26, farmer 75.

Pinney, R H Mrs., (Whitney's Point,) dress maker, Main.

Pratt O J., (Whitney's Point,) druggist, Collins.

Purdy, Samuel, (Whitney's Point,) carpenter and farmer leases of Mrs Dibble, 2

Richardson, Eugene, (Upper Lisle,) lot 12, farmer 74

Roberts, Esther Mrs., (Whitney's Point,) lot 64, farmer 106

ROBERTS, T H., (Whitney's Point,) principal of Whitney's Point Union School and Academy

Robinson, A C., (Whitney's Point,) lot 65, farmer 98.

Rockwell, Ann Mrs., (Upper Lisle,) lot 35, farmer 134

Rogers, Benj , (Whitney's Point,) farmer 300

ROGERS, C R., (Whitney's Point,) allo physician and surgeon

Rogers, Earlman, (Whitney's Point,) lot 65, farmer 180

Rogers, Jerry, (Whitney's Point,) farmer 100

ROGERS, MOSES, (Whitney's Point,) prop Rogers House, Main

Rogers, W H, (Whitney's Point,) prop livery stable and street commissioner

ROSS, D. T Rev , (Whitney's Point,) pastor First Baptist Church

ROUSE, JOEL & SONS, (Upper Lisle,) (*Lavoisian DeCalvus and Laroy Deloss,*) lot 35, farmer 300

ROUSE, LAROY DELOSS, (Upper Lisle,) (*Joel Rouse & Sons*)

ROUSE, LAVOISIAN DE CALVUS, (Upper Lisle,) (*Joel Rouse & Sons*)

Sanford, Geo. W., (Triangle,) lot 60, farmer 70

Sanford, Seymour, (Triangle,) lot 57, farmer 250

Saulsbury, Albertus, (Upper Lisle,) farmer leases of M L. Totman, 20

Saxton, Albert, (Smithville Flats, Chenango Co.,) lot 28, farmer 133

Saxton, Henry H., (Whitney's Point,) lot 42, farmer 180

SAXTON, ISRAEL, (Triangle,) boot and shoe maker, and farmer 5.

Scofield, E A Miss (Whitney's Point,) dress maker and milliner, Collins

Self, Joseph, (Triangle ) lot 53, farmer 60.

Seymour, C. A., (Whitney's Point,) farmer 4

SEYMOUR, FREDERICK R , (Whitney's Point,) lot 57, farmer 75

Seymour, G. W., (Whitney's Point,) (*Brewer & Seymour,*) farmer 65

SEYMOUR, HENRY A , (Whitney's Point,) farmer 100

Shipman, Frank, (Triangle,) wagon maker

Showers, Daniel, (Whitney's Point,) carpenter

SHUART JOHN S B., (Whitney's Point,) (*with Wm G*) farmer

SHUART, WM G, (Whitney's Point,) lot 65, farmer 50.

Sibley, G P., (Triangle,) lot 20, notary public and farmer 61.

SIMMONS BROS , (Triangle,) (*Rollin A. and E W ,*) dealers in hops.

SIMMONS, E W, (Triangle,) (*Simmons Bros ,*) (*Whitney & Co ,*) post master, dealer in groceries, boots, shoes, drugs and yankee notions, lumberman, hop grower and farmer 35

Simmons, H R , (Triangle,) lot 62, farmer 150

SIMMONS, ROLLIN A., (Triangle,) (*Simmons Bros ,*) farmer 150

Slater, Effa, (Triangle,) milliner and tailoress.

Sly, A , (Whitney's Point,) shoemaker

SMITH, CHAS. F., (Upper Lisle,) lot 25, farmer 138

Smith, Dennis, (Whitney's Point,) tannery

Smith, Erastus, (Upper Lisle,) lot 17, farmer 184.

Smith, E B , (Upper Lisle,) lot 11, farmer 143

SMITH, J L , (Lisle,) lot 3, secretary Stillwater Manuf Co and farmer 140

Smith, Silas, (Upper Lisle,) lot 10, farmer 224

Smith, Willie Jr , (Upper Lisle,) lot 20, farmer 43

SNOOK, COLLINS & CO , (Whitney's Point,) (*J M. Snook, Alonzo Collins and F D Gridley,*) manufa sash, blinds, doors and mouldings

SNOOK, J. M., (Whitney's Point,) (*Snook, Collins & Co* )

Southerland, Andrew, (Whitney's Point,) shoemaker, Main.

Spencer, Jason G., (Whitney's Point,) carpenter.

Stalker, Peter, (Upper Lisle,) lot 11, farmer 185

Standish, Chas., (Triangle,) lot 43, farmer 50

Standish, Cynthia Mrs , (Triangle,) lot 58, farmer 66

Starkey, Geo M , (Upper Lisle,) lot 26, farmer 133

Stearns, Gary, (Whitney's Point,) farmer 11

Stearns, H P Miss, Whitney's Point,) dressmaker Main.

STEVENS, ISRAEL, (Whitney's Point,) insurance agent and farmer 2¼, Main.

Stickney, Amos, (Upper Lisle,) lot 27, surveyor, carpenter and farmer 175

Stone, C H , (Triangle,) wagon maker

Stone, Francis B , (Triangle,) lot 59, farmer leases of Wm. G Guernsey, 108

STONE, STEPHEN N , (Whitney's Point,) dealer in hardware, stoves agricultural implements and glass, Main

Stowell, John M , (Whitney's Point,) lot 27, farmer 55.

Sweet, Eli, (Whitney's Point,) dentist.

Sweetland, Anson, (Triangle,) lot 59, farmer 85

Sweetland, Chas J., (Triangle,) lot 19, farmer 140

Sweetland, F. B , (Triangle,) constable and farmer.

Sweetland, Ira, (Triangle,) lot 23, carpenter and farmer 32

Tabei, Wm L , (Triangle,) lot 3, farmer 87.

Taft, Amos F , (Triangle,) blacksmith and farmer 8.

Taft, Asa, (Triangle,) lot 57, farmer 50.

Taft, Asa P., (Triangle,) lot 1, carpenter and farmer 27

Taft, Chas G , (Triangle,) lot 72, farmer leases of John, 208.

Taft, David, (Triangle,) lot 44, farmer 50.

Taft, Geo M., (Triangle,) lot 57, farmer 115.

Taft, Job, (Triangle,) lot 41, carpenter and farmer 92.

Taft, Lewis, (Whitney's Point,) cabinet maker

TAYLOR, A F , (Upper Lisle,) allo physician

Taylor, C. E. Rev , (Whitney's Point,) pastor M E Church at Chenango Forks and Kattelville, also insurance agent.

Terpening, Truman, (Whitney's Point,) (*Livermore & Terpening* )

Thurston, O. H., (Upper Lisle,) lot 26, farmer 50

Ticknor, Elisha, (Upper Lisle,) lot 14, farmer 50

Ticknor, Geo. S., (Triangle,) lot 55, farmer 128

Ticknor, Lewis M., (Upper Lisle,) farmer leases 200

Ticknor, Marietta Mrs., (Upper Lisle,) lot 29, farmer 155

Ticknor, Marion F., (Triangle,) lot 43, farmer leases 94

Ticknor, Nancy A. Mrs., (Whitney's Point,) lot 64, farmer 100

Ticknor, Samuel, (Triangle,) lot 54, farmer 120

Ticknor, Samuel 2d, (Upper Lisle,) lot 29, farmer 200.

Tillson, Stephen, (Whitney's Point,) lot 33, farmer 117

Todd, A., (Triangle,) prop Kinyon House

Triangle Cheese Co., (Upper Lisle,) H. S. Ballard, secretary; Francis Clough, treasurer; Harry Clough, salesman.

Turner, J. Clark, (Triangle,) carpenter and farmer 10.

Upper Lisle Lodge, F. & A. M., No. 388, (Upper Lisle,) meets every 2nd and 4th Thursdays of each month; Jasper Smith, W. M., R. O. Williams, secretary; L. B. Elliott, treasurer.

VanDerson, Isaac, (Whitney's Point,) (*Goodrich & VanDerson.*)

Vars, Samuel L., (Upper Lisle,) shoemaker.

Vroman, Jacob H., (Triangle,) blacksmith

Watrous, Alfred E., (Upper Lisle,) lot 28, farmer lease of Alex. Hodges, 200.

Webb, Samuel, (Upper Lisle,) lot 20, bark peeler and farmer 12

Webb, Stephen, (Whitney's Point,) lot 42, farmer 173.

Weld, Wm., (Upper Lisle,) lot 19, carpenter and farmer 50.

WHITCOMB, G. O., (Whitney's Point,) (*Perkins & Whitcomb.*)

WHITNEY, ABRAM T., (Triangle,) (*Whitney & Young,*) (*Whitney Bros.,*) farmer 1.

WHITNEY, ADELBERT R., (Triangle,) (*Whitney Bros.,*) engineer

WHITNEY BROS., (Triangle,) (*Abram T. and Adelbert R.,*) lot 74, farmer 100

WHITNEY, DOLPHUS, (Triangle,) (*Whitney & Young,*) farmer 130

Whitney, Elizabeth Mrs., (Whitney's Point,) farmer 175.

Whitney, Wm. D., (Triangle,) broom manuf

WHITNEY & YOUNG, (Triangle,) (*Dolphus and Abram T. Whitney, and Henry Young,*) lumbermen 3 acres

Wilber, John, (Triangle,) lot 45, carpenter and farmer 54.

Wilcox, F. T., (Whitney's Point,) farmer 224.

Wilcox, Wm. D., (Triangle,) lot 60, farmer 50

Williams, R. O., (Upper Lisle,) homeo. physician, minister and farmer 12.

Woodruff, Jolla Miss, (Whitney's Point,) dress maker

Wooster, A. B., (Whitney's Point,) oyster saloon, Collins

Yale, Ransom, (Whitney's Point,) lot 5, drover and farmer 102

Yarns, A. H., (Upper Lisle,) lot 20, farmer 50.

Yarns, Andrew J., (Triangle,) lot 41, farmer 20

YOUNG, HENRY, (Triangle,) (*Whitney & Young,*) collector

Youngs, John, (Triangle,) farmer.

---

# UNION.

## (Post Office Addresses in Parentheses.)

ABBREVIATIONS.—S D, School District: B P, Boston Purchase.

Adams, Joseph P., (Binghamton,) S D. 11, gardener and farmer 12

ADAMY, SOLOMON W., (Union,) dentist and dealer in musical instruments, over Eagle Drug Store, Nanticoke St.

Allen, Francis B., (Binghamton,) S. D 11, farmer 70

Allen, Lawrence, estate of, (Binghamton,) S D 11, 83 acres.

ALLEN, WILLIAM H., (Binghamton,) S D. 11, farmer 23, occupies estate of Lawrence Allen, 83

Anderson, John, (Binghamton,) S. D. 10, farmer 68

Anderson, Luther, (Binghamton,) S. D. 10, farmer leases 68

Andrews, Allen D., (Binghamton,) S. D. 17, farmer 5 and (*with Alonzo G.,*) 16.

Andrews, Alonzo G., (Binghamton,) S D 17, carpenter, farmer 8 and (*with Allen D. Andrews,*) 16

ANDREWS, EUGENE M., (Binghamton,) S D 17, farmer 25

ANDREWS, MILES C., (Binghamton,) S D. 17, farmer 20 and leases of Mrs. B. M Grant, 101

Angell, Barton, (Union,) farmer 40.

ARMSTRONG, ANDREW, (Union,) tailor, corner Main and Exchange.

Bacon, Solomon, (Union,) carpenter and farmer 35

Badger, Marcus M., (Union,) farmer 38, Main.

Baird, Samuel, (Union,) prop. of Railroad House corner Liberty and E R. R

Baker, Russell, (Union,) farmer 70.

# Riverside Gardens,

*(Half a Mile East of Water Works,)*

**BINGHAMTON, N. Y.**

OUR STOCK OF

# Plants, Bulbs, Trees,

## Ornament Shrubs and Seeds,

Embraces all that is new and rare in the several departments, and will be sold at reasonable prices.

*Orders for Plants, Trees, Shrubs, Boquets, Baskets, Crosses, Wreaths, Crowns and other Floral Designs,*

Also for **Flower and Vegetable Seeds**, will receive prompt attention.

**Cabbage and Tomato Plants and Asparagus Roots in their season.**

## D. C. McGRAW, Florist.

[Visitors Welome] (Successor to Mills & McGraw)

---

# The Daily Republican,

## Broome Weekly Republican,

AND

# The Binghamton Standard,

*(SEMI-WEEKLY)*

**BINGHAMTON, N. Y.**

## MALETTE & REID, - Proprietors,

*Republican Building, 98 Water Street.*

Aggregate Circulation greater than that of all the other Newspapers in this city.

**THE DAILY REPUBLICAN**

is a 32 column paper. The WEEKLY contains 48 columns. The STANDARD contains all the news of the Daily. These are the largest and best newspapers published in Southern Central New York, and have been established 24 and 50 years respectively.

---

## BOOK AND JOB PRINTING,

In every style of the Art! More extensive facilities than elsewhere in Binghamton.

Eagle Drug Store. Patent Medicines, Notions, Perfumery, &c. Sold cheap at L. D. Witherill's, UNION, Broome County, N. Y.

Go to HORTON, BROTHER & MYER'S, 32 Court Street, Binghamton, for your Stoves and Tinware. See advertisement. page 277.

BALCH, BENJAMIN, (Union,) justice of the peace and farmer 154, Nanticoke St.

BANKING HOUSE, (Union,) Chandler & Rockwell, Main.

BARDEN, PHILO, (Hooper,) farmer

BARNES, ANDREW J., (Union,) farmer 100.

BARNES, ELIJAH R., (Union,) supervisor and farmer 240, residence Main.

Barnes, Henry J., (Union Center,) S D. 9, farmer 40

Barnes, Jeremiah, (Union,) farmer 154.

Barnes, Jerry E., (Union,) painter, Main.

Barnes, Thomas J , (Union,) farmer 54

BARNEY, DARWIN D., (Union,) farmer 65¾

Barney, Paul, (Union,) farmer 60.

Barnum, Lucas, estate of, (Hooper,) S. D. 10, 80 acres

Bartle, Philip L., (Union,) blacksmith and farmer 32.

BARTON, CHANCELLOR, (Union,) butcher and farmer 42

Barton, Nathaniel W., (Union,) farmer 50.

Bassett, Stacy, (Union,) farmer 42.

Bayles, Theodore, (Union,) farmer 20.

Bean, Stephen, (Union,) farmer 181.

Beecher, Warren S , (Union,) farmer 60.

Benedict, Cephas, (Union,) farmer 14.

BENJAMIN, SAMUEL, (Binghamton,) joint S D. 14, farmer 50

BERGHAM, ELIJAH W., (Binghamton,) (*Wells & Bergham.*)

Berkley, Peter, (Union Center,) teamster and farmer 1.

BIDWELL, WILLIAM, (Binghamton,) S. D 11, farmer 43

Billings, Silas P., (Union,) (*Park & Billings.*)

Birch, John, (Union,) farmer 62.

Blakeslee, Jared D , (Hooper,) S D. 2.

BLAKESLEE, JOHN D., (Hooper,) S. D. 2, farmer 181, Hooper Station.

BLISS, CHARLES M., (Binghamton,) joint S D 14, dairyman and farmer 106.

Bolles, Charles H , (Hooper,) S D. 2, electric physician and farmer 160

Bostwick, Daniel, (Union,) farmer 54

BOSWELL, JOHN R., (Union Center,) lot 100, justice of the peace, assessor, notary public and farmer 80.

Bovee, Ira, (Hooper,) S D 16, farmer 218

Bovee, Rodney, (Hooper,) S D. 16, farmer 28 and leases of Wm B Stevenson, 88.

Boyd, Charles H., (Union,) harness maker and carriage trimmer, Main.

BRADLEY, ASEL, (Union,) farmer 70.

Bradley, Hanan M., (Union Center,) farmer 70

Bradley, Josiah, (Union Center,) farmer 50.

Bradley, Lewis, (Union Center,) speculator in farm produce and farmer 20.

Bradley, Seymour, (Union,) farmer 4.

Bradley, Silas W., (Union Center,) retired farmer.

Brick, Bryan, (Union,) farmer occupies 50.

Brigham, Josiah, (Union,) blacksmith, Nanticoke St.

BROAS, ISAAC V. W., (Hooper,) S. D. 9, farmer 194.

Broas, James P , (Hooper,) S. D. 9, farmer occupies for I V. W Broas.

Broas, Phebe, (Hooper,) S. D 16, weaver.

Brooker, LeRoy, (Union Center.)

Brooks, Law S., (Binghamton,) S. D 11, farmer

Brooks, Wesley, (Union Center,) general merchant and farmer, in Maine, 145

Brown, Alfred N , (Binghamton,) joint S D. 2, gardener and farmer 32

Brown, Brownell, (Hooper,) S. D. 10, retired farmer.

BROWN, BURRITT, (Binghamton,) joint S. D. 2, school teacher and farmer 55.

BROWN, GORDON M , (Choconut Center,) S D. 13, farmer 95.

Brown, L J , (Union,) dry goods, groceries and jewelry, Main.

Brown, Mary, (widow,) (Choconut Center,) S. D. 18, farmer 41.

Brown, Obadiah Z , (Choconut Center,) S D 18, farmer 100

Brown, Oliver C , (Choconut Center,) S D. 18, farmer 47

BROWN, WILLIAM B., (Hooper,) S. D. 10, farmer 65.

Buck, Benjamin, (Union,) farmer 25

Bunker, Stephen, (Binghamton,) farmer 11

BUNN, AMOS W , (Union,) carriage ironing and general blacksmithing, Main

Burdge, Morgan S., (Union,) shoemaker, Main

Burr, Charles H., (Hooper,) S. D. 2, painter and farmer 29

BURRILL, SILAS N., (Choconut Center ) S D 18, prop of steam feed mill, shingle mill, wagon and carriage maker, and farmer 1¼.

BURT, CHARLES W REV , (Union Center,) pastor of Congregational Church.

Butterfield, William H , (Choconut Center,) S. D. 18, lumber manuf. and farmer 40.

Cafferty, Chester, (Union,) farmer 25.

CAFFERTY, JOHN F., (Union Center,) lumberman and farmer 101.

Cafferty, Myron, (Union,) occupies estate of Enoch Cafferty Sen.

Cafferty, William, (Union,) prop. of Union Hotel, Main.

CAFFERTY, WILLIAM 2d, (Union,) (*Rockwell & Cafferty.*)

Campbell, Russell, (Union,) carpenter and builder, Nanticoke St.

Carhart, Susan B , (widow,) (Binghamton,) joint S. D. 2, farmer 8.

Carley, Alanson W., (Binghamton,) S. D. 11, farmer 50.

Carver, Angeline, (widow,) (Binghamton,) S. D. 17, farmer 135

Cary, Ezekiel, (Binghamton,) S. D. 6, farmer 25.

CARY, JOHN, (Union,) farmer 146.

Cary, Stephen, (Choconut Center,) S. D. 13, farmer 50.

Chalker, Oliver C , (Binghamton,) joint S D. 2, farmer 22 and leases 110

Chambers, Amos, (Binghamton,) S D. 11, retired farmer.

Chambers, Benjamin, (Binghamton,) S D 11, farmer 70.

Chambers, Charles, (Hooper,) S. D 16, farmer leases 73.

Chambers, Frank, (Binghamton,) S. D. 11, farmer leases 70.

CHAMBERS, JOSEPH, (Binghamton,) S. D 11, bonedust manuf and farmer 6¾

CHANDLER, DAVID R , (Union,) (*Chandler & Rockwell,*) farmer 40

CHANDLER, ETHAN A., (Union,) (*E. A Chandler & Son*)

*CHANDLER, E A & SON, (Union,) (*Ethan A and Ethan O,*) carriage makers and painters, E C M St

CHANDLER, ETHAN O , (Union,) (*E.A Chandler & Son.*)

CHANDLER, IRA E , (Union,) late dealer in groceries, provisions, confectionery, news &c., 2 Major Block, Nanticoke St

CHANDLER & ROOKWELL, (Union,) (*David R. Chandler and Martin C Rockwell,*) bankers and farmers 105, Main.

CHASE, ISAAC N , (Union,) carriage and sleigh manuf , dealer in village lots and farmer 24, Hannah

Chrysler, John A , (Union Center,) S D 9, farmer 74.

Cinnamond, Mary, (widow,) (Union,) farmer 64

Clark, Daniel, (Binghamton,) S D. 10, farmer 82

CLARK, JULIAN, (Union,) (*J & W Clark,*) assistant supt A & S. R R., residence Albany.

CLARK, J. & W., (Union,) (*Julian and William,*) props of the Vestal Tannery, (sheep skin,) lumber manufs. and farmers 365.

CLARK, WILLIAM, (Union,) (*J & W. Clark,*) residence Liberty St.

CLEAVELAND, ALANSON, (Hooper,) S D 16, boot and shoe maker and repairer, and farmer 35

Cleaveland, Alvin, (Hooper,) S D 16, farmer leases of Walter L Newland, 50

Cleaveland, Charles, (Hooper,) S. D. 16, farmer 125

Cleaveland, Joseph N., (Hooper,) S D. 16, farmer 64

Cleaveland, Rodolphna, (Hooper,) S. D 16, farmer 42

CLEAVELAND, WILLIAM H , (Hooper,) S D 10, farmer 58.

Cleveland, Sevahlon, (Hooper,) S. D 16, farmer leases 42

Clifford, Plant, (Binghamton,) S. D. 18, farmer 12.

COE, CHARLES M , (Union Center,) (*Smith & Coe,*) (*with G. Duane,*) farmer 9.

Coe, G Duane, (Union Center,) carpenter and builder and (*with Charles M ,*) farmer 9

Collard, William, (Union,) carpenter, Nanticoka St.

Cooper, Hoffman, (Binghamton,) S. D. 17, dairyman and farmer 100.

CORNELL, WILLIAM, (Union,) (*Sherwood, Cornell & Co*)

Cornish, W. O., (Union,) farmer 62 in Vestal, residence Liberty.

Cortright, Jervis, (Binghamton,) S D. 13, farmer 55

Cortright, Theodore, (Binghamton,) S. D. 13, cattle dealer, butcher and farmer 45.

Cortright, William, (Chocount Center,) S. D 18, dairyman and farmer 140.

COX, ANDREW J., (Binghamton,) joint S D 2, farmer 67

Crawford, Ezra, (Union Center,) farmer leases of Lewis Ketchum, 100

Crawford, John, (Union,) farmer 1 and leases 101.

CROCKER, ARTHUR E , (Binghamton,) S. D 11, (*A. E. & E Crocker,*) wholesale dealer in stationery and farmer 7¾

CROCKER, A. E & E, (Binghamton,) (*Arthur E. and Elias,*) dealers in lumber and railroad ties, and farmers 22

Crocker, Eli, (Binghamton,) S. D. 11, brick maker and farmer 10

CROCKER, ELIAS, (Binghamton,) (*A E. & E Crocker,*) S D 11, farmer 71

Crocker, George W , (Union,) resident, Main.

Crocker, Levi, (Binghamton,) S D. 17, broom manuf and farmer 30½.

Crocker, Oliver A., (Binghamton,) S. D. 11, farmer 9¾

CROCKER, OLIVER C. Hon , (Binghamton,) S D 11, farmer 200.

CROCKER, ROE, (Binghamton,) S. D 17, prop of saw mill, dealer in pine and hemlock lumber and farmer 70

Cummings, William H., (Hooper,) S. D 16, farmer 15

Cunningham, Joel, (Union Center,) farmer leases 70

Dart, Joseph, (Chocount Center,) S. D. 13, farmer 67.

Davis, Hopkins, (Hooper,) S. D. 16, farmer 1

Davis, John T , (Hooper,) S. D 9, farmer 123

DAVIS, LUTHER, (Hooper,) S. D. 2, farmer 170

Davis, Orlando L., (Hooper,) S. D. 2, farmer occupies 45

DAY, CHARLES M , (Union,) (*H. Day & Son*)

DAY, CHESTER, (Union,) farmer 139.

Day, Darwin Mrs., (Union,) farmer 40

DAY, HENRY H ,(Union,) (*H. Day & Son,*) farmer 200 in Windsor

DAY, H. & SON, (Union,) (*Henry H and Charles M ,*) props of Union Agricultural Works, Main

Decker, Elijah P (Union,) farmer 64

Decker, James, (Union,) farmer 160

Decker, Jesse D , (Union Center,) farmer 41¼.

Dedrick, Edwin C., (Chocount Center,) S. D 13, farmer 75

Dedrick, John P., (Chocount Center,) S. D 13, farmer 246

DEDRICK, MOSES, (Binghamton,) S D 6, cattle dealer, dairyman and farmer 222.

Delfendorf, Charles P., (Union,) house painter and farmer 10.

DeVOE, HENRY D., (Binghamton,) S. D. 11, farmer 48.

DeVoe, John, (Binghamton,) S. D. 11, farmer 5

Deyo, Richard, (Binghamton,) S D 18, farmer 112

DILLON, MORGAN, (Binghamton,) S. D. 13, dairyman and farmer 95

Dodge, Asa Rev., (Union Center,) farmer 50

DUDLEY, ROBERT, (Binghamton,) S. D. 11, farmer leases 80.

DUNCAN, WILLIAM, (Union,) farmer 135

Dunn, Amelia Mrs ,(Binghamton,) tailoress and dress maker, Ashery Corners.

Dunning. Dewitt L , (Hooper,) S. D 2, farmer 32½.

DUNNING, J. FRANK, (Hooper,) S D. 2, farmer 92.

DUNNING, WILLIAM H. H., (Hooper,) S D 10, farmer 60.

Eades, Henry, (Binghamton,) S D 11, farmer leases of Oliver C. Crocker, 200

*EAGLE DRUG STORE, (Union,) Nanticoke St , L D. Witherill, M. D , prop

Eastman, Daniel, (Union,) carpenter and farmer 10

Eastman, Jeremiah, (Union,) farmer 15.

Edson, William, (Union Center,) farmer 47

Evans, Elijah, (Union,) shoemaker, Exchange

Ferris, Aaron, (Hooper,) S. D. 10, farmer 184

Ferris, Harrison, (Hooper,) S. D. 2, farmer leases 100

FICAL, AARON, (Binghamton,) S D 11, dairyman and farmer leases 128

Finch, Joshua M , (Binghamton,) joint S D. 14, farmer leases 50

Finch, Munson, (Binghamton,) S. D. 17, farmer 86

Flint, Zaccheus, (Hooper,) S. D. 16, farmer 20

Foster, Fletcher, (Hooper,) S D. 9, farmer 50

FRAME, WILLIAM C , (Union Center,) tailor and farmer 1

Francis, Edwin A Rev , (Binghamton,) joint S. D. 6, Baptist evangelist and farmer 17.

Gardner, Elisha, (Union,) farmer 67

Gibbs, Ebenezer, (Hooper,) S D 9, farmer 40

Gibbs, Horatio M , (Union,) farmer 93

GIBBS, JONAS C , (Hooper,) S. D. 9, hop raiser and farmer 88

GIBBS, OLIVER A., (Hooper,) S D 9, farmer 56

Gilfoy Richard, (Union,) farmer 1.

GILLETT, ALMON S., (Binghamton,) foreman in Wells & Brigham's brick yard, residence New St., Binghamton

Goodell, Ira W., (Union,) retired farmer, Liberty

Gould, John, ( Union, ) billiard saloon, Nanticoke St

Grange, Thomas, (Union,) farmer 180

Gray, Christopher C , (Hooper,) S D. 2, farmer 165.

GRAY, HALA, (Hooper,) S. D. 2, farmer 80.

Gray, William, (Hooper,) S. D 2, farmer 130.

Green, Ezra, (Choconut Center,) S. D 13, farmer 80

Green, Lewis, (Binghamton,) S. D. 6, farmer 82½

Guyon, James Rev , (Union,) clergyman and farmer 104½.

Hagadorn, John D , (Union,) blacksmith, owns 4 acres, Main

Hagadorn, Sylvenus, (Union,) constable and farmer 9½, Main.

Hagadorn, William A., (Union,) carriage manuf , Main.

Hammond. Mary B., (widow,) (Hooper,) S D. 2, farmer 2.

Harrington, Samuel, (Choconut Center,) S. D. 18, butcher

HARRISON, JAMES E., (Union,) prop. of the Nanticoke Custom and Flouring Mill, and farmer 8

Harvey, Elias S , (Union,) billiard saloon, Main.

Hayes, James, (Union,) manuf of grain cradles, Main

HEATH, AARON, (Union,) manuf of hand rakes fork and hoe handles, and horse rake teeth, farmer 1½

Heath, Ogden R , (Union Center,) mechanic and farmer 1

Heller, Jesse, (Binghamton,) S D. 11, farmer 26½

HIGBEE, FREDERICK, (Hooper,) S D 16, farmer 84

HINDS, EDGAR, (Hooper,) S. D 18, farmer leases 70

Hodge, Faris, (Union,) boots and shoes, Nanticoke St.

Hodge, Lucinda A Mrs , (Union,) millinery, fancy goods and dress making, Nanticoke St

HOGG, JAMES, (Binghamton,) S. D 18, farmer 93

Holhater, Theron R , (Binghamton,) S D. 17, gardener and farmer 16¾

Hooper, Chester, (Hooper,) S. D. 2, farmer 70

HOOPER, FRANK, (Hooper,) S. D 2, postmaster, general merchant and farmer 14. Hooper Station

Hooper, W Wallace, (Hooper,) S D 2, farmer 55

Houghtaling, Henry, (Binghamton,) S D 11, carpenter and farmer 8

Houghtaling, Levi Mrs., (widow,) (Binghamton,) S. D. 17, farmer 2½

HOUGHTALING, MARTIN, (Binghamton,) joint S D 14, farmer 33½.

HOWARD, ALFRED L , (Binghamton ) (*with Colman B ,*) joint S. D. 14, farmer 70 and leases 60

HOWARD, BARZILLA, (Union Center ) (*J. C & B Howard,*) manuf of hand hay rakes and farmer 30.

HOWARD, COLMAN B , (Binghamton,) (*with Alfred L ,*) joint S. D. 14, farmer 70 and leases 60.

HOWARD, EDWIN, (Union Center,) farmer 40 and leases of S S Howard, 81.

HOWARD, JARVIS C , (Union Center,) (*J. C. & B Howard,*) general merchant and postmaster.

HOWARD, J. C. & B , (Union Center,) (*Jarvis C and Barzilla,*) props of Union Center Steam Saw Mill

Howard, Orren, (Union Center,) farmer 120

Howard, Stephen, (Union Center,) wagon maker and farmer 84

Howell, George B , (Union,) barber, Main

Howell, Joseph, (Binghamton,) S. D 6, farmer 2

Hubbell, Almeria, (Binghamton,) S. D 11, gardener and farmer 11

JEFFERS, ALVAH, (Binghamton,) S. D. 11, eclectic physician and farmer 20.

Jenison, Erskine P , (Binghamton,) S D 6., farmer leases 100

Jenison, Lewis, (Binghamton,) joint S. D 2, farmer 48.

Jenison, Luther, (Binghamton,) S D. 6, farmer 158.

Jewell, Charles H Rev , (Union Center,) pastor of M E Church.

Jewitt, Platt, (Union,) farmer 42

Johnson, Chas W , (Hooper,) S. D. 9, farmer 62

JOHNSON, JOHN E , (Binghamton,) joint S D 14, cattle dealer and farmer 119

Johnson, Malcom, (Binghamton,) joint S. D 14, farmer 75

KEELER ALEX P., (Union,) prop. of brick yard and farmer 85

Keeler, Edgar A., (Union,) traveling agent for D. M. & E. G Halbert, Binghamton, and farmer 30

Keeler, J. Mrs , (widow,) (Union,) farmer 30.

Keeler, Lasa E., (Union,) carpenter and farmer 50

Keeler, Lewis W., (Union,) broom manuf and farmer 160

KETCHUM, ALVA K., (Union Center,) farmer 100 and, in Maine, 120

Ketchum, Lnton H , (Union Center,) farmer leases of A. K. Ketcham, 220

Ketchum, Luther M , (Union Center,) farmer 60

King, Myron, (Union,) farmer 32.

Kipp, George D , (Union,) farmer 96.

Kipp, Jefferson, (Union,) farmer 120.

Kipp, Samuel, (Union,) farmer 1½

Kipp, Simeon, (Union,) sexton of M. E. Church and farmer, Main

Knapp, Theodore P., (Union,) homeo physician and surgeon, Main

LaGrange, Moses, (Union,) farmer 23, Main

Lashier, D Franklin, (Hooper,) (*with William*,) S D 9, farmer 50.

LASHIER, SOLOMON, (Union ) carpenter and builder, and dealer in village property, Prospect

Lashier, Theodore (Hooper,) S D 16, farmer 40½

Lashier, William, (Hooper,) butcher and (*with D Franklin*,) S D. 9 , farmer 50.

LATOURETT, JOHN, (Union,) farmer 26½ and occupies for Chandler & Rockwell, 105.

Latouretta, Andrewett, (Union,) farmer 52 and (*with Benjamin*,) leases 90

Latouretta, Benjamin, (Union,) (*with Andrewett*,) farmer leases 90

Latouretto, Eliza W , (Union,) farmer 50.

LATOURETTE, EUGENE, (Union,) farmer leases of William Witherill, 60, and of John Latonrette, 26½.

Latonrette, Mary Mrs., (Union ) farmer 90

LAWYER, EZRA, (Union Center,) physician and surgeon, and farmer 1¾

Lay, Johnathan W., (Binghamton,) S. D 17, milkman and farmer leases 135

Layton, Alonzo, (Choconut Center,) S. D. 18, blacksmith.

LeBarron, George, (Union,) farmer 101

LtBarron, Samuel, (Union,) stage prop., Union to Maine, and farmer leases 40.

LeBarron, Smith, (Union,) farmer 30.

Leonard, Marcus, (Hooper,) S D 9, farmer 27.

Lewis, D. H Crocker. (Choconut Center,) S. D 18, blacksmith and farmer 4

LEWIS, JUSTUS (Choconut Center,) S D. 18. live stock dealer, postmaster and farmer 97

Livingston, Peter, (Union,) farmer 220.

LONERGAN, JOHN, (Binghamton,) joint S D 2, butcher, live stock dealer and farmer 6

Lown, George, (Choconut Center,) S. D. 18, farmer 28

LUCE, WILLIAM H., (Union,) farmer 140.

Lyon, John S , (Union Center,) blacksmith and farmer 54

Maddison, Warren, (Choconut Center,) S D 18, farmer leases of Joseph Cushing, 114

MAJOR HOUSE, (Union,) F L Webb, prop Main

Manier, Alexander, (Binghamton,) S. D 17, farmer 2

Manluve, Solomon, (Union,) farmer 40.

MARTIN, HIRAM C , (Choconut Center,) S D. 18, farmer 16 and, in Maine, 29.

Martin, Mary, (widow,) (Binghamton ) S. D 17, farmer 1.

Mason, Cyrus O , (Union,) farmer 130

Mason, Mary Mrs , (widow,) (Union,) farmer 42.

Mason, Virgil, (Union,) farmer 45.

Mason, William M , (Union,) farmer 69

Matteson, Amos K., (Union,) saw mill in Newark and farmer 206, residence Nanticoke St.

McIntyre, Ebenezer (Binghamton,) S. D. 17, farmer 1¾.

McKeeby, William, (Hooper,) S D. 2, farmer 66

McNary, Mary, (Choconut Center,) S. D 18, farmer 9½

McWADE, H. ELBERT, (Union,) (*McWade & Mercereau*)

McWade, James, (Union,) blacksmith

McWADE & MERCEREAU, (Union,) (*H. Elbert McWade and John D. Mercereau*,) manufs and dealers in wagons, carriages &c., Main.

MERCEREAU, CHARLES L., (Union,) hardware, groceries &c., Main, residence Scranton, Pa., H. C. Mercereau, agent.

MERCEREAU, HENRY C , (Union,) town clerk and agent for Charles L. Mercereau, dealer in hardware, groceries &c., Main.

MERCEREAU, JOHN D , (Union,) (*McWade & Mercereau*)

Mericle, Marvin, (Union,) farmer leases 44.

Mersereau, Aaron, (Union,) groceries, boots, shoes, hats, caps &c., Main.

Mersereau, Christopher, (Union,) carpenter, Main

MERSEREAU, CORNELIUS, (Union,) carpenter and builder, Main

MERSEREAU, E. C., (Union,) general merchant, real estate dealer auctioneer, post master and farmer 50, Main

Mersereau, G. W., (Union,) general merchant, also commission merchant, Main.

Mersereau, Henry, (Union,) farmer 166.

MERSEREAU, HENRY, (Hooper,) S. D. 2, farmer 45

MERSEREAU, JOB L , (Union,) farmer 110, Main.

MERSEREAU, JOHN P., (Union,) railroad engineer and farmer 55

Mersereau, John S.,(Union,) (with Joshua,) farmer 95

Mersereau, Joshua,(Union,) (with John S,) farmer 95

Mersereau, Joshua 2d, (Union,) retired farmer, Main.

Mersereau, Putnam, (Union,) farmer, Nanticoke St

Mersereau, Robert T., (Union,) general merchant Main

MERSEREAU, SEYMOUR, (Union,) engineer, E R, and farmer 14, Main

MERSEREAU, S. AVERY, (Union,) farmer 151½

Mersereau, Timothy D., (Union,) farmer 15 and leases 110

Mersereau, William W, (Union,) commission dealer in butter, eggs &c, Main

Millan, Ann, (Union,) farmer 16.

Mineer, Jacob, (Union Center,) farmer 72

MOODY, EDWIN C, (Union,) attorney at law and fire insurance agent, Main

Moore, Daniel Y, (Hooper,) S D. 2, farmer 56

Morton, Wm A. Mrs, (Union Center,) farmer 70

Moulton, Alexis A, (Union,) farmer 50

NANTICOKE CUSTOM AND FLOURING MILL, (Union,) James E. Harrison, prop.

Nemire, Henry, (Union,) farmer 55.

NEWDALE ALBERT,(Binghamton,) joint S D 2, florist, market gardener and farmer 10

NEWELL, CHAUNCEY (Union,) fire insurance agent, Prospect.

NEWELL, JABEZ C, (Hooper,) S. D. 2, farmer 20 and estate of Charles H. Newell, 95.

NEWLAND, WALTER L, (Hooper,) S. D 2, general blacksmith and farmer 50.

Norton, Henry (Union Center,) farmer 48

Norton William A., (Union Center,) shoemaker

Oliver, Adam, (Union,) farmer 80,

Oliver, Marvin, (Union,) farmer leases 64

OLMSTED, WM JR, (Union,) (William Olmsted & Son)

OLMSTED, WILLIAM & SON, (Union,) (William Jr,) stoves and tinware, Nanticoke St

Orcutt, Ezra, (Union,) S. D. 2, farmer 105.

PALMER, DANIEL J, (Union,) drugs, medicines, fancy goods, chemicals &c, 1 Major Block, Nanticoke St

Parce Henrett, (Binghamton,) joint S D. 6, farmer 1½

Pardee, Alanson, (Binghamton,) S D., 11, gardener and farmer 2

Pardee John S., (Binghamton,) S. D. 11, prize lottery

Park & Billings, (Union,) (Gregory Park and Silas P. Billings,) props of the Major House Livery, Nanticoke St

Park, Eri, (Binghamton,) joint S. D 2, farmer 14.

Park, Gregory, (Union,) (Park & Billings.)

Parsons, Henry, (Union,) wagon maker and farmer 22

PARSONS, HENRY G, (Union,) carriage and wagon maker, and farmer 21½, Rail Road

Pelham Griffin E., (Hooper,) S. D. 2, cooper and farmer 40

PELHAM, ISAAC E., (Union,) carpenter

Pelham, John F, (Union,) bridge carpenter and farmer 80.

Pelham, William, (Union,) cooper and farmer occupies for John F Pelham, 80

Pierce, Isaac, (Union Center,) farmer 40

Pitkin, Chester, (Union Center,) farmer 12

Piatt, Stoddard, (Union Center,) physician and farmer 100

Ralyea, D. Mrs., (Union,) farmer 18, Main

Ralyea, Richard, (Hooper,) S. D 2, station agent, E R R, U S Express agent and farmer 1.

Randall, Seneca, (Union,) shoemaker, Nanticoke St

Redding, Thomas, (Binghamton,) joint S D 6, grocer

Rice, Henry, (Hooper,) (with Willis,) S D 9, shoemaker and farmer 75

Rice, Willis, (Hooper,) (with Henry,) S. D 9, shoemaker and farmer 75.

Richards, James A., (Binghamton,) S D 17, brick maker and farmer 1

Richards, Joel P., (Binghamton,) S. D. 17, farmer

RICKARD, GEORGE W., (Union,) broom manuf. and farmer 112.

ROBBINS, DENISON S, (Union,) mason and farmer 30

*ROBBINS, MOSE H., (Union,) editor and prop Union Weekly News, Main

Roberts, James L, (Hooper,) S. D 16, farmer 89.

Roberts, John H., (Hooper,) S. D 10, farmer 60

Robinson, Jesse, (Binghamton,) S. D. 10, milkman, dairyman and farmer 175

ROCKWELL & CAFFERTY, (Union,) (Martin C. Rockwell and William Cafferty 2d,) dry goods, groceries, boots, shoes &c, Main

ROCKWELL, CHAUNCEY G ,(Union Center,) lot 104, B P, farmer 33.

ROCKWELL, MARTIN C. (Union,) (Chandler & Rockwell,) (Rockwell & Cafferty,) (Sherwood, Cornell & Co,) justice of the peace.

RODMAN, E. Y., (Union,) farmer 156

Roe, Cyrus, (Union Center,) cooper and farmer 30.

Rogers, Atwell (Union Center,) blacksmith and farmer 1

Rogers, Simeon, (Union,) farmer 100

Root, Alton D (Union,) residence Oxford, Chenango Co, patent right dealer and (with Elam D,) hop raiser and farmer 41½.

Root Elam D., (Union) (with Alton D.,) hop raiser and farmer 41½

Round Hill Lodge, No 533 F & A M, (Union,) meets every Tuesday evening in Masonic Hall, Main

Rozell, Charles, (Choconut Center,) S D. 18, stone mason and farmer 112.

ROZELL, EDWARD S, (Binghamton,) general blacksmith and farmer 1, Ashery Corners

RUSSELL, HENRY, (Hooper,) S D 16, farmer 88

Russell, Martin, (Hooper,) S. D 10, farmer leases 63.

Rutherford, Amos, (Binghamton,) S D. 10, (*with Jacob A* ,) farmer
Rutherford, Jacob A , (Binghamton,) S. D. 10 farmer 84
Rutherford, William, J., (Hooper,) S. D 10, farmer 90
Sanford, William G , (Union Center,) farmer 6
Sayer, John H , (Hooper,) S. D. 2, farmer 100
Sayer, Joseph D , (Hooper,) S D 2 farmer 225
Scoville, Horace, (Union,) groceries, provisions, news room &c , carpenter and builder, 2 Major Block, Nanticoke St
Sharpe, James, (Binghamton,) S D. 6, baker and farmer 1
Shaw, Benjamin, (Union,) farmer leases of Lewis W Keeler, 112
Shaw, Jethro, (Union,) farmer leases of Elisha Gardner, 67
SHERWOOD, CORNELL & CO , (Union,) (*William H Sherwood, William Cornell and Martin C. Rockwell,*) props. of steam saw mill, manufs. and dealers in lumber and farmers 270 in Owego
SHERWOOD, WILLIAM H , (Union,) (*Sherwood, Cornell & Co.*)
Shippey, Robert C., (Union,) butcher and prop. of Union Market, Nanticoke St
SHORES, CHARLES, (Hooper,) S D 16, hop raiser and farmer 106
Shores, William, (Binghamton,) carpenter and farmer 72
Shute, Daniel, (Union Center ) farmer 50.
Sibley, Edgar Rev , (Binghamton,) pastor of Choconut Center M E Church
SKILLMAN, FRANK, (Union,) coal dealer, speculator and farmer 16, Railroad near Depot
Skillman, John M , (Union,) carpenter and builder, Liberty.
SMITH & COE, (Union Center,) (*Theron O Smith and Charles M Coe,*) props of Union Center Steam Planing Mill, lath manufs., planing, matching and sawing
Smith, Daniel, (Binghamton,) S. D 17, farmer 1
Smith, David, (Hooper,) (*with George and Frank,*) farmer 122.
Smith, F B , (Union,) attorney, Nanticoke
Smith, Frank, (Hooper,) (*with George and David,*) farmer 122
Smith, George, (Hooper,) (*with David and Frank,*) farmer 122.
Smith, Geo Wheeler, (Union,) farmer 49
Smith, John H , (Hooper,) S. D 2, farmer 29
Smith, J V N , (Union ) farmer 54.
Smith, Nathaniel, (Union Center,) farmer 44
Smith, Samuel, (Union,) (*S. Smith & Son* )
SMITH, SAMUEL F , (Union,) station agent E R R and U S Express agent, Union Station
Smith, S & Son, (Union,) (*Samuel and Warren D.,*) flour, feed, meal, groceries and lumber, Nanticoke St
SMITH, THERON O , (Union Center,) (*Smith & Coe* )
Smith, Warren D , (Union,) (*S. Smith & Son* )

SMITH, WILLIAM G., (Union,) W U. telegraph operator and baggage master, E. R R
Squires, Richard, (Binghamton,) watch maker and farmer 5
Stalker, Gershom, (Union,) farmer 75
Stevenson, William B , (Hooper,) S. D. 2, manuf lumber and farmer 113
Still, William H , (Union Center,) cooper
Stone, Hosea, (Union,) cooper, Exchange.
Stone, Uriah, (Binghamton,) S D. 18, blacksmith and farmer 12
SURDAM, SMITH, (Union,) farmer occupies estate of Ahram Bean, 128
SWARTWOUT, JACOB, (Binghamton,) S D 11. farmer occupies 132
Swartwout, Joel, (Binghamton,) S. D. 11, farmer 132
SWICK, JAMES M , (Union,) prop of Union Bakery, Main
SWIFT, MARTIN J., (Binghamton,) joint D 2, farmer 15
TAYLOR, ALLEN G , (Union,) cooper, manuf of tubs, firkins, barrels and all kinds of cooperage, Exchange
Taylor, Ambrose, (Union,) farmer 165 in Vestal, residence Main
THATCHER, C OTIS Rev , (Union,) pastor of First Presbyterian Church of Union, Main
Thompson, Florentine, (Binghamton,) farmer leases 80
Thompson, Hugh, (Union,) farmer 94
Thompson Lodge, No 633, I O G T , (Union,) meets every Wednesday evening in Rockwell Hall, corner Main and Nanticoke
Thorn, Emma C Mrs , (widow,) (Union Center,) farmer 84.
THORNTON, JOSHUA M., (Union,) basket maker and farmer 35
Thornton, Thomas, (Union,) basket maker and farmer 10
TILBURY, JAMES 2d, (Union,) carpenter and joiner, and farmer 83
Tilbury, Sally Miss, (Union,) farmer 3.
Tilbury, William, (Union,) farmer 60
Titus, Nelson N , (Union,) eclectic physician and surgeon, Prospect
Townsend, Harvey, (Binghamton,) S D 11, prop of East Union House and farmer 2
TRESTER, JOHN, (Union,) general blacksmith, horse shoeing, carriage ironing &c , Hannah
Tripp, Giles P., (Union,) watches, jewelry &c , Main.
TRUESDALE, AMBROSE, (Union,) justice of the peace and farmer 65, residence Main
Twining, Charles, (Hooper,) S. D 9, farmer 82
Twining, Emily, (widow,) (Hooper,) S. D 16, farmer 70
Twining, Philip, (Hooper,) S D 16, farmer 42
TWINING, WILLIAM, (Hooper,) S. D 10, farmer 105.
Twiss, George N , (Union Center,) constable and farmer 1
Twiss, William, (Union Center,) farmer 132
Tyler, Abraham, (Binghamton,) S D. 11, retired farmer 9.

Tyler, Benjamin F , (Binghamton,) S. D 11, farmer 60.

Tyler, James M., (Choconut Center,) S. D. 18, cooper and farmer 10.

Tyler, Silas B., (Binghamton,) S D. 11, farmer 40.

Tyrrell, Caroline, (widow,) (Union,) farmer 10

Ufford, Betsy and Maria, (Union Center,) farmers 6

UNION AGRICULTURAL WORKS, (Union,) H Day & Son, props , Main.

UNION BAKERY, (Union,) Main St , James M Swick, prop.

*UNION WEEKLY NEWS, (Union,) Moss B. Robbins, editor and prop., Main.

VanCLEFT, A. J. Rev., (Union,) pastor of M. E. Church, Nanticoke St.

Vandemark, Asa W., (Union,) farmer 64

VANDEMARK, ISAAC, (Hooper,) S. D. 9, farmer 81

Vandemark, Luke, (Hooper,) S D 9, farmer 86

Vandemark, Wilson, (Hooper,) S. D. 9, farmer 41½

VanName, William, (Union,) sea captain, residence Nanticoke St

VanName, William Mrs., (Union,) milliner and dressmaker, Nanticoke St

VanNOY, ELIAS, (Binghamton,) S. D. 10, farmer 185.

VanNOY, SAMUEL, (Binghamton,) S D 10 farmer 15.

VanPATTEN, JOHN J., (Union,) S. D. 9, hop raiser and farmer 112

VanWormer, Samuel Y., (Hooper,) S. D. 2, farmer 195

WARD, LUKE, (Union,) prop. of Ward's plaster mill, feed, flax and cider mill, and farmer 4

WARNER, J. M., (Union,) groceries, crockery and glassware, Main

Warner, Richard P , (Union,) farmer 20.

Warner, William, (Binghamton,) S D 18, ice dealer and farmer 51¾

WATERMAN, CHARLES H , (Union,) farmer leases of Charles H Bollee, 158.

Waterman, John C , (Union Center,) saw mill and farmer 64

WATERMAN, JOHN W , (Union Center,) lumber manuf. and farmer 86

WEBB, FRANK L , (Union,) prop of Major House, Main

Webb Stephen, (Union,) farmer 43.

Wedge, Wilson, (Binghamton,) S D. 17, farmer 87½

WELLS & BERGHAM, (Binghamton,) (John S. Wells and Elijah W Bergham,) brick manufs and farmers 60

WELLS, JOHN S , (Binghamton,) ( Wells & Bergham,) residence Binghamton City

WEST, MARTIN, (Union,) apiarian, lumber manuf. and dealer in cider vinegar and farmer 30.

West, Orman, (Union,) farmer 90.

Wheeler, Milton, (Union Center,) farmer 4

WHITFORD, CHESTER G.,(Binghamton,) harness maker, dealer in groceries, provisions &c , at Ashery Corners, 2½ miles north-west of city.

Whitney, Joseph S ,(Union,) physician and surgeon, and agent for the Howe Sewing machine, Nanticoke St

Whitney, William W , (Union,) surgeon and druggist, Nanticoke St.

Whittemore, Alonzo W , (Union,) (I V & A. W Whittemore )

Whittemore, Alvin, (Union,) farmer 62

Whittemore, Avery, (Union,) farmer 26½.

WHITTEMORE, EGBERT, (Union,) farmer 61

Whittemore, George, (Union,) farmer 63.

Whittemore, Isaac V , (Union,) (I. V. & A W. Whittemore.)

Whittemore, I V & A. W , (Union,) (Isaac V. and Alonzo W ,) planing mill, sash, door and blind manufs , furniture dealers and undertakers, Main

Whittemore, James S., (Union,) farmer leases 62.

Whittemore, Jasper, (Union,) farmer 46.

Whittemore, Mathew, (Union,) farmer occupies 80

Whittemore, Nathan, (Union,) farmer 4

Whittemore, Orm, (Union,) farmer 28½

WILCOX, FRANK, (Union Center,) farmer

Wilcox, Nathan, (Union Center,) carpenter.

Wilcox, Nathan Mrs., (Union Center,) farmer 12.

Wilkinson, William, (Hooper,) S. D. 2, farmer leases 100.

WILLIAMS, HARRY, (Union,) dealer in town and county rights for Griswold's fanning mill, and farmer 140.

Willis, Truman B., (Hooper,) S D 2, farmer occupies 120

WILSON, ALEXANDER (Choconut Center,) S D 18, dairyman and farmer 141

Winans, Maggie Miss, (Union,) dressmaker, Nanticoke St

Witherill, Hannah, (widow,) (Union,) owns farm 60, Nanticoke St

*WITHERILL, L D , M D , (Union,) physician and surgeon, and prop. of Eagle Drug Store, Nanticoke St.

WOOD, CHARLES D , (Union,) farmer 58

WOODCOCK, NICHOLAS, (Union,) broom manuf and farmer 23½

Woodward, Andrew J., (Union Center,) S. D 16, farmer 60

WOOSTER, JOHN P., (Hooper,) S D 16, farmer leases 185

Wooghter, Jesse, (Union,) farmer 35.

Wright, Isaac B., (Binghamton,) joint S D 14, farmer 7

Wright, Joseph M., (Hooper,) S D 9, farmer 110

Wright, Joseph M , (Binghamton,) joint S D 14, farmer 50

Wright, Martin V , (Binghamton,) joint S D. 14, farmer 50.

Yates, Samuel, (Union,) farmer 30.

Zimmer, Seymour E., (Union,) farmer 60.

# E. A. CHANDLER & SON,
## E. C. M. Street, UNION, N. Y.
### MANUFACTURERS OF
# Heavy and Light Carriages.
### PARTICULAR ATTENTION PAID TO
# Carriage Painting.
☞ *Repairing Promptly Done.*

---

# GEORGE VAN WORMER,
### MANUFACTURER OF AND DEALER IN

# HARNESS
### OF EVERY DESCRIPTION.
*All kinds of Horse Goods constantly on hand.*

Particular attention given to Repairing.
### 61 COURT STREET,
*BINGHAMTON, N. Y.*

Under B F. Sisson Sons' Dry Goods Store.

---

*Established.................. ...... .............1845.*

# Binghamton Democrat
## EVERY THURSDAY.
*GOOD ADVERTISING MEDIUM.*

# DAILY DEMOCRAT,
### IN ITS FOURTH YEAR.
## Issued Every Evening at 15 cts. per Week.
*Office, 89 Water St., "Grecian Building."*

# Job Printing and Advertising
AT LOW RATES.    Terms made known on application.

## W. S. & G. L. LAWYER, Proprietors.

# BURKE, FITZSIMONS, HONE & CO.,

## Importers, Jobbers and Retailers

OF

# DRY GOODS AND FANCY GOODS,

AND MANUFACTURERS OF

# WOOLEN GOODS,

## Nos. 53, 55 and 57 Main Street,

AND

### Nos. 1, 3, 5, 7 and 9 North St. Paul Street,

# ROCHESTER, - - - N. Y.

Having established the most extensive Dry Goods House in the State outside of New York City, we can offer advantages to buyers of Dry Goods unequaled by any other dealers in the country. We import directly and keep constantly on hand full lines of

Broche and Paisley Shawls; Pim Bros. Genuine Irish Poplins,
Black and Colored Silks; Irish Linens and Lace Curtains;
Lupins' Merinoes and Alpacas;

### Hilgers' Celebrated Broadcloths and Doeskins.

Our stock of the following goods is always full and complete:

Cloaks, Sacques and Mantillas; English, French and American Cassimeres; Genesee Falls Cassimeres, "our own make;"
Mohair and Cashmere Dress Goods;
Shaker and Ebenezer Flannels; White, Scarlet and Opera Wool Flannels; Damask Table Cloths and Towelings; Napkins, Doylies and Wine Cloths; Linen Sheetings and Pillow Casings;
3-4, 4-4, 5-4, 6-4. 7-4, 8-4, 9-4, 10-4 and 11-4 Cotton Sheetings.
French, American and Scotch Ginghams;
English, French and American Calicoes;
Woolen and Cotton Yarns, Blankets, Quilts and Counterpanes;
Real Laces and Embroideries; Swiss Nainsook and Victoria Muslins; Fancy Goods and Yankee Notions; Ribbons and Trimmings; Hosiery, Wrappers and Drawers; Balmoral and Hoop Skirts, &c, &c, &c., &c.

Our Jobbing business, which now extends from the Eastern portion of the State to the "Far West," offers inducements to city and country Merchants equal to any house in the United States. In addition to our advantages as Manufacturers and direct Importers, we have the sale of several makes of Brown Cottons and Woolen Mills in this locality.

Price Lists and Samples furnished on application, and orders sent by mail or entrusted to our agents, will receive prompt attention, and Dealers can rely upon purchasing of us the year around

## AT NEW YORK JOBBERS' PRICES.

R

# O. D. BEMAN,

## Watchmaker and Engraver,

### AND DEALER IN

## Gold & Silver Watches, Clocks, Jewelry and Silver Ware,

## 89 COURT STREET, - BINGHAMTON, N. Y.

Having located permanently in Binghamton, I respectfully solicit a share of your patronage, and offer the following inducements:

1st.—An experience of twenty years.

2nd.—No "jours" or apprentices.

3rd.—I have at great expense procured a complete outfit of machinery for manufacturing any part of a watch, new.

4th.—I have the ONLY absolutely perfect standard of time in this part of the State, viz., A fine Regulator Clock; and Marine Chronometer, by Frodsham, of London; also a Transit Instrument for taking the time directly from the sun or stars. By the use of the Transit any variation of the Chronometer amounting to only five-tenths of a second in a month, would be instantly detected.

5th.—I have but one rule in repairing fine Watches, viz., to repair it so that it is impossible to tell that it was ever broken.

☞ Refer by permission to Hon. JOB N. CONGDON, Ex-Mayor, Binghamton, and WM. H. COOPER, Banker, Montrose, Pa.

# O. H. GREEN,

# MERCHANT TAILOR,

## 79 BROAD STREET,

## Waverly, N. Y.

### A COMPLETE LINE OF

# CLOTHS & TRIMMINGS

### AND

## Gents' Furnishing Goods.

**First Class Artists in the Trade, and all Work Warranted.**

# VESTAL.

(Post Office Addresses in Parentheses.)

Adams, Harry, (Union,) farmer 53.
Aldridge, Frederick, (Vestal,) farmer 220.
Ames, James M , (Binghamton,) farmer 46½
Andrews, Judson, (Vestal,) farmer leases 220.
Angell, Laurana, (Tracy Creek,) farmer 7.
Babcock, Franklin, (Tracy Creek,) farmer 20
Baker, George, (Vestal,) farmer 30.
Baker, John, (Tracy Creek,) farmer 25
BAKER, R H., (Tracy Creek,) farmer 50
Baker, Sherman, (Tracy Creek,) farmer 41.
Baker, William, (Tracy Creek,) farmer 90.
Balcomb, Clarissa H., (Tracy Creek,) farmer 57.
Balcomb, Francis, (Tracy Creek,) farmer 8
Barlow, Morris Jr., (Vestal Center,) farmer 28
Barnum, Lucius, (Tracy Creek,) justice of the peace, shoemaker, tanner and farmer 4½
Bartholomew, Archibald, (Vestal,) farmer 53
Bartholomew, George, (Vestal,) farmer 55
Bartholomew, Henry, (Union,) farmer 100
Bartle, H P , (Union,) carpenter.
Barton, Alonzo, (Tracy Creek,) farmer 10
Barton, Orson, (Vestal,) farmer 30.
BATCHER, H V , (Vestal Center,) prop. of hotel
Baty, John, (Union,) farmer 70.
Baty, Ransom, (Vestal,) farmer 50.
Baty, Ransom, (Union,) farmer 81
Benjamin, Allen, (Union,) farmer 95.
Benjamin, Amaziah, (Tracy Creek,) blacksmith.
Benjamin, George A., (Vestal Center,) farmer 86
Benjamin, Minor, (Vestal Center,) farmer 30
Benn, Edwin, (Binghamton,) farmer leases 100.
Birdsall, Elemnel, (Binghamton,) farmer 153½.
Blackman, William, (Union,) farmer 22
Blakeslee, Wm , (Vestal,) physician.
Bloodgood, John D. Rev., (Vestal,) pastor M E Church
Boice, Henry, (Vestal,) farmer 25
Boren, Arthur, (Vestal Center,) farmer 107.
Borroughs, C. D., (Tracy Creek,) blacksmith and farmer 32
Borroughs, O. Mrs., (Vestal Center,) farmer 23
Bradley, John, (Vestal Center,) farmer 75
Bradley, Julian, (Binghamton,) farmer 80.
Bradley, Joshua, (Binghamton,) farmer 80.
Braman, James, (Hawleyton,) farmer 50
R

Brimmer, Abram P , (Vestal,) farmer 46½.
Brimmer, Daniel H., (Tracy Creek,) farmer 50
Brimmer, P W , (Vestal,) farmer 84
BRIMMER, SIDNEY J., (Tracy Creek,) farmer 30
Bronk, Erastus, (Vestal Center,) farmer 50 and leases of A Jenks, 50
Brown, Henry, (Vestal Center,) farmer 140.
Brown, James C., (Vestal Center,) town collector and farmer 62.
Brown, Samuel D., (Vestal Center,) general merchant.
Brown, Sanford S., (Vestal Center,) farmer 60 and agent for Aaron Healey of New York City, prop of French Tract, 2,900 acres.
Brown, Sylvenna, (Vestal,) farmer 50
Brown, William, (Vestal,) farmer 25
BROWN, WILLIAM H., (Vestal Center,) farmer 38½.
BULLOCK, BARNET, (Tracy Creek,) (Noyes & Bullock )
Campbell, A R , (Tracy Creek,) carpenter and farmer 70.
Card, Allyda E , (Tracy Creek,) farmer 117.
CARD, BENJAMIN G., (Tracy Creek,) farmer 74½
Card, Jason B., (Tracy Creek,) farmer 10.
Card, John R., (Tracy Creek,) farmer 50
Card, Jonathan (Tracy Creek,) farmer 34½
CARD, SYLVENUS, (Tracy Creek,) farmer 41.
Castleman, Nicholas, (Tracy Creek,) farmer 166.
Chamberlin, Samuel, (Vestal Center,) farmer 52½
Chandler, Nathan, (Union,) farmer leases 240.
Chase, William, (Vestal Center,) blacksmith
Chichester, ——  Mrs., (Vestal Center,) farmer 40
CHIDESTER, J D , (Tracy Creek,) carpenter and joiner
Chidester, John G., (Tracy Creek,) farmer 7
CHOCONUT MILLS, (Vestal,) Lee & Dewey, props
Clark, Patrick, (Vestal Center,) farmer 313
CLARK, SYLVESTER S , (Vestal Center,) carpenter and joiner, and farmer 1.
Clarke, Daniel M , (Vestal Center,) postmaster.
Clifford, Richard, (Vestal,) farmer 165.
Cobb, Eben, (Vestal Center,) farmer 20
Coffin, E C., (Tracy Creek,) farmer 101
Cogswell, George F , (Hooper,) farmer 4.

COLE, HENRY REV, (Tracy Creek,) pastor of Reformed Methodist Church

Cole, S W., (Tracy Creek,) local preacher and blacksmith.

COLLINS, JOHN, (Tracy Creek,) farmer 170.

Collins, Richard, (Vestal,) farmer 80.

Coon, John, (Hawleyton,) farmer 50

Cornell, H, (Binghamton,) farmer 121.

Cory, Carlos E, (Vestal Center,) farmer 50 and leases 50

Cory, Freeman, (Union,) farmer 30

Cory, Luther, (Vestal Center,) farmer 50.

Cox, I J, (Tracy Creek,) farmer 86.

Crane, Elias W., (Union,) farmer 130.

Crane, Ryason W., (Union,) wagon maker and farmer 13.

CROCKER, CHARLES, (Vestal,) blacksmith

Cronan, Edward, (Binghamton,) farmer.

Crom, J. C., (Tracy Creek,) farmer 40.

Daniels, Amos Rev., (Vestal,) pastor of Baptist Church and farmer 50

DAVENPORT, WILLIAM W, (Tracy Creek,) postmaster, overseer of the poor and farmer 145.

Davidson, William, (Tracy Creek,) farmer 50

Davis, Freeman, (Binghamton,) farmer leases 61.

DAVIS, GURTEN, (Binghamton,) farmer 50.

Day, John H, (Vestal Center,) prop of store and farmer 20

Decker, Horace, (Hawleyton,) farmer 100

DeGens, Alanson, (Tracy Creek,) farmer 40

DeGens, Harlow, (Tracy Creek,) farmer 1¼.

DeGens, Reuben, (Tracy Creek,) farmer 38

DeGROAT, H. BRADFORD, (Tracy Creek,) farmer 50.

DePuy, Charles, (Vestal,) farmer 73

DePuy, James, (Vestal,) farmer 90.

Denel, Abner, (Tracy Creek,) farmer 47.

DEWEY, M M, (Vestal,) (*Lee & Dewey*.)

DOREMUS, WILLIAM A., (Union,) farmer 55

Driscoll, William, (Vestal Center,) farmer 5.

Drum, Alexander, (Vestal Center,) farmer 55.

Drum, John T., (Vestal Center,) farmer 15.

Drum, Simon, (Vestal Center,) farmer 54.

Drum, Wm. A., (Binghamton,) farmer 40.

Dubois, Daniel, (Union,) farmer 80

Dubois, George, (Vestal,) farmer 50

DUBOIS, JOHN, (Union,) farmer 46.

Dunning, T. J., (Binghamton,) farmer 75.

Egleston, George H., (Tracy Creek,) farmer 100.

ELDREDGE, WARREN M., (Union,) town constable

Eldridge, Charles, (Union,) farmer 24.

Eldridge, G R., (Union,) (*with Lewis*,) farmer 180.

Eldridge, Lewis, (Union,) (*with G. R.*,) farmer 180

ELLIS, ALBERT R., (Vestal Center,) justice of the peace, civil engineer and farmer 57.

Ellis, Henry B, (Vestal Center,) saw mill and farmer 25

ELLSWORTH, WM. H., (Tracy Creek,) prop. of cooper shop

ENGLE, PAUL M., (Vestal Center,) farmer 125

Ensign, Charles, (Vestal,) farmer 60.

Ewell James, (Vestal) general merchant.

FAIRBROTHER, ALMON H., (Vestal Center,) farmer 85.

Fairbrother, Chester L., (Vestal Center,) farmer 60

Fairbrother, Thomas, (Vestal Center,) farmer 154

Fairbrother, William, (Vestal Center,) farmer 180

Fancher, J W., (Union,) farmer 106

Felter, George, (Binghamton,) saw mill

Flint, J F, (Tracy Creek,) farmer 3½.

Forker, J, (Binghamton,) farmer 63.

Fowler, Addison M., (Binghamton,) farmer 90.

Gage, William C., (Hawleyton,) farmer 54.

Gahagan, Thomas, (Hawleyton,) farmer 50

Gannane, Michael, (Vestal Center,) farmer 123.

Gardner, Delilah, (Tracy Creek,) farmer 58.

GARDNER, HIRAM H., (Vestal,) farmer 10.

Gardner, Issac, (Binghamton,) farmer 60

Garrison, Chester, (Vestal,) farmer 25.

Garrison, George, (Vestal,) contractor of railroad work and excavations.

Garrison, Richard, (Vestal,) farmer.

GATES, LEE C, (Binghamton,) farmer 187

GATES, LEVI S, (Binghamton,) farmer 45.

GATES, THOMAS R, (Binghamton,) farmer 50.

Gates, Washington, (Vestal,) farmer 9.

Goodnow, James S, (Tracy Creek,) farmer 170.

Goodnow, James S, (Tracy Creek,) farmer 135.

Goodnow, Jane, (Tracy Creek,) farmer 80.

Goodnow, Marcellus, (Tracy Creek,) farmer 10

GOODNOW, WALTER S, (Tracy Creek,) farmer

Green, Daniel, (Tracy Creek,) farmer 60.

Green, F., (Tracy Creek,) farmer.

Griffis, Mahlen, (Vestal Center,) farmer 137½.

Grippin, Leander, (Union,) farmer 25

Grippin, Nathan, (Union,) farmer 90

Groat, Ira, (Vestal Center,) farmer 48

Groat, Philip, (Vestal Center,) farmer 90

Gurney, Wm C., (Vestal Center,) butcher and farmer 7

Hagadorn, Job, (Union,) wagon maker, patent right agent and farmer.

Haight, Henry, (Union,) farmer 40.

Haight, Lydia, (Union,) farmer 16.

Halpine, John, (Vestal Center,) farmer 196

HANCE, ASHER C., (Hawleyton,) farmer 160.

Harding, William, (Tracy Creek,) farmer 15

Harris, Henry, (Vestal,) farmer 91

Harris, Thomas, (Vestal,) wagon maker and farmer 32.

Harrington, Richard D., (Vestal,) farmer 150

HARVEY, ISAIAH P., (Union,) farmer 87.

Harwood, Maurice, (Binghamton,) farmer 75.

Heath, Asa B., (Binghamton,) farmer 114

Hellygus, Peter, (Vestal Center,) farmer 63.

HEWETT, GEO. W., (Vestal Center,) shoemaker
Hill Delilah, (Vestal Center,) farmer 90.
Hines, George, (Vestal Center,) blacksmith and farmer 80.
Hines, Silas, (Binghamton,) farmer leases 206.
Hoak, Abimaaz, (Vestal,) farmer 25.
Holton, Henry, (Tracy Creek,) farmer 100.
Howard, Enos I., (Vestal Center,) farmer 70.
HOWARD, JERRY D, (Tracy Creek,) general dealer in dry goods, groceries and general merchandise.
Hull, James A., (Tracy Creek,) farmer 50.
INGRAHAM, JOHN L, (Binghamton,) farmer 100.
Jackson, George, (Vestal,) farmer 20
Jaycox, David, (Hawleyton,) farmer 27.
Jaycox, John, (Hawleyton,) farmer 61
Jenks, Harrison, (Tracy Creek,) farmer 86.
Jenks, Sabin, (Vestal Center,) farmer 50.
Jenks, Thomas J., (Vestal Center,) retired merchant.
Kallam, George L., (Vestal Center,) farmer 86.
Keator, Cyrus, (Binghamton,) (with John,) farmer 107.
Keator, John, (Binghamton,) (with Cyrus,) farmer 107.
Kellam, Bradford, (Vestal Center,) farmer leases 40
Kellam, Chester, (Vestal Center,) farmer 62½.
Kellam, Gilson, (Vestal Center,) farmer 82½.
Kelly, David, (Union,) farmer 7.
Kennedy, John, (Vestal Center,) farmer 55.
Kimball, Jacob, (Vestal,) farmer 11
Kimball, Joseph A., (Vestal,) farmer 30.
Kimball, Mary A., (Vestal,) farmer 50.
Kinney, Mathew, (Union,) farmer 50.
KNIGHT, AARON W., (Tracy Creek,) farmer 1.
Knight, J. L., (Tracy Creek,) farmer 52.
LaGrange, James S., (Union,) farmer 70.
LANDON, ALBIN, (Vestal Center,) farmer 150
Landon, Isaac, (Binghamton,) farmer 60.
LANDON, MARVIN, (Binghamton,) farmer 100.
LANDON, WILLIAM, (Vestal Center,) mason and farmer 50.
Lathrop, Ezekiel, (Vestal Center,) saw mill and farmer 30.
LATHROP, IRA, (Vestal Center,) sawyer and farmer 12.
Latonratte, Peter, (Vestal,) retired farmer.
Layton, Harriet M, (Union,) farmer 100.
Layton, Jacob, (Union,) farmer 28
LEE & DEWEY, (Vestal,) (H. F. Lee and M. M Dewey,) props. of Choconut Mills, dealers in flour, feed, hides, wool &c.
LEE, H F., (Vestal,) (Lee & Dewey.)
LeGrange, Moses, (Vestal,) farmer 75.
Lester, H W., (Vestal Center,) farmer 67¾.
Lewis, Page Mrs, (Binghamton,) farmer 300
Lillie, Benjamin, (Tracy Creek,) farmer 63.
Lindsey, Oren E., (Union,) farmer 40.
Loveland, Jay, (Vestal Center,) farmer 50.
Lynch, Daniel, (Binghamton,) farmer 50.
Marcle, Peter, (Vestal Center,) farmer 100.
Marine, Lucian, (Tracy Creek,) farmer 59.

Martin, James, (Binghamton,) farmer 75.
MASON, W. S., (Tracy Creek,) farmer 68.
McCain, Rose Mrs., (Binghamton,) farmer 206.
McEvoy, Michael, (Binghamton,) farmer 100.
McEvoy, Michael, (Binghamton,) farmer 40.
McIntyre, David, (Vestal Center,) farmer 90
McIntyre, Ezra, (Binghamton,) farmer leases 70.
Meddangh, Frank, (Union,) farmer 113.
Meeker, Henry, (Hawleyton,) farmer 120.
Meeker, Lorenzo, (Hawleyton,) farmer 50
Meeker, Norman, (Hawleyton,) farmer 50.
Merseran, Cornelius, (Vestal,) justice of the peace, shoemaker and postmaster.
Merseran, Daniel, (Union,) farmer 65.
Merseran, Eogene, (Union,) butcher.
Merseran, Wallace, (Union,) farmer 50
Monagan, Thomas, (Hawleyton,) farmer 194.
Moran, Patrick, (Vestal Center,) farmer 52.
Morris, Titus, (Binghamton,) farmer 53.
Morse, Amos, (Hooper,) farmer 116.
Morse, Eliza, (Hooper,) farmer 80.
Morse, Susan, (Hooper,) farmer 40.
Morton, George, (Tracy Creek,) blacksmith.
Murdock, Austin, (Vestal,) farmer 90.
Murphee, John A., (Vestal Center,) farmer 63.
Murphy, Catherine, (Vestal Center,) farmer 80.
Murphy, Daniel, (Vestal Center,) farmer 140.
Murphy, Jeremiah, (Vestal Center,) farmer 89
Murphy, Michael, (Vestal Center,) farmer 127½.
Murphy, Michael, (Vestal Center,) farmer 63.
Murphy, Timothy, (Vestal Center,) farmer 127.
Natswire, Wallace, (Vestal,) farmer 97.
Nelson, Daniel S., (Vestal Center,) farmer 45.
Nelson, Miner, (Vestal Center,) farmer 45.
Nemire, Simon P., (Tracy Creek,) farmer 25
Newcomb, Samuel, (Vestal Center,) farmer 50.
Nichols, Charles, (Vestal,) farmer 90
NOYES & BULLOCK, (Tracy Creek,) (James Noyes and Barnet Bullock,) props. of Tracy Creek Steam Saw Mill and manufs. of lath.
NOYES, JAMES, (Tracy Creek,) (Noyes & Bullock )
NOYES, SAMUEL H., (Tracy Creek,) farmer 336
O'Brien, Edward, (Binghamton,) farmer 130.
O'Brien, Patrick, (Binghamton,) farmer 45.
Osborn, Henry, (Binghamton,) farmer 11.
Osborne, Ashbill, (Binghamton,) farmer 47
Orsborne, Jacob S, (Vestal Center,) wagon maker and farmer 75
Osincap, Asbury, (Vestal Center,) farmer 143
OSINCUP, GILBERT, (Vestal Center,) farmer 100.
Page, Clinton F., (Binghamton,) saw and grist mills.
Palts, Eliza, (Union,) farmer 112.
Park, Smith, (Union,) farmer 115.

PARKER, HENRY S., (Vestal Center,) M E clergyman, justice of the peace and farmer 52½.

Parks, Arrin, (Binghamton,) farmer leases 10

PARKS, MILTON J., (Binghamton,) peddler.

PATRIE, ALEXANDER, (Vestal Center,) farmer 50

Peabody, H Eugene, (Union,) farmer 40.

Peabody, Hiram W , (Union,) inspector of election and farmer 100

Phelps, John A. Rev , (Vestal Center,) Baptist minister.

Pickett, Gideon, (Vestal,) carpenter

Pierce, Cornelius, (Vestal,) farmer 60.

Pierce, John, (Vestal,) farmer.

Pierce, Lyman, (Vestal,) farmer 65

PIERSON, CHARLES G., (Vestal Center,) (with William M ,) lumberman and farmer 538

PIERSON, ISAAC F , (Binghamton,) prop of steam saw mill, lumberman and farmer 398

PIERSON, MARY O , (Binghamton,) farmer 100

PIESON, WILLIAM M., (Vestal Center,) (with Charles G.,) lumberman and farmer 538

Platt, Epenetus, (Vestal Center,) farmer 24 and leases of Mrs O Burroughs, 22.

Plough, Abram, (Tracy Creek,) farmer 62.

PLOUGH, TOBIAS, (Tracy Creek,) commissioner of highways and farmer 100.

Post, William, (Vestal,) farmer 90

Potts, Furman, (Tracy Creek,) farmer 70

Potts, William, (Vestal,) farmer 45.

Powers, Catharine Mrs , (Vestal )

Prentiss, Malcom, (Union,) farmer 156

Preston, W H , (Vestal Center,) farmer leases 38½.

Price, Eyas W , (Vestal,) farmer 45.

Ralyea, William B , (Union,) saw mill and farmer 287

Randall, John, (Vestal,) farmer.

Randall, Samuel, (Vestal,) farmer 85

Randall, Theodore, (Vestal,) farmer 45.

Rathbun, J T , (Union,) farmer 137.

Razy, G R , (Binghamton,) carpenter and farmer 18

Reynolds, John, (Vestal Center,) farmer 69.

Rhinevalt, Orman C.,(Vestal Center,) blacksmith

Rhodes, David J , (Binghamton,) farmer 17.

Rhodes, Jacob K , (Binghamton ) farmer 20

Riley, Peter, (Hawleyton,) farmer 115

ROACH, PERRY, (Vestal Center,) farmer 104.

Robinson, James H , (Binghamton,) farmer 83.

Rockwell, Isaac R., (Union,) farmer 130.

Ross, G. E., (Union,) farmer 100.

Ross, T J., (Union,) farmer 50

ROUNDS, ALFRED, (Union,) prop of Vestal Blue Mills, custom and saw mills, and farmer 180.

Rounds, Amanda, (Vestal,) farmer 105

Rounds, Ira, (Vestal,) farmer leases 105.

ROUNDS, JACOB L , (Union,) supervisor and farmer 200

Rounds, John D., (Union,) lumberman and farmer 175

Rounds, Mima, (Union,) farmer 225

Rounds, Orrin, (Vestal,) farmer 119

Rush, W. D., (Binghamton,) farmer 12

Russell, Aaron S., (Union,) farmer 90

Russell, Andrew J , (Union,) farmer 35.

RUSSELL, AUSTIN, (Tracy Creek,) farmer 60

Russell, Green, (Tracy Creek,) farmer 82

Russell, Washington, (Tracy Creek,) farmer 75

Schemerhorn, Cornelius, (Vestal Center,) farmer 90.

Searles, Lorenzo, (Binghamton,) farmer 16

SEELEY, GEORGE W., (Hooper,) farmer 50.

Seeley, Polly, (Binghamton,) farmer 75

Seeley, William H , (Binghamton,) farmer leases 40

Seymour, Charles, (Binghamton,) farmer 80

Seymour, Chester, (Vestal,) farmer 336.

Seymour, Daniel, (Binghamton,) farmer 10.

Shae, Timothy, (Binghamton,) farmer leases 100

Sheldon, Henry A., (Binghamton,) farmer 180

Sigler, Peter H , (Vestal Center,) farmer 75.

Simmons, Isaac, (Vestal,) farmer 8

Simpson, Charles, (Hooper,) blacksmith

Smith, Andrew, (Binghamton,) farmer 100.

Smith, Christopher, (Vestal,) farmer 25

SMITH, FRANKLIN E., (Tracy Creek,) farmer 10

SMITH, JABEZ J., (Hawleyton,) farmer 87

Smith, John, (Vestal,) farmer 40.

Smith, Lewis, (Hooper,) farmer 80

Smith, Luther J , (Tracy Creek,) farmer 47.

Smith, Melancthon, (Vestal Center,) farmer 38.

Snedaker, Cornelius, (Binghamton,) carpenter and farmer 140.

Snyder, J. M., (Hooper,) farmer 40

Spalding, Alfred O , (Union,) farmer 60

Spalding, Reuben, (Union,) farmer 35

Spaulding, Frank, (Union,) farmer 60

Springer, Edmond T , (Binghamton,) farmer leases 180.

Stanbro, Hiram, (Vestal,) mason.

Stanley, Adam, (Binghamton,) sawyer and farmer 40

Stiles, Lewis L , (Vestal Center,) farmer 106½

Stone, Martin, (Binghamton,) farmer 216.

STRATTON, CORNELIUS, (Union,) constable and farmer 6

Sullivan, Daniel, (Tracy Creek,) farmer 60

Sullivan, John, (Tracy Creek,) farmer 75

Sullivan, Martin, (Tracy Creek,) farmer 30

Swan, Alma B Mrs , (Vestal Center,) farmer 145

SWAN, CHARLES T , (Vestal Center,) town clerk and farmer 62

SWAN, RYAS P , (Vestal Center,) butcher and farmer leases 145

Swartwood, Jacob, (Tracy Creek,) farmer 83

Tallmadge, Jonathan, (Binghamton,) farmer 180.

Taylor, Ambrose, (Vestal,) farmer 113

TAYLOR, DANIEL, (Union,) prop of steam saw mill and planer.

TAYLOR, EDWIN, (Vestal,) farmer leases 113

Taylor, Harvey, (Vestal Center,) farmer 170.

Thompson, Hamilton, (Vestal,) farmer 2.

Thompson, Reuben, (Binghamton,) farmer 5¼.

Tillbury, Jane Mrs., (Vestal Center,) farmer 107.

Timberman, John M., (Binghamton,) farmer 30.

TINN, PATRICK, (Binghamton,) farmer 58.

Towner, Ernest F., (Vestal Center,) saw mill and farmer 8½.

TRACY CREEK STEAM SAW MILL, (Tracy Creek,) Noyes & Bullock, props.

Travis, Ann, (Vestal,) farmer 45.

Truesdell, Davis D., (Vestal Center,) mill-wright, prop. saw mill and farmer 50.

Truesdell, Wilson J., (Vestal Center,) mill-wright and farmer 96.

TUCKER, J L., (Tracy Creek,) carpenter and builder.

Tuthill, John W., (Tracy Creek,) farmer 60.

Umsted, Mrs., (Binghamton,) farmer 150.

Underwood, Edward, (Tracy Creek,) farmer 104.

Vail, Alanson, (Vestal,) mason.

Van Vorss, Cornelius, (Hawleyton,) farmer 50.

VESTAL BLUE MILLS, (Union,) Alfred Rounds, prop.

Vosburg, Adam, (Hawleyton,) farmer leases 50.

Vosburg, Jacob, (Binghamton,) farmer 94.

Wakeman, Stephen, (Vestal Center,) farmer 100.

Walker, Lemuel, (Vestal Center,) farmer 82.

Walradt, Horace, (Tracy Creek,) farmer 60.

Weed, Irving, (Binghamton,) farmer 120.

WELLS, CHARLES C., (Vestal Center,) farmer 100.

WELLS, COE, (Vestal Center,) farmer 264.

Welsh, Margaret, (Binghamton,) farmer 75.

Welsh, Michael, (Binghamton,) farmer 20.

Welsh, Patrick, (Binghamton,) farmer 61.

Wendel, Henry, (Tracy Creek,) farmer 20.

WEST, DAVID B., (Binghamton,) lumber-man and farmer 220.

Western, William H., (Vestal,) farmer 40.

Westfall, Albert, (Vestal,) farmer 13¼.

Westfall, Simeon, (Binghamton,) saw mills.

Wheeler, John, (Vestal,) farmer 8¼.

WHEELER, LEE, (Tracy Creek,) prop. of planing mill and wagon shop.

Whitaker, Eliah R., (Union,) farmer 44.

Whitaker, John, (Tracy Creek,) farmer 58.

Whiting, Robert, (Vestal Center,) farmer 90.

Whittaker, Jasper, (Tracy Creek,) farmer 35.

WHITTAKER, SILAS, (Tracy Creek,) farmer 40.

Wilcox, Asa B., (Vestal Center,) farmer 60.

Wilcox, Oliver, (West Windsor,) farmer 50.

Wilcox, Silas, (Vestal Center,) farmer 41.

Wilcox, Wm R., (Vestal Center,) farmer 59.

Willis, Benjamin, (Hooper,) (*with Ryason*,) farmer 175.

Willis, Hannah, (Hooper,) (*with Sabrey*,) farmer 30.

WILLIS, JOHN, (Binghamton,) farmer 50.

Willis, Joseph, (Binghamton,) farmer 56½.

Willis, Ryason, (Hooper,) (*with Benjamin*,) farmer 175.

Willis, Sabrey, (Hooper,) (*with Hannah*,) farmer 30.

Winans, A. D., (Hooper,) farmer 69.

Worick, Daniel, (Tracy Creek,) farmer 80.

Worick, Daniel, (Tracy Creek,) farmer 60.

Wright, Ebenezer, (Binghamton,) lumber-man and farmer 100.

Wright, John, (Union,) farmer 30.

YATES, F M., (Vestal,) carpenter and farmer 64.

Yates, Johnson, (Hooper,) farmer.

---

# WINDSOR.

## (Post Office Addresses in Parentheses.)

ABBREVIATIONS —N P., Nicholas Patent; M. T., Morris Tract; A T, Allison Tract; L T, Lane Tract; G. T., Garnsey Tract; B. P., Binghamton Patent, N T, Norton Tract; R T., Randolph Township; C. T, Clinton Tract, H. T, Hooper Tract; S T, State Tract, F. T, Floyd Tract; H P, Hammond's Patent, G L., Gospel Lot; L L, Literature Lot, D. T., Doubleday's Tract.

Adams, Chas., (Windsor,) lot 106, farmer 121.

Adams, E. Mrs., (Windsor,) lot 13, Hommedien Patent, farmer 35.

Ainsworth, A., (West Windsor,) lot 7, Lawrence Tract, farmer 7.

Alden, Alanson, (West Windsor,) F. T., carpenter and farmer 54.

ALDEN, B F., (West Windsor,) F T., farmer 160.

Alden, Daton A., (Randolph Center,) lot 3, R. T, farmer 30.

Alden, Horatio, (West Windsor,) lot 12, Lawrence Tract, farmer 100.

ALDEN, JOHN C., (Randolph Center,) lot 3, R. T., farmer leases of Eri Kent, 114.

Alexander, Zina, (Randolph Center,) R T, farmer 52.

Alexander, Zira, (Windsor,) S.T., farmer 61.

ALLEN, CHAS. H., (Great Bend, Susquehanna Co., Pa.,) lot 13, R T, farmer 102.

ANDREWS, A. A., (Great Bend, Susquehanna Co., Pa.,) lot 10, R T, farmer 40.

ANDREWS, GEO W., (Great Bend, Susquehanna Co., Pa,) lot 9, R. T., farmer 250.

ANDREWS, R ALBRO, (Great Bend, Susquehanna Co , Pa ,) lot 10, R. T , farmer 108

ANDRUS, CHAS. Q., (Great Bend, Susquehanna Co., Pa ,) lot 9, R T , farmer 160

ANDRUS, ERASTUS, (Windsor,) N. P., farmer 74

Andrus, Joseph, (Windsor,) N. P., farmer 125

Andrus, Sherman P , (Windsor,) S T., carpenter and farmer 92

Ash, Robert, (Windsor,) L T , farmer 107

ATWELL, SAMUEL C , (Windsor,) lot 4, G T , farmer 127

ATWOOD, JOHNSON, (Randolph Center,) lot 9, R T , blacksmith and farmer 48.

AUSTIN, RUSSELL, (Windsor,) farm laborer

Baker, Benj H , (Windsor,) F T , farmer leases 148

Baker, Chas. M , (Windsor,) lot 13, Hommedien Patent, farmer 100.

Baker, Horace, (West Windsor,) lot 69, L. T , farmer 103

BALDWIN, HERMON, (Windsor,) mason

Ballard, James E , (Windsor,) N. P , farmer 27¾

Barnes, Joseph, (Windsor,) F T , teamster, constable, collector and farmer 80

BARNEY, ALBERT, (Windsor,) lot 4, A T , dealer in real estate and western land, and farmer 170

BARRETT, EDWIN L , (Windsor,) station agent

Bartholomew, Robert, (Windsor,) wagon maker

BARTON, ADNA B , (Windsor,) lot 10, Sherwood Tract, blacksmith and farmer 61.

Barton, Asal, (Windsor,) lot 2, Sherwood Tract, farmer 90.

Barton, Ezra P , (Windsor,) lot 9, Sherwood Tract, carpenter and farmer 20.

Barton, Hiram, (Windsor,) lot 10, Sherwood Tract, cabinet maker and farmer 40

BATHRICK, JOHN H., (Windsor,) (with William M Gregory,) N P , farmer 185

Baxter, Justin, (Great Bend, Susquehanna Co , Pa.,) lot 14, R T , farmer 85

BEAVAN, EDWARD D , (Great Bend, Susquehanna Co , Pa ,) lot 15, D T , lumberman and farmer 100

Beavan, Thos , (Great Bend, Susquehanna Co , Pa ,) lot 13, S. T., farmer 230.

Beckwith, N. B , (Windsor,) shoemaker.

BEDIENT, GEO. M , (Windsor,) A T., farmer leases of Nelson Minor, 100

Bedine, Martin, (Windsor,) S. T., farmer leases of Isaac Atwell, 55

Beebe, Charles, (Windsor,) lot 8, H. T., farmer 125.

BEEBE, CLARK, (Windsor,) lot 9, H T , farmer 121

BEEBE, LYMAN, (Windsor,) lot 9, H T , farmer 186

BEEBE, R. C., (Windsor,) lot 4, H T , farmer 105

Beebe, Simon, (Windsor,) N. T., farmer 70.

Beebe, ——, (Windsor,) physician

Belden, James R , (Windsor,) general merchant.

Bell, James W , (Randolph Center,) lot 4, R T , farmer 257

Benn, James, (Windsor,) G T , farmer 95.

*BENNETT, J E , (Windsor,) lot 5, R. T., general merchant and farmer 125

Bennett, L , (Randolph Center,) F. T , farmer 40.

Benson, Francis, (Cascade Valley,) (with James Hurbert,) lumberman and farmer 201.

BENSON, JAMES, (Cascade Valley,) (with Francis,) farmer 201.

Bevier, Joshua, (Windsor,) G T., broom manuf and farmer leases 170.

BICE, JEREMIAH, (Cascade Valley,) lot 10, farmer 115.

Bice, Nelson, (Cascade Valley,) B. P , farmer 198.

Birch, Christopher, (Great Bend, Susquehanna Co., Pa.,) lot 10, S. T , farmer 90

BIRD, BENJAMIN, (Windsor,) (Lewis Hurbert & Co.)

Blakesley, Warren, (Windsor,) lot 27, farmer 102

BLATCHLEY ALBERT C , (Great Bend, Susquehanna Co , Pa ,) lot 12, R. T., grist mill and farmer 120

Blatchley, Asa, (Great Bend, Susquehanna Co , Pa ,) lot 12, R. T., farmer leases 70

BLATCHLEY, A. P , (Great Bend, Susquehanna Co , Pa ,) prop. steam saw mill and millwright.

BLATCHLEY, ERASTUS R., (Great Bend, Susquehanna Co , Pa ,) lot 12, R. T., farmer 108

BLATCHLEY, FRANK A., (Great Bend, Susquehanna Co , Pa.,) lot 12, R T , sawyer and farmer 45.

BLATCHLEY, LEANDER, (Randolph Center,) lot 8, R T , farmer 50

BLATCHLEY LEE O , (Great Bend, Susquehanna Co , Pa ,) laborer in saw mill.

Blatchley, Rods M , (Great Bend, Susquehanna Co , Pa.,) lot 12, R. T , resident

BLATCHLEY, SOLON S , (Great Bend, Susquehanna Co , Pa ,) lot 12, R. T., carpenter and farmer 15

BLATCHLEY, URI E , (Great Bend, Susquehanna Co , Pa.,) lot 12, R. T., prop. steam saw mill and farmer 370.

BLATCHLY, NERI, (Randolph Center,) lot 8, R T , manuf of plows and farmer 270

Bourne, John, (Windsor,) lot 7, Hommedien Tract, farmer 75.

BRINK, GEO., (Kirkwood,) F T , farmer 85 and leases of Wm. M Weed, 160.

Brink, S Mrs , (Windsor,) N P., farmer 30

BRIZZEE, MELISCENT Mrs., (Windsor )

Brown, Allen, (Windsor ) lot 5, H T., farmer 80

Brown, Austin R., (Randolph Center,) (Brown Bros )

Brown Bros , (Randolph Center,) (Silas P and Austin R ,) lot 3, R T , farmer 50

BROWN, FRANK, (Kirkwood,) F T , farmer 110.

Brown, Joseph, (Randolph Center,) lot 3, R. T., postmaster and farmer 100.

Brown, Julius, (Great Bend, Susquehanna Co., Pa.,) lot 11, S. T., farmer leases of H. T. Gray, 90.

Brown, J. C., (Randolph Center,) F T., farmer 102.

BROWN, J S., (Randolph Center,) R T, farmer 35 and leases 150

Brown, Silas P, (Randolph Center,) (*Brown Bros*)

Brown, Thos , (Randolph Center,) lot 3, R. T., farmer 40

Brown, William D., (Cascade Valley,) wagon maker and farmer 70.

Brownell, Bennet, (Ouaquaga,) lot 74, H. P., farmer 300

Brownell, Chas , (Windsor,) lot 88, H P , farmer 60.

Brownson, E N , (Randolph Center,) F. T , farmer 150

BUELL, ALBERT, (Windsor,) G T., farmer 100 and on lot 14, R. T., 71.

BUELL, PLATT S , (Windsor,) patent right dealer, patentee and manuf of conical concave spring bed bottoms.

Bull, Henry, (Great Bend, Susquehanna Co , Pa.,) lot 13, R. T., farmer 41 and leases 160

BULLOCK, GEORGE E, (Windsor,) blacksmith.

Bullock, Jacob, (Windsor,) carriage maker and blacksmith

Burgess, S Rev., (Randolph Center,) pastor Wesleyan M E. Church.

BURHYT, JOHN M., (Cascade Valley,) lot 12, farmer 228.

Burnside, Thos , (Windsor,) A. T , farmer leases of H Manwarren, 250

Burt, Gideon, (Cascade Valley,) B. P., sawyer and farmer 36

Bute, J., (Windsor,) lot 18, Hommedieu Patent, farmer 100.

Butler, Edward W., (Cascade Valley,) lot 11, farmer 102.

Carl, Edgar, (Ouaquaga,) farm laborer.

CARRIER, ELIJAH, (Windsor,) N. P., farmer 120.

Chafee, Azotus, (Ouaquaga,) lot 77, farmer leases of Isaac Doolittle, 60

Chafee, Julius B , (Ouaquaga,) resident

CHAFFEE, J. M , (Windsor,) spoke maker and notary public.

Chamberlain, Chas., (Great Bend, Susquehanna Co., Pa.,) lot 14, D. T., farmer 60

CHAMBERLAIN, J. D , (Great Bend, Susquehanna Co., Pa.,) lot 15, D. T., butcher and farmer 56

Chapel, J C , (Windsor,) retired

Chase, David L , (West Windsor,) L L., farmer 86.

Chase, Jarius, (Windsor,) grocer.

Chase, S Mrs , (West Windsor,) lot 9, Lawrence Tract, farmer 83.

CHILD, ORRIN W., (Ouaquaga,) Harper Patent, farmer 182.

CLAPPER, SAMUEL, (Cascade Valley,) farmer leases 80

CLEARWATER, JOSEPH N , (Windsor,) cabinet maker and turner.

Coburn, A. W., (Windsor,) spoke and whip manuf

Cole, B. W., (Windsor,) N. P , farmer 26 and leases of Julia Woodruff, 24.

COMSTOCK, ABNER, (Windsor,) lot 6, A T , farm laborer.

COMSTOCK, BENJAMIN F., (Windsor,) (*with Philo,*) lot 7, A. T., farmer 500.

COMSTOCK, PHILO, (Windsor,) (*with Benj. F* ,) lot 7, A T , farmer 600

COMSTOCK, SABASTIAN, (Cascade Valley,) lot 8, postmaster and farmer 50.

Comstock, William, (Cascade Valley,) lot 8, farmer 50.

Conklin, Alvin, (Great Bend, Susquehanna Co ,) farmer 73

CRANDALL, DANIEL E., (Great Bend, Susquehanna Co., Pa.,) mason and carpenter.

Crandell, Richard, (Windsor,) (*with Salmon,*) L T , farmer 80.

Crandell, Salmon, (Windsor,) (*with Richard,*) L T , farmer 80

Cregan, John, (Cascade Valley,) N. P , farmer 90.

Cresson, Benjamin F., (Windsor,) N. T , farmer 108

CRESSON, SILAS S., (Ouaquaga,) lot 13, farmer 83

Cresson, William, (Windsor,) lot 12, A. T., farmer 60

Cresson, William G , (Windsor,) A. T , mason and farmer 60

Cronk, Nelson B., (Cascade Valley,) R T , farmer 90.

Cruse, Michael, (Windsor,) farmer 28 and leases of Eliza Adams, 56.

Cruse, Patrick, (Windsor,) lot 13, Hommedieu Patent, farmer 45.

Curtis, Geo., (West Windsor,) F. T., farmer 30

CURTISS, RILEY, (Windsor,) farmer leases of Henry Vanwarren, 225.

Darling, Henry A., (Cascade Valley,) lot 26, 2d Tract, saw mill and farmer 125.

DAVENPORT, GEO , (Windsor,) lot 14, R T , farmer 50

Davis, Abram, (Great Bend, Susquehanna Co , Pa ,) (*Spearbeck & Davis* )

DIBBLE, A. V , (Windsor,) lot 5, R. T., farmer leases of J. Bennett, 125

Dickinson, Morton, (Ouaquaga,) lot 11, C T., farmer 140.

DICKSON, CHAS T , (Windsor,) Moore Tract, farmer 72.

DOBSON, JACOB D , (Great Bend, Susquehanna Co , Pa ,) lot 4, D T., lumberman and farmer 46.

Doolittle, David, (Windsor,) N. P., farmer 120.

Doolittle, Dorman, (Ouaquaga,) lot 77, farmer 50.

DOOLITTLE, HARVEY P , (Ouaquaga,) lot 8, C. T., farmer 100.

Doolittle, Henry, (Windsor,) N. P., saw mill and farmer 180

Doolittle, Nelson E , (Ouaquaga,) lot 77, farmer 50

Doolittle, Orin, (Windsor,) N. P , farmer 100.

Drak, Levi, (Windsor,) farmer leases of L Doolittle, 30

DRAPER, EDMOND T., (Ouaquaga,) lot 11, C T , farmer 41

Dusenbury, George, (Windsor,) general merchant and farmer 2,000.

Dyer, Chas. W., (West Colesville,) lot 69, farmer 137

DYER, G L , (West Windsor,) lot 66, L. T , farmer 90

Eager, Wm , (Great Bend, Susquehanna Co., Pa ,) lot 8, N. T., farmer 137.

Edson, Elbert, (Windsor,) lot 102, H. P., carpenter and farmer 60.

Edson, M Mrs, (Windsor,) lot 13, Hommedieu Patent, farmer 20.

Edson, S C, (Windsor,) physician

EDWARDS, ADDISON, (Windsor,) farmer

Edwards, Alvin, (Windsor,) L T., farmer 160

Edwards, Alvin, (Windsor,) lot 4, A T, farmer 180

EDWARDS, HIRAM P., (Great Bend, Susquehanna Co, Pa,) lot 9, R T, farmer 80.

Edwards, John, (Windsor,) N P, farmer 134

Edwards, Judson, (Ouaquaga,) lot 74, farmer 112.

Edwards, Julius, (Windsor,) resident.

Edwards, Robert B., (Windsor,) lot 9, A. T., farmer 55.

EDWARDS, SIMON R., (Windsor,) N. P., farmer 50 and lessee of Mrs Polly Gillmore, 114

Edwards, Wm. E, (Windsor,) lot 9, A. T, farmer 55.

EGLESTON, MERRITT, (Ouaquaga,) lot 22, C T, farmer 71

Eighmy, Elias, (Windsor,) lot 12, D T. farmer 45

Ellis, Ira, (Windsor,) N P, agent for hay tedder and rake, and farmer 195

ENGLISH, ALBERT, (Ouaquaga,) lot 20, N T, farmer 130.

English, ——, (Windsor,) lot 88, H. P, farmer 150.

EVERETT, ROBERT, (Great Bend, Susquehanna Co., Pa.,) Hotchkiss Tract, farmer 77.

Evert, Lamont, (West Colesville,) G. L, farmer 163

FAIRCHILD, E. E, (Windsor,) farm laborer and engineer

Fairchild, George, (Cascade Valley,) lot 6, farmer 180

FAIRCHILD, P. B., (Randolph Center,) teacher.

Faulkner, Wm. R., (West Windsor,) F T, farmer 90

FISHER, ADELBERT P, (Great Bend, Susquehanna Co, Pa,) lot 6, D. T, lumberman and farmer 37½

FISHER, JAMES G, (Windsor,) lot 12, A T, lumberman and farmer 165.

Fisher, John E., (Windsor,) butcher

Fisher, M, (Windsor,) G T, lumberman and farmer 103

FISK, ABRAM, (Windsor,) sawyer.

Fletcher, A, (West Windsor,) lot 7, Hommedieu Tract, farmer leases 240.

Flint, D W., (Windsor,) F. T., stone mason and farmer 70

Flint, Elijah W., (Windsor,) lot 14, R T., farmer 40

Flint, Ephraim, (Great Bend, Susquehanna Co, Pa,) Hotchkiss Tract, farmer 45

Ford, A. M. Mrs., (Windsor,) A. T., farmer 11

Ford, J H, (Windsor,) shoemaker

Foreman, Emma Jane Mrs, (Great Bend, Susquehanna Co., Pa.,) lot 11, D T., farmer 20.

Fowler, Frederick, (Windsor,) lot 77, farmer leases 67.

Freeland, Russel, (Windsor,) lot 106, farmer 136

Freeman, Aaron, (Ouaquaga,) lot 11, farmer 44

Freeman, Andrew D., (Windsor,) lot 77, farmer 140.

Freeman, James W, (Windsor,) physician and surgeon.

Frost, Alberto, (Randolph Center,) lot 3, R T, farmer leases 86

FROST, C L, (Windsor,) lot 8, H. T., butcher and farmer 29

Frost, M, (Randolph Center,) F T, farmer 90.

Furgerson, Isaac, (Windsor,) lot 4, farmer 300

Gaphney, Patrick, (Cascade Valley,) 3d Tract, farmer 110

Gardner, Lucina, (Ouaquaga,) farmer 31

Garlick, Charles E, (Windsor,) (with Samuel R,) lot 8, A T, farmer 170.

Garlick, Samuel R, (Windsor,) (with Charles E,) lot 8, A T, farmer 170

GARLOW, E H, (Windsor,) hotel keeper and lumberman.

Garrett, W L, (Windsor,) lot 112, H. P., farmer 100.

Gates, Henry, (Windsor,) farmer 12

Gernsey, W, (West Windsor,) lot 13, Lawrence Tract, farmer 43

Goodell, E, (Windsor,) lot 5, R T, farmer 82.

Goodenough, Jonas, (Windsor,) lot 6, A. T, farmer 111.

GOODRICH, CHANCEY W, (Gulf Summit,) farmer, in Sanford, 45

Grace, James, (Kirkwood,) lot 2, R T, farmer 60

Gray, Sabin, (Great Bend, Susquehanna Co, Pa,) lot 4, R T., carpenter and farmer 46

GRAY, SILAS P., (Cascade Valley,) B P., carpenter and farmer 160

Green, Theadoah, (Great Bend, Susquehanna Co., Pa,) carpenter

GREGORY, WILLIAM M., (Windsor,) commissioner of highways and (with John H Bathrick,) N P, farmer 185

Griggs, Alvin, (Randolph Center,) lot 3, R T., farmer 50

Griggs, Bruce B, (Windsor,) lot 116, farmer 5.

GRIGGS, OLIVER, (Windsor,) lot 116, H. P, farmer 165.

Grosvant, P. S., (Windsor,) whip maker

GUERNSEY, ORLAN N, (Great Bend, Susquehanna Co., Pa.,) lot 13, R. T., farmer 150

Guernsey, Wm. M., (Windsor,) planing mill and carding machine.

Gurnsey, P and P Mrs, (Randolph Center,) R. T, farmer 150

Hagerty, Dennis, (Great Bend, Susquehanna Co., Pa.,) lot 7, R. T, farmer 80

Hagerty, John, (Great Bend, Susquehanna Co., Pa.,) lot 7, R T, farmer 30

Hall, Benj., (West Colesville,) lot 62, farmer 54

Hall, Caroline, (Windsor,) lot 62, farmer 83.

Hall, E, (West Windsor,) lot 22, Lawrence Tract, farmer 100.

Hall, Erastus, (Windsor,) lot 62, farmer 96

Hall, Samuel, (Windsor,) shoemaker
HALLOCK, FRED N, (Windsor,) lot 1, M T., farmer 45
HALLSTEAD, JOHN A., (Windsor,) wagon maker and laborer in mill.
HAMILTON, JAMES, (Windsor,) whip maker and foreman.
HAMLIN, GEO. H.. (Randolph Center,) wagon maker and blacksmith
Hammond, Alex., (Great Bend, Susquehanna Co., Pa,) lot 9, N. P., farmer leases 148.
Hams, Hiram, (Windsor,) lot 12, A. T., farmer 2¼.
HANES, ALSON, (Windsor,) N. P, farmer leases of George Deusenbury, 126
Hanson, Isaac B., (Windsor,) lot 14, A. T., farmer 200.
Hard, Alanson P., (Windsor,) lot 5, R. T., farmer 83.
Hargrave, Thos J., (Great Bend, Susquehanna Co, Pa,) lot 3, Sherwood Tract, boatman and farmer 100.
Harise, Truman, (Windsor,) lot 7, N. P., farmer 20.
Harris, Samuel W, (Windsor,) lot 4, A. T., farmer 80.
Harvey, Edward, (Ouaquaga,) lot 73, tin peddler and farmer 166
Hatch, Samuel, (Windsor,) teamster and peddler
Hawkins, Alfred, (Great Bend, Susquehanna Co., Pa.,) lot 13, N. P., farmer 20.
HAWKINS, EBEN, (Windsor,) N. P., carpenter and farmer 41.
Hawkins, Malcolm N., (Windsor,) lot 9, Sherwood Tract, farmer 60.
Hawkins, Nathan, (Great Bend, Susquehanna Co., Pa.,) lot 12, S T., farmer 25.
Hawkins, Thos, (Great Bend, Susquehanna Co, Pa.,) lot 12, S. T., saw mill and farmer 23
Haxton, Abram, (Great Bend, Susquehanna Co., Pa.,) lot 12, S. T., farmer 23.
Haynes, Wm. A., (Windsor,) hotel keeper
HAZARD, EDWARD A., (Great Bend, Susquehanna Co, Pa,) lot 7, N. P., farmer 170
Hazard, Franklin F., (Great Bend, Susquehanna Co, Pa,) lot 7, N P, farmer 41.
Hazard, Hiram C, (Great Bend, Susquehanna Co., Pa.,) lot 12, R. T., M. E. preacher and farmer 70.
HAZARD, JAMES G., (Great Bend, Susquehanna Co, Pa.,) Carpenter Tract, farmer 105
HAZARD, OLIVER P., (Great Bend, Susquehanna Co., Pa.,) lot 12, R T, farmer 140
Heath, Ervin, (Windsor,) lot 20, Hommedieu Patent, farmer 62.
Heath, Giles, (Windsor,) farmer leases of Chas. Lyons, 120
Heath, Isaac, (Ouaquaga,) farmer 80 and leases of Nathan Stockwell, 90.
Heath, Wallace N, (Ouaquaga,) lot 75, farmer 58
HENDRICKSON, SIMON, (Windsor,) L T, farmer leases of Lanson Simpkins, 136.
Hickcox, Gilgirt, (Ouaquaga,) lot 22, farmer 46.

HICKCOX, ROBERT, (Cascade Valley,) (*Watte & Hickcox*)
Higley, Isaac G, (West Windsor,) lot 18, Lawrence Tract, farmer leases 100
Hoadley, A A., (Windsor,) F. T., farmer 120
HOADLEY, EDWIN, (Windsor,) F. T., farmer leases 120
HOADLEY, JOHN W., (Windsor,) F. T., farmer 100.
Hoadley, Julian, (West Windsor,) lot 7, Lawrence Tract, farmer 113.
Hoadley, O, (Windsor,) F T., farmer 100
Hoadley, Samuel, (West Windsor,) lot 6, Lawrence Tract, farmer 97.
Hoadley, Thiron, (West Windsor,) lot 11, Lawrence Tract, farmer 70
Hoadley, Truman, (Windsor,) F T., farmer 80
Hoadley, U. R., (Windsor,) lot 15, Hommedieu Patent, farmer 100.
Hoadley, Walter, (Randolph Center,) lot 3, R. T., farmer leases of Wm. Bowman, 100.
Hoadley, Wm W., (Windsor,) F. T., farmer 100.
Holmes, Benj F., (Ouaquaga,) lot 73, brick mason and farmer 40
Homan, Oliver H. P., (Windsor,) grocer.
Hotchkiss, D. H, (Windsor,) miller, flour dealer and justice of the peace
HOTCHKISS, GEORGE, (Windsor,) lot 15, A T, farmer 100.
Hotchkiss, Harry, (Windsor,) N. P., flouring mill and farmer 33.
HOTCHKISS, THOMAS D, (Windsor,) lot 26, N. P., lumberman and farmer 75
HOTCHKISS, W. W., (Windsor,) lumber and bark dealer, and farmer 487
Howe, Samuel, (Windsor,) lot 7, N. P, farmer 38
Howell, Samuel, (Randolph Center,) R. T, farmer 76.
Hoyt, Coonrod, (Great Bend, Susquehanna Co, Pa.,) lot 18, R T., farmer 50.
Hubbard, Asa, (Windsor,) N. P, farmer 49.
Hubbard, Otis, (Windsor,) N. P., constable and farmer 126.
HUGABOOM, LEWIS, (Cascade Valley,) saw mill and farmer 60.
Hugaboom, Alvin, (Windsor,) lot 6, Hommedieu Tract, farmer leases of L Wooster, 94
HULBERT, LEWIS & CO, (Windsor,) (*Benjamin Bird,*) blacksmithing
Humaston, Grover, (Windsor,) lot 16, H. P., farmer 84.
HUMASTON, WILSON L., (Windsor,) harness maker.
HUMISTON, HENRY W, (Windsor,) N P., lumber dealer, farmer 40 and leases 180
HUPMAN, A. P., (Windsor,) G. T., farmer 210
Hupman, Geo S, (Windsor,) lot 14, R. T., prop of saw mill, farmer 149 and leases of Albert Buel, 100.
Hupman, John, (Windsor,) lot 7, H T, farmer 300
HUPMAN, M. P., (Windsor,) N. P, butcher and farmer 150
Hurlbert, A., (Windsor,) sewing machine agent.

HURLBURT, ANDREW W , (Center Village,) lot 11, Harper Tract, farmer 170

Jenkins, Benj. A., (West Coleville,) lot 60, farmer 157.

Jenkins, Willis, (West Coleville,) farmer leases of Mrs. Blatchley, 25.

Johnson, C. D , (Kirkwood,) lot 2, R. T , farmer 100

JUDD, ADBERT, (Great Bend, Susquehanna Co., Pa ,) lot 9, N. P., farmer 148

Judd, Allen S , (Randolph Center,) retired farmer.

Judd, Avery P , (Windsor,) Moore Tract, farmer 48.

JUDD BROS., (Randolph Center,) (*Leman N. and Wm H.*,) R. T , farmers 113

Judd, Daniel, (Randolph Center,) lot 9, R. T , farmer 83.

JUDD, GEO G , (Windsor,) N. P., justice of the peace and farmer 155.

JUDD, L D , (Randolph Center,) lot 9, R T , assessor, agent for mowing machines and wheel rakes, and farmer 130

JUDD, LEMAN N., (Randolph Center,) (*Judd Bros*)

JUDD, WM. H , (Randolph Center,) (*Judd Bros.*)

KENT, ERI, (Windsor,) R T , farmer 1000

KENYON, ELISHA, (Windsor,) G T., farmer 100

Kerr, Alexander, (Onaquaga,) C. T., farmer 220

KETCHUM, L F Rev , (Windsor,) pastor Randolph M. E. Church

Kayes, Chas C , (West Windsor,) lot 67, farmer leases of R. Sherwood, 96.

Keyes, Geo., (Windsor,) lot 108, H. P , farmer 90

KEYES, ISAAC P , (West Windsor,) (*with Levi*,) farmer.

Keyes, Levi, (West Windsor,) lot 17, Lawrence Tract, farmer 140

Killogg, M. Mrs , (Windsor,) lot 5, Hommedieu Tract, farmer 50

Knowlton, Gurdon, (Windsor,) N. P., farmer 100.

Knowlton, Henry M., (West Windsor,) lot 11, Lawrence Tract, stock dealer and farmer 40.

Knowlton, L W , (West Windsor,) lot 13, Lawrence Tract, commissioner of highways and farmer 68.

Knowlton, R. G , (West Windsor,) F T., farmer 80.

Knox, George, (Onaquaga,) farmer 10.

Knox, Merritt N , (Onaquaga,) C T , farmer 77.

KNOX, MILTON, (Onaquaga,) lot 15, C T., farmer 300.

LAMPMAN, JOHN, (Great Bend, Susquehanna Co., Pa.,) lot 13, R. T., farmer 50.

Langdon, Milo, (Windsor,) G. T., farmer 88.

LARABEE, B H ,(Randolph Center,) F T , inspector of elections, music teacher and farmer 62

Law, ——, (Windsor,) lot 4, Hommedieu Tract, farmer 200.

LEWIS, S. A , (Windsor,) dealer in hides, pelts, skins &c

Lord, Emery R , (Onaquaga,) lot 75, farmer leases 52.

LOVEJOY, IRA W., (Cascade Valley,) R. T., farmer 40.

LOVEJOY, LUTHER W., (Cascade Valley,) R T , farmer 40

Loveland, R J , (Great Bend, Susquehanna Co , Pa ,) lot 11, R. T , farmer 45.

Loveland, Wells, (Windsor,) lot 103, H. P., farmer 90.

Lovland, Silas, (Randolph Center,) lot 9, R. T., farmer 25.

Lynch, Albert E , (Windsor,) N P , lumberman and farmer 155

Madigan, John, (Cascade Valley,) 3d Tract, farmer 100.

Manning, Chancy, (Windsor,) lot 10, H. T., farmer 135

Manville, Henry E , (West Windsor,) lot 69, L. T , farmer 40

MANWARING, EDWARD S., (Windsor,) lot 11. A. T , farmer 400.

MANWARREN, ALBERT, (Windsor,) N P . meat market, grocery and farmer 92.

Manwarren, Henry, (Windsor,) farmer 1300.

Martin, Anthony, (Great Bend, Susquehanna Co., Pa.,) laborer.

Mason, Steroe, (Windsor,) lot 93, H. P., lumberman and farmer 185

Mathews, Chas. H., (Windsor,) N P , farmer leases 125

MATTESON, SPICER W., (West Windsor,) mason, justice of the peace and farmer 3

Mayo, Cyrus, (Windsor,) lot 2, A. T., farmer 25.

Mayo, Dennis, (West Windsor,) L. L, farmer 35.

Mayo, Ezra, (Great Bend, Susquehanna Co , Pa.,) lot 12, S T , farmer 18

Mayo, Geo , (West Windsor,) lot 3, Lawrence Tract, farmer 20.

MAYO, L BENNETT, (Windsor,) N. P., farmer 59

MAYO, LEVI, (Great Bend, Susquehanna Co., Pa ,) lot 13, R T , farmer 60.

Mayo, Warren, (Lanesborough, Susquehanna Co , Pa ,) B P , farmer 5

McCLURE, GEORGE W., (Windsor,) saw mill and millwright

McIntyre, Addison, (Windsor,) farmer leases of Henry English, 80.

McKUNE, GILBERT E , (Lanesborough, Susquehanna Co., Pa.,) B. P , farmer leases 160.

McKune, Joseph F , (Lanesborough, Susquehanna Co., Pa ,) B P , farmer 273

McMAHON, DANIEL, (Cascade Valley,) lot 22, farmer 160

MERRELL THOS. R., (Windsor,) lot 105, H. P., farmer 86.

MILLER, GEO., (Windsor,) boot and shoemaker

MOAT, ANTHONY B , (Windsor,) N P , cooper and farmer 25.

Moat, James S (Windsor,) cooper

MOORE, HENRY Y., (Windsor,) Moore Tract, farmer 100.

MOORE, RICHARD W., (Windsor,) lot 12, A T , farmer 8

MOORE, S. B., (Windsor,) F. T., farmer 111.

MORRIS, ORLANDO, (Ouaquaga,) farmer 80

Morrison, George, (Windsor,) lot 33, N. P, farmer 50

Morse, Russel, (Windsor,) lot 12, A. T., farmer 98.

Morse, William H., (Windsor,) lot 12, A. T., farmer leases 40

Murdock, Mathew, (Windsor,) N. P., farmer 100.

Newland, Frederick M, (Windsor,) N. T., blacksmith and farmer 15.

NEWTON, FRANCIS L., (Windsor,) lot 14, farmer 40.

Nichols, Elihu, (West Windsor,) lot 12, Lawrence Tract, farmer 137.

Nichols, Geo., (Kirkwood,) F. T, stone mason and farmer 8

NORTH, ALBERT, (Windsor,) (*U. T Wooster & Co.,*) N P, farmer 150.

OLIVER, JAMES W., (Windsor,) telegraph operator.

O'RORKE, PATRICK F., (Cascade Valley,) lot 5, 3d Tract, farmer 100

O'Rourke, Pater, (Cascade Valley,) farmer 104.

Ostrander, Warren, (Windsor,) lot 23, N P., farmer 114.

Ostrandler, George W., (Windsor,) N. P, farmer 110

Palmer, Chas A, (Randolph Center,) lot 8, R T., teamster and farmer leases 40

Pangburn, William, (Windsor,) lot 21, farmer 4.

PARKE, T. W, (Windsor,) N. P., mowing machine agent and farmer leases of E. Kent, 114

PARSONS, MARTIN S., (Windsor,) lot 9, D T., shoemaker and farmer 24

Parsons, Nilson, (Windsor,) N. P., farmer leases 100.

Peasall, Egbert, (West Coleaville,) lot 62, farmer 50.

PEASE, EDWARD, (Windsor,) lot 70, L. T, butcher and farmer 100.

PEET, HARLEY J., (Windsor,) G. T., money loaner and farmer 140.

Phelps, Myron, (Windsor,) lot 93, H. P., farmer 131

Phillipps, Isaac, (Great Bend, Susquehanna Co, Pa,) lot 13, R T., farmer 80.

Phillips, Daniel, (West Windsor,) lot 8, Lawrence Tract, wagon maker, blacksmith, postmaster and farmer 12

Phillips, Geo, (West Windsor) lot 69, L T, blacksmith and farmer 87½.

Phillips, Wm, (West Windsor,) lot 7, Hommedien Tract, blacksmith and farmer 65.

Phillips Z, (West Windsor,) lot 69, L T., farmer 87

Pierce, Sheldon, (Windsor,) N. P., farmer 96

PIERCE, WM., (Windsor,) lot 10, H. T, farmer 116.

Pike, Joseph, (Windsor,) N. P., farmer 40.

PLUNKETT, FRANK, (Cascade Valley,) lot 8, farmer 70

POMEROY, A C, (Windsor,) manuf. of spokes.

Pool, Robert, estate of, (Windsor,) S. T., 30 acres.

POOL, WM., (Windsor,) S T, carpenter, whip maker, blacksmith and farmer 60

PULZ, GEORGE J., (Windsor,) N P, prop saw mill, carpenter and farmer 100

Pulz, James S, (Windsor,) S T, farmer 120.

PULZ, WM A, (Windsor,) lot 14, S. T, lumberman and farmer 120.

Purkins, Augustin, (Windsor,) farmer 3

Purple & Son, (Great Bend Susquehanna Co., Pa,) lot 3, N P, farmer 150

Putman, Chas. E., (Windsor,) farmer leases 300

Quinn, Francis, (Great Bend, Susquehanna Co., Pa,) lot 2, S. T., farmer 87

RANDALL, RICHARD N, (Windsor,) (*Guernsey & Randall,*) foreman of whip factory,

REYNOLDS, JOHN L, (Windsor,) farmer leases of Geo. Dusenbury, 424.

RIDER, CHAS. A., (West Windsor,) general merchant.

RILEY, LEWIS, (West Windsor,) lot 14, Lawrence Tract, justice of the peace and farmer 159.

Roberts, James, (West Windsor,) lot 1, Lawrence Tract, farmer 269

Roberts, William Rev, (Windsor,) pastor of Zion Episcopal Church

Rockwell, James, (Randolph Center,) lot 3, R. T., farmer 5.

Rorke, Terence, (Cascade Valley,) lot 11, farmer 60

Rose, Chas, (West Windsor,) retired farmer

Rose, Geo S, (West Windsor,) lot 7, Lawrence Tract, farmer 150

Rose, Ira, (Great Bend, Susquehanna Co, Pa.,) lot 15, D. T., farmer 60

Rose, John, (Great Bend, Susquehanna Co, Pa,) Carpenter Tract, farmer 24..

Rose, Silas, (Great Bend, Susquehanna Co, Pa.,) lot 8, S. T., farmer 43.

RUGGLES, EDWIN A., (Windsor,) F. T., farmer leases 100

RUNYON, JOHN, (Windsor,) stage prop.

Russell, Henry, (Windsor,) cooper.

RUSSELL, P A, (Windsor,) post master and town clerk

Sage, Jeffrey, (Windsor,) lot 92, farmer 134

SALISBURY, JOHN, (Onaquaga,) lot 9, farmer 72

SANFORD, LAMBERT, (Windsor,) undertaker and farmer 15.

Saulsbury, O P, (Great Bend, Susquehanna, Co., Pa.,) lot 15, D. T., farmer 60

Saxby, James, (Great Bend, Susquehanna Co., Pa.,) lot 8, S. T., blacksmith and farmer 60

Schouten, Cornelius, (Windsor,) lot 11, N. P, carpenter and farmer 70

SCOVILLE, ANDREW F., (Windsor,) farmer 65 and leases of Dr Freeman, 117.

Shepardson, Edward, (Ouaquaga,) farmer 15.

Shepherd, Sally Mrs, (Windsor.)

SHERWOOD, THEODORE, (Kirkwood,) F T, farmer 60.

Sherwood, W B, (West Windsor,) lot 11, Lawrence Tract, carpenter and farmer 100.

SHUTTS, LEWIS E, (Susquehanna Depot, Pa.,) B P., farmer 150.

SIMPKINS, LEWIS J., (Windsor,) L. T , farmer 73
SIMPSON, GEO. W , (Windsor,) N P, farmer leases of Joseph W Simpson, 100
SLEEPER, AMOS S., (Windsor,) (H. L Sleeper & Son.)
SLEEPER, H L., (Windsor,) (H L. Sleeper & Son,) justice of the peace
SLEEPER, H L. & SON, Windsor, (Amos S.,) carriage makers and blacksmiths
Smith Bros , (Windsor,) (Ira W. and Sidney G ,) M P , farmers 85
Smith, Catlin,(Windsor,) farmer leases 172
Smith, E L , (Windsor,) shoemaker
SMITH, EDGAR O , (Windsor,) N P., farmer 200.
Smith, Edwin W., (Windsor,) lot 6, N. T , farmer 130
SMITH, FRANK S , (Windsor ) engineer and supt. of A W Coburn's spoke works.
Smith, Ira W., (Windsor,) (Smith Bros ,) gun and locksmith
Smith, James M , (Windsor,) lot 61, farmer 26
*SMITH, JAMES T., (Windsor,) foundry and machine shop, manuf of plows, cultivators, scrapers &c
Smith, Milo, (Windsor,) F. T , farmer 148
Smith, Nicholas, (West Windsor,) F T., farmer leases of Tracy Vail, 80
Smith, Sidney G., (Windsor,) (Smith Bros )
Smith, Spencer D , (Windsor,) lot 14, A T., farmer 195
Smith, Zina A , (Randolph Center,) N P , carpenter and farmer 10.
Snedaker, Chas. D , (Great Bend, Susquehanna Co., Pa.,) lot 1, D T , farmer 52½.
SNEDAKER, JOHN, (Great Bend, Susquehanna Co , Pa ,) lot 12, R T , lumberman and farmer 150.
Sornberger, George, (Windsor,) lot 15, A. T., dealer in butter and eggs, and farmer 71
Southard, Demetrius, (Windsor,) N P , farmer 60.
Southard, Henry, (Windsor,) N. P., farmer 40
Sparks, Loran, (Great Bend, Susquehanna Co , Pa ,) lot 13, R. T., farmer 55
Spearbeck, Andrew, (Great Bend, Susquehanna Co., Pa ,) lot 4, D. T., millwright, carpenter and farmer 104
Spearbeck, Andrew C., (Windsor,) N P., farmer 90
Spearbeck, Benj , (Great Bend, Susquehanna Co., Pa.,) (Spearbeck & Davis.)
Spearbeck & Davis, (Great Bend, Susquehanna Co , Pa ,) (Benj Spearbeck and Abram Davis,) Carpenter Tract, carpenters and farmers 71¼
Spearbeck, Henry, (Windsor,) N. P , cooper and farmer 3.
Spearbeck, Michael, (Great Bend, Susquehanna Co., Pa.,) lot 1, D. T., farmer 50.
SPEARBECK, SANFORD, (Windsor,) N P., farmer 84.
Sperring, Geo , (Great Bend, Susquehanna Co , Pa ,) Hotchkiss Tract, farmer 45
Spoor, Caroline, (Windsor,) lot 4, Sherwood Tract, farmer 80.

Spoor, Hiram A , (Windsor,) lot 3, Sherwood Tract, farmer 60.
Springsteen, Abram, (Windsor,) lot 18, C. T , farmer 96
SPRINGSTEEN, ELI H., (Windsor,) lot 2, N. T , farmer 112.
Springsteen, Gurley, (Windsor,) lot 10, farmer 87.
Springsteen, Jacob, (Windsor,) lot 17, N. T , farmer 113.
Springsteen, John, (Windsor,) lot 10, farmer 30.
Springsteen, M., (Windsor,) lot 88, H. P , farmer 50
Springsteen, Robert, (Windsor,) N. T., farmer leases of Almon Marshall, 163
Sparbeck, Robert H., (Windsor,) lot 27, farmer.
Squire, A. R , (Windsor,) farmer leases of D W., 100.
STANNARD, LOZELL D., (Windsor,) (Stannard & Son )
STANNARD, SAMUEL, (Windsor,) (Stannard & Son )
STANNARD & SON, (Windsor,) (Samuel and Lozell D.,) S T , saw mill and farmers 30.
Stannard, S. D , (Windsor,) lot 7, Sherwood Tract, farmer 200
Stevens, Philander, (Randolph Center,) lot 12, R T , farmer 43
Stewart, Minor, (Windsor,) lot 8, Sherwood Tract, farmer 30
Stilson, D , (West Windsor,) lot 2, Lawrence Tract, farmer 150.
Stilson, Hezekiah, (Ouaquaga,) farmer 40.
Stilwell, P. T , (Windsor,) lot 14, Hommedieu Patent, farmer 200
Stilwell, Thos., (West Windsor,) lot 68, farmer 80.
Stoddard, A R , (Great Bend, Susquehanna Co , Pa ,) lot 13, N P , farmer 70.
Stoddard, Ethel, (Windsor,) N. P , saw mill and farmer 80.
STOW, ELI H., (Windsor,) lot 10, R. T., farmer leases of E Kent, 109.
Stowe, H P., (Windsor,) lot 3, Hommedieu Tract, farmer 50.
Stowe, Merritt, (Windsor,) N. P., mason and farmer 283
Stringham, Warren D., (Windsor,) jeweler.
STRINGHAM, WILLIAM H , (Ouaquaga,) Harper Patent, farmer 180.
Stuart, Luman O , (Great Bend, Susquehanna Co , Pa ,) lot 3, N. P., farmer leases of Uriah Decker. 41.
SULLIVAN, JOHN, (Kirkwood,) lot 7, R. T., farmer leases 96.
Summerton, Thos., (Great Bend, Susquehanna Co., Pa ,) farmer 33 and leases 55
SUTLIFF, ADELBERT J , (Windsor,) (with Emory W.)
Sutliff, Emory W , (Windsor,) lot 10, R. T., farmer 108
SUTLIFF, HORATIO R., (Windsor,) lot 14, R T., farmer 50.
Suttle, Peter, (West Windsor,) lot 69, G L., farmer 230.
Suydam, Henry, (West Coleaville,) G. L., farmer 105
Swagart, William, (Lanesborough, Susquehanna Co , Pa ,) B. P., farmer 48.

Sweeney, Dennis, (Ouaquaga,) C. T., farmer 77.

SWINGLE, MATILDA, (Windsor,) L. T., farmer 5.

Taber, Jonathan, (Binghamton,) G. L., farmer 126.

Tarbox, James, (Great Bend, Susquehanna Co., Pa.,) lot 3, Sherwood Tract, boatman and farmer 40.

TIFFANY, WM. H., (Randolph Center,) lot 9, R T., farmer 127

Titus, L., (Windsor,) lot 6, Hommedieu Tract, farmer 90

Tompkins, Abel, (Windsor,) lot 20, C T, farmer 45

Tompkins, Abram, (Windsor,) N T., farmer 75.

Tompkins, Abram, (Ouaquaga,) lot 1, M. T, farmer 85

Tompson, Chas., (Great Bend, Susquehanna Co., Pa.,) N. P., grocer and farmer 30.

TWITCHELL, BETSEY Mrs.(West Windsor,) F. T., farmer 143

Ufford, John, (Great Bend, Susquehanna Co., Pa.,) lot 12, R T, farmer 40

Ufford, S B., (Great Bend, Susquehanna Co., Pa.,) lot 12, R T, farmer leases of Wm Parks, 10

VALENTINE, ANDREW J., (Windsor,) lot 14, R T, farmer 60

VALENTINE, GABRIEL, (Great Bend, Susquehanna Co., Pa.,) Hotchkiss Tract, farmer 94

Vanantwerp, C L, (Windsor,) lot 3, A. T, wagon maker and farmer 15

VanAntwerp, Daniel, (Windsor,) lot 3, A T, farmer 25

VanAntwerp, David H (Windsor,) lot 3, A T, farmer 85.

VanAntwerp, Wm E, (Windsor,) carpenter.

VANBARRIGER, H. P., (Windsor,) boot and shoemaker

Vanborager, John, (Ouaquaga,) lot 18, farmer 100.

VANORSDALE, MARCUS K., (Windsor,) L T., farmer 182

Vosburg, Levi, (Windsor,) farmer 69 and leases 193

Vroman Edmond, (Great Bend, Susquehanna Co., Pa.,) lot 9. S T, farmer 60

Vroman, Wm, (Great Bend, Susquehanna Co., Pa.) lot 14, D. T., shingle maker and farmer 5

WAITE & HICKCOX, (Cascade Valley,) (*I E Waite and Robert Hickcox*,) saw mill

WAITE, I E., (Cascade Valley,) (*Waite & Hickcox*.)

Warner, Elias, (Ouaquaga,) lot 21, N T, farmer 76.

Warner, John W, (Windsor,) lot 62, farmer 50.

Watrous, Almira J Mrs., (Ouaquaga,) lot 74, H. P., farmer 54

Watrous, Asa W., (Windsor,) N. P, farmer leases of Chas Stringham, 114.

Watrous, John B, (Lanesborough, Susquehanna Co., Pa,) B P, farmer 230.

WATROUS, WM. W., (Cascade Valley,) B. P., lumberman and farmer 86.

Watson, Henry L., (Windsor,) N P., farmer 165.

Watters, E., (Windsor,) lot 16, Hommedieu Patent, farmer 100

Way, Alonzo E., (Windsor,) L. T., farmer 136

WEBSTER, THOMPSON, (Ouaquaga,) saw mill

WEDGE, G. ALONZO, (Windsor,) lot 6, R T, farmer 108.

Weed, Egbert, (Kirkwood,) F T., farmer leases of Mary Hayes, 93.

Weed, Wm, (West Windsor,) lot 7, Lawrence Tract, farmer 174.

Week, Amos, (Windsor,) stock dealer.

WEEKS, HIRAM, (West Windsor,) lot 66, L L., farmer 58.

Weeks, P. Mrs., (West Windsor,) L. L., farmer 20

Welch, E, (Windsor,) N P, farmer 91

WELTON, LYMAN, (Great Bend, Susquehanna Co, Pa,) lot 11, R. T., farmer 140

Welton, Millard, (Great Bend, Susquehanna Co., Pa,) lot 11, R T, farmer leases of L Welton, 140

Wetmore, A. J., (Windsor,) F. T., farmer 50

WETMORE JAMES W, (Randolph Center,) F T., farmer 40

Wheeler, Franklin, (Windsor,) lawyer.

WHITE, ARBA, (Windsor,) lot 17, D. T., mechanic and farmer 55.

White, Charles E., (Windsor,) N. P., farmer 100

White, Harmony, (Windsor,) lot 7, N P., farmer 63.

WHITE, S J, (Windsor,) S. T., farmer 120

Whiteman, Geo. W., (West Windsor,) G L, farmer leases 100

Whitmore, Harvey P., (Ouaquaga,) lot 20, N T, farmer 62

WILCOX, OLIVER, (West Windsor,) F T, farmer 60 and leases of J N. Hoadley, 175

Wiles, H A. Mrs, (Windsor,) milliner.

WILES, J M, (Windsor,) saloon keeper and stage driver.

Williams, Henry, (Windsor,) lot 9, A T, farmer 30.

WILLIAMS, LEVI A, (Windsor,) lot 10, R T, commissioner of highways and farmer 80.

Wilmot, Clark, (Great Bend Susquehanna Co., Pa,) lot 15, D. T, farmer 21

WILMOT, D B, (Windsor,) lot 11, H. T, farmer 73

Wilmot, Mary, (Great Bend, Susquehanna Co, Pa,) lot 7, N P, farmer 38.

WILMOT, NATHAN W., (Great Bend, Susquehanna Co, Pa.,) Hotchkiss Tract, farmer 165.

Wilmot, Salura Mrs, (Great Bend, Susquehanna Co., Pa.,) lot 12, D. T., farmer 55

WINSOR, OLIVER, (Windsor,) carpenter

Witmore, Clark N, (West Windsor,) F. T., farmer leases of Lucy Alden, 101

Wolcot, Wm., (Great Bend, Susquehanna Co., Pa.,) lot 8, S T., farmer 30

WOOD, CHAS. S, (Windsor,) N P., farmer 88

Woodard, Geo., (West Windsor,) F. T., farmer 45

Woodard, James, (West Windsor,) F. T., farmer 25

Woodmancy, S., (Windsor,) N P , farmer 64

Woodruff, B H , (Windsor,) Moore Tract, farmer 40.

WOODRUFF, JEHIEL, (Kirkwood,) F T., carpenter, wagon maker and farmer 77

Woodruff, Jonah, (Windsor,) retired farmer

Woodruff, Lucian, (Windsor,) (*L. Woodruff & Son,*) tin and hardware.

Woodruff, Lucius, (Windsor,) (*L. Woodruff & Son* )

Woodruff L & Son, (Windsor,) (*Lucian and Lucius,*) general merchants and druggists

WOODRUFF, ORRIN, (Kirkwood,) F T, carpenter, wagon maker and farmer 33.

Woodruff, Simeon, (West Windsor,) F. T., farmer 40.

Wooster, David, (Windsor,) lot 7, farmer 80.

Wooster, T. L., (Windsor,) teamster and farmer 92½.

WOOSTER, U. T. & CO., (Windsor,) (*Albert North,*) general merchants.

Wooster, L Mrs , (West Windsor,) F. T , farmer 9

Yong, John, (Windsor,) N. P., farmer 2

# CITY OF BINGHAMTON.

## A.

Abbott, C. E., (*C. N. Abbott & Son* )
Abbott, C N. & Son, (*C E.,*) boots and shoes, 58 Washington.
Abbott, L. S , supervisor 1st Ward, office 52 Court.
Abels, A. Miss, dress maker, 14 Court.
Able, C Burdette, policeman.
Adams, Alonzo D , machinist and engineer, 5 Clinton Block, Clinton
Adams, Jennie Miss. Bon Ton, 5 Clinton Block, Clinton.
ALDRICH, SOLOMON, real estate dealer, 38 Washington.
Allen, Horace E , deputy U. S internal revenue collector, 26th dist , 77 Court.
Allen, Silas, (*Stack & Allen.*) second hand clothing, old No 6 Washington.
Allen, William, farmer, in Union, 80
American Hotel, Court corner Water, Moulter & Brown, props.
AMSBRY, CHAS. H., (*Amsbry & Morris.*)
AMSBRY & MORRIS, (*Chas H. Amsbry and Oliver A. Morris,*) hats, caps, furs, boots and shoes, 30 Court.
Anderson, John, (*Anderson & Tremain* )
Anderson & Tremain, (*John Anderson and Wm. Tremain,*) shoe manufs., 97 and 99 Water.
ANDREWS, ALEXANDER E., lawyer and recorder, 72 Court.
Andrews, A W K , physician, 89 Court
ANDREWS, G. R , boarding, sale and exchange stable, 10 Murray.
Andrews, M. S , telegraph operator.
Angell, A. C , blacksmith, Division
Angell, G. S., painter, 208 Court
Angell, James, wagon maker, 208 Court.
Arbor Hotel and Restaurant, Skillman & LaRose, props., Court corner Water.
Armsbry, Frank M , livery stable, rear Franklin House.
ARMSTRONG, ALBERT D , lawyer, 76 Court, over post office
ARMSTRONG, JAMES H., alderman 2nd Ward, supt of Chenango Canal, office 76 Court.
ARNOLD, CALVIN V., (*Arnold & Sons.*)
ARNOLD, ELLIS L , (*Arnold & Sons.*)
ARNOLD, SEYMOUR F , (*Arnold & Sons* )
ARNOLD & SONS, (*Calvin V , Seymour F. and Ellis L.,*) dry goods, 33 Court.
Arnott, James H , telegraph operator. W U and Erie.
Atlantic Garden, 66 Water, Henry Kaul, prop
AUSTIN & GALLAGHER, (*H C Austin and F. Gallagher,*) livery, hack and exchange stable, Collier near Fireman's Hall.
AUSTIN, H. C., (*Austin & Gallagher.*)
Avery, A. G , grocery, 109 Court

Ayers, D. S., (*Hallock, Cary & Co*)
*AYERS, E`, undertaker, 86 Washington

## B.

BABCOCK, JNO J.. (*Paige, Chaffe & Co.,*) owns farm 250 acres in Lisle
Bailey, M. T., general agent for Travelers Insurance Co , 51 Court.
BALCOM, RANSOM Hon., vice-president First National Bank and justice of the Supreme Court, office Court House.
Baldwin, John, shoemaker, Tow Path.
Baldwin, M. M. Mrs., dress cutting and fitting, and dealer in patterns and corsets, over 41 Court
BALLOU, ASA A., (*Wheaton & Ballou.*)
Banks, James H., shoemaker, Oak.
Barnes Bros & Blanding, (*J H. and G S. Barnes, and H. G. Blanding,*) props. Binghamton Marble Works, Chenango near Depot.
Barnes, G. S., (*Barnes Bros & Blanding.*)
Barnes, J H , (*Barnes Bros. & Blanding*)
BARNES, MORGAN L , (*Barnes & Myers,*) manager for Howe Sewing Machine Co
BARNES & MYERS, (*Morgan L Barnes and Jacob Myers,*) agents for Howe Sewing Machine, 39 Court.
Barnes, Newton, carpenter, West Cedar.
Barnes, Robert, boots, shoes and rubbers, 64 Washington.
Barsam, H , deputy sheriff, Court House
BARRETT, N P H., (*Shepard & Barrell*)
*BARRETT, S. W., pianos, organs, sheet music, watches, clocks, jewelry and silver ware, agent for the new Davis Vertical Feed Sewing Machine, 60 Court.
•BARTLETT, I. L., (*Blanchard, Bartlett & Co.*)
Bassett, Wm Dr , physician, 51 Carroll.
Baty, A. J.. bakery and saloon, Oak.
Bayless, John, (*Beman & Bayless*)
Beach, R. C., house painter and boarding house Division near Warren.
Beach, S D. & Co., Binghamton Coffee and Spice Mills, and Tea Warehouse, 44 Washington.
Beadle, Abram, carpenter, 17 Doubleday.
Bean, C., (*Marks & Bean.*)
Beardsley, Charles, (*Beardsley & Lane*)
Beardsley & Lane, (*Charles Beardsley and Caleb Lane,*) bowling saloon, 45 Washington.
Beardsley & Parker Lock Co , (*P A Hopkins and A. S Parker,*) 101 Water.
BECKER, GEO , lawyer, 63 Court.
BEDELL, MARCUS, teamster.
Beebe, Phineas W , farmer 16½, Grove.
*BEECHER, LYMAN G., photographer, 72 Court
Beman & Bayless, (*E. A Beman and John Bayless,*) coopers, near Chenango corner Frederick
Beman, E A , (*Beman & Bayless*)
*BEMAN, ORSON D., watches, clocks, jewelry and silverware, watchmaker and engraver, 89 Court.
BENEDICT, R K , (*Mead & Benedict.*)
BENNETT, ABEL, president First National Bank.
Bennett, Abel, farmer 100
Bennett, W H., carpenter, East Court
Bennett, Warren N , (*Wickham & Bennett.*)
Benson, B S , (*Benson & TenBrook*)
Benson, Edward J , (*Benson & Gillespie*)
Benson, F A., pianos and music, 10 Exchange
Benson & Gillespie, (*Edward J. Benson and James S. Gillespie,*) crockery, china, glassware &c., 68 Court.
Benson & TenBrook, (*B. S. Benson and R. W. TenBrook,*) shoe manufa. 95 Water.
Benton, O. A., restaurant, 47 Washington.
Berghoefer, F. H. G., manuf of birch beer, Main corner Clark.
BIGLER, WM , prop Otsenango Mills, Commercial Avenue.
Billings, Augusta Miss, dress maker, over 21 Court.
Bingham, E H , (*Bingham. Gay & Co*)
Bingham, Gay & Co., (*E. H. Bingham, Elbridge Gay and C. R Williams,*) soap manufa., 77 Washington.
*BINGHAMTON DAILY REPUBLICAN, 98 Water, Malette & Reid, publishers.
*BINGHAMTON DEMOCRAT, (daily and weekly, — Thursday,) 89 Water, Lawyer Bros , publishers
Binghamton Iron Works, Shapley & Wells, props , Hawley, office 52 Washington.
Binghamton Marble Works, Chenango near Depot, J. H. & G S Barnes, and H G. Blanding, props.
Binghamton Mills, 102 Washington, M. W. Bosworth & Co., props.

BINGHAMTON PLANING MILLS, Hawley corner Collier, Blanchard, Bartlett & Co., props.

Binghamton Savings Bank, Washington, next door north First National Bank, Fred Lewis, prest.; Wm. P. Pope and Wm. E. Taylor, vice-prests.; Harris G. Rogers, treas; Erasmus D Robinson, sec'y.

Binghamton Scale Works, H. B. Osgood & Co., props., Mary

Binghamton Skein & Axle Co, J C. Cushing, secretary, 96 Court.

Binghamton Soap and Candle Works, Winding Way, R. H Mcagley, prop.

*BINGHAMTON STANDARD AND SEMI-WEEKLY REPUBLICAN, 98 Water, Malette & Reid, publishers.

Binghamton Tannery, 12 Susquehanna, J B. Weed & Co., props.

*BINGHAMTON TIMES, (weekly, Thursday,) 38 Court, 3rd floor, A. L. Watson, prop. and publisher

Binghamton Water Cure, office 61 Court, O V Thayer, prop.

Binghamton Water Works, East end Court, office 45 Court

Bixbee, Fred A, amateur job and card printer, 21 Mill

BISHOP, FRANK G, lawyer, Court corner Washington

Bissell, A H, (*Bliss & Bissell*)

Blair, H. P, drugs, medicines, confectionery, stationery, notions &c., Chenango corner Doubleday

Blakely, Benjamin F., marble works, Water corner Ferry.

BLANCHARD, BARTLETT & CO, (*C N Blanchard, I L Bartlett and J. W. Rowlingson,*) props of Binghamton Planing Mill, Hawley corner Collier.

BLANCHARD, C N, (*Blanchard, Bartlett & Co*)

Blanchard, ——, (*Reynolds & Blanchard*)

Blanding, H G., (*Barnes Bros & Blanding*)

Bliss Aaron H, (*Bliss & Bissell*)

Bliss & Bissell, (*Aaron H Bliss and A. H. Bissell,*) Empire Livery Stable, Dwight.

Bloomer, A, (*Bloomer & Munsell.*)

BLOOMER, ELIJAH F, carpenter and builder, dealer in pine, cedar and hemlock shingles, lath, fence posts, roofing and sheathing, felt, pitch &c., Hawley corner Collier

Bloomer, James F, agent for Wheeler & Wilson Sewing Machine, over 31 Court.

Bloomer & Munsell, (*A Bloomer and G E Munsell,*) dry goods, 66 Washington.

Bodle, Daniel M., tobacconist, 44 Court

Bogardus, L M, boarding stables, lunch room and flour dealer, 34 Exchange

Bolles, L, supt of L Bolles Hoe and Tool Co, Walnut between R R and Clinton

Bolles, L Hoe & Tool Co, Walnut between R. R. and Clinton, S D Phelps, prest, T R Morgan, treas.; L Bolles, supt

Bone, Stephen L, groceries and provisions, Clinton corner Walnut

Booth, Wm. B, supervisor 4th Ward.

BOSS, HOMER B, (*Ely & Boss*)

BOSWORTH, MASON W. & CO., (*Frederick Lewis,*) grain dealers and props Binghamton Elevator, 4 North Depot.

*BOUCK, DAVID I., prop. of Bouck's Hotel, Chenango corner Pearne.

*BOUCK'S HOTEL, David I. Bouck, prop, Chenango corner Pearne.

BOWEN & CHITTENDEN, (*John B Bowen and Gus Chittenden,*) Empire Insurance Agency, 65 Court

BOWEN, JOHN B, (*Bowen & Chittenden*)

*BOWKER, NELSON, architect and builder, shop in J. S Wells' old stand, Main.

Bradley, H W, (*I S Matthews & Co*)

Bradley, Mary Miss, dress maker, 60 Washington

Bristol, D W, (*W P Gifford & Co,*) resides in Ithaca.

Brooks, James, physician and surgeon, 55 Front.

Brooks, Peletiah B, physician and surgeon, 56 Front.

Brooks, Walter A, physician and surgeon, 55 Front.

*BROOME REPUBLICAN, (weekly,) 98 Water, Malette & Reid, publishers.

Brown, Augustus M, carriage manuf, South Water, alderman 5th Ward

Brown, Charles, barber, opposite Erie Depot.

BROWN, H P, (*J. Pickering & Co*)

Brown, James E, (*I. N Hine & Co.*)

Brown, Robert, deputy sheriff, U S marshal and constable.

BROWN, T L, M D, homeo. physician, 45 Collier.

BROWNELL, CYRUS J, drugs, medicines, chemicals, varnish, oils, glass, dye stuffs and fancy articles, Court corner Washington.

BROWNSON, DAVID L, groceries, 67 Court, alderman 2d Ward

Bruce, Katie M Mrs., teacher of piano and organ, 10 Chenango

Bruce, O B, teacher, 10 Chenango

BRUNNER, CONRAD, lager beer saloon, 63 Washington.

Buffum, Lewis, groceries, provisions &c, 70 Washington

Bullis, Elizabeth A, cigar manuf, South Water.

Bullock, Seneca, photographer, 40 Court

Bump, N. H., (*with L Carr,*) hides, pelts and furs, 19 Commercial Avenue

S

BURNETT, J. W., builder and leases 26 acres, South Water
BURR, DAN S., (*G & D. S. Burr.*)
BURR, G. & D S , (*George and Dan S,*) physicians, 119 Court.
BURR, GEORGE, (*G & D S Burr*)
Burr, Nelson G , grocery, between Morgan and Allan.
Burrows, F Edward, lawyer, 46 Court
Burton, C. V , (*Burton & DeSanCorollo.*)
Burton & DeSanCorollo, (*C. V Burton and S. B. DeSanCorollo,*) sculptors and portrait painters, 64 Washington, up stairs
Butler, Charles, (*Butler, Smith & Co.*)
Butler, Lewis A , watchmaker and cigar manuf , 68 Court
BUTLER, REUBEN H , (*H Fish & Co.*)
Butler, Smith & Co., (*Charles Butler, Jeffrey Smith and Philo Wilcox,*) tobacconists, 72 Washington.
Byrnm, Josephus, cloth, dress and wool carder, foot Carroll.

## C.

CAFFERTY, CHARLES M , prop of Cafferty House and liveryman, Court corner Water.
CAFFERTY HOUSE, C. M. Cafferty, prop , Court corner Water.
Cahill, P , prop. of Franklin House.
Campbell, E R , billiard room, 99 Washington.
Campbell, E W., blacksmith, Chenango
CANOLL, W P , stoves, tin and sheet iron ware, house furnishing goods &c., 95 Washington.
CAPEN, JAMES W. Rev., Episcopal clergyman, in charge of Grace Church at Whitney's Point.
Carder, C W , tin, glass and japanned ware, and rag dealer, 122 Court.
*CARL, ABRAM W., prop and publisher of *Democratic Leader*, 3 Court
Carl, James F , (*Carl & Stoppard*)
Carl & Stoppard, (*James F. Carl and Moses Stoppard,*) book and job printers, 68 Court
Carlton, E M , Mrs , dress and cloak making, over 33 Court.
Carman, Thomas P , tobacconist, 2 Court
CARNS, E D , agent for Grover & Baker Sewing Machines, 3 Exchange.
CARR, A L., (*T. E. Carr & Co*)
Carr, L , (*with N. H. Bump,*) hides, pelts and furs, 19 Commercial Avenue
Carr, Royal R , allo physician and surgeon, over 19 Court, residence Front corner North, also farmer 165 in town of Chenango and 10 at Chenango Forks.
CARR, T E. & CO., (*A L Carr,*) meat market, 2 Main.
Carrier, W G , patent right agent
CARRINGTON, IRA M., (*Carrington & Porter*)
*CARRINGTON & PORTER, (*Ira M Carrington and T Edson Porter,*) stoves, tinware and house furnishing goods, 35 Court.
Carroll, John, tailor, 48 Washington.
Cary, J S , (*Hallock, Cary & Co*)
CARY, NASH & OGDEN, (*Solomon F Cary, Denison Nash and Charles Ogden,*) props. of Binghamton Paper Mills, office at S F Cary's store, 41 Court , mills located at Port Dickinson
CARY, SOLOMON F , (*Cary, Nash & Ogden,*) dry goods and clothing, agent for Florence Sewing Machine, 41 Court
CASEY, JAMES H , carpenter and joiner, Dickinson.
Casey, Michael, blacksmith, Water.
Castle, Elijah, meat market, Canal corner Court.
CHAFFEE, JOSEPH B , (*Paige, Chaffee & Co.*)
Chambers, Hannah Mrs., dyer and clothes cleaner, 69 Washington.
CHAPMAN & MARTIN, (*Orlo W Chapman and Celora E Martin,*) lawyers, 63 Court.
CHAPMAN, ORLO W , (*Chapman & Martin.*)
CHASE, F. N , publisher, 38 Court.
CHENANGO HOUSE, 73 Water, Chas Walee, prop.
Chenango Valley Mills, Commercial Avenue, Geo Q Moon, prop.
Chenango Valley Savings Bank, Sherman D. Phelps, president; Richard Mather and Benjamin N. Loomis, vice presidents; T. R. Morgan, treasurer; Phelps Building, corner Court and Chenango.
CHITTENDEN, GUS, (*Bowen & Chittenden*)
Chittenden, Joseph H., allo. physician, 68 Court.
Christopher, James H., (*Conine & Christopher.*)
CHUBBUCK, DAVID J. H , allo physician and druggist, 45 Court, residence 38 Main.
Chubbuck, H. W., (*Chubbuck & Saunders*)
Chubbuck & Saunders, (*H. W Chubbuck and C. L. Saunders,*) teas, coffees and spices, 44 Washington.
City Carriage Works, Eldridge near Erie Depot, Stockwell & McMahon, props

CITY GOVERNMENT.—*Mayor*, Hon. Sherman D. Phelps.  *Board of Aldermen*, 1st Ward, Mose T Morgan, Mathew Hays, 2d Ward, James H. Armstrong, David L Brownson, 3d Ward, Henry B Ogden, Z. L. Tidball, 4th Ward, Lowell Harding, Wm H Stilwell; 5th Ward, John H. Jessup, Augustus M Brown.  CITY OFFICERS —*Mayor*, Hon. Sherman D Phelps; *Clerk*, Wm. H Scoville; *Treasurer*, D. M. Worden; *Recorder*, A. E. Andrews, *Health Officer*, D. C. Jackson, M.D ; *Chief of Police*, Jas. Flynn, *Supt of Streets*, Thos. J. Clark; *Fire Marshal*, Perry P Rogers, *Chief Engineer Fire Department*, Ed A. Roberts; *Supt. of Poor*, Selah P Rood; *Sealer of Weights and Measures*, Frederick Welch; *Hay Weighers*, C M. Cafferty, H G. Blanding, H J Gaylord, *City Sexton*, Selah P. Rood.  POLICE DEPT.—*Chief of Police*, James Flynn; *Policemen*, Henry F. Stebbin, G. B. Darrow, M R. Hays, E. L. Dodge, C Burdette Able.

City National Bank of Binghamton, Chas. W Sanford, president, Wm. E Taylor, vice-president; Wm R Osborn, cashier; Court corner Washington

Clapp, John, lawyer, over 81 Court.

Clark, Daniel, restaurant, Rail Road Avenue

CLARK EDWARD K., attorney at law, notary public and commissioner of deeds, 54 Court

Clark, J W., carpenter, Clinton corner Jervis.

Clark, J. W., assistant engineer, extension of the Chenango Canal, office 51 Court

Clark, Lyman, liquors 5½ Collier.

Clark, Thos. J., supt. of streets.

Clarke, H R Rev., D D., presiding elder of Binghamton District and farmer 10, West end College.

Clock, Lyman, (*Kendall, Harrison & Co.*)

Cobb, George N, photographer, 77 Court

Coer, C T. Rev, chaplain of House of the Good Shepherd, South Water.

Coit, C. P Rev., pastor of North Presbyterian Church, residence 55 Prospect Avenue.

Coles, Charles, carpenter and builder, near Rockbottom Bridge

Collier, John A., lawyer and landholder, residence Prospect Avenue corner Eldredge.

Collins, Daniel, blacksmith, LeRoy Place.

Collins, Dennis, harness maker, 65 Washington.

Collins, Patrick F., tailor, over 33 Court

Conine & Christopher, (*Milton F. Conine and James H Christopher,*) groceries and provisions, Main corner Front

Conine, Milton F , (*Conine & Christopher.*)

CONKLIN, MOSES E , bill collector, 58 Court.

CONNER, JOHN H., (*Conner & Orr* )

*CONNER & ORR, (*John H Conner and Joseph W Orr,*) blacksmiths and manufs of Conner's Hoof Ointment, South Main corner DeRussey.

Conning, Thomas B , saloon, 65 Washington.

CONTINUOUS OIL REFINING CO , Hon. E C. Kattell, prest ; J S Wells, vice-prest.; Tracy R Morgan, secretary ; Wm. R. Osborn, treas ; manufs. cylinder, engine and lubricating oils for railway and steamship use, together with spindle machinery and woolens.

Coon, George, boot maker, 42 Court

Corbett, M. Miss, millinery and fancy goods, 55 Washington.

Cortesey, C , (*P. Cahill & Co* )

CORTESY, CARLOS, (*Cortesy & Hays* )

CORTESY & HAYS, (*Carlos Cortesy and Matthew Hays,*) dealers in groceries, lumber, sand &c , 50 Washington.

Cottage Hotel, Chenango corner North Depot, Burt J. Harris, prop.

COUTANT, CORNELIUS, (*Coutant & LeValley* )

COUTANT & LeVALLEY, (*Cornelius Coutant and F. LeValley,*) painters, Chenango near Doubleday.

Crafts, Edward G , physician and farmer 400, 99 Washington

Crandal, G L, (*J. F. Dohan & Co.*)

CRANDALL, A. J , prop. Ways Hotel, 116 and 115 Court.

Crary, Henry P., paper hanger and confectioner, Chenango.

Craver, George, (*Craver & Mersereau* )

Craver & Mersereau, (*George Craver and T. T. Mersereau,*) pork packers, dealers in wool, seeds &c , 93 Water

Crawford, H. C., carpenter, 89 Hawley.

*CRESSON, MILTON, livery, exchange and boarding stables, Carroll.

CROCKER, DAVID, (*Crocker & Ogden* )

CROCKER, LUTHER, (*Crocker & Ogden.*)

*CROCKER & OGDEN, (*Luther Crocker, D. H. Ogden and David Crocker,*) hardware and carriage goods, 91 Court

Crocker, S. G., harness, 43 Washington.

Crocker, Wm. S. G , hair dresser, 64 Court.

*CRONIN, DAVID E , lawyer, Deutscher Advocate, 43 Court.

Crosby, Wm. M., justice of the peace. 48 Court

Crozier & Hughes, (*Robert Crozier and ——— Hughes,*) painters and grainers, 63 Court

Crozier, Robert, (*Crozier & Hughes,*) supervisor 5th Ward.

Cumber, John, farmer leasee of Lewis heirs, 150.
Curran, B S , lawyer, 50 Court
Curtis, D. D , clerk Erie freight office.
Cushing, Joseph C., secretary of Binghamton skein and Axle Co , 96 Court.

## D.

Darrow, O B , policeman
Darrow, R S., (*Winton & Darrow* )
Davis, Alonzo, carriage shop Susquehanna corner Washington
DAVIS, A W , (*Newton & Davis* )
DAVIS BROTHERS, (*W P and D A.,*) carpenters and builders, Chenango near
  Pearne
Davis, B C & Co , (*Robert B Doubleday,*) Davis' patent blind rod cutters and staple
  drivers, and manfs of blind staples, Otseningo Mills, Commercial Avenue.
DAVIS D A , (*Davis Brothers* )
Davis, Elias, wood turner and manuf. wood work, Commercial Avenue
DAVIS, W P , (*Davis Brothers* )
Delaware & Hudson Coal Co., Chenango, Ford & Pope, agents.
Delaware, Lackawanna & Western Express Co , 93 Washington, W P Morgan, agent.
*DEMOCRATIC LEADER, (weekly, $1 50 per year,) 3 Court, Abram W. Carl, prop
  and publisher.
DeSanCorollo, S B , (*Burton & DeSan Corollo* )
DeVoe, Benjamin, internal revenue assessor, 26th dist , 77 Court.
DeVOE, JOHN G , (*J G DeVoe & Co* )
DEVOE, J G & CO , (*John G DeVoe and Samuel A Montgomery,*) props. of Ex-
  change Hotel, corner Court and Chenango Canal.
DEWITT, JEROME, (*Scovill & DeWitt,*) notary public, 49 Court.
DeWitt, Myra Mrs , dressmaker, 35 Hawley
Dexter, Chester, (*Richardson & Dexter* ) sawing and planing mill
Dickinson, Charles M., lawyer, 46 Court.
Dilley, Charles, carriage manuf , DeRussey.
Dillon, M. F., saloon, Division.
Doane, David, groceries, 183 Court
Dodge, E L , policeman
Dohan, J F & Co., (*G L Crandal,*) manufs of carriage curtain windows, Otseningo
  Mills, Commercial Avenue
Donley, A., groceries, provisions, seeds &c , old 43 Washington
DONLEY, JOHN H , (*Toohey & Donley* )
Donnelly, D D , cabinet ware, 50 Washington
DOOLEY, JAMES, saloon and tobacco store, 96 Washington.
Doolittle, Luke, flour, feed &c , foot of Carroll
Dorr, Alonzo E , agent National Express Co., 84 Washington
Dorr, Wm , physician, 14 North
DOUBLEDAY J W , (*Mason, Root & Co* )
Doubleday, Robert B , (*B C Davis & Co* )
DOUBLEDAY, WM B , piano tuning and repairer of musical instruments, 43 Court.
Douglas, Wm O , (*Sherman D Phelps & Co* )
DOWNING, JOHN, (*with Chas L. Seeley,*) brass foundry, 19 Commercial Avenue
Draes, S B., carpenter and builder, Susquehanna
Dudley, Ophelia C Mrs , dress maker, 103 Washington.
Dunham, Ephraim F , groceries, 25 Court
Dunmore H H , agent for A. B. Howe and American Sewing Machines, 49 Court, under
  City National Bank
Dunn, Cornelius E , (*James H Dunn & Co.*)
Dunn, James, shoemaker, 2 Sanford.
Dunn, James H , (*J H Dunn & Co.*)
Dunn, J H & Co , (*James H and Cornelius E Dunn,*) groceries, 118 Court.
Dunn, Patrick, prop. of Farmers' Saloon, Sisson's Block, Court
Durkee, Franklin A , lawyer and insurance agent, 77 Court
Dwight, Walton Col., ex-mayor of Binghamton, house Winding Way
DWYER, GEORGE, (*Smith & Dwyer.*)

## E.

Earle, Orlando W., manuf cigars, 58 Court
Edson. M O , flour, grain, feed, meal &c , 8 Commercial Avenue.
Edson, Newton W., school commissioner Western District, office at Court House.
EDWARDS, R O , boarding house and saloon, Canal near Depot.
EDWARDS, WILLIAM B , county judge and surrogate, office Court House, residence
  133 Oak
Eldridge, Hallam, farmer 30, Richmond

ELY & BOSS, (*Richard Ely and Homer B. Boss,*) general fire and life insurance agents, 47 Court, 2d floor.
ELY, RICHARD, (*Ely & Boss.*)
*ELY, S MILLS, wholesale grocer and dealer in Averill chemical paint, and Wheeler Melick & Co.'s threshing machine, Canal near R R , residence Washington corner Susquehanna
EMMONS, GEORGE W , (*Gillespy & Emmons.*)
Empire Livery stable, Dwight St , Bliss & Bissell, props.
EVANS, ALFRED J , (*Evans & Manning.*)
Evans, G R., (*Evans Sisters* )
Evans, H A , (*Evans Sisters* )
Evans, John, civil engineer, South Water.
EVANS & MANNING, (*Alfred J. Evans and R. T. Manning,*) watches, jewelry &c., 85 Washington.
Evans, Sarah A., (*Evans Sisters* )
Evans Sisters, (*Sarah A., G. R. and H. A.,*) human hair work and dressmaking, over 19 Court
Evans, Thomas T., instrumental music teacher, 12 Court.
*EVERETT. L W., manuf. of wagons and sleighs, Chenango north of the Depot
EXCHANGE HOTEL, corner Court and Chenango Canal, J G DeVoe & Co , props.

## F.

Fagan, Barvey, cigar maker, boats to let, South Main, south end Rockbottom bridge.
Farley, William, carpenter, Clinton.
Farley, William Mrs., dress and cloak maker, Clinton.
Farmers Saloon, Sisson's Block, Court, Patrick Dunn, prop.
FARNHAM, A. A., planing mill and general jobbing, Cedar.
Fee, Michael Capt , saloon, Chenango.
FELTER, DARWIN, practical millwright, South Water corner Mary.
Field, G S., assistant engineer, extension of the Chenango Canal, office 51 Court.
FIFTH WARD HOTEL, Mrs. Elizabeth Miles, prop., DeRussey.
Finch, Vincent, groceries, 10 Court.
Finley & Gorman, (*Philip Finley and Thomas Gorman,*) carriage makers, Hawley
Finley, Philip, (*Finley & Gorman* )
FINNEY, ERASTUS, groceries, 9 Court.
FIRST NATIONAL BANK, Court corner Washington, Abel Bennett, president, Ransom Balcom, vice-president ; George Pratt, cashier.
FISH, HENRY, (*H Fish & Co* )
FISH, H. & CO., (*Henry Fish and Reuben H. Butler,*) boots and shoes, 29 Court
Fisher, L. Mrs , dress maker, 100 Court.
Fitzgerald, Edward M , lawyer, 49 Court, over City National Bank.
Fitzgerald, Joseph, saloon, Susquehanna
Flanagan, John, (*Flanagan & O'Neil* )
Flanagan & O'Neil, (*John Flanagan and Matthew O'Neil,*) stoves, tinware &c., 47 Washington.
Flanders, Mary L Miss, tailoress, 69 Washington.
Flasher, John, shoemaker and prop. of boarding house, opposite Erie Depot
FLINT, NELSON B., grocer, 66 Court.
Floyd, L. C Rev , pastor of Centenary M. E Church, 5 Jay
Flinker, Jane, dress maker, Clinton.
Flynn, James, chief of police, 72 Court
Flynn, Wm., works in Weed's tannery and farmer 2, South Main.
Ford, Edward I , allo physician, Chenango corner Prospect.
Ford, L. C. Rev , pastor M. E. Church
Ford & Pope, (*R. A Ford and A. C. Pope,*) Delaware & Hudson Coal Co., Chenango
Ford, R A , (*Ford & Pope* )
Franklin House, P. Cahill, prop.
*FREAR, JOSEPH S., furnishing undertaker, coffin ware rooms, 6 Court
FREEMAN, EDWARD H., fire and life insurance agent, under First National Bank
Freeman, Reed B , (*Lyon & Freeman.*)
FRENCH, CLEMENT L., meat market, 120 Court, residence River near city limits.
Frisbee, John Rev., pastor of African M. E. Church, Starr Avenue.
Fuller, D. W , (*J. B. Weed & Co* )
Fuller, Joel, (*White & Fuller* )
FULTON, S. J., agent for C D Middlebrook, wholesale and retail dealer in Canada and western pine and black walnut lumber, Chenango near Union Depot.

## G.

Gage, Moses, agent for Watertown and Herkimer Co Insurance Co 's., 128 Court
Gaige, Moses, insurance agent, Robinson corner Cemetery.
GALE, A. C., (*Traver & Gale.*)

GALE, CHARLES, blacksmith, rear of Exchange Hotel.
GALLAGHER, F., (*Austin & Gallagher*)
Galloway, George W , groceries and provisions, Carroll corner Sonth
Gardner, Anna E Mrs , ladies' hair dresser, 30 Court
Gardner, O. P., prop. Gardner's Light Express
Gardner, Townsend S , clock repairer.
Garcy, David B , (*J. B. Weed & Co*)
GARRISON, E. M Mrs , millinery, ladies' furnishing goods and "Bazaar Patterns," 21 Court corner Water
Gay, Elbridge, (*Bingham, Gay & Co*)
Gaylard, H J , lumber dealer and agent for the Emmerson saw, South Main corner DeRussey
GENNET, A , groceries provisions and seeds, 49 Washington.
GERMON, JOHN H , carpenter and builder, Robert corner Virgil.
GERMOND, GEORGE, groceries, Chenango corner Pearne.
GIBBS, M H , tin peddler, 10 Mary
Gifford, Wm. P., (*W. P Gifford & Co*)
Gifford, W. P. & Co , (*Wm P. Gifford and D. W. Bristol, of Ithaca,*) ladies' furnishing and fancy goods, 31 Court.
Gillespie, James S., (*Benson & Gillespie.*)
GILLESPY, ELIPHALET N , (*Gillespy & Emmons*)
GILLESPY & EMMONS, (*Eliphalet N Gillespy and George W Emmons,*) druggists, 55 Court.
GILLETT, ALMON S , foreman Wells & Brigham's brick yard, New
Gilmore & Co , (*Lowell Gilmore and Addison V. Sanford,*) photographers, 68 and 70 Court
Gilmore, Lowell, (*Gilmore & Co*)
Glaser, John, boot maker and confectioner, 67 Water
Gleason, G W., groceries and provisions, 128 Court
Goff, Henry A , (*Lester Brothers & Co*)
Golder, F , ticket agent A. & S R R.
Goodsell, Thomas, chief engineer extension of the Chenango Canal, office 51 Court.
Gordon, William J , carpenter, 1 New
Gorman, Michael, boarding house, Main corner Front
Gorman, Thomas, (*Finley & Gorman*)
Grant, Duncan R , baker, 71 Court
Graves, Frank A , meat market, 183 Court
Green, Steward L., engineer Binghamton Water Works
Gregory, David D Rev. Presbyterian minister, east side Front.
Grieve, James, boot maker, 12 Fayette.
Griffin, Ellen Miss dressmaker, 102 Washington.
GRIFFIN, LANSING, physician and surgeon, 11 July.
Griffith, Sophia C Mrs , ornamental hair worker, 12 Court
Griswold, Horace, civil engineer. 49 Court
Griswold, Wm. L , lawyer and supervisor 2d Ward, 49 Court
Guilfoyle, John, groceries, provisions, books notions &c , 59 Henry
Guynone, Timothy, shoemaker, Liberty corner Pine

# H.

Hadley, Darius, boarding house, 16 Collier.
HALBERT, DeLANCEY M , (*D M & E G Halbert*)
*HALBERT, D M. & E. G , (*DeLancey M and Edwin G ,*) dry goods and carpets, 11 and 13 Court
HALBERT, EDWIN G., (*D M & E G Halbert*)
Hall, Charles S , U S commissioner, manager for R H Hall & Co., 34 Court.
Hall, Lucy A. Miss, teacher, 20 Collier
Hall, L M , fruit and confectionery, 114 Court
Hall, R. H. & Co., crockery, glassware and cutlery, 34 Court. Chas S Hall, manager
Hall, William H , dentist, Hagaman Block, Court corner Exchange
Hallock, Cary & Co , (*W. B. Hallock, J. S Cary, D. S Ayers, C. A and W. S. Weed,*) wholesale clothiers, 10 and 12 Chenango
HALLOCK, FREDERICK M , (*Hallock & Schefers*)
HALLOCK & SCHEFERS, (*Frederick M. Hallock and Jacob Schefers,*) custom tailoring, 62 Court.
Hallock, Wallace B., (*Hallock, Cary & Co.,*) hats, caps and furs, 64 Court
Hamlin, Amos, portrait painter, 54 Washington.
Hance, Jennie L. Miss, dress and cloak making, 14 Court
HANCOCK, JOHN D., prop. of Oyster Cove, oysters, wholesale and retail, 26 Court.
HAND, GEORGE F., (*S D. & G.F Hand*)
HAND, S. D., (*S D & G. F. Hand,*) farmer 110
HAND, S. D & G. F , (*George F.,*) physicians and surgeons, 20 Collier.
Hanes, Whitney, livery, boarding and sale stables, rear of Exchange Hotel, on Tow Path.

HANLON, WM , architect and builder, Fayette corner Whitney, residence Hawley corner Fayette.
HANRAHAN, JOHN, groceries, South.
Harding, A L , sash, doors, blinds and lumber, 130 Washington
Harding, Lowell, alderman 4th Ward.
Harding, L. & Son, (*T. A ,*) wool, hides, skins, bones and tallow, 91 Water.
Harding, T. A., (*L Harding & Son.*)
Harley, Connell, carpenter, Robinson.
Harris, Burt J., prop of Cottage Hotel, Chenango corner North Depot
Harris, Geo. M., retired merchant, 36 Court.
Harris, William, retired merchant, 36 Court.
Harrison, James, (*Kendall, Harrison & Co.*)
Havens, J. H , meat market, 51 Washington
Hawley, Charles W., hats, caps and furs, 50 Court
HAYES, SILAS C , groceries and provisions, 77 Chenango
HAYS, MATHEW, (*Cortesey & Hays,*) alderman 1st Ward.
Hays, M. R , policeman.
Hecox, William H., lawyer, 55 Court.
Hemmingway, Geo C., farmer 30, River
Herrick, C A , machinist, 18 Rutherford.
Heybeck, J V , bakery, 5 Division
Heyton, John C., boots and shoes, 126 Court.
Hickcox, Ambrose, (*Hickcox & Stiles.*)
Hickcox & Stiles, (*Ambrose Hickcox and Frederick Stiles,*) novelty machine shop, experimental machinery, Osteningo Mills, Commercial Avenue
Hicks, H. P , tree agent, South Water.
Hill, John, (*J. B Weed & Co.*)
Hine, Isaac N , (*I. N. Hine & Co.*)
Hine, I N & Co , (*Isaac N. Hine and Jas E Brown,*) dry goods, carpets &c , 59 Court.
HIRSCHMANN BROS., (*Sigmund J., Frederick J. and Lewis J.,*) dry goods, carpets, furs, millinery goods &c., 15 and 17 Court.
HIRSCHMANN, FREDERICK J., (*Hirschmann Bros.*)
HIRSCHMANN, LEWIS J , (*Hirschmann Bros.*)
HIRSCHMANN, SIGMUND J., (*Hirschmann Bros*)
Hitchcock, W A. Rev., rector Christ's Church, 2 Doubleday Place, Henry.
Hodge, H , dentist, 18 Chenango, residence 34 Henry
Holland & Brother, (*Schuyler and Lewis,*) meat market, 63 and 65 Court.
Holland, Lewis, (*Holland & Brother *)
Holland, Schuyler, (*Holland & Brother *)
HOLLENSWORTH, LEVI hair dresser at N. Y. State Inebriate Asylum.
Hollister, George B , fish, fruits and vegetables, 95 Court.
Hooton, William, groceries, 3 Division
Hopkins, P A , (*Beardsley & Parker Lock Co *)
HOPKINS, PETER W , lawyer and district attorney, 76 Court.
*HORTON, BROTHER & MYER, (*Henry W and Seymour S Horton, and Hiram M Myer,*) stoves, tin, heavy and shelf hardware, copper and sheet iron ware &c , 32 Court
HORTON, HENRY W , (*Horton, Brother & Myer *)
HORTON, SEYMOUR S., (*Horton, Brother & Myer.*)
Hotchkiss, Cyrus F., real estate broker and assistant assessor U S. internal revenue, 77 Court.
Hotchkiss, Giles W. Hon., lawyer, 46 Court.
Hourigan, James F Rev , pastor of St Patrick's Church, LeRoy
House of the Good Shepherd, South Water, Rev C T. Coer, chaplain ; Miss Jane A Loomis, matron
Howard, Schuyler, groceries, provisions &c., South Main corner DeRussey
HOWE SEWING MACHINE CO., M L Barnes, manager, 39 Court.
Howland, Rufus J., gunsmith, 67 Washington.
Hoyt, Bouton, builder, Exchange corner Whitney.
Hubbard, Henry B., dollar store, 89 Court
Hughes, ——, (*Crozier & Hughes.*)
Hull, Amos G., harness maker, 57 Court, up stairs, and manuf. of spokes, hubs &c., Hawley near Washington
Hull, John Jr , (*Hull, King & Co *)
Hull, King & Co , (*John Hull, Jr., John H. and Chas A King,*) cigar manufs , 86 Front.
HUNGERFORD, JOHN, groceries, provisions &c , Front near North
Hungerford, J. D , shoemaker, Tuder.
Hunt, Wallace P , lawyer, 66 Court.
HUNTER, JOHN, bricklayer and plasterer, Mary.

## I.

Insley, J , builder, Hawley.
Isbell, George E , assistant supt. of Binghamton City Water Works.

# MISS ELLA WOOD,
## ARTIST,
### 72 Court Street,
### Binghamton, N. Y.

**Miss Wood** respectfully informs her friends and the public, that she is now prepared to execute in the most tasteful and satisfactory manner, all work connected with the artistic department

**Oil Painting** of all descriptions, work neatly done with Water Colors and India Ink. Portraits painted from sittings or photographs

Particular attention given to all orders and satisfaction guaranteed in every case  At

## L. G. Beecher's Photographic Studio,
### 72 Court Street, Binghamton, N. Y.

# The Binghamton Times,

## PUBLISHED THURSDAYS,

BY

# A. L. WATSON,

*Publisher and Proprietor,*

## Court Street, (3d floor) Binghamton, N. Y.

# DAVID E. CRONIN, Editor.

## Terms of Subcription, $1.75 per Year.

# J.

Jackson, C. C., manuf of paper bags and flour sacks, 80 Front
Jackson, D. P , physician, 71 Front.
Jackson, D Post, physician, 73 Front
Jackson, —— Prof., school, over 43 Court.
Jarvis, Henry S , (*Marvin & Jarvis.*)
Jennings, A., boots and shoes, 79 Court.
Jessup, John H , alderman 5th Ward
Johnson, A , paints, oils &c., Exchange.
JOHNSON, BARNA R , lawyer 76 Court.
Johnson, Chas , supt Gas Works.
JOHNSON, INMAN, livery and boarding stable, Collier near Fireman's Hall.
JOHNSON, J M , county clerk, residence 90 Hawley
Johnson, J. H , deputy county clerk, residence 90 Hawley
Johnson, Lowell L., billiard parlor, 99 Washington.
Johnson, Thomas, constable and farmer in Union 40, Walnut.
Jones, Edward F., prop. of Jone's Scale Works, Starr Avenue
Jones, F A., tobacconist, 4 Collier.
Jones, Geo. C., (*G C Jones & Co.*)
Jones, G C & Co., (*Geo. C. and Joseph R. Jones,*) bonnet bleachers and manufs of straw goods
Jones, Joseph R (*G. C Jones & Co*)
Jones, Julia J Miss, millinery, over 15 Court.
JUDD, SOLOMON, lawyer, 57 Court

# K.

KANE, THOS. H , meat and fish market, 51 Washington
KATTELL, E. C. Hon., president Continuous Oil Refining Co.
KATTELL, E E., book keeper Continuous Oil Refining Co.
Kaul, Henry, prop of Atlantic Garden, 66 Water.
Kelley, Michael S , shoemaker, Oak.
Kellogg, Paulina Miss, dress maker, 51 Court.
Kendall, Harrison & Co., (*T. R. Kendall, James Harrison and Lyman Clock,*) tobacconists, 46 Washington.
Kendall, T R , (*Kendall, Harrison & Co*)
Kennedy, Peter K., (*with Geo. Penrie.*) manuf. hat conformitors, 19 Commercial Avenue.
Kennedy, Wm J , stoves and tinware, Main corner Front.
Kent, Brazilla, building mover, 53 Chenango.
Kent, E W., (*Kent & Stow.*)
Kent, G A , (*Westcott & Kent*)
Kent & Stow, (*E. W. Kent and Samuel Stow,*) groceries, Chenango north Depot.
Ketchum, A. J , groceries, Chenango.
Ketchum, C J., (*Jerry Ketchum & Son.*)
Ketchum, Jerry & Son, (*C. J.,*) groceries and provisions, Fuller Block, Chenango.
*KILMER, CHARLES, stoves, tin and sheet iron ware, and glass, 39 Hawley
King, Charles A , (*Hull, King & Co.*)
King, John H., (*Hull, King & Co*)
Kinney, Eugene H., (*Smith & Kinney.*)
Klee, Conrad, hair dresser, over 21 Court corner Water.
Klee, Sebastian & Peter, barbers, 54 Court.
*KNIBBS, GEO. G., manuf. of boots and shoes, 13 Lewis.
Kramm, Frederick, tailor, 40 Court.
Krauss, A., hides, skins, pelts and wool, 91 Water

# L.

LaConr, John W , confectionery, toys &c , 2 Court.
Lacy, J. R., (*Lacy & Peck*)
Lacy & Peck, (*J R. Lacy and Walter S. Peck,*) manufs. brackets, furniture carvings and picture frames, Commercial Avenue.
LaGrange, James, lawyer.
Lane, Caleb, (*Beardsley & Lane.*)
Lang, Richard G , scroll sawing and wood turning, 101 Water.
Laraway, Ed., agent, dealer in foreign wines and liquors, tobacco and cigars, 65 Court.
Larose, Andrew, (*Stillman & Larose.*)
*LAWTON, MARY A. Miss, dress maker and tailoress, 35 Hawley.
*LAWYER BROS , (*Wm. S. and George L.,*) publishers of the *Democrat,* 89 Water.
LAWYER, GEORGE L. (*Lawyer Bros.*)
Lawyer, Jacob H , photographer, 57 Court, up stairs
LAWYER, WM. S., (*Lawyer Bros*)
Leach, F , assistant engineer, extension of the Chenango Canal, office 51 Court.

Leach, F Jr , assistant engineer, extension of the Chenango Canal, office 51 Court.
Lee, Philo H , gents' furnishing goods, 50 Court.
Lee, Samuel, U S. gaoger.
Leet, A H , (*O. J. Rowe & Co*)
Leighton, James, grain, provisions and seeds Commercial Avenue.
Lemmerman, Cornelia Mrs , dress maker, 190 Washington
Lester Brothers & Co., (*Horace N and George W. Lester, and Henry A Goff,*) manufa. and wholesale dealers in boots and shoes, 5 and 7 Court.
LESTER, D A , house, sign and fresco painter, 14 LeRoy Place.
Lester, George W , (*Lester Brothers & Co.*)
Lester, Horace N , (*Lester Brothers & Co*)
Lester, J A Mrs , boarding house, 56 Hawley corner Carroll.
LESTER, RICHARD W., (*C. B Perry & Co*)
LeVALLEY, F., (*Coutant & Le Valley*)
Lewis, Cyrus, prop. Lewis House, Lewis corner Canal.
Lewis, E. L , liquors, 99 Washington.
LEWIS, FREDERICK, (*Mason W Bosworth & Co.,*) (*William Morris & Co.,*) prest. Binghamton Savings Bank.
Livermore, Wm. H , confectioner, 8 Chenango
Lloyd, John A., shoemaker, 59 Washington, up stairs.
LOCKWOOD, ALBERT W., (*Adam H. Rennie & Co*)
Loomis, Benj N , lawyer, commissioner of deeds, vice-president Chenango Valley Savings Bank and secretary of Susquehanna Valley Home for Indigent Children, 71 Court
Loomis, Charles W , lawyer and notary public, 71 Court.
Loomis, Jane A. Miss, matron of House of the Good Shepherd, South Water
Lovelace, Stephen B , boots, shoes, hats and caps, 85 Court
LOWELL, DANIEL W., principal of Lowell's Commercial College, Phelp's Block, Court corner Water
LOWELL'S COMMERCIAL COLLEGE, Phelps Block, Court corner Water, Daniel W Lowell, principal.
LUDDEN, WM. J., lawyer, over 43 Court.
Lyon & Freeman, (*Harry Lyon and Reed B. Freeman,*) clothing and gents' furnishing goods, 72 Court.
Lyon, Harry, (*Lyon & Freeman*)
Lyon, James, liquor store, Canal Bank near Court
Lyons, D , auctioneer and commission merchant, 71 Washington

## M.

Mable, C. H., plumber and gas fitter, 23 Liberty.
Maffit, S D , physician, 72 Hawley.
MALETTE, JAMES, (*Malette & Reid*)
*MALETTE & REID, (*James Malette and Geo. J. Reid,*) publishers *Binghamton Daily Republican, Broome Weekly Republican* and *Binghamton Standard and Semi-weekly Republican,* 98 Water
Mangan, Peter J., shoemaker, Henry.
Manier, Alex , jobber in liquors and wines, 5½ Collier. ·
Manier, James W , cashier Susquehanna Valley Bank.
Mann, Chas E. & Co., (*Harvey Way,*) New England Bakery, 109 Court
MANNING, R T., (*Evans & Manning*)
MANNING, W. J., metal roofer and general jobber in tin, sheet and galvanized iron, 12 Main
Marks, B , (*Marks & Bean*)
Marks & Bean, (*B. Marks and C Bean,*) wholesale grocers, 87 Washington
Marlla, Chas G , freight agent, D L & W R R., Syracuse and Binghamton.
MARTIN, CELORA E , (*Chapman & Martin.*)
Martin, Frederick W., sheriff, Court House
Martin, John, shoemaker, South Water.
Martin, Stephen D., wholesale produce and commission dealers, hides, wool, butter, cheese &c , 17 Commercial Avenue.
Marvin, Brazillai, commissioner of deeds, 45 Collier.
Marvin, Chauncy, (*Marvin & Jarvis.*)
Marvin & Jarvis, (*Chauncy Marvin and Henry S. Jarvis,*) merchant tailors and gents' furnishing goods, 28 Court.
Mason, A H , stock dealer
MASON, L M., Philadelphia Meat Market, Chenango, 2d door north of Depot
MASON, O. R , (*Mason, Root & Co.*)
*MASON, ROOT & CO., (*O R. Mason, C. O. Root and J W Doubleday,*) hardware, 83 Washington.
MASTEN, DANIEL, builder and jobber, Myrtle Avenue.
Mather, Richard, vice-president Chenango Valley Savings Bank
MATLACK, WM. D , carriage and sleigh trimmer, Susquehanna corner Washington
Matthews, I S. & Co , (*H. W. Bradley,*) agricultural implements, Commercial Avenue.

Muyell, Sanford, stoves, tinware and house furnishing goods, 23 Court corner Water.

MAYER, DAVID H., crockery, glass ware and house furnishing goods, 87 Court.

Mayo, W E., wholesale dealer in produce, provisions, seeds, grain, paper &c, 7 Commercial Avenue

McCall, S, dentist, Henry.

McDonald, Theodore F, lawyer, over postoffice

McElroy, J. J., (*McElroy & Watson.*)

McElroy & Watson, (*J. J. McElroy and D W Watson,*) wholesale and retail furniture dealers, 100 Washington.

McGlinn, M., boot maker, 84 Washington.

*McGRAW, D C, (successor to Mills & McGraw,) florist, prop of River Side Gardens, half mile east of Water Works

McHenry, Frank, traveling agent, residence Fuller Block, Chenango.

McIVOR, WM C, builder, Main

McKinney, Chas, (*McKinney & Phelps.*)

McKinney, Corliss, architect, over First National Bank, Court

McKinney & Phelps. (*Chas McKinney and Sherman D Phelps,*) coal dealers, Henry.

McKinney, Wm. A., lawyer, 44 Court.

McMahon, Michael, (*Stockwell & McMahon*)

McMahon, Thos. W., (*John O'Hara & Co*)

McNamara Bros, (*J P, D C and J A,*) wines and liquors, 5 Collier.

McNamara, D C., (*McNamara Bros*)

McNamara, J A, (*McNamara Bros*)

McNamara, J. P., (*McNamara Bros.*)

McNamara, Michael, farmer 6, Grove

MEAD & BENEDICT, (*J. O. Mead and R K. Benedict,*) manufs of ladies' and misses' fine shoes, 91 Water.

MEAD, J O, (*Mead & Benedict*)

Meagher, Jeffer, shoemaker, 77 Oak

Meagley, R H, prop Binghamton Soap and Candle Works, Winding Way.

Melina, F F. & Co, (*Wm Rowe,*) blacksmithing, Court.

Mercer, Verena Mrs, saloon, Hawley.

MERRIAM, ALBERT W, groceries, 12 Court

Merrick, H C, city surveyor, 79 Court, up stairs

Merrill, P A., manuf sash, blinds and doors, at the Railroad sash and blind shop, Chenango

MERSEREAU, G. W., (*J. Pickering & Co.*)

Mersereau, T. T, (*Craver & Mersereau*)

Michelbach, George, lager beer saloon, 48 Henry

MIDDLEBROOK, C. D., wholesale and retail dealer in Canada and Western pine and black walnut lumber, S J Fulton, agent. Chenango near Union Depot

MILES, ELIZABETH Mrs., prop. of Fifth Ward Hotel, DeRussey.

Milks, John, (*Milks & Watson*)

Milks & Watson, (*John Milks and E. H. Watson,*) spoke and hub manufs and carriage makers, South foot of Carroll.

Millard, S C, lawyer, 65 Court.

MILLER, JACOB M., merchant tailor, 69 Washington

Miller, William, clothing and furnishing goods, 18 Court

Miner, A. S, tinware manuf, 9 and 11 Commercial Avenue.

Monroe, Henry S., school commissioner Eastern Dist, and insurance agent, office at Court House.

MONTGOMERY, SAMUEL A, (*J G. De Voe & Co*)

MOON, GEO. Q., prop. of Chenango Valley Mills, Commercial Avenue

Moore, C F. & Brother, (*J P,*) farmers lease of John, 150, South Main

Morgan, J P., teller National Broome County Bank, fire and life insurance agent and agent for Cunard line steamships.

Morgan, Mose T., alderman 1st Ward

MORGAN, TRACY R., secretary Continuous Oil Refining Co., cashier National Broome County Bank, treasurer Chenango Valley Savings Bank and treasurer L. Bolles Hoe & Tool Co.

Morgan, W. P, D L & W Express agent, 93 Washington.

MORRIS, OLIVER A., (*Amsbry & Morris.*)

Morris, William & Co, (*Frederick Lewis,*) lumber dealers, 126 Washington

Morse, O. G., dyer and scourer, Washington corner Henry.

MOSHER, WM H, groceries and provisions, oysters at wholesale and retail, 107 Court.

Munsell, G. R, (*Bloomer & Munsell*)

Murphy, Ezra, (*E. Murphy & Brother*)

Murphy, E. & Brother, (*Ezra and William,*) photographers, 53 Court.

Murphy, William, (*E. Murphy & Brother*)

MYER, HIRAM M, (*Horton, Brother & Myer.*)

MYERS, JACOB, (*Barnes & Myers,*) owns farms 360, and 113 acres in Saratoga Co.

Mygatt, John T, wholesale coal dealer, 76 Court.

# N.

NASH, DENISON, (*Cary, Nash & Ogden*)
National Broome Co Bank, Cyrus Strong, president, Tracy R. Morgan, cashier; J P Morgan, teller; Phelps Bank Building, corner Court and Chenango
National Express Co, 84 Washington, Alonzo E. Dorr, agent.
Negus, A P, express, Morgan near Chenango
Negus, L R, hackman, 121 Court.
Negus, L R Mrs, dressmaker, 23 Fayette
Nelson, B H, groceries and confectionery, Chenango.
Nelson N B., carpenter, Court corner Water.
New England Bakery, 109 Court, Chas E Mann & Co., props.
NEWDALE, ALBERT, florist and market gardener, 1½ miles west of Court House
NEWELL, F T, dealer in groceries and provisions, flour, pork, lard, fish, clover and Timothy seed, 69 Washington
NEWMAN, M. A. DR, dentist, 10 Chenango.
Newman, Mary A, homeo physician, 10 Chenango.
NEWTON & DAVIS, (*S. S Newton and A W Davis,*) manufs and dealers in furniture, 90 and 92 Washington.
NEWTON, S S, (*Newton & Davis*)
Newton, Wm H, boots and shoes, 27 Court
Noxley, Lorenzo, stone quarry, South Prospect.
Noyes, E M & Brother, (*Joseph P,*) comb manufs, Ferry head of Water
Noyes, Joseph P., (*E. M. Noyes & Brother.*)

# O.

O'Brien, Julia Miss, milliner, 59 Court
OGDEN, CHARLES, (*Cary, Nash & Ogden*)
OGDEN, D H, (*Crocker & Ogden*)
Ogden, Henry B, alderman 3d Ward, carpenter and builder, Pine
O'Hara, John & Co, (*Thos W McMahon,*) clothiers and merchant tailors, 57 Court.
Olmsted, L. L, stoves and tinware, steam and gas fitter, 94 Washington
O'Neil Matthew, (*Flanagan & O'Neil.*)
ORR, JOSEPH W., (*Conner & Orr.*)
Orton, J G, physician, also president of Board of Managers, Susquehanna Valley Home for Indigent Children, Henry.
OSBORN, WM. R, treasurer Continuous Oil Refining Co, cashier City National Bank of Binghamton; treasurer Susquehanna Valley Home for Indigent Children and fire and life insurance agent.
Osborne, Frank L, sign and ornamental painter, 65 Court.
Osgood, H B & Co, props Binghamton Scale Works, Mary.
O'Shea, John, groceries, 70 Henry.
OTSENINGO MILLS, Commercial Avenue Wm Bigler, prop.
OYSTER COVE, 26 Court, John D. Hancock, prop

# P.

PADDOCK, Z. REV, D D, retired M E clergyman, 83 Hawley.
PAIGE, CHAFFEE & CO., (*Clinton P Paige, Joseph B Chaffee and Jno J Babcock,*) general insurance agents, agents for American Steam Safe Co and Babcock's Fire Extinguisher. 51 Court.
PAIGE, CLINTON P, (*Paige, Chaffee & Co*)
Parish Bros., (*H G and H,*) laundry, 5 Henry.
Parish, H, (*Parish Brothers*)
Parish, H G, (*Parish Brothers*)
Parker, A S, (*Beardsley & Parker Lock Co*)
Parks, Almira Mrs., dressmaker, South Water
Parmley, A. W., plumber and gas fitter 96 Water.
Parsons, J. H., real estate agent, 96 Washington
Parsons, James H, (*George Reed & Co*)
Patten, Alexander S, meat market, 84 Washington.
Patterson, James, mason, Griffith.
Patterson, U. H., mirrors, picture frames, window shades, artists' materials &c., 3 Collier.
PAYFAIR, JOSEPH E, out of business
Peabody, I W., homeo physician, 14 Court.
PECK, ALFRED C, (*Scudder & Peck*)
Peck, Walter S, (*Lacy & Peck*)
Peirce, C. J. Miss, dressmaker, Susquehanna.
PENRIE GEORGE W., (*Penrie & Wales*)
Penrie, Geo W., (*with Peter K Kennedy,*) manuf hat conformitors, 19 Commercial Avenue

PENRIE & WALES, (*George W Penrie and A. DeWitt Wales,*) attorneys and counselors at law, and real estate brokers, 75 Court
PEOPLE'S MARKET, 16 Court, John T. Whitmore, prop.
People's Market, 16 Chenango, W C & R S Tracy, props
Perkins, Allen, brick manuf. and farmer.
*PERKINS, C. A. Dr., dentist, 67 Court
PerLee, Henry, prop of PerLee House, 81 Washington.
PERRY, CHAS B, (*C. B. Perry & Co*)
PERRY, C. B. & CO, (*Chas B Perry and Richard W. Lester,*) dry goods, fancy and ladies' furnishing goods, 53 Court
Perry, H P, wall paper and confectionery, Chenango.
Perry, Isaac G., architect, over 11 Court
Persels, Henry, (*Smith & Persels*)
*PHELPS, A J, station agent for Erie R R., ticket agent for D L & W, S & B, U & C. V. R Re., agent for Hartford R. R. Insurance Co. and General Accident Insurance Co., house 127 Washington.
Phelps, Norman A, teller Susquehanna Valley Bank
Phelps, Sherman D Hon, (*Sherman D Phelps & Co,*) (*McKinney & Phelps,*) prest Susquehanna Valley Bank, prest. Chenango Valley Savings Bank, prest L Bolles Hoe & Tool Co, and mayor of City
Phelps, Sherman D. & Co., (*Wm O Douglas,*) wholesale dealers in hardware, 19 Court and 87 Water
PHILADELPHIA MEAT MARKET, Chenango, 2d door north of Depot, L. M Mason, prop
PHILLIPS, L C, general agent Washington Life Insurance Co, 69 Court.
Phillips, L C Mrs, milliner and dress maker, Cedar.
PICKERING, J. & CO, (*G. W Mersereau and H. P Brown,*) monuments, head stones and marble mantles, 126 Court.
Pickering, Orin, mechanic, residence 45 Pine.
Pine, Neri, lawyer, 69 Court
Piper, Eugene, wholesale liquor dealer, 62 Washington.
Pitts, Levi Rev., superannuated M E clergyman, agent for Way's sewer pipes, Frederick.
Pope, A C, (*Ford & Pope*)
Pope, A C & Co (*W P. Pope,*) coal dealers, Clinton.
Pope, W P. (*A C Pope & Co.*)
Pope, Wm P., (*W P Pope Jr & Co,*) vice-president Binghamton Savings Bank
Pope, W P Jr & Co., (*W P Pope,*) clothing, 4 Exchange
PORTER, T EDSON, (*Carrington & Porter*)
Post Office Bowling and Billiard Saloon, under Post Office, S Raymond, prop
Pratt, Eli, (*Pratt & Son*)
PRATT, GEORGE, cashier First National Bank.
PRATT, HALLAM E, books, stationery, paper hangings &c, 43 Court.
Pratt & Son, (*Eli and U D,*) lumber dealers, foot Carroll.
Pratt, U D., (*Pratt & Son.*)
Pratt, Wm. H, (*Whitney & Pratt*)
PRENDERGAST, JAMES, stoves, tin, copper and sheet iron ware, 51 Washington.
PRICE, LUCY A Mrs, ladies' hair dressing establishment, over 13 Court.
Prospect Iron Works
Pugsley, William, broom manuf., 6 Commercial Avenue.
*PURTELL, PATRICK W, baker, 8 Court.

## R.

Ragan, Wm., house painter, Hawley
*RAILROAD PLANING MILL, north of Erie R R Depot, Alonzo Roberson, prop
Railroad Restaurant Wm W. Walker, prop
Ramsbottom estate, fancy dyeing establishment, LeRoy Place
Randall, Nelson, liquor store, Canal Bank.
Rankin, John, resident, Front.
RAYMOND, S, prop. Post Office Bowling and Billiard Saloon, and mason, under Post Office
Reed, George & Co, (*James H Parsons,*) tobacconists and cigar manufs, 25 Court.
Reed, John M, (*Reed & Thomson*)
Reed & Thomson, (*John M Reed and M. M. Thomson,*) tobacconists, 129 Court corner Carroll
REID, GEO J., (*Malette & Reid.*)
Reid, John, (*Reid & Sherman*)
Reid & Sherman, (*John Reid and Martin Sherman,*) gents' furnishing goods, 39 Court.
RENNIE, ADAM H. & CO., (*Albert W. Lockwood,*) manufs boots, shoes and rubbers, 68 Washington
RENNIE, JOHN, boot maker, Front
RENNIE, M J, (*Royal & Rennie,*) prop of West Side Coal and Wood Yard corner Railroad and Walnut.

Reynolds & Blanchard, auctioneers, 18 Court.
REYNOLDS, J. GROSVENOR, (*Rogers & Reynolds* )
RICE, FREDERICK E , (*H M Rice & Son* )
RICE, HORACE M , (*H M Rice & Son* )
RICE, H. M  & SON, (*Horace M  and Frederick E.,*) grocers, 115 Court
Rice, J F., oyster and dining saloon, 6 Collier
Rice, M G , restaurant, Washington corner Hawley.
Rich H , telegraph operator
Rich, Tracy G Jr , (*T G Rich & Son* )
Rich, Tracy G Sr , (*T G Rich & Son* )
Rich, T G  & Son, (*Tracy G Sr and Tracy G Jr* ,) real estate agents, 69 Court
Richards, Daniel S., lawyer, 48 Court.
Richardson & Dexter, (*G W Richardson and Chester Dexter,*) manufs of flour, feed &c
Richardson, G W., (*Richardson & Dexter* )
Richeson, John, saloon, Canal Bank near Court
RICKS, GEORGE M , clothing, gents' furnishing goods, boots, shoes, hats and caps,
    79 and 81 Court.

*ROBERSON, ALONZO, wholesale and retail dealer in pine lumber, siding, flooring,
    ceiling, surfaced and otherwise, hemlock flooring, boards and scantlings, pine and
    hemlock shingles, lath, pickets, fence rails, oak plank and boards, chestnut and
    oak ceiling, Railroad Planing Mill, north of Erie R R Depot
Roberts, Ed A , chief engineer Fire Department
Roberts, Francis F , carpenter and joiner, 12 Myrtle Avenue.
Roberts, Wm , dyeing and cleaning, Canal near Court
ROBERTS, WILLIAM, stone ware manuf , Susquehanna, house 18 Collier.
Roble, J C., dentist and solicitor of patents, 79 Court, up stairs
*ROBINSON, E D , manuf and dealer in furniture, spring beds, mattresses &c , 88
    Washington, also secretary Binghamton Savings Bank
Robinson, J T  general ticket agent, opposite Erie R R Depot
Rockwell, Andrew H , horse trainer, 88 Hawley.
Rogers, Chas D , blacksmith, Water rear American Hotel.
Rogers, Geo , livery, rear Exchange Hotel
Rogers, Harris G , treas. Binghamton Savings Bank
ROGERS, ISAIAH, boarding house, 70 Water
Rogers P. P , lawyer, 76 Court.
ROGERS & REYNOLDS, (*Theo. S. Rogers and J Grosvenor Reynolds,*) groceries and
    provisions, 42 Court
Rogers, Samuel W , justice of the peace, 65 Court
ROGERS THEO S , (*Rogers & Reynolds* )
RONK, JOHN C , cabinet maker and jobber, Evans Basin
Rood, Selah P , supt of poor and city sexton
Rooney Brothers, (*M A and P F ,*) groceries and provisions, 72 Washington.
Rooney, M. A , (*Rooney Brothers.*)
Rooney P F , (*Rooney Brothers* )
ROOT, C O , (*Mason, Root & Co* )
ROOT, REUBEN H , lawyer and commissioner of deeds, 47 Court, 2nd floor.
Ross, Erastus, liquors, 70 Washington
Rounds, Louise A., dressmaker, Exchange corner Susquehanna
Rowe, D.J , (*O J Rowe & Co* )
Rowe, O J & Co , (*D J Rowe and A. H Leet,*) wholesale grocers and provision
    dealers, Chenango Block.
Rowe, Wm , (*F P Melus & Co* )
Rowland, C F , sexton of Spring Forest Cemetery.
ROWLINGSON, J. W., (*Blanchard, Bartlett & Co* )
*ROYAL & RENNIE, (*Robert F Royal and M. J. Rennie,*) hardware, stoves and house
    furnishing goods, 88 Court
ROYAL, ROBERT F., (*Royal & Rennie* )
Rummer, Hiram S , oyster and dining saloon, 53 Washington
Russell, William, blacksmith, Commercial Avenue
*RUSSELL, WHITNEY D , general agent Singer Sewing Machines, 89 Court.

## S.

Safford, LaFayette, book-binder, 43 Court
SALEM, PETER, boot and shoe maker, Fuller Block, Chenango.
Sampson, Daniel B , leather and findings, 47 Water
SANDERS, HIRAM, retail liquor dealer, 73 Washington.
Sanford Addison V , (*Gilmore & Co.*)
SANFORD, CHAS. W., president City National Bank of Binghamton.
Sanford, E N , watchmaker and jeweler, 56 Court
Saunders, C. L , (*Chubbuck & Saunders* )
Schad Henry, hair dresser, 61 Court.
SCHEFERS, JACOB, (*Hallock & Schefers* )

SCHEMHORN, JAMES, barber and hair dresser, 2 doors east of Way's Hotel, residence South.
Schloss, Aaron, merchant tailor, 62 Court
Schnell, Joseph Jr., manager W. U. telegraph office, 52 Court.
Scott, J. W , (*Scott & Truesdell.*)
Scott & Truesdell, (*J. W. Scott and R. B. Truesdell,*) stair builders and jobbers, Canal bank below Hawley
SCOTT, WM., manuf. of steam engines, saw mill, grist mill and tannery work, wood working machinery, shafting, hangers and pulleys, and all kinds of machinery made to order, Commercial Avenue near Court.
SCOVILL & DeWITT, (*Wm. H. Scovill and Jerome DeWitt,*) attorneys at law and solicitors in bankruptcy, 49 Court over City National Bank.
SCOVILL, WM H., (*Scovill & De Witt,*) commissioner of deeds, 49 Court
SCUDDER, CYRUS F , (*Scudder & Peck* )
SCUDDER & PECK, (*Cyrus F Scudder and Alfred C Peck,*) groceries and provisions, 105 Court.
Sears, A Mrs , dress maker, Chenango.
SEARS, CHARLES W., books, stationery, wall paper and news, 51 Court.
*SEARS, OLIVER W., books, stationery, news depot &c., 56 Court.
Sedgewick, Edwin, engineer, Binghamton Water Works
Sedgwick, Thomas A., supt. of Binghamton City Water Works.
Seeber, J E Miss, teacher in wax work, crosses, harps, flowers, fruit and statuary, corner North Liberty and Frederick
SEELEY, CHAS L , plumbing and gas fitting, 19 Commercial Avenue.
Sessions, Gilman L., lawyer 48 Court
Seward, Dudley, carpenter, 10 Eldridge
SEYMOUR, CHARLES J , physician and surgeon, 91 Court
Seymour, Lewis, lawyer, 46 Court.
Shafer, Henry, barber, 104 Court
Shapley, M W., (*Shapley & Wells.*)
Shapley & Wells, (*M W Shapley and J S Wells,*) props Binghamton Iron Works, iron and brass founders and machinists, Hawley, office 52 Washington.
Shaver, Norman E., sealer of scales at Jones' Scale Works.
SHAVER, N. E Mrs , fancy store, 113 Court
Shaw, Samuel T , shoemaker, Canal bank above Chenango
Sheak, M A , wholesale provision and produce dealer, 98 Washington
SHEPARD & BARRETT, (*E R. Shepard and N. P. H Barrett,*) manufs of American fluting irons and shelf hardware, 101 Water.
SHEPARD, E R , (*Shepard & Barrett* )
Sherman, Martin, (*Reed & Sherman.*)
Sherwood, Benj . 75 Court, up stairs
Simmons, Malinda Miss, tailoress, Eldridge.
SISSON, BENJ F , (*B F Sisson & Sons* )
SISSON, B F. & SONS, (*Benj F , Chas. F. and Will W ,*) dry goods, 61 Court
SISSON, CHAS F , (*B. F Sisson & Sons* )
SISSON, WILL W . (*B F Sisson & Sons.*)
Skillman, Elias S Jr , (*Skillman & Larose* )
Skillman & Larose, (*Elias S Skillman Jr. and Andrew Larose,*) props. of Arbor Hotel and Restaurant, Court corner Water
Sloan, Henry S., homeo. physician, 32 Court.
Slosson, H A , livery and boarding stables, 22 Carroll.
Slosson, Henry A , general agent for Mansfield's metalic paint, 77 Court
Smead, C A., (*Smead & Son* )
Smead, J. W , (*Smead & Son* )
Smead & Son, (*J W and C A.,*) blacksmiths, 69 Water
Smith, Augustus D . (*L L Smith & Son.*)
Smith, A E , (*Smith Brothers* )
Smith, Benjamin F . lawyer, clerk of the Surrogate Court and librarian of Supreme Court Law Library, office Court House
Smith Brothers, (*H. E. and A E.,*) boots and shoes, wholesale, opposite Erie R R. Depot
Smith Brothers, teas, coffees, spices and fine groceries, 36 Court.
Smith, Clark J , hardware, 59 Washington
Smith, Daniel B & Co., manuf sarsaparilla and lemon soda, 10 Commercial Avenue
SMITH, DAVID J., engineer Binghamton Water Works
SMITH & DWYER, (*Wm S Smith and George Dwyer,*) druggists and grocers, 54 Court.
Smith, Edgar B , (*L. B. Smith & Son* )
Smith, Edward P , (*Smith & Kinney.*)
Smith, Frank Mrs., boarding house, 54 Exchange
*SMITH, GEORGE H., looking glasses, picture frames, chromos, engravings &c., 101 Court.
SMITH, HENRY A , druggist, 77 Court
Smith, H. E., (*Smith Brothers* )
Smith, Ira W., gunsmith, 67 Washington, up stairs.

# P. W. PURTELL,

## BAKER,

*Bread, Crackers, Cakes, Pies, &c., &c.*

*FRESH EVERY DAY.*

**No. 8 Court St., LaFayette Block,**

Binghamton, N. Y.

☞ A Wagon will be run to all parts of the City each day

---

# F. H. STEPHENS,

DEALER IN

# Books, Stationery,

AND

# PAPER HANGINGS,

*GENERAL NEWS DEPOT,*

**52 Court Street, Binghamton, N. Y.**

---

# The Union Weekly News,

*(ESTABLISHED 1851.)*

## A Valuable Family Newspaper!

*Full of Reliable, Instructive and Interesting Reading Matter.*

☞ *Special attention given to Local Affairs.*

## PUBLISHED FRIDAYS.

## MOSE B. ROBBINS, Editor & Proprietor

ADVERTISERS will find the NEWS the Cheapest Weekly Paper for their use, because IT PAYS THE BEST! and costs the least in proportion to circulation of any paper in Broome County.

# Plain and Ornamental Job Printing

## Executed in the best style at lowest rates.

Smith, Jeffrey, (*Butler, Smith & Co*)
Smith, John H., (*Smith & Persels.*)
SMITH, JOSEPH S. Dr , dental surgeon, 134 Court.
Smith, Julius W , sign and ornamental painter.
Smith & Kinney, (*Edward P. Smith and Eugene H Kinney,*) wholesale notions and
    fancy goods, 103 Court.
Smith, Lyman B., (*L B Smith & Son*)
Smith, L B & Son, (*Lyman B. and Edgar B ,*) bakery, 68 Court.
Smith, L L & Son, (*Augustus D ,*) floor, feed &c , 49 Washington
Smith & Persels, (*John H. Smith and Henry Persels,*) saddlery hardware and manufs.
    harness &c , 68 Washington
SMITH WM S., (*Smith & Dwyer*)
Snell, Joseph, manager W U. Telegraph, 52 Court.
SNOW, E F & CO , (*Wm A Snow,*) dealers in stoves, tinware, house furnishing
    goods &c , also manufs boots and shoes, Fuller Block, Chenango
Snow, William, shoemaker, 42 Court.
SNOW, WM A , (*E F Snow & Co.*)
Southworth, —— Rev , pastor Free Methodist Church
SPAN, REUBEN R , whitewasher and plasterer, corner Spring and Chestnut
Sparkes, Samuel, shoemaker, LeRoy Place
Spaulding, Evander, supt. of poor, office Court House.
SPAULDING HOUSE, Warren F. Spaulding, prop , Chenango near Erie Depot
SPAULDING, WARREN F , prop of Spaulding House, Chenango near Erie Depot.
SPENCER, CYRENIUS D , physician and druggist, 100 Court
Squires, Richard, watchmaker, 71 Washington.
Stack & Allen, (*Patrick Stack and Silas Allen,*) groceries, old No 6 Washington
Stack, Patrick, (*Stack & Allen*)
Stebbin, Henry F , policeman
Stephens, Edward B., post master, Court corner Collier.
Stephens, Ephraim, carpenter and builder, corner Susquehanna and Carroll.
Stephens, E P , builder, 74 Susquehanna
*STEPHENS, F. H , books, stationery, wall paper and news office, 52 Court.
Stevens, Abram, hair dresser, 3 Court.
STEVENS BROS , (*David W. and Urbane S ,*) props. livery stable ; carriages to let at
    all hours, day and night ; stable in rear of Smith & Son's bakery, entrance from
    Court
Stevens, Charles, blacksmith, South corner Carroll.
Stevens, Columbus, mason, South Water
STEVENS, DAVID W., (*Stevens Bros*)
Stevens, Lewis, planing and scroll sawing, turning, chair and basket making, &c , 101
    water, up stairs
Stevens, Lina E. Miss, dress maker, Carroll corner Whitney
STEVENS O. L , groceries and meat market, 100 Chenango.
STEVENS, URBANE S., (*Stevens Bros*)
Stevenson, W. G., life insurance agent, 63 Court
Stewart, William, scale manuf , Ferry near Chenango River Suspension Bridge.
Stiles Frederick, (*Hickcox & Stiles*)
Stilwell, Wm H , alderman 4th Ward.
St. John, Vincent, farmer 50, Front corner River
Stockwell, A D , (*Stockwell & McMahon*)
Stockwell & McMahon, (*A D Stockwell and Michael McMahon,*) props City Carriage
    Works, Eldridge near Erie Depot
STONE, H. W , boarding house and dealer in hides and pelts, 77 Water
Stone, J M. & Co., manufs and wholesale dealers in boots and shoes, 109 Water.
Stone, Martin, supervisor 3d Ward.
Stoppard, H. S. Miss , dress maker, 91 Washington.
Stoppard, Joseph, tailor, 59 Washington, up stairs.
Stoppard, Moses, (*Carl & Stoppard.*)
Storm, Jane L , millinery and dress making, 69 Washington.
Stoutenburg, Benjamin F , groceries and provisions, 116 Court
Stow, Samuel, (*Kent & Stow*)
STRATTON, JAMES D , restaurant, 73 Court
Stratton, Jane C Mrs., ladies' hair dressing, 96 Washington.
STRINGHAM, C W , carpenter, 11 Robinson.
Strong, Cyrus, president National Broome County Bank, and farmer, in Union, 110.
Stryker, Alonzo, (*DeWitt C. Stryker & Son*)
Stryker, DeWitt C. & Son, (*Alonzo,*) groceries and provisions, 40 Court.
*STUART, CHARLES, firearms and sporting goods, 43 Washington.
Sullivan, D J , carpenter, Cedar
Sullivan, Thomas, grocer, 9 Whitney
Surdam, Charles M., millinery and fancy goods, 88 and 90 Court
Susquehanna Valley Bank, Phelps Building, corner Court and Chenango, Sherman D.
    Phelps, president ; James W Manier, cashier , Norman A. Phelps, teller

    **T**

Sweetland, Freeman B , (*Whitney & Sweetland* )
Swigert, J F , fruits, toys and confectionery, 1 Main

# T.

Taber, Susan J . M D , physician, 99 Court.
Taylor, Edward Rev , D D , pastor Congregational Church, Main.
TAYLOR, GEORGE, foreman in Young's cooper shop  Washington
Taylor, Wm. E., vice-prest. City National Bank of Binghamton , vice-prest Binghamton Savings Bank
TenBrook, R W , (*Benson & TenBrook* )
Thayer, G. A , allo physician, 75 Water.
Thayer, O V , physician and prop of Binghamton Water Cure, office 61 Court.
Thomson, M. M.. (*Reed & Thomson* )
Thorn, J S , assistant engineer extension of the Chenango Canal, office 51 Court
Tidball, Zan L , agent A & S R R Co , alderman 3d Ward
Titchenener, E C , confectionery manuf , 57 Washington
TOOHEY & DONLEY, (*Patrick J. Toohey and John H  Donley,*) dry goods and Yankee notions, 37 Court
TOOHEY, PATRICK J , (*Toohey & Donley* )
Topin, James, groceries, provisions and liquors, 9 Liberty
Tracy, W C & R S , props. People's Market, 16 Chenango.
TRAVER & GALE, (*John L. Traver and A. C. Gale,*) meat market, Clinton Block, Clinton
Traver, J. L.. meat market, Clinton near Walnut
TRAVER, JOHN L., (*Traver & Gale* )
Tremain Wm , (*Anderson & Tremain* )
Truesdell, R B , (*Scott & Truesdell* )
Truman, James C., general order and commission agency, under First National Bank, Court corner Washington
Turner, A. D , dentist, 70 Court.
Turner, Paul, groceries and provisions, Henry corner Liberty.
Tweedy, Asa R , hats, caps and furs, 75 Court.

# U.

Underwood, John N , plumber, 8 Liberty
United States Express Co., 91 Washington, E. VanTuyl, agent.

# V.

VANARSDALE, A. G , blacksmith, LeRoy Place.
Vandenbergh, Henry, carpenter, Chenango
VANDERVORT, CORNELIUS, planing, moulding and scroll sawing, Commercial Avenue
VanEpps, A C , teacher, Seminary Avenue
VanNORWICK, SARAH Mrs , steam laundry, Chenango
VanSlyck, W H , city bill poster and distributor, 71 Washington, up stairs
VanTuyl, E., agent U. S Express, 91 Washington.
*VanWORMER, GEORGE, harness, basement 61 Court
VanWormer, James, agent for Amos G Hull in harness shop
Vincent, Thos. W., manuf sarsaparilla, soda and birch root beer, 97 Chenango.
VOSBURY, D C , insurance agent, 18 Jay
VROOMAN, J H , boarding house, meals at all hours, board by the day or week, 50 Lewis.

# W.

Wadhams, W. M., billiard parlor, 54 Washington.
WALES, A DeWITT, (*Penrie & Wales.*)
WALES, CHARLES, prop of Chenango House, 78 Water.
Wales, Stephen S Rev , pastor of Zinn's Church, (colored,) Whitney
Walker, Alfred, agent for Canton Tea Co , 67 Washington.
Walker, A E , Canton Tea Co , Alfred Walker, agent, 67 Washington.
Walker, William, confectionery and toys, 97 Court
Walker, W. J. & Co., manuf. sash locks, Commercial Avenue.
Walker, Wm W. W., prop. R R. Restaurant
Walnut, James A., billiard rooms, Post Office Block, and boarding house, Hagaman Block, Court corner Exchange

WALRATH, SILAS, carpenter, 12 Sand.
WARNER, ISAAC, prop. Warner House, Chenango corner Pearne.
Waterman, Thomas W , lawyer, 49 Court.
Waterman, Wm. M , lawyer, 49 Court.
WATSON, A. L., (*Purdy & Watson* )
Watson, D. W , (*McElroy & Watson.*)
Watson, E H., (*Milks & Watson.*)
WATSON, MATTHEW, boot maker, LeRoy Place.
Way, Harvey, (*Chas. E Mann & Co* )
WAY'S HOTEL, A. J Crandall, prop., 113 and 115 Court.
Weaver, Wm., (*Weaver & Wilson.*)
Weaver & Wilson, (*Wm. Weaver and Geo. R. Wilson,*) cigar manufs , 38 Court.
Webster, C H., apothecary, 72 Front.
Webster, Cornelius H. Jr., ready made clothing and gents' furnishing goods, 62 and 64 Court.
Weed, C. A., (*Hallock, Cary & Co* )
Weed, F M , (*J B. Weed & Co.*)
Weed, J B & Co , (*F M Weed, John Hill, David B. Garey and D. W. Fuller,*) props. of Binghamton Tannery, 12 Susquehanna.
Weed, W. S., (*Hallock, Cary & Co* )
WEEKS, BENJAMIN W , restaurant, warm meals at all hours, opposite Erie Depot.
Wellington, Acil, blacksmith, Chenango.
Wells, J. S , (*Shapley & Wells* )
WELLS, J. S., vice president Continuous Oil Refining Co.
Wentz, J E., carpenter and builder. 22 Collier.
Weesel, Elizabeth A. Miss, dressmaker, 66 Washington.
West, George J , confectionery and toys, 14 Court.
WEST, LEWIS, prop. of West's Lager Beer Brewery and Mount Prospect Iron Spring, and farmer 12, Prospect
WEST SIDE COAL AND WOOD YARD, cor. Railroad and Walnut, W. J. Rennie, prop.
Westcott, H , (*Westcott & Kent.*)
Westcott & Kent, (*H. Westcott and G. A. Kent,*) wholesale tobacconists, 3 Commercial Avenue
Western Union Telegraph Office, Joseph Snell, Jr., manager, 52 Court
WHEATON & BALLOU, (*Washington W. Wheaton and Asa A Ballou,*) dentists, 96 Court.
Wheaton, Thos J., dentist, 184 Court.
WHEATON, WASHINGTON W., (*Wheaton & Ballou,*) eclectic physician and surgeon, 96 Court.
Wheeler, Benj., dealer in paper hangings and paper hanger, 94 Hawley.
Wheeler, Dan, wines and liquors, above Slosson's Block, opposite Canal Lock
Wheeler, Henry W , billiard parlor, 43 Washington.
*WHITE, ALFRED, confectioner and fancy cake baker, 99 Court.
White, Frederick, dry goods, confectionery &c , 59 Main
White & Fuller, (*L. S. White and Joel Fuller,*) brewers, Collier.
White, L. S , (*White & Fuller* )
White, Nancy M. Mrs., boarding house, 6 Henry.
WHITE, R Mrs., hair dresser, 39 Hawley.
WHITMORE, JOHN T , prop of People's Market, 16 Court
Whitney, C A., (*Whitney & Pratt.*)
WHITNEY, GEORGE, attorney and counselor at law, 44 Court
WHITNEY, JOSHUA, Whitney Place, between Court and Robinson, near Griswold, farmer 26.
WHITNEY, J H., foreman of the Continuous Oil Refining Co.
Whitney, Newell D , lawyer, 63 Court.
Whitney & Pratt, (*C. A Whitney and Wm H. Pratt,*) wholesale dealer in flour, provisions and seeds, Henry corner Commercial Ave.
Whitney & Sweetland, (*Wm D. Whitney and Freeman B. Sweetland,*) agents for Weed sewing machines, 109 Court
Whitney, Thomas W., watches and jewelry, Court corner Washington.
Whitney, Wm D , (*Whitney & Sweetland.*)
Wickham, Alvan, (*Wickham & Bennett.*)
Wickham & Bennett, (*Alvan Wickham and Warren N. Bennett,*) insurance agents, 53 Court.
Wilcox, Philo, (*Butler, Smith & Co* )
Wilkinson Brothers, (*W. H. and C. A.,*) manufs. of card and upper leather, foot of Carroll
Wilkinson, C A , (*Wilkinson Brothers* )
Wilkinson, W. H., (*Wilkinson Brothers.*)
Williams, A , boots, shoes and confectionery, 114 Court corner Cedar
Williams C R , (*Bingham, Gay & Co.*)
Wilson, Geo. R , (*Weaver & Wilson* )
WILSON, JOSEPH, saloon, 44 Washington.

# Geo. H. Smith,

## MANUFACTURER OF

# LOOKING GLASSES,

## Picture Frames,

# CHROMOS,

# Engravings, &c.

## 101 Court Street, Binghamton, N. Y.

*Regilding and Repairing of Old Frames Done to Order.*

# The Democratic Leader!

## PUBLISHED EVERY FRIDAY,

### BY

# A. W. CARL,

## 63 and 65 Court Street,

## BINGHAMTON, BROOME COUNTY, N. Y.

## Terms $1.50 per Year, in Advance.

☞ *Advertising Rates Reasonable.*

# BOOK & JOB PRINTING,

*Executed with Neatness and Dispatch.*

Wilson, Robert J., livery, North Depot.
Wilson, W. N., wholesale dealer in cloth, cassimeres &c., 84 Court.
Winslow, J. Ancrum, lawyer and commissioner of deeds, 76 Court.
Winton & Darrow, (*M. T. Winton and R. S. Darrow,*) manfs. of children's carriages, sleighs and toy goods, office and salesroom, 18 Chenango, manufactory Rockbottom Dam.
Winton, M. T., (*Winton & Darrow.*)
Wiser, F. X., saloon, Main corner Front.
WOOD, ABRAM R., boots, shoes, leather and findings, 70 Court.
*WOOD, ELLA Miss, artist in oil and water colors, 72 Court.
WOOLSEY, E. (*E. Woolsey & Co.,*) residence 44 Susquehanna.
WOOLSEY, E. & CO., (*G. A. Woolsey,*) house, sign and ornamental painting and paper hanging, 47 Washington.
WOOLSEY, G. A., (*E. Woolsey & Co.*)
Worthing, John P., painter and grainer, 65 Court, and justice of the peace and coroner, 63 Court.
Wright, George H., barber, 72 Washington.
Wright, Lyman Rev., pastor Baptist Church, 49 Chenango.

# Y.

Youmans, Chasloy, gardener, Front corner Prospect.
Youngs, William F., cooper, Washington.

# Z.

Zimmer, Charles, hair dresser, 40 Court.

# TIOGA COUNTY
# BUSINESS DIRECTORY.

### EXPLANATIONS TO DIRECTORY.

Directory is arranged as follows    1  Name of individual or firm.    2  Post office address in parenthesis    3  Business or occupation

A Star (*) placed before a name, indicates an advertiser in this work.  For such advertisement see Index

Figures placed after the occupation of *farmers*, indicate the number of acres of land owned or leased by the parties.

Names set in CAPITALS indicate subscribers to this work

The word *Street* is implied as regards directory for the villages.

**For additions and corrections see Errata, following the Introduction.**

## BARTON.

(See Index to Business Directory )

## BERKSHIRE.

(Post Office Addresses in Parentheses.)

ABBREVIATIONS.—S. D , School District.

ABBOTT, GEORGE, (Berkshire,) S. D. 4, general blacksmith.

AKINS, LYMAN P , (Speedsville, Tompkins Co ) S D 7, farmer 30

Akins, Stephen B , (Berkshire,) S. D. 6, farmer 190

Aldrich, David, (Jenksville,) S. D 5, farmer 7

Andrews, George, (Berkshire,) S. D. 1, farmer 87

Ball, Alvah, (Berkshire,) dealer in eggs and butter, and (*with Martin H ,*) farmer 10.

Ball, Anson, (Berkshire,) (*Ball & Waldo* )

Ball, Asa, (Berkshire,) S. D. 4, assessor and farmer 150

Ball, Jno , (Berkshire,) S. D. 4, prop. of saw mill and lumberman

Ball, Levi, (Berkshire,) S. D. 4, farmer 66.

Ball, Martin H., (Berkshire,) (*with Alvah,*) farmer 10.

Ball & Waldo, (Berkshire,) (*Anson and E. B Waldo,*) dealers in flour, feed, coal, plaster &c.

Ballou, Aldin C , (Berkshire,) (*with Reuben A ,*) farmer 97.

Ballou, Reuben A , (Berkshire,) (*with Aldin C.,*) farmer 97.

Bancroft, Wm H , (Newark Valley,) S, D 2, farmer 55.

Barrett, James M , (Berkshire ) S D 1, principal of Berkshire Graded School

BATES, OTIS L , (East Berkshire,) S. D 8, farmer 81.

Belcher, A P , (Berkshire,) S. D 1, farmer 150.

Belcher, H. P., (Berkshire,) S. D. 1, (*with A P ,*) farmer

Benton, Charles W., (Speedaville, Tompkins Co ,) S D 6, farmer 62.

BERKSHIRE HOTEL, (Berkshire,) Ira Crawford, prop

Bidwell, Hiram, (Berkshire,) S. D. 1, justice of the peace.

Bidwell, Samuel O., (Berkshire,) justice of the peace and farmer 33

BLACKMAN, ABRAM, (Berkshire,) S. D. 5, stock dealer and farmer 160

BLACKMAN, JUDSON, (Speedaville, Tompkins Co ,) S. D 3, (*with Keith,*) farmer 250

BLACKMAN, KEITH, (Speedaville, Tompkins Co ,) S. D 3, (*with Judson,*) farmer 250.

Blanchard, Joseph A , (Speedaville, Tompkins Co.,) S. D, 7, farmer leases 200

Borthwick, Joseph, (Jenksville,) S D 5, farmer 75

Boyce, Stephen, (Speedaville, Tompkins Co ,) S D 7, farmer 400.

Boyle, Charles, (East Berkshire,) S. D. 8, farmer 66.

Brainard, C E , (Berkshire,) S. D. 8, farmer 280.

BROWN, DUYGAN & CO , (Berkshire,) (*Ransom Brown, James W Duygan and Charles O. Clark,*) props of saw mill and lumbermen

BROWN, EDWIN B., (Berkshire,) S D 1, carpenter and farmer 1½

BROWN, F H., (Berkshire,) S D 1, farmer 150

BROWN, ISAAC, (Berkshire,) S. D. 1, farmer 222

Brown, I. L., (Berkshire,) S D 1, carpenter.

Brown, Levi B , (Berkshire,) S. D. 1, carpenter.

Brown, Mary W. and T. C., (Berkshire,) S. D. 1, farmer 100

Brown, Myron, (Berkshire,) S. D. 1, carpenter.

BROWN, RANSOM, (Berkshire,) (*Brown, Duygan & Co*)

Brown, Robert C., (Berkshire,) S. D. 1, farmer 118.

Bunnell, Henry J , (East Berkshire,) blacksmith.

BUNNELL, JOHN G , (East Berkshire,) S D 8, farmer 115.

Carl, Foster C., (Berkshire,) S. D. 6, farmer 200.

Carpenter, George, (Berkshire,) S. D. 6, farmer 120

Chappius, Mark, (Berkshire,) S. D. 6, farmer 50.

CHURCH, ELIJAH C , (East Berkshire,) S. D. 8, farmer 48

CLARK, AUSTIN, (Ketchumville,) S. D. 2, farmer 125.

CLARK, CHARLES O., (Berkshire,) S. D. 1, (*Brown, Duygan & Co.*)

Clark, G. W , (Ketchumville,) (*with Austin,*) farmer 125.

Clark, Sanford H , (Berkshire,) S. D 1, farmer 43.

Coats, Charles, (East Berkshire,) S. D. 8, farmer 108.

Coher, Isaac, (Wilson Creek,) S. D. 11, farmer 50.

COLLINS, AMBROSE H , (Berkshire,) S. D. 4, carpenter and farmer 2.

Collins, Junius, (Berkshire,) S D 4, capitalist and farmer

Cooper, Anna Mrs ,(Ketchumville,) S D 2, farmer 144

COOPER, THOMAS G., (Ketchumville,) (*with Mrs Anna,*) farmer

Cortright, Darius, (East Berkshire,) S. D 2, farmer 34.

Cortright, Henry H , (East Berkshire,) S. D 2, farmer 30.

Cortright, James H ,(East Berkshire,) S D. 2, farmer 80.

CRAWFORD, IRA, (Berkshire,) prop of Berkshire Hotel and farmer 400

CROSS & HOLCOMB, (Berkshire,) (*Wm. O. Cross and J. W. Holcomb,*) props of ax factory.

Cross, James O ,(Berkshire,) S. D. 4, tailor

CROSS, WM. O , (Berkshire,) (*Cross & Holcomb* )

Davidge, Horton & Co , (Berkshire,) (*John Davidge, Lucian Horton and James Davidge,*) lumbermen and tanners

Davidge, James, (Berkshire,) (*Davidge, Horton & Co* )

Davidge, John, (Berkshire,) (*Davidge, Horton & Co.*)

Denison, Dileverge, (Ketchumville,) S. D. 2, farmer 64

Denison, John, (Wilson Creek,) farmer 89.

DENSMORE, SAMUEL, (Speedaville, Tompkins Co.,) S. D. 3, farmer leases of Mrs. Clark, 100.

Dewey, Charles J , (Berkshire,) (*Dewey & Darbonnier,*) S D 4, town clerk

Dewey & Darbonnier, (Berkshire,) S. D. 4, general merchants.

Driggs, John F , (Berkshire,) (*with Lorenzo J.,*) saw and grist mills, and lumber dealer

Driggs, Lorenzo J , (Berkshire,) (*with John F.,*) saw and grist mills, and lumber dealer

Duell, Benjamin, (Jenksville,) S D 5 , farmer 170 and (*with R M Jenks,*) 220

DUYGAN, JAMES W., (Berkshire,) (*Brown, Duygan & Co*)

EDWARDS, MERRITT P.,(Ketchumville,) S D 2, farmer 50.

Everitt, Henry, (East Berkshire,) S D 8, farmer 144

FOOTE, WM. B., (Berkshire,) S D. 10, steam mill and farmer 273

FORD, GEORGE, (Berkshire,) S. D. 6, farmer leases of Charles B., 130

Ford, George R , (Berkshire,) S. D. 6, farmer 107.

Ford, John R , (Berkshire,) S. D. 6, farmer 162.

Ford, Marcus J., (Berkshire,) S. D. 4, farmer 82.

FORD, WM W., (Berkshire,) S D 4, farmer 82

Freeland, Lewis A , (Newark Valley,) S D 3, farmer 53

Freeman, Nancy J. Mrs , (Berkshire,) S. D 4, planing mill

Gleezen, Silas P , (Berkshire,) farmer 9.

Goold, Joel, (Ketchumville,) S D. 2, farmer 138.

GREEN, TIMOTHY, (East Berkshire,) S. D 8, carpenter and joiner, and farmer 5

Gross, L , (East Berkshire,) S D 8, farmer 114

Gummerson, DeForreet P., (Berkshire,) S. D 4, author

HAIGHT, FOWLER Mrs , (Berkshire,) farmer 28

Hartwell, Bishop A , (Berkshire,) S. D 6, farmer leases of Mrs. Robinson, 110

HARTWELL, LEVI, (Ketchumville,) S D 2, farmer 100

Harvey, Andrew J , (Wilson Creek,) farmer leases 40 and (*with Martin V. B.,*) 183

Harvey, Martin V. B , (Wilson Creek,) S. D 11, (*with Andrew J .*) farmer 183.

Hayden, John, (Speedsville, Tompkins Co ,) S. D. 6, farmer 74.

Higgins, John, (Speedsville, Tompkins Co ,) S D 7, farmer 55

HOLCOMB, J W , (Berkshire,) S D 1, (*Cross & Holcomb*)

Holland, James J., (East Berkshire,) S. D 8, farmer 21.

Hollenbeck, Alonzo D., (East Berkshire,) S D 8, farmer 50.

Horton, Lucian, (Berkshire,) (*Davidge, Horton & Co*)

Houghtaling, Wm. M., (Berkshire,) S. D 4, carriage maker

*HULL, WARREN A , (Berkshire,) S. D 4, general blacksmith.

Hutchinson, Harvey, (Wilson Creek,) S. D. 10, farmer 106

Hutchinson, Williams, (Wilson Creek,) S D, 11, carpenter and farmer 5

Jackson, Wm H , (Ketchumville,) S D 2, town assessor and farmer 123

JAPHET, ELIJAH, (East Berkshire,) S. D. 8, farmer 30.

Japhet, George W , (East Berkshire,) S D 8, farmer 88

JAPHET, LEVI B., (East Berkshire,) S. D 8, overseer of the poor, owns right in town of Richford for Trumbull's patent churns and farmer 54

JAPHET, SYLVESTER W., (East Berkshire,) S D. 8, farmer 22 and leases 66

Jenks, Calvin, (Jenksville,) S D 5, (*with Franklin A.,*) farmer 200.

Jenks, Franklin A , (Jenksville,) S. D. 5, (*with Calvin,*) farmer 200.

Jenks, R. M , (Jenksville,) (*with Benjamin Duell,*) farmer 220

Jewett, A., (Speedsville, Tompkins Co.,) S. D 3, farmer 80

JEWETT, WALTER, (Berkshire,) S. D. 10, farmer 120.

Johnson, Carlisle P , (Berkshire,) S D. 4, general merchant and postmaster

JOHNSON, EUGENE F , (Berkshire,) S. D 4, farmer 220

Johnston, John, (Berkshire,) S. D 4, shoemaker

Jones, Wm , (Speedsville, Tompkins Co ,) S. D 3, farmer 91½

Judd, John N., (Berkshire,) S. D. 4, farmer leases 100

KEENY, WILLOUGHBY L , (Speedsville, Tompkins Co ,) S D. 7, farmer 112

KIMBALL, JOHN F., (Wilson Creek,) S. D 11, farmer 200

KIMBLE, JAMES S , (Berkshire,) S D 4, lumberman and farmer leases of Ira Crawford, 200

Lacy, Thomas J , (East Berkshire,) S D 8, farmer 52½

LANING, CHARLES, (Berkshire,) S. D 4, physician and surgeon

Lawrence, Oscar S., (Speedsville, Tompkins Co ,) (*with Wm S and Wm ,*) farmer 350

Lawrence, Wm , (Speedsville, Tompkins Co ,) S D 7, (*with Oscar S and Wm S.,*) farmer 350.

Lawrence, Wm S., (Speedsville, Tompkins Co ,) (*with Oscar S and Wm .,*) farmer 350

Legg, David E , (Speedsville, Tompkins Co ,) S D 7, farmer 90

LEGG, LARNARD, (Speedsville, Tompkins Co ,) S D 3, farmer 7

Legg, Layton J , (Jenksville,) S. D 5, (*with O A .*) farmer 110

LEGG, O. A , (Jenksville,) S. D 5, (*with Layton J.,*) farmer 110.

LEONARD, CATHARINE A Mrs , (Berkshire,) S D 4, gardener

Leonard, Charles T , (Berkshire,) farmer 33.

Leonard, George F., (Berkshire,) S. D. 4, farmer 313

Leonard, Hannah Mrs., (widow,) (Berkshire,) S D 4, farmer 185.

Leonard, Joseph W , (Berkshire,) S. D. 4, farmer 90

Lynch, Theodore, (Berkshire,) S. D. 4., farmer 175

Manning, Chas S ,(Berkshire,) S D 1, farmer 175.

Manning, Ralph, (Berkshire,) S D. 4, farmer

MARSH, RODNEY, (Berkshire,) S D 4, farmer leases of C. T Leonard, 143

MARSHALL, WM. H , (Berkshire,) S D. 4, laborer

Masters, John, (East Berkshire,) S. D 8, farmer 50.

Mayor, Theodore, (Berkshire,) S D 1, farmer 300

McMahon, Patrick, (Berkshire,) S. D. 10, farmer 19

MEEKS, EDMUND, (Speedsville, Tompkins Co ,) S D 7, farmer 108.

Merrell, Wm M , (Berkshire,) S. D 1, farmer leases 40

Northrup, James E , (Berkshire,) saw mill.

Oliver, Louis, (Berkshire,) S. D. 1, handrake factory.

Orton, Demas, (East Berkshire,) S. D 8, farmer 41.

Orton, James, (East Berkshire,) (*with Demas,*) farmer 41.

Owen, James K , (Ketchumville,) S. D. 8, farmer 24

OWEN, MOSES, (Speedsville, Tompkins Co ,) S D 3, prop. of machine cooperage and saw mill

Palmer, S. E Rev , (Berkshire,) pastor of Congregational Church

Parsons, Chauncy, (Berkshire,) S D. 4, farmer 85

Payne, Demming A , (Berkshire,) S. D. 6, farmer 20

PIERCE, ALPHEUS, (East Berkshire,) S. D 8. farmer 57½.

Pierce, Loren M., (Ketchumville,) S. D. 2, farmer 43.

PIERCE, SYLVESTER, (Ketchumville,) S D 2, farmer 180

Prentice, George B., (Wilson Creek,) S. D 11, farmer 68

Prentice, Irving B , (Newark Valley,) S D 6, farmer 97.

Prentice, Joseph, (Newark Valley,) S. D. 3, farmer 113.

Prentice, Orlando, (Newark Valley,) (with Joseph,) farmer.

Qyall, Robert, (East Berkshire,) S. D. 8, farmer

REED, SHERMAN, (Ketchumville,) S D 2, farmer leases of Dr Gates, 107.

Reynolds, N. S. Rev., (Berkshire,) S. D. 4, pastor of M E Church

Rightmire, Squire, (Berkshire,) S. D. 4, carpenter

Robinson, Newel, (Berkshire,) S. D. 10, farmer 118

Rockwell, Peter, (Berkshire,) S. D. 11, farmer 115

ROCKWOOD, LORENZO F., (Berkshire,) S D 1, prop of horse-rake factory and planing mill.

ROYCE, DEODATUS, (Berkshire,) S. D. 4, farmer 150.

Royce, George C., (Berkshire,) farmer leases 270.

Royce, John B., (Berkshire,) S. D. 4, farmer 500.

Royce, John L., (Berkshire,) farmer leases 280

Ranball, Anson M , (Wilson Creek,) S. D 11, justice of the peace, postmaster and farmer 35

Sargent, Silas, (Wilson Creek,) S D 11, farmer 43

Scott, Charles, (Berkshire,) S. D. 6, (with Edmund F ,) farmer 247.

Scott, Edmund F., (Berkshire,) S. D. 6, (with Charles,) farmer 247.

Shaff, Frederick, (East Berkshire,) S. D 8, farmer 180

Shaff, Joseph, (East Berkshire,) S. D. 8, farmer 125.

Shaff, Wm. H., (Berkshire,) S. D. 8, farmer 84.

Shaw, William T., (Berkshire,) S. D. 10, farmer 265

SHERMAN, EDWARD A , (Ketchumville,) S. D 2, farmer 105.

Sherman, J. W , (Berkshire,) S D 8, farmer 30

Simmons, Alpheus, (Berkshire,) S. D 10, farmer 255

SIMMONS, SYLVESTER, (Berkshire,) S. D. 5, farmer 133

Sliter, Wm H. (Berkshire,) S D. 4, farmer leases of Nathan Rightmire, 140

Smith, Charles R , (Berkshire,) S. D. 10, farmer 41

Smith, Edwin, (Berkshire,) S D. 10, farmer 350

Smith, Edwin, (Berkshire,) S. D 10, farmer 50

SMITH, EMORY J., (Berkshire,) S D. 3, farmer 88.

STANNARD, LORENZO J., (Wilson Creek,) S. D 11, (with John F. Kimball,) farmer.

Stephens, Andrew, (Berkshire,) S D 4, currier and farmer 35

Swan, Silas F , (Ketchumville,) S D 2, farmer 60

Sykes, Horatio, (Berkshire,) S. D. 1, farmer 114

Thorn, Henry M., (Wilson Creek,) S D. 11, farmer 50

TORREY, JOHN, (Berkshire,) S. D. 4, carpenter.

TORREY, JNO. 2D., (Berkshire,) S D 6, farmer 100.

Waldo, E B., (Berkshire,) (Ball & Waldo,) station agent.

Waldo, Robert E., (Berkshire,) S D 11, road commissioner, farmer 123 and leases 40.

Walter, Joseph S., (East Berkshire,) S. D. 8, physician and farmer 87

Walton, George, (Newark Valley,) S. D. 11, farmer 93

WATKINS, AMOS G , (Speedsville, Tompkins Co ,) S D 3, farmer 127

Wavel, Peter, (East Berkshire,) S D 8, farmer 112

Whitaker, Charles P., (Wilson Creek,) S D. 11, farmer 106.

WILLIAMS, GEORGE, (Berkshire,) S. D. 4, general merchant.

Williams, Harvey, (East Berkshire,) S D 8, farmer 100.

Williams, Lewis, (Ketchumville,) S D 2, engineer, sawyer and farmer 69

Winship, George, (Berkshire,) S D 1, farmer 100

Wiswell, Jerome, (Ketchumville,) S. D. 2, farmer 50.

Witter, F A. & G. B., (Berkshire,) hardware merchants

Wood, Joseph, (East Berkshire,) S D. 8, farmer 65

Youngs, Peter, (East Berkshire,) S. D 8, farmer 107

# CANDOR.

### (Post Office Addresses in Parentheses.)

ABBREVIATIONS —S. D., School District.

Adams, Gaylord W., (Candor,) patent dealer, Spencer St

Adams, Geo., (West Candor) farmer 200.

Ainger, Hannah A., (Candor,) S. D. 17, farmer 9

Allen, B. L., (Candor,) constable, lumber agent for James Bishop, of Owego, and farmer 3

Allen, Charles, (Weltonville,) joint S. D. 24, blacksmith

Allen, C W., (Candor,) cabinet maker and undertaker, Front

Allen, Increase, (Candor,) S. D. 22, agent for James Bishop.

Allen, J K., (Candor,) restaurant and billiard rooms, Front

Allen, James L., (Wilseyville,) S D 8, farmer 31½

Allen, William, (Wilseyville,) S. D 8, carpenter

Ames, Daniel S. & H. C., (Candor,) S D. 14, farmer 197.

Anderson, Charles L., (Candor,) S D. 7, farmer 75

Anderson, Edwin S., (Owego,) S. D. 11, farmer leases 150

ANDERSON, JAMES M., (Catatonk,) S D 1, dealer in agricultural implements and farmer 50.

Anderson, Joel, (Owego,) S. D. 11, farmer 111

Anderson, L., (Owego,) S D 11, farmer 75

Anderson, Marshall, (Catatonk,) S D 1, farmer 51

Anderson, Philander, (Owego,) S. D. 11, farmer 250

Anderson, Stephen, (Catatonk,) S. D. 1, cooper and farmer.

Andrews, Levi, (Owego,) S D 11, farmer 125

Andrews, Philetus, (Owego,) S D 11, farmer 200

Andrews, Wm. H., (Candor,) grocery and news room.

Armitage, Alfred, (Candor,) mason, Owego St

BACON, DANIEL, (Candor,) S D 14, notary public and farmer 57

Bacon, George Q., (Candor,) music teacher and farmer.

Bacon, Harvey D., (Candor,) (with Daniel,) farmer

BACON, JOHN G., (Candor,) union S. D. 9 and 18, farmer 95

Baird, James L., (Speedsville, Tompkins Co.,) joint S. D. 5, farmer 112

Baker, Aaron, (Candor,) S. D. 15, farmer 62½

Baker, Isaac, (Candor,) S D 15, farmer 85

Bangs, Wm. L., (Candor,) S D. 14, farmer 100

Banks, Alanson, (Wilseyville,) S. D. 21, farmer 140

Barber, John, (Candor,) S. D 10, farmer 100.

Barber, Sterling J., (Candor,) S D 8, farmer 100

BARDEN, ROBERT S., (Candor,) S. D. 7, mechanic and farmer leases 100

Barett, Knowlton V., (Weltonville,) joint S D 24, mechanic and farmer 10

BARNES, HUGH S., (Catatonk,) S. D. 1, (with Thomas,) farmer 108.

Barnes, James D., (Candor,) farmer 250, Church.

BARNES, THOMAS, (Catatonk,) S D. 1, (with Hugh S.,) farmer 108

Barnes, William, (Candor,) S D. 10, farmer 100

BARRETT, JUSTUS, (Weltonville,) joint S D 24, justice of the peace and farmer 80.

Barrett, Simeon L., (West Newark,) joint S. D. 12, farmer 500.

Barrett, Stephen R., (Jenksville,) S. D. 17, farmer 223

BARROTT, AMIAL W., (Weltonville,) (with Samuel R.) S D 24, lumberman, jobber, dealer in flour, apiarian, dairyman and farmer 300.

BARROTT, SAMUEL R., (Weltonville,) (with Amial W.,) S. D. 24, lumberman, jobber, dealer in flour, apiarian, dairyman and farmer 300

Barrott, Simeon W., (Weltonville,) joint S D 24, farmer 265

Barrott, V. N., (Weltonville,) joint S D. 24, farmer 12½

Barto, Simeon, (Wilseyville,) S. D. 6, farmer 25

Barton, Husted, (Wilseyville,) S. D. 6, farmer 50.

BAYLOR CHAS. F., (Candor,) S. D. 15, blacksmith and farmer

BAYLOR, DANIEL H., (Candor,) (Baylor & Slawson)

BAYLOR & SLAWSON, (Candor,) (Daniel H Baylor and James G. Slawson,) blacksmiths

Batterson, Andrew J., (Wilseyville,) S D. 6, farmer leases of M. A. White, 240

Beach, Charles, (Wilseyville,) S. D 20, farmer leases of Mrs Hull, 27.

Beadle, Jared J., (Candor,) S. D. 15, farmer 50 and leases of Joel Starkweather, 70.

Beebe, A., (Candor,) miller for Halsey & Hexson of Ithaca, Mill

Beebe, Abram, (Candor,) (*Beebe & Co*)

Beebe, Clark W, (Candor,) engineer and mechanic, Owego St

Beebe & Co., (Candor,) (*Abram Beebe and Alex B. Crane* ) S. D. 22, lumberman

Beers, Chas. H., (Catatonk,) S D 1, lumberman and farmer 109.

Best, Geo , (Strait's Corners,) joint S. D. 18, farmer 100

Blakeslee, Geo. H. Rev., (Candor,) pastor M E Church.

BLANCHARD, ARNOLD, (Jenksville,) joint S. D. 5, farmer 100.

Blewer, Levi, (Weltonville,) joint S D 26, farmer 95

Blinn, Burdett, (Candor,) S. D 7, farmer.

BLINN, ELI, (Candor,) S. D 7, (*with Sherman* ) farmer 124.

Blinn, Lewis, (Candor,) S. D 7, carpenter and farmer 93.

Blinn, Martha J , (Candor,) S. D. 7, farmer 47 and occupies 75.

Blinn, Philo, (Candor,) carpenter and builder, Railroad.

BLINN, SAMUEL E, (Candor,) S. D 5, farmer 62

BLINN, SHERMAN, (Candor,) S. D. 7, (*with Eli,*) farmer 124

Boeck, Edward S , (Catatonk,) S. D. 12, teacher, farmer 75 and leases 40.

Bogart, Lawrence, (Wilseyville,) S. D. 6, mechanic and farmer 15¾

Bogart, William, (Strait's Corners,) S D 12, farmer 112

Bogart, Wm. E , (Candor,) S. D 2, preacher, Owego St.

Bogert, Peter, (Candor,) (*Tuttle & Bogert,*) farmer 100.

BOOTH, ABEL H., (Candor,) S. D. 8, farmer 400.

BOOTH, DENNIS, (Candor,) S. D. 3, counts lumber at Strait's mill and farmer 215

BOOTH, EDWIN, (Candor,) (*E. R. & H F Booth,*) S. D. 3, farmer 265.

BOOTH, EDWIN A , (Candor ) (*Potter, Booth & Co.,*) prest. First National Bank of Candor

Booth, E. A. & H. T., (Candor,) iron founders.

Booth, Geo D , (Candor,) (*with Abel H.*)

BOOTH, HORACE, (Candor,) justice of the peace, residence and office Main.

BOOTH, H. FRANK, (Candor,) (*Horace Booth & Son,*) asst. postmaster, Main

BOOTH, HORACE & SON, (Candor,) (*H Frank,*) lumbermen and farmers 160

Booth, Jesse F., (Candor,) (*with Lorin,*) lumberman, manuf. lumber, lath &c.

Booth, J. W., (Candor,) asst cashier First National Bank of Candor.

BOOTH, LORIN, (Candor,) S D 3, lumberman and farmer 482

Booth, Norman C., (Candor,) (*with Abel H* )

Booth, Orange, (Candor,) S. D. 8, farmer 255

Booth, Theron S , (Candor,) (*with Loring.*)

Braman, Jesse, (Candor,) mason, Bank

BRAMAN, JOSEPH W , (Candor,) joint S. D 9 and 18, carpenter and joiner, and farmer 1.

Brearley, Harry, (Candor,) carpenter, Main

Brearley, L. M., (Candor,) millinery and dress making, Main

Briggs, Julius, (Owego,) S D 11, farmer leases of Austin Rogers, 50

Briggs, Lyman S , (Weltonville,) S. D 26, farmer 45

Brink, Calvin, (Candor,) S D 17, farmer 25.

Brink, Elihu, (Candor,) S. D 18, farmer 53.

Brink, Homer, (Weltonville,) S D 17, farmer 81

BRINK, JAMES, (Weltonville,) S D. 26, farmer 50

Brink James S., (Candor,) S. D. 18, farmer leases 30.

BRINK, JOHN J., (Weltonville,) S. D 26, farmer leases 175

Brink Stephen T., (Weltonville,) S D 17, farmer 70

Brink, Wilman C , (Candor,) S. D. 7, farmer 300

BROOKS, GEO. T., (Candor,) S D 2 mechanic and cabinet maker, Owego St

Brown, E S., (Wilseyville,) S D 20, farmer 48.

Brown, James, (Candor,) S D 3, farmer leases 185

Brown, John J., (Candor,) farmer, Owego St

Brownell, John C., (Owego,) joint S. D. 2, bridge builder

Brundage, Emmet R , (Candor,) station agent and coal dealer.

Buckley, Frederick E , (Candor,) union S D. 9 and 18, carpenter, Main

BUNNEL, MANSFIELD, (Candor,) union S. D. 9 and 18, brick manuf and farmer 78

Bunnell, Wm , (West Candor,) S D 22, tinner, hotel keeper and deputy post master

Burchard, Jason, (Owego,) joint S D 2, farmer 150.

Burleigh, Eban, (Candor,) S D 15, carpenter

Burleigh, Hezekiah, (Candor,) S. D 15, farmer 46.

Burleigh, James E , (Candor,) S. D 15, jobber.

Burleigh, Maria, (Candor,) S. D 15, farmer 50,

BURT, GEORGE, (Catatonk,) S. D. 1, farmer 50

Bush, Abram R , (Wilseyville,) S D 6., general merchant and apiarian.

Bush, I L , (Candor,) S. D. 2, well driver, Owego St

Butler, Jacob, (West Candor,) S. D. 23, farmer 100.

Cable, Philip, (Catatonk,) S D 1, farmer 52.

CAMPBELL, ALBA, (Candor,) S D. 14, farmer 20.

Campbell, Chas B., (Candor,) telegraph operator, Thompson.

Campbell, John A , (Candor,) S. D. 14, farmer leases 39 and (*with Jenus R. Eoston,*) prop of threshing machine

CANDOR FREE ACADEMY, (Candor,) Prof Lemnel D. Vose, principal.

*CANDOR FREE PRESS, (Candor,) Main, Benj. B F. Graves, editor and prop.

Candor Lodge, No 411, F. & A. M., (Candor,) communications 1st and 3d Wednesday evenings of each month

Card, Alonzo, (Candor,) farmer

Card, E L Nathan, (Candor,) blacksmith, Mill

Card, Timothy A , (Candor,) lumberman.

Carl, Peter, (Candor,) millwright and farmer, Owego St.

Carlton, Amasa T , (Catatonk,) S. D. 12, farmer occupies 56

Carman, Andrew, (Owego,) S. D. 11, farmer 52

Carroll, Thomas, (Candor,) S. D. 14, farmer occupies 70 owned by wife

Caple, Adam, (Candor,) S D 10, farmer 125

Case, Samuel, (Strait's Corners,) S. D. 23, farmer 192

Case, Wm , (Strait's Corners,) (with Samuel,) farmer

Case, Z , (Wilseyville,) S D 5, farmer 10

*CENTRAL HOUSE, (Candor,) Main, Wm Murray, prop

Chandler, Michael, (Catatonk,) S D 1, farmer 27

Chandler, Wm., (Catatonk,) S. D 1, farmer 70

Chapman, Amos C , (Candor,) S. D. 7, farmer 150.

CHAPMAN, FRANCIS A , (Candor,) (with Amos C ,) farmer

Chedsey, Hermon L., (Candor,) S. D. 2, harness maker and farmer

Chidsey, Leonard, (Candor,) speculator, Owego St , also constable

Chidsey, Lucy, (Candor,) S D 2, farmer 21

Clark, Hiram J., (Candor,) S. D. 7, farmer 173

Cleavland, Joseph, (Wilseyville,) S D 6, carpenter.

Clerk, Richard, (Candor,) union S. D. 22, blacksmith.

Cleveland, Geo., (Wilseyville,) S. D. 6, millwright and farmer 8

Clover, Geo., (Wilseyville,) shoemaker.

Cochran, Robert, (Catatonk,) S D 11, farmer 103

Coffin, Wm , (Candor,) S D 11, farmer 50.

Cogswell, Joel, (Candor,) farmer 20, Owego St

Cole, Wm J , (Candor,) carpenter and builder, Main

COMSTOCK, EPHRAIM, (Jenksville,) joint S. D 5, farmer 170

Comstock, Wm I , (Jenksville,) joint S D 5, lumberman and farmer 125

Cook, John, (Strait's Corners,) joint S D 18, farmer occupies 113.

Cook, Nelson, (Catatonk,) S D 1, sawyer and farmer 50

Cookingham, Geo., (Wilseyville,) S. D 20, farmer 50

COOPER, CHAS. W., (West Candor,) farmer

COOPER, FENNIMORE H., (Candor,) student.

Cooper, John H Jr., (West Candor,) grocer.

CORTRIGHT, CHARLES H., (Weltonville,) joint S. D 26, farmer 80.

Cortright, Jacob, (West Newark,) S D 24, farmer 78

Cortright, James, (Weltonville,) S. D 25, farmer 31

Cortright, James F , (Weltonville,) S. D. 26, farmer 120.

CORTRIGHT, SAMUEL, (Weltonville,) S D 25, farmer 130

Cortright, Simeon, (Weltonville,) S D 25, stock broker, commissioner of highways and farmer 55

Cortright, Simeon, (Weltonville,) S D 26, farmer 112

CORTRIGHT, THEODORE, (Weltonville,) S D 24, farmer 150

Coryell, Edward S , (Candor,) physician and surgeon, Front.

Coarsen, John M , (Candor,) S. D. 10, farmer 173

Coarsen, John M , (Strait's Corners,) S. D. 12, farmer 183.

Coarson, Thos. H., (Candor,) S. D. 14, farmer 40

COURTRIGHT, HENRY A , (West Newark,) town constable and (with Levi,) farmer.

Courtright, Herbert N., (Weltonville,) joint S. D. 24, boot maker and poor master.

Courtright, Jacob A., (West Newark,) (with Jacob,) farmer

Courtright, Levi, (West Newark,) joint S. D. 24, farmer 125.

Courtright, Leroy M., (Candor,) S D 2, music teacher and farmer 1½

Cowles, Daniel F., (Candor,) S D. 2, farmer 45

Cowles, George, (Candor,) S. D. 14, farmer 41.

Cowles, Horace, (Candor,) mason and building mover, Railroad

Cowles, James, (Candor,) S D. 2, farmer 55.

Cowles, James, (Candor,) S. D. 2, farmer 71

Cowles, J Harvey, (Candor,) S D. 14, farmer 57

Crane, Alex. B., (Candor,) (Beebe & Co )

Crane, Sarah, (Candor,) farmer 3

CRINE, STEPHEN D., (Candor,) S. D. 5, farmer 194½.

Cronk, Byron E., (Weltonville,) S. D 17, carpenter.

Crum, LaFayette, (West Candor,) S D 23, farmer 126

Crum, McDonough, (West Candor,) S. D. 23, farmer 80.

Culden, Henry, (Catatonk,) S. D. 1, farmer 38.

Coller, Geo D , (Candor,) union S D. 9 and 18, farmer 34.

Curtis, Abel, (Wilseyville,) farmer 12

Custard, Anson, (Weltonville,) joint S. D 24, farmer 33

Dean, Geo , (Wilseyville,) (with Samuel H ) farmer.

Dean, Hatfield, (West Candor,) farmer 210.

Dean, Samuel H., (Wilseyville,) S D. 5, farmer 43½

DECKER, OLIVER H P , (Candor,) S D. 18, farmer 50.

Decker, Samuel, (Candor,) S. D. 18, farmer 57

DELANY, EVERETT H , (Jenksville,) S D 13, dairyman and farmer 121

DENNIS, ALBERT, (Candor,) S. D. 17, farmer 118

DENNIS, ALFRED, (Candor,) S D. 17, farmer 200

DENNIS, GEORGE, (Candor,) S D 16, farmer 50.

Densmore, Richard, (Catatonk,) S. D. 1, farmer 10.

Dereamer, Enos, (Wilseyville,) S D. 6, mechanic.

Deuel Chas., (Catatonk,) S D 2, carpenter and builder.

Dewey, Daniel, (Candor,) S. D. 25, farmer 1.

Deyo, Alma E., (Weltonville,) joint S D 26, (with Chas. T. Humphrey,) farmer 27

Deyo, Charles L , (Candor,) S. D. 17, farmer 84

Dickinson, Albert, (Catatonk,) S. D. 1, farmer occupies 148.

Dixon, John C , (Candor,) physician, corner Owego and Front

Dorn, E B , (Wilseyville,) (with G M. Mulks,) S. D 19, farmer 20

Doty, Chas , (Candor,) carpenter, Owego St.

DOTY, CHAS. H., (Candor,) carpenter, Owego St

DOTY, JAMES, (Candor,) S. D. 5, farmer 195¾

DOUGLASS, GEORGE, (Strait's Corners,) S D 12, commissioner of highways and farmer 132

DOUGLASS, JOHN, (Strait's Corners,) S D 12, farmer 133.

Douglass, Wm., (Strait's Corners,) S. D 25, farmer 70

Downes, Joshua, (Candor,) S. D 17, farmer 30

DOWNING, S S , (Candor,) S D 18, farmer 110.

DOWNS, WM., (Candor,) S D 14, (Knapp & Downs )

DOYLE, MICHAEL, (Candor,) journeyman tanner

Draper, Manzo V , (Catatonk,) S. D. 1, farmer 70

Drew, Geo , (Catatonk,) S. D. 1, farmer 75

Duell, Gilbert, (Candor,) Union S. D. 9 and 18, farmer 10

Duff, Alexander, (Strait's Corners,) S. D. 12, farmer 90

Duncan, James, (Catatonk,) S. D. 21, farmer 50.

Dorfey, Frederick, (Wilseyville,) farmer occupies 21

Dorfey, Harriet, (Wilseyville,) S D 6, farmer 45

Dykeman, James F., (Candor,) (Dykeman & Snyder )

DYKEMAN, ORIN, (Candor,) S D 3, saw mill

Dykeman & Snyder, (Candor,) (James F. Dykeman and Edward E. Snyder,) physicians, Mill

Eastham, Nathan, (Strait's Corners ) joint S D. 18, farmer 153

Eastham, Thomas, (Strait's Corners,) (with Nathan,) farmer.

Eastman, Amos, (Wilseyville,) S D 6, farmer 125

Eastman, Ebenezer, (Candor,) union S D 9 and 18, farmer 80.

Eastman, John N , (Wilseyville,) S. D. 6, carpenter and farmer 80.

Easton, Jeuus R , (Candor,) S D 14, (with John A Campbell,) prop. of threshing machine

Ebert, John, (Wilseyville,) S. D. 5, farmer 11

Edmonds, Northrup, (Candor,) S. D. 14, farmer 15.

Eighmey & Co , (Candor,) (Thos Eighmey, Warren Willsey and James Holley,) boots, shoes and groceries, Spencer

Eighmey, Thos., (Candor,) (Eighmey & Co )

Eignor, James W , (Candor,) joint S. D 9 and 18, farmer 56, Owego Turnpike.

Eignor, Wm., (Candor,) farmer 56, Owego St

Elmendorf, Geo. E., (Strait's Corners,) S D 23, farmer

Elmendorf, Jonah, (Strait's Corners,) S D. 23, farmer 110

Embody, Abram, (Catatonk,) farmer 40

EMBODY, JACOB, (Candor,) wagon maker, Spencer St

Emerson, Chester, (Strait's Corners,) S D 12, farmer 56

Evans, Richard, (Strait's Corners,) S D 12, blacksmith and farmer 50

Evans, Stephen C , (Strait's Corners,) S D 12, farmer 5

Evelien, Alfred, (Strait's Corners,) S. D. 10, farmer

Evelien, Christopher, (Strait's Corners,) joint S. D. 18, farmer 220

Farley, Daniel M , (Speedsville, Tompkins Co ,) S. D. 13, farmer 75

Farley, Eli J., (Speedsville, Tompkins Co ) S D 7, carpenter and farmer 10

FENDERSON, F M , (Weltonville,) S. D. 17, lumberman and farmer 50.

Ferris, Richard R , (Candor,) S. D. 21, farmer 50.

Fessenden, Chas. H , (Candor,) (with Wm,) cabinet maker.

FESSENDEN, WM L & SON, (Candor,) S D 2, cabinet makers and undertakers, Owego St., wareroom Front

FIELD, RICHARD, (Candor,) union S D 9 and 18, mason, Mountain Avenue

Fitch, C. S , (Candor,) S D 7, farmer 114

Foot, Wm , (Candor,) S. D 14, farmer leases 140.

Forsythe, Geo , estate of, (Candor,) S. D. 25, 41 acres.

Foster, Cyrus A , (Candor,) S. D. 15, farmer 70

FOSTER, ELBERT C , (Candor,) sawyer and farmer 30, Royal.

FOSTER, JAMES S , (Jenksville,) joint S. D. 5, farmer 175.

Franks, Geo , (Candor,) merchant tailor, Owego St.

Frought, Henry, (Candor,) meat market, Front

Fuller, Alvah, (Candor,) S. D. 5, farmer 176

Fuller, Jacob, (Wilseyville,) S D. 6, farmer 119.

Fuller, Marvin, (Candor,) S D. 5 farmer 64⅝

Fuller, Radeker J , (Candor,) S. D 17, farmer 90.

Fuller, Robert, (Candor,) S D 17, farmer 70.

FULLER, SAMUEL G., (Candor,) S. D. 17, town assessor and teacher
Gage, Ezra, (Owego,) S D 11, farmer 50
Gage, Henry, (Candor,) S D 14, farmer 20.
Galleger, John, (Weltonville,) S. D. 26, farmer 120
GALLEGHER, JOHN, (Candor,) employe of Humboldt Tannery.
Galpin, Abel F, (Weltonville,) S. D. 26, farmer 150
Galpin, James, (West Candor,) S. D. 22, farmer 205
Galpin, James T., (Weltonville,) S D 17, farmer 130.
Galpin, Jasper, (Weltonville,) S. D. 17, farmer 65
Galpin, Jerusha, (Candor,) S. D. 17, farmer 49
Galpin, Luzern, (Weltonville,) S. D 17, farmer 55
Galpin, Samuel F., (Weltonville,) S. D. 17, farmer 71
Galpin, Stephen, (Candor,) S D. 17, teacher
Gardner, C H., (Candor,) prop Dr J O Hill's Family Medicines, Main.
Gardner, Charles, (Candor,) S D. 14, farmer 150
Gardner, Eliza, (Candor,) union S D 9 and 18, farmer 150.
Gates, Luzerne, (Candor,) painter and paper hanger
Gay, Daniel (Jenksville,) joint S D 12, farmer 82
Gay, Isaac W., (Jenksville,) farmer and graduate of Eclectic Medical University
German Cyrus B , (Candor,) carpenter and builder, Kinney Avenue
Gilkey, Elbert, (Candor,) insurance agent, Owego St
GILKEY, ORRIN T , (Candor,) insurance agent, Owego St.
Gilman, Truman, (Wilseyville,) farmer 50
Goodwin, Lois Ann, (Candor)) tailoress, Foundry
GRANT, JAMES M , (Candor,) S. D. 14, farmer 50
*GRAVES, BENJ B F., (Candor,) editor and prop *Candor Free Press* Main
Gridley, Chas T., (Candor,) (*with Wm C ,*) farmer.
Gridley, Newton S , (Candor,) S D 21, farmer 120
GRIDLEY, WM C , (West Candor,) S. D. 22 farmer 900.
GRIDLEY, WM C. JR , (West Candor,) agent for agricultural implements and farmer 125.
Griffin, Lewis, (Wilseyville,) S. D. 19, farmer 210
Griffin, Lewis, (Candor,) mason, Railroad.
Griffin, Nehemiah, (Wilseyville,) S. D 20, farmer 75
Griffin, Smith, (Candor,) joint S D. 9 and 18, farmer 6
GRIMES JOHN M. Rev , (Flemingsville,) M E. clergyman and owns 152 acres.
Haddock, George, (Speedsville, Tompkins Co ) joint S D 5, farmer leases 72
HADDOCK, JOHN V , (Candor,) S D 13, farmer 61 and leases of J Rich, 30
Hale, John L , (Candor ) S. D. 15, farmer 14
Hale, L B , (Candor,) S D. 10, farmer 100

Hale, Simeon, (Candor,) S D. 10, farmer 62
Hall, Edward, (Wilseyville,) S. D. 6, farmer
Hall, Lewis, (Wilseyville,) S. D 6, farmer 5 and in Danby, 100
Hallett, Chas , (Wilseyville,) S D 16, farmer 23
Hammond, Seth, (Strait's Corners,) S D 28, farmer 67.
HARDING, C N , (Owego,) S D 1, dairyman and farmer leases of R. H. Sackett, 200
Harding, Chas O , (Wilseyville,) carpenter.
Harding, Hubert, (Wilseyville,) S. D 8, blacksmith
Harlin, John J , (Strait's Corners,) S. D. 12, farmer 200
HARLIN, SAMUEL, (Strait's Corners,) S. D. 12, farmer leases 130
Hart, Abel, (Candor,) inspector of elections and farmer 280, Owego St
Hart, Daniel, (Candor,) joint S. D. 9 and 18 farmer 63, Owego St
HART, GEO H , (Candor,) cabinet maker, prop plaster mill, turning lathe, planing, scroll sawing, cross cut and slit saws Mill
Hart, Gilbert, (Candor,) union S D. 9 and 18, farmer 57
Hart, Horace, (Candor,) (*with Norman,*) farmer 50 Owego St
HART, JONATHAN B , (Candor,) deacon of the Congregational Church, cabinet maker and farmer 57
Hart, Morris, (Candor,) S D 21, farmer 91.
Hart, Norman, (Candor,) (*with Horace,*) farmer 80, Owego St
HART OLIVIA M Mrs , (Candor,) union S D 22, farmer 106
Hart, Selah (Candor,) joint S D 9 and 18, farmer 190, Owego St
Hart, Wm , (Candor,) S D 21, farmer 85
Haskell, T. A , (Jenksville,) joint S. D. 5, farmer 50
*HASKIN, ABNER A , (Wilseyville,) S. D. 6, general merchandise
Hatch, Josiah, (Weltonville,) S D 17, farmer 50
Hatch, Russell, (Candor,) wagon repairer, Railroad
Hawkins, Orin, (Candor,) S D. 5, farmer leases 160
Hazen, Daniel, (Strait's Corners,) S D 23, farmer 100.
Head, A P , (Candor,) hotel prop and farmer, Owego St
Head, Emmet W , (Wilseyville,) S D. 6, farmer 87.
Head, Isaac, (Wilseyville,) S. D 20, farmer 75 and leases of L Griffin, 180
Heath, Edward E , (Candor,) tinsmith.
*HEATH, H D , (Candor,) dealer in hardware tinware, stoves and agricultural implements, Main.
Heath, James H , (Wilseyville,) S. D. 6, dealer in pumps and churn thermometers
Hedges, Daniel A , (Wilseyville,) S. D. 6, shingle factory and farmer 112
Hedges, J J , (Candor,) (*Hedges & Smith.*)
Hedges & Smith, (Candor,) (*J J Hedges and Alanson Smith,*) boots and shoes, Front

Henderson, Charles, (Weltonville,) S. D 17, farmer 95

Henderson, Hiram, (Weltonville,) (*with Wm. P.,*) S D. 17, farmer 50

Henderson, Jesse W, (Candor,) foreman Humboldt Tannery, Foundry

Henderson, Theodore, (Weltonville,) S. D. 17, farmer 40

Henderson, Wm P, (Weltonville,) (*with Hiram,*) S D 17, farmer 50.

Henry, Wm Jr., (Speedsville, Tompkins Co.,) drover and farmer

Herrick, Alfred W., (Catatonk,) (*with Stephen H ,*) farmer

Herrick, Edward P., (Weltonville,) S. D 26, farmer

HERRICK, PERLEE, (Catatonk,) S. D. 1, dealer in agricultural implements and farmer 130.

Herrick, Stephen H , (Catatonk,) S. D. 1, farmer 100.

Herrick, Walter, (Weltonville,) joint S. D. 26, farmer 116.

Hodge, Andrew C , (Catatonk,) S D 1, farmer 45.

Hodges, George, (Candor,) S D 5, painter and farmer 220

Hodges, James, (Candor,) S. D. 5, ornamental painter and farmer.

Hodges, Samuel, (Candor,) S. D 5, ornamental painter and farmer

Holden, H., (West Newark,) joint S D 12, farmer leases 50.

Hollenbeck, David J., (Catatonk,) S. D. 12, farmer 107

Hollenbeck, James, (Candor,) union S. D 9 and 18, farmer 48.

Hollenbeck, John, (Catatonk,) S. D. 12, farmer 40.

HOLLENBECK, John R., (Candor,) carpenter and jobber, Bank

Hollenbeck, Mary E., (Candor,) farmer 5

Holley, James, (Candor,) (*Eighmey & Co.*)

Hollister, Harvey, (Speedsville, Tompkins Co ,) (*with Septus H .*) farmer.

Hollister, Septus H , (Speedsville, Tompkins Co ,) S D. 13, farmer 50.

Holly, Morris M Jr , (Candor,) telegraph operator, Main.

Holmes, Job. (Candor,) joint S D. 9 and 18, Owego St.

Holmes, Samuel, (Candor,) S D. 2, capitalist and farmer 25

Hoose, Chas , (Wilseyville,) S. D. 19, farmer 100.

Horton, Andrew, (Candor,) S. D. 15, peddler and farmer 45

Honk, Geo E , (Candor,) S. D 14, farmer leases of Dana Robinson, 80.

Hovei, Benjamin, (West Newark,) joint S D 12, farmer 127

Hover, Cornelius, (Weltonville,) S. D. 26, saloon keeper.

HOVER, COURT L , (West Newark,) S D 17, farmer 41½

HOVER, GEO., (Candor,) moulder, Owego St

Hover, Henry, (Weltonville,) S D. 26, resident

Hover, Henry 2nd, (Weltonville,) S. D. 17, farmer 83.

Hover, Leander, (Weltonville,) S. D. 14, farmer 31.

HOVER, SOLOMON, (Candor,) S. D 7, farmer 114

Hover, Wm P., (Candor,) S D 18, farmer 12½

HOWARD, CHAS. C., (Owego,) S. D 11, farmer 108.

Howard, Hiram, (Candor,) S D 14, farmer 92.

Howard, Loring P., (Candor,) S D 11, farmer 100.

HOWARD, SAMUEL G., (Candor,) S D 21, farmer 230

HOWARD, STEPHEN, (Wilseyville,) S D. 21, farmer 200

Howell, Wm , (Wilseyville,) S. D. 6, farmer 30

Hoyt, Adoniram, (Candor,) S. D. 15, farmer occupies 77

Hoyt, Geo., (Weltonville,) S D 14, farmer

Hoyt, Stephen J., (Candor,) S D 15, farmer 88

Hoyt, Wm , (Catatonk,) S D. 1, farmer 50.

Hubbard, Albert C., (Candor,) S D 14, farmer 57

Hubbard, Eli B., (Candor,) dentist, Front

HUBBARD, W H. & J F , (Candor,) S D. 14, manufs and dealers in lumber, lath &c., and farmers 350

Hull, Asa D., (Candor,) S D 17, brick maker and farmer 127

Hull, Daniel, (Weltonville,) S D. 17, farmer occupies 70

Hull, Leonard, (Candor,) S. D 2, farmer 6

Hull, Nathan T , (Candor,) union S. D. 9 and 18, farmer 92.

Hulslander, Wm , (Candor,) union S. D. 9 and 18, farmer 60.

Humiston, Horace N Rev , (Candor,) S. D. 7, minister and farmer 10.

HUMISTON, MORRIS, (Candor,) harness maker, Front, over Sackett's store, residence corner Humiston and Railroad

Humphrey, Chas. T , (Weltonville,) joint S. D. 25, (*with Alma E Deyo,*) farmer 27

Humphrey, Erastus E , (Speedsville, Tompkins Co.,) S. D. 13, mechanic and farmer 20.

HUMPHREY, JAMES F , (Weltonville,) S. D 25, farmer 65

Hunt, Wm N ,(Candor,) homeo. physician, Owego St.

Hunter, Jason E , (Candor,) physician, corner Main and Rich.

Hurd, John W., (Wilseyville,) S D 6, inspector of elections and farmer 126

Ide, William P., (Wilseyville,) S D 6, physician

Isenburg, Wm , (Candor,) S D. 14, teamster and farmer 5

IVORY, JAMES, (Candor,) carpenter.

Jackson, Joseph, (Candor,) S. D. 21, farmer 100.

Jacobs, Hiram C Rev , (Weltonville,) S D. 17, Baptist preacher and farmer 51

JACOBS, JAMES, (Candor,) S D 7, farmer 96

Jacobs, John W , (Candor,) S D. 7, farmer 135

JACOBS, OLIVER, (Candor,) S. D 15, farmer 72.

Jacobs, Thomas, (Candor,) S. D. 15, farmer 80.

# CANDOR HARDWARE STORE!

# H. D. HEATH,

### Near the Depot, - CANDOR, N. Y.

DEALER IN

*Heavy and Shelf*

# HARDWARE

## STOVES

*Of all desirable Kinds.*

## Tin, Sheet Iron

AND

## Copper Ware,

*Agricultural Tools,*
*Pumps, Saws, Cut-*
*lery, &c., &c.*

All Job work promptly attended to.

# The Owego Times,

## PUBLISHED WEEKLY,

### *At OWEGO, N. Y.*

*Circulation one-third Larger than any other Paper in the County.*

*Republican in Politics, and Official Town and County Paper.*

*Superior Inducements Offered to Advertisers.*

# The Jobbing Department

*of this office is second to none on the line of the Erie Railroad.*

## WILLIAM SMYTH, Proprietor.

**WILLIAM SMYTH,** } **Editors.**
**WM. A. SMITH,**

Jacob, Thomas P., (Candor,) S. D. 15, farmer 72.

JARDEN, OSCAR, (Candor,) S. D. 15, lumberman and farmer 6.

Jennings, Abigail, (Wilseyville,) occupies Jennings estate

Jennings, Albert, (Candor,) union 8 D 9 and 18, carpenter.

Jennings, Chas., (Wilseyville,) farmer, Jennings estate

Jennings, Edwin, (Candor,) carpenter, Church

JENNINGS, J L. & SON, (Candor,) (*Randolph*,) flour, feed and groceries.

JENNINGS, RANDOLPH, (Candor,) (*J. L Jennings & Son*)

JENNINGS, W. E. & J. H, (Candor,) druggists, Front.

Johnson, Allen C., (Candor,) carpenter.

Johnson, C. H, (Candor,) Owego St.

Johnson, Chas. N., (Strait's Corners,) joint S. D. 18, farmer 132

Johnson, Chester, (Candor,) S. D. 2, farmer 35

Johnson, D, (Candor,) boots and shoes, leather and findings, Mill.

Johnson, Harmon, (Strait's Corners,) S. D. 12, farmer 120

Johnson, John, (Strait's Corners,) joint S. D. 18, farmer leases 100.

Johnson, Leroy N, (Candor,) S. D. 14, farmer 1½.

Johnson, Obadiah, (Candor,) S D 7, farmer 50

Johnson, Orange, (Candor,) S D 7, farmer 13

Jorden, Hannah, (Candor,) S. D. 5, farmer 50

Joslin, Edward A., (Weltonville,) S D. 26, cabinet maker and farmer leases of Mrs Herrick, 111.

JUDD, WM, (Candor,) tailor and farmer 54, Owego St.

Keith, Luther P, (Speedsville, Tompkins Co,) S. D. 13, farmer 62.

Kelsey, John, (Candor,) S. D. 14, farmer 250.

Kershaw, Hannah M., (Candor,) S. D. 15, farmer 12

Ketchum, Chas, (Owego,) S. D 11, farmer 50

KETCHUM, WM P, (Candor,) carpenter and joiner, Mill

KINNEY, HENRY J, (Candor,) carpenter and joiner, Main.

Kinney, Isaac,(Candor,) mason, Thompson.

KINNEY, J, S, (Candor,) dealer in groceries and hardware, and builder, Mill

Kirby, Geo, (Speedsville, Tompkins Co.,) joint S D 5, farmer 25.

KIRK, JOHN, (Candor,) S. D. 15, farmer 100

Knapp, Dan. H, (Candor,) S. D. 7, farmer 104¾.

KNAPP & DOWNS, (Candor,) (*R. Knapp and Wm. Downs*,) S D 14, blacksmiths

Knapp, Ezekiel, (Candor,) (*with Dan H*,) farmer.

KNAPP, I. E, (Candor,) S D 7, carpenter and farmer works Homer Knapp estate, 119

KNAPP, R., (Candor,) S D 14, (*Knapp & Downs*.)

**U**

Knapp, Sarah A, (Candor,) S. D. 7, Homer Knapp estate

Krom, Abram H, (Candor,) union S. D. 9 and 18, farmer leases of Peter I., 114

Kyle, Samuel F., (Catatonk,) S. D. 11, farmer 100.

Kyle, Thomas, (Owego,) S D. 11, farmer 225.

Lake, Augustus, (Weltonville,) (*with Geo.*,) S. D. 17, farmer 140.

Lake, Ebenezer, (Candor,) S D 17, farmer

Lake, George, (Weltonville,) (*with Augustus,*) S D 17, farmer 140.

Lake, Thomas B., (Weltonville,) S. D. 25, farmer 98.

LAMPHIER, DAVID H, (Candor,) S. D 3, lumberman and farmer 110.

Lamphier, Emmet G., (Candor,) S. D 3, farmer 50

LANE, CHARLES E, (Weltonville,) S. D. 17, mechanic and farmer 1½

LANE, GEO A ,(Weltonville,) (*with Levi,*) farmer 30.

LANE, GEO. F., (Weltonville,) S. D. 17, blacksmith, grocer and farmer 45.

Lane, Geo S., (Candor,) cartman, Thompson

Lane, George W, (West Candor,) farmer 25.

LANE, LEVI & SON, (Weltonville,) S. D 17, farmer 80

Lane, Stephen, (Strait's Corners,) S D 23, farmer 52.

Larcom, William, (Candor,) S D. 17, saw mill and farmer 15.

Larkin, Hugh, (Catatonk,) S. D. 1, farmer 99½.

Larkin, John, (Catatonk,) S. D. 1, farmer 50.

Lawrence, Benjamin M., (Wilseyville,) (*with John,*) blacksmith.

Lawrence, John, (Wilseyville,) S. D. 6, blacksmith and farmer 62

Leach, John, (Weltonville,) S D. 24, farmer 73

Leet, Julius C., (Speedsville, Tompkins Co,) S. D. 7, farmer 100

Leet, Norman L., (Speedsville, Tompkins Co.,) carpenter.

Leet, Samuel, (Speedsville, Tompkins Co.,) carpenter

Legg, Geo W, (Speedsville, Tompkins Co,) S D 13, farmer 107.

Legg, Leonard C., (Speedsville, Tompkins Co.,) S. D. 13, farmer 180

LEGG, MONTGOMERY, (Flemingsville,) S D. 26, butcher and farmer leases 10

Lewis, Lucas, (Candor,) S D 14, farmer 10.

Lewis, Thos. N., (Candor,) union S. D 9 and 18, lumberman and farmer 150.

Little, Susan M, (Candor,) union S D 9 and 18, farmer 12

Little, Thos B, (Candor,) overseer of the poor and farmer 44

LOCEY, ISAAC V., (Candor,) mechanic and farmer 64, Mill

Loring, Horace W., (Candor,) joint S D 9 and 18, farmer 10.

LOUNSBURY, DANIEL, (Candor,) S. D. 10, farmer 250.

Lovejoy, Aaron, (Candor,) farmer, Owego St

Lovejoy, Elom, (Candor,) S D. 15, painter, carpenter and farmer 5.

Lovejoy, Geo W., (Candor,) S D 13, farmer 130

Lovejoy, James M., (Candor,) blacksmith, Owego St.

LYNCH, WM H., (Candor,) S. D. 18, farmer leases 70

Magee, John P., (Candor,) physician, Front

Maine, Wm F, (Wilseyville,) S D 6, farmer 8.

Manning, Mahlon, (Wilseyville,) S D 21, farmer 50.

Manning, Robert, (Wilseyville,) S. D. 21, farmer 75.

Marshall, John H., (Candor,) S D 3, manuf Speedy Relief and farmer 250.

Masten, Geo. W., (Candor,) S. D. 2, farmer 70

Matthews, Mrs, (Candor,) dressmaker.

Mayo, Hiram, (Wilseyville,) S D. 8, lumberman and farmer 60.

McArthur, John, (Owego,) joint S D 2, farmer 2.

McCapes, Spencer, (Candor,) joint S. D 9 and 18, carpenter, Owego Turnpike

McCarty & Co., (Candor,) (John W, John and F A. McCarty,) general merchants and produce dealers, corner Main and Mill

McCarty, F A, (Candor,) (McCarty & Co)

McCarty, John, (Candor,) (McCarty & Co)

McCarty, John W., (Candor,) (McCarty & Co,) post master

McCOY, NATHANIEL, (Jenksville,) joint S D 12, farmer 100.

McCoy, Oliver A, (Jenksville,) (with Nathaniel,) farmer.

McIntire, John J., (Catatonk,) S. D 14, farmer 32

Mead, Alanson, (Weltonville,) S. D. 17, farmer 29

MEAD, ASA E., (Candor,) S D. 18, farmer 60.

Mead, Charles, (Candor,) S D. 14, farmer 43.

Mead. D. P., (Candor,) wagon repairer, Main

Mead, E H., (Weltonville,) S. D. 17, farmer 63

Mead, Holloway, (Owego,) joint S D 2, farmer 90.

Mead, H. J, (Candor,) lawyer, town clerk and notary public, Main

Mead, John, (Weltonville,) S D 17, farmer leases 112

Mead, Josephus, (Catatonk,) farmer leases of Wm Coyle, 55.

Mead, J G, (Candor,) tinner, Mill

Mead, Lewis L., (Weltonville,) S. D. 17, farmer 52½

MEAD ROGERS D, (West Newark,) joint S D 6, farmer 260.

Mead, Russell J., (Weltonville,) S D. 17, inspector of elections, carpenter and farmer 83.

Mead, Saloman, (Candor,) farmer 82.

MEAD, WILLIAM R, (Jenksville,) joint S D. 12, farmer leases 140

Meier, Fred, (Candor,) S. D. 7, farmer 62.

Mericle, Henry, (Candor,) S D 15, threshing machine and farmer 80.

Merrick, Abner, (Speedsville, Tompkins Co.,) S. D. 13, mason and farmer 70.

Merrill, Marlin M., (Wilseyville,) S D. 6, carpenter, prop saw and feed mill and farmer 12

MERRITT, ABRAM, (Candor,) S. D. 18, farmer leases 45

Middaugh, Asa, (Weltonville,) S. D. 10, farmer 25.

Miller, Augustine, (Weltonville,) S D. 26, farmer 50 and leases of J Mead, 172

Miller, D S, (Candor,) (Miller & Wardwell,) physician and surgeon, residence on Railroad St

Miller, Nathaniel B, (Candor,) S.D 17, farmer 85

Miller & Wardwell, (Candor,) druggists, Main

Mix, Miles C., (Wilseyville,) S D 6, blacksmith and farmer 15

Monell, Samuel A, (Wilseyville,) S D 6, farmer 100

Morrison, James, (Candor,) S. D. 14, farmer 33

Mory, Benj S., (Candor,) farmer 50.

Mory, Edward A., (Candor,) S D 18, farmer 50.

Mulks, G M., (Wilseyville,) (with E. B. Dorn) S D 19, farmer 20

Munroe, Henry W., (Candor,) union S. D 22, farmer 97

Munroe, James, (Candor,) farmer leases 39.

*MURRAY, WM, (Candor,) prop Central House and livery, Main.

Mustoe, Martin, (Candor,) S D. 18, farmer 30.

Nelson, Caleb D., (Candor,) farmer 25 in Spencer and leases 50

Nelson, Wilham B, (Candor,) S D. 10, farmer lessee of Chas W Allen, 78.

NEWMAN, ABRAHAM, (Candor,) S. D. 17, farmer 125

Newman, Alonzo M, (Candor,) carpenter

NEWMAN, JAMES, (Jenksville,) S D 17, farmer 132.

Nicholds, Vincent, (Strait's Corners,) S D 12, blacksmith

NICHOLS, H. J, (Candor,) S D. 12, farmer occupies 200

Nixon, Wm., (Jenksville,) joint S. D. 5, farmer 100.

North, George, (Candor,) shoemaker

O'Neil, John, (Catatonk,) S. D 1, farmer 50

Orcutt, James E, (Catatonk,) S D 1, blacksmith.

ORCUTT, WM C, (Candor,) mason, Foundry

Osburn, William, (Speedsville, Tompkins Co,) joint S. D. 5, apiarian and farmer 26.

Owen, Abel C, (Candor,) S. D. 10, carpenter and farmer 50

Owen, Daniel R, (Candor,) S D. 10, farmer 108

Owen, John D, (Wilseyville,) S. D. 8, grocer and farmer 5

Owen, Wm, (Wilseyville,) S D. 8, saw mill and farmer 32

Palmatier, John, (Candor,) union S D 9 and 18, butcher and carpenter

Palmer, Geo W, (Jenksville,) joint S D. 5, stock broker and farmer 180.

PARK, BEVERLEY R., (Owego,) joint S. D. 2, farmer 100.

Park, Geo W., (Weltonville,) S. D. 26, assistant postmaster and grocer

Parmele, John C., (Candor,) justice of the peace, Front.

Pass, Peter, (Strait's Corners,) S D 23, farmer 90

PELTON, GEO. A Rev , (Candor,) pastor Congregational Church, Main.

PERRINE, DANIEL H , (Catatonk,) joint S D. 21, farmer 195

Perry, Solomon & Son, (Candor,) blacksmiths

PERSONEUS, SOLOMON, (Candor,) joint S D 9 and 18, farmer 49

Personius, Chauncey, (Candor,) mason, Mill.

PERSONIUS, ALANSON, (Wilseyville,) S D 6, farmer 53

Personius, Ephraim, (Candor,) S. D. 5, retired farmer

Personius, Ira, (Candor,) S. D. 5, farmer 140

PETERS, CHAS G , (Candor,) union S. D. 9 and 18, farmer 180.

Peters, Richard, (Candor,) union S. D. 9 and 18, carpenter.

Phelps, Asa, (Flemingaville,) joint S D. 2, farmer 97.

PHELPS, DAVID, (Candor,) S D 25, farmer leases 66

Phelps, Herrick J , (Flemingaville,) (with *Jesse*,) farmer

Phelps, Jesse, (Flemingaville,) joint S. D. 2, farmer 100

Phelps, Wm., (Catatonk,) S. D. 1, farmer 35.

Pierce, John, (Wilseyville,) farmer 70

Potter, Harvey, (Candor,) farmer 250, Main

Potter, Henry P , (Candor,) (with *Harvey*,) farmer

Preston, Frank F., (Candor,) general merchant and farmer 6, Mill.

Pultz, Lewis, (Owego,) S. D 11, farmer 105

QUICK, DANIEL F., (Candor,) S. D. 5, farmer leases 50

REASOR, JAMES B , (Weltonville,) joint S D 26, cooper and farmer 1.

REES, JACOB S., (Jenksville,) joint S. D. 5, farmer 26.

Reeves, Moses, (Candor,) (*Reeves & Young*.)

Reeves & Young, (Candor,) (*Moses Reeves and Daniel O Young*,) props Eagle Hotel and livery

Reynolds, Frank, (Candor,) S D. 18, farmer 25

RICH, JOSIAH, (Candor,) real estate broker, prop. woolen factory and 140 acres.

Richardson, Henry, (West Newark,) joint S D 12, farmer 100.

Richardson, Jerome, (Candor,) billiard saloon, restaurant, confectionery &c , Front.

ROBBINS, JOHN E., (Candor,) S. D. 7, farmer 82½.

Robinson, A A , (Candor,) insurance agent, Main.

Robinson, Aldia A , 2d, (Candor,) (with *Joel*,) farmer

ROBINSON, JOEL, (Candor,) S. D. 14, retired carpenter and millwright, and farmer 10, aged 86 years.

Robinson, Joel O., (Candor,) S D 3, farmer leases 80

Robinson, John Sanford, (Candor,) S D. 14, miller and millwright

Rockwell, Lucy, (Jenksville,) S. D. 13, farmer, occupies Peter Rockwell estate

ROCKWELL, RUFUS, (Jenksville,) S. D. 18, farmer 45

Roe, Gamaliel, (Wilseyville,) S. D. 8, farmer 140.

Roe, Wm. F., (Candor,) S. D. 7, farmer 104

Ross, Emily Mrs., (West Candor,) farmer 103

Ross, Harry, (Wilseyville,) S. D 19, farmer 250

Ross, James D., (Candor,) S. D. 22, farmer 250

Royall, Morris B , (Candor,) farmer 30

RUMPFF, ADOLPHUS F. Rev , (Candor,) rector St Mark's Church, Front.

Rumpff, John H., (Candor,) lawyer, Front.

Ryan, John, (Candor,) tanner, Mill

Sackett, J. J., (Candor,) general merchant, Front.

Sackett, ——, (widow,) (Candor,) dress maker, Owego St

Salisbury, Wm , (Wilseyville,) S. D 21, farmer leases of Alanson Banks, 100

SANFORD, BARLOW, (Wilseyville,) S D 6, justice of the peace and farmer 175.

Sanford, E., (Wilseyville,) S D. 5, farmer 7

Sanford, Herman, (Wilseyville,) S D. 6, farmer leases of Josiah Rich, 50

Sarson, Agnes Mrs., (Wilseyville,) farmer 50.

Sarson, John, (Wilseyville,) S. D, 19, farmer 80

Scott, E. O., (Candor,) lawyer and notary public, Main.

SEAMAN, JOEL, (Candor,) S D 14, stock broker and farmer 60.

Searle, Chas M , (Candor,) carpenter and farmer 70.

Shafer, Joseph, (Catatonk,) S D 1, farmer 100

Sherwood, Wm. K , (Candor,) photographer and portrait painter, Front

Shoienburgh, Horace M., (Candor,) S. D 10, farmer 2

Silvernail, John, (Strait's Corners,) S D 25, farmer 75

Skellinger, Robert, (Speedaville, Tompkins Co ,) S. D 13, farmer 8.

SLAWSON, JAMES G., (Candor,) (*Baylor & Slawson*,) residence Railroad.

Smith, Alanson, (Candor,) (*Hedges & Smith*,) town collector

Smith, Alanson , (Catatonk,) S. D 1, farmer 27¾.

Smith, Edgar M , (Candor,) carpenter and farmer, Owego St.

Smith, Frank N , (Candor,) S D 2, farmer

Smith, Geo. B , (Candor,) S. D. 17, farmer 45

Smith, James, (Candor,) S. D. 2, farmer 70.

Smith, James, (Wilseyville,) S. D 16, farmer 15

Smith, Jared, (Candor,) farmer 150, Owego St.

Smith, Jesse A., (Candor,) wagon maker

Smith, Lucina, (Candor,) S D 2, carpenter.

## CENTRAL HOUSE,
### *Above the Depot,*
# CANDOR, N. Y.

## WM. MURRAY, Proprietor.

This House is on the line of the D. L. & W. R. R., Cayuga Division. No pains will be spared that will contribute to the comfort of Guests.

There is a good LIVERY connected with the House. Trusty Horses, fine Carriages and a careful Driver always in readiness to convey people to any part of the country.

☞ CHARGES REASONABLE.                ☞ GIVE US A CALL.

# JOHN D. SWART,
# House and Ornamental Painting,

# Paper Hanging, Kalsomining, Graining,
## LETTERING ON GLASS,
*Tints or Color, & Carriage Painting promptly attended to.*

P. S.—Parties desiring anything in the Painting line, please give me a call. Satisfaction guaranteed.

## Candor, Tioga County, N. Y.

Smith, M. H., (Candor,) carpenter and farmer, Owego St.

SMITH, WAKEMAN B., (Wilseyville,) S. D. 6, post master and farmer 265.

Smith, Wm., (Candor,) S D 17, farmer 25.

Smullen, Patrick, (Weltonville,) joint S. D. 26, blacksmith.

Snover, J. F., (Candor,) joint S. D. 9, joiner and farmer 19.

Snyder, Benjamin C., (Candor,) S D 5, farmer 141.

Snyder, Edward E., (Candor,) (Dykeman & Snyder).

Snyder, William C., (Candor,) S D. 5, retired farmer.

Sofield, Truman, (Candor,) S. D 22, farmer 115.

Soules, Luther, (Candor,) carpenter, Owego St.

Southwick, Aaron B., (Strait's Corners,) S D. 12, farmer 53.

Spaulding, Catharine, (Wilseyville,) S. D 19, farmer 84.

SPAULDING, U. P., (Candor,) (U. P. Spaulding & Co.,) supervisor, prop. grist and flouring mill, and farmer 29, Main.

SPAULDING, U P & Co., (Candor,) (W F Young,) millers and grain dealers, coopers and real estate brokers, Main.

Spellman, Michael, (Catatonk,) S. D 1, farmer 80.

Stafford, Horace G., (Strait's Corners,) S.D. 12, dairyman, farmer 55 and lessee 157.

Starks, James, (Wilseyville,) S. D. 20, farmer 175.

Starks, James O., (Wilseyville,) S. D. 20, farmer 50.

Starkweather, Charles, (Candor,) S. D. 15, farmer 60.

Starkweather, Henry, (Candor,) S D 20, farmer 61.

Steenbergh, Theodore, (Wilseyville,) S. D. 21, carpenter and farmer 25.

Stephens, Amos, (Candor,) farmer, Foundry.

Stephens, Edson L., (Wilseyville,) S. D. 6, farmer 25.

Stephens, James M., (Wilseyville,) S. D. 6, shingle maker and farmer 25.

Stephens, Levi, (Wilseyville,) S. D. 6, farmer 85.

Stephens, Louise D.; (Wilseyville,) S. D. 6, farmer 9.

STEVENS, EDSON J., (Wilseyville,) S. D 5, operative dentist.

Steward, Chas., (Candor,) barber, Front.

Stewart, Henry, (Candor,) S. D. 14, farmer 10½.

STINARD, SAMUEL, (Jenksville,) S. D. 17, dairyman and farmer 231.

STINARD, WM. H., (Candor,) farmer, Royal.

STONE, CHARLES E., (Candor,) S. D. 15, (with Lewis Wheeler,) farmer.

STOWELL, ALMOND F., (Candor,) sexton Congregational Church and carpenter and joiner, Railroad.

STRAIT, GEO. F., (Candor,) S. D 25, lumberman, prop. Strait's mill and farmer 50.

Strong, Charles S., (Candor,) (with Joel C.,) farmer.

Strong, Hebron, (Candor,) S. D 7, farmer 50.

Strong, Isaac B., (Candor,) S. D. 5, farmer 141.

Strong, J., (Candor,) S D 7, farmer 88.

STRONG, JOEL C., (Candor,) S. D. 7, farmer 135.

Strong, J. H., (Candor,) (Strong & Tuttle.)

Strong, Josiah C., (Candor,) dealer in agricultural implements and farmer 40.

STRONG, ORIN, (Candor,) S D. 7, farmer 121.

STRONG, SILAS H., (Candor,) S. D. 7, farmer 24.

STRONG, TAYLOR, (Candor,) S. D. 7, farmer 76.

Strong & Tuttle, (Candor,) (J. H. Strong and B. F. Tuttle,) bakers and grocers, under Sackett's store.

‡SWART, JOHN D., (Candor,) sign and ornamental painter and paper hanger, Owego St.

Tanner, John H., (Weltonville,) S. D. 26, physician.

Tasy, Alex, (Candor,) mechanic, Railroad.

Taylor, Abram, (West Newark,) joint S D. 12, farmer 378½.

Taylor, Chas. D., (Candor,) (with John M.,) farmer.

Taylor, Gillie, (Candor,) farmer 15.

Taylor, Isaac A. Rev., (Candor,) S D. 2, Baptist clergyman.

Taylor, John M., (Candor,) S. D 10, mechanic and farmer 75.

Taylor, Martin, (West Candor,) S. D. 25, farmer 32.

TAYLOR, SAMUEL E., (Weltonville,) joint S. D. 26, farmer 175.

TAYLOR, W. J., (West Newark,) joint S. D 12, farmer occupies 378½.

Terwilliger, Chas., (Candor,) Owego St.

Terwilliger, Solomon E., (Catatonk,) S. D 1, blacksmith.

Terwilliger, Andrew J., (Candor,) S D 25, farmer 84.

TERWILLIGER, ROBERT, (Strait's Corners,) S. D 25, farmer 78.

Thomas, Geo. H., (West Newark,) joint S D. 24, farmer 40.

Thomas, Miles B., (West Newark,) joint S. D. 24, farmer 40.

Thompson, Emeline, (Wilseyville,) farmer 25.

Thompson, Jerome, (Candor,) cashier First National Bank of Candor and prest Board of Education Candor Free Academy.

Thompson, Wm. Walter, (Wilseyville,) shoemaker.

Throop, John G., (Wilseyville,) farmer 100.

Tidd, John, (West Candor,) S D. 22, farmer 1.

TRIPP, SEAMORE C., (Candor,) watch maker and jeweler, Front.

TRUMAN, FRANK W., (Catatonk,) (G. Truman & Co.,) (L. Truman & Bros.) postmaster, farmer 333 and (with Orin,) in Owego, 210.

TRUMAN, G & CO., (Catatonk,) (Geo. Orin, Lyman and Frank W Truman, and T L. Smull,) tanners and grocers.

TRUMAN, LEVI B., (Owego,) joint S. D. 2, farmer 128.

Truman, Lyman R., (Owego,) *(with Levi B.)* farmer.

Truman, Wm S., (Catatonk,) S D. 1, foreman of and has an interest in Catatonk Tannery

TUBBS, EBENEZER, (Candor,) *(with Isaac)* farmer.

Tubbs, Isaac, (Candor,) S D 7, farmer 25

Tucker, A H, (Candor,) carpenter and bridge builder, Owego St

Tucker, Seth, (Candor,) Candor Union District, carpenter and farmer 100

Tucker, Wm, (Wilseyville,) farmer 108

Turner, Geo, (Strait's Corners,) S. D. 12, farmer 70

Tuttle & Bogert, (Candor,) *(Ehada Tuttle and Peter Bogert,)* general merchants, Front

Tuttle, B F, (Candor,) *(Strong & Tuttle.)*

Tuttle, Ehada, (Candor,) *(Tuttle & Bogert)*

Tuttle Joel, (Wilseyville,) S D 6, farmer 107

TUTTLE, WARREN H, (Candor,) S D 10, hay dealer and farmer 75

Tuttle, Wm H, (Wilseyville,) S D 8, farmer occupies 60

UPSON, EDWARD C, (Candor,) S D 15, farmer 94

VanBuren, John W, (Candor,) S. D 13, farmer leases 50

VanDebogart, Peter, (Candor,) dealer in agricultural implements, agent for Grover & Baker Sewing Machine and farmer 150, Mill

VanDermark, Peter, (Candor,) S D 10, farmer 10.

VanEtten, Geo., (Wilseyville,) S D. 8, farmer 80

VanGlone, Stillman, (Candor,) S. D. 13, farmer 41.

VANKLEECK, CHAS H, (Candor,) S D 21, agent for agricultural implements, mowing machines &c, and farmer 100

VanKleeck, John M, (Candor,) S. D. 21, retired farmer

VanLuven, Samuel E, (Strait's Corners,) S D 12, farmer 170

VanLuven, Simon, (Candor,) S D 2, commissioner of highways and farmer 75

VANSCOY, BURT R, (Jenksville,) S D 17, farmer 43

VANSCOY, ISAAC D, (Jenksville,) S D 17, farmer 130

VanScoy, Knowlton, (Candor,) S. D. 15, farmer 90.

VanValcalner, Jacob, (Candor,) S. D 14, farmer 80.

VanValknar, Geo F., (Candor,) S. D. 14, farmer 50 and leases 80

VanVLEET, THEODORE, (Wilseyville,) S D 6, farmer 150

VanWert, Lebbeus B., (Candor,) S D 21, farmer 240

VanWoert, Hermon, (West Candor,) farmer 75

VanZile, Stephen, (Candor,) S. D. 18, farmer 20

Vergason, David, (Strait's Corners,) S D 23, farmer 92

Vergason, George, (Strait's Corners,) *(with David.)* farmer.

VERGASON, SOLOMON, (Candor,) S. D 10, farmer 237.

VERGASON, STEPHEN, (Strait's Corners,) S D. 23, farmer 125.

Vorce Henry, (Weltonville) S D 17, school teacher, inspector of election and farmer leases 132

Vorce, Volney, (Weltonville,) S. D. 17, farmer 72

VOSE, LEMUEL D. PROF, (Candor,) union S D 9 and 18, principal of Candor Free Academy.

Wake, James, (Candor,) *(with William,)* farmer

WAKE, WILLIAM, (Candor,) union S D. 9 and 18, farmer 140

Walts, Conrad, (Candor,) S D. 25, farmer 60.

Wanzer James, (Candor,) mechanic

Ward, Elmma Miss, (Candor,) millinery, Front

Ward, Harvey H, (Candor,) S. D. 4, farmer 100 Owego St

Ward, Hiram, (Candor,) S D 2, farmer 60

WARD, WM, (Candor,) manuf woolen goods, Main.

WASHBURN, RANSOM A REV, (Weltonville,) S D 24, pastor of Owego Creek Baptist Church

Watson, Seth, (Candor,) S. D 2, harness maker and egg dealer, Owego St

Weaver, John S, (Candor, farmer 22, Railroad.

Webster, Edwin, (Owego,) joint S D. 2, stock broker, butcher and farmer

WEED, JOHN D, (Candor,) manuf. lumber, planing mill &c., and farmer 50, Mill

Wentworth, Charles, (Candor,) painter, Church

Wentworth, John, (Candor,) *(with Chas.,)* painter

Wentworth, Noyea, (Candor,) *(with Chas,)* painter

Werner, John C., (Candor,) farmer 50

Wheeler, Abram, (Candor,) S D 14, R. R. bridge builder

Wheeler, Chas T, (Owego,) S D 11, farmer 83

Wheeler, John H., (Candor,) S D 10, fireman.

Wheeler, Lewis, (Candor,) S. D. 15, farmer 53

Wheeler, Olra E, (Candor,) union S. D 9 and 18, farmer 208.

White, Abel, (Strait's Corners,) S D 23, farmer 90.

WHITE, MORGAN A., (Wilseyville,) S. D. 6, hotel keeper, grocer, broker, express and freight agent, D L & W. R R, and farmer 1,000 in Tompkins and Tioga Counties.

Whiteley, George M., (Wilseyville,) S. D. 8, farmer 54

WHITLEY, AARON S REV, (Wilseyville,) S. D. 20, Baptist minister and farmer 128.

Whitley, Andrew J, (Wilseyville,) S D. 20, farmer 139

WHITLEY, WARREN P., (Wilseyville,) S D 20, farmer 50 and leases 128

Whitmarsh, A., (Catatonk,) S. D. 1, farmer 33

Whitmarsh, Ambrose, (Catatonk,) farmer 62¼.

Whitmarsh, Edward, (Catatonk,) S. D. 1, farmer 62½

Whitmarsh, Laura, (Catatonk,) S. D. 1, farmer 17.

Whitney, Joseph S , (Candor,) S. D. 14, farmer 96

WHITNEY, PERRY B , (Candor,) S. D. 14, farmer 50 and leases 49.

Whitney, Thompson, (Candor,) S. D 14, farmer 25.

Wilber, Wm H., (Speedsville, Tompkins Co ,) joint S. D. 5, farmer 200.

Wilcoxen, Abram Rev , (Candor,) S. D. 14, retired clergyman and farmer 6

Willett, Edward S., (Candor,) speculator, Church

Williams, Chas , (Catatonk,) S. D. 11, farmer 50

Williams, E S., (Candor,) clothing, gents' furnishing goods, hats, caps &c , Front.

Williams, LaFayette, (Catatonk,) S D. 11, farmer 90

Williams, William I., (Catatonk,) S D 1, farmer 64.

Willsey, Gaylord, (Candor,) joint S D. 9, retired, Spencer St

WILLSEY, JACOB T., (Wilseyville,) S. D. 6, town assessor and farmer leases of Warren, 200.

Willsey, Martin, (Candor,) (with Warren )

WILLSEY, WARREN, (Candor,) (Eighmey & Co ,) farmer 375, Spencer St

WILLSEY, WM W., (Wilseyville,) S. D. 6, farmer 200

Winfield, James, (Stralt's Corners,) S D 12, farmer 10

WOOD, BENJ., (Candor,) carpenter and millwright, Thompson.

Woodbridge, E H Mrs , (Catatonk,) S. D 1, farmer 148.

Woodford, Chas., (Candor,) S D 3, retired farmer

Woodford, Chauncey B , (Candor,) S D 22, stock dealer and farmer 148.

WOODFORD, CHAUNCEY T., (Candor,) county supt. of poor and farmer 100, Owego St.

Woodford, Elbert C., (Candor,) S D 22, farmer 200.

Woodford, Geo , (Candor,) agent for agricultural implements and farmer 200.

Woodford, John R., (West Candor,) post master, overseer of West Candor Hotel and farmer 35.

Woodford, Luther, (Candor,) S D. 9, farmer 130

Woodford, Myron L , (Candor,) S D. 22, farmer 129

Woodford, Romanta & Sons, (Candor,) S. D 3, farmer 260

Woodford, Sylvester, (Candor,) union S. D. 9 and 18, farmer 100.

WOODRUFF, TIMOTHY T , (Wilseyville,) S. D. 21, farmer 95.

Woods, John, (Owego,) joint S. D 21, farmer 54.

Wool, Joseph D , (Wilseyville,) S D. 16, saw mill and farmer 126.

Wright, Calvin, (West Candor,) S. D. 25, farmer 52

Wright, Charles H., (Candor,) S. D 25, farmer 137.

Wright, Jenny, (Stralt's Corners,) S D 12, farmer 50

Wright, John, (Candor,) S D 25, farmer 50

Wright, John T , (Candor,) S. D. 27, moulder and farmer 50.

Wright, Wm. A., (Candor,) S. D 3, farmer 60

Yerks, Catharine, Mary and Clarissa, (Catatonk,) S. D. 1, farmers 87.

Young, Daniel O., (Candor,) (Reeves & Young.)

YOUNG, W F , (Candor,) (U. P. Spaulding & Co )

YOUNG, WM F , (Candor,) (Young & Spaulding )

Youngs, Andrew, (Wilseyville,) S D. 20, farmer 40.

YOUNGS, LEWIS, (Wilseyville,) S D 6, carpenter and joiner

Zimmer, Ira, (Jenksville,) S. D. 7, farmer 95.

# NEWARK VALLEY.

### (Post Office Addresses in Parentheses.)

ABBREVIATIONS.—S. D., School District.

Ackerman, Joseph, (Newark Valley,) S D 3, carpenter and farmer 103¾

Alden, Timothy P , (Newark Valley,) S. D. 2, tinware, stoves and hardware.

ALEXANDER, CHAS S REV , (Newark Valley,) S. D 2, pastor M. E. Church.

Allen, James, (Newark Valley,) S D 4, cooper and farmer 1½

Allen, Samuel N , (Newark Valley,) S. D. 4, wagon maker and farmer 18

Allen, Sylvester S., (Newark Valley,) S. D 4, traveling agent and farmer leases of Mrs Nancy Allen, 68

Allison, George H , (Newark Valley,) S. D. 2, (Allison & Sherwood,) (Allison & Crary )

Ames, Stephen W , (Newark Valley,) S. D. 3, farmer 100

Andrews, Chester C , (Newark Valley,) S. D. 18, farmer 33

Andrews, C & L Misses, (Newark Valley,) S D 18, farmers 20

Andrews, Daniel, (Newark Valley,) S. D. 18, farmer 50

Andrews, Heman W , (Newark Valley,) (with Judson,) S. D 2, farmer 80

Andrews, Jesse, (Newark Valley,) S.D. 2, mechanic and farmer 4.

Andrews, Judson, (Newark Valley,) (with Heman W ) S D 2, farmer 80

Andrews, Luther, (Newark Valley,) joint S D 11, farmer 300

ARMSTRONG, WM H , (Jenksville,) joint S D 5, prop Jenksville Creamery and Cheese Factory, dairyman and farmer leases of Geo J Pompelley, 515

Arnold, Isaac, (Newark Valley,) S. D. 10, farmer 142½.

Arnold, James, (Ketchumville,) S. D. 7, farmer 25.

ARNOLD, JAMES Jr., (Newark Valley,) S D 10, farmer 88

Ashley, Francis D., (Newark Valley,) joint S D 11, farmer leases of Gershom Clark, 100

Avery, Samuel M , (Jenksville,) post master and justice of the peace

Bailey, Hiram C., (Maine, Broome Co ,) S. D 5, farmer 110.

Bailey, Margaret Mrs., (Newark Valley,) S. D 5, farmer 80

BAKER, ALBERT A , (Newark Valley,) S. D. 1, marble dealer in the State of Alabama and farmer 350.

Ball, Augustus R , (Newark Valley,) S D. 4, farmer leases 140

Ball, Franklin, (Newark Valley,) S. D. 3, farmer 4.

Ball, Wm W., (Newark Valley,) S D 4, farmer 140.

Ballard, Levi & Sons, (Newark Valley ) (Wm H. and Lewis W ,) operate saw mill for Davidge, Landfield & Co.

Ballard, Lewis W , (Newark Valley,) (Levi Ballard & Sons )

Ballard, Wm. H., (Newark Valley,) (Levi Ballard & Sons )

Barber, Edbert M., (Newark Valley,) S. D. 2, farmer 40

Barber, Philander L., (Weltonville,) joint S D 26, farmer 1.

Barber, Royal, (Newark Valley,) S D 10, farmer 78

Barbour, Elbridge L., (Newark Valley,) S. D 3, farmer 167.

Barden, Oscar L , (Ketchumville,) blacksmith and farmer leases 50

Barnes, Lewis N., (Newark Valley,) S. D. 4, carpenter and farmer 52

Barrott, Josephus, (Weltonville,) joint S. D. 24, farmer 88.

Beacher Clark, (Newark Valley,) S. D. 2, farmer 1

Beecher, Lambert, (Newark Valley,) S D. 2, harness maker.

Belcher, A Bement, (Newark Valley,) S. D 2, (C & A B Belcher )

Belcher, Chas , (Newark Valley,) S D 2 (C. & A. B. Belcher,) agent for Sprague Mower

Belcher, C & A. B., (Newark Valley,) (Chas and A Bement,) S. D 1, farmer 220

Belcher, J. Waldo, (Newark Valley,) S. D. 2, painter

Belcher, Sidney, (Newark Valley,) S D. 1, saw and shingle mills, and farmer 100.

Bement, Egbert, (Newark Valley,) S. D. 2, saw mill &c , and farmer 150

Benham, Martinna L., (Newark Valley,) S D 7, farmer 72.

Berkley, Egbert, (Union Center, Broome Co ,) farmer 100

Besaac, Fayette B., (Berkshire,) S D. 4, farmer 143

Bieber, Henry, (Newark Valley,) S. D. 13, farmer 62.

Bieber, Philip, (Newark Valley,) S D 13, farmer 55.

BISHOP, CURTIS L , (Newark Valley,) S D 2, dealer in musical instruments, agent for sewing machines and fire and life insurance

BISHOP, FRANCIS M , (Newark Valley,) (*L D. Bishop & Son*,) jeweler.

BISHOP, LEWIS D., (Newark Valley,) (*L D Bishop & Son*,) justice of the peace

BISHOP, L D. & SON, (Newark Valley,) (*Lewis D. and Francis M.*,) S. D. 2, general merchants and manufs lumber in McKean Co., Pa., 1113 acres of wood land.

Blackman. Wm. G., (Weltonville,) joint S D. 26, farmer 82

Blair, Alfred, (Newark Valley,) S. D. 10, blacksmith and farmer 180.

Blair, Milo, (Newark Valley,) S D 2, farmer 1

Blewer, Chas , (Weltonville,) joint S.D. 26, farmer 95.

BLEWER, JOHN F., (Weltonville,) (*with Wm H.*,) joint S. D 26, farmer 210.

BLEWER, WM H , (Weltonville,) (*with John F.*,) joint S. D 26, farmer 210.

Borthwick, Alex , (Jenksville,) joint S D. 5, commissioner of highways and farmer 44

Borthwick, Daniel J , (Jenksville,) joint S. D 5, farmer 165

Borthwick, Geo H , (West Newark,) joint S D. 12, farmer leases 112½

Bowles, Jason, (Maine, Broome Co.,) S. D. 8, farmer 30.

Bowles, Wallace, (Maine, Broome Co ,) S D. 8, farmer leases 30.

Boyle, James, (Ketchumville,) joint S. D. 5, farmer 80

Bradley, Lambert, (Newark Valley,) S D. 4, farmer 6.

Brick, Thos., (Newark Valley,) S. D 3, laborer.

Brigham, James E , (Newark Valley,) S D 4, carpenter and farmer leases 96.

Brockway, Joseph B., (Berkshire,) S D 4, farmer 74½

Brooks, Jesse, (Maine, Broome Co.,) S D. 9, prop stallion "Messenger," and farmer 100

BROOKS, NELSON, (Maine, Broome Co.,) farmer leases 100.

Brougham, Wm., (Newark Valley,) S. D. 13, farmer 53.

Brown, Elmina Mrs., (Newark Valley,) S. D 2, farmer 27

BURCHARD, HARVEY J.,(Ketchumville,) (*Dean & Burchard*,) physician and surgeon, photographer and dealer in sewing machines

BURR, WM. J , M D., (Newark Valley,) S. D 2, physician and surgeon.

Bushnell, Calvin, (Newark Valley,) joint S D 11, farmer 83.

Bushnell, Edwin G., (Newark Valley,) S. D. 7, farmer 47.

Bushnell, Francis G., (Newark Valley,) joint S. D. 11, farmer 93½.

Bushnell, Henry T., (Newark Valley,) joint S.D. 11, farmer 62

Bushnell, Wm. B., (Newark Valley,) S. D. 11, farmer 50.

BUSHNELL ZINA H., (Newark Valley,) joint S D 11, farmer 75.

BUTLER, JOHN, (Newark Valley,) S. D. 2, farmer 300.

Buttler, Wm R , (Newark Valley,) S. D 2, mechanic.

Caldwell, Wm J , (Newark Valley,) S. D 2, notary public

Cameron, John, (Newark Valley,) S. D. 2, farmer leases 80

Cameron, Wm H , (Newark Valley,) S. D. 2, farmer 52½

Cargill, Geo , (Newark Valley,) S D 2, retired farmer 4.

Cargill, Heman, (Newark Valley,) S D 2, retired farmer 7½.

CARGILL, WM , (Newark Valley,)(*Moors, Cargill & Co.*)

Carpenter, H Lyman, (West Newark,) joint S. D. 12, farmer 160.

Cary, Thos A., (Newark Valley,) S D. 2, farmer 208

Cattell, Esken, (Newark Valley,) S D. 7, farmer 50.

Cattle, John H., (Maine, Broome Co.,) farmer 40.

Chamberlain, Daniel, (Newark Valley,) S. D. 4, farmer 83.

Chamberlain, Stephen S., (Newark Valley,) S. D. 2, boot maker and farmer 4

Chapman, Albert, (Newark Valley,) S. D. 7, farmer 50

Chapman, Edgar E , (Newark Valley,) S D. 2, carpenter.

CHAPMAN, GEO. M., (Newark Valley,) S. D 2, house builder and farmer 1½

Chapman, Lyman F., (Newark Valley,) S. D. 2, grocer and house builder

Chapman, Noyes P., (Newark Valley,) S D 2, carpenter.

Chittenden, A Jackson, (Newark Valley,) S. D 13, farmer 40

Chittenden, Lester, (West Newark,) joint S D. 12, farmer 35

Clark, Chas. A., (Newark Valley,) S. D. 2, lawyer, county judge and farmer 1

CLARKE, JOHN, (Newark Valley,) joint S D 11, farmer 50

Clifford, John M., (Newark Valley,) S. D 7, farmer 118.

CLINTON & ELWELLS, (Newark Valley,) (*Royal W Clinton, Morris and Wm. Elwell*,) S D. 2, general merchants, lumber and coal dealers

CLINTON, HENRY, (Newark Valley,) (*R W. & H Clinton*)

Clinton, Julian S., (Newark Valley,) S. D. 2, farmer 130

CLINTON, MORRIS D., (Newark Valley,) S D 2, farmer 82.

CLINTON, ROYAL W., (Newark Valley,) S D. 2, (*Clinton & Elwells*,) (*R W. & H Clinton*,) R. R. commissioner and lumber dealer.

CLINTON, R W. & H., (Newark Valley,) (*Royal W. and Henry*,) joint S. D. 11, saw mill.

Cole, Anson L., (Ketchumville,) farmer 120

Cole, Loren P , (Ketchumville,) mechanic and farmer.

Cole, Orlando, (Ketchumville,) farmer 47.

Congdon, George, (Newark Valley,) S D. 2, stage prop. and farmer, in Maine, 55.

Cook, Harry M , (Ketchumville,) farmer 20.

Cooley, Benj. F , (Newark Valley,) S. D. 2, agent for Harvey Cooley, sheep skin tannery, and farmer 20.

Cooley, John, (Ketchumville,) farmer 28

Cooper, Chas , (Flemingsville,) farmer 62.

Corboy, Wm , (Newark Valley,) S D. 2, farmer 50

Cortwright, Franklin, (West Newark,) joint S D 12, farmer 196

Cortwright, Josephus, (Weltonville,) joint S D 12, farmer 65.

Cortwright, L Eltıng, (West Newark,) joint S D 2, farmer 37½

Cortwright, Wm. C (West Newark,) joint S D 12, farmer 90

Councilman, David, (Newark Valley,) S. D 7, farmer 40

Councilman, Timothy S , (Newark Valley,) S D 3, farmer 90.

Courtright, Alva M , (Newark Valley,) S D 2, teacher Union School

Curlhair, Henry, (Maine, Broome Co.,) S. D 9, farmer 5

CURTIS & HOOKER, (Newark Valley,) (*Isaac Curtis and Chas B Hooker,*) S D. 2, props Newark Valley Nursery

CURTIS, ISAAC, (Newark Valley,) S. D. 2, (*Curtis & Hooker.*) farmer 7

Curtis, Mark H., (Newark Valley,) S. D. 2, farmer 30

Duggett, Barney, (West Newark,) joint S D 12, farmer 86

DAVIDGE, JAMES, (Newark Valley,) (*Davidge, Landfield & Co* )

DAVIDGE, JOHN, (Newark Valley,) (*Davidge, Landfield & Co.,*) S D 2, farmer 130.

DAVIDGE, LANDFIELD & CO , (Newark Valley,) (*John Davidge, Sherwood B Davidge, Jerome B Landfield, Lucian Horton and James Davidge,*) S. D 2, manufs. sole leather and lumber, dealers in general merchandise, agents for A B Howe Sewing Machine and U S Express Co.

DAVIDGE, SHERWOOD B., (Newark Valley,) (*Davidge, Landfield & Co* )

DAVIS, ASA, (Newark Valley,) (*Davis Bros* )

DAVIS BROS , (Newark Valley,) (*Franklin and Asa,*) S D. 10, props circular saw mill.

DAVIS, FRANKLIN, (Newark Valley,) (*Davis Bros.,*) farmer, in Maine, 72.

Davison, David H , (West Newark,) joint S D. 12, cooper and farmer 2

DEAN & BURCHARD, (Ketchumville,) (*Chas H Dean and Harvey J Burchard,*) general agents for the Eureka Mowing Machine

DEAN, CHAS H , (Ketchumville,) (*Dean & Burchard,*) justice of the peace, dealer in stock, skins, &c , and farmer 125.

Dean, Franklin G , (Newark Valley,) S D 2, farmer 80.

Dean, Reuben, (Ketchumville,) saw mill and farmer 140.

DeGaramo, James, (Newark Valley,) joint S D 11, farmer 51

DeGARAMO, LORENZO,(Newark Valley,) S D 2, (*with Wm.,*) farmer

DeGaramo, Peter, (Newark Valley,) joint S. D 11, farmer 135

DeGaramo, Wm., (Newark Valley,) S. D. 2, farmer 57½

Delaney, John, (Newark Valley,) S D. 10, farmer 124

Denison, Joseph H , (Newark Valley,) S D 4, mason and farmer 38

Dickinson, Lyman, (Newark Valley,) S D. 2, farmer 80.

Dickson, George M., (Newark Valley,) joint S. D 11, farmer leases 50.

DIMMICK, OSSIAN, (Newark Valley,) (*Dimmick & Young,*) telegraph operator.

Dimmick, Simeon L Rev , (Ketchumville,) pastor Reformed Methodist Church

DIMMICK & YOUNG, (Newark Valley,) (*Ossian Dimmick and Hiram Young,*) S D. 2, props. Dimmick House, opposite Depot.

Dobe, Geo., (Newark Valley,) S D 2, mason and farmer 11.

Donahue, Patrick, (Newark Valley,) S D 2, farmer 50

Doney, Saloma C. Mrs., (Newark Valley,) S D 2 farmer 114.

Dooly, John, (Newark Valley,) S. D 2, farmer 50

Dunning, Peter S., (Jenksville,) joint S D 5, grist, saw and cider mills, and farmer 5

Elison, John T., (Jenksville,) joint S D 5, farmer leases 10

ELWELL, MORRIS, (Newark Valley,) (*Clinton & Elwells.*)

ELWELL, WM , (Newark Valley,) (*Clinton & Elwells* )

Fairchild, Edward S , (Newark Valley,) S. D 3, mason.

Fairchild, Hiram, (Newark Valley,) S D. 3, mason and farmer 1

Faroe, Henry, (Newark Valley,) S D. 2, farmer 33

FELLOWS, RUSSEL S., (Newark Valley,) S D 2, dentist

Fivaz, Jules, (Newark Valley,) S. D 2, farmer 38.

Fivaz, Mark Rev , (Newark Valley,) retired clergyman

Fogle, Jacob, (Maine, Broome Co.,) farmer 50.

Ford, Horace, (Maine, Broome Co ,) farmer 25

Ford, Ichabod A., (Newark Valley,) S D. 2, farmer 118.

Freeland, Lyman, (Newark Valley,) S. D. 3, farmer 100

Gaskell, Levi C , (Newark Valley,) S. D. 1, mechanic and farmer 50

GATES, NORTON S , (Newark Valley,) S. D. 2, carpenter

Gibson, Edwin, (Maine, Broome Co.,) S D 9, farmer leases of J Hollenbeck, 50.

GLEAZEN, GEO. D., (Newark Valley,) S. D 2, carpenter and joiner.

Gleazen, Julia Miss, (Newark Valley,) (*with Miss Sabrina,*) S D 2, farmer 3.

Gleazen, Sabrina Miss, (Newark Valley,) (*with Miss Julia,*) S D 2, farmer 3

Glines, Alden, (Flemingsville,) farmer 30.

Gould, Ephraim D., (Ketchumville,) farmer leases of Ephraim Ketchum, 4

Gould, Joel S., (Ketchumville,) farmer leases of Geo J. Pumpelly, 313

Gregory, Hezekiah, (Maine, Broome Co ,) S. D 5, farmer 200

Grenell, James C , (Ketchumville,) S. D 7, farmer 47

Griffin, Hiram, (Newark Valley,) S D. 2, farmer 105.

Guy, Albert, (Newark Valley,) S D 2, carpenter and carriage maker.

Guyon, Chas. S, (West Newark,) joint S D 12, farmer 1½.

Guyon, Henry B, (Newark Valley,) S D 3, farmer 70.

HAGEN, W. HENRY, (Jenksville,) joint S D 5, blacksmith and farmer 1.

Hall, Abner G., (Newark Valley,) S D. 3, farmer 71½.

Hammond, Ansel H., (Newark Valley,) S D 4, farmer 90.

Hammond, Levi B., (Newark Valley,) S D 4, farmer.

Hammond, Melville F., (Newark Valley,) S. D 4, carpenter and farmer 54.

Hand, Delmar C., (Newark Valley,) S D 2, farmer leases 4.

Hardendorf, Henry D., (Ketchumville,) carpenter and farmer 30.

Harding, Ford, (Newark Valley,) S. D 1, farmer leases 200.

Harris, John, (Newark Valley,) S. D 4, carpenter and farmer 45.

Harris, Washington, (Newark Valley,) joint S. D 11, farmer 42.

HAVENS, GEO., (Newark Valley,) S D 2, boot and shoe maker.

HAYNE, HENRY J., (Newark Valley,) (*Moore, Cargill & Co.*)

Heaton, Carlton R , (Newark Valley,) S D. 2, physician.

Henderson, Alex , (Newark Valley,) S D. 3, farmer 100.

Hess, David, (Newark Valley,) S D 10, farmer leases of Bradford Phelps, 45.

Hicks, James, (Ketchumville,) farmer 50.

Higbe, Chas., (Newark Valley,) S D. 2, farmer 90.

Hibgae, Chas , (Maine, Broome Co ,) S D 5, farmer 7.

Hoff, Erastus, (Newark Valley,) S. D 3, farmer 165.

Holden, Hiram, (Flemingsville,) farmer leases 275.

Hollenbeck, Jacob, (Maine, Broome Co.,) S D 9, farmer 282.

HOLLENBECK, JOHN, (Newark Valley,) S D 3, mason and farmer 45.

Hollister, Chas. G , (Ketchumville,) clergyman, shoemaker and farmer 2.

HOOKER, CHAS. B., (Newark Valley,) S D 2, (*Curtis & Hooker*,) farmer 8.

HORTON, LUCIAN, (Newark Valley,) (*Davidge, Landfield & Co*)

Hotchkin, Marshal, (Newark Valley,) S D 3, farmer 145.

Hover, Albert (West Newark,) joint S. D 12, farmer 85.

Hover, Silas, (West Newark,) joint S. D. 12, farmer leases 100.

HOWLAND, ARTEMAS, (Newark Valley,) (*A. & H. Howland.*)

HOWLAND, A. & H , (Newark Valley,) (*Artemas and Harper*,) S. D. 2, meat market.

HOWLAND, HARPER, (Newark Valley,) (*A & H Howland*)

Holslander, Levi S , (Maine, Broome Co ,) S. D 9, farmer 90.

Hunt, Lewis, (Newark Valley,) S. D 2, prop saw mill, manuf. grain cradles and farmer 9.

Hyden, Chas , (Ketchumville,) farmer 70.

JAPHET, MILO G , (Ketchumville,) road commissioner, carpenter and joiner, agent for Eureka Churn and farmer 75.

Jayne, Henry F., (Newark Valley,) S D. 3, dairyman, farmer 50 and leases 290.

Jenks, Calvin M , (Newark Valley,) farmer 109.

Jenks, Theodore, (Jenksville,) joint S D 5, farmer 10.

Johnson, John R., (Newark Valley,) S D 3, farmer 68.

Jones, Alva I , (Newark Valley,) S D 2, mechanic.

Joslin, Daniel, (Flemingsville,) saw mill and farmer 96.

Kenyon, Chas E , (Newark Valley,) S. D 13, farmer 38.

KENYON, LORENZO, (Newark Valley,) S D 4, farmer 42.

Kershner, Belthasss,(Newark Valley,) foreman Davidge, Landfield & Co's tannery.

Ketchum, Seneca, (Ketchumville,) post master, general merchant, live stock dealer and hotel keeper.

Kirk, Henry, (Newark Valley,) S D 2, chair maker.

Kittle, Harmon, (Newark Valley,) S D 2, farmer 100.

KNAPP, MUNSON G , (Newark Valley,) S D 2, prop saw mill and farmer, for Mrs Knapp, 50.

Knapp, Wm. T., (Newark Valley,) S D 2, carding machine and farmer 96.

Knapp, —— Mrs., (Newark Valley,) S. D. 2, farmer 50.

Lainhart, Aaron, (Maine, Broome Co ,) S. D. 8, farmer 144.

Lainhart, Abram, (Newark Valley,) S. D. 13, farmer 90.

Lainhart, Elias, (Union Center, Broome Co.,) farmer 96.

Lainhart, John, (Maine, Broome Co.,) S D. 5, cider mill and farmer 50.

Lamb, Ira, (Newark Valley,) S. D. 2, farmer 32¼.

Lamb, Ira D., (Newark Valley,) S D 2, farmer leases 175.

Lamb, J Bruce, (Maine, Broome Co ,) joint S D 5, farmer 105.

LANDFIELD, JEROME B , (Newark Valley,) (*Davidge, Landfield & Co* ,) S D 2, post master and supervisor.

Lawrence, Geo. S , (Newark Valley,) farmer 3¼.

Lawrence, Horace F., (Newark Valley,) farmer 23.

Lawrence, Wm. J , (Newark Valley,) S. D. 4, farmer 52 and leases 25.

LEONARD, AUGUSTUS N , (Newark Valley,) S. D. 3, farmer 120.

Leru, Geo , (Maine, Broome Co ,) S. D. 9, farmer 30.

Lincoln, Edwin B , (Newark Valley,) S. D. 2, prop. hotel.

Lindsley, S Rev , (Speedsville, Tompkins Co ,) pastor Alpha M. E. Church, Jenksville.

LIPE, ALBERT, (Newark Valley,) S. D 7, farmer 92.

Lipe, David, (Newark Valley,) S. D. 13, farmer 45.

Lipe, Jacob Jr , (Newark Valley,) S D. 13, carpenter and farmer 125.

Lipe, John W., (Newark Valley,) S. D. 13, farmer 145.

Loomis, W Rowe, (Maine, Broome Co.,) S D 8, farmer leases of Anson, 190.

Loring, Wm T, (Newark Valley,) S. D 1, brick yard and farmer 175

Macnab,Wm. Rev.,(West Newark,) joint S. D 12, pastor Congregational Church

Maher, John J, (Newark Valley,) S. D. 10, farmer 78

Marinos, David, (Newark Valley,) S D 3, wagon maker and farmer leases of E L. Barbour.

Mattison, Amos K, (Maine, Broome Co.,) (*Amos K Mattison, Son & Co.,*) saw mill and farmer 173

Mattison, Amos K, Son & Co, (Maine, Broome Co.,) (*Freeman Mattison and Harrison Zimmer,*) S D 9, saw mill

Mattison, Freeman, (Maine, Broome Co.,) (*Amos K Mattison, Son & Co,*) (*Mattison & Zimmer*)

Mattison & Zimmer, (Maine, Broome Co.,) (*Freeman Mattison and Harrison Zimmer,*) S D 9, operate saw mill and farm for Amos K Matteson.

McCoy, Stiles, (Weltonville,) joint S. D. 26, farmer 50.

McCullough, Lorenzo D, (Newark Valley,) S D 14, farmer 150

McCollough, Wm, (Newark Valley,) S. D. 13, farmer 100

McLAIN, ROBERT, (Newark Valley,) S D 2, lumberman and farmer leases 19

Mead, Levi, (Weltonville,) joint S D. 12, farmer 175.

Mead, Martin, (Newark Valley,) S. D 3, farmer 167

Mead, Russel S., (West Newark,) joint S D. 12, farmer 95.

Merrill, Abel, (Newark Valley,) S. D 4, farmer 25

Millen, Elisha, (Jenksville,) joint S. D. 12, farmer 70

Miller, Daniel H., (Newark Valley,) S D 4, carpenter and farmer 24

Miller, Robert, (Newark Valley,) S. D. 2, cigar maker

MOORE, CARGILL & CO, (Newark Valley) (*Chas. H. Moore, Wm Cargill, Lucius E Williams and Henry J Hayne,*) S D 2, manufs and dealers in lumber, carriage and wagon builders, and undertakers

MOORE, CHAS. H, (Newark Valley,) (*Moore, Cargill & Co*)

Moore, R Frank, (Newark Valley,) S D 2, civil engineer.

Moseman, Naomi Mrs, (Newark Valley,) S D. 2, dressmaker.

Moses, Philander P., (Newark Valley,) S D 2, millwright and miller

Moses, Samuel, (Newark Valley,) S D 2, cabinet maker.

Muzzy, Chas, (Newark Valley,) S. D. 3, farmer 22

Muzzy, Henry M, (Berkshire,) S D. 4, carpenter and joiner, and farmer 84½

Mynard, Benajah, (Newark Valley,) S D 4, farmer leases of S S. Watson, 235

Nearing, Ira S, (Maine, Broome Co,) S D 8, farmer 230

NELSON, ORVILLE, (West Newark,) joint S. D. 12, farmer leases 95.

Newark Valley Lodge, F & A M, No 614, (Newark Valley,) regular communications 2d and 4th Mondays of each month.

Nicholson, H. Col, (Newark Valley,) joint S D 11. farmer 35.

Niefer, Philip, (Newark Valley,) S D. 13, farmer 126.

Nixon, Chas., (Newark Valley,) S. D. 1, farmer 19

Nixon, Ephraim, (Newark Valley,) S D 1, farmer 73

Nixon, John G, (Jenksville,) joint S D 5, local preacher and general merchant.

Noble, David W, (Newark Valley,) S D. 2, farmer 90

NOBLE, E GEO, (Newark Valley,) S D. 2. (*with W A. and James T,*) W T Noble's estate.

Noble, James T, (Newark Valley,) S D 2, (*with E. Geo and Washington A.,*) W. T. Noble's estate.

Noble, Washington A, (Newark Valley,) S D 2. (*with E. Geo and James T.,*) W. T. Noble's estate.

Noble, W T, estate of (Newark Valley,) S D. 2, (*E Geo., Washington A and James T Noble,*) 90 acres.

Noon, John, (Newark Valley,) S D 2, farmer 30.

North, Frederick D, (Ketchumville,) S. D. 7, farmer 41

Nowlan, Edward G, (Newark Valley,) S. D 2, blacksmith and coal dealer

OAKS, JEROME, (Ketchumville,) farmer 95.

Pake, John, (West Newark,) joint S. D. 12, produce commission agent

Parker, Alonzo, (Ketchumville,) farmer 100.

Patrick, Leroy, (Maine, Broome Co,) S D 8, farmer leases 129

Patridge, Jane Mrs.,(Jenksville,) joint S. D. 12, farmer 4.

Patterson, Alfred, (Newark Valley,) S. D 2, farmer 102.

PATTERSON, D. WILLIAMS, (Newark Valley,) S. D. 2, dentist by profession, farmer and genealogist by practice, farmer 50

Payne, Anson W, (Maine, Broome Co.,) S. D. 9, prop. Payne's patent hook and swivel, combined evener, mechanic and farmer 90.

Pellett, George, (Jenksville,) joint S D. 5, cooper and farmer 22

Pellett, Wm M, (Newark Valley,) joint S. D 12, farmer 83

PERRY, CEPHAS, (Ketchumville,) farmer 33¾.

Perry, Nathan L., (Ketchumville,) farmer leases of Erastus Town, 100

Phelps, Jason, (Newark Valley,) S. D. 2, retired farmer 3.

Pierson Wm., (Newark Valley,) S D 4, farmer 70

Pitcher, David, (Newark Valley,) S D. 5, farmer 180

Pitcher, Eli, (Maine, Broome Co,) S D 9, farmer 72.

Pitcher, Harrison, (Newark Valley,) S. D. 7, farmer 116

Pitcher, John W, (Ketchumville,) farmer leases of C. H. Dean, 130.

Pitcher, Silas, (Maine, Broome Co.,) S.XD 9, farmer 90

Prentice, Sarah Mrs.,(Newark Valley,) joint S D 11, farmer 200.

Prentice, Wm F., (Newark Valley,) S. D. 3, farmer 109

Prentice, Wm G., (Newark Valley,) S. D. 1, farmer leases 176.

Pumpelly, Chas F, (Ketchumville,) farmer, agent for Geo J

Race, Wheaton, (Newark Valley,) S.D. 2, retired farmer

Randall, Oscar S., (Newark Valley,) S D. 4, farmer 200

Reed, Timothy C., (West Newark,) joint S. D. 12, farmer 110.

Rees, Sarah J Mrs , (West Newark,) joint S. D 12, farmer 1

Reeves, John, (Newark Valley,) joint S. D. 12, farmer 75.

Reeves, Wm J , (Newark Valley,) S. D. 3, farmer 85 and leases 75.

Rewey Elbridge, (Newark Valley,) S. D. 2, farmer 132.

REWEY, OLIVER, (Newark Valley,) S D. 2, blacksmith and farmer 7

Rich, Geo E., (Newark Valley,) S D.1, farmer 220

Richardson, Fred W , (Newark Valley,) S D 3, farmer 200

Richardson, Herbert, (West Newark,) joint S D 12, post master and farmer 200

RILEY, ANDREW B , (Ketchumville,) carpenter and joiner, and agent for Eureka Churn

Riley, Wm ,(Ketchumville,) blacksmith and farmer 25

Robbins, Harlow, (Newark Valley,) S. D. 3, farmer 218

Robinson, Thos. A., (Newark Valley,) S D. 2, resident.

Rogers, Elias H , (Newark Valley,) S.D 2, wood worker

Rogers, Washington, (Newark Valley,) S. D 1, machinist and farmer leases 100

Ross John, (Maine, Broome Co.,) S. D. 5, farmer 95.

ROULET, ALFRED, (Newark Valley,) S D 2 watchmaker and farmer 185

Roulet, Felix, (Newark Valley,) S D 10, agent for agricultural implements and farmer leases of Alfred, 140.

Roys, Alpheus D , (Newark Valley,) S D 2, tree agent and farmer 90

Russell, Henry, (Maine, Broome Co ,) S. D. 13, farmer 100.

Russell, J Goldsmith,(Maine, Broome Co.,) S D. 13, shingle weaver

Russell, Whiting, (Newark Valley,) resident.

Saddlemire, Adam, (Newark Valley,) S. D. 7, farmer 66

Saddlemire, Alex., (Newark Valley,) S. D. 7, farmer 88

Saddlemire, Daniel J , (Newark Valley,) S. D. 7, carpenter and farmer 25.

Saddlemire, David, (Newark Valley,) S. D. 7, farmer 75

Saddlemire, Elias, (Newark Valley,) S D. 18 farmer 204.

Saddlemire, Ephraim,(Maine, Broome Co.,) S D. 9, farmer 61

Saddlemire, Frederick, (Newark Valley,) S. D. 13, saw mill and farmer 125

Saddlemire, Jacob, (Newark Valley,) S. D. 5, farmer 109

Saddlemire, Jacob H., (Newark Valley,) S D 10, farmer 78.

Saddlemire, Joseph, (Newark Valley,) S. D 13, farmer 111

SADDLEMIRE, NOYES P., (Newark Valley,) S D. 7, farmer 88

Saddlemire, Peter, (Newark Valley,) S D. 7 farmer 100.

Schoolcraft, Adam, (Maine, Broome Co.,) S D 9, farmer 99

Schoolcraft, J Henry, (Newark Valley,) S D 13 farmer 60 and leases 40

Schoolcraft, Lawrence, (Newark Valley,) S D. 13, mechanic and farmer 40.

SCHOOLCRAFT, MINER, (Newark Valley,) S. D 13, farmer occupies land of Lawrence

Schoolcraft, Paul, (Newark Valley,) S. D. 7, farmer 19

Schoolcraft, Perry, (Newark Valley,) S D 4, laborer.

Searles, Ezra, (Newark Valley,) farmer 50.

Sears, Heart B., (Newark Valley,) S D 2, town collector and tailor

Sears, Martin N , (Newark Valley,) S D 2, upholsterer and carpenter

SETTLE, DAVID, (Newark Valley,) S D 7, farmer 272.

Settle, Geo. B., (Newark Valley,) farmer leases of David, 86

Settle, Ira, (Newark Valley,) S. D 7, farmer leases 175

Settle, John, (Newark Valley,) S D. 7, farmer 200.

SETTLE, JOHN W., (Newark Valley,) S. D. 7, farmer 86

Settle, Peter, (Newark Valley,) S. D. 7, farmer 256

Shaffer, Simon, (Newark Valley,) S. D. 10, farmer 181

Sharp, Peter, (Ketchumville,) carpenter and farmer 2

Sharp, Robert G , (Ketchumville,) blacksmith, wagon maker and farmer 40.

Shear, David J , (Newark Valley,) S. D. 7, farmer leases 66

Shear, John I , (Newark Valley,) S D 7, carpenter and farmer 66

Sheldon, Harley G , (Newark Valley,) S. D. 4, assessor and farmer 74½

Sherman, Hiram L., (Ketchumville,) mechanic and agent for Eureka Churn

Sherwood, Warren D , (Newark Valley,) S. D 2, boots and shoes.

Shoultes, Geo J., (Newark Valley,) S. D. 13, farmer 64½

Shoultes, Ira, (Newark Valley,) S. D. 13, farmer 175.

Shoultes, Ira A., (Maine, Broome Co.,) S. D 8, farmer 40.

Shoultes, Wm H, (Newark Valley,) S D. 7, farmer 75

Simmons, Joseph, (Newark Valley,) S D. 2, farmer 1½

Slosson, Geo W., (Newark Valley,) S. D. 2, station agent S. C R R

SMITH, ALFRED, (Jenksville,) joint S D 5, miller, carpenter and farmer leases of D. L. Jenks, 40.

Smith, Edwin F , (Newark Valley,) S. D. 4, farmer 75

Smith, Harvey B , (Newark Valley,) S D. 4, farmer 20 and leases of Mrs. Sally Smith, 24

Smith, Jeanette Mrs , (Newark Valley,) S D 1 farmer 93 and occupies 100

Smith, Joel, (Newark Valley,) S D 4, farmer 12

Smith, John E , (Newark Valley,) S. D. 1, farmer 100.

Smith, Randolph L., (Newark Valley,) S D 1, farmer 67

SMITH, WM H , (Newark Valley,) S D 4, carpenter and joiner, and farmer 45

Snapp, George, (Newark Valley,) S D 13, farmer 150

Snapp, Jacob Jr , (Newark Valley,) S D 13, farmer 25.

SPAFFORD, RUSSEL H. REV , (Newark Valley,) S D 2, pastor Baptist Church

Spaulding, Julius H , (Newark Valley,) S D 2, police constable and farmer 1.

Spaulding, Lucius W , (Newark Valley,) (M & L Spaulding )

Spaulding, Luther J , (Newark Valley,) S D 1, farmer 140

Spaulding, Marcus F , (Newark Valley,) (M & L Spaulding )

Spaulding, M & L , (Newark Valley,) (Marcus S and Lucius W.,) S. D. 1, farmers 300

Sprague, Henry A , (Newark Valley,) S D 3, farmer 111

Stanard, Albert & Sons, (Newark Valley,) (John M and Aretus R ,) S. D. 10, farmers 104

Stanard, Aretus R , (Newark Valley,) (Albert Stanard & Sons )

Stanard, Henry C , (Newark Valley,) S D 10, farmer 100.

Stanard, John M , (Newark Valley,) (Albert Stanard & Sons,) S. D. 10, agent for Stanard's machine for turning log on a carriage

Stanton, Abel, (Weltonville,) joint S. D. 26, farmer 50

Stevens, Allen C , (Newark Valley,) S D 2, mechanic

Straight, Joseph, (Newark Valley,) S. D 4, teamster

Strong, B J , (Jenksville,) joint S. D. 6, cheese maker.

Sturtevant, David M,, (Newark Valley,) S D 2, grist mill and farmer 32.

SUTTON, GEO B , (Newark Valley,) S D 2, artist and farmer 80

Sykes, Edward F., (Newark Valley,) S D. 4, farmer 129

Tappan, Asher C , (Newark Valley,) S D 2, farmer 84.

Tappan, John C , (Newark Valley,) S D 2, physician and farmer 220.

TAPPAN, RILEY A., (Newark Valley,) S D 2, farmer 150

TIBBITTS, ELI D , (Newark Valley,) S D 13, farmer 82

Todd, Elizabeth Mrs., (Newark Valley,) joint S. D. 11, farmer 50

Tracy Jonathan, (Newark Valley,) S D 2, retired farmer 1½

Tubbs, Moses N , (Newark Valley,) S. D. 3, photographer and farmer leasee of Henry F Jayne, 50.

Tulloch, James A., (Union Center, Broome Co ,) S D 13, farmer leasea of John Lambart, cider mill and 50

TURNER, HENRY , (Maine, Broome Co ,) S D 8, farmer 270.

Turner, Russel, (Maine, Broome Co ,) S. D 8. farmer 115

Vandemark, John, (Weltonville,) joint S. D 26, farmer 37

Wade, Wm H , (Newark Valley,) S D. 1, farmer 86.

Waldo, Dwight, (Berkshire,) S D 4, farmer 124

Walworth, Clark, (Newark Valley,) S D 3, farmer 135

Walworth Lorenzo D , (Newark Valley,) S D 3. farmer 98

Waring, Norman K., (Newark Valley,) S D. 2, prop. Newark Valley Trout Ponds and Pic Nic Grounds

WATKINS, ALBION H , (West Newark,) joint S D 12, painter and farmer leases 200

Watkins, Foster W., (West Newark,) (Wm. Watkins & Son )

Watkins, Wm & Son, (West Newark,) (Foster W.) joint S D 12, farmer 123

Watson, Samuel S , (Newark Valley,) S. D. 2, farmer 476.

Wells, Frederick T , estate of, (Newark Valley,) S D 2, (Henry L., Lucius E and Wm F. Wells ) 118 acres

Wells, Henry L , (Newark Valley,) S D 2, (with Lucius E. and Wm. F.,) Wells estate.

Wells, Lucius E , (Newark Valley,) S D. 2, (with Henry L and Wm. F ,) Wells estate

Wells, Wm F., (Newark Valley,) S. D 2, (with Lucius E and Henry L.,) Wells estate

Westfall, Joseph F , (Newark Valley,) S D. 4, farmer 90.

Westfall, Walter, (Newark Valley,) S D. 13, farmer 20.

Whitmore, Horace L., (Newark Valley,) S. D 2, supt lumber yard

WILLIAMS, CHAS H , (Maine, Broome Co ,) S D 8, prop threshing machine, agent for Young Warrior Mower and farmer 52

WILLIAMS, LUCIUS E., (Newark Valley,) (Moore, Cargill & Co,) farmer 4

Williams, Oliver G , (Newark Valley,) S. D 2, farmer 125

Williams, Royal R., (Newark Valley,) (R R & W B Williams )

Williams, R R & W B , (Newark Valley,) (Royal R and Wright B.,) S D 2, farmers 85

Williams, Theodore, (Newark Valley,) S D 2, carpenter

Williams, Wm. T., (Newark Valley,) S. D. 2, saw mill and farmer 120

Williams, Wright B , (Newark Valley,) (R R & W B Williams.)

Willis, Horace P , (Maine, Broome Co ,) S. D 9, farmer 16.

Winship, Chas B , (Newark Valley,) S. D. 2, blacksmith

Winship, Henry, (Newark Valley,) S D 2, blacksmith

Woodward, Allen R., (Ketchumville,) (Elias H Woodward & Son )

Woodward, Ellas H. & Son. (Ketcham-ville,) (*Allen E.,*) farmers 201.

Young, Edward W., (Newark Valley,) S. D. 2, carpenter.

YOUNG, HIRAM, (Newark Valley,) (*Dimmick & Young*)

Young, Hiram S., (Newark Valley,) joint S. D. 11, carpenter and farmer leases 200.

Youngs, John H., (Union Center, Broome Co.,) shingle weaver and farmer 96.

Zimmer, Almon, (Newark Valley,) S. D. 2, carpenter.

Zimmer, Anthony M., (Newark Valley,) S. D. 2, farmer 91.

Zimmer, Chas., (Newark Valley,) S. D. 7, farmer 142.

Zimmer, Daniel H., (Newark Valley,) S. D. 13, farmer 60.

Zimmer, Elias, (Newark Valley,) S. D. 13, farmer 270.

Zimmer, Harrison, (Maine, Broome Co.,) (*Amos K. Mattison, Son & Co.,*) (*Mattison & Zimmer.*)

Zimmer, Henry, (Newark Valley,) S. D. 13, farmer 107.

Zimmer, Henry S., (Newark Valley,) S. D. 2, farmer leases of Elias, 75.

Zimmer, Jacob, (Newark Valley,) S. D. 7, farmer 26.

ZIMMER, JOHN E., (Newark Valley,) S. D. 7, shingle weaver and farmer 50.

Zimmer, John J., (Newark Valley,) S. D. 7, farmer 44.

Zimmer, John M., (Newark Valley,) S. D. 13, farmer leases 107.

ZIMMER, MINER S., (Newark Valley,) S. D. 13, shingle maker and farmer 54.

Zimmer, Nathaniel, (Maine, Broome Co.,) S. D. 9, shingle weaver and farmer 90.

Zimmer, Paul, (Newark Valley,) S. D. 7, shingle weaver and farmer 1.

Zimmer, Peter B., (Newark Valley,) S. D. 7, farmer 150.

Zimmer, Ransom J., (Newark Valley,) S. D. 7, farmer 90.

---

# NICHOLS.

## (Post Office Addresses in Parentheses.)

ABBREVIATIONS.—S. D., School District.

Adams, Absalom, (Hooper's Valley,) S. D. 7, farmer 140.

AMERICAN HOTEL, (Nichols,) Frederick A. Jakway, prop., corner Wappasening and River.

ANNABLE, JARVIS B., (East Nichols,) (*with John B.,*) S. D. 5, farmer 75.

ANNABLE, JOHN B., (East Nichols,) (*with Jarvis B.,*) S. D. 5, farmer 75.

Armstrong, Jeremiah, (Nichols,) S. D. 3, farmer 55.

Arnold, Andrew, (Hooper's Valley,) S. D. 1, farmer 70.

Atwood, Ira, (Nichols,) farmer, River.

BABCOCK, ISAAC, (Nichols,) S. D. 2, carpenter and joiner, and cabinet maker.

BARR, JOHN, (Hooper's Valley,) S. D. 12, farmer 127.

BARSTOW, MARY L., (Nichols,) farmer 5, River.

BARSTOW, OLIVER A., (Nichols,) S. D. 1, supervisor, justice of the peace and farmer 60.

Bartlett, Lyman H., (Nichols,) tobacco raiser and farmer leases of S. Horton, 8, River.

BENNETT, ABRAHAM, (Hooper's Valley,) S. D. 12, farmer 30.

Bennett, Elijah, (Hooper's Valley,) S. D. 10, farmer 125.

Bixby, Schuyler, (Nichols,) (*with Joseph Reynolds,*) S. D. 11, farmer.

Bliven, C. V. S., (Nichols,) wagon maker and farmer 5, River.

Blossom, Benj., (Owego,) S. D. 8, farmer leases of Mrs. Thos. Barton, 15.

Bonham, Jonas H., (Nichols,) shoe maker, Wappasening.

BRADLEY, MARCUS, (Nichols,) S. D. 1, farmer.

Briggs, Brightman Jr., (East Nichols,) S. D. 5, farmer 61.

Briggs, David, (Nichols,) S. D. 11, farmer 97.

Briggs, Ebenezer, (East Nichols,) S. D. 5, farmer 106.

Briggs, Edward W., (East Nichols,) S. D. 5, farmer 91.

Briggs, Elihu S., (East Nichols,) S. D. 5, farmer 71.

Briggs, Herman J., (Nichols,) S. D. 2, farmer 50.

BRIGGS, IRA, (Nichols,) S. D. 5, farmer 73.

BRIGGS, MILO A., (East Nichols,) S. D. 5, farmer leases 116.

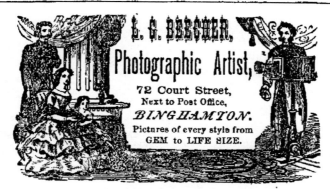

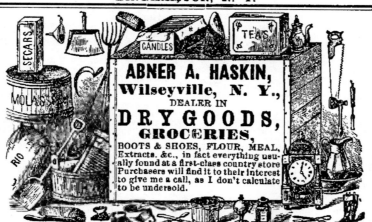

Briggs, Oliver C., (East Nichols,) S D. 5, farmer 110

Brink, Leonard M., (Nichols,) S. D. 1, dairyman and farmer.

Brown, Fanny Mrs., (Nichols,) S. D 6, farmer 2

Brown, James M., (Nichols,) S D. 6, carpenter

BROWN, PETER, (Hooper's Valley,) S D 12, farmer 120.

BROWN, SELAR O., (Hooper's Valley,) S. D 12, farmer

Buttolph, LeRoy, (Nichols,) S. D. 11, farmer 96

CADY, GEORGE M , (Nichols,) (*G M & G P Cady* )

CADY, G M. & G P., (Nichols,) (*George M and George P*,) physicians, surgeons and druggists, Wappasening

CADY, GEORGE P., (Nichols,) (*G M & G. P. Cady*,) coroner, River

CADY, HENRY, (Nichols,) postmaster and agent for G M & G. P. Cady, druggists, Wappasening.

Campbell, David S., (Owego,) S. D. 9, cooper and farmer.

Campbell, Robert S., (Nichols,) S. D. 11, farmer 31.

Catlin, Nathaniel R., (Owego,) S. D 8, shoemaker

CHUBBUCK, AARON, (Hooper's Valley,) S D. 1, farmer 90.

CLAPP, SAMUEL, (Nichols,) farmer 60, River

Coburn, Eliza Mrs , (Nichols,) farmer 26, River

Coffin, German L , (Owego,) S D 3, farmer 87.

Cole, Horace, (Hooper's Valley,) S D 10, farmer.

Cole, Truman, (Nichols,) S D 10, farmer 128

Coleman, Coe, (Nichols,) groceries and crockery, Wappasening

COMFORT, GEORGE Rev., (Nichols,) pastor of M. E. Church, Wappasening

Conaut, Luther, (Nichols,) boots and shoes

CORYELL, EMANUEL, (Hooper's Valley,) S D 7, postmaster and farmer 65

CORYELL, FREDERICK C., (Hooper's Valley,) S D. 7, dairyman, stock raiser and farmer 330, Riverside Farm.

CORYELL, HENRY P , (Hooper's Valley,) S D 7, dairyman and farmer 230

Dalrymple, Mary M , (Nichols,) tailoress, Wappasening

DEAN, NATHAN S., (Hooper's Valley,) S. D 1, town assessor, tobacco raiser and farmer 40

Densmore, Hiram, (Owego,) S D 8, stock dealer and farmer 50

Deosmore, John L., (Owego,) S. D. 8, (*with Hiram*,) farmer

Deuel, George W., (East Nichols,) S. D. 5, farmer

DEVENPORT, ABRAHAM N , (Hooper's Valley,) S. D 12, farmer 25

Devenport, George, (Hooper's Valley,) S D 12, farmer 100

DEVENPORT, JOEL, (Nichols,) grist and saw mills, and lumber dealer

Doty, William A., (Hooper's Valley,) S D. 10, farmer leases of Mrs G. H Vandemark, 35

V

Douglass, Charles, (Owego,) S D 8, farmer.

Dunham, Albert W , (Hooper's Valley,) S D. 1, (*w'th Eben*,) farmer 270

Dunham, Anson, (Owego,) S. D. 9, farmer 100.

Dunham, Benjamin, (Nichols,) S. D. 9, carpenter and farmer 76

Dunham, Dailey J , (Nichols,) S D 2, farmer 140.

DUNHAM, EBEN, (Nichols,) (*Dunham & Latham*,) insurance agent, (*with Wright*,) farmer 200 and (*with Mrs. Wm B* ,) 270.

Dunham, Harvey W , (Nichols,) S D 2, farmer 122.

DUNHAM, ISAAC, (Nichols,) farmer 144 and leases 132, River

Dunham, James D , (Nichols,) farmer 5, River.

Dunham, John, (East Nichols,) S. D. 3, Owego, farmer 95.

DUNHAM & LATHAM, (Nichols,) (*Eben Dunham and Sidney B Latham*,) dry goods, groceries, grain, flour, feed &c., Wappasening

Dunham, Nehemiah, (Owego,) S. D. 9, farmer 50

Dunham, Norman C., (Nichols,) S. D. 6, farmer 50

Dunham, Platt, (Owego,) S D 9, farmer 248

Dunham, Samuel, (Owego,) S. D. 9, farmer 4

Dunham, Samuel, (Nichols,) S. D. 6, farmer 75.

DUNHAM, STEPHEN H., (Nichols,) (*Willson & Dunham*.)

Dunham, William H., (Nichols,) farmer 100, River.

Dunham, Wright, (Nichols,) S D. 6, grist and saw mills, and farmer 120

EDSALL, DAVID, (Hooper's Valley,) apprentice at wagon making

EDSALL, JOHN R , (Hooper's Valley,) S. D. 7, wagon maker and blacksmith, River Road

Edwards, Birt, (Hooper's Valley,) S. D. 7, farmer leases.

Ellis, George, (Hooper's Valley,) S. D. 12, farmer 50

Ellis, George, (Hooper's Valley,) S. D. 7, carpenter.

Ellis, Jesse, (Hooper's Valley,) S. D 12, farmer 33

Ellis, John, (Hooper's Valley,) S D. 7, farmer, River Road.

Ellsworth, Francis H , (Nichols,) carpenter and farmer 90, River Road.

Evans, Chas , (Owego,) S. D. 3, farmer 48.

Evans, Cyrus, (Owego,) S D. 3, farmer 123

Evans, Stephen W , (Owego,) S. D 3, farmer 53.

Evans Ziba Rev , (Owego,) S. D 8, farmer 75

EVERETT, FREDERICK M., (Nichols,) tinman, Wappasening

EVERITT, ELMER, (Nichols,) farmer 1.

EVERITT, HARVEY C., (Nichols ) farmer 85, Wappasening

EVERITTE, JOHN, M D , (Nichols,) retired physician and farmer 85

Farnham, Edwin M , (Nichols,) S D 6, carpenter.

Farnham, Oscar E., (Nichols,) S D 6, wood turning and bracket sawing, prop of cider mill

Ferris, Horace, (Owego,) S. D 4, farmer 50

Fisher, William D , (Nichols,) S D 10, farmer 75.

FORMAN, JOHN, (Nichols,) S D 2, dairyman and farmer 200

Forman, Stephen P , (Nichols,) S D 2, farmer 170

Gardner, Frederick J., (Hooper's Valley,) S D. 1, farmer

Gitchell, William, (East Nichols,) S D 5, farmer leases of Jonathan Hunt, 20.

Goodsell, William S , (Hooper's Valley,) S. D 1, farmer 50

Goodsell, Zina, (Hooper's Valley,) S. D. 12, farmer 186

GOULD, JOEL, (Hooper's Valley,) S D 1, farmer

GOULD, JOHN N Jr , (Hooper's Valley,) S. D. 7, farmer.

Hamel, Clark B , (Owego,) S. D. 8, gardener

Hancock, Eliza M. Mrs , (Nichols,) S D 6, school teacher.

Harford, Edward C , (Nichols,) S D 2, farmer 42

HARRIS, NATHANIEL B , (Nichols,) (O P & N B Harris.)

HARRIS, OLIVER P , (Nichols,) (O P & N B Harris,) attorney at law, justice of the peace and notary public, Wappasening

HARRIS, O P & N B , (Nichols,) (Oliver P. and Nathaniel B ,) general merchants and farmers 100, Wappasening.

HERRICK, HANNAH Mrs , (Hooper's Valley,) S. D. 12, farmer 37

Hill, Morris M , (Nichols,) S D 6, farmer

Hilligass, Jacob, (Nichols,) S. D. 6, farmer 4

Horton, Stephen S , (Nichols,) mail contractor, prop. of stage route and farmer 155

Hover, William, (Owego,) S D 8, farmer.

Howell, Arthur M., (Nichols,) S. D. 6, (with Robert,) farmer

HOWELL, JOHN J., (Nichols,) (J L Howell & Son )

HOWELL, JOHN L , (Nichols,) (J. L. Howell & Son,) prop. of saw mill and farmer 294

HOWELL, J. L & SON, (Nichols,) (John L. and John J.,) dry goods, groceries, boots, shoes hats, caps, grain, flour, meal and feed

HOWELL, ROBERT, (Nichols,) S D 6, farmer 155

Hoot, Brown, (Waverly,) (with Samuel,) S D 1, farmer 90

Hunt, Ebenezer, (Nichols,) S D. 3, farmer 60

Hunt, Enos, (Nichols,) S D 3, (with Seth,) farmer.

Hunt, Ezra C , (Owego,) S D 8, farmer 110.

Hunt, Harvey, (Owego,) S. D. 9, farmer 194

Hunt, Jonathan, (Tioga Center,) S. D 3, farmer 400

Hunt, Jonathan Jr., (Owego,) S. D. 9, (with Harvey,) farmer.

Hunt, Samuel, (Waverly,) (with Brown,) S. D 1, farmer 90.

HUNT. SETH Sr , (Nichols,) S D 3, farmer 139.

Hunt, Seth Jr , (Nichols,) (with Seth Sr ,) S D 3, farmer

Hunt, Thos. J , (Owego,) S D 4, farmer 85

Hunt, Williston, (Nichols,) S D 2, farmer 113

HYRES, JERRY W., (Nichols,) cooper, River

JAKWAY, FREDERICK A., (Nichols,) prop of American Hotel and livery, corner Wappasening and River

Johnson, Charles E., (Nichols,) S D 2, farmer 44

Johnson, John E., (Nichols,) S. D. 2, farmer 15

Johnson, Parley Jr., (Nichols,) S D 2, farmer 23

JOHNSON, WILLIAM W , (Hooper's Valley,) S D 7, dairyman and tobacco raiser, River Road

Jones, James, (Nichols,) S. D. 5, farmer 100

JONES, LEWIS, (Nichols,) S D. 5, (with James,) farmer

JONES, PERMELIA, (Nichols,) S D 29, farmer 2.

JOSLIN, ALMIRA T., (Nichols,) milliner, Wappasening.

JOSLIN, HERM T , (Nichols,) sub-insurance agent and constable, office Howell's Block, Wappasening

Keech, Stephen, (Nichols,) S. D. 11, farmer 50

Ketcham, Abijah, (Owego,) S. D. 8, farmer 8

Ketcham, Alexander H., (Nichols,) wagon maker, Wappasening

Ketcham, Eli G , (Owego,) S D. 9, farmer 97

KETCHAM, JONAS S , (Hooper's Valley,) S D. 7, dairyman and farmer leases 4

Ketcham, William, (Nichols,) butcher and dealer in hides, Wappasening

KIRBY, SELIM, (Nichols,) general merchant, dealer in grain of all kinds and farmer 52, Wappasening

Kuykendall, Peter, (Hooper's Valley,) S D 7, farmer 2.

Lamonte, Samuel M , (Owego,) S. D. 3, farmer 82

Lane, Amos, (Owego,) S. D. 4, farmer 175

Lane, David J., (Owego,) S. D 4, farmer

Lane, George S., (Owego,) S. D. 3, farmer 180

Lane, Warren A , (Owego,) S. D. 4, (with Amos,) farmer 175

LATHAM, SIDNEY H., (Nichols,) (Dunham & Latham.)

Lee, Lydia Miss, (Nichols,) dress maker, Wappasening.

Leonard, Chauncey, (Owego,) S. D. 4, farmer 7

Lockwood, Charles, (Hooper's Valley,) S. D 7, farmer 90, River Road.

Lounsberry, Benj , (Owego,) S. D. 3, farmer 138

LOUNSBERRY, CHARLES, (Nichols,) (C Lounsberry & Brother,) S. D. 8, farmer 324

*LOUNSBERRY, C. & BROTHER, (Nichols,) (*Charles and John,*) props of steam, saw and grist mills, manufs and dealers in lumber, lath, shingles and pickets, also in all kinds of grain, flour and feed

Lounsberry, George, (Tioga Center,) S D 3, farmer 50.

Lounsberry, Horace, (Tioga Center,) S. D. 3, farmer 361.

Lounsberry, Horace 2d, (Tioga Center,) S D 3, (*with Horace,*) farmer.

Lounsberry, James, Sen , (Tioga Center,) S D 3, farmer 150.

Lounsberry, James Jr., (Tioga Center,) S. D 3, farmer 113

LOUNSBERRY, JOHN, (Nichols,) (*C. Lounsberry & Brother,*) S. D 8, farmer 160

Lounsberry, Platt, (Tioga Center,) S D 3, farmer 221

Lounsberry, William, (Tioga Center,) S. D. 3, farmer 122

Loveland, Lewis, (Nichols,) S. D. 1, farmer 86

LOWMAN, FREDERICK C., (Hooper's Valley,) S D 7, dairyman and farmer 204, River Road.

Lynch, DeWitt C., (Nichols,) S. D. 2, mason

MALLERY, JOHN L. Rev., (Owego,) S. D 9, local preacher, carpenter and joiner, and farmer 25.

Mallory, Harris, (Owego,) S. D. 4, farmer 68

Manning, Job R., (Hooper's Valley,) S. D. 7, farmer 200, River Road

Marshall, Samuel Major, (Nichols,) S. D. 11, farmer 63.

Marshall, Timothy B., (Nichols,) S. D. 11, farmer 50

MASTIN, ROBERT J., (Nichols,) S D. 10, farmer 12

Matthews, Hiram P., (Nichols,) S D 11, farmer 112

MATTHEWS, STEPHEN P , (Owego,) S D 8, physician and farmer 45.

McDOWELL, McKEAN, (Hooper's Valley,) S. D. 7, farmer 180.

McMaster, Arial Rev., (Nichols,) pastor of Presbyterian Church, Cady Avenue

McNiel, Arthur B., (Owego,) S. D 9, farmer 50

Measer, Ernest H , (Hooper's Valley,) S. D 12, farmer 70

Middaugh, Jacob, (Hooper's Valley,) S. D. 7 farmer

MIKELS, JAMES HENRY, (Nichols,) S. D 2, farmer

Mills, Francis, (Nichols,) (*with Joseph Reynolds,*) S D 11, farmer

Mills, William F , (Nichols,) S. D. 5, assessor and farmer 104.

Mollet, Peter, (Owego,) S. D. 8, farmer 45

Moody, George H., (Hooper's Valley,) S. D 10, farmer 45

Moore, Edwin T., (Owego,) S D 9, farmer 114

Moore, Geo., (Nichols,) S D 11, farmer 151.

Moore, Hezelton N , (Owego,) S D 9, drover and farmer 170

Moore, Nathaniel, (Owego,) S. D 9, farmer 148.

Moore, Richard, (Owego,) S. D. 9, (*with Nathaniel,*) farmer 148

Morey, Robert H , (Nichols,) (*with Wm ,*) S. D. 8, farmer 200

Morey, William, (Nichols,) (*with Robert H ,*) S. D. 6, farmer 200.

Morley, David C , (Nichols,) tailor, Wappassening

Neal, Henry C , (Hooper's Valley,) S. D. 12, farmer 52

NEAL, LOVINUS 2d , (Nichols,) S D 10, farmer 80.

Neal, Nehemiah E , (Nichols,) carpenter, painter and constable, Cady Avenue

Newman, George, (East Nichols,) S D 5, dealer in sheep and cattle, and farmer 232

NICHOLS HOTEL, (Nichols,) Jonathan Platt, prop , River.

Nichols, James A., (East Nichols,) S. D. 3, Owego, farmer 73.

Northrop, Charles T., (East Nichols,) S D 3, Owego, farmer 23

Northrop, Zimri P., (East Nichols,) S. D 3, Owego, farmer 50.

OLMSTED, FREDLAW, (Nichols,) S. D. 6, (*with Joseph,*) farmer

OLMSTEAD, JOSEPH, (Nichols,) S D 5, farmer 151.

Orsburn, Miars, (Hooper's Valley,) S D. 1, farmer 250

Osborn, Henry B., (Nichols,) harness maker, Wappassening.

O'Sullivan, Dennis, (Nichols,) mason, Cady Avenue

Palmer, Lewis, (Hooper's Valley,) S D 1, farmer 200.

Paris, Peter P., (Tioga Center,) (*with Sidney V.,*) S D. 8, farmer.

Paris, Sidney V., (Tioga Center,) (*with Peter P.,*) S D 3, farmer

Parks, Ira J., (Hooper's Valley,) S D 7, deputy post master and miller, River Road

Pearl, Daniel, (Owego,) S. D. 9, farmer 153.

Pearl, Walter H , (Owego,) S. D. 4, farmer 69

PEARSALL, GILBERT, (Hooper's Valley,) (*G. Pearsall & Son,*) S D 7, lumberman.

PEARSALL, G & SON, (Hooper's Valley,) (*Gilbert and Luther B.,*) lumberman and farmers 350

PEARSALL, LUTHER B , (*G. Pearsall & Son,*) S D 7, farmer 350, River Road

Pettis, Joshua, (Nichols,) S. D. 6, farmer 50

Phillips, James H , (Owego,) S D 9, farmer 23.

Pitcher, Harvey, (Owego,) S. D. 8, farmer 112.

Pitcher, Heman, (Owego,) S D 8, farmer 130

Pitcher, Leroy H., (Owego,) S. D 8, (*with Harvey,*) farmer

PLANTS, WILLIAM L , (Nichols,) farmer leases of N B Harris, 100

PLATT, JONATHAN, (Nichols,) prop of Nichols Hotel, River

Plum, Oliver J., (Nichols,) cabinet maker, Howell

Quetschenbesch, Walter B., (Owego,) S D 3, farmer 20

Reed, Ezra, (Owego,) S. D. 4, justice of the peace, carpenter and farmer 25.

# Alexander A. Swinton,
## NICHOLS, N. Y.

DEALER IN

# HARDWARE
# STOVES,
## Tin, Sheet Iron, Copper, Iron, Nails,
### PUMPS,
OF DIFFERENT KINDS

Agent for the Cayuga Chief Mower & Reaper.

Agent for the American Base Burner.

Agent for the American Cook Stove.

Agent for E. M. Bailey Plows.

Twenty years a manufacturer of Tin and Copper Ware. **Peddlers Supplied.**

---

# C. LOUNSBERRY & BRO.,
## PROPRIETORS OF
# STEAM SAW AND GRIST MILLS,
*Two Miles South-East of the Village of*
## NICHOLS, N. Y.,

KEEP CONSTANTLY ON HAND A SUPERIOR STOCK OF

## Lumber, Lath, Shingles, Pickets, &c.,
Which we offer for sale at Wholesale or Retail

## All kinds of Long Timber Sawed to Order.

Also Manufacturers and Dealers in

## Flour, Meal and Feed, and dealers in all kinds of Grain.

P. O. Address,—NICHOLS, N. Y.

CHAS. LOUNSBERRY.                      JOHN LOUNSBERRY.

Reed, George H., (East Nichols,) S. D. 5, farmer 58.
Reynolds, Daniel C., (Nichols,) S. D. 11, farmer.
Reynolds, Geo., (Nichols,) S. D. 11, farmer 31.
Reynolds, Henry, (Hooper's Valley,) S D 12, farmer.
REYNOLDS, JOSEPH, (Nichols,) farmer 136.
REYNOLDS, STEPHEN, (Hooper's Valley,) S D 12, farmer 48.
REYNOLDS, STEPHEN T., (Nichols,) S D. 6, farmer 113
Reynolds, Wm , (Hooper's Valley,) S D. 12, carpenter and farmer 48
Riddell, Frederick, (Hooper's Valley,) S D 12, farmer 34
RIDDELL, HENRY, (Hooper's Valley,) S. D 12, carpenter and joiner, and painter.
Robertson, Albert, (Owego,) (with John White,) S D 3, farmer
ROBINSON, WILLIAM O, (Nichols,) tobacco raiser and farmer 21, River
Rogers, Marshall S, (Nichols,) shoemaker, Wappasening.
Rose, Leonard B , (Nichols,) cabinet maker and undertaker, Wappasening
Russell, Justin A , (East Nichols,) S. D. 3, Owego, farmer 69
Sackett, Daniel B , (Owego,) S. D. 8, carpenter and farmer.
Seymour, Herrick H , (Owego,) S. D 3, farmer 175.
Sharp, Henry, (Hooper's Valley,) S. D. 10, farmer 16
Sharp, Rufus G., (Nichols,) S D 6, miller.
SHERWOOD, JAMES O., (Hooper's Valley,) (with Silas,) S. D 7, farmer 70.
SHERWOOD, SILAS, (Hooper's Valley,) (with James O.,) S D. 7, farmer 70.
Sherwood, Wesley W , (Tioga Center,) S. D. 3, blacksmith and farmer 2.
Shipman, Edmund, (Nichols,) S. D. 10, lumberman and farmer 80.
Shoemaker, Edgar, (Hooper's Valley,) S D 1, commissioner of highways and farmer 97
SHOEMAKER, HIRAM W , (Hooper's Valley,) S D. 1, farmer 320.
SHOEMAKER, HORACE A , (Nichols,) farmer leases of Dewitt C. Olmstead, 8.
Shoemaker, William R., (Nichols,) S. D. 1, farmer 180.
SISK, JOHN, (Nichols,) S. D. 6, blacksmith
Slawson, Phebe Mrs., (Hooper's Valley,) S. D 1, farmer 108.
Smith, Charles H., (Owego,) S. D. 4, farmer 115.
Smith, Harvey R , (Owego,) S. D. 4, musician
Smith, John, (Owego,) S. D 4, farmer 137
Smith, John Jr., (Owego,) S. D. 4, farmer 157.
Smith, Joseph W., (Owego,) S. D 4, farmer 87.
SMITH, OLIVER P , (Hooper's Valley,) S. D. 7, general blacksmith, town poormaster and farmer 1¼, River Road
Smith, Samuel B., (Nichols,) S D. 3, farmer 250.
Smith, Silas H., (Owego,) S. D 4, farmer 26.

Smith, Warren A., (Nichols,) (with Samuel B .) S D 3, farmer 250.
SMITH, WASHINGTON, (Hooper's Valley,) S D. 1, farmer 124
Smith, William H., (Nichols,) S. D. 6, mason.
Stanton, Joshua, (Hooper's Valley,) S D 10, farmer 25.
Stanton, Silas, (Owego,) S D 8, farmer
Steward, Jacob, (Hooper's Valley,) S D 1, farmer 147
Steward, Thaddeus, (Hooper's Valley,) S D 7, farmer 100, River Road.
*SWINTON, ALEX A., (Nichols,) dealer in hardware, stoves, nails, iron, pumps &c., and agent for Cayuga Chief Mower and Reaper. Wappasening.
Tanner, Horace, (Nichols,) S D 2, farmer
Thomas, David B , (Owego,) S D 9, farmer 60.
Thomas, Seymour, (Owego,) S. D. 4, farmer 22
Tripp, Peleg, (East Nichols,) S D 3, Owego, farmer 20.
Vandermark, Casper, (Hooper's Valley,) S D 7, farmer
Vandermark, Frederick, (Hooper's Valley,) S D 7, farmer leases 14, River Road
Vandermark, Josiah, (Hooper's Valley,) S. D 10, farmer 14
Vangarder, Aaron, (Hooper's Valley,) S. D. 12, farmer 80
VanNess, Myron, (Hooper's Valley,) S D 7, farmer 150, River Road
Wait, Jefferson, (East Nichols,) S. D 3, Owego, farmer 73
Walker, Elliot, (Owego,) S. D. 8, farmer 50
Ward, Abraham B , (East Nichols,) S D. 5, farmer 42
Ward, Ezra, (Owego,) S D 8, mason.
Warner, Frederick, (Hooper's Valley,) S D. 10, farmer 2.
Warner, James R , (East Nichols,) S D 3, Owego farmer 1.
WASHBURN, JOHN H , (Hooper's Valley,) S. D. 12, farmer
Washburn, Joshua, (Hooper's Valley,) S. D. 12, farmer
Washburn, Nicholas, (Hooper's Valley,) S. D 12, farmer 136
Waterman, Alonzo C., (Nichols,) farmer 180
Waterman, Benjamin M , (Nichols,) blacksmith, Wappasening.
Waterman, Ethelinda Mrs , (Nichols,) resident, River
*WAYMAN, WILLIAM, (Nichols,) manuf. and dealer in harness, blankets, whips &c., Wappasening, also farmer 1.
WAYMAN, WM MRs , (Nichols,) milliner, Wappasening.
WESTBROOK, LEVI S., (Nichols,) farmer 180.
Whipple, Andrew G , (Owego,) S. D. 8, (with Eben W .) farmer.
Whipple, Eben W., (Owego,) S. D. 8, farmer 212
White, Daniel, (East Nichols,) S. D. 5, farmer 100.
White, Enoch, (East Nichols,) S D 5, postmaster and farmer 50.
White, Ferdinand P., (Owego,) S D. 9, farmer 1.

White, George, (East Nichols,) S. D. 5, farmer 60

White, Henry, (East Nichols,) S. D. 5, farmer 168.

White, John, (Owego,) S D 3, farmer 70

WHITE, JOHN LAWRENCE, (Owego,) S D 9, constable, collector and farmer 47.

White, Joseph, (Owego,) S D 8, farmer 88

White, Joseph W , (East Nichols,) S. D 3, Owego, farmer 171.

White, Leonard, (East Nichols,) S D. 5, farmer 71

WHITE, WELLINGTON, (East Nichols,) S D. 5, (*with Henry*,) farmer.

WHITE, WILLIAM, (East Nichols,) S D 5, farmer 140

WHITE, WILLIAM W., (Owego,) S. D. 8, farmer 86

WIGGINS, ABSALOM J , (Nichols,) shoemaker, Wappasening

WIGGINS, GEORGE F , (Hooper's Valley,) S D 10, carpenter and joiner, and farmer 25.

Wiggins, Silas, (Nichols,) shoemaker, Wappasening

Willbor, Jonathan, (East Nichols,) S D 3, Owego, farmer 62

Willbur, Weston, (East Nichols,) S D. 3, Owego, (*with Jonathan*,) farmer

Williams, Stephen E , (Nichols,) mason, Cady Avenue.

WILLSON, CHARLES H , (Nichols,) (*Willson & Dunham*,) town clerk.

WILLSON & DUNHAM, (Nichols,) (*Chas. H Willson and Stephen H. Dunham*,) dry goods, groceries, flour, feed &c , Wappasening

Wood, Albert, (Nichols,) farmer 80, River Road.

Wood, N Allen, (East Nichols,) S D. 5, farmer

Wright, Ward S , (Nichols,) tobacco raiser and (*with Lewis Loviland*,) farmer 91, River.

---

# OWEGO.

(Post Office Addresses in Parentheses.)

ABBREVIATIONS—S. D., School District.

Abbott, John, (Owego,) S D 25, farmer leases of Warren Reeves, 17

Adrience, Albert, (Union, Broome Co ,) S D 5, farmer 50

*AHWAGA CHIEF, (Owego,) Main, Horace A Brooks, editor and prop

AHWAGA HALL, (Owego,) Geo W Fay, prop

Ahwaga Lodge, No 587, F. & A M., (Owego,) 19 Lake, meets every Tuesday evening.

Aldrich, Aaron, (Apalachin,) S D 18, farmer 26.

Aldrich, Frederick, (Apalachin,) S D. 18, farmer 254

Aldrich, Olney, (Owego,) S D 18, farmer 50

Aleport, Nathaniel, (Apalachin,) S. D. 29, farmer 104.

Allen, Alexander P., (Owego,) S. D 37, farmer 100.

Allen, Reuben, (Flemingville,) S. D. 23, farmer 23

Allen, R. Mrs , (Owego,) dressmaker, North Avenue

Allen, Sarah M. Mrs., (Owego,) S. D. 8, farmer 113.

Andraws, Geo. C. Rev., (Campville,) pastor M E Church

Annevelle, Chas , (Owego,) S. D 25, farmer 46.

Anson Amos, (Owego ) S. D. 3b, farmer 45

ARCHIBALD, ALMEN W , (Owego,) S D. 39, prop saw mill, manuf and dealer in lumber, and farmer 160

ARCHIBALD, SAMUEL, (Owego,) prop. Owego Upper Leather Tannery, manuf. and dealer in boots and shoes, and farmer 143, south of River Bridge

Armstrong, A Theron, (Owego,) homeo. physician, 6 Park

Ayer, Isaac, (Apalachin,) S D 15, shoemaker and farmer 45.

Ayer, Warren, (Apalachin,) S. D 13, farmer 125

Ayer, Warren L , (Owego,) physician, 33 Main

Ayers, Henry, (Owego,) conductor Erie R. R , Main.

Babcock, J. B. G , (Owego,) (*Babcock & Pitcher*,) (*with Wm D* ,) farmer, in Pennsylvania, 275.

Babcock & Pitcher, (Owego,) (*J B G Babcock and Daniel M. Pitcher*,) wool, pelts and hides, Front

Babcock, Zach , (Owego,) baggage master S. C R R

Bacon, Cornelius G., (Apalachin,) S. D. 19, farmer leases 21
Bacon, Nathan, (Apalachin,) insurance agent and farmer 21
Bailey, Alex , (Owego,) tanner, Fifth Avenue
Bailey, James, (Owego,) S. D. 37, farmer 60
BAILEY, THOMAS, (Owego,) S. D 37, farmer 84
Bailey, William, (Owego,) S D. 37, farmer 130
Bakeman, Abram, (Campville,) (*with Jacob,*) S D 7, farmer 40
Bakeman, David, (Flamingaville,) S. D. 11, farmer 23
Bakeman, Isaac, (Campville,) S. D. 7, farmer
Bakeman, Jacob, (Campville,) S D. 7, farmer 40
Bakeman, Philip I, (Owego,) S. D 30, farmer 75
Baker, E. V , (Flemingaville,) S D 11, farmer 50
Baker, Frank M., (Owego,) station agent, S. C R R
Baker, James R , (Owego,) farmer 104, North Avenue.
Baker, John G , (Flemingaville,) S. D. 23, farmer 90
BAKER, ROMEO W., (Owego,) (*S. S. Truman & Baker*)
BALL HIRAM S REV., (Apalachin,) S. D 36, pastor First F W. Church of Owego
Ball, M B Mrs , (Owego,) agent for Dalton's Knitting Machine, Spruce.
Ballou, Andrew J., (Campville,) S D 17, carpenter.
Ballou, H., (Owego,) S D. 15, farmer 50.
BALLOU, STEPHEN, (Campville,) S D. 17, basket maker and farmer 10
Bandler, Robert, (Owego,) clothing and gents' furnishing goods, 28 Lake.
Barden, Ebenezer, (Owego,) S D. 18, farmer 40
Barker, Chauncey, (Apalachin,) S D. 31, farmer leases of Aaron Steele, 212.
Barker, Jacob, (Apalachin,) S D.31, farmer 40.
Barner, Amariah, (Owego,) S. D. 19, farmer 28
Barnes, Reed A , (Owego,) S D 36, farmer 75
Barney, Allen, (Apalachin,) S D. 34, farmer 7.
Barney, Fred , (Gaskill's Corners,) S D 20, blacksmith
Barney, Ransom, (Apalachin,) S. D 19, farmer 34
Barry, John & Co., (Owego,) carriage makers, North Avenue.
Barton, Albert, (Apalachin,) (*A Barton & Son,*) farmer 11.
Barton, A & Son, (Apalachin,) (*Albert and Chas L.,*) S. D 34, dealers in live stock and country produce.
Barton, Chas. L., (Apalachin,) (*A. Barton & Son,*)
Barton, E Mrs , (Owego,) S. D. 26, prop. of Lamont ferry boats.
*BARTON, GEO. W., (Owego,) cigar manuf., 23 Main.

Barton, Isaac, (Apalachin,) S. D 29, farmer 104.
Barton, Mary E., (widow) (Apalachin,) fruit grower and farmer 2¾.
Barton, Priscilla, (widow,) (Apalachin,) (*with John S Giles,*) S D 34, farmer 81.
BARTON, RENSSELAER, (Owego,) S D. 26, runs ferry boats at Lamont Ferry
Barton, Robert Mrs., (Apalachin,) S. D 22, farmer 2½.
Barton, Smith Jr., (Apalachin,) S D 29, farmer 62
BARTON, SMITH G , (Apalachin,) S. D 15, school teacher and fruit grower
Barton, Thos W , (Apalachin,) S D 34, justice of the peace and farmer 11
Bateman, Jacob, (Union, Broome Co.,) S D. 5, farmer 84.
Bates, E H Miss, (Owego,) allo. physician and agent for Mutual Life Insurance Co , 11 Park
BATES GILFORD, (Apalachin,) S. D. 31, farmer 40
Bates, James, (Owego,) carpenter and farmer 4, Main.
BATES, WM R., M D., (Owego,) allo physician, 1st door south of Congregational Church, 11 Park. This property for sale
Bauder, G M., (Owego,) S.D. 2, shoemaker
Beach, Darius, (Owego,) groceries and cordage, 24 North Avenue.
BEACH, GEO W., (Apalachin,) physician and surgeon, and dealer in drugs, medicines, paints, oils &c., Main.
Beach, Nathan, (Owego,) S D 32, farmer 37
BEACH, WILLIAM A., (Gaskill's Corners,) S D 20, supt of Gaskill's Corners Cheese Factory and farmer 86.
Beaman, Warren, (Little Meadows, Susquehanna Co., Pa ,) S D 38, farmer 1.
BEAN, HENRY L , (Owego,) justice of the peace, insurance and claim agent, Front.
Beardslee, Wm L., (South Owego,) S D 16, farmer 115
Becker, Chas. E , (Owego,) (*with Fayette A and Jacob,*) S D 30, farmer 257
Becker, Fayette A., (Owego,) (*with Jacob and Chas. E ,*) S D 30, farmer 257
Becker, Jacob, (Owego,) S D 30, (*with Fayette A and Charles E ,*) farmer 257.
BEEBE, HIRAM A., (Owego,) (*Beebe & Kingman*)
*BEEBE & KINGMAN, (Owego,) (*Hiram A Beebe and Leroy W. Kingman,*) editors and props. *Owego Gazette*, 30 Lake
BEEBE, REUBEN, (Apalachin,) S D 36, farmer 119
Beecher, Isaac S., (Owego,) S D. 37, farmer 71½
Beers, Chas , (Owego ) agent for L. Green Plow, 41 East Main.
Beers, Chas M , (Owego,) S. D 17, carpenter and farmer 35
Beers, Chas. Mrs , (Owego,) millinery, 41 E Main.
Beers, Frank J., (Owego ) grocery and eating saloon, corner North Avenue and Depot.
Beers, John J.,*(Owego,) S. D 8, farmer 112.

BELKNAP, JOHN J., (Campville,) (*Truman & Belknap,*) farmer 120

Benedict, Henry B., (Owego,) clothing, corner Main and Lake.

Benjamin, Albert, (Owego,) S D 25, farmer 55

Benjamin, James, (Owego,) S D 25, farmer 90

Benjamin, James U., (Owego,) S. D 25, dairy and farmer 165

Benner, Philip, (Apalachin,) blacksmith.

Benton, George F., (Owego,) variety store, 41 Lake

Benton, John B, (Owego,) physician and owns 200 acres in Tioga, 41 Lake

Bergin, Deming & Co, (Owego,) (*Michael Bergin, Horace R. Deming and John Jones,*) wholesale and retail grocers, north side Front, nearly opposite River Bridge

Bergin, Michael, (Owego,) (*Bergin, Deming & Co.*)

Berry, Franklin, (Owego,) (*Snider & Berry*)

Berry, Joseph, (Owego,) (*Spooner, Carlson & Berry*)

Beat. James, (Owego,) mail agent, S C R R

Bill, Alonzo, (Apalachin,) S D 31, farmer 31.

Billings, Chas Jr, (Little Meadows. Susquehanna Co, Pa.,) S. D. 38, carpenter and builder, and farmer 3

Billings, Chauncey, (Apalachin,) S D 15, farmer

Billings, Clinton, (Apalachin,) S D 31, manuf lumber and farmer 100

Billings, Henry, (Owego,) conductor D L. & W R. R, Chestnut.

Billings, Henry W, (Owego,) (*Billings & VanBunschoten*)

Billings & VanBunschoten, (*Henry W. Billings and Hiram VanBunscholen,*) fish market. 12 North Avenue

Bills, Amriah, (Apalachin,) S. D. 31, farmer 25

Bills, Cynthia, (widow,) (Apalachin,) S. D. 34, farmer 1.

Bills, James H, (Owego,) S. D 25, farmer 100

Bills, Paul, (Apalachin,) S D 34, farmer 5

Bills, Warren A, (Apalachin,) S D 31, farmer 62.

Bishop, Gilbert, (Apalachin,) carpenter

Bixby, Wm Rev, (Owego,) pastor M. E. Church, Chestnut.

Blair, Wm. H., (Owego,) boots and shoes, Court.

BLISS, ANGELINE Mrs, (Owego,) clairvoyant physician, Fifth Avenue

Bliss, Frank, (Owego,) (*Nichols, Bliss & Co*)

Bliss, Francis A, (Owego,) (*Nichols & Bliss.*)

Blow, Francis, (Owego,) S D 3, farmer 70

Blow, Henry, (Owego,) S D. 18, farmer 95.

BODINE, JAMES, (Campville,) S D 7, farmer 42

Bodle, Sarah Mrs., (Owego,) S. D. 32, farmer 96½.

BOOTH, EDWIN A, (Owego,) (*Potter, Booth & Co,*) prest First National Bank of Candor, residence Candor.

Bornt, Frederick, (Owego,) S D 26, farmer 80 and leases of Ann Bornt, 30.

Bornt, Levi, (Campville,) S. D 17, farmer 50 and leases 80

Bornt, Lyman, (Campville,) S. D. 7, farmer

Bornt, Samuel, (Campville,) S D. 7, farmer 65

Bostwick, Curtis, (Owego,) farmer

Bostwick, Joel, (Owego,) S D 25, farmer leases 80

BOSTWICK, MARTIN, (Owego,) S D 27, manuf and dealer in lumber, and farmer 163.

Bostwick, Oliver, (South Owego,) S D 3, farmer 50

Bostwick, Thos M, (Owego,) S. D. 25, farmer 150

Boughton, Sarah A., (Owego,) S. D. 17, farmer 13

Bowen, Cyrus F, (Windham, Bradford Co., Pa.,) S D 3, farmer 100

BOYCE. NICHOLAS, (Apalachin,) S D 28, farmer 110.

Boynton, John, (South Owego,) S D 3, farmer 54.

Bradley, Elisha I., (Owego,) S D. 32, farmer 43

Bradt, Anthony, (Owego,) S D 21, farmer 54.

Bradt, John, (Owego,) S D 21, farmer 105

Bradt, Peter, (Owego,) S. D 21, farmer 86.

Brainard, Polly, (widow,) (South Owego,) S D 22, farmer 60

BRANCH, ANDREW E., (Campville,) S D 33, shoemaker and farmer 8

BRANT BROS, (Owego,) (*Hiram H. and Nelson,*) wholesale liquors, Main.

BRANT, HIRAM H., (Owego,) (*Brant Bros*)

BRANT, NELSON, (Owego,) (*Brant Bros*)

Bredley, Frank, (Owego,) saloon and confectionery, 30 North Avenue

BRIGGS HOUSE, (Owego,) North Avenue, corner South Depot, Samuel R. Briggs, prop

Briggs, James A., (Union Center, Broome Co.,) S. D 15, farmer 64

BRIGGS, SAMUEL R, (Owego,) prop. Briggs House, North Avenue corner South Depot

Brink, John, (Union, Broome Co.,) S. D. 4, farmer 77

BRINK, NELSON, (Owego,) fruit garden, 8 acres, near east end of Main

Brink, Ruth, (Campville,) S D 33, farmer 26

Bristol, Geo. W., (Owego,) (*Bristol Iron Works*)

Bristol Iron Works, (Owego,) (*Wheeler H. Bristol, Chas. F. Johnson Jr, Edwin Ellis and Geo W Bristol,*) corner of Temple and Central Avenue.

Bristol, Wheeler H, (Owego,) (*Bristol Iron Works,*) (*Post, Bristol & Co,*) farmer 100, resides in Tioga.

Bromaden, W., (Flemingsville,) S. D. 11, farmer 33.

*BROOKS, HORACE A., (Owego,) county clerk and editor and prop *Ahwaga Chief,* Main.

Brooks, John, (Owego,) S D 17, farmer 6.

Brooks, Lizzie D, (Owego,) dress maker, 45 Lake.

Broagham, Anthony, (Union Center,) S D 15, farmer 80.

Brougham, Cornelius, (Gaskill's Corners,) S D 13, farmer 38

Brougham, John I., (Union Center, Broome Co.,) S D 15, farmer 53.

Brougham, John, (Flemingsville,) S. D. 11, farmer 140.

Brougham, Lewis, (Flemingsville,) S. D. 11, farmer 35

BROWN, BENJ. W., (Owego,) (*Ross, Brown & Howes*)

Brown, David D., (Little Meadow, Susquehanna Co., Pa.,) S. D. 38, farmer 109.

BROWN, FRANK L., (Apalachin,) general dealer in dry goods, groceries and general merchandise, Apalachin.

Brown, Geo., (Apalachin,) S. D 13, house painter and farmer 50.

Brown, John, (Owego,) hotel and restaurant, Main

Brown, R., (Owego,) dealer in village lots and farmer, North Avenue.

Brown, Royal S., (Apalachin,) S. D. 31, farmer 118.

Brown, Simeon, (Apalachin,) S. D 15, farmer 28.

Brown, Sylvenus, (Owego,) cabinet maker and farmer 38.

Brown, Thomas, (Union, Broome Co.,) S D 5, farmer leases of James Armstrong, 50.

Brown, Wesley, (Owego,) S. D. 6, farmer 100.

Brownell, B. W., (Flemingsville,) S. D. 2, farmer 50

BRUSH, JOHN B., (Owego,) cashier First National Bank and County treasurer.

Buck, Alonzo D., (Owego,) S. D. 26, farmer 47¾.

Buckbee, Ezra S., (Owego,) (*Stone & Buckbee*)

Buffington, Oliver, heirs of, (Owego,) S. D 25, farmers 2

BUFFUM, EDWARD R., (Apalachin,) dealer in dry goods, groceries, boots, shoes &c

Bunza, John, (Owego,) S. D 30, farmer 49.

Bunzey, Charles, (Gaskill's Corners,) S. D. 20, farmer 65.

BURROWS, JAMES, (Owego,) prop. Burrows Rock Brewery, North Avenue.

BURTON, BENJ., (Apalachin,) S. D. 13, farmer 125

Burton, Nathaniel T., (Owego,) baker, North Avenue.

BURTON, OBADIAH B., (South Owego,) S. D. 22, farmer 100 and leases 118.

Burton, Oliver, (South Owego,) S. D. 16, farmer 50

Busteed, John K., (Union, Broome Co.,) S D 7, farmer 44

CABLE, FREDERICK O., (Owego,) (*Davis, Corey & Co*)

Cafferty, Thomas, (Campville,) S D. 33, farmer 65

Caine, Edwin, (Owego,) S. D. 2, carpenter.

Calkins, Charles B., (Owego,) S. D. 32, farmer 90

Cameron, Geo. F., (Owego,) news, confectionery, cigars &c., also notary public, 47 Lake

Cameron, Robert, (Owego,) wholesale and retail grocer and dealer in grain, coal, lime and farm produce, 1 and 2 Park.

Camp, Asa, (Apalachin,) prop. of grist mill and farmer 120.

Camp, Geo. Sidney, (Owego,) attorney, Front

CAMP, HENRY W., (Owego,) iron founder, manuf agricultural implements and Cornell's Prize Corn Sheller, Front

Camp, James F., (Apalachin,) S. D. 35, farmer 140.

Camp, John, (Campville,) S. D. 33, farmer 70

Camp, Oliver, (Campville,) S. D. 33, farmer 92

Camp, Roswell, (Campville,) retired farmer

CAMP, ROSWELL 2D, (Apalachin,) S. D. 35, farmer 94

Camp, Sylvester, (Campville,) S. D. 33, retired farmer 130.

Campbell, Arba & Co., (Owego,) (*Chas.*) sheep skin tannery and dealers in wool

Campbell, Chas., (Owego,) (*Arba Campbell & Co*)

Card, David, (Apalachin,) S D 29, farmer 32

Card, Eliza A., (widow,) (Tracy Creek, Broome Co.,) S D. 29, farmer 24.

Card, Geo. H., (Little Meadows, Susquehanna Co., Pa.,) S D 24, farmer leases of Bullock, 150, and of Reuben Simone, 75

Card, I W., (Flemingsville,) S D 9, engineer

Carlson, Otto M., (Owego,) (*Spooner, Carlson & Berry*)

Carpenter, Joseph S., (Owego,) S. D. 25, dairyman and farmer 134

Carr, Richard J., (Gaskill's Corners,) S D. 20, road commissioner and farmer

Carr, Sarah J., (Gaskill's Corners,) S D. 29, farmer 60

Carroll, James, (Little Meadows, Susquehanna Co., Pa.,) S D 38, farmer 140.

Cart, Peter E., (Owego,) S. D 33, farmer 63.

CARTER, ANDREW, (Owego,) general blacksmith.

Case, Daniel, (Campville,) S D. 33, farmer leases 154.

Case, Hiram, (Campville,) S D. 17, farmer 50.

CASE, PETER, (Campville,) S. D. 21, farmer leases 60

Case, Zenas, (Campville,) S D. 33, farmer 114.

Casterline, Moses J., (Owego,) S. D. 18, farmer leases of Geo. O Kile, 130

Catlin, Frederick H., (Owego,) S. D. 19, farmer leases 80

CATLIN, GEORGE L., (Apalachin,) S D 35, farmer 66

Catlin, Jacob, (Apalachin,) S. D 35, farmer 73

Catlin, Nathaniel, (Apalachin,) S D. 35, farmer 98

Chaffee, Elizabeth, (widow,) (Owego,) S. D. 18, farmer 30.

Chamberlin, Lee N., (Owego,) manuf and jobber in boots and shoes, 19 and 21 Lake, up stairs.

Chandler, E A., (Owego,) carriage painter, Temple opposite Bristol Iron Works.

Chapman, Horace, (Owego,) S D 25, farmer 7.

Chatfield, John R., (Owego,) (*Storrs & Chatfield*)

Chatfield & Jones, (Owego,) (*Thos I Chatfield and Frank L Jones,*) props Cannewana Sheep and Calf Skin Tannery.

CHATFIELD, THOS I, (Owego,) (*Chatfield & Jones,*) State Senator, wholesale and retail grocer, south side Front

Chicester, Samuel, (Little Meadows, Susquehanna Co, Pa ,) S D 24. farmer 60

*CITY LAUNDRY, (Owego,) Mrs. M. J. Crandall, prop

CLAPP, JAMES H., (Owego,) (*J H Clapp & Co*)

CLAPP, J. H. & CO, (Owego,) (*James H. Clapp and Chas Dana,*) manufs men's and boys' coarse and fine boots, Front, south side

CLARK, CHAS A, (Owego or Newark Valley,) county judge, surrogate, attorney &c, residence Newark Valley, office over Tioga National Bank, Front.

CLARK, JAMES, (Owego,) S D. 27, dairy and farmer 84

Clark, Samuel T Rev., (Owego,) pastor First Presbyterian Church, Front

Cleft, Lemuel, (Owego,) S D 17, farmer 111.

Cleveland, Albert, (Owego,) conductor S. C. R R, North Avenue

Coakley, James, (Owego,) telegraph operator

Coburn, Andrew, (Owego,) (*A & E Coburn*)

Coburn, A & E, (Owego,) (*Andrew and Ebenezer,*) photographers, dealers in picture frames and farmers, in Pennsylvania, 300, Front corner Court

Coburn, Ebenezer, (Owego,) (*A & E Coburn*)

Coburn, Geo, (Apalachin,) S. D 19, farmer 40

Cochran, John, (Owego,) S D 18, farmer

Cochran, John Mrs., (Owego,) S. D. 18, farmer 17.

Cochran, Mary E Miss, (Owego,) (*with Miss Lorinda E Leasure,*) dressmaker, 49 Lake corner Main

Codner, Hiram, (Owego,) S D 27, farmer 90

Codner, John, (Owego,) S D. 27, farmer 42 and leases 90

Codner, Nelson, (Owego,) S D 27, farmer 82.

Coe, Jesse, (Gaskill's Corners,) S. D. 30, farmer 260

Cofferty, Burdett, (Union, Broome Co,) (*with James Jr*) farmer leases 264

Cofferty, James, (Union, Broome Co,) S D 4, farmer 324

Cofferty, James Jr, (Union, Broome Co,) (*with Burdett,*) farmer leases 264

COFFIN, FERNANDO D, (South Owego,) S D 16, dairyman and farmer 132

Coffin, Harvey, (Owego,) S. D 17, boatman.

COFFIN, MILTON, (South Owego,) S D. 22, dairy and farmer 90.

Coffin, Wm H, (Apalachin,) S. D. 31, farmer 70

Cole, Abram, (Flemingsville,) S. D 2, farmer 100.

Cole, Wm H, (Owego,) school commissioner, Court House

Comfort, Melville L, (Owego,) jeweler and optician, 23 Front

Conant, Emory, (Little Meadows, Susquehanna Co, Pa ,) S. D 38, farmer 80

Conant, Simeon, (Owego,) S D 25, blacksmith.

Conklin, Alfred, (Owego,) S D 8, farmer leases 100

Conklin, Amaziah, (Owego,) S. D 19, farmer 40.

Conklin, Charles H, (Owego,) farmer leases of David M LaMonte, 77.

Conklin, Joseph, (Owego,) S D 36, farmer 30

Conklin, Lewis D., (Owego,) S. D 39, mason and farmer 13

Conklin, Wm, (Owego,) S D. 8, engineer and farmer 3½

Conover, Isaac, (Flemingsville,) S. D 9, farmer 140.

Constantine, Michael, (Owego,) saloon, Green

Cook, Chas., (Owego,) conductor Erie R. R, Temple

Cooper, Byron, (Flemingsville,) S D 11, farmer 60

Cooper, C H, (Union, Broome Co,) S D 5, farmer 70

COOPER, GEO, (Apalachin,) S D 13, justice of the peace, justice of sessions and (*with Samuel,*) prop. steam grist and saw mills, manuf and dealer in lumber, and farmer 410

COOPER, SAMUEL, (Apalachin,) S D 13, (*with Geo,*) prop steam grist and saw mills, manuf and dealer in lumber, and farmer 410.

COREY & THOMPSON, (Owego,) (*Wm H Corey and Sidney Thompson,*) wholesale dealers in pressed hay, South Depot.

COREY, WM. H., (Owego,) (*Davis, Corey & Co.,*) (*Corey & Thompson,*) general R R ticket agent, South Depot.

Cornell, Daniel, (Union, Broome Co.,) S. D. 6, farmer 128

Cornell, Eli, (Union, Broome Co ,) S D 6, resident.

Cornell, Henry, (Owego,) S D 32, groceries, provisions and notions, also blacksmith

Cornell, Wm, (Union, Broome Co.,) S D 6, farmer 100.

CORNICK, JOHN, (Owego,) S. D 14, farmer leases of A. VanPatten, 56

Cornwell, Jennie Miss, (Owego,) dressmaker, Franklin.

Corsaw, Harrison, (Campville,) S. D. 4, farmer 20

COURTRIGHT, JOHN J., (Apalachin,) S. D. 15, dealer in live stock, butcher and farmer 38¾.

Cragan, John, (Apalachin,) mason and contractor.

*CRANDALL, M J MRS, (Owego,) prop City Laundry, dressmaker and paper hanger

Crater, Adelbert L., (Owego,) (*F E & A. L Crater*)

CRATER, CHAS. H., (Owego,) agent for F E & A L Crater, baker, 18 North Avenue.

Crater, Frederick E., (Owego,) (*F E & A. L. Crater*)

Crater, F E & A. L., (Owego,) (*Frederick E and Adelbert L ,*) bakery, 18 North Avenue

Crater, Samuel, (Owego,) S. D. 25, farmer 50

Crawford, Albert, (Union Center, Broome Co ,) S. D 15, saloon keeper

Crawford, Joseph, (Owego,) S. D. 32, farmer 45

Crawford, Robert, (Union Center, Broome Co ,) S. D 15, farmer 32

CROSBY, JAMES, (Owego,) S D. 27, charcoal burner and farmer 50

Crotz, Orrin, (Owego,) S D 5, farmer 2

Crouce, John H., (Owego,) S D 12, farmer 160

Crounse, Harriet Mrs , (Owego,) dress maker, St. Patrick.

Curtis, Frank, (Gaskill's Corners,) S D 20, farmer

Curtis, George R , (Owego,) S D 20, prest of Owego Butter and Cheese Manufactory, dairyman and farmer 850

Curtis, Harmon, (Owego,) S D 20, farmer 70.

Curtis, Harvey, (Owego,) S. D 26, nurseryman and farmer 1½.

DANA, CHAS , (Owego,) (*J. H Clapp & Co* )

DANA, FOSTER, (Owego,) farmer 22, south of River Bridge.

Danford, George, (Owego,) S. D 21, farmer 2

DANIELS, DARWIN H , (Owego,) S. D. 15, farmer 93.

DANIELS, EZEKIEL, M. D., (Owego,) physician and surgeon, 89 Main corner Church

DANIELS, GUSTAVUS N., (Owego,) S D. 14, farmer leases of A. Schoolcraft, 195

DANIELS, O R , (Owego,) farmer.

Darby, Frank B , (Owego,) dentist, north side Front

Darling, Mary E., (widow,) (Little Meadows, Susquehanna Co., Pa ,) S. D 38, farmer 70

DARLING, SELIM, (Apalachin,) contractor and builder, Apalachin.

DAVIS, BURR J , (Owego,) (*Davis, Corey & Co.,*) prop. Central House, corner Lake and Main

DAVIS, COREY & CO., (Owego,) (*Burr J. Davis, Wm. H. Corey and Frederick O. Cable,*) wholesale oyster dealers, Lake

Davis & Easton, (Owego,) (*Nathaniel W Davis and David T. Easton,*) lawyers, south side Front.

Davis, James, (Owego,) S D 18, painter.

Davis, James Mrs , (Owego,) S. D. 18, farmer 20.

DAVISON, JOSIAH L., (Apalachin,) (*with Wm ,*) S D 13, farmer 170.

Davison, Lucius, (Apalachin,) S. D. 13, farmer 96.

Davis, Nathaniel W , (Owego,) (*Davis & Easton,*) notary public and farmer, in Tioga, 135

DAVISON, WM., (Apalachin,) (*with Josiah L.,*) S D. 13, farmer 170.

Davy, Charles, (Owego,) auction store, 16 Lake

Day, Ithimer, (Owego,) S. D 32, farmer 10.

Day, Thomas, (Owego,) S. D 32, farmer 55.

DAY, WARREN, (Owego,) (*Jackson & Day* )

Dean, Calvin B , (Owego,) town clerk and prop North Avenue Livery Stable, 21 North Avenue

DEAN, HORATIO NELSON, (Owego,) (*H. N Dean & Sons,*) deceased, August 10, 1872

DEAN, H N & SONS, (Owego,) (*Horatio Nelson, Ransom B. and Isaac N.,*) props. Deans' Tannery, (upper leather,) North Avenue

DEAN, ISAAC N., (Owego,) (*H N Dean & Sons* )

Dean, James A , (Owego,) carpenter and builder. Main corner Spencer Avenue.

DEAN, RANSOM B , (Owego,) (*H N Dean & Sons.*)

Dearbourn, Asa, (Owego,) shoemaker, 16 North Avenue.

Decker, Alex., (Owego,) farmer 3, Fifth Avenue

Decker, Anson, (Owego,) wholesale wines and liquors, owns 68 acres, Main

DECKER, CORNELIUS, (Apalachin,) prop Eagle Hotel and farmer 55, Apalachin

Decker, David, (Owego,) S. D. 26, farmer leases of Anson, 63

Decker, Edmund W , (Apalachin.)

Decker, Emanuel, (Union, Broome Co ,) S D 5, farmer 160

Decker, Gideon, (Owego,) S D 37, farmer

Decker, John, (Apalachin,) S D. 38, carpenter, millwright and farmer 2

Decker, John, (Union, Broome Co ,) S. D. 7, farmer leases of Peter Livingston, 165

Decker, John W , (Owego,) S D 37, farmer 85.

Decker, Joseph, (Owego,) S D 2, (*with David Moulee,*) farmer leases of John J Horton, 100

Decker, Morgan, (Owego,) S D 32, farmer leases of Alexander, 40.

Decker, Moses Mrs , (Apalachin,) S D. 29, farmer 30

Decker, Samuel, (Owego,) S D 37, farmer 40

Dedgroat, John, (Owego,) S D 8, farmer leases of John Carmichael, 118

Dedgroat, Wm C., (Owego,) S. D 8, mechanic.

DeGaugh, Delinda Mrs , (Apalachin,) S. D 28, farmer 25.

DeGroat, J. DeWitt, (Owego,) S D 39, farmer 59.

DeGROAT, J FIELDS, (Owego,) S. D 39, produce dealer and farmer 121

DeGroat, Lorenzo N., (Owego,) S. D. 36, farmer 52

Deming, Horace R , (Owego,) (*Bergin, Deming & Co* )

Denison, Henry, (Owego,) S. D. 27, farmer 60.

Dennis, Edmund, (Flemingsville,) S D 9, cooper.

Densmore, Eli, (Owego,) S. D. 25, farmer 50.

Denel, Augustus S , (Owego,) S D 3, farmer 140.

DeWitt, Old Joe, (Owego,) prop Metropolitan Hotel and restaurant, and dealer in confectionery, south side Front

Dexter, Francis, (Owego,) S. D 26, farmer 40

Dickerson, Ira W., (Campville,) S D 7, farmer 43

Dingman, John Jr , (South Owego,) S D 16, farmer 160

Dinga, Adam C , (Owego,) brick maker.

Dobson, Wm., (Little Meadows, Susquehanna Co., Pa ,) S D 38, grocer

Dodd, Thos , (Owego,) conductor Erie R. R , Main

Dodge, A J , (Owego,) (with Joseph N.,) S D 14, farmer 100

DODGE, DANIEL S , (Owego,) S. D. 39, farmer 122½

Dodge, Edmond, (Campville,) S. D 33, carpenter

Dodge, John, (Owego,) S D. 32, fireman.

Dodge, Joseph N , (Owego,) (with A J.,) S D. 14, farmer 100

Dolan, Henry, (Owego,) S D 23, (with John ) farmer 72

Dolan, John, (Owego,) S. D. 23, (with Henry,) farmer 72

Doty, Elijah, (Owego,) tailor, 5 Lake.

Doty, Geo W , (South Owego,) S D 22, farmer leases 95.

Dougherty, James R , (Owego,) (Houk, Dougherty & Trusdell,) owns 52 acres in Candor.

Drake, Chas., (Apalachin,) S. D 19, farmer 13

Drake, Eli B , (Owego,) cooper, Temple

Drake, Noble, (Apalachin,) S D 34, farmer 18.

Drake, Tamar, (widow,) (Apalachin,) S. D. 19, farmer 15.

Duane, Burr, (Owego,) S. D. 22, saw mill and farmer 63

Duane, John, (Owego,) S D 22, farmer 33½

Duane, Timothy, (Owego,) S D. 22, farmer 65

DUELL, BYRON B., (Owego,) (Duell & Skym.)

DUELL & SKYM, (Owego,) (Byron B Duell and John Skynn,) manufa root beer, 5th Avenue

Dugan, Hugh, (Owego,) prop Exchange Hotel and farmer 26, Front

DUNHAM, ASA, (Owego,) S. D. 27, farmer 131½

Dunham, James, (Owego,) S D 25, farmer.

Dunham, Sylman, (Apalachin,) S D. 31, farmer 95

Durussel, Louis F., (Owego,) jewelry &c., 27 Lake

DWELLE, JEFF. C., (Owego,) (Dwelle & Link.)

Dwelle, Jed E , (Owego,) groceries and provisions, corner Main and North Avenue.

DWELLE & LINK, (Owego,) (Jeff C. Dwelle and Chas A Link,) merchant tailors and clothiers, Front.

EAGLE HOTEL, (Apalachin,) Cornelius Decker, prop , Apalachin

EASTABROOK, HENRY O., (Owego,) (Howell & Eastabrook )

Easton, David T , (Owego,) (Davis & Easton,) notary public and farmer 125

EDWARDS, EDSON, (Apalachin ) general dealer in dry goods, boots, shoes, groceries &c., Apalachin.

EDWARDS, IRA, (Apalachin,) butcher, Apalachin.

Edwards, Ira, (Apalachin,) S. D 15, farmer 38

Eldred, Samuel, (Owego,) S. D 2, farmer 2

Eldrid, Nelson, (Owego,) S D 6, farmer 56.

Elliott, Henry W., (Owego,) druggist, 3 Lake.

Ellis, Alex D , (Owego,) tailor, Front

Ellis, Edwin, (Owego,) (Bristol Iron Works,) agent Western New York Life Insurance Co

ELLIS, WM. W., (Owego,) (G B Goodrich & Co)

Ely, Ann S , (widow,) (Owego,) owns farm 500.

Ely, Bros , (Owego,) (Chas C and Mrs. Ann S ) druggists, 33 Lake

Ely, Chas C , (Owego,) (Ely Bros )

Evans, Chas , (Union, Broome Co ,) S D. 6, farmer leases of Mrs Mary A. Wales, 200

Evans, Erastus, (Owego,) soap factory, corner Temple and Liberty

Evans, Truman, (Campville,) S D. 33, carpenter

Fairbanks, Samuel, (Apalachin,) S D. 31, farmer 47½.

FARNHAM, CHAS , (Owego,) agent Glens Falls Insurance Co , Central Avenue

Farrington, Thos , (Owego,) lawyer, Tioga Bank Building, Front.

Faulkner, Fanny Mrs , (Owego,) dressmaker, Main, east of Railroad.

FAY, GEO W., (Owego,) general insurance and real estate agent, and prop Ahwaga Hall, Ahwaga Block, Front.

Fenderson, John, (Owego,) S. D. 6, retired farmer.

Fennison, John, (Owego,) S. D 6, farmer 60.

Ferguson, Eugene, (Flemingaville,) S. D. 23, farmer 112.

Ferguson, Wm , (Flemingaville,) S. D. 23, farmer 84.

FERRISS, LEMUEL W., (Owego,) pattern maker and farmer 3, south of River Bridge

Field, B. Frank, (Owego,) agent for Elias Howe Sewing Machine, 3 Park.

Fields, Wm B., (Owego,) conductor Erie R. R , George

Finch, J S , (Owego,) S D 37, farmer 80.

FIRST NATIONAL BANK, (Owego,) Front, capital $100,000; Lyman W. Truman, prest.; John B Brush, cashier; Clarence A. Thompson, teller.

Fisher, J , (Owego,) (with J. Wilson,) prop Park Livery, corner Central Avenue and Main.

Flemming, Luke, (Flemingaville,) S. D. 28, farmer 50.

Flemming, Robert S , (Flemingaville,) S. D 9, farmer 450.

Follett, James, (Owego,) S D. 25, farmer leases 20.

Ford, Edgar A , (Gaskill's Corners,) S D 30, farmer 100.

Ford, George L., (Gaskill's Corners,) S D 30, farmer 400.

Ford, Lewis, (Gaskill's Corners,) S. D. 20, speculator and farmer 60.

Foster, Charles M , (Owego,) S D. 17, farmer leases 100

Foster, Daniel R., (Owego,) S. D. 17, retired farmer

Foster, David, (Apalachin,) S. D. 15, farmer 1

Foster, Evahne, (Owego,) shoemaker, corner Front and Farm

**FOSTER, LEONARD,** (Owego,) S D. 17, manuf and dealer in lumber, and farmer 147½

Foster, Willard, (Campville,) S D. 17, saw mill, grist mill and farmer 190

Foster, —— Mrs , (widow,) (Apalachin,) farmer 8

**FOX, ALLEN,** (Owego,) S. D. 25, farmer 125

Fox, Charles, (Owego,) S D 36, farmer 30

Fox, Fred , (Owego,) S D 36, farmer leases farm of Mrs F H Pumpelly.

Fox, Geo , (Apalachin,) S. D. 31, farmer leases 40.

Fox, Geo , (Owego,) S D. 36, farmer 60

Fox, Harvey, (Apalachin,) S. D. 15, carpenter and farmer 1.

Fox, Harvey, (Apalachin,) S. D 35, farmer 83

Fox, Ira, (Apalachin,) S D 13, farmer 62

Fox, Ira W , (East Nichols,) S D. 3, farmer leases 47½

Fox, James (Apalachin,) S. D. 31, farmer 10

Fox, John S., (Apalachin,) S D 19, farmer 50.

Fox, Joseph, (Flemingeville,) S D 9, engineer

Fox, Olive, (widow,) (East Nichols,) S. D. 3, farmer 47½

Fox, Orson S , (Apalachin,) wagon maker

Fox, Russel, (Apalachin,) S. D 31, farmer 50

**FRANK, JOHN,** (Owego,) eclectic physician, 14 Front.

Frear, John, (Owego,) S. D 26, farmer 48

Freeman, John, (Owego,) barber, under Park Hotel

Friendship Lodge, No. 153, F. & A. M , (Owego,) 19 Lake, meets every Wednesday evening.

Friment, Casper, (Owego,) ball alley, North Avenue

Fullmer, Peter, (Owego,) S. D. 20, farmer 140.

Fulmer, Philip, (Owego,) S. D. 37, farmer 80

**GAEHDE, ALBERT F.,** (South Owego,) S. D. 22, school teacher and farmer 50

Gage, E M , (Owego,) S. D. 14, butcher and farmer 50.

Gage, Jeremiah, (Owego,) S. D 26, carpenter.

Galpin, A Mrs., (Owego,) S D. 12, farmer 40

**GARRISON, DAVID R.,** (Little Meadows, Susquehanna Co., Pa.,) S. D 38, prop steam saw and cider mills, farmer 240 and (with Chas. DePuy,) in Vestal, 56.

Garrison, Seneca, (Tracy Creek, Broome Co ,) S D 29, farmer 25.

Gaskill, H Mrs., (Owego,) S. D. 32, farmer 6

Gaskill, James, (Union, Broome Co.,) S. D. 6, farmer 9

**GASKILL, NATHAN W ,** (Gaskill's Corners,) S. D 20, carpenter, wagon maker and repairer, prop. turning lathe and farmer leases 110

**GASKILL, PAUL,** (Gaskill's Corners,) S. D 20, farmer 110.

Gaskill, Wilder J , (Apalachin,) prop, Apalachin Steam Mills, custom grinding, saw and plaster mills.

Gavell & Taylor, (Owego,) cigar manufs.

Gere, Eugene B , (Owego,) lawyer, district attorney and notary public, Front.

Gibson, David, (Little Meadows, Susquehanna Co., Pa.,) S. D. 34, farmer 15

**GIFFORD, DAVID S ,** (South Owego,) S. D 22, farmer 100.

**GIFFORD, RUSSEL D ,** (South Owego,) S D. 22, farmer 84.

Gile, Horton, (Owego,) S. D 11, farmer 10.

**GILES, JOHN S ,** (Apalachin,) S. D 34, grower of small fruits, farmer 35 and (with Mrs Priscilla Barton,) 81

**GLANN, CHAS.,** (Apalachin,) S D 13, farmer 177.

Glann, Geo , (Apalachin,) S D 13, farmer 102 and (with James H ,) 234

Glann, James H., (Apalachin,) S. D. 13, farmer 160

Glann, Martin V., (Apalachin,) S D 31, farmer 46

Glann, Wm., (Apalachin,) S D. 15, farmer 210.

**GLOVER, ANSON B ,** (Apalachin,) S. D. 31, grower of small fruits and farmer 90

Goodale, L. C. Mrs., (Owego,) milliner, 7 Franklin

Godenow, Abram, (Apalachin,) (with John and Henry,) farmer leases 208

**GOODENOW, ALANSON,** (Apalachin,) S. D. 31, saw mill, manuf. of lumber and farmer 64½

Goodenow, Albert, (Apalachin ) S. D 34, farmer 208

Goodenow, Chauncey, (Apalachin,) S. D. 34, farmer 25

Goodenow, Henry, (Apalachin,) (with John and Abram,) farmer leases 208.

Goodenow, John, (Apalachin,) (with Abram and Henry,) farmer leases 208

Goodenow, John W., (Apalachin,) S D 34, rake maker and farmer 1

Goodenow, Julia Mrs., (Apalachin,) S D 34, farmer 1.

Goodrich, Albert E., (Owego,) S. D. 25, farmer 54.

**GOODRICH, CHAS. P.,** (Owego,) S. D. 2, keeper of Tioga Co. Alms House

Goodrich, David, (Owego,) town assessor, wool dealer and farmer 5, north side Front

Goodrich, Edwin, (Owego,) S D 35, farmer 141

**GOODRICH, GEO B ,** (Owego,) (G B Goodrich & Co )

GOODRICH, G. B. & CO., (Owego,) (Geo B Goodrich, Wm. W. Ellis and James W Goodrich,) dry goods, carpets and oil cloths, 28 Front

GOODRICH, JAMES W., (Owego,) (G. B Goodrich & Co)

Goodrich, John E., (Owego,) (Starr & Goodrich)

Goodrich, Mathew, (Owego,) S D. 25, farmer leases 90

Goodspeed, Alden, (Owego,) S D. 3, farmer leases 150.

Goodspeed, James, (East Nichols,) S D 3, farmer 175

Goodspeed, Joel J., (Owego) farmer 50, south of River Bridge.

GOODSPEED, NATHANIEL, (Owego,) S D 3 farmer 150.

Goodwill, M Mrs., (Owego,) hair dresser, Central Avenue

Gordon Samuel, (Owego,) S. D. 8, farmer

Goss, Seward, (Owego) conductor Erie R. R., Main

Gould, Almon W., (Owego,) policeman.

GOULD, ANDREW C., (Owego,) S D 27, farmer 82.

Gould, Chas., (South Owego,) S. D. 22, farmer 25

GOULD, ELON N., (South Owego,) S D 25, farmer 237

Gould, Joel M., (South Owego.) S D 22, wagon maker, turning lathe &c

Gould, Morris P., (Owego,) blacksmith, 64 Temple

Gould, Rutta Mrs., (Owego,) dress maker, 14 Lake

Gould, Smith, (South Owego,) S D 22, dairyman and farmer 150.

Gould, Stanley H., (South Owego,) S D 22, farmer 17

Gould, Wilbur D., (South Owego,) S. D. 28, farmer 270

Gower, Thomas, (Union Center, Broome Co.,) S D 15, farmer 65

Gower, Thomas B., (Union Center, Broome Co.,) S D 15, farmer 125

Graham, John B., (Owego,) (Graham & Woodward)

Graham & Woodward, (Owego,) (John B. Graham and Joseph Woodward,) horse shoers, Court

GRAVES, CHESTER, (South Owego,) S. D 22, dairyman and farmer 217.

Graves, Horace, (Little Meadows, Susquehanna Co., Pa,) S D 38, farmer 104

Green, Allen, (Gaskill's Corners,) S D 20, wagon maker

Green, Carlton, (Gaskill's Corners,) S D 20, mechanic

Green, Clark S., (Gaskill's Corners,) S. D. 20, postmaster and farmer

Green, Nathan J., (Apalachin,) S D 19, farmer 40

GREENE, NATHANIEL W., (Gaskill's Corners,) S D. 20, house painter

Greenleaf, John T., (Owego,) physician, 20 Main.

GREENWOOD, WM G., (Owego,) boot and shoe maker, prop nursery, gardener and farmer 3, south of River Bridge

Grem, Augustus, (Owego,) S D 8, retired farmer

Griffin, Alfred, (Owego,) S. D. 32, retired carpenter.

Griffin, Alvah, (Gaskill's Corners,) S. D 30, farmer 50

Griffith, Upton, (Owego,) barber, 38 Lake

Griswold, Geo. N., (Owego,) S D 39, farmer 91½.

Griswold, Josiah, (Apalachin,) S D 38, farmer 10

Griswold, T P., (Owego,) principal Academy and supt' Owego Union School

Groat, Abram W., (Owego,) cabinet maker and saw filer, Court

GROESBECK, CORNELIUS, (Owego,) S D 36, farmer 70.

Groesbeck, Cornelius 2d, (Owego,) farmer 13

Groesbeck, Isaac W., (Owego,) S. D 86, farmer 141

Guile, Ebenezer S., (Owego,) S D 16, farmer 50

Guiles, Abram, (Little Meadows, Susquehanna Co, Pa·,) S D 38, farmer 60

Guiles, Alex, (South Owego,) S. D 16, farmer 82.

Hagadorn, Wm A., (Owego,) S D 18, farmer 83½

Halnes, Sarah Mrs., (Owego,) S D 8, farmer 3

Hakes, Catherine Mrs., (Tracy Creek, Broome Co,) S D 20, farmer

Hakes, Hannah Mrs., (Little Meadows, Susquehanna Co., Pa,) S. D 24, farmer 17.

Hale, John P., (Owego,) prop Hale's Hotel, nearly opposite Erie Depot

HALL, JANE Mrs., (Owego) millinery and dress making, south side Front

Hall, Wm D., (Little Meadows, Susquehanna Co., Pa,) S D 38, farmer 56

Hancock, Delos O., (Owego,) lawyer, 5 North Avenue.

Hand, Jacob, (Owego,) saw mill and farmer 150

Hauvy, Hugh, (Owego) S D. 21, farmer 60.

Harder, Emmett, (Owego,) boots and shoes, 19 Lake.

HARRIS, DAVID, (South Owego,) S D. 22 farmer 50.

HARRIS, ISRAEL, (Apalachin,) S. D. 38, farmer 106

Harris, Scott, (Owego,) agent U S Express Co, 28 Lake

Harrison, Wm L., (Owego,) harness, 17 North Avenue.

Hart, Allen, (Owego,) confectionery, fruits &c, 44 Lake

Haskins, Thomas, (Owego,) S D 37, farmer 50

Haskins, Thos., (Owego,) farmer leases 100

Haskins, Thomas O., (Owego,) S D 37, farmer leases of Wm Smyth, 75

HASTINGS, JAMES M., (Owego,) (Hastings & Pendleton.)

HASTINGS & PENDLETON, (Owego) (James M Hastings and Gurdon E Pendleton,) dry goods and groceries, south side Front.

Haviland, Geo., (Owego,) R R engineer and farmer 1, south of River Bridge

HAYES, IRA P., (Owego,) S. D. 19, farmer 30

Hayes, Julia F; (Apalachin,) dress maker.

HAYNER, DAVID H , (Campville,) S. D.
17, farmer 221
Hayner, Levi J , (Owego,) S D. 18, farmer
47
Hayner, Mathew W., (Owego,) S. D. 25,
farmer 49
HAYWOOD, CHAS. M , (Owego,) (*Haywood & White.*)
HAYWOOD & WHITE, (Owego,) (*Chas
M Haywood and Chas White,*) marble, slate and granite works, 26 North
Avenue
Heald, Edward, (Apalachin,) S D. 38, farmer 50
Heath, Watson A., (Apalachin,) manuf.
hand and horse rakes.
Hemstrought, Charles, (Campville,) S D. 7,
farmer 20.
Hemstrought, Harvey, (Campville,) S. D.
33, farmer 26
Hemstrought, Jacob Jr , (Campville,) S D
33, brakeman and farmer 28.
Hemstrought, James, (Campville,) S. D. 33,
wagon maker and farmer 27
Hemstrought, Joseph, (Campville,) S. D. 7,
farmer 57
Hemstrought, Wm., (Campville,) S. D. 33,
farmer 1
Herrington, Russell, (Owego,) S. D. 25, carpenter and farmer 42
Herzig. John, (Owego,) dyer and scourer,
13 North Avenue.
HEWITT, BENJ F., (South Owego,) S. D.
21, postmaster, dairyman and farmer
150
Hibbard, Ralph W., (Owego,) cabinet
maker, 5 Park
HIBLER LEVI G , (Apalachin,) S. D 15,
attorney and counselor at law, and farmer 5¾
HICKEY, JOHN, (Apalachin,) S D. 34,
farmer 111½
Hickey Patrick, (Owego,) prop Owego
House opposite Depot, Depot St
Hickey, Thomas, (Owego,) S D 37, shoemaker
Hiersteiner, Moses, (Owego,) prop. Washington Market. North Avenue
Higby, George, (Owego ) S. D. 17, farmer
125
Hillerty, Harmon, (Gaskill's Corners,) S D.
20, shoemaker
Hill, Chas F , (Owego ) electro plater and
manuf silver spoons
Hills, Asel, (Apalachin,) S D 31, farmer 30.
Hills, Chas S., (South Owego,) S D. 22,
farmer 63
Hills, Geo H., (South Owego,) S. D. 22, farmer 67
Hilton, Walter, (Apalachin,) S. D. 35, farmer 130
HINES, JESSE A , (Apalachin,) S D 38,
farmer 108
Hitchcock, E , (Owego,) S D 32, farmer 1.
Hoagland, Wm , (Owego,) S D 32, farmer
60.
Hodge, Wm , (Owego,) S. D. 8, tanner and
farmer 3
Holbrook, Chas. R , (Owego,) news, fruit
and variety store, 15 North Avenue
Holbrook, Geo. W , (Owego,) farmer 3.
Holden, Edward P., (Owego,) S D. 12, dairyman and farmer 100.

Holden, Jonathan, (Flemingsville,) S D 9,
farmer
Holden, Oliver, (Flemingsville,) S D 9,
farmer 100
Holder, Thos , (Owego,) prop Ahwaga
Restaurant, fruits and confectionery,
17 Main
*HOLDRIDGE, EDGAR P ,(Owego,) clothier and merchant tailor, south side
Front.
Holland, Daniel, (Little Meadows, Susquehanna Co , Pa ,) S D 38, farmer 45
Hollenback, Geo F , (Owego,) (*G. W. Hollenback & Sons* )
Hollenback Geo. W , (Owego,) (*G W. Hollenback & Sons,*) owns 540 acres
Hollenback, G W & Sons, (Owego,) (*Geo
W., Geo. F. and John G ,*) crockery
and groceries, 10 Front
Hollenback, John G., (Owego,) (*G. W.
Hollenback & Sons* )
Hollensworth, Jeremiah M., (Owego,)
barber, 24 Lake
Hollister, E , (Owego,) S. D 14, farmer 90.
Hollister, Julius, (Owego ) silverware
manuf. and agent Davis Sawing Machine, North Avenue.
Holmes, Asher, (Apalachin,) S. D 15, farmer 89
Holmes, Chas., (Owego,) S D 19, farmer
80
Holmes, Elston, (Owego,) S D 36, farmer
110
HOLMES, GILBERT, (Apalachin,) S. D. 15,
farmer.
Holmes, James, (Apalachin,) (*Holmes &
Townsend* )
Holmes, John, (Apalachin,) S. D. 15, farmer
200
Holmes & Townsend, (Apalachin,) (*James
Holmes and John P Townsend,*) produce dealers.
Hooker, John J , (Owego,) supt E. R R
bridge shop, McMaster and E. R R
Hooker, Warren, (Owego,) foreman Erie
R R. bridge shop
Hopkins, C , (Union, Broome Co ,) S D 5,
farmer 90
Hosford, Thomas, (Owego,) S. D. 30, farmer 30.
Hoskins & Isbell, (Owego,) (*Watson L
Hoskins and Wells Isbell,*) jewelry and
fancy goods, 15 Front
Hoskins, Watson L , (Owego,) (*Hoskins &
Isbell* )
Hotchkiss, Geo , (Apalachin,) S D 31,
farmer leases 106
Houk, Dougherty & Trusdell, (Owego,)
(*Lewis C Houk, James R Dougherty
and Lewis W. Trusdell,*) plumbers, gas
fitters, dealers in stoves hardware &c.,
Main foot North Avenue
Houk Jonathan S., (Owego,) (*Keeler &
Houk.*)
Houk, Lewis C , (Owego,) (*Houk Dougherty & Trusdell* )
HOUSE, EPHRAIM H , (Owego,) coal
dealer, corner McMaster and West
Avenue
Hover, Loadwick, (Flemingsville,) S. D. 12,
shoemaker
Hover, Samuel, (Owego,) S D 27, farmer
25.

# PATRICK MALONEY,

## DEALER IN

# GROCERIES, PROVISIONS,

## Wines and Liquors.

AND AGENT FOR THE

## Inman and National Lines of Steamers,

**Page Street, Near E. R. R., Owego, N. Y.**

# The Owego Gazette,

## Established in 1813.

*The oldest and best Family Newspaper published in Southern New York, and*

# The Best Advertising Medium

*IN TIOGA COUNTY.*

**Subscription, $2.00 per Year, in Advance.**

# Beebe & Kingman,

*Editors and Publishers.*

Howard, Albert D., (Union, Broome Co ,) S. D 4, farmer 50

Howe, Sylvester, (Owego,) S. D 32, farmer

HOWELL & EASTABROOK, (Owego,) (*Roger B. Howell and Henry O. Eastabrook*,) dealers in musical instruments and merchandise, 45 Lake

HOWELL, GEO. W , (South Owego,) S. D 22, horse shoeing and general blacksmithing.

HOWELL, ROGER B , (Owego,) (*Howell & Eastabrook* )

Howes, Joshua F., (Owego,) S D. 39, farmer 70.

HOWES, MILES F., (Owego,) (*Ross, Brown & Howes*,) architect, Delphine near S C R R Depot

Hoxie, Raymond, (Apalachin,) S D. 28, farmer 25

HUBBARD, TRUMAN M , (Owego,) furniture dealer and undertaker, 27 Main opposite Central House

Hull Bros , (Gaskill's Corners,) (*George W. and Willis D* ,) S D 30, manufs. and dealers in lumber, and farmers 105

Hull, Clark, (Gaskill's Corners,) S D 30, (*with Wellington G* ,) farmer 80

HULL, FREDERICK K , (Owego,) (*Platt & Hull*,) supervisor town of Owego

Hull, George W , (Gaskill's Corners,) (*Hull Bros* )

Hull, Orange, (Owego,) S D. 6, foreman of Houck & Keeler's brick yard

Hull, Wellington G , (Owego,) (*with Clark*,) S D. 30, farmer 80.

Hull, Willis D., (Gaskill's Corners,) (*Hull Bros* )

Humphrey, Lucius, (Owego,) S. D. 37, farmer 100.

Hungerford, Chauncey, (Owego,) groceries, provisions and meat market, North Avenue

HUNT, AMOS T , (Owego,) farmer 75

Hunt, A Tylor, (Owego,) S D 25, farmer 70

Hunt, Emily J. Mrs.,(Owego,) dress maker, 18 Lake

Hunt, Hattie Miss, (Owego,) teacher.

HUNT, JOHN, (Owego,) S. D. 21, dairy and farmer 224

Hutchinson, Horace W., (Owego,) tinware &c , corner North Avenue and Fox

HYDE, OTIS B., (Owego,) (*Newell & Hyde* )

Hyde, Samuel W., (Owego,) insurance agent, 5 North Avenue.

Ingersoll, Charles, (Owego,) S D 32, farmer 44.

Ingersoll, Clinton, (Owego,) (*with Geo.*,) S D 32, farmer leases 470.

Ingersoll, Eugene, (Owego,) S. D. 32, farmer 58½

Ingersoll, Geo., (Gaskill's Corners,) S. D. 20, farmer.

Ingersoll, George, (Owego,) (*with Clinton*,) S. D. 32, farmer leases of W. Ingersoll, 470.

Ingersoll, Harry, (Owego,) S. D. 17, farmer 100.

Ingersoll, James, (Owego,) S. D. 32, farmer 100

Ingersoll, James Jr , (Owego,) S. D 32, farmer leases of C. Kellogg, 70

Ingersoll, Mary E. Mrs , (Owego,) dress maker, south side Front.

Ingersoll, Moses, (Owego,) S D 32, farmer 147

Ingersoll, Wm., (Owego,) S. D 32, dairyman and farmer 550

IRA, WM , (Owego,) blacksmithing, Temple, opposite Bristol Iron Works.

Isbell, Wells, (Owego,) (*Haskins & Isbell* )

JACKSON & DAY, (Owego,) (*Edmund W. Jackson and Warren Day*,) eating saloon, 20 North Avenue

JACKSON, EDMUND W., (Owego,) (*Jackson & Day*)

Jackson, John, (Owego,) photographer and dentist, 12 Lake

James, Russell, (Owego,) S. D. 13, farmer 150.

Jenks, Byron J , (Owego,) S. D. 27, dairyman and farmer 213.

Jenks, Daniel L , (Owego,) S. D 37, speculator and farmer 150.

Jewett, Chas W , (Apalachin,) S D 34, school teacher and farmer 15½.

Jewett, Harry, (Owego,) groceries and provisions, Front

Jewett, Ira W , (Apalachin,) S. D 15, blacksmith

Jewett, Moses W , (Apalachin,) S D 35, farmer 30.

Jewitt, George, (Apalachin,) S. D. 19, farmer 56

Jewitt, John W., (Union, Broome Co.,) S. D 4, farmer 112.

Johnson, Chas F Jr , (Owego,) (*Bristol Iron Works* )

JOHNSON, CLARK H., (Owego,) S D 37, farmer 50

Johnson, Edward J , (Owego,) blacksmith, North Avenue

Johnson, Henry M , (Owego,) S D 26, farmer 100 and works estate of John Camp, 50.

Johnson, Philo, (Owego,) farmer leases 120, south of River Bridge

Johnson, Stillman J , (Owego,) S D 2, blacksmith

Jones, Edward A , (Apalachin,) S D. 13, carpenter and farmer 31¼

JONES, FRANK L , (Owego,) (*Chatfield & Jones*,) (*Jones & Stebbins*,) postmaster

Jones, John, (Owego,) (*Bergin, Deming & Co* )

Jones, Myron H , (Owego,) (*Platt, Jones & Co* )

JONES & STEBBINS, (Owego,) (*Frank L Jones and Barney M. Stebbins, Jr* ,) general insurance agents, 11 E Front

Jones, Sullivan, (Little Meadows, Susquehanna Co , Pa.,) S D. 24, farmer 56

Jopp, Frederick, (Owego,) silversmith and farmer 1¼, south of River Bridge.

Joslin, D. T , (Flemingville,) S. D 23, farmer 74

Judge, Thos., (Little Meadows, Susquehanna Co , Pa ,) S D. 24, farmer 26.

Judge, Thos. Jr., (South Owego,) S D. 3, farmer 50

Kaley, John, (Owego,) S D. 30, farmer 100

Keath, Jack, (Campville,) S D. 7, farmer leases 40.

Keeler, Albert H , (Owego,) (*Keeler & Houk* )

*KEELER, CHAS. H , (Owego,) editor and prop. of *Tioga Co. Record*, sooth side Main.

Keeler & Houk, (Owego,) (*Albert H Keeler and Jonathan S Houk*,) brick, lath, lime, cement &c., Contr.

Keeler Joseph, (Union, Broome Co.,) S D 5, farmer 10

Kellogg, Mary, (Apalachin,) S D 34, farmer 5

Kellum, Ambrose, (Apalachin,) carriage maker

KELLUM, ORRIN, (Apalachin,) wagon maker.

Kelly, John, (Owego,) (*Wall & Kelly*)

Kelly, Michael, (Union, Broome Co.,) S D. 7. farmer 40

Kenyon, Henry B , (Newark Valley,) S. D. 15, farmer 70

Ketcham, Adelbert, (Owego,) farmer leases 40

Ketchum, Adelbert, (Owego,) S. D. 25, farmer leases 35

Kettle, William H , (Union Center, Broome Co ,) S D 15, farmer 28.

Kidder, James H Rev , (Owego,) rector Episcopal Church

Kile, Geo O., (Owego,) millwright and farmer 131, south of River Bridge

Kile, Sarah, (Owego,) carpet weaver, south of River Bridge.

KIMBALL, ABRAM, (Apalachin,) S D. 38. farmer 182½

King, Geo A. (Owego,) (*W A King & Co*)

King, Wm. A., (Owego,) (*W A King & Co*)

King, W. A & Co , (Owego,) (*Wm. A and Geo A King*,) books, stationery and wall paper, 17 Lake.

King, Wm B , (South Owego,) S. D 16, farmer 76

King, Wm H Rev , (Owego,) pastor First Baptist Church, Front

KINGMAN, LEROY W , (Owego,) (*Beebe & Kingman*.)

Kipp, Clinton, (Owego,) S D 32, farmer 60

Kipp, Geo , (Owego,) meat market and farmer, in Tioga, 82, Main

Kipp, Wallace, (Owego,) S. D. 32, farmer 30

Kittle, John B , (Owego,) miller

Knapp, Amos, (Apalachin,) S D 16, farmer 257

Knapp, Fred. J., (Owego,) telegraph manager

KNAPP, IRA, (Apalachin,) S. D. 29, farmer 80

Knapp, Joel, (Apalachin,) S D 38, farmer leases 33

Knapp, Solomon, (Apalachin,) S. D. 38, farmer leases 106.

Knapp, Theodore Mrs., (Owego,) S D 39, farmer 20

Kneeland, Abner, (Owego,) S D 21, farmer 15

Knights, Wm. G., (South Owego,) S D 16, farmer 50

Krom, Dana, (Owego,) conductor Erie R. R , boards Central House.

Kyle, Thomas 2d, (Owego,) S D 32, farmer 1d2.

Ladd, Isabelle, (widow,) (Owego,) S. D. 36. farmer 22

Lainhardt, Simon M., (Owego,) S D 20, farmer 84.

LAINHART, ADAM, (Owego,) (*with John*,) S D 14, farmer 400

Lainhart, Ephraim, (Gaskill's Corners,) S D. 20, mechanic.

Lainhart, Geo., (Owego,) (*Ogden & Lainhart*)

LAINHART, JOHN, (Owego,) (*with Adam*,) S D 14, farmer 400

Lamb Geo W , (South Owego,) S. D 22, farmer 100.

LaMONTE, CYRENIUS M., (Owego,) S. D 26, commissioner of highways, agent for Harder's Empire Agricultural Works and farmer 240

LaMONTE, DAVID M , (Apalachin,) S D. 15, farmer 83½.

LaMONTE, FRED. S , (Apalachin,) S D. 35, dealer in live stock and farmer 90

Lamoreux, John W , (Owego,) harness, 26 Lake

Lane, Aaron L., (Apalachin,) S D 35, farmer leases from heirs of David Mereereau, 175

Lane, Chas , (Owego,) S D. 8, currier and farmer 15

LANE, ISAAC, (Owego,) S D 39, farmer 90

LANEHART, ADDISON, (Gaskill's Corners,) S D. 14, farmer 60.

LANGAN, PATRICK J., (Apalachin,) blacksmith and wagon maker, Apalachin.

Lawrence, Peter, (Owego,) S D 32, farmer 10 and leases 10

Leach, B C , (Flemingsville,) S. D 9, blacksmith and farmer 2.

Leach, Eva L. Miss, (Owego,) dress maker.

LEASURE, JOSEPH, (South Owego,) S. D. 22, farmer 10

Leasure, Lorinda E. Miss, (Owego,) (*with Miss Mary E Cochran*,) dress maker, 49 Lake corner Main

LEONARD, GEO. S , (Owego,) insurance and real estate agent, and notary public, 3 Ahwaga Block, Front.

Letts, F M , (Owego,) S. D 17, farmer 12.

LEWIS, C. H , (Gaskill's Corners,) dealer in groceries, provisions and notions, also blacksmith

Lewis, Hiram, (Apalachin,) S. D. 85, farmer 112.

Lewis, Isaac W , (Apalachin,) S. D. 15, physician.

Lewis, J , (Owego,) S D 32, blacksmith.

LEWIS, JAMES, (Apalachin,) S D. 35, manufacturer and wholesale dealer in brooms and brushes

Like, George, (Owego,) S. D. 19, farmer 73

Like, Nathaniel, (Owego,) S. D. 19, shoe maker and farmer 20

Like, Peter H., (Campville,) S. D 33, farmer 84

Lillie, Darius, (Apalachin,) S D 29, farmer 14.

Lillie, Darius, (Apalachin,) S. D. 29, farmer 24

Lillie, Jared, (Owego,) saloon, 18 Lake.

Lillie, Nancy, (Apalachin,) S. D 29, farmer 88.

Lillie, Wm Mrs., (Apalachin,) S. D. 29, farmer 63½

LINCOLN, CHAS K , (Owego,) (*Lincoln & Napier*)

LINCOLN & NAPIER, (Owego,) (*Chas K Lincoln and Henry B Napier,*) drugs and medicines, Main corner North Avenue.

Lindsley, D E Rev , (Owego,) presiding elder M. E. Church.

LINK, CHAS. A., (Owego,) (*Dwelle & Link.*)

Linsday, Hiram, (Owego,) S D. 2, carpenter

LIVERMORE, JAMES M , (Owego,) S. D. 15, dairyman and farmer 500

Livingston, Henry W., (Campville,) (*with Mortimer,*) S D 33, farmer 83

Livingston, John, (Campville,) S. D. 33, lawyer

LIVINGSTON, MICHAEL, (Campville,) S D 33, carpenter and farmer 81

Livingston, Mortimer, (Campville,) lawyer and (*with Henry W.,*) S. D. 33, farmer 83

LIVINGSTON, WILLIAM, (Campville,) S D 35, auctioneer and farmer 26

Long, Jeremiah, (Owego,) clothing, 20 Lake

Loun, Abner, (Owego,) S D 32, farmer lessee of B. Woodford, 190

LOVELAND, MARTIN, (Owego,) saloon, North Avenue.

Lovless, James J., (Campville,) S. D. 33, farmer leases 120

Lown, Jacob, (South Owego,) S.D. 3, farmer 227

Lown, John W , (Owego,) farmer 14.

Lowry, David, (Apalachin,) S. D 31, farmer 54

LUCE, E. P , (Owego,) wholesale and retail dealer in hats, caps, furs &c , 8 Lake, under supervision of David C Anthony

Lynch, Michael, (Owego,) S. D 21, farmer 100

Maberry, E , (Owego,) S. D 12, farmer 50

Mack, John, (Campville,) S. D 33, night watchman, Erie Depot.

Mackley, Frank S., (Owego,) book-binder. Lake over Express office

Maloney, Jeremiah, (Apalachin,) S. D. 19, farmer leases 90

Maloney, John Jr., (Owego,) prop. Park House at Canawana and dealer in village lots.

*MALONEY, PATRICK, (Owego,) groceries, provisions, wines and liquors, 68 Paige.

MANNING, HENRY, (Owego,) carpenter and millwright, North Avenue

Manning, Marvin L. Mrs , (Owego,) millnery, 14 Lake

Marine, Mark, (Owego,) conductor Erie R. R., North Avenue.

Marine, Simeon, (Owego,) S. D. 17, farmer 110.

Marsh, Dwight W Rev., (Owego,) pastor Congregational Church, Main

Marsh, Geo. B , (Owego,) S. D. 2, shoemaker.

MARSH, JOEL K , (Apalachin,) mail carrier.

Martin, David H., (Apalachin,) S D. 38, farmer 76.

MARTIN, WM. M , (Owego,) S D 22, boot and shoe maker, and farmer 85 Stop at the "Old Mount Vernon House."

Mason, Albert G , (Owego,) S. D 6, farmer 60.

Mason, Albert G Jr., (Owego,) S. D 6, farmer 60

MASON, SAMUEL, (Owego,) S D 37, (*with Thomas,*) farmer 76

MASON, SAMUEL E , (Owego,) S D 37, brakeman, N. C. R R "Collar bone broken while coupling cars at Trout Run, May 31st, 1872."

MASON, THOMAS, (Owego,) S D 37, (*with Samuel,*) farmer 76

Mason, Wm , (Owego,) S D 6, farmer 97.

Masten, James, (South Owego,) S D 3, farmer 50.

Matson, John L , (Owego,) furniture dealer and undertaker, 13 Front.

Mayhew, Geo. W., (Little Meadows, Susquehanna Co , Pa ,) S D, 38, farmer 50.

Mayor, Edward A,, (Owego,) dentist, north side Front.

McAlpin, Wm , (Owego,) prop McAlpin's Hotel, 6 North Avenue.

McCANN, HARVEY A., (Campville,) S D. 33, brakeman E R R. and farmer 6.

McCann, Wm., (Campville,) S. D. 33, farmer 44

McCarthy, Benj. B., (Owego,) boots and shoes, 6 Front

McCaslin, Alex , (Owego,) blacksmith and farmer 30, south end of River Bridge

McClary, Del, (Owego,) physician, McClary's Hotel, Main.

McClary, Rexford, (Owego,) prop. McClary's Hotel and Restaurant, 19 Main

McCORMICK HENRY, (Owego,) S. D 39, farmer 100.

McCulloch, David, (Owego,) shoe maker, 4 Lake

McHenry, Francis B., (Apalachin,) S. D 19, farmer 50

McHenry, Thomas, (Apalachin,) S. D. 19, farmer 92

McLain, Marilla Mrs., (Owego,) S. D 2, farmer 130.

McLane, Charles, (Owego,) S. D. 12, farmer 95.

McNEIL, ROSWELL C., (Campville,) S D 33, station and general stock agent E R R , saw, plaster, lath and shingle mill, notary public, stock raiser and farmer 460.

Meacham, Erastus, (Owego,) blacksmith, North Avenue

Mead, Edward, (Flemingaville,) S. D 9, farmer 82.

Mead, Edwin, (Owego,) S D 36, farmer 2

Mead, George, (Owego,) S D, 36, farmer 2 and leases farm of James Travis

MEAD, ISAAC, (Owego,) S. D. 12, farmer 83

Mead, Joshua, (Flemingaville,) S. D. 9, farmer 264

Mead, Josiah, (Apalachin,) farmer 20.

# CITY LAUNDRY

## AND

# Dress Making Emporium,

### CENTRAL AVENUE,

## Nearly Opp. Park Hotel, Owego, N. Y.

☞ All Orders Promptly Attended to. ☜

## All orders will be executed with Neatness and Dispatch.

# MRS. M. J. CRANDALL.

# TIOGA COUNTY RECORD,

## OWEGO, N. Y.

# A LIVE LOCAL PAPER.

Read by many thousands, and has the largest circulation in village where published, which speaks well of its popularity where it is best known

## BUSINESS MEN AND FARMERS

### CAN GET ALL KINDS OF

# JOB PRINTING

Executed in the best manner, on short notice, and at the lowest living prices

## Terms for Record, $1.50 a Year in Advance.

### Advertising Rates lower than any other paper in the village

# C. H. KEELER, Proprietor.

Mead, Peter, (Little Meadows, Susquehanna Co  Pa ,) S  D  24, farmer 60.

MEAD, STEPHEN B., (Flemingsville,) S. D  12, sheep breeder, stock dealer, dairman and farmer 175.

MEAD, WILLIAM E., (Gaskill's Corners,) S. D  20, farmer 80

Mead, William H , (Flemingsville,) S. D. 9, speculator

MEADE, FAYETTE, (Owego,) S. D. 12, farmer

MERICLE, JACOB, (Owego,) S  D. 3, dairy and farmer 105.

MERICLE, JOHN, (Owego,) (*with  Wm. H  ,*) S. D  27, farmer 162.

MERICLE, WM  H , (Owego,) (*with John,*) S. D. 27, farmer 162.

Merrick, Geo , (Owego,) S. D. 18, farmer 83

Mersereau, David, estate of, (Apalachin,) S  D  35, 175 acres.

Mersereau, George J , (Owego,) S  D. 35, farmer 90.

Metcalfe, Azel E , (Owego,) physician, 35 Main

Metcalfe, Geo  W , (Owego,) physician, 35 Main

MILLER, ABRAM H., (Owego,) dry goods and carpets, and owns 620 acres in Spencer, 16 Front.

MILLER, ALEXANDER, (Owego,) S. D. 15, farmer 50

Miller, John, (Owego,) S  D  21, farmer 50

MILLREA, THOMAS, (Owego,) S. D. 37, farmer 110

Millrea, William A , (Owego,) S. D. 37, butcher.

Mills, Henry, (Union, Broome Co ,) S. D. 6, farmer.

Moak, R. F  Mrs , (Owego,) boarding hall, St Patrick

Moe, Ezra, (South Owego,) S  D  16, farmer 56

Moe, Silas, (Little Meadows, Susquehanna Co , Pa ,) S  D  38, farmer 38

Moeller, Frederick C , (Owego,) barber, Front, under Ahwaga House

Montanye, Buffum D., (Campville,) S. D. 33, farmer 65

Moore, Bruce G , (Flemingsville,) S  D  9, farmer

Moore, Chas. H., (Owego,) (*Spaulding & Moore.*)

MOORE, ROBERT E , M  D., (Owego,) physician and surgeon, 21 Park.

Moot, Peter, (Owego,) S  D  12, farmer 60

Morehouse, Elijah, (Owego,) shoemaker, West Avenue.

Morgan, Alexander, (Union, Broome Co.,) S. D. 6, farmer 40

Morrison, Benj , (Owego,) restaurant and saloon, Front opposite Church

MORRISON, JAMES, (Little Meadows, Susquehanna Co , Pa ,) S. D. 38, farmer 108½

Morton, John, (Owego,) currier and farmer 2, south of River Bridge.

Morton, Levi, (Apalachin,) retired shoemaker

Mott, Israel D., (Campville,) S  D. 26, farmer leases of S  G. Tousley, 70.

Monles, David, (Owego,) S  D. 2, (*with Joseph Decker,*) farmer leases of John J Horton, 100.

Munger, Alanson, (Owego,) lawyer and justice of the peace, Front corner Court

MUNGER, CHAS  A , (Owego,) attorney at law, corner Front and Court

MURPHY, EDWARD, (Apalachin,) S. D. 15, owns Eagle Hotel, tailor and farmer 24

Muzzy & Warren, (Owego,) (*Wm H. Muzzy and Robert H. Warren,*) livery, 32 and 34 Lake.

Muzzy, Wm. H , (Owego,) (*Muzzy & Warren.*)

Myers, Joseph H., (Owego,) S  D  36, farmer leases 22.

NAPIER, HENRY B., (Owego,) (*Lincoln & Napier.*)

New Jerusalem Chapter, No 47, R. A  M , (Owego,) 19 Lake, meets 1st and 3d Mondays of each month

NEWELL, FRIEND G., (Owego,) (*Newell & Hyde* )

Newell, Gilbert, (Owego,) supt Newell & Hyde's Spoke Works.

NEWELL & HYDE, (Owego,) (*Friend G. Newell and Otis B. Hyde,*) manufs. and dealers in hubs, spokes, shafts, poles, felloes &c., Delphine near S. C. R. R. Depot

Newman, Nelson S. Mrs , (Tracy Creek, Broome Co ,) S  D. 29, farmer 34.

Newman, Wm., (Flemingsville,) S  D  23, farmer 20

Nichols & Bliss, (Owego,) (*Thos. M Nichols and Francis A  Bliss,*) millers and dealers in flour, feed and grain, Front

Nichols, Chas., (Owego,) S  D  36, farmer 67.

NICHOLS, CHARLES I., (Campville,) S  D. 32, veterinary surgeon, manuf of medicines and hair invigorator

Nichols, Enos, (Owego,) S  D  19, farmer 30

NICHOLS, GEO , (Owego,) S. D. 39, farmer 84

Nichols, John, (Campville,) S. D. 32, peddler, manuf  of medicines and hair invigorator, and farmer 5.

Nichols, Justus, (Owego,) S. D  11, farmer 80

Nichols, Simeon, (Owego,) S  D  19, retired farmer.

Nichols, Thos  M , (Owego,) (*Nichols & Bliss.*)

Nichols, Washington, (Owego,) S. D. 19, farmer 37.

NICHOLS, WILLIAM, (Apalachin,) S  D. 35, farmer 40

Nicket, Geo , (Apalachin,) S. D. 15, shoemaker.

NICKET, JOHN Jr , (Apalachin,) wagon and carriage maker, and blacksmith, Apalachin

NICKET, JOSEPH, (Apalachin,) manuf. and dealer in boots, shoes and rubbers, fine boots a specialty, Apalachin.

Noteware, Daniel, (Apalachin,) S  D  31, farmer 86.

Noteware, Frederick H., (Apalachin,) S  D. 31, farmer 74

Noteware, Geo  W , (Apalachin,) S  D  38, farmer 211

Nutt, David, (Apalachin,) S  D  35, farmer 20

Oakley, Lewis Dr., (Owego,) S. D 30, farmer 600.

Oakley, Timothy, (Owego,) S D 30, manuf and dealer in lumber

O'Brien, Daniel M., (Owego,) barber, North Avenue.

Ogden, Aaron, (Owego,) tobacconist, 5 Lake.

Ogden, Isaac, (Apalachin,) S. D 34, farmer 35

Ogden & Lainhart (Owego,) *(Walter Ogden and Geo Lainhart,)* variety store and manufs fire arms, Front opposite Ahwaga House

Ogden, Walter, (Owego,) *(Ogden & Lainhart )*

OLMSTEAD, AUGUSTUS, (Apalachin,) S D. 13, R R engineer and farmer 126

Olmstead, Avery, (Apalachin,) S. D. 13, farmer 222

Olmstead, Daniel B , (Apalachin,) S D 18, farmer leases 80

Olmstead, Julia M , (widow,) (Apalachin,) S. D. 13, farmer 80.

Orford, Chas , (Apalachin,) S D 15, carpenter

Orford, David, (Apalachin,) S. D. 15, shoemaker.

Owego Gas Light Co , (Owego,) corner Front and Lake, A. P. Storrs, prest.

*OWEGO GAZETTE, (Owego,) 30 Lake, Beebe & Kingman, editors and props

*OWEGO TIMES, (Owego,) 21 Main, Wm. Smyth & Son, editors, Wm Smyth, prop

Owen, Ellas H , (Owego,) conductor S C R R , Main

Paggett, Edward, (Owego,) S D 32, farmer 30

Paris, Stephen, (Owego,) billiard rooms, 25 Lake.

Parker, Chas. E., (Owego,) lawyer, Front opposite Ahwaga House

PARKER, JOHN M , (Owego,) judge of the Supreme Court, opposite Ahwaga House, Front

Parmelee, Colburn S , (Owego,) telegraph manager, Erie Depot

PARTRIDGE, JOHN F., (Owego,) S D 2, shoemaker, and farmer leases 60

Patterson, Elizabeth, (widow,) (Apalachin,) S D 13, farmer 25.

Payne, Thomas, (Owego,) saloon, North Avenue

PEARL, LORING C., (Owego,) S. D 18, farmer 126.

Pearl Thos F , (Owego,) sheriff, Main

Pearsall, C S Mrs , (Owego,) S. D. 2, farmer 28.

PEARSALL, CHAS. W., (Apalachin,) S D 15, farmer 55

Pearsall, Geo T., (Apalachin,) prop. saw, lath, shingle and planing mills, and farmer 75

PEARSALL, JOHN W , (Apalachin,) S. D 15, farmer 82

PEASE, CHAS , (Apalachin,) prop Steele's Hotel, Apalachin.

PEASE, GEORGE, (Flemingsville,) S D 9, prop of Pease's Hotel and farmer 12

Peck, J. K Rev., (Flemingsville,) pastor of M E Church.

PENDLETON, GURDON E., (Owego,) *(Hastings & Pendleton.)*

Pendleton, Jenks, (Little Meadows, Susquehanna Co , Pa ,) S. D. 24, farmer 50.

Pendleton, Newell N , (Little Meadows, Susquehanna Co , Pa.,) S. D. 24, farmer 55½

Perkins, Barney P , (Owego,) S. D. 19, farmer 4½

Perkins, Julia, (Apalachin,) S D 19, dress maker

Perry, Hiram, (Apalachin,) S. D 34, farmer 14

Perry, Wm H , (Owego,) S. D. 39, carpenter and builder, and farmer 100.

Peterson, Peter C , (Owego,) *(Truman, Thompson & Co )*

Peterson, —— Rev., (Owego,) pastor African Zion M. E Church, Fox

Pettigrove, John , (Owego,) S D. 8, prop. of Red Mills

Pettigrove Sewell, (Owego,) S D 8, miller at Red Mills

Phelps Ezekiel B , (Owego,) physician and farmer, 59 Front.

Philips, Betsey, (Owego,) S D 14, farmer 64

Philips, James, (Owego,) S. D. 14, farmer 36

PINNEY, HAMMON D., (Owego,) drugs, books and wall paper, south side Front

Pitcher, Daniel M., (Owego,) *(Babcock & Pitcher,)* deputy assessor internal revenue, 11 Front

Platt, Frederick E , (Owego,) *(Platt, Jones & Co )*

PLATT FREDERICK E , (Owego,) cashier Tioga National Bank.

PLATT & HULL, (Owego,) *(Thos C. Platt and Frederick K Hull,)* drugs, medicines, paints, oils &c., Front corner Lake.

Platt, Jones & Co , (Owego,) *(Frederick E Platt, Myron H. Jones and Henry R. Wells,)* bankers, loan and real estate agents, and dealers in Government securities, 21 Lake

PLATT THOS C , (Owego,) *(Platt & Hull,)* prest Tioga National Bank, engaged in lumbering in Michigan

Pomeroy, Chas R , (Owego,) liquor dealer, 42 Lake.

PORTER, RUFUS W , (Campville,) S D 7, dairyman and farmer 98.

Porter, Stratton, (Campville,) S D 7, farmer

Post, Bristol & Co , (Owego,) *(Ira A Post, Wheeler H. Bristol and Linus E Post )* props. Owego Steam Flouring Mill, Central Avenue

POST, GARDNER S., (Apalachin,) S D 31, carpenter and joiner and farmer 60.

Post, Ira A., (Owego,) *(Post Bristol & Co.)*

Post, Linus E , (Owego,) *(Post, Bristol & Co )*

POTTER, ASA N , (Owego,) *(Potter, Booth & Co )*

POTTER, BOOTH & CO , (Owego,) *(Asa N. Potter, Edwin A Booth and Oliver L Ross,)* dry goods, south side Front

Potter, Henry, (Owego,) millwright and farmer 3, south of River Bridge.

Potter, Levi E., (Owego,) S D. 17, insurance agent and farmer 85.

Powell, John Henry, (Owego,) S D 17, farmer leases 2b.
Pratt, Marshall D , (Owego,) policeman.
Price, Chas H., (Owego,) restaurant, E R R Depot.
Prichard, Albert, (Flemingaville,) S D 23, farmer 25
Prichard, Calvin P., (Flemingaville,) S. D 9, farmer 90
Prichard, Lyman, (Flemingaville,) S. D. 9, farmer 50
Prichard, Saul, (Flemingaville,) S D 23, farmer 80.
Prichard, S H , (Flemingaville,) S. D 23, farmer 133
Probasco, Samuel, (Owego,) S. D. 30, farmer 75.
Pumpelly, Frederick Mrs., (Owego,) farmer 631.
PULTZ, FRED , (Flemingaville,) S. D 14, farmer 100.
PULTZ, RANSOM, (Owego,) S D. 12, farmer 73
Pultz, Zachariah, (Flemingaville,) S. D. 14, retired farmer.
Pumpelly, Frederick H. Mrs., (Owego,) farmer 120.
Pumpelly, Geo. J., (Owego,) land office.
Pumpelly, Josiah C., (Owego,) (*Settle & Pumpelly*)
Quimby, John L , (Owego,) stone mason and farmer 1.
Randall, Henry, (Owego,) S D 17, farmer 100.
Raymond, Chauncey L., (Owego,) (*W P. Raymond & Sons*)
Raymond, Wm. B., (Owego,) (*W. P. Raymond & Sons*)
Raymond, Wm P , (Owego,) (*W P. Raymond & Sons,*) farmer 128
Raymond, W. P , (Owego,) S. D. 8, grocer and farmer 100
Raymond, W. P. & Sons, (Owego,) (*Wm. P , Wm. B and Chauncey L.,*) groceries, provisions and meat market, 25 Main
Recodon, L , (Flemingaville,) S. D. 11, farmer 90.
Redding, John, (South Owego,) S D. 22, farmer leases of John C. Manning, 154
Reed, James L., (Flemingaville,) S. D 23, blacksmith and farmer 2½.
Relyea, Andrew, (Owego,) carpenter, 8 Fulton
Reynolds, Peter E , (Owego,) carpenter, West Temple.
REYNOLDS, SAMUEL F , (Owego,) prop Arcade Restaurant, evening concerts, orchestra of six instruments, 29 Front.
Rhinevault, Myron, (Owego,) S D 2, blacksmith.
Richardson, Jerome B., (Owego,) S. D. 22, farmer 35.
Richardson Josephus, (Owego,) S. D 17, farmer 90.
Riley, George, (Owego,) (*G. Riley & Son*)
Riley, G. & Son, (Owego,) (*Geo and James,*) horse shoeing, North Avenue corner Temple.
Riley, James, (Owego,) (*G. Riley & Son*)
Riley, James, (Owego,) S D. 32, farmer leases 75
Rising, John, (Gaskill's Corners,) S D 30, farmer 123.

Rising Joseph H , (Gaskill's Corners,) S D 30, farmer 110.
Rising, William, (Gaskill's Corners,) S D 30, farmer 57 and leases 123.
Robbins, E. L., (Owego,) master locomotive dept , S. C R R.
Robbins, E O , (Owego,) S. D 17, farmer 104.
Robertson, Edward P , (Owego,) S D 18, farmer 40
Robertson, Jay, (Owego,) policeman
ROBERTSON, PETER, (Owego,) florist, gardener and farmer 5, Main near Fulton
Robertson, Timothy, (Owego,) chief of police, Main.
Robinson, Benjamin B , (Owego,) S D. 32, farmer 346
Robinson, Edward P , (Owego,) farmer 10
Robinson, Henry, (Union, Broome Co.,) S. D 4, farmer 64.
Robinson, John, (Owego,) farmer 21
Robinson, John J , (Owego,) S D 37, farmer.
Robinson, Matthew, (Owego,) S. D. 37, farmer 118.
ROBISON, ALEXANDER, (Flemingaville,) S, D 14, farmer leases of Simeon Marquet, 50.
Rockwood, Charles, (Owego,) S D 8, farmer 5.
Rodman, Charles H , (Owego,) S D 35, farmer 77
Rodman, Nichols, (Owego,) S. D 35, retired farmer
Rogers, James Rev., (Owego,) pastor St Patrick's (Catholic) Church and principal Sacred Heart Academy, Main
Rogers, Jeremiah, (Campville,) S D 33, farmer 3,
Rogers, Susan Mrs , (Owego,) ladies' hair dresser, Front.
Roman, Benjamin, (Owego,) S D 6, farmer 2.
Roman, Chas., (Owego,) S. D 6, farmer 80
ROSS, AMOS, (Owego,) (*Ross, Brown & Howes.*)
ROSS, BROWN & HOWES, (Owego,) (*Amos Ross, Benj W Brown and Miles F Howes,*) manufs. sash, blinds and doors, and dealers in lumber, Delphine near S C R R. Depot
Ross, John S , (Owego,) carriage maker, North Avenue near Erie Depot
ROSS, OLIVER L , (Owego,) (*Potter, Booth & Co*)
Rourke, Thos , (Owego,) liquors and groceries, 22 Lake
Rowe, Julius, (Owego,) S D. 26, gardener and farmer 14.
Rondell, Roswell R., (Owego,) photographer, 6 Lake
Russell, Chas., (Owego,) S. D. 21, farmer leases 160
Russell, Elbridge, (Flemingaville,) S D 12, farmer 75.
Rutherford, Levi L , (Campville,) S D. 26, farmer 50.
Ryan, James, (Apalachin,) S D. 19, farmer 40
Ryan, Walter, (Owego,) S. D 18, farmer 40

Sackett, Chas. R., (Owego,) saw and placing mills, and lumber yard, corner Temple and Central Avenue

Sacred Heart Academy, (Owego,) in charge of Sisters of Mercy, Rev Jas Rogers, principal

SADLER, EDWARD P., (Owego,) (Stone & Sadler)

Sampson, J. A., (Owego,) conductor Erie R R, boards Park Hotel

Sanford, Oliver, (Owego,) S D 25, farmer 80

Saunders, Adaline A. Miss, (Owego,) dress maker, 43 Lake.

Sawyer, Nathan W., (Owego,) S. D. 26, farmer 50

Sawyer, William, (Owego,) S. D 26, farmer 60

Schouten, Chas M., (Owego,) groceries and provisions, 10 North Avenue

Scott, Alonzo, (Owego,) S D 2, farmer 40

Scott, Frederick, (Flemingsville,) S D 23, farmer 35

Scott, W R., (Owego,) restaurant and billiard rooms, North Avenue

Scrofford, John, (Gaskill's Corners,) S. D 14, farmer 42

Scott, Melinda, (Owego,) farmer 20

Searle, E F., (Owego,) S D 32, (with E S.) farmer 115

Searle, E S., (Owego,) S D 32, (with E. F.) farmer 115

Searles, Alfred, (Campville,) S D. 17, farmer 30

Searles, A P., (Flemingsville,) S D 23, farmer 60

Searles, Chester, (Flemingsville,) S D 23, farmer 15

Searles, Geo. M., (Owego,) (Stearns & Searles)

Searles, Ira, (Flemingsville,) S. D. 23, farmer 52

Searles, John B., (Owego,) manuf. sash, doors, blinds, agricultural implements &c, corner Temple and Central Avenue

Searles, John T., (Flemingsville,) S D 23, farmer 80

Searles, Lott, (Flemingsville,) S D 23, farmer

Searles, Nathan, (Flemingsville,) S. D. 23, mason and farmer 75

Settle, Lyman, (Owego,) (Settle & Pumpelly,) police justice, 5 Lake.

Settle & Pumpelly, (Owego,) (Lyman Settle and Josiah C Pumpelly,) lawyers, 5 Lake.

SEVERSON, GEORGE S, (Campville,) S. D 33, general blacksmith

Severson, Henry, (Campville,) S D 33, farmer leases of Henry Billings, 17

SHAFER, ABRAHAM, (Owego,) S. D. 12, farmer 140

SHAFER, EGBERT, (Owego,) S D. 12, farmer leases 57.

Shannon, Cornelius, (Owego,) S D. 14, farmer 33

Shaw, Delinda, (widow,) (Owego,) farmer leases 100.

SHAW, HIRAM D, (Owego,) S. D 22, dairyman and farmer 135

Shay, Hiram, (Owego,) meat market, 32 North Avenue.

SHELDON, ERASTUS, (Owego,) saw filing, key fitting, umbrella and general repairing, North Avenue

Sheldon, Geo. R., (Owego,) S D 39, farmer 100

Sherley, John, (Owego,) S D 14, farmer 20

Sherley, Jonathan, (Owego,) S D 21, farmer 13

Sherley, Riley, (Owego,) S D 21, farmer 30

Sherley, Samuel, (Owego,) S. D 21, farmer 40.

Sherman, John, (Owego,) S D. 17, farmer leases of B Robinson, 90

Sherwood, Elijah, (Apalachin,) S D. 19, farmer 99

SHERWOOD, GEO J, (Apalachin,) S D 34, school teacher and farmer 60.

Sherwood, John, (Apalachin,) S D. 35, farmer 25

Sherwood, Nathaniel, (Apalachin,) S D 19, farmer 51

Sherwood, William H., (Apalachin,) S D. 19, farmer 95.

Shopp, Peter, (Owego,) stone cutter and farmer 2, south of River Bridge

Short, George R., (Apalachin,) S. D 19, farmer 18½

Short, Uriah, (Apalachin,) S. D. 19, farmer 154

Short, Uriah Jr, (Apalachin,) S D. 31, farmer leases 47.

Sibley, Samuel, (Owego,) S. D 25, farmer 200.

Signor, Sarah Mrs., (Owego,) S. D. 36, farmer 50.

Skinner, Chas F., (Owego,) telegraph operator, Erie Depot.

SKYM, JOHN, (Owego,) (Duell & Skym.)

Slawson, Geo, (South Owego,) S D 16, farmer 70

SLAWSON, MILTON, (Owego,) S D 16, dairyman and farmer 272

Slocum, Humphrey C, (Owego,) S. D. 26, carpenter.

Smead, David, (Owego,) S. D. 27, farmer leases of Asa Stanton, 90.

Smith, Chas F., (Owego,) S D 11, farmer 107

Smith, Chas. O., (Owego,) S D. 25, farmer 15

Smith, Cyrus T, (Owego,) prop. Ahwaga House Front corner Church.

Smith, Edward, (Apalachin,) S. D. 34, farmer 47½.

Smith, Elmer T, (Little Meadows, Susquehanna Co., Pa.,) S. D 24, farmer 180

SMITH, GEORGE A, (Owego,) S. D. 25, speculator and farmer 88

SMITH, HENRY W, (Owego,) S D 39, dairyman, farmer 55 and leases of Dr Ezekiel B. Phelps, 100

Smith, Isaac W., (Owego,) policeman.

SMITH, JAMES M, (Owego,) S D. 14, stock dealer, dairyman and farmer 236

Smith, Jane A, (Owego,) (with Mary N.,) dressmaker, 20 Lake

Smith, Jerome, (Campville,) S. D. 7, farmer 10

Smith, Laban J., (Apalachin,) S D 15, farmer 78

Smith, Mary N., (Owego,) (with Jane A.,) dress maker, 20 Lake.

Smith, Robert C., (Owego,) S. D 14, farmer leasee of W P Stone, 110.
SMITH, ROYAL Y., (Apalachin,) S. D. 15, assessor and farmer 64.
Smith, Samuel L., (Owego,) hats, caps &c., 6 Lake.
Smith, Stephen W., (Owego,) S. D. 26, farmer 95.
*SMYTH WM , (Owego,) (*Wm Smyth & Son*,) prop *Owego Times* and owns farm 100, 21 Main.
SMYTH, WM A , (Owego,) (*Wm. Smyth & Son.*)
*SMYTH, WM. & SON, (Owego,) (*Wm A .*) editors *Owego Times* 21 Main.
Snell, Robert, (Owego,) S. D 25, farmer 50
Snider & Berry, (Owego,) (*Geo. Snider and Franklin Berry,*) wholesale and retail wines and liquors, also dealers in produce and fur, south side Front
Snider, Geo , (Owego,) (*Snider & Berry*)
Snyder, Edwin D , (Owego,) cabinet maker, Court.
Southwick, George, (Flemingsville,) S. D. 23, farmer 110
Spaulding, Enoch R , (Owego,) (*Spaulding & Moore*)
Spaulding & Moore, (Owego,) (*Enoch R. Spaulding and Chas. H Moore,*) barbers, 40 Lake.
Spencer, Brioton W., (Owego,) S D 21, auctioneer and farmer 85
Spencer, Judson, (Owego,) S D 32, farmer leasee 300.
Spencer, Wakely, (Owego,) farmer 310, Paige
Spencer, Will, (Owego,) sewing machines, 31 Lake
Spooner, Carlson & Berry, (Owego,) (*Frank Spooner. Otto M. Carlson and Joseph Berry,*) music dealers.
Spooner, Frank, (Owego,) (*Spooner, Carlson & Berry.*)
SPRAGUE, EZRA B , (Owego,) homeo physician and surgeon, 40 Lake.
Springstein, Brainard C , (Owego,) machinist and model maker, 3 Park.
Sprong, John B , (Owego,) grocer, Adelline corner McMaster.
Stalker, Samuel, (Owego,) S. D. 32, farmer 10.
STANBROUGH, JOHN B , (Owego,) (*Stanbrough & Strattons.*)
STANBROUGH & STRATTONS, (Owego,) (*John B. Stanbrough, Geo and Edwin Stratton,*) dealers in hardware, doors, sash, blinds and carriage makers' supplies, Front opposite First National Bank
Stanton, Almira, (widow,) (Owego,) S. D. 18 farmer 60
STANTON, ASA, (Owego,) S. D 18, farmer 114 and occupies 60 for Almira Stanton
Stanton, Edward, (Owego,) S D, 17, farmer 150.
Starr, Chas P., (Owego,) (*Starr & Goodrich.*)
Starr & Goodrich, (Owego,) (*Chas. P. Starr and John E. Goodrich,*) jewelers, 29 Lake
Stearns, Henry M , (Owego,) (*Stearns & Searles.*)

Stearns & Searles, (Owego,) (*Henry M Stearns and Geo M. Searles,*) carriage makers, Temple opposite Bristol Iron Works.
STEBBINS, BARNEY M. JR , (Owego,) (*Jones & Stebbins* )
Stebbins, Wm M , (Owego,) insurance agent, 70 Front
Stedman, L., (Flemingsville,) S. D. 9, farmer 60.
Stedman, M Adaline Mrs , (Owego,) millinery and fancy goods, Ahwaga Block, Front
STEELE, AARON, (Apalachin,) postmaster, dealer in general merchandise and farmer 400.
STEELE, AARON W , (Owego,) S D 39, farmer 220.
Steele, George, (Owego,) S D 32, carpenter and farmer 27.
Steele, John F , (Owego,) harness, 38 Lake
Steele, Philetus, (Owego,) S. D. 39, (*with Aaron W ,*) farmer
Steele, Ransom, estate of, (Apalachin,) 115 acres
Steele, Wm , (Owego,) S D 39. farmer 110
STEELES HOTEL, (Apalachin,) Charles Pease, prop , Apalachin.
Steenburg, Isaac, (Apalachin,) S D 31, farmer 32.
Stephens, Chester, (Owego,) S D 8, mechanic.
STEPHENS, HENRY W., (Apalachin,) S D. 38, farmer 25.
Stephens, Samuel,(South Owego,) S. D 22, farmer 34½
STEPHENS, THOS. B , (Apalachin,) S D 38, farmer 100.
STEVENS, ALLAN, (Owego,) dealer in boots, shoes, leather and findings, south side Front.
Stevens, Richard, (Campville,) S. D. 33, farmer 1
Stever, David, (Flemingsville,) S. D. 9, prop of hotel
Stiles, Chas L , (Owego,) physician, Front.
Stilson, Hiram, (Apalachin,) S D 15, carpenter
Stockwell, Lorenzo, (Little Meadows, Susquehanna Co., Pa ,) S D 38, farmer 75
Stone & Buckbee, (Owego,) (*Wm P Stone and Ezra S. Buckbee,*) dry goods, carpets and millinery, 22 Front
Stone, Chas , (Owego,) S D 27, farmer 30
STONE, ELI W , (Owego,) teller Tioga National Bank,
STONE, GEORGE, (Owego,) (*Stone & Sadler* )
STONE & SADLER, (Owego,) (*Geo Stone and Edward P Sadler,*) dealers in boots, shoes, leather and findings, and general agents for the Weed Sewing Machine, 31 Lake
Stone, Wm P , (Owego,) (*Stone & Buckbee* )
Storrs, Aaron P., (Owego,) (*Storrs & Chatfield,*) farmer 60
Storrs, A. P., (Owego,) prest. Owego Gas Light Co.
Storrs & Chatfield, (Owego,) (*Aaron P Storrs and John R. Chatfield,*) hardware, 19 Front corner Lake
Stont, Richard, (Owego,) policeman.

STRAIT, EDWARD E., (Owego,) asst post master, Lake
STRATTON, EDWIN, (Owego,) (Stanbrough & Strattons.)
STRATTON, GEO , (Owego,) (Stanbrough & Strattons )
Stratton, Richard, (Owego,) S D. 2, carriage manuf
Strong, Lewis, (Gaskill's Corners,) S D. 20, carpenter
Swank, John Rev , (Apalachin,) pastor Baptist Church
Swartout, Abram, (Owego,) conductor Erie R R, Temple.
Sweet, George W., (Owego,) boots, shoes, glass, china ware, cutlery, trunks, valises &c , 4 North Avenue
Swick, Samuel M , (Owego,) saloon and shoemaker, 15 North Avenue
Talcott, Geo. B., (Owego,) S D. 8, farmer 87.
Talcott, George L , (Owego,) dealer in village lots and farmer, Talcott
Talcott, Joel, (Owego,) S D, 8, farmer 200
Talcott, William C., (Owego,) S D 2, farmer 124
Talcott, William H., (Owego,) S D 2, wagon maker and farmer 60
Tallmadge, Ezra, estate of, (South Owego,) S D 22, 118 acres
TALLMADGE, EZRA W., (Owego,) S. D. 22, farmer 115
Taylor, David, (Flemingaville,) S D 23, farmer 2
TAYLOR, JOHN J, (Owego,) prest Southern Central R. R., corner Front and Court
Taylor, John L , (Owego,) S. D 32, farmer 200
Taylor, Susan Mrs.,(Owego,) boarding hall, 56 Fox
Taylor, ——. (Owego,) (Gavell & Taylor )
TERBUSH BROS , (South Owego,) (Hiram and Clark,) S D 22, dealers in carriage and coach horses, and farmers 188.
TERBUSH, CLARK, (South Owego,) (Terbush Bros )
TERBUSH, HIRAM, (South Owego,) (Terbush Bros )
Thomas, Jesse Mrs., (Owego,) S D 18, farmer 49
Thompson, A Chase, (Owego,) (Truman, Thompson & Co.)
Thompson, Anthony D., (Owego,) conductor Erie R. R. and agent D. & H Coal Co., Fox.
THOMPSON, CLARENCE A , (Owego,) teller First National Bank
THOMPSON, EDWARD B, (Owego,) W U telegraph operator, Main
THOMPSON, SIDNEY, (Owego,) (Corey & Thompson )
THOMPSON, WM , (Apalachin,) contractor and builder, Apalachin
Thompson, Wm H , (Owego,) telegraph operator S C R R office
THORNTON, GEORGE E , (Gaskill's Corners,) S. D 20, laborer
Thornton, James A., (Owego,) S D. 6, farmer 39.
Thornton, Jeremiah, (Campville,) S. D 17, farmer 38.

Thurston, Geo , (Owego,) planing mill and scroll sawing, North Avenue
Tilbury, Hermon M., (Campville,) S D 4, farmer leases of Chas Dodge, 68
Tilbury, James, (Campville,) S. D. 33, farmer 103
Tilbury, Richard, (Union, Broome Co ,) S D. 4, farmer 100
*TIOGA COUNTY RECORD, (Owego,) south side Main, Chas H Keeler, editor and prop. , Ozias S Webster, asst editor
TIOGA NATIONAL BANK, (Owego,) Tioga National Bank Building, Front, capital $150,000, Thos C Platt, prest, Frederick E. Platt, cashier, Eli W. Stone, teller.
TOUSLEY, S G., (Campville,) S. D. 23, dealer in dry goods, groceries &c., town assessor, postmaster and farmer 50
Townsend, John P., (Apalachin,) (Holmes & Townsend,) S D 34, agent for Cayuga Chief Mower and farmer leases of Geo S., 127
Towsend, Michael, (Owego,) S D 3, farmer 91
Tracy, Benj , (Apalachin,) S. D. 15, farmer 7
Tracy, Harvey J., (Apalachin,) S D 15, farmer 79.
Tracy, W Harrison, (Apalachin,) S D 31, farmer 124
Travers, Frederick, (Union, Broome Co ,) (with Robert,) S. D 5, farmer leases of Isaac Thompson, 32.
Travers, Robert, (Union, Broome Co ,) (with Frederick,) S D 5, farmer leases of Isaac Thompson, 32.
Travis, James, (Owego,) S. D 36, farmer 50.
Tripp, Daniel, (Owego,) watch maker, piano and organ tuner, 10 Lake
Tripp, Lovina, (Owego,) dress maker, West Avenue.
Truesdell, Jonathan, (Campville,) S D. 33, retired farmer
Truman, Aaron, (Gaskill's Corners,) farmer leases 128
Truman, Aaron B., (Gaskill's Corners,) S. D. 14, farmer 128.
TRUMAN & BELKNAP, (Owego,) (John B Truman and John J Belknap,) hay dealers, West Avenue near Erie Depot
Truman, Chas E., (Flemingaville,) S. D. 9, justice of the peace, postmaster and farmer leases 92.
Truman, Chas. F., (Flemingaville,) S. D. 9, farmer
Truman, Elias W , (Gaskill's Corners,) S D 14, farmer 80.
TRUMAN, FRANK W., (Owego,) (L. Truman & Bros.,) farmer 383 and (with Orrin,) 210.
TRUMAN, GEO , (Owego,) (L Truman & Bros ,) (Truman, Thompson & Co ,) (G. Truman & Co )
TRUMAN, JOHN B , (Owego,) (Truman & Belknap )
TRUMAN L & BROS , (Owego,) (Lyman W , Orrin, Frank W. and Geo ,) farmers, in Spencer, Candor, Owego, Tioga and Lisle, Broome Co., 2,143.

Truman, Lyman B , (South Owego,) S. D. 22. farmer leases 224½

TRUMAN, LYMAN W , (Owego,) (*L Truman & Bros.,*) prest. First National Bank of Owego and farmer, in Richford, 62½

TRUMAN, ORRIN, (Owego,) (*L Truman & Bros .*) (*G Truman & Co ,*) farmer 128 and (*with Frank W.,*) 213

TRUMAN, STEPHEN S , (Owego,) (*S. S. Truman & Baker.*)

TRUMAN, S. S. & BAKER, (Owego,) (*Stephen S Truman and Romeo W Baker,*) dry goods, millinery, notions, groceries &c , 14 Front.

Truman, Thompson & Co., (Owego,) (*Geo. Truman, A Chase Thompson and Peter C Peterson,*) dry goods, 20 East Front.

Trusdell, Lewis W ,(Owego,) (*Houk, Dougherty & Trusdell.*)

TUCK, GEO , (Owego,) clothing and gents' furnishing goods, 31 Front

Tunison, Kittie, (Owego,) dress maker, North Avenue

Tuttle, Joel A , (Apalachin,) S D 28, farmer 80

Ulmsted Seth, (Owego,) S D. 2, farmer.

VANAUKEN, ALVIN, (Owego,) S. D. 2, dealer in hay

Vanauken, Jacob, (Owego,) S. D. 2, farmer leases of B. R. Park, 30.

VANBUNSCHOTEN, GEO. W , (Apalachin,) S D. 34, horse dealer and prop. grey stallion Miltonian

VanBunschoten, Hiram, (Owego,) (*Billings & VanBunschoten*)

VanBunschoten, Isaac Mrs , (Owego,) S D 18, farmer 77.

VanCampen, John, (Owego,) S. D. 32, farmer leases 45.

VanGorder, Almon, (Owego,) (*with Isaac,*) farmer 44

VanGorder, Ezra, (Apalachin,) S D 31, farmer 5

Vangorder, George, (Apalachin,) S D 19, farmer leases 47.

VanGorder, Isaac, (Owego,) (*with Almon,*) farmer 44

Vangorder, Joseph, (Apalachin,) S D. 19, farmer 72

Vangorder, Reuben, (Campville,) S. D. 7, farmer 50

VanKirk, Clarence C , (Owego,) prop City Bath Rooms, 45 East Main

VanKirk, Harriet P , (Owego,) prop Owego Cure, 45 East Main

VANKLEECK, JOHN J., (Owego,) deputy Co clerk, Court

VANPATTEN, ANDREW, (Owego,) S. D. 11, farmer 90

VanPatten, Frederick, (Owego,) S. D. 37, farmer leases of George Hollenback, 250.

VanRiper, Morris, (Owego,) S D 19, farmer 28

VanTuyl, Ebenezar, (Campville,) S D. 33, agent U S. Express Co. at Binghamton and farmer 112.

VanWormer, Frederick, (Owego,) S. D. 30, retired farmer.

Vickery, Sarah E. Mrs , (Owego) hoop skirts, 21 Main.

VOSBURGH, STEPHEN H., (Owego,) S. D 3, saw filer and general jobber.

VOSE, GEORGE, (Owego,) S D 3, dealer in horses and farmer.

Wade, Chas , (Flemingaville,) S D 23, saw mill and farmer 15.

Wade, George N , (Owego,) meat market and groceries, North Avenue

Wade, O D , (Flemingaville,) S D 11, farmer 115

Wait, Chas B , (Owego,) S D. 3, farmer 91

Wait, Christian, (Owego,) S. D. 3, farmer leases of Henry O , 50

Wait, Henry, (Owego,) S D 3, farmer 112

Wait, John, (Owego,) S D 26, farmer 50

Wait, John H , (Owego,) S. D 3, farmer 130.

Wait, Wm., (Owego,) S. D. 3, farmer 330

Walker, George D , (Union, Broome Co ,) S. D. 6, farmer 128.

Walker, Henry, (Flemingaville,) S D. 23, carpenter and farmer leases 90.

Walker, Ransom, (Owego,) dentist, Front

Walker, Rial, (Owego,) S D 32, farmer 40.

Wall, Chas , (Owego,) (*Wall & Kelly*)

Wall & Kelly, (Owego,) (*Chas Wall and John Kelly,*) boots and shoes, south side Front.

Walter, Artamna, (Gaskill's Corners,) S D 20, farmer 245

WALTER, GEO W., (Gaskill's Corners,) S D 20, dairyman and farmer 280

Walter, Jas , (Gaskill's Corners,) S D. 30, (*with Wm ,*) farmer 100

WALTER, WM , (Gaskill's Corners,) S D 20, saw mill, lumber dealer and farmer 400

Walter, Wm. H., (Owego,) S. D 14, farmer

Ward, Henry, (Owego,) S. D 18, carpenter and farmer 40.

WARD, ORLANDO, (Gaskill's Corners,) S. D 20, farmer

Ward, Richard, (Owego,) S. D. 17, farmer 55

Ward, Wm., (Owego,) S. D. 17, farmer 40.

Warner, Frederick W , (Owego,) agent American Sewing Machine, 45 Lake.

Warner, John W., (Owego,) S D 25, farmer 53

Warren, Robert H , (Owego,) (*Muzzy & Warren*)

Warrick, Peter, (Owego,) S D 32, farmer 190

Warrick, Samuel, (Union, Broome Co.,) S. D. 5, farmer 44

Waugh, Andrew, (Gaskill's Corners,) S. D. 20, farmer 95

WEBSTER, OZIAS S.,(Owego,) asst editor *Tioga Co Record*, south side Main

Webster, Russell, (Owego,) S. D 14, farmer 4

Welch, Henry H., (Owego,) S D 21, farmer 40 and leases 69

Welch, Hiram, (Owego,) S. D 21, farmer 87½

Welch, John, (Owego,) groceries and provisions, Main head of North Avenue

Wells, Henry R , (Owego,) (*Platt, Jones & Co*)

Wemple, Isaac S., (Union, Broome Co ,) S D. 6, farmer leases 80

Wenn, John, (Campville,) S. D 4, dairyman and farmer 99.

Wescott, Wm., (Flemingaville,) S. D 23, farmer leases 29.

OWEGO.

WESTERN UNION TELEGRAPH OF-
FICE, (Owego,) south side Main, Ed-
ward B Thompson, operator.
Whaley, David K , (Owego,) carpenter and
farmer 40
Whitaker, Richard, (Flemingaville,) S D
12, farmer leases of H. Burgett, 70
WHITE, ANDREW, (Apalachin,) S. D 34,
farmer 85
WHITE, CHAS , (Owego,) (Haywood &
White )
White, Edwin, (Owego,) wholesale and re-
tail confectionery, North Avenue
White, Geo , (Little Meadows, Susquehan-
na Co , Pa ,) S. D 24, farmer leases 25
White, Horace, (Little Meadows, Susque-
hanna Co , Pa ,) S D 24, farmer 25
Whitney, David H , (Campville,) S. D 33,
farmer 27
WHITTEMORE, VIRGIL, (Owego,) S D.
17, dairyman, stock raiser and farmer
140.
Whittemore, Wm ,(Union Center, Broome
Co ,) S D 15, farmer 70
Whittimore, Alvin, (Union, Broome Co.,)
S, D 6, farmer leases 155.
Whittimore Charles, (Union, Broome Co ,)
S D. 6, farmer 47
Whittimore, Jason, (Union, Broome Co ,)
S D 6, farmer leases 66
Whittimore Lyman, (Union, Broome Co ,)
S D 6. farmer 117
Whittimore, Stanley, (Union, Broome Co ,)
S D. 6, farmer 50.
WICKS, LUCIUS M., (Owego,) S D 26,
tobacco raiser, farmer 8 and leases of
Stephen B. Leonard, 13
WIGHTMAN, ALFRED, (South Owego,)
S D. 16, farmer 68½.
Willard, Lewis D., (Owego,) (L. D & T F
Willard )
Willard, L D & T F, (Owego,) (Lewis D.
and Theodore F ,) props. Park Hotel,
Main corner Central Avenue
Willard, Theodore F., (Owego,) (L. D &
T F Willard )
Williams, Daniel M., (Owego,) S D. 39,
farmer 15
Williams, Geo E , (South Owego,) S D
16, farmer leases of Obadiah B Burton,
100
Williams, Harrison, (Apalachin,) S D 31,
farmer 25
Williams, Henry, (Owego,) confectionery,
Fox
Williams, Jacob, (Owego,) S D. 27, farmer
110
WILLIAMS, JOHN E , (Apalachin,) har-
ness maker and constable.
Williams, Lucy, (widow,) (Owego,) farmer
100 Liberty
Williams, Stephen L., (Owego,) S D. 18,
farmer 47 and leases 49
WILLIAMSON, EZRA M., (Owego,) S D.
37, farmer 80
WILLIAMSON, WILLIAM, (Flemingaville,) S D 14, farmer 80
Wilsie, Otis, (South Owego,) S. D. 22, farmer 150
Wilson, James, (Owego,) retired physician, owns Wilson Hall, prop crystal
door plate and (with J Fisher,) prop
Park Livery, corner Central Avenue
and Main

Winans, Orlando, (Owego,) S D 25, far-
mer 112
Winne, Walter V., (Gaskill's Corners,) S.
D 14, farmer 195
Winship, Frank, (Flemingaville,) S D 23,
horse trader and farmer 14
Winship, Samuel, (Flemingaville,) S D.
23, farmer 2
Witter, Lyman, (Owego,) S. D. 27, farmer
40.
Wolcott, Aaron, (South Owego,) S. D. 16,
threshing machine and farmer 50
Wood, Andrew J., (Owego,) S D 25, far-
mer 42
Wood, Catharine E , (widow,) (Apalachin,)
S D 28, farmer 75
Wood, Edmond, (Owego,) (with Royal P ,)
S D 2, farmer 100.
WOOD, GEO H , (Apalachin,) S. D. 34,
horse shoeing and general blacksmith-
ing, one-half mile south of Post Office
Wood, M E Miss, (Owego,) dress making,
Talcott.
Wood, Royal P., (Owego,) S. D. 2, (with
Edmond,) farmer 100
Wood, Wm , (Apalachin,) S D 13, farmer
71¼.
Woodward, Joseph, (Owego,) (Graham &
Woodward )
Worrick, Freeman, (Apalachin,) S. D. 28,
farmer 72.
WORRICK, LEANDER, (Apalachin,) S.
D 28, farmer 89½
Worrick, Nathaniel S , (Owego,) S D. 17,
farmer 36
Worthington, John C , (Owego,) general
ticket agent E. R. R and coal dealer,
corner West Avenue and McMaster.
Woughter, Andrew, (Campville,) S D 7,
farmer leases of Mary Billings, 80.
Woughter, Avery, (Campville,) (with
Charles,) S D. 4, farmer leases 67.
Woughter, Charles, (Campville,) (with
Avery,) S D 4, farmer leases 67
Woughter, Chester, (Campville,) S. D. 7,
farmer 25 and leases 25
Woughter, Cornelius, (Campville,) S D 7,
farmer 25
Woughter, Geo V., (Owego,) S D 26, far-
mer 20 and leasee of Abigail Woughter,
46
Woughter, John, (Campville,) S D 7, far-
mer 30
Woughter, Joseph, (Campville,) S D. 33,
farmer leases 117.
Woughter, Orson L , (Owego,) S D 26,
agent for agricultural implements.
WRIGHT, ALBERT G , (Owego,) harness
maker and carriage trimmer, North
Avenue corner Temple
Wright, John, (Owego,) S. D 11, farmer 60.
Wright, Jonathan H., (Owego,) S D. 39,
mason and farmer 4½
Writer, Gabriel M., (Owego,) conductor
Erie R. R , Main
YAPLE, CHARLES E , (Owego,) S. D. 37,
farmer leases 106
Yates, Alanson, (Owego,) S D 36, farmer
96.
Yates, Alonzo L , (Apalachin,) S D. 19,
farmer leases 70.
Yates, John 2nd, (Owego,) S. D. 36, farmer
70.

YATES, JOHN S, (Apalachin,) S D 15, farmer 100

YATES, TRACY, (Apalachin,) S. D. 31, farmer 51

Yearsley, John, (Campville,) S D 33, farmer leases of Thomas Cofferty, 118.

Young, George, (Owego,) S D 26, farmer 95.

YOUNG JOSEPH, (Owego,) S. D. 17, farmer 35 and leases of C Spring, 75.

Young Men's Christian Association, (Owego,) Lake, corner Main, Peter C Peterson, prest., Frank M Baker, vice-prest, Frank B Darby, corresponding secretary, Frank Slater, recording secretary, Edgar P Holdridge, treasurer

YOUNG, THOS B, (Owego,) S D 22, dairyman and farmer 166

Zimmer, Albert, (Flemingville,) S D 23, farmer.

ZIMMER, ALONZO, (Newark Valley,) S. D. 15, farmer 29.

# RICHFORD.

## (Post Office Addresses in Parentheses.)

ABBREVIATIONS.—S D , School District.

ABBEY EDWARD H., (Caroline, Tompkins Co ,) S D 4, farmer occupies 134

Allard, Jonathan S , (Harford Mills, Cortland Co.,) joint S. D 5, farmer 50

Allen, Carlton E ,(Caroline,Tompkins Co ,) S. D. 4, carpenter

Allen, Henry C , (Caroline, Tompkins Co ,) S. D. 4, farmer 37

Allen, James Jr , (Richford,) S. D 6, physician and surgeon

Allen, Sidney B ,(Caroline, Tompkins Co.,) S D 4, farmer leases 68.

ALLEN, STEPHEN M , (Caroline, Tompkins Co ,) S D 4, farmer 134

Allen, William, (Richford,) S D 6, carpenter

Arnold, Clement, (East Berkshire,) joint S. D 10, farmer 80

Ayers, Elias, (Richford,) S. D. 11, farmer 231

Ayers, James W , (Richford,) S. D. 6, shoemaker and farmer 28

Ayers, Job (Richford,) S D. 3, farmer 163.

AYERS, PHEBE Mrs.,(Richford,) S D 11, farmer 92

Ayers, Rudolph, (Richford,) S. D 3, farmer 128

Barden, Ezra S , (Richford,) S. D 6, farmer 117

BARKER, GEO W., (Slaterville, Tompkins Co ,) joint S D 1, farmer 289

Barnes, Grant W , (Richford,) S D. 6, agent for Eclectic Life Insurance Co., harness maker and farmer 14

Bayette Brothers, (Richford,) (*Morat M and Moran M* ,) manufs and dealers in cigars leaf tobacco &c

Bayette, Moran M , (Richford,) (*Bayette Brothers* )

Bayette, Morat M , (Richford,) (*Bayette Brothers* )

Beebe, Philo, (Center Lisle, Broome Co ,) farmer 44

Belden, Edgar F., (Richford,) joint S D 10, farmer occupies 100

Belden, Frederick C., (Richford,) S D 6, farmer 157

Belden, Wm F , (Richford,) S D 6, prop saw mill, lumber manuf and farmer 165.

Berry, Benjamin,(Caroline, Tompkins Co ,) S. D. 4, farmer 75

Blaksman, Asahel, (Harford Mills, Cortland Co ,) S, D 1, farmer 95

Blakeman, William, (Harford Mills, Cortland Co ,) S D 9, farmer 124

Bliss, Hiram R., (Harford Mills, Cortland Co.,) joint S D 5, saw mill, sash, door and blind factory

Bolster, Truman E , (Harford Mills, Cortland Co , S D 3, farmer 30

Boyce, Abraham, (Harford Mills, Cortland Co ) (*with William*,) S D. 9, farmer 95

Boyce, James E ,(Richford,) S D 6, wagon maker and farmer 5

Boyce, William, (Harford Mills, Cortland Co ,) (*with Abraham*,) S D 9, farmer 95

Boyce, William H , (Harford Mills, Cortland Co,) S D 9, farmer leases 102.

Brainard, Payson A., (Richford,) S D 6, stoves, tinware &c.

Brigham, Bostwick, (Richford,) S. D. 8, farmer 115.

Brookins, Charles, (Center Lisle, Broome Co.,) S. D 12, farmer

Brookins, Charles Jr , (Center Lisle, Broome Co ,) S D 12, agent for the sale of dry goods and farmer 62

Brooks, James L., (Richford,) S D 8, farmer 12

Brummage, John, (Speedsville, Tompkins Co.,) joint S. D. 3, farmer 3

Burleigh & Owens, (Richford,) (*Rufus S Burleigh and Levi Owens,*) blacksmiths

Burleigh, Rufus S ,(Richford,) (*Burleigh & Owens*)

Callender, Dewey & Co , (Richford,) (*E Elmore Callender, Henry A Tobey and Silas S Dewey,*) S D 11, props. saw mill, lumber manufs and own 240 acres

Clark, Abram, (East Berkshire,) joint S D 10, farmer 103½.

Clark, Edward, (Richford,) S. D. 6, insurance agent

Clark, Jonathan D , (Harford Mills, Cort-Co ) S D 3, shoemaker and farmer 8

Cleveland, Clinton, (Richford,) S. D 6, lumberman and farmer 126

Cole John, (East Berkshire,) joint S D 10, farmer 44.

Colliton, John B , (Richford,) S. D 11, farmer

Conger, Harmon S , (Richford,) S D. 8, agent for Smiley's Churn Thermometer, lumberman and farmer 143

Corey, Lewis, (Richford,) S. D 11, farmer 16

Crandall, Ira S , (Caroline, Tompkins Co ,) S D 4, carpenter and farmer 117

Crapo, Job, (Richford ) S D 11, farmer 43

Crapo Reuben, (Richford,) S D 11, farmer occupies 43

CROSS, ALBERT R , (Richford,) S D. 6, farmer 50

Crumb George W , (Harford, Cortland Co ,) S D 4, farmer 185

Curtis. Charles F., (Richford,) S D 6, farmer 185.

Daniels, Heman Jr , (Harford Mills, Cortland Co ,) joint S D 5, farmer 282

Daniels, Samuel H., (Harford Mills, Cortland Co.,) S. D. 5, engineer and surveyor

Darlin, Joseph, (Slaterville, Tompkins Co ) joint S D 1, farmer 12.

Darlin, Philo, (Slaterville, Tompkins Co.,) joint S D 1, farmer 3.

Darlin, Preston, (Slaterville, Tompkins Co ,) joint S. D. 1, farmer 2

Davis, Alfred (Harford Mills, Cortland Co ,) S D 6, farmer 160

Davis, John M , (Richford,) S. D. 12, farmer 71

Davis, Lewis B., (Richford,) S D. 12, farmer 86½

Decker, Catherine Mrs., (Harford Mills, Cortland Co ,) S D 9, farmer 102

Decker, James M , (Harford Mills, Cortland Co ,) S D 9 farmer 1½

Decker, Stephen, (Harford Mills, Cortland Co.,) S D. 9, farmer 56.

Delrymple, Samuel A , (Harford Mills, Cortland Co ,) S D 8, farmer 100

Deming, John H , (Richford,) S D 6, retired merchant and supervisor

Dewey, Silas S , (Richford,) (*Callender, Dewey & Co.*)

Dill, Solomon W., (Richford,) S. D. 6, wagon maker.

Dodge, Charles E., (Richford,) S. D 1, farmer 120

Donn, John Jr , (East Berkshire,) joint S. D. 10, farmer 50

Duel, David D , (Harford Mills, Cortland Co ,) joint S. D 5, farmer 104.

Dye, Dwight D., (Richford,) S D 3, farmer 77½

Dye, Milton R , (Harford Mills, Cortland Co ,) S D 1, farmer 81.

Earsley, Richard, (Caroline, Tompkins Co ) S D 8, farmer 123

Edmister, Henry, (Center Lisle, Broome Co.,) S. D. 12, saw mill and farmer 94½

Evans, Elizabeth Mrs , (Richford,) S D 8, farmer 17½

Fellows, Edward, (Caroline, Tompkins Co ) S D 4, farmer 100.

Fellows, Egbert M , (Harford Mills, Cortland Co ,) S. D 3, farmer 94

Finch, Clarence W., (Richford,) (*H S & C. W Finch,*) carpenter

Finch, E , (Richford,) S. D 6, foreman of H S Finch's log and lumber yard

Finch, Hotchkiss S., (Richford, (*H S & C W Finch,*) provisions, flour and feed, lumber dealer and farmer 396

Finch, H S & C. W., (Richford,) (*Hotchkiss S and Clarence W.,*) S D 6, saw and planing mills

Foote, Edwin W , (Speedsville Tompkins Co .) joint S D 3, farmer 10½

Foxgate, George, (Harford Mills, Cortland Co ,) S D 9, shoemaker and agent for Blanchard Foxgate, 72 acres

Foster, Bruce, (Center Lisle, Broome Co.,) S D. 12, farmer 62 and leases 62

Foster, James F , (Harford Mills, Cortland Co ,) S. D. 9, mason and farmer 122

Freeland, Joseph, (Richford,) S D 8, farmer 8

Freeland, Squire D , (Speedsville, Tompkins Co ,) joint S D 3, farmer 150

Fries, James M , (Harford Mills, Cortland Co.,) farmer 25.

Fundis, John, (Richford,) S. D. 3, farmer 250

Gee, Leroy, (Richford,) S D 1, farmer 25.

Gee, Mary A. Mrs , (Richford,) S D. 11, farmer 25

Gee, Philemon, (Richford,) S D 1, farmer 115.

GEER, GEORGE M , (Richford,) S D. 6, clerk and farmer 200

Geer, H C Mrs , (Richford,) S D 6, farmer 10.

Geer, Ichabod H , (Richford,) S D 11, farmer occupies 200

Gilbert, Milo Mrs., (Center Lisle, Broome Co ,) farmer 60

Glezen, Charles A , (Center Lisle, Broome Co ) farmer 200

Goodrich, William S , (Richford,) S D 3, farmer 167.

Griswold, William Rev , (Richford,) S D 9, Free Methodist clergyman and farmer 120.

Hale, Samuel B., (Richford,) S. D 11, farmer 120.

Hamilton, Alexander, (Richford,) S D 12, shingle weaver and farmer 20.

Hamilton, James L., (Richford,) S D 12, farmer 30

Hamilton, Luther B., (Harford Mills, Cortland Co ) S D 9, farmer 124

Hand, Horace, (Caroline, Tompkins Co ,) S. D. 4, carpenter and farmer 34

Haynes, Sylvester C., (Richford,) S. D. 11, farmer 100

Heath, Nathaniel, (Richford,) S. D. 6, carpenter

Heath, Seymour, (Richford,) S. D. 8, carpenter and farmer 37½

Hill, Wilson J., (Richford,) S. D. 3, farmer 40

Hoag, David, (Richford,) S. D 6, resident

Hoaglin, Walter, (Richford,) S. D. 6, farmer 50.

Holcomb, Harriet Mrs., (Richford,) S. D. 12, farmer 40.

Holcomb, John E., (Richford,) S. D. 11, farmer 50.

Holcomb, Milton, (Richford,) S. D. 12, farmer 75

Horton, Stephen, (Richford,) S. D. 11, farmer 50

Houck, Benjamin, (Richford,) S. D. 8, farmer 128.

Howland, James B., (Center Lisle, Broome Co.,) saw mill and farmer 380.

Howland, W Harrison, (Center Lisle, Broome Co.,) farmer 168.

Hudson, Ruth Mrs., (Richford,) S. D 1, farmer 85½.

Hyde, Seymour, (Harford Mills, Cortland Co.,) S. D. 3, farmer 200

Jayne, Amzi L., (Richford,) S D 3, farmer 112

Jayne, Samuel A., (Richford,) S D 3, farmer 150.

Jenkins, Evan, (Richford,) S D 6, farmer 70

Jennings, Henry A., (Center Lisle, Broome Co.,) S D 12, farmer 200.

Jennings, Justus, (Richford,) S D 8, farmer 135.

Jennings, William H, (Richford,) S. D. 8, farmer 170.

Jewett, Caroline Mrs., (Richford,) joint S. D. 10, farmer 93

Jewitt, Oliver, (Richford,) S D 8, farmer 100

Johnson, James B, (Richford,) S. D. 6, farmer 92

Kendall, John, (Richford,) S. D. 6, farmer 11

Keyes, Thomas S, (Richford,) S. D 11, farmer 68.

Lacy, James, (Richford,) S D 3, farmer 137½ and leases 145

Leach, Myron, (Richford,) joint S. D. 10, farmer 22

Leonard, Buien C., (Richford,) S. D. 11, foreman and head sawyer for Callendar, Dewey & Co

Leonard, John B, (Richford,) S. D 12, mechanic and farmer 25

Lowe, James, (Richford,) S. D. 8, farmer 90

Mallory, Loyal N, (Richford,) S. D. 8, farmer 6

Marsh, Aaron, (Richford,) S. D. 12, farmer 50

Marsh, Burr, (Center Lisle, Broome Co.,) farmer 44

Marsh, Burr Jr., (Center Lisle, Broome Co.,) farmer 100

Marsh, Washington, (Richford,) S. D 6, farmer 25

Matson, Isaac, (Caroline, Tompkins Co.,) (with Seth,) S. D. 4, farmer 90.

Matson, Orren, (Harford, Cortland Co.,) S D 3, farmer 88

Matson, Seth, (Caroline, Tompkins Co.,) S. D 4, mason and (with Isaac,) farmer 90

Matson, Silas, (Harford, Cortland Co.,) S D 2, farmer 25.

McIntyre, John, (Richford,) S D 3 farmer

McIntyre, Matthew, (Richford,) S. D 3, farmer 117

McVean, Charles U, (Richford,) S. D. 1, farmer 37.

Meachan, Orin N, (Richford,) S D 11, carpenter and farmer 60

Meloy, Charles T, (Richford,) S D 12, farmer.

Meloy, Timothy, (Richford,) S D 12, farmer 145

Millen, Andrew D, (Harford Mills, Cortland Co.,) S. D. 9, farmer leases 150

MOORE, ELIJAH, (Richford,) S. D 11, farmer 112.

MOORE, OSCAR D. REV, (Richford,) S. D 11, pastor of First Freewill Baptist Church, East Richford, and farmer 15

Moore, Richard, (Richford,) S D 8, farmer 150

More, Samuel, (Richford,) S D 11, farmer 26

Mcreuna, Chauncey, (Richford,) S D 12, farmer 130

Moreuna, John P., (Richford,) S D 12, farmer 77½

Myers, Harrison F., (Harford Mills, Cortland Co.,) S. D. 1, farmer 30

Myers, John S., (Harford Mills, Cortland Co.,) S D 1, farmer 50

Nash, E B, (Richford,) S D 6, justice of the peace

NASH, PHILANDER, (Richford,) S D 6, general blacksmith

Newton, Dela, (Richford,) S. D. 6, farmer 46

Northrup, George W., (Richford,) S. D. 8, physician and farmer leases 2½

O'Bryan, Edward, (Richford,) S D 3, farmer 125

Osborn, James F, (Richford,) S. D. 8, farmer 137

Owens, Levi, (Richford,) (Burleigh & Owens)

Parker, William W., (Harford Mills, Cortland Co.,) S D 5, farmer 100

Perkins, Frederick, (Harford Mills, Cortland Co.,) joint S D 5, mechanic and farmer 2½.

Perry, Ebenezer, (Caroline, Tompkins Co.,) S D 4, threshing machine and farmer 19½

Perry, Edwin A., (Richford,) S. D 8, mechanic and farmer

Perry, Francis G., (Richford,) S D 8, music teacher and farmer.

Perry, Maria Mrs., (Richford,) S. D. 8, farmer 133

Perry, Norman, (Richford,) S D 8, farmer

Phillips, Charles M, (East Berkshire,) farmer 100

Pierce, Benjamin C, (Harford, Cortland Co.,) S D 4, farmer 60

Polley, Amos, (Richford,) S D 11, farmer 25

Polley, Hiram, (Richford,) S D 11, farmer 70.

# GEORGE W. BARTON,

## MANUFACTURER OF CIGARS,

WHOLESALE AND RETAIL DEALER IN

## Tobacco and Smokers' Articles,

### No. 23 Main Street, - OWEGO, N. Y.

---

# ALFRED WHITE,

## ORNAMENTAL

# CONFECTIONER,

AND

## Fancy Cake Baker,

### No. 99 Court St., Binghamton.

**Parties and Weddings** supplied with Plain and Fancy Cakes, Ice Creams, &c   A fine assortment of Ornaments for Cake kept on hand

---

# The Ahwaga Chief,

# HORACE A. BROOKS,

## Editor and Proprietor.

*Publication Commenced February 23rd, 1872,*

—AT—

## OWEGO, TIOGA COUNTY, N. Y.

### Circulation July 1st, 1872, - 1,600.

*A Weekly Paper, 28 by 42 Inches, Devoted to Politics, Literature and Reform.*

Polley, Lemuel, (Richford,) S. D 6, farmer 40

Polley, Lemuel D , (Richford,) S. D. 11, farmer 207

Polly, Solomon, (Richford,) S D. 11, farmer 62

POWELL, ELIJAH, (Richford,) S. D. 6, physician and surgeon

Powell, H. A. Mrs , (Richford,) S D. 6, millinery and fancy goods

Powell, William H , (Richford,) S D 6, supt. of Bayette Bros cigar manuf

Rawley, Daniel, (Richford,) S D 6, prop Eagle Hotel and farmer, in Solon, Cortland Co , 227

Rawley, Hiram B , (Richford,) S. D. 6, town clerk, groceries and provisions.

Rich, Chauncey D , (Richford,) (*C D & G. L Rich,*) postmaster

Rich, C D. & G. L , (Richford,) (*Chauncey D and George L ,*) S. D. 6, general merchants

Rich, Chauncey L., (Richford,) S D. 6, railroad commissioner

Rich, George L., (Richford,) (*C. D & G L Rich,*)

Rich, Lucian D., (Richford,) S D 6, station agent, S C R. R and U. S. express agent

RICHFORD HOTEL, (Richford,) Hiram W Sheleman, prop.

Robinson, Calvin J , (Richford,) S D 6, farmer 100

Robinson, Emily Mrs , (Carolina, Tompkins Co ,) S. D 8, farmer 180

Robinson, Isaac N., (Richford,) S D. 3, farmer 60

Robinson, Martin, (Richford,) S D. 8, farmer 264

Rockefeller, Jacob S , (Caroline, Tompkins Co ,) S D. 4, charcoal burner, butcher, cattle dealer and farmer 82½

Rockefellow, Egbert, (Harford Mills, Cortland Co.,) S D 9, farmer 135.

Roe, Moses M., (Slaterville, Tompkins Co.,) joint S.D. 1, saw mill and farmer 225

Rogers, Solomon, (Harford Mills, Cortland Co ,) (*with Walter L ,*) S. D. 9, farmer 80

Rogers, Walter L , (Harford Mills, Cortland Co ,) (*with Solomon,*) S D. 9, farmer 80.

Root, Daniel Jr., (Center Lisle, Broome Co.,) farmer 86

Root, Reuben, (Richford,) S D. 11, farmer

Roper, James M , (Caroline, Tompkins Co.,) S D 4, farmer 20

Ruscher, William, (Carolina, Tompkins Co.,) S D 4, farmer 38 and leases 68

Satterly, James, (Richford,) S. D 1, farmer 50

SATTERLY, LYMAN J , (Richford,) S. D. 11, carpenter and farmer 3.

Sears, Diocleason, (Richford,) S D 1, justice of the peace and farmer 131½

Sears, James M , (Richford,) S D. 12, farmer 100.

SEARS, PHILLIP, (Richford,) (*with Quincy A ,*) S. D 1, farmer 105

SEARS, QUINCY A., (Richford,) (*with Phillip,*) S D. 1, farmer 105

X

Sexton, Oscar, (Harford Mills, Cortland Co ,) (*with Ransom,*) S D 6, farmer 200

Sexton, Ransom, (Harford Mills, Cortland Co ,) (*with Oscar,*) S D 5, farmer 200.

Sheldon, Henry B., (Harford, Cortland Co ,) S. D 3, farmer 146

SHELEMAN, HIRAM W., (Richford,) S D 6, prop of Richford Hotel.

Sherwood, Isaac, (East Berkshire,) joint S D 10, farmer 50

Smith, James E , (Richford,) joint S D 10, farmer occupies 130

Smith, James S., (Richford,) joint S.D. 10, farmer 104

SMITH, JULIUS C , (Richford,) S D 6, wagon maker, undertaker and farmer 1½

Smith, Nicholas E., (Harford Mills, Cortland Co ,) S D 9, farmer 52

Smith, Ralph P., (Richford,) S D 12, farmer 100

Smith, Robert, (Harford, Cortland Co.,) S D 2, farmer 138

SMYTH, SAMUEL M , (Harford, Cortland Co ,) S D. 2, farmer 53 and occupies 138.

Stanley, Anson, (Center Lisle, Broome Co ,) farmer 50

Stanton, Elisha W , (Harford Mills, Cortland Co ,) S D 2, farmer 55.

Steele, Clark, (Harford Mills, Cortland Co ,) S D 9, sawyer

Surdam, Francis M , (Richford,) S D 3, farmer leases 93

Sweet, William B , (Richford,) S D 6, farmer 30.

Talbot, David W., (Richford,) S D 6, farmer 165

Talcot, George, (Richford,) S D 1, farmer 70

Tarbox, Benjamin, (Harford Mills, Cortland Co.,) S D 5, farmer 40

Tarbox, David, (Harford Mills, Cortland Co.,) S. D 3, farmer 120

Thomas, William W., (Slaterville, Tompkins Co ,) joint S D 1, farmer 97.

Thomson, Samuel, (colored,) (Harford Mills, Cortland Co.,) S. D. 1, farmer 79

Thurston, Andrew P , (Richford,) S D 1, farmer occupies 25

Tryon, Miner M , (Harford Mills, Cortland Co.,) S D 9, farmer 42½.

Tryon, Oliver, (Harford Mills, Cortland Co ,) S D 1, farmer 60.

Tubbs, Elbert, (Richford,) S D. 1, farmer

Tubbs, Gamaliel, (Center Lisle, Broome Co.,) S D 12, lumberman and farmer 250.

Tubbs, Gamaliel Jr , (Center Lisle, Broome Co ,) S D 12, farmer 50.

Tubbs, Robert B , (Richford,) S D 1, mechanic and farmer 50

Tyler, Erastus, (Richford,) S D 11, shoemaker

Vincent, Peter D , (Harford Mills, Cortland Co ,) S D 5, farmer 140.

Walker, Erastus T , (Richford,) joint S D 10, farmer 86

Walker, Lyman, (Richford,) S. D. 6, farmer 87½

Walker, Orin, (Richford,) S D. 6, farmer 111 and leases 125.

Welch, Luther H., (Caroline, Tompkins Co ,) S D 4, farmer occupies 165.

Welch, Rufus H ,(Caroline, Tompkins Co ,) S D 4, farmer 128.

Welch, Thomas, (Caroline, Tompkins Co.,) S D 4, farmer 165

Wheaton, Mason S , (Harford Mills, Cortland Co ,) S D 3, farmer 60.

Wilcox, Gardner (Harford Mills, Cortland Co ,) S. D. 5, farmer 160

Wilcox, Smith, (Richford,) S D 3, farmer 70.

Willsey, John P., (Richford,) S. D. 1, farmer 40.

Willsey, Simon P., (Richford,) S D 12, farmer 275

Wilson, Josiah, (Richford,) S D 13, farmer occupies 44

Witter, Asa, (Richford,) joint S. D. 10, farmer 106

Woodard, John, (Richford,) S. D. 6, farmer 100

Young, Saloma Mrs , (Caroline, Tompkins Co ,) S D. 4, farmer 63

Zee, Holmes, (Richford,) S. D. 12, farmer 28

---

# SPENCER.

### (Post Office Addresses in Parentheses.)

ABBREVIATIONS —S D , School District

Abbott, Andrew, (North Spencer,) S D 8, farmer 100

Abbott, Reuben H , (Spencer,) S. D. 4, mail carrier and freightman

Ackler, Truman, (Spencer,) S D 8, farmer 2

Adams, Frank, (North Spencer,) (*with Wm. H ,*) farmer.

Adams, Wm H., (North Spencer,) S. D. 8, farmer 113¾.

Austin, Alvah, (Spencer,) S D 4, farmer 27¾

BAILEY, OLIVER P , (Spencer,) S. D. 16, farmer 50

BANGS & BRO., (West Candor,) (*Elbert L. and John A ,*) lumbermen, manufs. and dealers in lumber of all kinds.

BANGS, ELBERT L., (West Candor,) (*Bangs & Bro* )

BANGS, JOHN A., (West Candor,) (*Bangs & Bro* )

Barber, Adaline, (widow,) (Spencer,) S D 2, farmer 50

BARBER, FRED C , (Spencer,) farm laborer.

Barber, Hiram, (Spencer,) S D 14, cooper.

Barden Bros., (Spencer,) S. D. 4, meat, fish and hides.

Barden, Chas. H., (Spencer,) (*Barden Bros* )

Barnes, John S., (Spencer,) S. D. 4, shoe maker.

Bartron, John P., (Halsey Valley,) S. D 2, farmer 100.

BARTRON, MOSES, (Halsey Valley,) S D 2, (*with John P ,*) farmer 100.

Bassett, Shepard, (Spencer,) S D. 4, shoemaker

Bassett, —— Misses, (Spencer,) S. D. 5, farmers 90.

Beadle, Geo , (Spencer,) S. D 12, farmer leases of Truman Scofield, 115

Bell, Alfred, (Spencer,) S. D 5, carpenter

Bennett, Peter K , (Spencer,) farmer leases 175.

BENNETT, PETER K., (Spencer,) S. D. 4, farmer 185

Benton, Carmi, (Spencer,) D. S 8, farmer 80.

Benton, James L , (Spencer Springs,) S D. 6, farmer 100

Benton, Wm. H , (Spencer,) S.D. 6, farmer 50.

Berry, Nathaniel, (North Spencer,) S D 3, farmer 8 and leases of Harvey Lake

Bidlack, Ransom, (Spencer,) S. D. 2, farmer 175

Bingham, I. Augustus, (Spencer,) S D 6, farmer 100

Birchard, Lyman, (Spencer,) S. D. 7, farmer 18.

Birchard, Stephen, (Spencer,) carpenter

Blinn, Samuel D., (Spencer,) S. D. 4, farmer 50

Bliss, Theodore F , (Spencer,) allo. physician

Bliven, Chas. D , (Spencer,) (*with Luther H.,*) S D 4, farmer 49¾.

Bliven, Luther H., (Spencer,) (*with Chas. D ,*) S D 4, farmer 49½

BODA, FREDERICK C , (Spencer,) S D. 6, farmer 50.

BODA, GEO , (Spencer,) S. D. 6, farmer leases of Chas , 150

Bogart, Isaac, (Spencer,) S D 10, lumberman and farmer 128.

Borden, Simon, (Spencer,) S. D. 4, (*Borden Bros* )

Bostwick, LeRoy, (Spencer,) principal Union School.

Bowen, Daniel, (Spencer,) S D 14, farmer leases 50.
BOWEN, FRANK, (Spencer,) (with Daniel) S. D 14, farmer
Bowen, James G., (Spencer,) S. D. 14, farmer 45
Bowen, Seth, (Spencer,) S. D. 13, farmer 129
Bradley, Calvin W., (Spencer,) S D 4, farmer 225
Bradley, Chas E , (Spencer,) general merchant
Bradley, Lyman, (Spencer,) S. D 4, proprietor village property.
Brink, Alvadore, (Spencer,) S D. 2, farmer 25
Brink, James, (Spencer,) S. D. 14, farmer 100
Brock, DeWitt C., (Spencer,) S D. 5, farmer 50
Brock, Etheal, (Spencer,) S. D 14, farmer 140.
Brock, John, (Spencer,) S. D 8 lumberman, cattle dealer and farmer 117½.
Brock, Thos , (Spencer,) cattle dealer
Brooks, Chas. L., (Spencer,) S. D. 12, farmer 75
BROOKS, DANIEL, (Spencer,) S D 13, farmer 85.
BROOKS, DANIEL C , (Spencer,) S D 13, commissioner of highways, agent for Meadow King Mowing Machine and farmer 100
Brown, Geo W., (North Spencer,) S D 3, farmer 75
Brown, Margaret A., (widow,) (Spencer,) S. D. 8, farmer,2.
Brown, Wm T., (North Spencer,) S. D. 8, carpenter.
Brundage, DeWitt C., (Spencer,) S D. 4, carriage maker
BURHYTE, ANDREW Rev., (Spencer,) S D 4, M. E clergyman and farmer 147
Buttler, Morden U , (VanEttenville, Chemung Co ,) S. D. 1, farmer 75.
Butts, Andrew P , (Spencer,) S. D. 4, egg dealer and farmer 3
Butts, Chas E , (Spencer,) S. D 4, tannery and farmer 57.
Butts, Hyatt B , (Spencer,) S. D. 4, farmer 50.
Butts, Sarah M , (widow,) (Spencer,) S. D. 4, farmer 45
CARPENTER & NICHOLS, (Spencer,) (Wm C Carpenter and John A Nichols,) S D 4, manufs. sash, blinds and doors.
CARPENTER WM. C , (Spencer,) (Carpenter & Nichols,) S. D. 4, carpenter and joiner.
Cashaday, John, (Halsey Valley,) S. D. 2, farmer 83
CLAPP, WALKER G , (Spencer,) S. D. 4, photograph artist.
Clark, Dennis, (Halsey Valley,) S. D. 2, carpenter
Clark, Franklin, (North Spencer,) S. D. 3, farmer 50
Clark, Howard, (Spencer,) S. D. 4, house builder and farmer 29
Clark, John C , (Spencer,) S D. 7, farmer leases of Mrs. E. P. Goodrich, 250.

Clark Leverett J , (Spencer,) S. D. 6, farmer 215.
Clark, Lewis, (Spencer,) S. D. 4, carriage ironer
Clark, Theodore A , (Spencer,) S D 6, farmer 50
Clay, John, (Spencer,) S D 13, farmer 40.
Clinton, DeWitt C., (Spencer,) wheelwright and carpenter
Close, John E , (Spencer,) S D 4, harness maker.
COGGIN, ALBERT, (Spencer,) S D. 12, farmer 100.
Coggin, John V., (Spencer,) S D. 4, harness maker.
COGGIN, LOAMA T , (Spencer,) S D 4, farmer leases 210.
Converse, Theodore E , (Spencer,) S. D. 10, carpenter and farmer 97
Cook, M. A., (Spencer,) (with Thos.,) S D. 8, farmer 40
Cook, Thos , (Spencer,) (with M A ,) S D 8, farmer 40
COOPER, CHAS W , (West Candor,) hop grower, gardener and dealer in plants.
Cooper, John H Sen , (West Candor,) S D 22, farmer 5.
CORNELL, NATHAN T , (VanEttenville, Chemung Co ,) S. D. 4, farmer 100 and, in VanEtten, 70
Cortright, Ayres D , (Halsey Valley,) S D 2, farmer 16.
Cortright, Elbert, (Spencer,) S. D. 16, farmer 30.
CORTRIGHT, JOSEPH, (Spencer,) S. D. 4, cattle and wool dealer, lumberman and farmer 126
Cowell, Benj., (Spencer,) S D 4, carpenter.
Cowell, Chas , (North Spencer,) S. D 3, farmer 150
Cowell, Edward, (North Spencer,) S. D. 3, commissioner of highways and farmer 100
Cowell, James, (North Spencer,) S D 3, farmer 50.
Cowell, John A , (North Spencer,) S D 3, farmer 96
Cowell, Lewis, (North Spencer,) S. D. 3, farmer 50
Cowles, Aaron, (North Spencer,) S. D. 3, farmer leases 100
COWLES, JASON, (Spencer,) S. D. 18, farmer 50.
Cowles, Lewis, (North Spencer,) S D 3, farmer 102.
Cronin, Cornelius, (Spencer,) S. D. 5, farmer 131.
Crosson, Geo T. Rev., (Spencer,) S D 7, Baptist clergyman and farmer 40.
Davenport, Henry, (Spencer,) S. D. 2, carpenter
Davenport, Sherman, (Spencer,) S D 16, farmer 50.
Dawson, Chester W., (Spencer,) S D 12, farmer 180
DAWSON, JOHN, (Spencer,) S D 5, farmer leases 120
Dawson, Nelson, (Spencer,) S D 12, farmer 107.
Dawson, Phebe, (Spencer,) (with Maria Emory,) S D 13, farmer 50
Dawson Seth W , (Spencer,) S. D. 13, farmer leases of Geo. Brooks, 100.

# M. B. FERRIS,

## SPENCER, N. Y.

### DEALER IN

# Staple and Fancy Dry Goods,

## Hats, Caps, Boots, Shoes,

# Groceries,    Queensware,    Hardware,

## IRON, NAILS, GLASS,

# Drugs & Medicines, Paints, Oils,

*Family Medicines, Dye Stuffs, Perfumery,*

and **NOTIONS** generally. Our Goods have been bought low, for Cash, selected with the greatest care, and will be sold at the very lowest prices.

☞ **Call and Examine before Purchasing Elsewhere.**

---

### Mr. F. M. JEWETT

would respectfully announce to the people of Spencer and vicinity that he has rented the

# BLACKSMITH SHOP!

formerly occupied by S O SABIN, and is now prepared to do all kinds of work pertaining to the business.

# HORSE SHOEING

MADE A SPECIALTY Persons owning horses with contracted or flat feet will find it to their interest to give him a call. MR JEWETT, being a VETERINARY SURGEON of many years' practice, is also prepared to treat all diseases of the Horse

**F. M. JEWETT,    -    SPENCER, N. Y.**

---

# CHAS. STUART,

### DEALER IN

# Guns, Pistols,

### AND

## Sporting Articles Generally,

Fixed and Loose Ammunition,

☞ Fine Breech-Loading Shot Guns,

**43 Washington Street,**

Opposite Franklin House,

# BINGHAMTON, N. Y.

Dawson, Wm. A., (Spencer,) S. D 12, farmer leases of Mrs. Mary A. Dawson, 100

Day, John, (Spencer,) S. D 4, hardware, house furnishing goods, agricultural implements &c

Day, Wm S, (Spencer,) S. D. 8, blacksmith and farmer 49

Dean, John F, (Spencer,) S D. 5, farmer 58 and leases 126

DEAN, JUDSON, (North Spencer,) S. D. 3, farmer 7½.

Deming, Augustus C, (Spencer,) S.D. 4, farmer 47.

Deming, Wm. B., (Spencer,) S D. 4, farmer 48½.

Deming, Wm H, (Spencer,) S. D 4, stump puller and farmer 50

Deyo, Casper, (Spencer,) S. D. 16, farmer 20

Deyo, Chancey, (Spencer,) S. D. 14, mason and farmer 2½

DIKEMAN, GEO R., (Halsey Valley,) S. D 17, farmer 52

Dikeman, Michael P., (West Candor,) joint S D 4, farmer 5.

Dodge, Alvin, (Spencer,) S. D. 10, carpenter and farmer 50

DODGE, EDWIN, (Spencer,) S D 4, manufacturer of flour, feed and meal, manuf. and dealer in lumber, millwright, dairyman, 18 cows, farm and timber land 600.

Drew, Samuel, (Spencer,) S. D. 6, farmer leases of Leverett J Clark, 215.

Dutton, Ansel H, (North Spencer,) S D 9, farmer 197.

Eastham, John, (West Candor,) S D 17, farmer 20

EASTHAM, ROBERT, (West Candor,) S D. 17, farmer 113.

Eastham, Thos, (West Candor,) S. D. 17, farmer 52

Edwards, Philo, (Halsey Valley,) S. D. 10, farmer 75.

Emery, David, (Spencer,) S. D. 12, mason and farmer 65

Emery, James C, (Spencer,) S D 6, lumber manuf

Emmons Bros., (Spencer,) S D 4, general merchants

Emory, Marla, (Spencer,) (*with Phebe Dawson,*) S D 13, farmer 50.

Eunis, Samuel, (Halsey Valley,) S. D. 2, farmer 107

Evelin, Stephen H., (Spencer,) S. D 16, farmer 50

Farnsworth, Edgar, (Spencer,) S. D. 4, farmer 30

Farnsworth, Edgar, (Spencer,) S D. 8, farmer 29

Ferris, Andrew, (Spencer,) farmer leases 166

Ferris, Daniel, (Halsey Valley,) S. D. 10, farmer 30.

Ferris, Daniel Jr, (Halsey Valley,) S. D. 10, farmer 63

FERRIS, DAVID A., (Halsey Valley,) S D 10, (*with Edmund,*) farmer.

Ferris, Edmund, (Halsey Valley,) S D 10, lumberman and farmer 127.

Ferris, Geo. C., (West Candor,) S D. 7, farmer 108.

Ferris, Geo H, (Spencer,) S. D. 4, egg dealer, liveryman and farmer 10

Ferris, James, (Spencer,) S D 2, farmer 50 and leases 70

Ferris, James H., (Spencer,) S D 10, farmer 58

Ferris, John, (Spencer,) S. D. 2, farmer 90

Ferris, Joshua H., (Spencer,) S. D. 4, constable

Ferris, Myron, (Spencer,) S. D. 4, farmer leases of John McQuigg, 250

*FERRIS, MYRON B., (Spencer,) S D 4, general merchant.

Fish, Daniel T, (Spencer,) S D 7, stock broker, pension agent and farmer 90

Fisher, Chas B, (Halsey Valley,) S D 17, farmer 25

Fisher, Chas. J., (Spencer,) S. D. 4, druggist

Fisher, Clarence C., (Halsey Valley,) S. D 17, farmer 25

Fisher, John P.,(Spencer,) (*with Robert H,*) S D. 5, dairyman, 35 cows, and farmer 477½

Fisher, Leonard, (Spencer,) S D 4, farmer 150

Fisher, Luther W., (Spencer,) S. D. 8, farmer 90

Fisher, Marvin D., (Spencer,) coal, flour, feed &c.

FISHER, ROBERT H, (Spencer,) (*with John P,*) S D 5, dairyman, 35 cows, and farmer 477½.

Fleming, Wm H, (Spencer,) S D 16, lumberman and farmer 275

Foresyth, Henry, (Spencer,) (*with Silas Stone,*) S. D. 7, farmer 77.

Forsyth, Henry B., (Halsey Valley,) S. D. 17, farmer 60.

FOSTER, CHAS., (Spencer,) S D 7, farmer 113.

Fulton, Frederick, (Spencer,) S D 16, farmer 95

Furman, Horace, (North Spencer,) S. D. 3, farmer 80

Garatt, Corinth & Sons, (Spencer,) S D 7, farmer 136

Garey, A. Lafayette, (Spencer,) S. D 4, carriage dealer

Garey, Augustus T., (Spencer,) S. D. 4, resident.

Garey, Henry, (Spencer,) S. D. 4, farmer 50.

Gay, Patrick, (Spencer,) S. D. 7, farmer 150.

GAY, WHEELER B, (Spencer,) (*with Patrick,*) S D 7, farmer

Gibbs, Barzillia B Rev, (Spencer,) pastor Baptist Church.

Goodrich, Calvin E, (Spencer,) S D 4, farmer 85.

Goodrich, Calvin J., (Spencer,) S D 4, stone mason and teamster.

Goodsell, Jared H, (Spencer,) S D 14, farmer.

Griffith, Absalom, (Spencer,) S D 5, farmer 66.

Guinnip, Dempster M, (Spencer,) (*G & D M Guinnip*)

Guinnip, Geo., (Spencer,) (*G. & D M. Guinnip*)

Guinnip, G & D M., (Spencer,) (*Geo. and Dempster M* ) house and carriage painters.

Hagadoro, David B , (Halsey Valley,) S D 17, farmer 63 and leases of James, 160

Hall. Hervey S , (Spencer,) S D. 5, farmer 531

HALL, LEONARD F., (Spencer,) S. D. 8, carriage maker and carpenter.

Hallock, John, (Spencer,) S. D 4, lumberman and farmer 88

Hamilton, Joseph A , (Halsey Valley,) S D 16, farmer leases of I & L Manning, 105

Hanyan, David, (Spencer,) S D 17, farmer leases 80

HARRIS, JAMES M., (Van Ettenville, Chemung Co ,) S D 1, farmer 16.

HAYWARD, CHAS , (Spencer,) S D. 13, farmer 80

Hayward, Leonard, (Spencer,) S D 13 farmer leases 129

HEDGES, ROBERT F , (Spencer,) S D 10, farmer 75

HENDERSON DARIUS, (Spencer,) S. D 4, justice of the peace

Hodridge, Amos, (Spencer,) S. D. 2, farmer 217

Holdridge, Felix, (Van Ettenville, Chemung Co ,) S D 1, farmer 50.

Holmes, John, (West Candor,) lumberman, drover and farmer 230.

HOUCK ISRAEL, (Spencer,) S D 4, (*Houck & Snook,*) dealer in bees, honey, honey boxes, American side-opening bee hives with movable comb &c , also, S. D. 16, owns farm 50.

HOUCK & SNOOK, (Spencer,) (*Israel Houck and David L Snook,*) S D 4, manufs and dealers in harness, saddles, whips, robes, blankets &c.

House, Judge R , (Spencer,) S D 3, farrier and farmer 53

House, Lewis M , (North Spencer,) S. D. 3, farmer 45 and leases 33

House, Oakley A , (Spencer ) S D 4, liveryman, horse farrier, hackman and farmer 134.

Hover, Merritt L , (Halsey Valley,) S D 17, farmer 63

Howell, Henry B , (Spencer,) S. D. 4, farmer 31.

Howell, Ira M., (Spencer,) carpenter.

Howell, J , (widow,) (Spencer,) S D 4, farmer 15

Howell John D , (Spencer,) S D 16, farmer leases of Isaac H , 11

Howell, Jonathan F., (Spencer,) S. D. 16, farmer 1

Hubbard, —— , (widow,) (Spencer,) S. D. 6, farmer 10

Huddle, Jacob B , (Halsey Valley,) S D 17, farmer 56½

HUGG, HORACE A., (North Spencer,) (*Hugg & Mowers,*) S D 3, farmer 233.

Hugg, Luman H., (Spencer,) S D 8, farmer 121½.

HUGG & MOWERS, (North Spencer,) (*Horace A Hugg and Henry Mowers,*) S D. 3, manufs and dealers in lumber

Hulburt, Luther, (North Spencer,) S. D. 3, lumberman and farmer leases 256.

Hull, Eben, (Spencer,) S. D. 4, blacksmith and farmer 19

Hull, James B , (Spencer,) (*with Loring W.,*) S D 8, farmer 124

Hull, Loring W , (Spencer,) (*with James. B ,*) S D 8, farmer 124

Humphrey, Richard C., (Spencer,) S D. 8, shoemaker

Hunt, Isaiah, (Spencer,) S D 10, farmer 97.

Hutchings, Eli M., (Spencer,) S. D 4, carpenter

Hutchins, Chas. H , (Spencer,) S D 14, overseer of poor and farmer 60.

Hyatt, Wm W , (Spencer,) S. D. 4, farmer 14

Hyser, James T , (Spencer,) S D. 4, harness maker.

*JEWETT, FRANK M , (Spencer,) S. D. 4 veterinary surgeon and horse shoer.

JOHNSON, ALMANZA D., (Spencer ) S. D. 4 machinist.

Johnston, David O , (North Spencer,) S. D. 3, farmer 90

Johnston, John C., (North Spencer,) S D 3, farmer 42

Joy, Abel, (Spencer,) S D 7, farmer 47

Joy, Alvah, (Spencer,) S D. 6, farmer 50.

Joy, Daniel, (Spencer,) S. D. 4, brick manuf and farmer 70

Kirk, Chas , (Halsey Valley,) S. D. 17, farmer 74

Kirk, Henry, (Spencer,) S. D. 17, farmer 170

Kirk, Parker, (Halsey Valley,) S D 17, farmer leases of Samuel Clark, 76

Kirk, Stephen, (Halsey Valley,) S D 17, farmer 118.

Kouppenborg, Myron, (Spencer,) farmer leases of Ansel B Tallman, 100

Lake, Harvey, (North Spencer,) S. D. 3, farmer 162

Lake Rufus E , (North Spencer,) (*Lake & Vorhis,*) S D 3, postmaster and farmer 100

Lake & Vorhis, (North Spencer,) (*Rufus E Lake and Andrew C' Vorhis,*) general merchants

LANG, FREDERICK W , (Spencer,) S D 6, farmer 175

Larow, Bartlett, (Spencer,) S. D 10, farmer

Lawrence, Sevellan F , (Spencer,) S. D. 4, farmer 75

Leonard, Michael, (Spencer,) S. D 4, farmer 71

Lewis, Benj F , (Spencer,) (*with Wm ,*) S. D 8, farmer 300

Lewis, Wm , (Spencer,) (*with Benj F.,*) S D 8, farmer 300.

Lott, Benj (Spencer,) S. D 4, carpenter and farmer 74

Lott, Isaac M , (Spencer,) house painter

Lotz, Hartman Jr , (North Spencer ) S. D. 3, farmer 100.

Lotze, Betheney, (widow,) (North Spencer,) S. D. 8, farmer 50

Mabee Daniel, (Spencer,) S D 4, blacksmith

Mabee, Franklin H., (Halsey Valley,) S. D. 2, farmer 103

Mabee, Roderick B., (Spencer,) S D 13, farmer leases of Edward Cowell, 100

Mabee, Theodore, (Spencer,) S D 6, farmer 160.

Maine, C. I , (Spencer,) physician.

Maine, Christopher V , (Spencer,) S D. 4, physician and farmer 116.

Maine, Ira L , (Spencer,) S D 4, carpenter and farmer 57½

Manley, Geo S , (Halsey Valley,) S. D. 17, farmer 116.

Manning, Levi, (Halsey Valley,) S. D. 16, (*I. & L Manning* )

Manning, Robert, (Halsey Valley,) S. D 10, farmer 82.

Manning, Wm. H , (Spencer,) S D 6, farmer 74

Martin, Ira, (Spencer,) S D. 6, dairyman, 25 cows, and farmer 850.

Martin, I Woodford, (Spencer,) (*with Ira,*) farmer

McMaster, James, (Spencer,) S D 10, farmer leases 97

McMaster, Jeremiah T , (Spencer,) S D. 4, farmer 151 and, in Tioga, 100

Mead, John, (North Spencer,) S. D. 8, farmer 100

Mead, Lewis, (North Spencer,) farmer leases 100.

MESSENGER, CHANCEY S., (Spencer,) sawyer.

Miller, Elizabeth, (widow,) (Spencer,) S D 4, resident.

Moffitt, Daniel S., (Spencer,) S D 7, farmer 40

Monroe, James H , (Spencer,) carpenter.

Moody, Chas., (Spencer,) S D 4, farmer 99

Morse, Sidney E , (West Candor,) joint S. D 4 , farmer 23.

Mosher, Hiram, (Spencer,) S. D. 6, farmer 90.

MOWERS, HENRY, (North Spencer,) (*Hugg & Mowers* )

Nelson, James, (Spencer,) S D. 14, justice of the peace and farmer 127.

Nelson, Nathaniel, (Spencer,) S. D. 7, farmer 50

News, Gabriel B., (Spencer,) S. D. 2, farmer 97

NICHOLS, JOHN A., (Spencer,) (*Carpenter & Nichols,*) director, station and express agent, Ithaca & Athens R R , prop steam saw and planing mills, farmer 60 acres and 150 acres timber land in S D 4.

Norris, Alonzo, (Spencer,) S. D 4, physician, breeder of Jersey cattle and Essex swine, and farmer 250.

ODELL, FREEMAN, (Spencer,) S. D. 10, farmer 98.

Odell, James, (Spencer,) S D 2, farmer 85.

OLMSTEAD, DAVID, (Candor,) S D 6, farmer 75

OSBORN, ELIJAH, (Spencer,) S D 4, manuf light and heavy wagons, sleighs, cutters &c . also owner of farm 105 acres in District 2.

Osborn, Jabez, (Spencer,) S. D. 7, farmer 140.

Osborn, Phineas, (Spencer,) S. D. 7, farmer 76

Osborn, Ransom, (Spencer,) S D 7, farmer 15.

Palmer, J Hawley, (Spencer,) S. D. 8, carpenter and farmer 45

Park, Anthony, (Spencer,) S D. 8, farmer.

Patrie, Ostrander, (Spencer,) S D. 7, farmer.

Perrin, Alex., (Spencer,) S. D. 4, farmer 60.

Perrio, Wm H , (Spencer,) S. D 4, blacksmith

Petty, Gesper, (Spencer,) S D 16, farmer 105

Pierson, Geo E , (West Candor,) S. D 7, farmer 152½

Pierson, Silas, (North Spencer,) S. D 3, carriage builder and farmer 54

PLATT, J RUFUS, (Spencer,) prop. Spencer Hotel.

Platt, Jerome R., (Spencer,) (*Stanclift & Platt* )

Post, Robert L., (Spencer,) town clerk.

Post, Thos F , (Spencer,) S. D. 4, blacksmith

Post, Thos. L , (Spencer,) S. D 4, clothier

Post, Wm , (Spencer,) clothier

PRAY, EPHRAIM, (Spencer Springs,) S D 6, prop Spencer Springs Hotel

Pray, Wm. H., (Spencer Springs,) S. D. 6, post master and farmer 200

Quick, Elijah E , (Halsey Valley,) S. D. 17, farmer 50

Quick, Erastus, (Spencer,) S. D. 17, farmer leases of Harrison Vasbinder, 80.

Randall, David, (Spencer,) S D 3, farmer 60

Raub, Barnett, (Spencer,) S. D 16, farmer 105

Raub, Henry S , (Spencer,) S D 16, farmer 150

REEVE, AARON D., (Spencer,) S. D. 4, farmer

REMSEN, ABRAM, (Spencer,) S. D. 4, general laborer.,

Remsen, M. J. Mrs., (Spencer,) millinery and dress making.

Riker, Anthony, (Spencer,) S D 7, inspector of elections and farmer 100.

Riker, Captain L , (Spencer,) S D. 7, carpenter.

Riker, James L., (Spencer,) justice of the peace and carpenter.

RIKER, OLIVER P., (Spencer,) S. D. 7, farmer 100

Riley, John, (Spencer,) S. D 4, farmer 60.

RIPLEY, LORENZO D., (Spencer,) S D 7, farmer 80

ROBINSON, DANA F., (Spencer,) town assessor, millwright, carpenter and joiner, and farmer, in Candor, 86.

Rolfe, James K., (Spencer,) S D 2, farmer 50

Rosekrans, Geo., (Spencer,) S. D 4, wagon maker.

Rumsey, Johnson, (Halsey Valley,) S. D. 17, farmer 73

SABIN, EDGAR D , (North Spencer,) (*with Philo,*) S. D. 3, farmer.

Sabin, Philo, (North Spencer,) S. D. 3, lumberman and farmer 125

Sabin, Seth, (Spencer,) S D 7, farmer 25

Sabin, Seth O , (Spencer,) S. D 4, blacksmith, farmer 125 and 300 acres timber land

Sager, Cornelius E , (Halsey Valley,) S. D. 17, lumberman and farmer 52½

Sanford, James H , (Spencer,) S D 4, manuf wood pumps and farmer 65.

Saunders, Randall M., (Spencer,) S. D. 6, farmer leases 150.

Saunders, Zaccheus M., (Spencer,) S D 6, farmer 150.

Sawyer, Ezra O , (Spencer,) carpenter.
Scofield, Horace, (Spencer,) S D 11, farmer 64
SEELEY, A & BRO , (Spencer,) (*Alfred S and Seymour,*) manufs and dealers in lumber of all kinds, also lath and shingles.
SEELY, ALFRED S (Elmira, Chemung Co ,) (*A Seely & Bro.*)
SEELY, SEYMOUR, (Spencer,) (*A. Seely & Bro*)
Shaw, Joseph B., (West Candor,) farmer 100.
Shaw, Wm A , (Spencer,) S. D 2, mason and farmer 80
Shepard, Alva A , (Spencer,) wagon maker
Shepard, John Q., (Spencer,) S. D 4, farmer 250.
Shepard, Mary Mrs , (Spencer,) S D 7, farmer 55
Shepard, Myra A., (widow,) (Spencer,) S. D. 7, (*with heirs,*) farmer 137
SHEPARD, SILAS J , (Spencer,) (*S. & S. J Shepard*)
SHEPARD, SILVENES, (Spencer,) S D 4, postmaster and farmer 75.
SHEPARD, S. & S J , (Spencer,) (*Sylvenus and Silas J ,*) dealers in dry goods, groceries, drugs &c
SHEPHARD, EDWIN A., (Spencer,) tall sawyer.
SIGNER, ADANIGER, (North Spencer,) (*with Albert,*) lumberman and farmer
Signer, Albert, (North Spencer,) S. D. 15, lumberman and farmer 300
SIGNER, PETER, (North Spencer,) S D 3, farmer 49.
Smith, Joshua S , (Halsey Valley,) (*with Jared Van Marter,*) S. D. 2, lumber manuf.
Smith, Philemon N., (North Spencer,) S D 9, farmer 100
Smith, Wm., (Spencer,) S D 4, mail carrier and farmer leases of Garrett R House, 6
SNOOK, DAVID L , (Spencer,) (*Houck & Snook*)
Snyder, Sely H., (Spencer,) S. D. 2, farmer 130
SOUTHWELL, EDWIN B , (Spencer,) S. D. 14, farmer 160.
Southwick, Albert, (Halsey Valley,) S D 17, farmer 83
Southwick, Orange L , (Spencer,) S D 10, farmer 50
Spaulding, Benj., (Spencer,) S. D. 4, farmer 200.
SPAULDING, CHAS W , (Spencer,) (*with Benj ,*) farmer 200.
Spaulding, John C , (Spencer,) S. D. 16, farmer 99.
SPAULDING, SMITH, (Spencer,) (*with Benj ,*) farmer
Spaulding, ——, (widow,) (Spencer,) S D 4, resident
SPENCER HOTEL, (Spencer,) J. Rufus Platt, prop
SPENCER SPRINGS HOTEL, (Spencer Springs,) S D 6, Ephraim Pray, prop
Stanclift, Isaac S , (Spencer,) (*Stanclift & Platt,*) supervisor
Stanclift & Platt, (Spencer,) (*Isaac S Stanclift and Jerome R. Platt,*) S. D. 4, general merchants.

Stark, Cain B , (Spencer,) S. D. 8, cooper
Stark, Chas , (Spencer,) S D 8, cooper
Stark, Stephen, (Spencer,) cooper
STEVENS, CHAS W , (North Spencer,) S D 3, farmer 64
Stevens, David, (Spencer,) S. D. 6, farmer 75.
Stevens, Harmon, (Spencer,) S D 6, farmer 158
STEVENS, JACOB, (Spencer,) S D 7, commissioner of highways and farmer 65
Stevens, John, (Spencer,) S D 6, farmer 12½.
Stevens, Thos J , (Spencer,) S D 3, farmer 49
Stewart, Ira, (North Spencer,) S D 8, lumberman and farmer, in Newfield, 64
Stilson, James L , (West Candor,) joint S. D 4, farmer 58.
STILSON, NELSON T , (West Candor,) joint S D. 4, teacher and farmer
STINARD, JOSEPH, (Spencer,) miller in E Dodge's grist mill
Stone, Silas, (Spencer) (*with Henry Foresyth,*) S. D. 7, farmer 77
Stow, John M , (Spencer,) S D 4, furniture dealer and undertaker.
Strait, Sylvester, (West Candor,) lumberman
Strong, Austin C., (Spencer,) S D 7, farmer 50.
Stryker, Jacob, (Spencer,) S. D. 7, farmer 42½.
Swartout, Marcus L., (Spencer,) S D 5, farmer leases of Leonard Fisher, 140
Swartout, Thos T , (Spencer,) S. D. 6, farmer 75.
Tallman, Charlotte, (widow,) (Spencer,) S. D 13, farmer 112.
Tompkins, James, (Spencer,) S D 7, farmer 269
Tompkins, Joshua, (Spencer,) S D 4, farmer 40
Towner, Martin L., (Spencer,) S. D. 7, meat dealer.
Troy, John, (Spencer,) S D 5, farmer 70
Troy, Wm , (Spencer,) S. D. 5, farmer 84
Tucker, Horace, (West Candor,) (*with Wm ,*) S D 7, farmer 125
Tucker, William, (West Candor,) (*with Horace,*) S D 7, farmer 125.
Turk, David, (North Spencer,) S. D. 15, farmer 70.
TURK, STEPHEN D., (North Spencer,) S. D. 8, blacksmith
Tyler, Luzern, (Halsey Valley,) S. D. 17, farmer 132.
Valentine, Elvin, (West Candor,) S D 7, farmer 30
Valentine, John, (West Candor,) shoemaker.
Valentine, Wm., (Spencer,) S D. 2, farmer 104.
VanKleek, Jesse, (Spencer,) carpenter
VanMarter, Enos, (Spencer,) S. D. 2, farmer leases
VanMarter, Jared, (Halsey Valley,) (*with Joshua S. Smith,*) S. D. 2, lumber manuf.
VanMarter, Milo D., (Spencer,) farmer
VanMartin, Jared, (Halsey Valley,) S D. 2, farmer leases 103.

Vannatta, John, (Spencer,) S D 16, farmer 105.

Vannatta, John D , (Spencer,) S D. 16, lumberman and farmer 43½.

VanNostrand, Peter, (Spencer,) S. D 16, farmer 35.

VanWoert, Lewis J , (Spencer,) S. D. 6, farmer 175.

VanWOERT, SAMUEL D , (Candor,) S D 6, farmer 75.

VanWoret, Wm., (Spencer,) S D 12, farmer 60.

VENABLE, EDWARD W., (Spencer,) telegraph operator at Depot.

Vergason, Iddo, (West Candor,) S. D. 17, farmer 56.

Vorhis, Andrew C., (North Spencer,) (*Lake & Vorhis,*) S D, 3, station agent 1. & A R R and farmer 324.

Vorhis, Catharine, (Spencer,) S D. 13, farmer 36.

VORHIS, TRUMAN P., (North Spencer,) S. D. 3, farmer 100

VORHIS, WM. R., (North Spencer,) S D 3, farmer 50

Voris, Stephen Rev , (Spencer,) pastor Congregational Church

VOSE, EPHRAIM, (Spencer,) S D 6, carpenter and joiner

Vose, Alfred, (West Candor,) town assessor and farmer 100.

Vose, John P , (Spencer,) S D 4, groceries, provisions, crockery &c

VOSE, THOS , (Spencer,) S D 6, farmer 240

Vose, Wm H , (West Candor,) surveyor, grocer and farmer.

Wait, Geo W., (Spencer Springs,) S. D 6, farmer 50

WALLING, WM. O , (Spencer,) S. D. 14, boot and shoe maker.

Washburn, Paschal P , (Spencer,) shoemaker.

Watkins, David, (Spencer,) S. D. 6, farmer 75.

Watson, John, (Spencer,) S. D. 8, carpenter.

WATSON, OLIVER, (Spencer,) manuf and dealer in furniture

Weeks, Stephen M , (Spencer,) S D. 14, farmer 84.

Wells, Josiah, (Spencer,) S. D 4, blacksmith.

West, Albert, (Spencer,) S D 2, farmer leasee of Elijah Osborn, 114.

West, Marshall C., (Spencer,) S D 2, wagon maker and farmer 60

Wheeler, Jesse A., (Spencer,) S D. 4, farmer 61

White, Gilbert G , (Spencer Springs,) S D 6, farmer 100

Willerby, Major P , (Spencer,) cooper

Williams, John F. Rev , (Spencer,) pastor M E Church

Woodford, Cyrus, (Spencer,) S. D 7, farmer 168

Woodford, —— Misses, (Spencer,) S.D 10, farmer 113

WOODRUFF, THOS , (Spencer,) S. D. 8, farmer 90

Wright, Hanford B , (Spencer,) S. D. 4, (*Hugg & Wright,* Van Ettenville,) farmer 6½ and, in Danby, 90

# TIOGA.

(Post Office Addresses in Parentheses.)

ABBREVIATIONS.—S. D., School District

Adkins, R M., (Owego,) S. D. 17, farmer leasee 166.

AHART, CHARLES, (Strait's Corners,) S D 16, (*with George,*) farmer

Ahart, George, (Strait's Corners,) S. D. 16, farmer 45.

Algin, Elam, (Owego,) S. D. 2, cooper

Anderson, Ezra F., (Owego,) S D 15, farmer 125

APPLINGTON, SARAH M., (Smithsborough,) milliner.

Armstrong, A Mrs , (Owego,) joint S. D. 8, farmer 49.

Armstrong, James R , (Smithsborough,) S. D 8, refused information

AYERS, CHARLES, (Owego,) S. D. 1, manuf. and dealer in family medicines.

AYERS, THOS F , (Owego,) S D 15, farmer 65.

BABCOCK, JOSHUA, (Smithsborough,) carpenter

Badger, Lucius A., (Owego,) S D. 10, farmer 62.

BAKER, EPAPHRAS W , (Halsey Valley,) S D 10, farmer 51

Baker, Melvin J , (Tioga Center,) S D. 3, carpenter

BARRETT, C. A W., (Tioga Center,) S D 3, butcher

BARTRON, MOSES, (Smithsborough,) S. D 5, farmer 75.

Batron, Alonzo, (Smithsborough,) S D 6, farmer.

Baner, Christian, (Strait's Corners,) S D 16, millwright, carpenter and farmer 131

BEDELL, WM H , (Smithsborough,) S. D 5, assessor and farmer 140

Best, Phila Mrs , (Tioga Center,) S D 7, farmer 50

Bidwell, —— Mrs , (Strait's Corners,) S. D. 16, farmer 35.

Bignall, B B , (Owego,) farmer 26.

Blake, Wm , (Tioga Center,) S D 3, foreman in tannery

Bogart, Peter V , (Smithsborough,) S D. 19, farmer 120

BOGET, HENRY, (Owego,) S. D. 17, farmer 36.

Bonham, Morris,(Smithsborough,) S D 19, farmer 52.

Bowers, Adam, (Strait's Corners,) S D 16, farmer 63½

Bowman, Zebulon, (Smithsborough,) S. D. 8, farmer 20.

Brayton, Mary D Mrs , (Owego,) S D 1, farmer 20.

Brink, Joseph S , (Owego,) S D 9, farmer 90

Brink, Wm , (Owego,) S D 2

Bristol, George, (Owego,) S. D. 1, farmer 92

BRISTOL, WHEELER H , (Owego,) S D 1, farmer 110.

Brooks, Benjamin J., (Tioga Center,) S. D. 3, farmer 150

Brooks, Charles (Tioga Center,) S D. 3, farmer leases 50.

Brooks, George, (Tioga Center,) S D. 3, tanner.

Brooks, James, (Tioga Center,) S D. 7, farmer

Brooks, Lot M., (Tioga Center,) S D. 3, tanner and farmer 10

Brooks, Wm , (Tioga Center,) S. D. 3, farmer 55

Brown, Ethan, (Owego,) S. D. 2, farmer 250.

BROWN, GABRIEL, (Halsey Valley,) S. D 13, agent for Ithaca Agricultural Works and farmer 132

BROWN, GEORGE Rev (Tioga Center,) S D 3, Baptist clergyman.

BROWN, JOHN V., (Owego,) S D 9, farmer 48

BUCHANAN, JAMES H., (Halsey Valley,) S D 10, farmer leases of John, 165

Buchanan, John K., (Halsey Valley,) S. D 10, farmer 165.

BURLINGTON, JOSEPH, (Owego,) S D 17, blacksmith and farmer 185.

Burlington, Robert, (Owego,) S. D. 16, farmer 150

Burns, Robert, (Owego,) S. D. 2, farmer 26

Cable, Silas, (Tioga Center,) S D 10, farmer leases of W H Best, 75.

Candall, Samuel, (Smithsborough,) S. D. 19, farmer 40

Canfield, Amos, (Smithsborough,) S. D. 4, farmer 250

Capel, John, (Catatonk,) S D 17, night hand in Catatonk tannery and farmer 25

Caple, Chrisjohn, (Strait's Corners,) S D. 16, farmer 38

Caple, Philip W , (Catatonk,) S. D. 16, farmer 50.

CARLETON, EDWARD D , (Owego,) S. D. 15, farmer 160

Carmer, Thomas H , (Halsey Valley,) S D. 19, farmer 102

Carpenter, Jesse C , (Smithsborough,) S. D 4, dairyman and farmer 200

CARPENTER, PETER R , (Smithsborough,) S D 19, dairyman and farmer 76

Casterline, John, (Halsey Valley,) S D 10, blacksmith.

Casterline, Warren J., (Smithsborough,) S D 19, farmer 72.

CATLIN, BENJAMIN F., (Owego,) S. D. 9, farmer 150.

Catlin, Emeline Mrs , (Owego,) farmer 50

Catlin, George, (Owego,) S D 9, wagon maker and farmer 16

Catlin, Mary J , (Owego,) S. D. 9, farmer 26.

Catlin, Nathan, (Owego,) S D 9, farmer 44

CHAMPION, JAMES H , (Strait's Corners,) S. D 18, lumberman

Champlain, Joshua, (Owego,) (with Robert,) joint S. D. 8, farmer 8.

Champlain, Robert, (Owego,) (with Joshua,) joint S D 8, farmer 8

Chapman, George M , (Tioga Center,) S. D. 3, carpenter and farmer 20

Chase, Gideon O , (Smithsborough,) station agent E R R

Clark, Alexander H , (Strait's Corners,) S. D 16, farmer 47

Clune, James, (Smithsborough,) S D. 19, farmer 49

Cole, Benjamin F , (Owego,) S D. 6, miller and farmer 50

Cole Dennis R , (Tioga Center,) S. D. 3, engineer.

COLE, FRANK E , (Smithsborough,) joint S D 1, farmer leases of R C , 100

Cole, John, (Tioga Center,) S D 3, farmer

Collin Nathan S , (Smithsborough,) farmer 70

Colman, James, (Tioga Center,) S D. 11, farmer leases of Mrs Leonard, 100

Conklin, John, (Tioga Center,) farmer 2

Cook, Esther Mrs , (Strait's Corners,) S D 18, farmer 55

Cook, Fernando, (Strait's Corners,) S D 18, farmer leases 82.

COONS, DANIEL, (Strait's Corners,) S. D. 7, lumberman, prop of saw mill, commissioner of highways and farmer 172.

Coons, Elias, (Tioga Center,) S D. 7, farmer 53

Coons, Johnson E., (Tioga Center,) S D 7, farmer 200.

COONS, WALTER, (Strait's Corners,) S D 7, farmer 94

COOPER, FRANCIS A., (Halsey Valley,) S D 10, farmer leases of Samuel Gilkey, 65.

Cooper, Wesley, (Halsey Valley,) S D 10, farmer 52

Cortright, Elias, (Tioga Center,) S D 3, resident.

Courtright, Charles, (Owego,) S. D. 2, farmer

CRANDALL, BENJAMIN, (Halsey Valley,) S D 13, farmer 25 and leases of Wm. Gilss, 126.

Crater, Warren W , (Tioga Center,) S. D 3, farmer 125

CRAWFORD, ABRAM, (Owego,) S D 17, farmer

Culli, Adam, (Strait's Corners,) S D. 16, cooper and farmer 50

Cunningham, Daniel, (Owego,) S. D. 9, farmer 82 and leases 32

Daily, Daniel, (Barton,) joint S. D. 12, farmer 273.

Daniels, John, (Tioga Center,) S D. 10, painter and farmer 100.

Davenport, Albert, (Barton,) joint S D 12, farmer 30

Davenport, Alonzo, (Barton,) joint S D 12, farmer 45

Davenport, Ann Mrs., (Halsey Valley,) farmer 84.

Davenport, Henry, (Strait's Corners,) joint S D 12, farmer 50.

Davenport, Jackson, (Smithsborough,) S. D 5, farmer 45

DAVIS, ALBERT, (Smithsborough,) blacksmith.

Davis, Nathaniel W Jr , (Owego,) S D 2, farmer 117.

Delano, Chas , (Owego,) S D 1, mason.

Delano, Reuben, (Owego,) S D. 1, mason

Dexter, Geo , (Owego,) S. D. 15, (with Stephen,) farmer 55.

Dexter, Nathaniel T , (Owego,) S D. 1, manuf boots and shoes, prop planing mill and inspector of elections.

Dexter, Stephen, (Owego,) S. D. 15, surveyor and farmer 55.

Dexter, —, (Owego,) (Farnham & Dexter )

Deyo, Charles, (Owego,) S. D. 6, farmer

Deyo, Wm , (Owego,) S D 6, farmer 33

Dinehart, Thomas, (Tioga Center,) S D 8, tanner and farmer

Doane, David, (Smithsborough,) S D 19, farmer 50

DOANE, TIMOTHY N., (Strait's Corners,) S. D 18, farmer 73

Drake, Ezra E., (Halsey Valley,) S D 18, farmer.

Drake, George P., (Smithsborough,) tinner

DRAKE & POOLE, (Smithsborough,) (W J Drake and E V Poole,) dealers in general merchandise, hardware and tin

DRAKE, W J., (Smithsborough,) (Drake & Poole )

Duff, Alexander L., (Tioga Center,) S. D. 7, farmer 150

Duff, Andrew, (Tioga Center,) S D. 7, farmer 65

Duff, James, (Owego,) S. D 9, farmer 75.

Duff, John, (Halsey Valley,) S. D. 7, farmer 68.

Duff, Robert H.,(Tioga Center,) S D 7, farmer 50.

Duncan, Alexander, (Owego,) S. D. 6, farmer 115.

Duncan, George, (Strait's Corners,) joint S. D. 12, shoemaker

Dundun, Thomas, (Owego,) S. D. 6, farmer 50.

Earll, David, (Tioga Center,) S D. 3, farmer 130

EASTHAM, PETER, (Strait's Corners,) S. D 18. farmer leases of Thomas Robinson, 65

EATON, AMBROSE P., (Smithsborough,) attorney and counselor at law.

Eberhart, Peter, (Owego,) S. D 17, farmer 42

ECKERT, GEORGE F , (Smithsborough,) S D 19, farmer 150.

Edwards, Christopher, (Halsey Valley,) S. D. 18, farmer 25.

Edwards, Samuel, (Owego,) S D 15, farmer 11.

Ellis, Wm H., (Smithsborough,) S D 8, farmer

Emerson, Jonathan, (Strait's Corners,) S. D 15, farmer 90

Emerson, Robert H , (Strait's Corners,) S. D. 7, assessor and farmer 167

EMERSON, SAMUEL H , (Strait's Corners,) S D. 16, farmer 87½

Emerson, Stephen, (Strait's Corners,) S. D. 15, farmer 50.

Emerson, Wm , (Strait's Corners,) farmer 70.

Estep, J , (Smithsborough,) S D 11, blacksmith.

Evans, Thomas, (Strait's Corners,) S D 17, farmer 52

Evlin, Benjamin, (Strait's Corners,) S D. 18, farmer 94

FARNHAM, ANDREW O , (Owego,) S D 15, commissioner of highways and (with Sylvester,) farmer 65

Farnham, Chas , (Owego,) S. D 15, agent Glens Falls Insurance Co and farmer 58

Farnham & Dexter, (Owego,) planing mill

Farnham, Enos S., (Owego,) S D. 1, farmer 75

FARNHAM, FREDERICK A , (Owego,) joint S. D 8, Owego and Tioga, wheelwright, wool carder and farmer 140

FARNHAM, GEO. A , (Owego,) S D 1, farmer 33.

Farnham, Orin, (Smithsborough,) blacksmith.

Farnham, Sylvester, (Owego,) (with Andrew O ) S D 15, farmer 65.

Fenderson, Isaiah C., (Tioga Center,) S D 3, manuf of lumber, shingles and lath, and farmer 10

Finn, Patrick, (Owego,) S. D. 15, farmer 200

Fitzgerald, Edward, (Owego,) S. D 2, farmer

Foote, Jared, (Owego,) S D 1, farmer 25

FOOTE, JARED A., (Owego,) S. D. 1, overseer of poor and farmer 13.

Foote, Lyman B., (Owego,) S D. 1, farmer 38

FORD, OLIVER P,, (Owego,) S. D. 9, dairyman and farmer 57

FRANKLIN, B. B., (Tioga Center,) S D 3, prop of Tioga Center Flouring Mill and farmer 8.

FRENCH, JEREMIAH, (Tioga Center,) S D 3, manuf. boots and shoes, and deputy postmaster

Fuller, Joseph A., (Tioga Center,) S D 10, groceries

GARLAND, FREDERICK J., (Smithsborough,) S D 5, farmer

Garvey, Isaac, (Strait's Corners,) joint S. D 12, farmer 308.

Geer, Rezin J , (Strait's Corners,) S. D 7, farmer 82

Gile, Leonard, (Tioga Center,) S D. 8, farmer 68

GILE, SOLOMON H., (Halsey Valley,) S D 13, farmer 52

Giles, Wm W , (Halsey Valley,) notary public and farmer 150

Gilkey, Peter P., (Halsey Valley,) S. D 10, farmer 108½

Gillson, Jehial, (Owego,) S D 9, farmer 44.

Gillson, Nathan S., (Owego,) S. D 2, farmer lessee of Henry Younge, 150

Giltner, Wm. V., (Barton,) S D 5, farmer 100

GOODENOUGH, DELOSS, (Smithsborough,) manuf. and dealer in boots and shoes, and postmaster.

Goodrich, Andrew J , (Owego,) S. D 14, farmer 160

GOODRICH, EPHRAIM, (Owego,) S. D 14, farmer 160

Goodrich, G. L., (Owego,) S D 14, farmer 135

Goodrich, Herman, (Owego,) S D 9, farmer 35.

Goodrich, John A , (Owego,) S D 2, farmer 160

Goodrich, Noah, (Owego,) S D 14, farmer 47

Goodrich, Stephen, (Owego,) S. D. 14, farmer 100

Gray, George, (Owego,) S. D. 6, painter and farmer 5

GRAY, JOHN C , (Smithsborough,) dealer in coal, lime, plaster &c , station agent S. C. R R

Gray, ——, (Smithsborough,) (*Tuttle & Gray.*)

Greene, Calvin E , (Strait's Corners,) S D 18, sawyer and farmer 3

Greene, J G , (Owego,) S. D. 2, carpenter

Greene, Stephen, (Strait's Corners,) S. D. 18, shoemaker and farmer 2

Guyles, Daniel, (Strait's Corners,) S. D 18, farmer 25

Guyles, Rufus, (Strait's Corners,) S D 18, farmer 30

Haldin, Daniel, (Tioga Center,) S D 11, farmer lessee of Walace & Horton, 50.

Hamilton, Theodore A , (Halsey Valley,) S D 10, carpenter

Hanbury, Adam, (Strait's Corners,) S. D 16, farmer 42

HANBURY, ADAM Jr., (Strait's Corners,) S D 16, farmer 50 and lessee of James Bates, 55

HANBURY, EZRA, (Strait's Corners,) S. D 16, farmer 58¾

HAND, EDWARD, (Tioga Center,) S. D. 7, lumberman, farmer 100 and lessee of Morris Best, 153

Hann, Martin, (Tioga Center,) S D 10, shoemaker

Hanna, John, (Smithsborough,) joint S D 1, farmer 80.

Harding, Adna, (Catatonk,) S. D. 1, farmer 4½

HARDING, JOHN, (Owego,) S D 1, carpenter and joiner, millwright and farmer 1.

Harlie, Wm , (Strait's Corners,) joint S D 12, farmer 130.

Harris, Reuben T , M. D , (Smithsborough,) drugs, medicines and jewelry

Hart, Henry, (Smithsborough,) S D 8, farmer 7

Hawes, Oliver, (Owego,) S D 1, farmer

Higby, Alanson B , (Tioga Center,) (*with Forman S ,*) farmer 96½

Higby, Forman S , (Tioga Center,) postmaster and (*with Alanson B ,*) farmer 96½

Hill, Abner J , (Tioga Center,) S D 3, sawyer

Hill, Thomas, (Smithsborough,) S. D. 4, mason.

Hinkley, Cornelius B , (Tioga Center,) S D. 11, farmer 25.

Hobler, Peter, (Strait's Corners,) S D 16, farmer 27

Hobler, Peter Jr , (Strait's Corners,) S. D 16, farmer 52.

Hoff, Cornelius D., (Tioga Center,) S. D 7, farmer 80.

HOFF, HIRAM S , (Tioga Center,) S D 7, farmer 98

Hoff, Sanford, (Tioga Center,) S D. 7, lumberman and farmer 40.

Hoglen, Peter, (Owego,) S. D. 2, farmer.

HOLLISTER, WM H , (Halsey Valley,) S D 10, farmer 95

Holmes, John, (Tioga Center,) S D 3, farmer 50

Holt, Wm. H , (Smithsborough,) joint S. D 1, farmer 75.

Hoover, David T , (Smithsborough,) S D. 19, farmer lessee of E. Dubois, 50

Horton, Abram, (Owego,) S D 14, farmer 125

HORTON, BENJAMIN, (Owego,) S. D. 2, farmer 90

Horton, Charles, (Owego,) S D. 1, (*with Daniel B.,*) farmer 136

Horton, Daniel B., (Owego,) (*with Charles,*) S D. 1, farmer 136

Horton, Geo M., (Smithsborough,) cabinet maker and undertaker

Horton, Gurdon, (Owego,) S. D. 2, farmer 100

Horton, G S , (Owego,) S. D 2, farmer 100

Horton, Isaac S., (Owego,) S. D 2, lumberman and farmer 100

HORTON, THEODORE, (Owego,) S. D. 14, farmer 100

Houghtaling, W. R., (Owego,) S. D. 15, farmer 14.

Hoyt, Ira, (Halsey Valley,) S. D. 10, cooper.

Hoyt, James, (Halsey Valley,) S D 10, grocer

Hyatt, John D , (Owego,) S. D 17, farmer 55

HYATT, JOHN M , (Owego,) S. D. 17, mail carrier and farmer 55

HYDE, HENRY, (Owego,) S D 1, cooper and farmer 1.

Hyers, Charles, (Halsey Valley,) S. D 10, cooper and farmer 2.

JEWETT, CHAS F., (Catatonk,) S. D. 15, lumberman and farmer 100

Jewett, Harris, (Catatonk,) S. D. 15, farmer 140.

Jewett, Wm. A , (Catatonk,) S D 15, farmer lessee 30.

JOHNSON, ARTHUR A , (Smithsborough,) S. D. 5, farmer.

Johnson. Charles F , (Owego,) S D. 2, farmer 230
Johnson, J J , (Smithsborough,) S. D 5, farmer 75
Johnson, John S., (Smithsborough,) S. D 5, farmer 120.
Johnson, Julius, (Barton,) S D 5, farmer 100
Johnson, Peter, (Tioga Center,) S. D 8, mechanic
Johnson, Wm. H., (Smithsborough,) S. D. 5, farmer 100
Jones, Horace, (Owego,) S D. 1, farmer 45
Jones. Stephen W., (Owego,) S D. 1, farmer 45
Jones, Wm. H , (Owego,) joint S D 8, farmer 74
Keeler, Egbert, (Owego,) S D 1, miller
Keeney, S B. Rev , (Tioga Center,) M. E. clergyman
Keith, George W , (Halsey Valley,) S D 10, farmer leases of O T. Gilkey, 146½.
Kies, Peter S , (Strait's Corners,) S D. 13, farmer 50
King, Adam, (Owego,) S. D. 16, farmer 35
KING, ADAM Jr , (Strait's Corners,) S. D 17, farmer 156.
King, John W , (Smithsborough,) S D 4, farmer leases 125.
Kipp, George, (Owego,) S D 1, farmer 80
Krapp, Sylvester Jr , (Smithsborough,) S D. 8, physician and surgeon.
Kuykendall, Samuel, (Tioga Center,) S D. 3, farmer 86.
KYLE, DANIEL Y , (Tioga Center,) S. D. 3, farmer leases of J G. Smith 150
Lamonte, Seth D , (Tioga Center,) S. D 11, lumberman and farmer 115
Landers, Wm., (Owego,) S D. 9, farmer 100
LANE, CHARLES T , (Owego,) S D 9, farmer 80 and leases of Noah Goodrich, 30
LANE, WALTER N , (Owego,) S D. 1, farmer leases of Geo J Pumpelly, Glen Mary Farm
Leach, Stephen W , (Owego,) S D 1, prop of Leach's Mills and farmer 40.
Leach, W H , (Owego,) S D 1, farmer 25
Leonard, George, (Tioga Center,) S D. 3, mason and farmer 50
Leonard, John H., (Owego,) S. D. 2, farmer 63
Lewis, Martin V., (Owego,) S. D 6, farmer 103
Lawlor, Patrick, (Owego,) S D 6, farmer 80
Light, Eli, (Smithsborough,) S D 4, farmer 137.
Light, Henry, (Smithsborough,) S D 4, farmer 73.
Link, Joseph, (Tioga Center,) S D 11, farmer.
LOUNSBERRY, AMOS L., (Smithsborough,) S D 8, farmer 100
LOUNSBERRY, BENJAMIN Jr (Smithsborough,) S D 8, farmer 125
Lounsbery, Harvey Rev , (Smithsborough,) S. D 5, W M. clergyman and (with S.,) farmer 129
Lounsbery, S , (Smithsborough,) S D 5, (with Harvey,) farmer 129
Lounsbury, Clark, (Tioga Center,) S. D. 8, farmer 82

Lounsbury, Lewis, (Tioga Center,) S D 3, farmer 150
LUCE, PERMELIA Mrs., (Tioga Center,) S. D 5, farmer 225.
Luddington, J A., (Smithsborough,) S D 11, farmer 83
LUM, LYMAN S , (Tioga Center,) S D 5, farmer 108½
LYONS, JOHN, (Smithsborough,) shoemaker
Martin, Fred , (Tioga Center,) S. D. 3, general merchant.
Mead, Albert, (Tioga Center,) S D 3, farmer
Mead, James R , (Owego,) S. D. 6, farmer 150.
Merchant, C. W., (Owego,) S D 2, commercial traveler and farmer 20
Meeple, Joshua, (Owego,) S. D 17, farmer 80
Middaugh, James E., (Owego,) S D 1, farmer.
MIDDAUGH, LORENZO T , (Smithsborough,) S. D 8, mechanic
Middauh, Elijah, (Owego,) S D 6, farmer 70.
Miller, Ezra, (Smithsborough,) S D 4, farmer 195
MOFFIT, ROBERT J., (Smithsborough,) S. D 11, farmer 50
Morton, Geo. E., (Owego,) joint S D 5, farmer
Mulock, David, (Smithsborough,) S D 8, farmer 150.
Munson, Heman, (Owego,) S D 1, farmer leases 87
Myers, John H , (Smithsborough,) telegraph operator
NEALLY, JOHN F , (Owego,) S D 14, farmer 216
Nichols, George J , (Tioga Center,) (Nichols & Ross )
Nichols & Ross, (Tioga Center,) (George J Nichols and John W Ross,) S D 7, props. of Beaver Meadows Steam Mill and farmers 250
Nickerson, Amos V , (Catatonk,) S D. 15, farmer leases of J. O McMaster, 50
NOBLE, ASA S , (Halsey Valley,) S D 10, carpenter and painter
O'Connell, Barney, (Owego,) S. D 15, dairyman and farmer leases of P K Bennett, 163
O'Connor, Joseph, (Owego,) S D. 6, farmer 19.
Ohart, Moses, (Tioga Center,) S D 3, prop of Tioga Center Hotel and town clerk
Orcutt, Eliza Mrs., (Owego,) S D 1, resident
Padgett, George W , (Tioga Center,) S D 3, farmer.
Pearsall, John O., (Smithsborough,) S D 4, carpenter and farmer 3
Papard, Jackson S , (Smithsborough,) S. D 19, farmer 50
PEPPER, JOHN T , (Smithsborough,) S. D 19, farmer 100
Perry, Albert A , (Smithsborough,) S. D. 11, carpenter and farmer 56
Pickering, Josiah, (Smithsborough,) general merchant and supervisor
PICKERING, JOSIAH Jr , (Tioga Center,) S D. 3, dealer in general merchandise

Platt, Houston, (Smithsborough,) S D. 8, farmer 12

POOLE, E V , (Smithsboro·gh,) (*Drake & Poole*,) owns 20 acres.

Post, A W , (Tioga Center,) S D. 3, physician and surgeon

Preston, Silas, (Owego,) S D 2, farmer leases of J Goodrich, 140

Price, —— Mrs , (Smithsborough,) S D. 8, farmer 3.

Quirn, J G & J , (Tioga Center,) props of Tioga Center Tannery

Randsll, Walter C , (Smithsborough,) grocer, justice of the peace and farmer 25

Ransom, E D., (Tioga Center,) S D. 3, groceries &c.

Ransom, Wm , (Tioga Center,) S D 3, lumberman and farmer 1400

Ranson, Chas E , (Tioga Center,) S D 3, station agent, Erie Depot, and farmer 285

RAUCH, GEORGE, (Strait's Corners,) S D 16, farmer 82

Reed, Paul, (Owego,) S D 6, farmer 95

Richards, Benjamin, (Smithsborough,) S. D 19, farmer 170

Rider Amos L , (Strait's Corners,) S D 7, farmer 90

Rider, Charles F , (Tioga Center,) S D 7, farmer leases of Stephen, 180.

Rider, Dana B , (Halsey Valley,) S. D 10, farmer 90

Rider, Jacob S , (Tioga Center,) farmer 50

Rider, Stephen, (Tioga Center,) S D 7, farmer 180

RIDER, STEPHEN J., (Strait's Corners,) S D 7 prop of saw mill, lumberman and farmer 135

Rise, Chauncy, (Owego,) S D 6, farmer leases of James Taylor, 80

ROBERTS, JAMES M , (Owego,) S D. 15, farmer leases of John Link, 18

Robertson Robert, (Barton,) farmer 50½

Robertson, Thomas, (Smithsborough,) S D 19 farmer 73.

Ross, Ellis H., (Smithsborough,) S. D. 5, farmer 250

Ross, John W , (Tioga Center,) (*Nichols & Ross* )

Rumsy Nelson, (Halsey Valley,) S D 10, farmer 40.

Russell, Holmes W., (Owego,) S. D. 17, farmer 145

Russell, VanNess, (Owego,) S D 17, dairyman and farmer 166

Schoonover, A. L & S L , (Smithsborough ) joint S D. 1, farmers lease of N M 272

SCHOONOVER, CHARLES P ,(Tioga Center,) S D 13, lumberman, blacksmith, prop of stone quarry and farmer 147.

Schoonover, Jackson F , (Tioga Center,) S D 13, millwright and mechanic.

Schoonover, James T , (Tioga Center,) S D 13, river pilot and fox hunter

Schoonover, Martin V , (Owego,) S. D. 9, farmer 19

Schoonover, Nicholas, (Tioga Center,) S. D. 3, farmer 140.

Schoonover, Samuel, (Tioga Center,) S D 3 farmer 234

SCHOONOVER, SMITH , (Tioga Center,) S D 3, farmer 74

Schutt Chas., (Halsey Valley,) S D 10, general merchant.

Segar, George, (Halsey Valley,) S D. 13, farmer 40

Severn, George W , (Smithsborough,) grocer

Sharp, Wm , (Smithsborough,) joint S D 1, farmer 75

Shear, Jeremiah, (Halsey Valley,) S. D, 7, farmer 100

Shipman, George H , (Barton,) S. D 19, farmer leases of Mrs Rose, 100.

Shorter, Harriet, (Halsey Valley,) S D 13, farmer 108

Signor, Charles, (Tioga Center,) S D 10, lumberman and farmer 60

SIGNOR, GEO H , (Tioga Center,) S. D. 10, lumberman and farmer

Sisson, George, (Owego,) S D 1, constable and farmer 20

SLATE, NELSON, (Owego,) S. D. 6, farmer leases of D L Durphy, 300

Smith, Cornelius D , (Tioga Center,) S. D. 3, farmer 97

Smith, Cynthia A , (Smithsborough,) S. D. 5, farmer 100

Smith, David T , (Owego,) S. D 3, farmer 100.

Smith, George, (Tioga Center,) S D. 10, farmer 240

Smith, Horace K , (Tioga Center,) S D. 19, pump maker and farmer 76

Smith, James T , (Tioga Center,) S D 3, lumberman and farmer 120

SMITH, JOHN G , (Tioga Center,) S D. 3, lumberman and farmer 843

Smith, John Y , (Smithsborough,) S D 5, farmer 250

Smith, Michael, (Smithsborough,) S. D 5, farmer 185.

SMITH, SAMUEL A , (Smithsborough,) carriage maker

Smith, Spencer E., (Owego,) S. D 9, farmer 40

Smith Stephen H , (Owego,) S D 9, carpenter

Snyder Adam, (Strait's Corners,) S D 16, farmer 46

Snyder, Nicholas, (Owego,) S. D 16, farmer 55

Snyder, Nicholas M., (Strait's Corners,) joint S D 12, saw mill and farmer 8

Snyder, Peter, (Strait's Corners,) joint S. D 12, farmer 67

Snyder, Peter J. (Strait's Corners,) joint S. D. 12, farmer leases 67

SOLOMON, WM C , (Owego,) S D. 1, carpenter and joiner, and farmer 76

Spaulding, Eliza Mrs , (Owego,) S D 17, farmer 100

Spencer, Alvah, (Owego,) S. D. 9, farmer 128

Spencer, Charles H., (Owego ) S D 9, farmer 07

Spencer, David, (Owego,) S D 6, farmer 1½

SPENDLEY, ANDERSON, (Smithsborough,) (*R & A Spendley*.)

SPENDLEY, RICHARD, (Smithsborough,) (*R & A Spendley* )

SPENDLEY, R. & A., (Smithsborough,) (*Richard and Anderson*,) S D. 4, manufs. brooms and farmers 370.

Stalker, Wm. P., (Owego,) S D. 1, wagon maker and farmer 25

STEELE, JAMES, (Owego,) S D 6, farmer 190

STELLER, STOKES, (Tioga Center,) S D 10, prop of saw mill and farmer 227.

Stewart, John, (Smithsborough,) S. D 19, farmer 100.

STILES, B C, (Owego,) S D. 14, general agent for Bristol Iron Works and farmer 20.

STILES, F H., (Owego,) S. D. 14, farmer 20.

STIMSON, CHARLES W., (Smithsborough,) cooper.

Strait, Alvinza, (Strait's Corners,) joint S. D 12, farmer

Strait, David, (Strait's Corners,) joint S D. 12, post master and farmer 67¾

Strait, John G , (Strait's Corners,) joint S. D 12 peddler

SWARTWOOD, ANDREW, (Halsey Valley,) S D 10, shoemaker

Swartwood, Edmond, (Owego,) S. D. 2, farmer 28

Swartwood, Edwin, (Owego,) S D 6, farmer leases of Ephraim Goodrich, 100

Taylor, Alexander, (Owego,) S D 9, farmer 45.

Taylor, Charles E , (Halsey Valley,) S D. 10, postmaster and farmer 26.

Taylor, Fred H , (Halsey Valley,) S D 10, prop saw mill, agent for Halseyville plow and farmer.

Taylor, Gideon, (Owego,) S D. 2, carpenter

Taylor, Ira, (Halsey Valley,) S. D 10, farmer 105.

Taylor, Jairus A , (Owego,) S. D. 9, farmer 60

Taylor, John T., (Owego,) S. D. 2, farmer 62¾

TAYLOR, NORMAN G , (Owego,) S. D. 9, farmer 91.

Taylor, Rodney, (Smithsborough,) S. D. 5, farmer 80.

TERBUSH, LANCELOTT B , (Strait's Corners,) S D 14, prop of Grove Steam Mill, lumberman and farmer 100

Terrell, Charity, (Smithsborough,) hotel keeper.

Thayer, Frank A., (Barton,) joint S D. 12, carpenter and farmer leases of Sally Daily, 150.

Thayer, Jerome B , (Tioga Center,) S D. 7, lumberman and farmer 66

Thayer, Wm., (Tioga Center,) S D. 3, saw mill

THAYER, WM S., (Smithsborough,) harness manuf.

Thorn, Warren, (Owego,) farmer 50

Tiffany, A F., (Owego,) S D 1, painter and farmer 6

TRACY, JAMES R , (Owego,) S D 1, sawyer

Tribe, John, (Halsey Valley,) S. D. 13, farmer 104

Truesdal, David S , (Owego,) S D. 9, farmer 57

Truesdal, Jeremiah, (Owego,) S. D. 9, farmer 80.

Truesdal, Wm. L , (Owego,) S D. 9, tanner and farmer leases 25.

Truman, Gilbert, (Owego,) S. D 2, farmer 120

Turner, James, (Tioga Center,) S D 7, farmer 100

TURNER, PETER, (Strait's Corners,) S. D. 18, farmer 115

Tuttle & Gray, (Smithsborough,) flour, feed, plaster. lime &c

Ulrick, John, (Owego,) S D 17, farmer 48.

Valentine, —— Mrs., (Strait's Corners,) S. D 16, farmer 51.

Vandemark, George, (Smithsborough,) joint S D. 1, farmer 50.

Vandermark, A. Mrs , (Smithsborough,) tailoress and prop. of saloon.

Vanduzer. Henry, (Catatonk,) S D. 15, farmer 20

VanGorder Elias, (Tioga Center,) S D 10, farmer 57

VanInven, Elias, (Strait's Corners,) joint S. D. 12, farmer 80

Vanoostran, John, (Smithsborough,) S. D. 3, farmer 56

Vanostrand, James, (Smithsborough,) S D. 11, farmer 40.

VanRiper, George, (Halsey Valley,) S. D. 13, farmer 50

VanWert, Smith R , (Tioga Center,) S D. 11, farmer leases of Dr. Benton, 80

Vasbinder, Eliza Mrs , (Halsey Valley,) S. D 10, farmer 150.

Vasbinder, James H., (Halsey Valley,) S. D 10, school teacher and farmer.

VERMILYA, ABRAM, (Owego,) S. D. 1, farmer 172.

Vosburg, Henry P., (Halsey Valley,) S. D. 10, physician

Walden, Joseph H , (Halsey Valley,) S.D. 10, farmer 1

Wallace, David, (Owego,) S D 2, farmer 175.

Wallace, David B., (Owego,) S D 2, (with David,) farmer

Watkins, John, (Smithsborough,) S D 4, farmer 30

Weber, Philip, (Owego,) S. D 16, farmer 40

WEBER, PHILIP Jr., (Owego,) S D 16, farmer 51½

Weiss, Sebastian, (Owego,) S D 6 farmer 100.

West, Charles, (Halsey Valley,) S D 10, farmer 75.

WEST, LUTHER B , (Halsey Valley,) S. D 10, speculator, dealer in merchandise, justice of the peace and sessions, dairyman and farmer 468.

Wheeler, Benjamin, (Strait's Corners,) S D 18, farmer 69.

Wheeler, Hendrick S., (Tioga Center,) joint S. D 18, farmer

Whitcomb, John M., (Smithsborough,) S D 19, farmer 52

WHITE, BARNEY H , (Owego,) S. D 17, farmer 128

White, Dudley, (Strait's Corners,) S. D. 16, farmer 55

White, Lewis, (Smithsborough,) S. D. 8, farmer 52

Whitley, Joel S., (Catatonk,) S D 15, farmer 140

Whitmarsh, Abram, (Owego,) S D 1, farmer 74

Whitmarsh, Daniel, (Owego,) S D 1, farmer 1

Whitney, I N , (Owego,) S. D 6, farmer leases of J Goodrich, 63

Whyte, George A., (Owego,) S. D. 6, butcher and farmer 30

Wiggins, Henry, (Tioga Center,) S D 10, farmer 42

WIGGINS, NORMAN L , (Tioga Center,) farmer.

Wiggins, Silas 2d, (Tioga Center,) S D 10, blacksmith

Wilbur, Everett A., (Halsey Valley,) S D 10, blacksmith

Willmott, James R , (Owego,) S D.1, saw, plaster and cider mills

Wilmot, George W , (Owego,) S D 17, farmer

Wilmot, William, (Owego,) S D 17, farmer 105

Wilson, Wm., (Owego ) S D 9, farmer 1

Winters, Joseph, (Smithsborough,) S D 8, prop of Smithsborough Creamery and farmer 150.

Wolcott, George, (Smithsborough,) S D 5, farmer

Wood, Charles O , (Halsey Valley,) farmer leases of L. B West, 425

WOOD, GEORGE, (Strait's Corners,) S D 18, farmer 97.

Wood, Joseph, (Strait's Corners,) S. D 18, farmer 75.

WOOD, PETER, (Halsey Valley,) S D 10, lumberman and farmer 175

Wood, Spencer, (Halsey Valley,) S D 13, farmer 50

Woodburn, David P , (Smithsborough,) S D 3, farmer

Wright, S Y., (Tioga Center,) S D 3, blacksmith.

Young, Henry, (Owego,) S D 2, farmer 200

Zorn, George, (Owego,) S D 16, farmer 40.

Zorn, Jacob, (Owego,) S D 17, farmer 27

Zorn, John, (Strait's Corners,) S D 16, farmer 15

# PUBLISHER'S NOTICES.

**G. G. Knibbs,** manufacturer of Boots and Shoes, 13 Lewis Street, Binghamton, N Y , publishes a humorously illustrated card on page 216 We do not hesitate to say that the conception of the artist only justly conveys the idea of the reasonable figures at which the goods of Mr Knibbs are disposed of The culprit in the picture, all will agree, deserves a good *booting*, and all will likewise agree that Mr. K. is an adept in that profession. If he don't get *fits* to *boot*, we are mistaken in our estimate of the ability of Mr Knibbs

**Conner & Orr,** General Blacksmiths and Horse Shoers, Binghamton, print a card on page 228. Messrs. C. & O. do a general Blacksmithing and Horse Shoeing business, and are prompt and reliable in the execution of all orders Mr Conner is the proprietor of Conner's Celebrated Hoof Ointment, which is said, by those who have tried it, to be unexcelled as a remedy for diseases of the Hoof

**Miss Mary A. Lawton,** Fashionable Dress Maker and Tailoress, 35 Hawley Street, Binghamton, publishes a card on page 212 Those requiring her services in either of the above branches, will find her prompt and careful in executing their orders.

**Dr. C. A. Perkins,** Dentist, 67 Court Street, Binghamton, N. Y., thoroughly understands his business and will perform all operations in a manner to suit the customer Nitrous Oxide Gas will be administered when desired See card on page 212

**Hobbs Bros.,** manufacturers of Fine Carriages, Nineveh, N Y , print a card on page 216 Their work is all manufactured from the best material by competent workmen, and always gives satisfaction They also deal in Carriage Goods

**Chas. Kilmer,** dealer in Stoves, Tinware &c , Crosby Block, 39 Hawley Street, Binghamton, keeps a good assortment of all wares in his line If you want a good Cook or Parlor Stove at a reasonable price, call on Mr. K. Peddlers are supplied at the lowest rates See card, page 216

**John Riley,** dealer in Dry Goods, Groceries, Boots, Shoes, Flour, Feed, &c , Castle Creek, N Y , is prepared to supply his customers with a great variety of goods at reasonable prices See his advertisement on page 212.

**D. I. Bouck,** proprietor of Bouck's Hotel, at Binghamton, makes his bow on page 230 This is a new Hotel, recently opened, and has been fitted up with every convenience for the comfort of guests. It is conveniently located, near the Erie Depot, and under the management of Mr Bouck, is giving good satisfaction A good Livery is connected with the house, also stabling for the accommodation of horses

**Nelson Bowker,** Builder, Binghamton, N Y , prints a card on page 228 Mr. B. gives his personal supervision to the erection of all buildings entrusted to his care, and being an experienced workman, he allows no work to go out of his hands imperfectly executed Jobbing promptly attended to. His shop is in J S Wells' old stand, on Main Street, first door west of the Congregational Church.

**J. S. Frear,** Furnishing Undertaker, 8 Court Street, Binghamton, N Y , publishes a card on page 228 He keeps a good assortment of Undertaking goods of all kinds, including Masonic, Odd Fellow and Fire Department Emblems and will serve his customers to their entire satisfaction

# BARTON.

(Post Office Addresses in Parentheses.)

ABBREVIATIONS—S D , School District

AITCHISON, THOMAS, (Barton,) S. D 6, farmer 278

Akins, George, (Waverly,) S D 13, farmer 50

Albright Adam, (Barton,) S. D. 6, farmer 70

Albright Hiram C , (Barton,) S. D. 1, general merchant

Albright, Isaac D., (Barton,) S. D. 5, farmer 285 and leases of J Albright, 168.

Albright, John L., (Barton,) S. D. 6, farmer leases

Albright, Josiab, (Barton,) S D 5, farmer 50

Allen, A G , (Waverly,) lawyer, real estate broker and farmer 23½, room 5 Exchange Block, Broad

ALLEN & BEEKMAN, (Waverly,) (*John Allen and F. E. Beekman,*) groceries and provisions, 49 Broad

ALLEN, JOHN, (Waverly,) (*Allen & Beekman* )

ALLEN, W. H. & CO , (Waverly,) (*Henry Shriver,*) wholesale dealers in illuminating and lubricating oils and benzine, Rail Road, 2d door east of Fulton

ANDRE, ABRAM T., (Bingham's Mills,) S D 3, farmer 65

Andre, George A., (Factoryville,) S D 2, farmer leases 80.

ANDRE, ISAAC J , (Factoryville,) S. D. 13, prop Manning's Mills

ANDRE, JACOB, (Bingham's Mills,) S. D 3, farmer 75.

ANDRE, J H , (Bingham's Mills,) S. D 3, (*with Jacob,*) farmer

Andrus, Richard, (Bingham's Mills,) S D 3, farmer leases of Mrs M D Andrus, 44

Angell, E J , (Waverly,) portrait painter and farmer 4, Chemung.

Armstrong, Joseph, (Barton,) S D 1, groceries, boots, shoes, hides &c

Atwater Bros , (Waverly,) (*Wm V and DeWitt C ,*) livery, sale and boarding stables, Clark near Broad

Atwater, DeWitt C , (Waverly,) (*Atwater Bros* )

Atwater, Wm. V., (Waverly,) (*Atwater Bros* )

BABCOCK, EDWARD M , (Halsey Valley,) machinist, boiler maker and farmer leases 103

BAKER, ALONZO, (Bingham's Mills,) S D 16, farmer 56.

BAKER & SHANAHAN, (Waverly,) (*W R Baker and P H Shanahan,*) dealers in teas, sugars, coffees, spices, wines, liquors and a general assortment of groceries, provisions &c., 92 Broad

BAKER, W. R., (Waverly,) (*Baker & Shanahan.*)

Baldwin, H T , (Waverly,) manager Opera House, Fulton St.

Barden, Aaron P , (Barton,) S D 6, farmer 45

Barden, Charles, (Barton,) S D 25, farmer 43.

BARDEN, GEORGE W .(Bingham's Mills,) S D. 3, farmer leases of L. H. Barner, 200

Barden, Z , (Barton,) S. D. 1, farmer leases 50

Bardon, Ira, (Barton,) S D 18, farmer leases of C. Spear.

Barker, John Mrs., (Factoryville,) farmer 25.

BARNUM, SAMUEL B , (Bingham's Mills,) S D 16, farmer 55

BARROWS, JOHN W , (Bingham's Mills,) farmer 480 and leases of L Edgcomb, 400

Bartron, Joseph, (Barton,) S D 1, farmer 80

Bartron, Philip, (Barton,) S. D. 1, blacksmith.

Beackman, ——, (Factoryville,) farmer 40

Beams, Marvin, (Barton,) saw mill.

BEEKMAN, F E., (Waverly,) (*Allen & Beekman* )

Bellis, May Miss, (Waverly,) dress maker, 82 Broad

BEMENT, JOHN M , (Waverly,) farmer leases 150.

Bennett, Amos, (Waverly,) S D 16, farmer leases of Charles Sawyer, 137

Bennett, Stephen, (Waverly,) druggist, Broad.

Bensley, Daniel, (Barton,) S. D. 1, farmer 180

Besemer, Daniel V., (North Barton,) S D 11, farmer 110.

Besemer, Jacob D , (North Barton,) S D 11, farmer 200

Bingham Charles, (Factoryville,) farmer 120, Main

*BINGHAM, GEO W , (Bingham's Mills,) S D 3, postmaster and prop Bingham's saw and grist mills.

Bingham, Jefferson, (Waverly,) prop Union Marble Works, Broad

*BINGHAM JEFFERSON, (Bingham's Mills,) S. D 3, prop of shingle, plaster and lath mills, lumberman and farmer 112

BINGHAM, JNO , (Bingham's Mills,) farmer 25

Blake, C A & Co , (Waverly,) J F Dewitt, agent, miners and shippers of Anthracite coal, Fulton corner Rail Road

Bogart, Charles, (Barton,) S D 5, farmer 90

Bogart. George W , (Barton,) S D 5, farmer 6

Bogart, James, (Factoryville,) S. D. 9, farmer 48

Bogart, James V 2d, (Bingham's Mills,) S D 15, lumberman and farmer leases of J. Bogart, 100

BOGART, JOSEPH V , (Bingham's Mills,) S. D 3, farmer 100 and (with Peter V ,) prop of saw mill.

Bogart, Joseph V D , (Barton,) S D 15, blacksmith and farmer 20

BOGART, MERRITT D , (Waverly,) S D 15, farmer 85

Bogart, Peter V , (Bingham's Mills,) farmer 200 and (with Joseph V.,) prop of saw mill

Bogart, Wm (Barton,) S D. 5, farmer 60.

Bogert L , (Waverly,) farmer leases 125

BONNELL, B W , (Waverly and Factoryville ) (Westfall & Bonnell,) town clerk

Bowman, Absalom, (Waverly,) S D 9, farmer 118

BREARLEY, JOHN W., (Halsey Valley,) S D. 10, carpenter and joiner

Brewster, D S., (Waverly,) carpenter, 106 Broad

Brink, Chas (Waverly,) S D 5, farmer leases of Jas. Swartwood, 80.

BRINK, JACOB, (Waverly,) S D. 4, farmer 80

Bristol, Nathan, (Waverly ) farmer 10, Chemung

BROCK, JOSEPH, (Waverly,) S D. 3, farmer 128

BROCK, LEWIS, (Bingham's Mills,) S. D 14, farmer 35

BROOKS, C C , (Waverly,) (C C Brooks & Co ) (C C Brooks & Taylor,) deputy sheriff

Brooks, C. C. & Co , (Waverly,) (W. S Drew,) fire, life and lightning insurance agents, 72 Broad

BROOKS C C & TAYLOR, (Waverly,) hair dressing rooms and props. Taylor's Invigorating Hair Gloss, Opera House Block

BROUGHAM, WESLEY H., (Factoryville ) groceries, confectionery &c , Main corner Ithaca

Brown. Avery, (North Barton,) S D. 17, farmer 133

Brown, Charles, (Spencer,) S. D. 20, farmer 50

BROWN, CHESTER, (North Barton,) S. D 11. farmer 76

Brown, Ezra (Waverly ) S D 13, farmer 90

BROWN, GEORGE M , (North Barton,) S D 17, (with Avery,) farmer 133

BROWN, GEORGE W ,(Halsey Valley,) S D. 13, farmer 136.

Brown Jacob J., (Halsey Valley,) S D. 13 farmer 57.

BROWN, MENSON E , (Halsey Valley,) S. D 13, farmer 100

BROWN, M J (Waverly,) billiard parlor, Gilbert Block, Broad

Brown, Shubael C , (North Barton,) S D 12, farmer 124

BRUSTER, DANIEL K , (North Barton,) S D 11, farmer 95

Bruster, John E , (North Barton,) S. D 11, farmer 150

Bruster, Oliver M , (Waverly,) S D 9, farmer 150

Bryant, J N Mrs ,(Factoryville,) farmer 2.

Buck, J T (Waverly,) ticket agent for E & L. V R R., Erie Depot.

Buck, Lyman, (Waverly,) (with G. W Hanna,) farmer 65

Buley, James, (Waverly,) S D. 9, farmer 160

Buley, J D , (Waverly,) (Snuffin & Buley,)

Buley, Joseph M , (Waverly,) blacksmith

BUNNELL, HENRY, (Waverly,) farmer 155

BUNNELL, HENRY J , (Waverly,) S D 18, farmer 140 and leases 90

Burdick, J W., (Waverly,) manager W. U. Telegraph, Erie Depot

BURLING, J Dr , (Waverly,) homeo. physician and surgeon, special attention paid to chronic diseases, 89 Broad

Bush, J G , (Waverly,) (H M Wilcox & Co )

Butts, Henry S , (Waverly,) musical instruments and patent medicines, Pensylvania Avenue

Calph, John, (Waverly,) carpenter, 49 Waverly

Campbell Bros , (Waverly,) (W. B., E. J. and F J.,) general merchants, 62 and 64 Broad

Campbell, E J., (Waverly,) (Campbell Bros )

Campbell, F J., (Waverly,) (Campbell Bros )

Campbell, W B , (Waverly,) (Campbell Bros )

Canfield, Amos, (Waverly,) S D 9, farmer 100

CARPENTER, S C , (Waverly,) (Stowell & Carpenter )

Cary, Leonard, (Barton,) S D 19, farmer 113

CARY, SAMUEL, (Barton,) S. D. 6, farmer 310.

Case, John, (Waverly,) carpenter, Howard.

Cashaday, Horace, (Halsey Valley,) S D 12, farmer 50

Casterline, Wm , (Waverly,) S D 9, farmer 50

Cayuta Chapter, No 245, R A M , (Waverly,) regular convocations 2d and 4th Mondays in each month, at Masonic Hall, corner Broad and Waverly

Chadsey, C H (Waverly,) sewing machine agent, 68 Broad

Clark, B B., (Waverly,) retired merchant, corner Pennsylvania Avenue and Providence

Clark, Warren, (Waverly ) carpenter and builder, Rail Road corner Pennsylvania Avenue.

Clark, W, M, (Waverly,) carpenter, Waverly.

Clendenney, Theodore, (Waverly,) news dealer, 1¾ Opera Block, Fulton.

Clock, Clarence E, (Factoryville,) station agent, Ithaca & Athens R. R.

Coleman, Alfred, (Barton,) S D. 6, farmer 30

Coleman, Benjamin J, (Barton,) S D. 12, carpenter and farmer 30.

Coleman, E Mrs, (Barton,) S D 6, farmer 160

Coleman, Gabriel, (Barton,) S D 20, farmer 80

Coleman, George, (Waverly,) S D 16, farmer 60

Coleman, John B, (Barton,) S D 1, carpenter and farmer

Coleman, John P, (Barton,) S. D. 1, carpenter and farmer 10

Coleman, Joshua, (Barton,) farmer 46.

COMSTOCK, A B,, (Waverly,) (*Pratt & Comstock*)

Cooley, Harvey L, (Factoryville,) tanner, Main.

Cooley, Robert R, (Bingham's Mills,) S. D 11, farmer 50

Cornell, Wm., (Barton,) S. D. 1, general merchant

Cortright, Abram, (Halsey Valley,) S D 9, farmer 152 and leases of Wm. Corey, 120

Corwin, O B & Son, (Waverly,) (*William,*) butter dealers, 1 Harneden Block, Waverly

Corwin, Wm, (Waverly,) (*O. B. Corwin & Son.*)

Cowen, H S, (Waverly,) book-keeper, 12 Clark.

COWEN, THADDEUS C., (Waverly,) wholesale and retail dealer in crockery, glassware and notions, auction and commission merchant, 53 Broad, boards at 12 Clark

Crans, R G, (Waverly,) (*Goldsmith & Co ,*) variety store, 2 Opera Block, Fulton

Crotsley, Lewis M, (Barton,) S D. 5, farmer 125.

Cumber, Solomon, (Barton,) farmer 15.

CURTIS BROS., (Waverly,) (*Edward P. and Fred E ,*) dry goods and carpets, 81 Broad.

CURTIS, EDWARD P., (Waverly,) (*Curtis Bros )*

CURTIS, FRED E., (Waverly,) (*Curtis Bros )*

Curtis, Levi, (Waverly,) (*Phillips & Curtis )*

CURTIS, ROBERT, (Factoryville,) S. D 18, farmer 70

Davenport, David, (Barton,) S D. 6, farmer 70

Davenport, George, (Barton,) (*with David,*) farmer 70

Davenport, Leonard, (Barton,) S D. 6, farmer leases 15.

DAVIES, JOHN, (Waverly,) boot and shoe manuf., Broad

Davis, Cornelius, (Factoryville,) miller, Main

Davis, Joel A, (North Barton,) farmer leases of Merrit D Bogart, 85

Davis, John Rev, (Waverly,) S. D. 9, pastor of M E Church.

DAVIS, SAMUEL H, (Bingham's Mills,) S. D 21, agent for Yankee Mowing Machine and farmer 600.

Davis, W H, (Waverly,) agent for E L Hedstrom, wholesale coal dealer, Exchange Block

Decker, James, (Waverly,) S D. 18, farmer leases of J. P Hyatt, 40

DeFOREST, CHARLES, (Halsey Valley,) S D 17, road commissioner and farmer 100

Dennis, Moses, (Halsey Valley,) S D 12, farmer 110

DeWitt, J F., (Waverly,) supervisor

Dewitt, J F & Co., (Waverly,) coal yard, Rail Road.

DeWITT, WM., (Factoryville,) (*Van Gaasbeck & DeWitt )*

DEXTER, J N, (Waverly,) attorney at law, 87 Broad

Dickerson, Archibald, (Barton,) S D 5, farmer 80

Doan, Benjamin, (Waverly,) S D 5, farmer 45

Dorsett, Samuel, (Waverly,) (*Faulkner & Dorsett )*

Doracy, W. L., (Waverly,) hair dresser, Broad.

Doty, Asa, (Barton,) S. D. 15, lumberman and farmer 50.

DOTY, E W, (Factoryville,) S D. 15, shingle manuf. and teacher of vocal music

Doty, Jesse J, (North Barton,) S D 11, (*with Stephen McKinney,*) farmer

Doud, Augustus, (Factoryville,) gardener, florist and farmer 1¾, Main.

Doyle, Jacob, (Barton,) S D 5, farmer 147.

Doyle, John, (Barton,) S D 5, farmer 8

Drake, Betsey Mrs, (Barton,) S. D. 6, farmer 90.

DRAKE, JAMES, (Barton,) S D 6, farmer 100

Drake, James H, (Barton,) S D 6, (*with Mrs. Betsey,*) farmer 90.

DREW, W. S, (Waverly,) (*C C. Brooks & Co )*

Dubois, Wm L, (Waverly,) S D 4, farmer leases of J. V. Solomon, 76.

Dunham, J J, (Waverly,) wagon maker, Broad

Dunn & Field, Misses, (Waverly,) Ladies' furnishing and fancy goods, Broad

Durkee, Charles, (Waverly,) S D 5, farmer 150

Durkee, C. A, (Factoryville,) (*J. W. Knapp & Co ,* Waverly,) farmer 150, Main

Eccleston, John S, (Halsey Valley,) S D 16, farmer 58

Edgcomb, Frederick G, (Factoryville,) (*with George G ,*) farmer 230

Edgcomb, George G, (Factoryville,) S D 9, farmer 230

Edgcomb, Gilbert, (Factoryville,) S D 9, farmer 10

Edgcomb, Hubbard, (Factoryville,) S. D. 9, farmer 120

Edgcomb, Foote & Co, (Waverly,) (*Le Roy Edgcomb, Gilbert E Foote and S. H Howell,*) coal dealers, Erin

Edgcomb, LeRoy, (Waverly,) (*Edgcomb, Foote & Co ,*) farmer 450

EDWARDS, JAS H., (Halsey Valley,) S. D 12, (*with Mrs Mary A ,*) farmer 50.

Edwards, Mary A Mrs., (Halsey Valley,) S. D. 12, farmer 50

Elliott, Wm B., (Factoryville,) chair maker, carpenter and farmer 9

Ellis, Christopher, (Factoryville,) S D. 9, farmer 44

Ellis, Ebenezer, (Waverly,) book store and news room, Post Office Building.

Ellis, F. A., (Barton,) S D. 7, prop Barton Saw and Grist Mills

Ellis, Gilbert S., (Waverly,) S. D 18, farmer 40

Ellis, Hiram, (Waverly,) (*W Manners & Co.*)

Ellis, Ira D., (Factoryville,) S D 18, farmer 50

ELLIS, JOHN, (Factoryville,) S D 18, farmer.

Ellis, Lewis B., (Factoryville,) S D 18, farmer 15.

Ellis, Thaddeus, (Factoryville,) S D. 2, farmer 128.

ELLIS, WM., (Factoryville,) S D. 18, farmer 200

ELLISON, JOHN, (Waverly,)carpenter and joiner, Pleasant

ELLISON, SAMUEL W., (Bingham's Mills,) S D 16, farmer 118

ELLISON, WM B., (Bingham's Mills,) S. D 11, farmer 62

ELMENDORF, DAVID E.,(Halsey Valley,) S D 17, farmer leases 100.

Elmer, Howard, (Waverly,) prest. First National Bank of Waverly

Elmer, R A., (Waverly ) cash. First National Bank of Waverly

Eleton, Julius, (Barton,) S D 6, farmer 88

ELWELL, ORLANDO, (Van Ettenville, Chemung Co.,) S. D. 14, millwright and machinist.

EMERSON, WM. H., (Bingham's Mills,) S D. 14, general mechanic and farmer leases of T. Hartford, 60

Emery, J., (Waverly,) prop. of Bradford House, Loder corner Rail Road

Esch, J. Frederick Rev., (Waverly,) rector Grace Church, Park Avenue

Estep, Jacob, (Smithsborough,)blacksmith

Evelin, Samuel, (Halsey Valley,) farmer 210.

Evenden, Robert, (Barton,) S. D. 24, farmer 60

Evenden, Robert, (North Barton,) S. D. 12, farmer 82.

FACTORYVILLE GRIST MILL, (Factoryville,) Main. Westfall & Bonnell, props.

Fairman, Jared P., (Waverly,) variety store, Fulton

Faulkner & Dorsett, (Waverly,) (*Lyman Faulkner and Samuel Dorsett,*) meat market, 67 Broad

Faulkner, Lyman, (Waverly,) (*Faulkner & Dorsett*)

Ferguson, H M & Co., (Waverly,) (*E W Horton*,) cigar manufs, 21 Chemung.

Ferguson, P T., (Waverly,) prop. of Lehigh Valley House, Rail Road.

Ferris, Moses T., (North Barton,) S D. 17, farmer 40.

Field, J. Emery, (Barton,) S D 15, (*Hubbell & Field*,) prop of Barton Saw Mill.

Field, Noah, (Bingham's Mills,) S. D 16, farmer 66.

Field —— Miss, (Waverly,) (*Misses Dunn & Field*)

Fields, Maj., (Waverly,) prop of Fields' Hotel, opposite Erie Depot

Finch, Amasa, (Factoryville,) carriage maker, Main.

FINCH, WILBER F., (Factoryville,) (*Manning & Finch*)

First National Bank of Waverly, (Waverly,) Broad corner Fulton, Howard Elmer, prest, R A. Elmer, cashier

Fisher, Horace A. (North Barton,) S D. 19, farmer 66

Fisher, Thomas D., (North Barton,) S. D. 19, farmer 108

Fitch, M P., (Waverly,) manuf. sash, doors and blinds, prop planing mill and lumber dealer, corner Railroad and Pennsylvania Avenue

Floyd, Jacob B., (Waverly,) lawyer, Exchange Block

Follett, Josiah, (Waverly,) brickmaker and farmer

Foote, Gilbert E., (Waverly,) (*Edgecomb, Foote & Co*,) constable

Forman, Edmund M., (Barton,) S D 1, music dealer and farmer 103.

Forsyth, Henry E., (Halsey Valley,) farmer 60

Foster, Horace, (Factoryville,) S D 2, farmer leases of Isaac Raymond, 10

Franklin, H. M., (Waverly,) barber, 79 Broad.

French, George, (Waverly,) baggage master Erie Depot

Frisbey, Wm R., (North Barton,) S D 11, farmer 157

Frisbie, Charles, (Halsey Valley,) S D 17, farmer 150

Gay, John S., (Waverly,) (*Gay & Mullock*)

Gay & Mullock, (Waverly,) (*John S Gay and Corwin Mullock,*) drugs, medicines and chemicals, 83 Broad

Gee, Wm., (Halsey Valley,) S D 19, carpenter and farmer 150

GENUNG, ADAM S., (Waverly,) S. D 18, carpenter and joiner.

Genung, George W., (Waverly,) S. D 18, shingle mill

Genung, Nathaniel, (Waverly,) S D 15, farmer 70

Genung, Salmon A., (Waverly,) S D 18, farmer 70.

Gibbs, W B., (Waverly,) prop. American Hotel, Broad

GILLAN, B R., (Factoryville,)blacksmith, Main corner Chemung

Giltner, Dexter E., (Barton,) (*with Edward W* ) farmer 100

GILTNER, EDWARD W., (Barton,) S D 6, (*with Dexter E*,) farmer 100

GILTNER, EZRA A., (Barton,) S D 6, (*with Francis,*) farmer 100.

GILTNER, FRANCIS, (Barton,) S D 6, farmer 174

Giltner, John, (Barton,) S D 6, farmer 100

GILTNER, JOHN A., (Barton,) S. D. 6, farmer 76

Godwin, Floyd H., (Bingham's Mills,) S D 16, farmer 63

GOLDEN, BENJAMIN, (Factoryville,) S D 16, superintendent of the poor, lumberman and farmer 180

GOLDEN, NATHANIEL, (Bingham's Mills,) S. D. 16, general cooper

Goldsmith & Co., (Waverly,) (*W H. Goldsmith and R G Crans,*) liquors and cigars, corner Railroad and Fulton

Goldsmith, W. H., (Waverly,) (*Goldsmith & Co*)

Graft, George H., (Factoryville,) farmer 400 Main

Green, E L., (Waverly,) prop. Arbor Restaurant, 73 and 75 Broad

*GREEN, O. H., (Waverly,) merchant tailor and dealer in gents' furnishing goods, 79 Broad

Green, O. H. jr., (Waverly,) (*Mulock & Green*)

*GREEN, STEPHEN DELOSS, (Bingham's Mills) S. D. 3, grocer and shoemaker

Hall, John, (Barton,) S D 6, farmer 80.

Hall, S O Prof., (Waverly,) principal Union School, 66 Waverly

Hallett, Hatfield, (Waverly,) (*VanDuzer & Hallett.*

Hamilton, David Henry, (Halsey Valley,) S D 17, farmer leases 30

Hamilton, Simeon V., (Halsey Valley,) S D 17, farmer 100

HAMILTON, S V N, (Halsey Valley,) carpenter and joiner, blacksmith, carriage maker and farmer 95

HAMILTON, THOMAS A., (Halsey Valley,) S D 17, prop of Biker, Holmes & King e Celebrated Cream Strainer and farmer 95

Hancock, Jeremiah, (Waverly,) farmer 40

Hanford, Henry, (Factoryville,) S D 20, farmer 150

Hanford, Noah, (Factoryville,) S. D. 20, (*with Henry,*) farmer

Hanna, Adelbert, (Factoryville,) S D 2, farmer 100.

Hanna, Edward R., (Factoryville,) S D 2, (*with Mrs Jane,*) farmer

Hanna, Fred K., (Factoryville,) S D 2, farmer 200

Hanna, George I., (Factoryville,) S D 2, farmer 100

HANNA, GEORGE W., (Factoryville,) S D 13, farmer 300

Hanna, J Mrs., (Factoryville,) S. D 2, farmer 70

Hanna, Nancy M. Mrs., (Factoryville,) dress maker, Main

HANNA, SELAH S., (Factoryville,) S D 18, farmer 140.

Harding, Benjamin, (Factoryville,) S D 4, farmer 60

Harding, Ira, (Factoryville,) S. D. 4, farmer 75

Harding, James E., (Waverly,) S D 4, farmer 115

HARDING, JOHN, (Barton,) S D 5, farmer leases 83

HARDING, SHERMAN, (Waverly,) carpenter and joiner, Broad

Harnden, D. D., (Waverly,) physician, 5 Harnden's Block, Waverly.

Harris, D N., estate of, (Waverly,) jewelry, 63 Broad.

Harsh, Charles, (Waverly,) refused information.

Harsh, C M., (Waverly,) tinware, &c, Broad.

HAVENS, A. B., (Waverly,) shoemaker, Rail Road.

HAVENS, L. Mrs., (Waverly,) dress maker, Rail Road

HAYDIN, BERT, (Waverly,) freight clerk, P & N Y. R R

Hayes, H H., (Waverly,) (*Slaughter & Hayes.*)

Head H Mrs., (widow,) (Halsey Valley,) S D 12 farmer 100

HEAD, THERON, (Halsey Valley,) S. D. 12, (*with Mrs H,*) farmer 100

HEDGES, CHARLES C, (North Barton,) S D 11, carpenter and farmer 180

HEDGES, JOHN B., (North Barton,) S D. 20, prop. of saw mill and farmer 150.

Hedges, Sylvanus D., (Bingham's Mills,) S D 14, farmer 60

Hedstrom, E L., (Waverly,) wholesale coal dealer, W. H. Davis, agent, Exchange Block.

Herrick, George, (Waverly,) cashier Waverly Bank

Herrick, H T., (Waverly,) pres Waverly Bank

Hess, Jacob, (Halsey Valley,) S. D. 17, farmer 50

Hess, Samuel, (Halsey Valley,) S. D. 12, carpenter and farmer 81

HESS, SYLVESTER N., (Halsey Valley,) S. D. 17, farmer 32

Hewit, Henry, (Factoryville,) S D 9, farmer leases of A. J Lyons, 139.

HILDEBRAND, A., (Waverly,) manufacturer and dealer in boots and shoes, 68 Broad

Hill, Ira G., (Factoryville,) farmer 28

Hill, John G., (Factoryville,) S D 2, farmer 123

Hoffman, Mary Mrs., (Barton,) S. D. 19, farmer 48

Hollenbeck, Harry, (Barton,) farmer 160.

Hollenbeck, George, (Spencer,) S D 20, farmer 100

Hollenbeck, Lieman C., (Spencer,) S. D. 20, (*with George,*) farmer

Holt, Charles, (Barton,) S D 1, farmer 850

HOPKINS, HENRY, (Barton,) S. D. 1, constable and farmer 48

HOPKINS, SAMUEL H., (Barton,) S D 1, farmer 60

Horton, E W., (Waverly,) (*H. M. Ferguson & Co.*)

Horton, M Mrs., (Factoryville,) S D 9, farmer 45.

Houver, Wm., (Halsey Valley,) S D 12, farmer 50.

Howard, Clark, (Waverly,) tobacco store and restaurant, 51 Broad

Howell, S L., (Waverly,) (*Edgecomb, Foote & Co.,*) farmer 70

Hoyt, Edmund H., (North Barton,) postmaster and (*with Sylvanus H.,*) farmer 80.

Hoyt, Fred, (Halsey Valley,) S D 10, (*with Nathan A Lamoreaux,*) prop Halsey Valley Mill

Hoyt, John L., (Waverly,) S D 2, farmer leases of F Hanna, 100.

Hoyt, Sylvanus H., (North Barton,) dealer in Rumsey & Updike plows, and (*with Edmund H,*) farmer 80.

Hoyt, Warren J., (Halsey Valley,) S D. 17, cooper and canvassing agent.

Hubbell, Elmer S, (Factoryville,) (*with Volney,*) lumberman and farmer 105

Hubbell, Shadrach D., (Factoryville,) S. D. 11, farmer 86

Hubbell, Volney, (Factoryville,) S. D 16, lumberman and farmer 105

Hugg, Lyman D , (Waverly,) (*Pierce Bros. & Co*)

Hulett, John, (Factoryville,) S D. 4, farmer 66

Hulett, Milo J., (North Barton,) S. D. 17, farmer 35

Hungerford. Jerome, (Waverly,) (*Persons & Hungerford*)

Hyatt, John P., (Waverly,) S D 2, farmer 130 and leases 90

Hyatt, Pierre V. C., (Waverly,) S. D. 9, farmer 90

Jackson, James H . (Waverly,) hackman, Field's Hotel. Broad

Jackson, Wm , (Factoryville,) prop. Jackson House, Main.

Johnson, Cyrus, (Factoryville,) S D. 9, farmer 106

Johnson, P A , (Waverly,) eclectic physician, 13 Waverly

Johnson, W E , (Waverly,) physician, 8 Waverly

JONES, WM. L., (Waverly,) joiner, Chemung corner Athens

Joyce, Michael, (Factoryville,) S D 9, blacksmith.

KELSEY, HORACE Rev., (Barton,) S. D 6, Baptist minister

Kennedy, James, (Waverly,) S D 9, farmer 140

Kern, David O., (Factoryville,) S. D. 4, farmer leases 280.

Kerry, David, (Barton,) S D 4, farmer 50.

Kimly, Wm. H , (Factoryville,) farmer.

King, Charles C , (Barton,) S D. 13, (*with Henry A.,*) farmer 105

KING, CLAYTON G , (Bingham's Mills,) S D 16 farmer 100

KING, GEORGE, (Factoryville,) S. D. 13, lumberman and farmer 500

King, Henry A , (Barton,) S. D 13, (*with Chas. C.,*) farmer 105

King, Solomon D , (Barton,) S D 6, dealer in butter, grain &c , and farmer 130.

King, Warren, (Bingham's Mills,) S D 20, carriage maker and farmer leases of C. Hanford, 175

King, Willard, (Factoryville,) farmer 33

Kingsworth, Leonard, (Waverly,) S. D. 11, farmer 150

KINNER, SELEY, (Waverly,) S. D. 4, farmer 200

Kinney, Newton, (Waverly,) carriage making, Broad

KINNEY, O H P , (Waverly,) (*Polleys & Kinney,*) editor of *Waverly Advocate*

KISHPAUGH, JONAS, (Barton,) S. D 19, farmer 90.

KLASE, T J , (Waverly,) agent for P & N Y. R. R Co , Fulton corner Rail Road.

Knapp, D D , (Waverly,) watches, jewelry &c., 65 Broad

Knapp, J. W & Co , (Waverly,) (*Chas. A Durkee,*) bakery, groceries and provisions, 80 Broad.

LAGEMAN, E W , (Waverly,) groceries and provisions, Fulton south side E R R.

*LAGRANGE, DELLA & THERESA Misses, (Waverly,) hair dressing and hair jewelry, 8 Harnden's Block, Waverly

LAIN, WILLIAM A , (Waverly,) manuf of churns, butter firkins, tubs &c., corner Chemung and Pine

LAMBART, JOHN, (North Barton,) S. D. 12, farmer 100.

Lambart, John L., (North Barton,) S. D. 12, (*with John,*) farmer

Lamont, Allen, (Factoryville,) S. D. 9, farmer 116

Lamont, Allen, (Factoryville,) farmer 40

Lamoreaux, Nathan A , (Halsey Valley ) S D 10, (*with Fred Hoyt,*) prop. of Halsey Valley Mill

Lanard, A., (Factoryville,) refused information

Lawler, John, (Bingham's Mills,) S. D. 21, mason and farmer 5.

Lee, Henry B., (Waverly,) S. D. 9, farmer 35.

Lemon, James, (Waverly,) foundry, Broad

Lewis, Peter, (Factoryville,) S D 4, farmer 150.

Little, Richard, (Factoryville,) S. D. 18, farmer 100

LOTT, GEO W , (Factoryville,) S. D. 14, prop Lott's mill, lumberman and farmer 400.

Lott, Isaac S , (Factoryville,) S D. 14, farmer 95.

LOTT, PERRY, (Factoryville,) carpenter and joiner, and farmer 18

Louterback, Henry, (Barton,) S. D. 6, farmer 30.

Lowman, H E , (Waverly,) lumbering

Loyd, H S Rev , (Waverly,) Baptist minister Tioga

Lubers, Theodore, (Factoryville,) tanner, Main

Lyons, C T. Dr , (Waverly,) drugs, medicines, crockery, wines and liquors, 95 Broad.

Lyons, C T Mrs., (Waverly,) dress maker, 95 Broad.

Lyons, Francis, (Factoryville,) wines and liquors, Main

Lyons, Henry, (Bingham's Mills,) S D 3, farmer 46

MACK, S F , (Waverly,) hardware and house furnishing goods, 94 Broad, residence Pennsylvania Avenue

Mackesey, P. J., (Waverly,) shoe maker, Broad

Macknay, W. D., (Waverly,) grocer, Broad

Malloy, Isaac S., (Factoryville,) S. D. 9, farmer 3½.

Malloy, Peter, (Factoryville,) S. D. 9, farmer 16.

Manners, Alonzo, (Waverly,) (*W. Manners & Co.*)

Manners, Robert N., (Waverly,) (*Van Velsor & Manners*)

Manners, W. & Co , (Waverly,) (*Alonzo Manners and Hiram Ellis,*) grocery and bakery, 61 Broad.

Manning, Alfred, (North Barton,) S D 11, farmer leases of H. Edgcomb, 80.

MANNING & FINCH, (Factoryville,)(*Gurdon G Manning and Wilber F. Finch,*) general merchants. Main corner Ithaca.

MANNING, GURDON G., (Factoryville,) (*Manning & Finch,*) farmer 118
Manning, John, (Barton,) S D 6, farmer 84
Manning, John, (Halsey Valley,) S. D. 17, farmer 46.
Manning, Reuben C., (Barton,) S. D. 6, thrasher and farmer 57½.
Manning & Sawyer, (Factoryville,) (*G G Manning and James Sawyer,*) dealers in grain, coal, salt and plaster, at Ithaca & Athens Depot
Manoca Lodge, No. 219, I. O. O. F., (Waverly,) meets every Tuesday evening at Parshall's Block, Broad, W B Campbell, N. G.; G H Powers, secretary.
Mansfield, Josiah J., (Barton,) S. D. 19, horse dealer and farmer 200
Masterson, Samuel, (Barton,) S. D. 5, farmer 30
Masterson, Urial, (North Barton,) S. D 19, farmer 14
McCarty, John, (Factoryville,) S D 13, farmer leases of R Parshall, 275
McDonald, Alex, (Waverly,) dry goods, boots and shoes, hats, caps &c, Broad
McElwain, Alex, (Waverly,) shoemaker, Broad
McGuffie, M, (Waverly,) agent for J. F Dewitt & Co, coal yard, corner Rail Road and Fulton
McKINNEY, STEPHEN, (North Barton,) S D 11, farmer 140
Mead, Montgomery, (Waverly,) photographer, 66 Broad.
Masterson, E I, (Barton,) S D. 1, cooper
Merriam, H. G., (Waverly,) hardware, stoves &c,, wholesale and retail, 89 Broad and 3 Waverly.
Merril, Jackson, (Factoryville,) S D 18, farmer 27.
Miller, James, (Factoryville,) teamster, Chemung.
Miller & Murray, (Waverly,) (*S W. Miller and John H Murray,*) groceries, provisions and meat market, Broad foot Park Avenue
Miller, S W, (Waverly,) (*Miller & Murray.*)
MILLS, J H., (Waverly,) grain, flour and feed, Broad foot Park Avenue
MILLS, WM G., (Waverly,) S D 4, farmer 120
Minick, Benjamin, (Factoryville,) S. D. 19, farmer leases of George Graft, 130
MITCHELL, S N., (Waverly,) (*Murray & Mitchell,*) attorney at law, over First National Bank.
Mix, A. M, (Waverly,) joiner and stair builder, east side Pine, 2d house above Chemung.
Morgan, D S., (Waverly,) house and carriage painter, Loder.
Morse, J E, (Waverly,) (*with J. R. Rowland,*) sign writer.
Mott, A S, (Waverly,) tailor, 78 Broad
Mullock, A., (Waverly,) (*Mullock & Weatherly.*)
Mullock, Corwin, (Waverly,) (*Gay & Mullock*)
Mullock, G L., (Waverly,) (*Mullock & Sliter.*)
Mullock & Sliter, (Waverly,) (*G. L Mullock and J B Sliter,*) manufs carriages, west end Broad

Mullock & Weatherly, (Waverly,) (*A Mullock and P. Weatherly,*) coal dealers, Erin
Mulock, A J., (Waverly,) (*Mulock & Green,*) agent Home Sewing Machine, 79 Broad.
Mulock & Green, (Waverly,) (*A. J. Mulock and O H Green jr,*) agents Weed Sewing Machine, 79 Broad.
MULOCK, L W., (Waverly,) justice of the peace and farmer 6.
Mum, George H, (Factoryville,) S D. 18, carpenter
Murdock, John K, (Waverly,) agent for U. S & Central Express Co., Erie Depot.
MURRAY, JAMES S, (Waverly,) (*Murray & Mitchell,*) real estate agent and justice of the peace in South Waverly, Pa., over First National Bank
Murray, John H, (Waverly,) (*Miller & Murray.*)
*MURRAY, JOHN R, (Waverly,) fire, life and accidental insurance agent, special attention given to farm property, over Corner Drug Store, 87 Broad
MURRAY & MITCHELL, (Waverly,) (*James S Murray and S N Mitchell,*) insurance agents, over First National Bank
Murray Wm T, (Waverly,) (*Slmey & Murray*)
Myers, L D, (Waverly,) Opera Restaurant, 4 Opera Block, Fulton
Newland, David, (Barton,) S. D. 1, (*with Daniel Odell,*) farmer 100
Newland, Samuel M, (Barton,) general merchant.
Newman, P. Mrs, (Barton,) S. D 24, farmer 80
NICHOLS, CHAUNCEY S, (North Barton,) dealer in Reynolds & Co 's plows, farmer 82 and leases of Mrs H A. Nichols, 65
NICHOLS, JACOB E, (Bingham's Mills,) S D 14, farmer leases of P Hedges, 100
Nichols, Oliver, (Waverly,) merchant tailor, 59 Broad.
NICOL, W R, M D. O. M, (Waverly,) physician, over Gay & Mullock's drug store, Broad corner Waverly.
Nobles, Ezekiel, (Barton,) S. D 6, blacksmith and farmer
Odell, Daniel, (Barton,) S D. 1, (*with David Newland,*) farmer 100.
Olin, —— Rev, (Waverly,) pastor M. E Church, Waverly.
O'NEAL, MICHAEL, (Factoryville,) manuf and repairer of boots and shoes, Main
Orange, G W, (Waverly,) station agent, Erie Depot.
Osborn, J T, (Factoryville,) groceries and provisions, Main
Paine, Chancey, (Barton,) S D. 15, farmer 98.
Park, John, (Barton,) S. D 15, farmer 245
Parker, James E, (Factoryville,) S. D. 9, prop of stallion *Young Blackhawk* and farmer 104.
Parks, Daniel, (Barton,) S D 1, farmer 100
Partridge, Anson J, (North Barton,) S D 11, farmer leases of F. Brown, 148
Patten, T J Mrs, (Waverly,) millinery, 96 Broad

Payne, F. Y, agent, (Waverly,) Waverly Furniture and Undertaking Store, Broad

Peironnet, John, (Factoryville,) farmer 10, Main

Pembleton, Charles, (Factoryville,) S D 18, farmer 124

PEMBLETON, J E, (Waverly,) secretary of Waverly Paper Mills.

Perry, Chancy, (Barton,) S. D. 6, millwright and (*with Edward Tilbury,*) farmer 58

Persons, E D, (Waverly,) (*Persons & Hungerford*)

Persons & Hungerford, (Waverly,) (*E. D Persons and Jerome Hungerford,*) wholesale and retail dealers in crockery, glassware, groceries, provisions &c, Broad corner Fulton

Phillips & Curtis, (Waverly,) (*T. J. Phillips and Levi Curtis,*) props. Cayuta Flouring Mills

Phillips, T. J., (Waverly,) (*Phillips & Curtis*)

Pierce, Bros & Co, (Waverly,) (*Gilbert and Marion Pierce, and Lyman D. Hugg,*) groceries and provisions, Broad corner Clark

Pierce, Gilbert, (Waverly,) (*Pierce Bros. & Co*)

Pierce, Marion, (Waverly,) (*Pierce, Bros. & Co*)

Pierce, W. R, (Waverly,) allo. physician, Waverly

PIFHER, CALVIN D., (Waverly,) S. D 13, farmer leases of J Follett, 250.

*POLLEYS & KINNEY, (Waverly,) (*Wm Polleys and O H P Kinney,*) publishers of *Waverly Advocate.*

POLLEYS, WILLIAM, (Waverly,) (*Polleys & Kinney,*) postmaster

Pool, Daniel, (Factoryville,) blacksmith and farmer 50

Pool, Franklin, (Halsey Valley,) S. D. 17, blacksmith and farmer 39

Pool, George, (Halsey Valley,) farmer leases of Daniel, 50.

Post, H W., (Waverly,) cutter, 59 Broad.

Post, John, (Waverly,) baggage master, Erie Depot

Powers, G H., (Waverly,) (*Waverly Marble Works*)

*PRATT & COMSTOCK, (Waverly,) (*M C Pratt and A. B. Comstock,*) photographers, 76 Broad.

PRATT, M. C., (Waverly,) (*Pratt & Comstock.*)

Pray, Robert, (Bingham's Mills,) S D 16, farmer 109

PRIMROSE, JAMES, (Barton,) S. D 1, manuf of all kinds of matched and surface lumber

Raymond, Isaac L, (Factoryville,) S D. 2, farmer 360

Reed, Alfred, (Waverly,) butter dealer and farmer 200, Broad

Reed, Eugene N ,(North Barton,) S. D 11, farmer 77.

RENIFF, ABISHA B, (Waverly,) (*A. B Reniff & Sons*)

RENIFF, A B & SONS, (Waverly,) (*Abisha B, Wm J and Solomon R,*) props. of saw and shingle mills, and farmers 480.

RENIFF, SOLOMON R., (Waverly,) (*A. B. Reniff & Sons*)

RENIFF, WM. J, (Waverly,)(*A B Reniff & Sons*)

Richards, Horace, (Waverly,) S D. 2, farmer leases of Sela Hanna, 100.

RICHARDSON, I L, (Waverly,) (*L S. Richardson & Son.*)

RICHARDSON, L S & SON, (Waverly,) (*I L,*) wholesale and retail dealers in foreign and domestic liquors, 98 Broad.

Root, Silas, (Barton,) S D 24, farmer 38

ROWEN, HIRAM, (North Barton,) farmer 30

Rowland, G R, (Waverly,) house, sign and carriage painter, 98 Broad, up stairs

Ruse, Daniel B, (Barton,) station agent E. Rail Road.

Sager, James A., (Barton,) S. D. 12, farmer 116

Sagar, Mark B., (Waverly,) S. D. 15, farmer 50.

Sager, Elijah, (Barton,) S D. 18, farmer 52

Sager, Philander A., (Halsey Valley,) farmer 200

Sager, Simon, (Barton,) S. D 24, farmer 48.

Santee, J. B Rev, (Barton,) pastor of M. E Church

Saunders, Christopher, (Waverly,) S. D. 2, farmer 100.

SAUNDERS, GEORGE W, (Waverly,) S. D. 2, (*with Christopher,*) farmer 100.

Saunders, Nathan, (Factoryville,) S. D. 18, farmer 39

SAWYER, CHAS. H., (Waverly,) farmer 234, Chemung

Sawyer, James, (Factoryville,) (*Manning & Sawyer*)

Sawyer, M, (Waverly,) clothing, hats, caps and gents' furnishing goods, 66 Broad

Sawyer, Moses, (Factoryville,) farmer 164

Saxton, James A Rev., (Halsey Valley,) S D 12, farmer 61

Schuyler, Philip C., (Barton,) S. D 15, farmer 255

Schuyler, Spear T., (North Barton,) S. D. 19, farmer 21.

*SCUDDER, F T, (Waverly,) editor and prop. of *Waverly Enterprise,* Fulton corner Rail Road

Seamans, D O, (Waverly,) Washington Market, Broad

Searles, Cornelius, (Factoryville,) S D. 15, (*with Emanuel,*) farmer 100.

Searles, Elias, (Factoryville,) S. D. 15, (*with Emanuel,*) farmer

SEARLES, EMANUEL, (Factoryville,) S. D 15, lumber dealer and farmer 100

Seely, Charles, (Factoryville,) S D 4, farmer leases of Moses Sawyer, 187

Segar, Oliver, (Factoryville,) carpenter, Main

Severn, Lemuel, (Barton,) S. D. 24, farmer 80

Shafer, Sanford, (Bingham's Mills,) S. D. 16, farmer 100

SHANAHAN, P H, (Waverly,) (*Baker & Shanahan.*)

SHAW, E A. & R. R., (Waverly,) manufs and dealers in harness, saddles, trunks, traveling bags, robes, blankets, curry combs, whips &c, 45 Broad.

Shelp, Charles, (Factoryville,) S D 9, farmer 25

Shelp. Freeman, (Factoryville,) farmer 25

SHEPARD, C H., (Waverly,) vice-president of Waverly Paper Mills and farmer 5, in Chemung Co. 150, and in Bradford Co., Pa., 300.

SHEPARD, W W Hon., (Waverly,) president of Waverly Paper Mills and farmer 200

Shipman, Harvey D, (North Barton,) S. D 19, farmer 108 and leases of S. Howell, 70.

Shipman, Shaler, (Barton,) S. D 15, farmer 179.

Shoemaker, Aaron, (Barton,) S D 15, farmer 76.

Shoemaker, Daniel D, (Barton,) S. D. 15, farmer 50

Shoemaker, Henry, (Barton,) S D 15, farmer 70.

SHRIVER, HENRY, (Waverly,) (*W. H. Allen & Co*)

Shulenburgh, F P, (Waverly,) barber, 3 Opera Block, Fulton.

Signer, George, (Factoryville,) S D 16, farmer leases 249

Simons. Wm R, (Factoryville,) S. D. 9, farmer 143

Simpson, J D, (Waverly,) blacksmith, Broad corner Pennsylvania Avenue.

Skilling, John W, (Halsey Valley,) S. D. 10, farmer 52

SKILLING, SAMUEL G., (Halsey Valley,) S D 10, millwright and farmer 35.

Slaughter & Hayes, (Waverly,) (*S. W Slaughter and H. H. Hayes*,) props Corner Drug Store, druggists and booksellers, Broad corner Waverly

Slaughter, S. W, (Waverly,) (*Slaughter & Hayes*)

Sliney, Chas. H, (Waverly,) (*Sliney & Murray*.)

Sliney & Murray, (Waverly,) (*Chas H Sliney and Wm T Murray*,) bakery, groceries, fruits &c, 82 Broad

Sliter, Harvey, (Waverly,) S. D. 4, farmer 50.

Sliter, J B, (Waverly,) (*Mullock & Sliter*)

Sliter, James M., (Factoryville,) S. D. 4, farmer 124

Smith, Charles B., (Waverly,) S D 18, farmer 60

Smith, Chas. O., (Waverly,) pump manuf., Chemung

Smith, Daniel, (Bingham's Mills,) S. D. 16, farmer 50

Smith, David Mrs, (Halsey Valley,) S D. 17, farmer 200

Smith, D. & B., (Waverly,) S. D. 4, farmer 30

SMITH, E A, (North Barton,) S D 12, school teacher.

Smith, John jr., (North Barton,) farmer 80

Smith, John G, (Factoryville,) farmer 50, Main

Smith, J S, (Waverly,) dentist, 72 Broad.

Smith, Levi P, (Bingham's Mills,) S D.16, farmer 66

SMITH, LORENZO, (Factoryville,) S. D. 21, farmer leases of G King, 300.

Smith, Rufus, (North Barton,) S D. 12, farmer leases of J Smith, 80.

Smith, Rushton, (Waverly,) S. D 18, surveyor and (*with Charles B.*,) farmer.

Smith, R M Mrs, (Bingham's Mills,) S. D 14, farmer 125

SMITH, SCHUYLER F, (Halsey Valley,) S D 17, lumberman and (*with Mrs David*,) farmer

SMITH, WM E., (North Barton,) S D 12, farmer leases of John Crisfield, 90

Smith, W W, (Waverly,) carpenter, 10 Tioga

Sniffin & Buley, (Waverly,) (*H H Sniffin and J D Buley*,) grain, feed, produce and coal, Broad

Sniffin, H. H, (Waverly,) (*Sniffin & Buley*.)

*SNOOK, F M. Dr., (Waverly,) dentist, Broad corner Waverly.

Snyder, Wm, (Barton,) prop of Barton Hotel, agent for Kirby Mower and Reaper, seed sower and Tompkins Co Wheel Rake

Solomon, George, (Waverly,) S. D. 4, farmer 90

SOPER, EDWARD A, (Bingham's Mills,) S D 14, farmer leases of A Vail, 110

Southwick, Aaron C, (Halsey Valley,) saw mill and farmer 108

Spanish Hill Encampment, No 52, I O O. F, (Waverly,) meets at Odd Fellow's Hall on the 2d and 4th Fridays of each month; John Mahony, W.C.P, W B Campbell, H.P.

Spalding, M T Mrs., (Factoryville,) dress maker, Main

SPEAR, BARNEY, (Bingham's Mills,) farmer leases 130

Spear, Samuel, (Barton,) S D 6, farmer leases of I O Albright, 120

Spencer, C. F., (Waverly,) boots and shoes, 84 Broad

Spencer, Joseph, (Halsey Valley,) S D 17, mason and farmer 31.

Stahl, S., (Waverly,) (*Unger & Stahl*)

Star Chapter, No 9, (Waverly,) regular meetings 2d and 4th Wednesdays in each month, at Masonic Hall, corner Broad and Waverly.

Stebbins, Lemuel, (Waverly,) S D 11, farmer 100

Stebbins, Marcus M, (Waverly,) S D 9, stone quarry and farmer 115

Stebbins, O Harrison, (Waverly,) S D 11, (*with Lemuel*,) farmer 100

Stebbins, Wm H, (Waverly,) owns 200 acres western land

Stewart, Cornelius, (Barton,) S. D. 15, millwright, carpenter and farmer

St John, Miner, (Waverly,) carpenter, Chemung

Stone, L D., (Waverly,) physician, Waverly

Stone, W P, (Waverly,) (*Waverly Marble Works*)

*STOWELL & CARPENTER, (Waverly,) (*H L Stowell and S C Carpenter*,) dealers in boots and shoes, Harnden's Block, 3 Waverly.

STOWELL, H L, (Waverly,) (*Stowell & Carpenter*)

Struble, Henry, (Factoryville,) S. D.9, (*with John*,) farmer.

STRUBLE, JOHN, (Factoryville,) S D 9, farmer leases of George Graft, 300

Swain, Lester, (Factoryville,) farmer 60

Swartwood, Ezekial, (Barton,) S D 1, farmer 96

Swartwood, H Mrs , (Factoryville,) S. D 18, farmer 43.

Swartwood, John P , (Barton,) S D 2, farmer 120

Swartwood, Wm , (Barton,) S. D. 5, farmer 60

Sweet, Wesley, (Waverly,) furniture dealer and undertaker, 97 Broad corner Park Avenue

Swort, Geo , (Waverly,) S D 9, farmer 133

Taoner, John J , (Waverly,) carpenter, 50 Chemung

Tannery, Ida Miss, (Waverly,) milliner and fancy goods, 98 Broad

Tatevet, Oscar, (Barton,) S. D. 24, farmer 105

Taylor, Daniel W , (Halsey Valley,) S D 17, (*with Orrin*,) farmer 100

Taylor, Edwin, (Halsey Valley,) S D 17, (*with Orrin*) farmer 100

Taylor, Eli, (Halsey Valley,) S. D 17, farmer 90

Taylor, George, (Halsey Valley,) S. D 17, farmer 25

Taylor, John P , (Factoryville,) tin peddler and farmer 3.

Taylor, Orrin, (Halsay Valley,) S. D. 17, farmer 100.

TAYLOR, ——, (Waverly,) (*O. C. Brooks & Taylor*)

Terry, J J , (Waverly,) clothing and gents' furnishing goods, Broad

Thatcher, N N , (Waverly,) boots and shoes, 90 Broad

Thrall, Charles E , (Bingham's Mills,) S D 8, farmer 24

Tilbury, Edward, (Barton,) S D 6, farmer 58

TOZER, ALMERIN H , (Factoryville,) S. D 18, farmer 126

Tozer, Edward, (Factoryville,) farmer 50

Tozer, Franklin, (Waverly,) blacksmith, Broad

Tozer, Henry, (Factoryville,) farmer 45

TOZER, WM H , (Bingham's Mills,) S D 3, millwright and farmer 40

Tracy, E. G , (Waverly,) (*Waldo & Tracy*).

Tribe, James P , (Barton,) S. D 5, farmer leases of Chas. Hall

Tuthill, Burton, (Factoryville,) shoemaker, Ellistown Road

Tuthill, Elvira Mrs , (Waverly,) S D. 9, farmer 180

Tutle, Nelson, (Factoryville,) S. D 18, farmer leases of C Ellis, 80.

Tyrell, A , (Waverly,) allo physician, 78 Broad

Unger, A , (Waverly,) (*Unger & Stahl*)

Unger & Stahl, (Waverly,)(*A. Unger and S. Stahl*,)tobacconists, Spaulding's Block, Broad

Updike, Archibald, (Waverly,) painter and gardener, Clark

Vail, Alonzo V C , (Waverly,) prop Dean Creek Steam Mill, lumberman and farmer 800

Vanatta, Adam, (Factoryville,) S D 4, farmer 50

VANATTA, BENJAMIN, (Barton,) S. D 5, farmer 104

Vanatta, Oscar H,, (Barton,) S. D. 5, farmer 79 and leases 52

VANATTA, PETER, (Barton,) S. D 5, farmer 52

Vandemark, Henry, (Barton,) S. D. 6, farmer 65

VanDusen, Daniel, (Waverly,) livery stable, Fulton

VanDuzer & Hallett, (Waverly,)(*R D Van Duzer and Hatfield Hallett*,) wholesale and retail lumber dealers and props. planing mills, Exchange Block

VanDuzer, R. D., (Waverly,) (*VanDuzer & Hallett* )

Vanetten, Elisha, (Barton,) S D 24, farmer 89

Vanetten, Lorenzo F , (Barton,) (*with Elisha* ) farmer

Vanetten, Richard E., (Barton,) S. D. 19, farmer 52

VANGAASBECK & DEWITT, (Factoryville,) (*John VanGaasbeck and Wm DeWitt*,) manufs. sarsaparilla and soda water, Main

VANGAASBECK, JOHN, (Factoryville,) (*VanGaasbeck & DeWitt* )

VanMarter, Elijah, (North Barton,) S D 17, farmer 60.

VanMarter, Freeman W., (Halsey Valley,) S D 17, (*with Elijah*,) farmer 60

VanMarter, Joseph, (North Barton,) S. D. 11, farmer 125

VanSteenburgh, Alfred H., (North Barton,) S D 11, farmer 58

VanVelsor, Geo B , (Waverly,) (*Van Velsor & Manners* )

VanVelsor & Manners, (Waverly,) (*Geo B VanVelsor and Robert N Manners*,)merchant tailors, dealers in hats, caps and gent's furnishing goods, 70 Broad.

Vasbinder, Lewis M , (Halsey Valley,) farmer 100

Vredenberg, Charles, (Bingham's Mills,) S D 20, farmer 78

Walden, Jno. N , (North Barton,) S. D. 12, farmer 50

Walden, Thomas, (Factoryville,) S. D 9, farmer 28.

Waldo, G F , (Waverly,) (*Waldo & Tracy* )

Waldo & Tracy, (Waverly,) (*G F Waldo and E G Tracy*,) drugs, books, wall paper &c., 86 Broad.

Walker, Leander, (Waverly,) S. D 9, farmer 170

Walker, Loren A , (Spencer,) farmer 109

Walker, Thaddous S , (Factoryville,) farmer 70.

WALKER, WILLARD C., (Spencer,) S. D 20, farmer 75

Walling, Joseph, (Waverly,) S D. 1, post master at Barton

Walsh, Mike, (Waverly,) billiard room, Broad corner Fulton

Warford, Cyrus, (Waverly,) prop. Snyder House, Broadway nearly opposite Erie Depot

WARNER, F. R & CO , (Waverly,) (*Watrous Bros & Co*,) (*W L and Addison Watrous*,) dealers in groceries and provisions, wholesale and retail, Broad corner Waverly

Warner, Milton J , (Waverly,) lawyer, over Waldo's drug store 86 Broad.

Warner, Wm. F , (Waverly,) lawyer, 59 Broad

Washburne, Chas F , (Halsey Valley,) farmer 100

Washburne, Ozias F , (Barton,) S D 6, farmer leases 15

Washburne, Paschal jr , (Bingham's Mills,) S D 20, farmer leases of Mrs L. Hoyt, 160

Wasson, Stanley, (Waverly,) shoe maker, Broad

WATROUS, ADDISON, (Waverly,) (*Watrous Bros & Co*,) (*F R Warner & Co*)

WATROUS BROS. & CO , (Waverly,) (*F R Warner & Co*,) (*Addison and W L Watrous, and F R. Warner,*) dry goods and carpets, 91 Broad

WATROUS, W. L , (Waverly,) (*Watrous Bros & Co*,) (*F R. Warner & Co*)

Watts, Robert A ,(Bingham's Mills,) farmer leases of Cory Lyons, 300

*WAVERLY ADVOCATE, (Waverly ) Polleys & Kinney, publishers, O H P. Kinney, editor

Waverly Bank, (Waverly,) 72 Broad, H. T. Herrick, pres , George Herrick, cashier

*WAVERLY ENTERPRISE, (Waverly,) F T Scudder. editor and prop , Fulton corner Rail Road

Waverly Lodge, No. 407, F & A M , (Waverly,) regular communications 1st 3d and 5th Mondays in each month, at Masonic Hall, corner Broad and Waverly.

Waverly Marble Works, (Waverly,) (*W P Stone and G. H. Powers,*) Broad corner Pennsylvania Avenue

WAVERLY PAPER MILLS (Waverly,) Hon W W Shepard president , J E Pembleton, secretary , C H Shepard, vice-president , W W. Shepard, treasurer , office Broad

Weatherly, P , (Waverly,) (*Mullock & Weatherly* )

WEAVER, M B Dr , (Waverly,) clairvoyant physician, Octagon Place, Chemung

West, Andrew L , (Halsey Valley,) farmer 78

WESTFALL & BONNELL, (Waverly and Factoryville ) (*Levi Westfall and B W Bonnell,*) grain, flour, feed &c office and store 108 Broad mills at Factoryville

WESTFALL, JOHN, (Barton,) S D 1, farmer leases of Charles H Sawyer, 104

Westfall, John V , (Barton,) S. D. 1, farmer 110

WESTFALL, LEVI,(Waverly and Factoryville,) (*Westfall & Bonnell,*) justice of the peace

Wheeler, Grant, (Waverly,) S D 5, farmer 100

WHIPPLE, SOLOMON (Waverly,) S. D. 5, farmer 127. This place for sale

Whitaker, Lewis M., (Factoryville,) S. D. 18, farmer 130

White, Geo H , (Waverly,) policeman, Waverly

Wilber, Wm. P , (Halsey Valley,) S. D. 12, farmer 64

Wilcox, H M & Co , (Waverly,) (*J. G. Bush,*) dry goods, boots and shoes, 2 Union Block, 76 Broad.

Wilkinson, Charles S , (Factoryville,) S. D 2, (*with Joseph G* ,) farmer 111

WILKINSON, JOSEPH G , (Factoryville,) S D 2, farmer 111

Williams, Gabriel, (Waverly,) saloon, 47 Broad.

Williams, Justus A , (Bingham's Mills,) S D 16, carpenter and farmer 104

WILLIS, SYLVESTER, (Barton,) farmer leases of Wm , 160

WILLIS, WM , (Waverly,) S D 1, assessor and grain dealer.

Wilson, Stephen, (Barton,) farmer 18

WOOD, HENRY A., (Factoryville,) manuf boots and shoes, Main corner Chemung

WOOD, O P , (Factoryville,) manuf boots and shoes, Main corner Chemung

WRIGHT, J M , (Waverly,) joiner, 10 Tioga

Wright, Sylvenus, (Factoryville,) S D. 18, farmer 41

Wrigley, James, (Factoryville,) tailor, Main

YATES, ARTHUR JUDGE, (Waverly,) dealer in real estate and surveyor, Park Avenue

Yates Thos jr , (Factoryville ) post master and carriage maker, Main

# PUBLISHER'S NOTICES.

**The Binghamton Times,** advertised on page 302, is an able weekly paper, advocating the principles of the Republican party. Since their card was printed, this paper has undergone some change, both in its form and management. Mr Watson has retired from the proprietorship, though still having charge of the Job Department of the office and contributing to the Local columns of the paper, and has been succeeded by Messrs E H Purdy and D. E Cronin, under the firm name of Purdy & Cronin, the latter having charge of the Editorial columns. The *Times* is now issued in an enlarged form, in folio style, instead of quarterly as formerly and presents a very creditable appearance. The variety and character of its reading matter give evidence that the publishers are endeavoring to make it a live "family paper," and their efforts will no doubt be appreciated by the citizens of Broome County and vicinity.

**Alex. A. Swinton,** Nichols, N Y, dealer in Hardware Stoves, Tinware &c, advertises on page 346. His stock of Hardware, Tin, Copper &c, is varied and complete and if you cannot get a Stove to suit you here, both as to quality and price, you must be hard to please. Among his stoves will be found the celebrated American Cook Stove and American Base Burner. Mr S is also agent for the Cayuga Chief Mower and Reaper, and E M Bailey Plows.

**C. Lounsberry & Bro.,** proprietors of Steam Saw and Grist Mills, situated two miles south-east of the village of Nichols, in Bradford Co, Pa, print a card on page 346. These mills are newly built and are fitted up throughout with the most approved machinery, which is driven by an engine of 75 horse-power. Their facilities therefore, it will be seen, are quite ample to fill all orders in their different lines in a prompt and satisfactory manner. Call and see for yourself.

**Patrick Maloney,** better known as "Pat Maloney," dealer in Groceries, Provisions, Wines and Liquors, Page Street, Owego, advertises on page 356. We take pleasure in calling the attention of our patrons to this store, as they can always find a good assortment of Groceries and Provisions at prices as low as at any other place in Owego. Mr Maloney is also agent for the Inman and National lines of steamers. In his card you may see a picture of the ship that brought him over.

**Mrs. M. J. Crandall,** proprietor of City Laundry and Dress Making Emporium, Central Avenue, Owego, N Y is prepared to wash and do up the soiled linen of our patrons in a manner to suit the most fastidious. In the line of Dress Making, we need only refer our readers to any of her numerous patrons, to convince them that Mrs C is no novice in the art of getting up ladies' neat and fashionable dresses and suits. Her card appears on page 362.

**The Ahwaga Chief,** published at Owego, by Horace A Brooks, is comparatively a new candidate for public favor. Its publication was commenced February 23, 1872, and by referring to its card on page 374, it will be seen that it has already secured quite a good circulation. In one item the *Chief* excels, viz.—Its Literary matter, a considerable amount of which is contributed, while at the same time its Local and Editorial columns are by no means deficient. We commend the *Chief* to our patrons as a good family paper.

**M. B. Ferris,** Spencer, N Y, publishes a card on page 378, to which we would call the special attention of our readers. Mr F keeps a first-class country store, where Dry Goods, Groceries, Hats, Caps, Boots Shoes, Hardware, Drugs, Medicines and everything usually found in such establishments, are disposed of at a small advance on cost. Mr. Ferris evidently intends that the wants of this community, as far as he can supply them, shall be fully satisfied. If you doubt it, call and inspect his establishment and you will be convinced of the truth of our statement.

**F. M. Jewett,** Spencer, N Y., advertises on page 378. Mr J is prepared to do all kinds of Blacksmithing and Horseshoeing in a workmanlike manner. As a Horseshoer his reputation is established. Mr J. is also a Veterinary Surgeon of many years experience, and is quite competent to treat all the ills that horse flesh is heir to. Try him.

**Chas. Stuart,** 43 Washington Street, Binghamton, N Y, prints a card on page 378. He keeps on hand a large assortment of Guns, Pistols and sporting articles generally. Call on him when you want anything in his line.

**Geo. W. Barton,** 23 Main Street, Owego, N Y, manufactures Cigars of a superior quality and deals in articles pertaining to the wholesale and retail Tobacco trade. If you will use the *weed* we advise you to patronize Mr Barton. Card on page 374.

**Wm. Murray,** proprietor of the Central House, Candor, Tioga Co, N Y, prints his card on page 330. The Central House, under his management, is meeting the wants of this community in such a manner as to convince all its patrons that Mr M. "can keep a hotel." A good Livery is connected with the house, where fine horses and carriages can always be had at moderate rates. Those traveling this way will find a *home* with Mr Murray.

**F. H. Stephens,** Bookseller &c, 52 Court St., Binghamton, N. Y, prints a card on page 310. Mr. S. keeps a fine assortment of everything in the Book and Stationary line, also a good selection of Paper Hangings. Don't fail to call and see his stock. It will pay you.

**The Binghamton Democrat.** (Daily and Weekly,) published at Binghamton, by W S & G L Lawyer, are Democratic journals of no ordinary merit. The Daily is now in its fourth year of publication, and both papers enjoy a good circulation, the latter fact, business men should make a note of Job Printing is here done at very moderate rates. See card, page 276.

**John D. Swart,** House, Ornamental and Carriage Painter, Paper Hanger &c, at Candor, prints an illustrated card on page 330 Mr Swart is prepared to do all kinds of work pertaining to his trade In a manner which will prove satisfactory to his patrons Being a first class mechanic himself, his work is always well executed We have no hesitation in commending Mr. Swart to the favorable notice of our patrons

**E. A. Chandler & Son,** Carriage makers, Union, N. Y., print a card on page 276 Messrs C select their materials with great care and employ first class workmen, consequently their work is of a substantial character. They pay particular attention to Carriage Painting.

**Abner A. Haskin,** at Wilseyville, prints a card on page 342 Mr H keeps a store well stocked with a large and varied assortment of all goods required for a country trade He is an honorable, fair dealing man, and bound not to be undersold. Try him once and you will call again.

We have much pleasure in calling public attention to the advertisement of **Ketchum's Hotel,** on page 244 Few, if any, country hotels can bear favorable comparison with this establishment In the specialty of Horses, Messrs. Ketchum & Hathaway have earned for themselves a wide-spread and well-merited reputation for honorable dealing, and buyers would do well to give them a call before purchasing elsewhere

**D. C. McGraw,** successor to Mills & McGraw, Florist, proprietor of Riverside Gardens, a half mile east of the Water Works Binghamton, N Y, advertises on page 268 These Gardens embrace all kinds of Plants, Bulbs, Trees, Ornamental Shrubs, Seeds &c Persons interested in the culture of Plants and who have pleasure grounds to ornament, will find it for their advantage to order of Mr McGraw, as he will be able to fill the entire orders of his customers. Visitors are always welcome

**J. E. Bennett,** dealer in Dry Goods, Groceries, Hats, Caps, Boots Shoes, Crockery &c, and all goods usually kept in a first-class country store, advertises on page 248 Mr Bennett is located in the thriving village of Windsor, Broome Co., and judging from appearances he thoroughly understands the wants of the community and is determined that no one shall be compelled to go out of town for good goods at low prices. We commend him to the patronage of all interested, feeling assured that they will find what they want here at as low prices as at any other store

**The Tioga County Record,** published at Owego, N Y, by C H Keeler, is advertised on page 362, The *Record* is a 28 column paper, neatly printed, neutral in politics, and is an interesting local family paper. Although it is only in its second year, its management has drawn to it a very creditable circulation The Job facilities of the office are ample, and the prices as low as any Long may the *Record* wave

**Alonzo Roberson,** Binghamton, N Y, wholesale and retail Lumber Dealer, advertises on page 342 Mr R is doing an extensive business in the Lumber line and fills all orders promptly at reasonable rates Try him

**H. D. Heath,** dealer in Hardware, Stoves, Tinware, Agricultural Implements &c, Candor, N Y, advertises on page 326. He keeps on hand a good assortment of the best Stoves in the market, which he is selling at prices to suit the times His stock of Hardware, Tinware, Agricultural Implements, Pumps &c, is very complete In short everything pertaining to the above lines may be found at the Candor Hardware Store.

**Wm. Wayman's** Harness Shop, at Nichols, Tioga County, N. Y., is the center of attraction for all those who wish to dress their horses out in the best style Mr. Wayman has one of the handsomest harness shops to be found in this section of the country, and he keeps it well stocked with as good a selection of goods in his line to be found in any country place. He has had an experience of thirty years in the business, and employing the most skilled workmen and using only the best oak-tanned leather, he is enabled to get up anything in the harness line equal to the best His prices too are so low that every own who owns a horse can afford to have a good harness Good clothing is as important for a horse as a man. He also keeps a good variety of Saddles, Trunks, Valises, Whips, Blankets, Robes &c, which he sells cheap as the cheapest Let those who want anything in his line call on him. He publishes an attractive card on page 6, facing the Introduction.

**Milton Cresson's** Livery, Exchange and Boarding Stable, Carroll Street, Binghamton, is advertised on page 244 Pleasure or business parties will here find a supply of good Horses and Carriages at all times and at moderate rates. Horses boarded by the day or week We commend Mr. C to those wanting anything in the Livery line

**Stowell & Carpenter,** Boot and Shoe dealers, Waverly, N Y, advertise on page 398 A good *booting*, such as the above gentlemen can inflict, is more of a pleasure than a punishment, as many a victim is ready to testify Those fine hand-sewed Boots and Shoes for which Messrs S & C have the exclusive sale, are *just the thing* If you don't believe it try a pair. They make ladies' fine shoes a specialty

**The Daily Republican, Broome Weekly Republican, and Binghamton Standard,** (semi-weekly,) published at Binghamton, N Y, by Malette & Reid, are advertised on page 268 These are old established journals, ably edited and worthy champions of the cause of the Republican party Their large circulation makes them an excellent advertising medium, of which fact business men are not slow to take advantage. Book and Job Printing, in every style of the art, is also executed at this office

**L. W. Everett,** proprietor of the Railroad Carriage Shop, Binghamton, N Y, advertises on page 244 Mr E manufactures all styles of Carriages, Wagons and Sleighs, and uses only the best timber and iron, which, being put together by first-class mechanics, is sure to give satisfaction; We commend Mr. E and his work to the favor of our patrons.

**Heath & Norton,** manufacturers of Hand Rakes, Fork, Hoe and Broom Handles &c, Maine, N Y, advertise on page 248 This firm do an extensive business in the above lines, as well as Wood Turning, Planing and Jobbing generally. They are good mechanics and always give satisfaction Try them

**S. Mills Ely,** Canal Street, Binghamton, wholesale Grocer and Provision dealer, advertises on page 248 Mr Ely keeps a good supply of everything in the above lines. He also keeps the celebrated Averill Chemical Paint, all colors ready mixed for the brush, and deals in Wheeler, Melick & Co 's Combined Threshers and Cleaners Give him a call

**J. T. Smith,** Windsor, N Y, manufacturer and dealer in Plows, Cultivators, Corn Plows &c, advertises on page 248 The implements of Mr Smith's manufacture always give satisfaction, as those who have used them are ready to testify Mr S also does custom and machine work to order Call on him.

**Stephen D. Green,** Bingham's Mills N Y, keeps a choice assortment of Groceries, Provisions &c, to which we would call public attention In the Boot and Shoe line also you can always get suited here, and if your *understanding* wants repairing, Mr G is the man to do it. See card on page 394

**Geo. H. Smith,** manufacturer and dealer in Looking Glasses, Picture Frames, Chromos &c, at 101 Court Street, Binghamton, keeps on hand at all times a splendid assortment of goods from which the most fastidious customer cannot fail to find a choice. While visiting his store we priced several of his articles and were struck at the cheap rates at which he offered them We advise the citizens of Broome and Tioga Counties to call on Mr Smith for new goods in his line, or for repairing and regilding of old frames &c He advertises on page 314

**The Owego Times,** published at Owego by Wm Smyth, is a sterling family newspaper which for twenty years has proved a welcome visitor at the homes and firesides of a large number of patrons Its columns, editorial, local and miscellaneous are well sustained, exhibiting carefulness and attention in the management of the several departments A good Job office is connected with the establishment See card on page 326.

**L. G. Beecher,** of 72 Court Street, Binghamton, is now engaged in taking a picture on page 342 of this book He has had extensive experience and his Photographs are pronounced excellent Let those who would see themselves as others see them, repair to his gallery and "secure the shadow ere the substance fades " Miss Ella Wood, the *artiste*, is engaged in this Gallery

**W. D. Russell,** makes his headquarters at 89 Court St, Binghamton, and employs his time and talents in making converts and customers for the *musical* Sewing Machine. Some people call it the "*Singer*," and isn't a Singer musical ? It has been supposed by some people that this is one of the most popular machines in the country, but the *absurdity of the idea* will be apparent to all on hearing that the *actual sales* of these machines in 1871 was only the trifling number of 181,260, which was only about 50,000 more than the sales of any other machine This machine has been too long in the market and is too well known to require comment or praise from us It has stood the test for years and has more friends today than ever before. Mr Russell has engaged a lady *to sit on page* 294, where she may be seen now busily sewing.

**L. D. Witherill,** proprietor of the Eagle Drug Store, Union, N Y, advertises on foot lines between pages 260 and 277. Mr W is at all times prepared to supply his customers with the best quality of Drugs, Medicines, Paints, Oils, Perfumeries, Toilet Articles, Dye Stuffs, Glass &c, to be found in the market, and at as reasonable rates as they can be procured anywhere in the country Give him a call and you will be convinced of the truth of our statement

**P. W. Purtell,** makes nice Bread, Crackers, Cakes, Pies, &c, every day, at No 8 Court St, Binghamton Leave your orders there if you want to be well served He is now busy at work on page 310

**S. W. Barrett,** dealer in Jewelry, Watches, Silver and Plated Goods, Music and Musical Instruments, at No. 60 Court St, Binghamton, can show his customers as fine an assortment of goods in his line as may be found anywhere outside the large cities. His goods are selected with taste, bought low for cash and will be sold at bottom figures Call and see if what we say is not true His store is new and so are his goods See advertisement on foot lines.

# POPULATION OF BROOME & TIOGA COUNTIES.
## Census Returns for 1860, 1865 and 1870, showing the Increase and Decrease in the last decade.
### BROOME COUNTY.

| TOWNS. | 1860. | 1865. | 1870. | Increase. | Decrease. | Rate per cent. increase or decrease. |
|---|---|---|---|---|---|---|
| Barker | 1090 | 1339 | 1396 | 306 | ..... | 28 + * |
| Binghamton† | 9919 | 10092 | 2066 } | 4839 | ...... | 49— |
| Binghamton City | ...... | ...... | 12692 } | ...... | ...... | ..... |
| Chenango | 1841 | 1671 | 1680 | ...... | 161 | 9— |
| Colesville | 3250 | 3202 | 3400 | 150 | .... | 5— |
| Conklin | 1146 | 1282 | 1440 | 294 | ...... | 26— |
| Fenton | 1345 | 1503 | 1499 | 154 | ...... | 11— |
| Kirkwood | 1389 | 1440 | 1402 | 13 | ... | .9+ |
| Lisle | 1791 | 2066 | 2525 | 734 | ...... | 41— |
| Maine | 1609 | 2061 | 2035 | 426 | ...... | 26 + |
| Nanticoke | 797 | 972 | 1058 | 261 | ...... | 33— |
| Sanford | 3061 | 3262 | 3249 | 188 | ...... | 6+ |
| Triangle | 1693 | 1875 | 1944 | 251 | ...... | 15— |
| Union | 2092 | 2532 | 2538 | 446 | ...... | 21 + |
| Vestal | 2211 | 1939 | 2221 | 10 | ...... | .5— |
| Windsor | 2672 | 2697 | 2958 | 286 | ...... | 11— |
| Totals | 35906 | 37933 | 44103 | 8197 | ...... | 23— |

### TIOGA COUNTY.

| | | | | | | |
|---|---|---|---|---|---|---|
| Barton | 4234 | 4077 | 5087 | 853 | ...... | 20 + |
| Berkshire | 1151 | 1073 | 1240 | 89 | ...... | 8— |
| Candor | 3840 | 4103 | 4250 | 410 | ..... | 11— |
| Newark Valley | 2169 | 2133 | 2321 | 152 | .... | 7 + |
| Nichols | 1932 | 1778 | 1663 | ..... | 269 | 16 + |
| Owego | 8935 | 8865 | 9442 | 507 | ...... | 6— |
| Richford | 1404 | 1283 | 1434 | 30 | ...... | 2 + |
| Spencer | 1881 | 1757 | 1863 | .... | 18 | 1— |
| Tioga | 3202 | 3094 | 3272 | 70 | ...... | 2 + |
| Totals | 28748 | 28163 | 30572 | 1824 | ...... | 6 + |

* As it is not convenient to give the decimal expressing the exact rate per cent, when the remaining fraction is less than one-half, we have made use of the plus sign to indicate that the true rate per cent is greater than that expressed, and when the remaining fraction is greater than one-half, one has been added to the integer, and the minus sign used to indicate that the true rate per cent is greater than the number by which it is expressed.

† Binghamton City was incorporated April 9, 1867, and the indicated increase represents the increase in the population of the city and town combined.

z

# Agricultural Statistics for Broome and Tioga Counties from Census of 1865 and 1870.

## BROOME COUNTY.

| TOWNS | Winter Wheat, bush harvested '64 | Oats, bushels harvested 1864 | Indian Corn, bushels harvested 1864 | Potatoes, bushels harvested 1864 | Tobacco, pounds harvested 1864 | Hops, pounds harvested 1864 | Apples, bushels harvested 1864 | Milch Cows, number of, 1865 | Butter, pounds made, 1864 | Horses, two yrs old and over, 1865 | Sheep, number shorn, 1865 |
|---|---|---|---|---|---|---|---|---|---|---|---|
| Barker | 200 | 8,239 | 9,061 | 12,539 | 3,100 | 2,000 | 10,597 | 2,576 | 155,519 | 378 | 2,641 |
| Binghamton | 1,728 | 17,508 | 15,353 | 27,592 | 48,454 | 9,450 | 11,417 | 1,123 | 76,352 | 654 | 1,746 |
| Chenango | 2,626 | 31,506 | 21,159 | 25,688 | 1,000 | | 11,951 | 1,245 | 151,030 | 461 | 2,229 |
| Colesville | 603 | 38,544 | 19,507 | 31,843 | 2,657 | 1,000 | 31,212 | 2,341 | 278,215 | 794 | 5,843 |
| Conklin | 1,204 | 10,615 | 8,992 | 9,230 | 2,700 | | 3,288 | 558 | 51,413 | 183 | 1,029 |
| Fenton | 1,866 | 15,501 | 9,912 | 14,685 | 11,900 | 3,000 | 6,996 | 888 | 99,509 | 324 | 2,080 |
| Kirkwood | 2,888 | 20,591 | 11,791 | 16,040 | 600 | 335 | 7,914 | 878 | 124,053 | 347 | 2,878 |
| Lisle | 203 | 8,838 | 6,158 | 11,777 | | 724 | 16,312 | 1,234 | 169,080 | 443 | 2,823 |
| Maine | 412 | 18,302 | 11,184 | 29,061 | 6,100 | 7,976 | 8,046 | 1,276 | 138,327 | 447 | 2,711 |
| Nanticoke | 49 | 4,067 | 3,524 | 8,389 | | 1,950 | 5,921 | 708 | 92,168 | 193 | 1,224 |
| Sanford | 12 | 11,609 | 4,469 | 19,204 | 376 | 6,835 | 10,281 | 1,927 | 212,547 | 535 | 3,512 |
| Triangle | 407 | 9,126 | 17,727 | 13,031 | 1,300 | 11,492 | 20,832 | 1,800 | 263,685 | 471 | 2,842 |
| Union | 6,747 | 43,145 | 29,132 | 41,916 | 6,480 | 4,650 | 10,121 | 1,419 | 190,895 | 555 | 2,172 |
| Vestal | 3,315 | 29,328 | 15,769 | 31,131 | 4,500 | 3,270 | 3,682 | 877 | 90,590 | 413 | 2,670 |
| Windsor | 1,479 | 20,075 | 13,409 | 23,021 | | | 12,625 | 1,846 | 107,955 | 507 | 5,135 |
| Total | 23829 | 287204 | 197243 | 314747 | 89,727 | 52,082 | 180195 | 20,699 | 2,291,268 | 6,615 | 41535 |

## TIOGA COUNTY.

| TOWNS | Winter Wheat | Oats | Indian Corn | Potatoes | Tobacco | Hops | Apples | Milch Cows | Butter | Horses | Sheep |
|---|---|---|---|---|---|---|---|---|---|---|---|
| Barton | 5589 | 51977 | 29043 | 21258 | 2470 | | 12996 | 1698 | 170513 | 682 | 3658 |
| Berkshire | 63 | 9837 | 8069 | 13065 | | | 17976 | 882 | 113974 | 311 | 3504 |
| Candor | 3423 | 44616 | 28009 | 40734 | | 1600 | 26093 | 2046 | 247247 | 910 | 7322 |
| Newark Valley | 605 | 26367 | 17107 | 27563 | 2150 | 876 | 13742 | 1399 | 169160 | 583 | 5190 |
| Nichols | 5540 | 45669 | 26690 | 21923 | 58500 | | 12585 | 1074 | 100703 | 548 | 2525 |
| Owego | 7644 | 79441 | 47012 | 88138 | 9905 | | 25664 | 2415 | 250893 | 1191 | 5890 |
| Richford | 145 | 7314 | 8211 | 8355 | | | 12409 | 802 | 100601 | 272 | 2410 |
| Spencer | 2350 | 23596 | 15612 | 12062 | 3600 | | 13278 | 992 | 125229 | 398 | 4349 |
| Tioga | 4338 | 43424 | 24008 | 30381 | 35563 | | 16130 | 1404 | 118850 | 771 | 4086 |
| Total | 29757 | 331743 | 205291 | 258479 | 112248 | 2476 | 151833 | 12672 | 1432650 | 5656 | 40434 |

## ADDITIONAL STATISTICS FROM CENSUS OF 1870.

In addition to the above extracts we give the following *totals* for the Counties, as per returns for the several heads mentioned

### BROOME COUNTY.

*Cash Value of Farms,* $17,653,310, *of Farming Implements,* $699,028, *Wages Paid,* (including value of board,) $354,546, *Value of all Farm Productions,* (including betterments and additions to stock,) $3,828,791, *Value of all Live Stock,* $2,898,638; *Value of Home Manufactures,* $15,616, *Value of Animals Slaughtered or sold for Slaughter,* $408,032, *Tons of Hay Produced,* 101,955, *Rye,* bushels harvested, 10,708, *Barley,* bushels harvested 2,465; *Buckwheat,* bushels harvested, 136,085, *Wool,* pounds shorn, 72,137, *Cheese,* pounds made, 31,540, *Hops,* pounds harvested, 164,809, *Maple Sugar,* pounds made, 65,560, *Honey,* pounds gathered, 32,493; *Value of Orchard Products,* $67,570, *Value of Market Garden Products,* $40,395, *Value of Forest Products,* $189,636, *Working Oxen,* number of, 1,986; *Other Cattle,* number of, 13,001, *Sheep,* number of, 20,134; *Swine,* number of, 8,201

# TIOGA COUNTY.

*Cash Value of Farms*, $13,431,805, *of Farming Implements*, $450,065, *Wages Paid*, (including value of board,) $415,016; *Value of all Farm Productions*, (including betterments and additions to stock,) $2,932,907, *Value of all Live Stock*, $2,072,537, *Value of Home Manufactures*, $9,334; *Value of Animals Slaughtered or Sold for Slaughter*, $301,855, *Tons of Hay Produced*, 65,078, *Rye*, bushels harvested, 14,643, *Barley*, bushels harvested, 5,320, *Buckwheat*, bushels harvested, 167,674, *Wool*, pounds shorn, 79,432, *Cheese*, pounds made, 73,204, *Hops*, pounds harvested 800, *Maple Sugar*, pounds made, 15,444, *Honey*, pounds gathered, 42 095; *Value of Orchard Products*, $62,825, *Value of Market Garden Products*, $8,680, *Value of Forest Products*, $135,277, *Working Oxen*, number of, 933, *Other Cattle*, number of, 8,460, *Sheep*, number of, 19,668; *Swine*, number of, 6,130

**The Waverly Enterprise**, published at Waverly, N Y, by Frank T Scudder, is advertised on page 398 This excellent local paper is as enterprising as its title signifies, and is worthy of it by its numerous patrons The Job Department of this office is very complete, the facilities for doing all kinds of Job Printing being equal to any in the County As an advertising medium this journal has merits which business men should not overlook.

**Crocker & Ogden**, dealers in Hardware, Carriage Goods, Mechanics' Tools &c, at 91 Court St, Binghamton, are prepared to supply all who are in want of their kind of goods, from the best hoes the market affords and at as reasonable prices This firm makes Carriage Goods and Mechanics' Tools, specialties Their stock is very large at all times Our readers will study their own interests by calling on this firm when in town Their advertisement may be found in various marginal lines

**George Van Wormer**, manufacturer of Harness, and dealer in Horse Goods of all kinds, advertises on page 276 Mr Van Wormer's shop is new and well stocked We assure our friends that no where else can they be better suited Call and see him at No. 61 Court Street, Binghamton

**Alfred White**, Ornamental Confectioner and Fancy Cake Baker, at No 99 Court St, Binghamton, publishes an illustrated card on page 374 Mr White has had long experience in this line of business, his place is always clean and neat and it is a real pleasure to visit his rooms to see the array of nice things, even it one is not in want of his goods Call and see for yourselves, if you are proof against temptation

**E. Ayers**, Undertaker, at 86 Washington Street, Binghamton, has had eight years experience at his profession He keeps a splendid hearse and is prepared to furnish all kinds of goods in his line at lowest prices and on short notice Card on page 212

**The Union Weekly News** is published at Union, Broome County, every Friday, by Mose B Robbins It is an independent sheet, ably managed, neatly printed and enjoying an extended circulation. The Job Department has good facilities for doing Book and Job Work with neatness and dispatch See card on page 310

**The Buckeye Mowing and Reaping Machines.**—When the great U. S Trial of Mowers and Reapers was held at Syracuse in 1857, this admirable machine, which had just been brought out, surprised everybody by its novelty and many excellencies, and won the highest awards At that time the valuable patents under which it was built were secured for several States by the enterprising firm which now continues its manufacture, Adriance, Platt & Co. At the second great trial of Mowers and Reapers, made by the N Y State Agricultural Society in 1866, the Buckeye again carried off the highest honors, showing that in the years intervening it had not gone backward in the race for superiority. Every new suggestion is thoroughly weighed, *improvements* only are adopted The verdict of the people is nearly as unanimous as that of the learned and practical committees who made those awards, for its sales far exceed those of any other machine in the sections supplied by Adriance, Platt & Co In fact they increase so *fast*, that the demand is almost always in excess of the supply The Self-Raking Attachment on the Buckeye Machine has met with a success corresponding to that of the Mower, and has surpassed all others in the perfection of its operation One great secret of the success of Adriance, Platt & Co, as manufacturers, has been in the conscientious manner in which they have built their machines, and the great durability of the Buckeye machine has been largely due to the excellence of the material used and the mechanical perfection of the workmanship See advertisement on Map

**Oliver W. Sears** sells Books, News papers, Stationery, Wall Paper, Croquet Goods &c, at 56 Court Street, Binghamton Mr Sears is a young man just entering upon the race for business fame He has had the best of tutilage however in the business at which he is engaged, and is and will be at all times prepared to furnish his friends and customers with the *latest news*, most popular books, or anything else in his line at the lowest prices See his advertisement on page 204 and on margins

**Jefferson Bingham**, Bingham's Mills, N Y, in a card on page 894, calls attention to the fact that he deals in all kinds of Lumber also Cayuga Plaster. Mr B. we are assured, is a man who will do just what he advertises His terms are as reasonable as can be had anywhere.

# STARTLING NEWS FROM
# GEO. W. BINGHAM!
## WHAT IS IT?
### WHY, HE HAS OPENED A
# SAW & FLOURING MILL,
## On the Ithaca and Athens R. R.,
### AND IS SELLING
# LUMBER OF ALL KINDS,
### AND
# FLOUR, FEED, Etc.,

For CASH, cheaper than any-one else  He also pays highest cash price for all kinds of Grain  Give him a call, buy of him and save your money

Mr BINGHAM would like to prove to those having custom work to do in his line that he can satisfy the most fastidious   GEO W. BINGHAM.

# THE DEMOCRATIC LEADER!
## PUBLISHED EVERY FRIDAY,
### BY
# A. W. CARL,
## No. 3 COURT STREET,
# Binghamton, Broome County, N. Y.

*Terms, $1.50 per Year, in Advance.  Advertising Rates Reasonable.*

# BROOME COUNTY OFFICERS.

**Clerk of Board of Supervisors.**

| | P O ADDRESS |
|---|---|
| T. F. McDonald ... | ...Binghamton |

**Coroner.**

| | |
|---|---|
| John P Worthing .... | Binghamton |

**County Clerk.**

| | |
|---|---|
| Joseph M. Johoson | ... .Binghamton |
| J Humphrey Johnson, Deputy | Binghamton |

**County Judge and Surrogate.**

| | |
|---|---|
| Wm B Edwards . . | Binghamton |

**County Treasurer.**

| | |
|---|---|
| Alonzo C. Mathews..... | Binghamton |

**District Attorney.**

| | |
|---|---|
| Peter W. Hopkins.. | Binghamton |

**Justices of Sessions.**

| | |
|---|---|
| Ruff Finch . . . | Kirkwood |
| Addison Miller........ . . . | Fenton |

**Keeper of Poor House.**

| | P. O. ADDRESS |
|---|---|
| M B Payne . . . ... | Binghamton |

**Loan Commissioners.**

| | |
|---|---|
| Sylvester D. Parsons .. ... | Harpersville |
| John H. Smith. . ........ | Binghamton |

**Member of Congress, 26th District.**

| | |
|---|---|
| Milo Goodrich | Dryden, Tompkins Co |

**School Commissioners.**

| | |
|---|---|
| Newton W Edson ...... | Binghamton |
| Henry S Monroe . . | Binghamton |

**Sheriff.**

| | |
|---|---|
| Frederick W Martin .. ... .. | Binghamton |
| Henry H Merrill, Under Sheriff | Binghamton |

**State Senator, 24th District.**

| | |
|---|---|
| Thos I Chatfield .. | Owego |

**Superintendent of the Poor.**

| | |
|---|---|
| Evander Spaulding . ... | ..Binghamton |

---

# TIOGA COUNTY OFFICERS.

**Coroners.**

| | P. O. ADDRESS |
|---|---|
| Theodore S. Armstrong......• . | Owego |
| Geo P Cady . . .. | .... Nichols |
| Edward C Coryell | . . ... .Candor |

**County Clerk.**

| | |
|---|---|
| Horace A Brooks . . | Owego |
| John J. VanKleeck, Deputy.. . . | Owego |

**County Judge and Surrogate.**

| | |
|---|---|
| Chas. A. Clark ...... .. ... | Owego |

**County Treasurer.**

| | |
|---|---|
| John B. Brush . .. .. | Owego |

**District Attorney.**

| | |
|---|---|
| Eugene B Gere... ... . . | Owego |

**Justices of Sessions.**

| | |
|---|---|
| Geo Cooper.. . . ... | ..Apalachin |
| Luther B. West ... . | Halsey Valley |

**Loan Commissioners**

| | |
|---|---|
| David M Goodrich . . | ....Owego |
| Chas. E. Ransom. . | ... Tioga Center |

**Member of Assembly.**

| | . O ADDRESS |
|---|---|
| Wm. Smyth ................ | ...Owego |

**Member of Congress, 26th District.**

| | |
|---|---|
| Milo Goodrich | .Dryden, Tompkins Co |

**School Commissioner.**

| | |
|---|---|
| William H Cole . ... | ......Owego |

**Sheriff.**

| | |
|---|---|
| Thos F. Pearl. . . .. . | Owego |

UNDER SHERIFF.

| | |
|---|---|
| Harvey P Lane. . . | Owego |

DEPUTY SHERIFF.

| | |
|---|---|
| Chas C Brooks . . . . | Waverly |

**Special County Judge.**

| | |
|---|---|
| J. Newton Dexter | .. Waverly |

**State Senator, 24th District.**

| | |
|---|---|
| Thos. I. Chatfield . ... | Owego |

**Superintendents of the Poor.**

| | |
|---|---|
| Benj. Golden . . | Waverly |
| Chauncey T Woodford.. .... ..... | Candor |

# TERMS OF COURT--1872-3.

—

## *BROOME COUNTY.*

### TO BE HELD AT THE COURT HOUSE IN BINGHAMTON

—

#### GENERAL TERM
First Tuesday in September.

#### CIRCUIT COURTS AND COURTS OF OYER AND TERMINER.

| | 1872 | 1873 |
|---|---|---|
| Third Monday in March | MURRAY, Justice | BALCOM, Justice |
| Third Monday in June | BOARDMAN, Justice | MURRAY, Justice |
| Fourth Monday in November | MURRAY, Justice | BOARDMAN, Justice |

#### SPECIAL TERM—SUPREME

| | 1872. | 1873 |
|---|---|---|
| Second Tuesday in July | BOARDMAN, Justice | MURRAY, Justice |

#### FOR MOTIONS ONLY.

| | |
|---|---|
| Fourth Tuesday in October. | BALCOM, Justice |

#### COUNTY COURTS AND COURTS OF SESSIONS

W B EDWARDS, COUNTY JUDGE

| | |
|---|---|
| Last Monday in January | Jury |
| Second Monday in May | No Jury |
| Fourth Monday in September | Jury |
| Third Monday in November | No Jury |

—◆—

## *TIOGA COUNTY.*

### TO BE HELD AT THE COURT HOUSE IN OWEGO

—

#### CIRCUIT COURTS AND COURTS OF OYER AND TERMINER

| | 1872 | 1873 |
|---|---|---|
| Last Monday in February | MURRAY, Justice | BOARDMAN, Justice |
| First Monday in December | BOARDMAN, Justice | BALCOM, Justice |

#### SPECIAL TERM—SUPREME

| | 1872 | 1873. |
|---|---|---|
| Last Tuesday in April. | BALCOM, Justice | BOARDMAN, Justice |

#### COUNTY COURTS AND COURTS OF SESSIONS

CHAS. A CLARK, COUNTY JUDGE

| | |
|---|---|
| Last Monday in March. | Law Term |
| First Monday in June | Sessions |
| First Monday in September | Sessions |
| Last Monday in November | Law Term |

BROOME COUNTY TABLE OF DISTANCES

# Broome County Table of Distances,

*Showing Distances in Miles and Tenths of Miles, between the Villages, Measured on the nearest Public Roads.*

| VILLAGES | Binghamton. | Castle Creek. | Chenango Forks | Deposit | Glen Aubrey | Glen Castle | Harpersville. | Hawleyton. | Killawog | Kirkwood | Lisle | Maine | Nineveh | North Sanford. | Osborn Hollow. | Oquaga | Port Crane | Sanford. | Triangle | Union | Union Center | Upper Lisle | Vallonia Springs | Vestal | Vestal Center | Whitneys Point |
|---|---|---|---|---|---|---|---|---|---|---|---|---|---|---|---|---|---|---|---|---|---|---|---|---|---|---|
| Binghamton | | | | | | | | | | | | | | | | | | | | | | | | | | |
| Castle Creek | 9.6 | | | | | | | | | | | | | | | | | | | | | | | | | |
| Chenango Forks | 11 2 | 4 2 | | | | | | | | | | | | | | | | | | | | | | | | |
| Deposit | 28 4 | 33 1 | 28 9 | | | | | | | | | | | | | | | | | | | | | | | |
| Glen Aubrey | 13 0 | 7 0 | 10 5 | 39.4 | | | | | | | | | | | | | | | | | | | | | | |
| Glen Castle | 6.1 | 3 5 | 7 7 | 31 7 | 9 2 | | | | | | | | | | | | | | | | | | | | | |
| Harpersville | 17 2 | 17 8 | 13 6 | 15 3 | 24 1 | 16 4 | | | | | | | | | | | | | | | | | | | | |
| Hawleyton | 5 6 | 15 2 | 16 8 | 30 8 | 18 6 | 11.7 | 22 8 | | | | | | | | | | | | | | | | | | | |
| Killawog | 23 7 | 14 1 | 14 9 | 43 8 | 11 2 | 17.6 | 28 5 | 29 3 | | | | | | | | | | | | | | | | | | |
| Kirkwood | 9 2 | 18 1 | 16 0 | 28 3 | 22 2 | 15 3 | 16 3 | 7 5 | 30 9 | | | | | | | | | | | | | | | | | |
| Lisle | 20 0 | 10 4 | 11 2 | 40.1 | 7 5 | 13 9 | 24 8 | 25 6 | 3 7 | 27 2 | | | | | | | | | | | | | | | | |
| Maine | 18.0 | 9 0 | 13 2 | 41 1 | 6 3 | 9 4 | 25 8 | 18 6 | 15 8 | 22 2 | 12 1 | | | | | | | | | | | | | | | |
| Nineveh | 18 9 | 19 5 | 15 3 | 15 4 | 25 8 | 18 1 | 1 7 | 24 5 | 30 2 | 18 0 | 26.6 | 27 5 | | | | | | | | | | | | | | |
| North Sanford | 30 0 | 30 7 | 26 3 | 7.8 | 36 8 | 29 1 | 12 7 | 33 3 | 41.2 | 25 8 | 37 6 | 38 5 | 12 7 | | | | | | | | | | | | | |
| Osborn Hollow | 10 2 | 11 8 | 9 7 | 23.0 | 18 8 | 8 7 | 7 7 | 15 8 | 24.6 | 10 4 | 20 9 | 18 1 | 9 4 | 20 4 | | | | | | | | | | | | |
| Oquaga | 14 8 | 19 0 | 15.6 | 16 8 | 26 0 | 16.9 | 4 1 | 19 5 | 30 4 | 12 0 | 26 7 | 25 3 | 5 8 | 16 0 | 7 2 | | | | | | | | | | | |
| Port Crane | 7 0 | 8 1 | 6 0 | 26 7 | 15 1 | 6 0 | 11 4 | 12 6 | 20 9 | 10 0 | 17.2 | 14 4 | 13 1 | 24 1 | 1 3 | 10 9 | | | | | | | | | | |
| Sanford | 28 0 | 28 6 | 24 4 | 4 3 | 34 9 | 27 2 | 10 8 | 29 3 | 39.3 | 21.8 | 35 6 | 36 6 | 10 9 | 4 0 | 18 5 | 12 0 | 22 2 | | | | | | | | | |
| Triangle | 18 9 | 9 0 | 7 7 | 35 6 | 10 9 | 12.5 | 21 3 | 24 5 | 10 7 | 23 7 | 7 0 | 16 2 | 23 0 | 34 0 | 17 4 | 23 2 | 13 7 | 31 1 | | | | | | | | |
| Union | 8 7 | 16 0 | 18 1 | 37 1 | 12 5 | 13 6 | 25 9 | 12 2 | 23 0 | 7 2 | 27 6 | 38 6 | 18 9 | 23 5 | 15.7 | 36 7 | 23 4 | | | 4.0 | | | | | | |
| Union Center | 9 3 | 11 2 | 15 4 | 37 7 | 8 5 | 11 2 | 26 5 | 14 9 | 19 0 | 18 5 | 15 3 | 3 2 | 28 2 | 39 2 | 19 5 | 24 1 | 16 3 | 37 | 19 4 | 4.0 | | | | | | |
| Upper Lisle | 22 0 | 13 0 | 13 8 | 42 7 | 11 3 | 16 5 | 27 4 | 28 2 | 4 6 | 29 8 | 4 4 | 16 6 | 29 9 | 41 4 | 16 6 | 6 1 | 14 3 | 10 0 | 18 0 | 7 2 | 27 9 | | | | | |
| Vallonia Springs | 23 8 | 24 4 | 20 2 | 11 7 | 30 7 | 23 0 | 6.6 | 29 4 | 35 1 | 21.3 | 31 4 | 33 4 | 6 6 | 11 4 | 14 8 | 8 1 | 18 2 | 6 0 | 27 9 | 32 6 | 33 1 | 34 0 | | | | |
| Vestal | 8 7 | 16 3 | 18 4 | 37 1 | 13 6 | 12 8 | 25 9 | 11.1 | 24 1 | 17 9 | 20 4 | 8 3 | 27 6 | 38 6 | 18 9 | 28 5 | 15 7 | 36 7 | 24 5 | 1 1 | 5 1 | 24 9 | 32 6 | | | |
| Vestal Center | 8.0 | 17 6 | 19 2 | 36 4 | 17 9 | 14 1 | 25 2 | 6 9 | 28 4 | 14 3 | 24 7 | 12 6 | 26 9 | 37 9 | 18.2 | 22 8 | 15 0 | 36 0 | 26 9 | 5 4 | 9 4 | 29 2 | 31 8 | 4 3 | | |
| Whitneys Point | 17 6 | 8 0 | 8 8 | 37 7 | 6 3 | 11 5 | 23 4 | 23 2 | 6 1 | 24 8 | 2 4 | 11 6 | 24 1 | 35 1 | 18 5 | 24 3 | 14 8 | 33 2 | 4 6 | 18 8 | 14 8 | 5 6 | 29.0 | 19 9 | 24 2 | |
| Windsor | 14 9 | 21 5 | 19 0 | 13 5 | 28 5 | 18 4 | 8 4 | 17 3 | 33 9 | 9 8 | 30 2 | 27 9 | 10 1 | 16 0 | 9 7 | 4 3 | 13 4 | 12 0 | 26 7 | 23 6 | 24 2 | 32 8 | 11 6 | 23 6 | 22 9 | 27 6 |

## Tioga County Table of Distances,

### In Miles and Tenths of Miles, Between the Principal Villages.

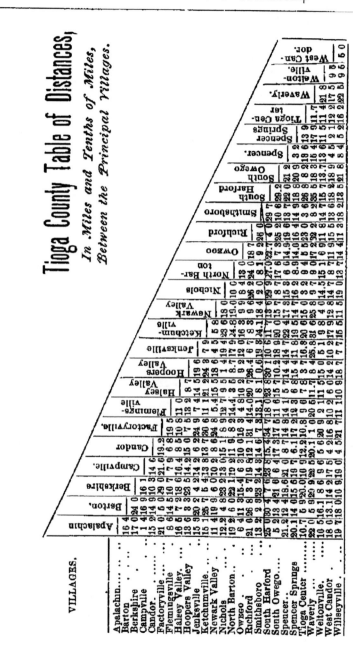

VILLAGES.

Apalachin
Barton
Berkshire
Campville
Candor
Factoryville
Flemingsville
Haley Valley
Hoopers Valley
Jenksville
Ketchumville
Newark Valley
Nichols
North Barton
Owego
Richford
Smithboro
South Harford
South Owego
Spencer
Spencer Springs
Tioga Center
Waverly
Weltonville
West Candor
Willseyville

# PRATT & COMSTOCK,

*(Successors to W. G. Singhi.)*

# PHOTOGRAPHERS,

AND DEALERS IN

## Stereoscopes, Views,

## Fancy Card Pictures,

### Albums, Frames, etc.

*Old Pictures of every descrip-
tion Copied and Enlarged,
and Colored in*

## Oils, Water Colors and India Ink.

*Satisfaction Guaranteed.*

## 76 Broad St., - Waverly, N. Y.

M. C. PRATT. A. B. COMSTOCK.

---

CALL AT

# ROBINSON'S

## SOUTHERN TIER

# FURNITURE EMPORIUM,

### No. 83 WASHINGTON ST.,

### BINGHAMTON, N. Y.

Where you will find a Larger and
Better Assortment of all kinds of

# FURNITURE

*Than at any other Establishment in Binghamton, and which will be*

## SOLD AT THE VERY LOWEST CASH PRICES.

### All Goods Warranted as Represented.

#### REMEMBER THAT WE CANNOT BE UNDERSOLD.

Z 2

Breinigsville, PA USA
23 January 2011
253880BV00003B/81/P